VOLUME ONE
ECONOMY
AND
SOCIETY

Translators: *EPHRAIM FISCHOFF*

HANS GERTH

A. M. HENDERSON

FERDINAND KOLEGAR

C. WRIGHT MILLS

TALCOTT PARSONS

MAX RHEINSTEIN

GUENTHER ROTH

EDWARD SHILS

CLAUS WITTICH

Max Weber

ECONOMY
AND
SOCIETY

AN OUTLINE OF INTERPRETIVE SOCIOLOGY

Edited by Guenther Roth
and Claus Wittich

University of California Press
Berkeley • Los Angeles • London

Economy and Society is a translation of Max Weber, *Wirtschaft und Gesellschaft. Grundriss der verstehenden Soziologie*, based on the 4th German edition, Johannes Winckelmann (ed.), Tübingen: J. C. B. Mohr (Paul Siebeck), 1956, pp. 1–550, 559–822, as revised in the 1964 paperback edition (Köln-Berlin: Kiepenheuer & Witsch), with appendices from Max Weber, *Gesammelte Aufsätze zur Wissenschaftslehre*, 2nd rev. edition, Johannes Winckelmann (ed.), Tübingen: J. C. B. Mohr (Paul Siebeck), 1951, pp. 441–467 (selected passages), and Max Weber, *Gesammelte politische Schriften*, 2nd expanded edition, Johannes Winckelmann (ed.), Tübingen: J. C. B. Mohr (Paul Siebeck), 1958, pp. 294–394.

The exclusive license to make this English edition has been granted to the University of California Press by the German holder of rights, J. C. B. Mohr (Paul Siebeck), Tübingen.

The English text includes (with revisions and with addition of notes) material previously published and copyrighted by these publishers:

Beacon Press:
Ephraim Fischoff, trans., *The Sociology of Religion* (Boston: Beacon Press, 1963), pp. 1–274. Copyright © 1963 by Beacon Press. Reprinted by arrangement with Beacon Press.

Oxford University Press:
Hans Gerth and C. Wright Mills, trans. and eds., *From Max Weber: Essays in Sociology* (New York: Oxford University Press, 1946), pp. 159–244, 253–262. Copyright 1946 by Oxford University Press, Inc. British Commonwealth rights by Routledge and Kegan Paul Ltd. Reprinted by permission.

The Free Press of Glencoe:
Ferdinand Kolegar, trans., "The Household Community" and "Ethnic Groups," in Talcott Parsons *et al.*, eds., *Theories of Society* (New York: The Free Press of Glencoe, 1961), vol. 1, pp. 296–298, 302–309. Copyright © 1961 by The Free Press of Glencoe. Reprinted by permission.

Talcott Parsons, ed. (A. M. Henderson and T. Parsons, trans.), *The Theory of Social and Economic Organization* (New York: The Free Press of Glencoe, 1964; originally published by Oxford University Press, 1947), pp. 87–423. Copyright 1947 by The Free Press of Glencoe. Reprinted by permission.

Harvard University Press:
Max Rheinstein, ed. (Edward Shils and Max Rheinstein, trans.), *Max Weber on Law in Economy and Society* (20th Century Legal Philosophy Series, Vol. VI; Cambridge, Mass.: Harvard University Press, 1954), pp. 11–348. Copyright, 1954 by the President and Fellows of Harvard College. Reprinted by permission.

Correspondence about these sections of the English translation should be directed to the above publishers. See editors' preface for details about their location in this edition.

SUMMARY CONTENTS

APPENDICES

INDEX

ANALYTICAL CONTENTS

Part One: CONCEPTUAL EXPOSITION

Chapter III

THE TYPES OF LEGITIMATE DOMINATION 212

Chapter IV

STATUS GROUPS AND CLASSES

Chapter XI

Chapter XVI

THE CITY (NON-LEGITIMATE DOMINATION)

Appendices

List of Abbreviations

Some of the extant translations were extensively annotated by the original translators. This annotation was to the largest part retained, and in some cases complemented by the editors; we also used some of the annotation provided for the 4th German edition of *Wirtschaft und Gesellschaft* by Johannes Winckelmann. The unsigned notes in Part One, chs. I–III are by Talcott Parsons, in Part Two, chs. VII–VIII by Max Rheinstein, and elsewhere by one of the editors as identified at the head of each section of notes. The following abbreviations were used to identify the authors of other notes:

(GM): Hans Gerth and C. Wright Mills
(R): Guenther Roth
(Rh): Max Rheinstein
(W): Johannes Winckelmann
(Wi): Claus Wittich

In the editorial notes, a number of abbreviations were used for works (or translations of works) by Max Weber; these are listed below. A group of further bibliographical abbreviations used only in Max Rheinstein's annotation to the "Sociology of Law" is given in Part Two, ch. VIII:*i*, n. 1 (pp. 658–661 below).

AfS or *Archiv*
   Archiv für Sozialwissenschaft und Sozialpolitik. Tübingen: J. C. B. Mohr (Paul Siebeck). (A scholarly periodical edited by Max Weber, Edgar Jaffé and Werner Sombart from 1904 on.)

Agrargeschichte
   Die römische Agrargeschichte in ihrer Bedeutung für das Staats- und Privatrecht. Stuttgart: Ferdinand Enke, 1891. (Weber's second dissertation.)

"Agrarverhältnisse"
   "Agrarverhältnisse im Altertum," in *Handwörterbuch der Staats-*

[xxv]

wissenschaften, 3rd ed., I (1909), 52–188. Reprinted in *GAzSW,* 1–288. (Page references are to this reprint.)

Ancient Judaism or AJ
> *Ancient Judaism.* Translated and edited by Hans H. Gerth and Don Martindale. Glencoe, Ill.: The Free Press, 1952. (A translation of "Das antike Judentum," Part III of "Die Wirtschaftsethik der Weltreligionen," first published in *AfS,* 1917–19, and of a posthumously published study, "Die Pharisäer," both in *GAzRS,* III.)

Economic History
> *General Economic History.* Translated by Frank H. Knight. London and New York: Allen & Unwin, 1927; paperback re-issue, New York: Collier Books, 1961. (A translation of *Wirtschaftsgeschichte.* Page references in ch. VIII are to the 1927 edition, elsewhere to the 1961 paperback.)

Fischoff
> *The Sociology of Religion.* Translated by Ephraim Fischoff, with an introduction by Talcott Parsons. Boston: Beacon Press, 1963.

GAzRS
> *Gesammelte Aufsätze zur Religionssoziologie.* 3 vols. Tübingen: J. C. B. Mohr (Paul Siebeck), 1920–21; unchanged re-issue 1922–23.

GAzSS
> *Gesammelte Aufsätze zur Soziologie und Sozialpolitik.* Tübingen: J. C. B. Mohr (Paul Siebeck), 1924.

GAzSW
> *Gesammelte Aufsätze zur Sozial- und Wirtschaftsgeschichte.* Tübingen: J. C. B. Mohr (Paul Siebeck), 1924.

GAzW
> *Gesammelte Aufsätze zur Wissenschaftslehre.* 2nd ed. revised and expanded by Johannes Winckelmann. Tübingen: J. C. B. Mohr (Paul Siebeck), 1951. (1st ed. 1922.)

Gerth and Mills
> *From Max Weber: Essays in Sociology.* Translated and edited by Hans H. Gerth and C. Wright Mills. New York: Oxford University Press, 1946.

GPS
> *Gesammelte Politische Schriften.* 2nd ed. revised and expanded by Johannes Winckelmann, with an introduction by Theodor Heuss. Tübingen: J. C. B. Mohr (Paul Siebeck), 1958. (1st ed. München: Drei Masken Verlag, 1921.)

Handelsgesellschaften
> *Zur Geschichte der Handelsgesellschaften in Mittelalter.* (Nach

südeuropäischen Quellen). Stuttgart: Ferdinand Enke, 1889. Reprinted in *GAzSW*, 312–443. (Page references are to the reprint. This was Weber's first dissertation.)

Protestant Ethic
The Protestant Ethic and the Spirit of Capitalism. Translated by Talcott Parsons, with a foreword by R. H. Tawney. New York: Charles Scribner's Sons, 1958 (first publ. London, 1930). (A translation of "Die protestantische Ethik und der Geist des Kapitalismus," *GAzRS*, I, 1–206; first published in *AfS*, 1904–05.)

Rechtssoziologie
Rechtssoziologie. Newly edited from the manuscript with an introduction by Johannes Winckelmann. ("Soziologische Texte," vol. 2.) Neuwied: Hermann Luchterhand Verlag, 1960 (2nd rev. ed. 1967). (This is the German edition of the "Sociology of Law" underlying the revised translation in Part Two, ch. VIII, below.)

Religion of China
The Religion of China. Confucianism and Taoism. Translated and edited by Hans H. Gerth. New edition, with an introduction by C. K. Yang. New York: Macmillan, 1964 (1st ed. Free Press, 1951). (A translation of "Konfuzianismus und Taoismus," Part I of "Die Wirtschaftsethik der Weltreligionen," first published in *AfS*, 1916, reprinted in *GAzRS*, I, 276–536.)

Religion of India
The Religion of India. The Sociology of Hinduism and Buddhism. Translated and edited by Hans H. Gerth and Don Martindale. Glencoe, Ill.: The Free Press, 1958. (A translation of "Hinduismus und Buddhismus," Part II of "Die Wirtschaftsethik der Weltreligionen," first published in *AfS*, 1916–17, reprinted in *GAzRS*, II.)

Rheinstein and Shils
Max Weber on Law in Economy and Society. Translated by Edward Shils and Max Rheinstein, edited and annotated by Rheinstein. Cambridge, Mass.: Harvard University Press, 1954.

Shils and Finch
The Methodology of the Social Sciences. Translated and edited by Edward A. Shils and Henry A. Finch. Glencoe, Ill.: The Free Press, 1949. (A translation of three methodological essays, "Die 'Objektivität' sozialwissenschaftlicher und sozialpolitischer Erkenntnis," *AfS*, 1904; "Kritische Studien auf dem Gebiet kulturwissenschaftlicher Logik," *AfS*, 1906; "Der Sinn der 'Wertfreiheit' der soziologischen und ökonomischen Wissenschaften," *Logos*, 1917/18; reprinted in *GAzW*, 146–214, 215–290, 475–526.)

Theory

The Theory of Social and Economic Organization. Translated by A. M. Henderson and Talcott Parsons, edited with an introduction by Parsons. New York: The Free Press, 1964 (first publ. New York: Oxford University Press, 1947).

Wirtschaftsgeschichte or *Universalgeschichte*

Wirtschaftsgeschichte. Abriss der universalen Sozial- und Wirtschafts-geschichte. Edited from lecture scripts by Siegmund Hellmann and Melchior Palyi. München: Duncker & Humblot, 1923. (2nd ed. 1924; 3rd rev. ed. by Johannes Winckelmann, 1958.)

WuG and *WuG*-Studienausgabe

Wirtschaft und Gesellschaft. Grundriss der verstehenden Soziologie. 4th edition, revised and arranged by Johannes Winckelmann. 2 vols. Tübingen: J. C. B. Mohr (Paul Siebeck), 1956. *WuG*-Studien-ausgabe refers to the licensed paperback edition (2 vols.; Köln-Berlin: Kiepenheuer & Witsch, 1964) which already incorporates some of Winckelmann's further revisions for the forthcoming definitive 5th German edition.

Preface to the 1978 Re-issue

After several years of being out of print, during which time it rapidly attained the status of a bibliophilic rarity, *Economy and Society* is now for the first time available in this country and abroad as a hardcover and a paperback, thanks to the cooperation of the American publishers who have separately published segments of the work in older versions.

The present re-issue is identical with our 1968 edition, although some errata are eliminated. In the meantime, Professor Johannes Winckelmann, on whose fourth German edition of 1956 and 1964 our own edition is based, has completed his fifth and final edition with three hundred pages of annotations—a feat that only a member of his scholarly generation could have accomplished (Tübingen: Mohr-Siebeck, 1976). When the English editors prepared their own edition, they cooperated closely with Winckelmann in clarifying many dubious passages in the posthumously published work and in identifying literary and historical references, but unfortunately, the new annotations of the fifth edition could not be included in the present English re-issue.

Several important Weber translations have appeared since 1968. Edith E. Graber translated Weber's essay "On Some Categories of Interpretive Sociology" (M.A. thesis, Department of Sociology, University of Oklahoma, 1970). This essay, the most important definitions of which appear here in Appendix I, was a fragmentary first draft of the general conceptual underpinnings for the work, but Weber decided to publish it separately in 1913. Just before conceiving the idea of *Economy and Society* Weber finished his great encyclopedic essay on the economic and political history of antiquity, which Alfred Heuss, one of the most respected German classicists, has called "the most original and illuminating study yet made of the economic and social development of antiquity." This work, discussed here in relation to *Economy and Society* in the introduction (xlii–lvii), has now been translated by R. I. Frank under the title *The Agrarian Sociology of Ancient Civilizations* (London: New Left Books, 1976).

Most of Weber's methodological critiques, which prepared the way for the positive formulation of his sociology in *Economy and Society*, have now been translated. Guy Oakes translated and edited *Roscher and Knies: The Logical Problems of Historical Economics* (New York: The Free Press, 1976) and *Critique of Stammler* (New York: The Free Press, 1977). An excursus on the Stammler critique is found in *Economy and Society*, pp. 325–32 below. Oakes has also translated and edited Georg Simmel's *The Problems of the Philosophy of History* (New York: The Free Press, 1977), to which Weber refers in his prefatory note to ch. I, p. 3 below. Louis Schneider translated "Marginal Utility Theory and the So-Called Fundamental Law of Psychophysics," *Social Science Quarterly*, 56:1, 1975, 21–36. This leaves untranslated only Weber's demolition of the "energeticist" theories of culture of the famed chemist and natural philosopher Wilhelm Ostwald, and some scattered but important methodological observations in his substantive writings.

The 1968 introduction by Roth was intended in part as a supplement to Reinhard Bendix's *Max Weber: An Intellectual Portrait* (1960), which for the first time presented comprehensively the substance of Weber's comparative sociology of politics, law and religion as it is found in *Economy and Society* and the *Collected Essays in the Sociology of Religion* (containing the studies of the Protestant ethic and sects in relation to the spirit of capitalism and in contrast to the religious and social order of China, India and Ancient Judaism). This well-known study too was re-issued in 1978 by the University of California Press with a new introduction by Roth, which covers the Weber literature accumulated since 1960. One further yield from Bendix's and Roth's concern with Weber was a joint volume, *Scholarship and Partisanship*, also published by the University of California Press in 1971. Moreover, Roth has continued his methodological exploration of *Economy and Society* in three other essays, "Socio-Historical Model and Developmental Theory," *American Sociological Review*, 40:2, April 75, 148–57; "History and Sociology," *British Journal of Sociology*, 27:3, Sept. 76, 306–18; and "Religion and Revolutionary Beliefs," *Social Forces*, 55:2, Dec. 76, 257–72.

An up-to-date bibliography of the almost limitless secondary literature is Constans Seyfarth and Gert Schmidt, eds., *Max Weber Bibliographie: Eine Dokumentation der Sekundärliteratur* (Stuttgart: Enke, 1977), 208 pp. For the latest bibliography of Weber's own writings, see Dirk Käsler, "Max-Weber-Bibliographie," *Kölner Zeitschrift für Soziologie*, 27:4, 1975, 703–30.

For the present re-issue the editors are greatly indebted to the unflagging interest and efforts of Mr. Grant Barnes of the University of California Press and to the support of Mr. Georg Siebeck, of the firm of Mohr-Siebeck in Tübingen, the German publisher of Weber's works.

Finally, we dedicate with sorrow this edition to the memory of Carolyn Cain Roth (1934–1975), who for several years lived with the burden of our intense labors, showing great forebearance and retaining the salutary distance of an artistic vision, which should always balance the sober concerns of scholarship.

BAINBRIDGE ISLAND, WASHINGTON   *Guenther Roth*
Scarsdale, New York   *Claus Wittich*
February 1977

Preface

This is the first complete English edition of *Economy and Society*. All hitherto unavailable chapters and sections have been translated and the annotation has been considerably expanded. The Appendix contains a brief terminological supplement and one of Weber's major political essays. All previously translated parts used here have been thoroughly revised and many passages have been rewritten. The original translators of these chapters are absolved from all responsibility for the present version of their work. We would like to thank Ephraim Fischoff for going over our revision of his translation of the "Sociology of Religion" (Part Two, ch. VI) and for making further suggestions and offering other help. However, he too should not be held responsible for the final version.

A number of extant translations were completely replaced: in Part One, ch. IV, "Status Groups and Classes"; in Part Two, ch. III:3, "The Regulation of Sexual Relations in the Household," ch. IV:3, "The Oikos," ch. XIV:*i–ii*, "Charisma and Its Transformations," and ch. XVI, "The City." This last book-length chapter was newly translated by Wittich; all other new translations were first done by Roth. Our strategy of translation is explained in the Introduction.

The following earlier translations of sections of *Wirtschaft und Gesellschaft* have been used and revised with the permission of the publishers, which is gratefully acknowledged.

Ephraim Fischoff, trans., *The Sociology of Religion* (Boston: Beacon Press, 1963), pp. 1–274; now Part Two, ch. VI;

Hans Gerth and C. Wright Mills, trans. and eds., *From Max Weber: Essays in Sociology* (New York: Oxford University Press, 1946), pp. 159–244, 253–262; now Part Two, chs. IX:3–6, XI, and XIV:*iii*;

Ferdinand Kolegar, trans., "The Household Community" and "Ethnic

Groups," in Talcott Parsons *et al.*, eds., *Theories of Society* (New York: The Free Press of Glencoe, 1961), vol. I, pp. 296–298, 302–309; now Part Two, ch. III:1, ch. IV:2, and ch. V:2;

Talcott Parsons, ed. (A. M. Henderson and T. Parsons, trans.), *The Theory of Social and Economic Organization* (New York: The Free Press of Glencoe, 1964; originally published by Oxford University Press, 1947), pp. 87–423; now Part One, chs. I–III;

Max Rheinstein, ed. (Edward Shils and Max Rheinstein, trans.), *Max Weber on Law in Economy and Society* (Cambridge, Mass.: Harvard University Press, 1954), pp. 11–348; now Part Two, ch. I, chs. VII–VIII, ch. IX:1–2, and ch. X.

Without the dedication and hard labor of the previous translators the present edition might never have been undertaken. Hans Gerth, who spent a singular amount of time on the translation of Weber's works, deserves special recognition. The broadest contribution to the reception of Weber's thought has clearly been made by Talcott Parsons' translations and writings.

Our special gratitude goes to Prof. Johannes Winckelmann, the German editor of Weber's works and head of the Max Weber Institute at the University of Munich, who gave us access to his text revisions for the forthcoming 5th edition of *Wirtschaft und Gesellschaft* and always freely shared his thoughts on textual and other problems.

Finally, we want to thank Hans L. Zetterberg, who combines scholarship and entrepreneurship; he held out the challenge, patiently waited for the manuscript, and then saw it through to its publication. We are also grateful to Mr. Robert Palmer for preparing the index and to Mr. Sidney Solomon of the Free Press for supervising the technical preparation of the work and for designing the volumes.

BERLIN AND NEW YORK

March 1968

Guenther Roth

Claus Wittich

INTRODUCTION
by Guenther Roth

We know of no scientifically ascertainable ideals. To be sure, that makes our efforts more arduous than those of the past, since we are expected to create our ideals from within our breast in the very age of subjectivist culture; but we must not and cannot promise a fool's paradise and an easy road to it, neither in thought nor in action. It is the stigma of our human dignity that the peace of our souls cannot be as great as the peace of one who dreams of such a paradise.

Weber in 1909

1. A Claim

This work is the sum of Max Weber's scholarly vision of society. It has become a constitutive part of the sociological imagination as it is understood today. *Economy and Society* was the first strictly empirical comparison of social structure and normative order in world-historical depth. In this manner it transcended the plenitude of "systems" that remained speculative even as they claimed to establish a science of society.

Decades have passed since the manuscript was begun and left unfinished, yet few works in the realm of social science have aged so little. Its impact has been considerable over the years, although in a fragmented and erratic fashion as the various parts became available only piecemeal to the English reader or remained altogether out of reach. Weber's ideas on social action and sociological typology, on instrumental and substantive rationality, on formal and material justice, on bureaucracy and charisma, on religious beliefs and economic conduct, have been gradually assimilated by social scientists—by way of accurate reception, imaginative adaptation and, not too infrequently, inventive misinterpretation.

The renaissance of comparative study in the nineteen-sixties has restored some of the original intellectual setting of *Economy and Society*.

This has given a new pertinency to the work and is one reason for the complete English edition; another is the hoped-for correction of the uneven influence exerted by the isolated parts. Now the work has a fair chance to be understood as a whole, and its readers have a better opportunity to comprehend it—this will be a test for both.

Economy and Society is Weber's only major didactic treatise. It was meant to be merely an introduction, but in its own way it is the most demanding "text" yet written by a sociologist. The precision of its definitions, the complexity of its typologies and the wealth of its historical content make the work, as it were, a continuous challenge at several levels of comprehension: for the advanced undergraduate who gropes for his sense of society, for the graduate student who must develop his own analytical skills, and for the scholar who must match wits with Weber.

Economy and Society is part of the body of knowledge on which Weber drew in his unwitting testament, his speeches on "Science as a Vocation" and "Politics as a Vocation," which he delivered shortly after the end of the first World War before a small number of politically bewildered students. By now thousands of students have read these two rhetorical masterpieces with their poignant synopsis of his philosophical and political outlook as well as of his scholarly animus. Yet the very compactness of the two speeches impedes easy comprehension. *Economy and Society* elaborates much that is barely visible in them. However, it minimizes the propagation of Weber's own philosophical and political views, since it wants to establish a common ground for empirical investigation on which men of different persuasions can stand; in contrast to some of the methodological polemics, *Economy and Society* is meant to set a positive example. Yet there is more to it than is readily apparent. The work contains a theory of the possibilities and limitations of political democracy in an industrialized and bureaucratized society, a theory that Weber considered not only empirically valid but politically realistic as against a host of political isms: romanticist nationalism, agrarianism, corporate statism, syndicalism, anarchism, and the Marxism of the time. Hence, there is in the work an irreducible element of what Weber considered political common sense, but this does not vitiate the relative value-neutrality of the conceptual structure. Moreover, the work is full of irony, sarcasm and the love of paradox; a dead-pan expression may imply a swipe at the *Kaiser*, status-conscious professors or pretentious *littérateurs*.[1] And finally, with all its seemingly static typologies, the

---

1. Ironic formulations and wordplays are hard to render in translation, and it would have been self-defeating pedantry to explain more than a fraction in the editorial notes.

work is a sociologist's world history, his way of reconstructing the paths of major civilizations.

2. Sociological Theory, Comparative Study and Historical Explanation

Economy and Society builds a sociological scaffolding for raising some of the big questions about the origins and the possible directions of the modern world. Weber set out to find more specific and empirically tenable answers to those questions than had been given previously. He belonged to the small number of concerned men who shared neither the wide-spread belief in Progress, which was about to be shattered by the first World War, nor the new philosophical irrationalism, which had begun to appeal to many younger men.

Weber's image of "economy and society" is so widely shared today among research-oriented students of society that in its *most general* formulation it no longer appears exceptional, unless we remember that it drew the lines against Social Darwinism, Marxism and other isms of the time. Weber rejected the prevalent evolutionary and mono-causal theories, whether idealist or materialist, mechanistic or organicist; he fought both the reductionism of social scientists and the surface approach of historians, both the persistent search for hidden "deeper" causes and the ingrained aversion against historically transcendent concepts. He took it for granted that the economic structure of a group was one of its major if variable determinants and that society was an arena for group conflicts. He did not believe, however, in the laws of class struggle, jungle or race; rather, he saw men struggle most of the time under created laws and within established organizations. Given the incomplete reception of his work, the roles he attributed to force and legitimacy have been overemphasized in isolation. *Economy and Society* clearly states that men act as they do because of belief in authority, enforcement by staffs, a calculus of self-interest, and a good dose of habit. However, Weber was not much interested in master-key statements on the nature of Society and was set against the "need for world-formulae" (*Weltformelbedürfnis*). Unlike Engels, he saw no grounds for assuming an "ultimately determining element in history." *Economy and Society* demonstrates the rather concrete level on which he wanted to approach sociological theory and historical generalization.

After 1903 Weber clarified his methodological position toward the cultural and social sciences in half a dozen essays.[2] But in *Economy and*

2. Cf. 1. *Roscher und Knies und die logischen Probleme der historischen Nationalökonomie* (1903/6), 145 pp.; 2. *Die "Objektivität" sozialwissenschaft-*

Society he focussed on those concepts and typologies that would directly aid the researcher. He developed his sociological theory—his *Kategorien-lehre,* as he sometimes called it—as an open-ended, yet logically consistent formulation of fundamental aspects of social action, on the one hand, and of historical types of concerted action ("general ideal types") on the other. The construction of such trans-epochal and trans-cultural types as, for example, enterprise and *oikos* or bureaucracy and hierocracy, makes sociological theory historically comparative. In this way sociological theory provides the researcher with the dimensional concepts and empirical types that are prerequisites for the kind of comparative mental experiment and imaginative extrapolation without which causal explanation is impossible in history.

Weber's sociological theory, then, grew out of wide-ranging historical research and was meant to be applied again to history, past and in the making. In addition to theory in this generically historical sense, he employed substantive theories of differing degrees of historical specificity:

1. Theories explaining a relatively homogeneous historical configuration ("individual ideal type"), such as the spirit of capitalism;

2. Theories about relatively heterogeneous, but historically interrelated configurations, such as the "economic theory of the ancient states of the Mediterranean";

3. Theories ("rules of experience") that amount to a summary of a number of historical constellations, without being testable propositions in the strict sense: for example, the observation that foreign conquerors and native priests have formed alliances, or that reform-minded monks and secular rulers have at times cooperated in spite of their ineradicable antagonism. The occurrence of the former kind of collaboration, as in ancient Judaism, or its failure to come about in Hellas, due to the battle at Marathon,[3] may have far-reaching historical consequences—one reason for the scholar's interest in such historical "summaries."

---

licher und sozialpolitischer Erkenntnis (1904), 68 pp.; 3. *Kritische Studien auf dem Gebiet der kulturwissenschaftlichen Logik* (1905), 75 pp.; 4. *Stammlers "Überwindung" der materialistischen Geschichtsauffassung* (1907), 68 pp., with a posthumously published postscript (20 pp.); 5. *Die Grenznutzlehre und das "psychophysische Grundgesetz"* (1908), 15 pp.; 6. *"Energetische" Kulturtheorien* (1909), 26 pp.; 7. *Über den Sinn der "Wertfreiheit" der soziologischen und ökonomischen Wissenschaften* (1917/18), prepared as a memorandum for a meeting of the *Verein für Sozialpolitik* in 1913. All are reprinted in *GAzW* (for this and other abbreviations used for Weber's works, see the list following this Introduction). For English versions of essays 2, 3, and 7, see Max Weber, *The Methodology of the Social Sciences* (Edward A. Shils and Henry A. Finch, trans. and eds.; Glencoe, Ill.: The Free Press, 1949).

3. On the battle of Marathon and the category of objective possibility, cf. Weber in Shils and Finch (eds.), *Methodology . . . ,* 174.

Of course, the explanation of any specific historical event also remains "theoretical" in that it subsumes many discrete actions and is merely plausible, because unverifiable in the manner of the experimental sciences. Weber was acutely aware of this difficulty, which was exacerbated by the scarcity and unreliability of the sources in most areas of his investigations, ancient and modern.

Sociologists live, and suffer, from their dual task: to develop generalizations and to explain particular cases. This is the *raison d'être* of sociology as well as its inherent tension. It would be incompatible with the spirit of Weber's approach to value the transhistorical ("functionalist") generalizations of any formal sociological theory more highly than the competent analysis of a major historical phenomenon with the help of a fitting typology. The sociology of *Economy and Society* is "Clio's handmaiden"; the purpose of comparative study is the explanation of a given historical problem. Analogies and parallels, which at the time tended to be used for evolutionary and morphological constructions and spurious causal interpretations, had for Weber merely instrumental purpose:

> Whoever does not see the *exclusive* task of "history" in making itself superfluous through the demonstration that "everything has happened before" and that all, or almost all, differences are matters of *degree*—an obvious truth—will put the stress on the *changes (Verschiebungen)* that emerge in spite of all parallels, and will use the similarities only to establish the *distinctiveness (Eigenart)* vis-à-vis each other of the two orbits [i.e., the ancient and the medieval]. . . . A genuinely critical *comparison* of the developmental stages of the ancient polis and the medieval city . . . would be rewarding and fruitful—but only if such a comparison does *not* chase after "analogies" and "parallels" in the manner of the presently fashionable general schemes of development; in other words, it should be concerned with the *distinctiveness* of each of the two developments that were finally so different, and the purpose of the comparison must be the causal *explanation* of the difference. It remains true, of course, that this causal explanation requires as an indispensable preparation the isolation (that means, abstraction) of the individual components of the course of events, and for each component the orientation toward rules of experience and the formulation of *clear concepts* without which causal attribution is nowhere possible. This should be taken into account especially in the economic field in which inadequate conceptual precision can produce the most distorted evaluations.[4]

Weber had in mind men like Wilhelm Roscher, Ranke's pupil, for whom

4. "Agrarverhältnisse im Altertum," in *GAzSW*, 257, 288. (Cf. below, n. 27.)

peoples are "generic biological entities"—as Hintze put it quite adequately. Roscher has explicitly stated that for science the development of peoples is in principle *always the same,* and in spite of appearances to the contrary, in truth nothing new happens under the sun, but always the old with "random" and hence scientifically irrelevant admixtures. This obviously is a specifically "scientific" (*naturwissenschaftliche*) perspective.[5]

Weber's comparative approach was directed against theories of historical sameness as well as theories of universal stages. He opposed in particular the interpretation of Antiquity, including ancient capitalism, as a "modern" phenomenon; this interpretation was advanced by "realistic" historians reacting against the humanist tradition with its idealization of classic Greece and Rome. Weber equally rejected the contemporary stage theories of rural and urban economic development. He, too, believed in a "general cultural development," but he focussed on the dynamics of specific historical phenomena, their development as well as their decline. For this purpose he employed several comparative devices (which will be illustrated below, p. xliii): (a) the identification of similarities as a first step in causal explanation; (b) the negative comparison; (c) the illustrative analogy; (d) the metaphorical analogy.

The ideal type too has a comparative purpose. It was Weber's solution to the old issue of conceptual realism versus nominalism, but in the context of the time it was his primary answer to the scientific notion of law and to the evolutionary stage theories. Weber wrote much more on the logical status of the ideal type than on his comparative strategy. This imbalance is reflected in the literature; a great deal has been written about the ideal type, but very little that is pertinent to the art of comparative study. As historical "summaries" of varying degrees of specificity, ideal types are compared with slices of historical reality.[6] For the researcher the issue is not whether the ideal type is less "real" than other historical concepts; rather, his task consists in choosing the level of conceptual specificity appropriate for the problem at hand. Weber's ideal types, as the reader can himself see, involve a theory about the dynamics and alternative courses of the phenomena involved. They are not meant

5. "Roscher und Knies . . . ," in *GAzW,* 23.

6. "All expositions for example of the 'essence' of Christianity are ideal types enjoying only a necessarily very relative and problematic validity when they are intended . . . as the historical portrayal of facts. On the other hand, such presentations are of great value for research and of high systematic value for expository purposes when they are used as conceptual instruments for *comparison* and the *measurement* of reality. They are indispensable for this purpose." Weber in Shils and Finch (eds.), *Methodology . . . ,* 97.

to fit an evolutionary scheme, but they do have a developmental dimension.

Ideal types are constructed with the help of historical rules of experience, which are used as heuristic propositions. For example, Weber's theory of monarchy includes the observation that monarchs throughout the ages, from ancient Mesopotamia up to Imperial Germany, have been welfare-minded because they needed the support of the lower strata against the higher; however, these higher strata, nobility and priesthood, usually remain important to the maintenance of monarchic power and legitimacy. Hence, the stability of monarchy rests in part on the ruler's ability to balance the two groups. It is from such observations, which permit the necessary specification, that the ideal type of patrimonialism (Part Two, ch. XII below) emerges.

Weber's comparative strategy was directed toward establishing, with the aid of his typologies, (1) the *differences* between modern and older conditions, and (2) the *causes* of the differences. This involved the exploration of secular phenomena that had "dropped out" of history (for example, ancient capitalism) but that were culturally important in themselves or useful for identifying modernity; it also involved the search for the "causal chains" of history.

In the absence of a reductionist one-factor scheme and of historical "one-way streets," the relationship of economy, society and polity became for Weber a multi-faceted set of problems encompassing the interplay of organization and technique of production, social stratification, civil and military administration, and religious and secular ideology. Apart from the issue of the uniqueness of Western civilization, this perspective too led Weber to a comparative interest in the workings of civilizations.

Such a comprehensive program of research required broad knowledge and expertise in several fields. The historical content of *Economy and Society* rests on a large body of scholarly literature, but also on Weber's previous research. In drawing on historical sources and secondary literature, Weber had an advantage over those historians whose training had been mainly philosophical and philological, partly because he was a trained jurist and economist, partly because he had developed a sociological framework within which he could address precise questions to the secondary literature.

An adequate understanding of *Economy and Society* should encompass Weber's previous research and writings and perceive the close links. Since Weber rendered no systematic account of his strategy of comparative study or of the intellectual development that led him

to the writing of *Economy and Society*, it appears worthwhile to trace
here the methodological and substantive lines of reasoning that con-
verge in the later work; since almost all of the earlier writings are
untranslated, they will be quoted more extensively than would otherwise
be desirable.[7]

3. The Legal Forms of Medieval Trading Enterprises

Even for a man of Weber's generation it was rare to gain competence
as historian of both Antiquity and the Middle Ages, and then to combine this with the study of contemporary concerns—industrialization,
bureaucratization, democratization. Weber began his career in legal and
economic history as both a "Romanist" and "Germanist"; he transcended
the ideological antagonism of the two schools that so sharply divided
German jurisprudence in the 19th century. Weber wanted, first of all, a
good grasp of the varieties of legal and economic arrangements; hence
he emulated the tremendous learning of an Otto Gierke, but he was
out of sympathy with the persistent inclination of the Germanists to
reduce European history to the dichotomy of Romanized authoritarian
organization (*Herrschaftsverband*) and Germanic egalitarian association
(*Genossenschaft*).

From the beginning of his academic career Weber addressed himself
to two broad historical questions: The origins and nature of (1) capitalism in Antiquity, the Middle Ages and modern times, (2) political
domination and social stratification in the three ages. His dissertation of
1889 dealt with legal institutions of medieval capitalism, his *Habilitation*
of 1891 (that is, the second doctorate required for academic teaching)
with the relationship between Roman politics and capitalism.

The dissertation was a "Germanist" study, *On the History of the
Medieval Trading Companies*, written under Levin Goldschmidt.[8]
Based largely on printed Italian and Spanish sources, it dealt with
various forms of limited and unlimited partnership that emerged with
the revival of maritime and inland trade and urban craft production.

---

7. In the following, attention will be given particularly to those studies that
were omitted in Reinhard Bendix, *Max Weber: An Intellectual Portrait* (New
York: Doubleday, 1960), Anchor edition, xxiii; see chs. I and II on Weber's early
activities, his scholarly and political response to the problems of industrialization
in Germany, especially the agrarian issue in Prussia east of the Elbe river (East
Elbia). The present introduction is an effort to supplement Bendix' work and the
introduction by Hans Gerth and C. Wright Mills in *From Max Weber: Essays
in Sociology* (New York: Oxford University Press, 1946).

8. *Zur Geschichte der Handelsgesellschaften im Mittelalter* (*Nach südeuropäischen Quellen*) (Stuttgart: Enke, 1889), reprinted in GAzSW, 312–443.

Medieval capitalism required legal institutions for implementing the sharing of risk and profit and defining the liabilities and responsibilities of the parties to a joint venture. Weber investigated the differences between the partnership forms originating from the institutions of overseas trade in cities like Genoa and Pisa and those that emerged from the family craft enterprises of inland cities like Florence. The former were typically *ad hoc* associations for trading ventures, the latter more commonly continuous households, with family and other members, often surviving several generations. The partnership forms of overseas trade (*commenda, societas maris*) were only concerned with delimiting responsibilities and benefits, but the household enterprises long combined capitalist and communist modes of operation, before internal closure set in and they disintegrated as units of commercial enterprise.

A few Weberian guidelines can already be perceived in this highly technical analysis. Economic and legal development are intertwined, yet "law follows criteria that are, from the economic viewpoint, frequently extraneous";[9] it may regulate economic conditions far removed from its own dogmatic and social origins—this was a critique of correspondence theories, especially of the economically determinist variety. The insistence on the importance of the legal order for economic action is also the starting point of the first chapter of *Economy and Society* (Ch. I: 1 of the older Part Two). Here the consistency of Weber's basic perspectives over time is indicated. But the strength of the dissertation lay less in such a general position than in the vivid and detailed treatment and the ability to argue firmly with the historical opinions of renowned scholars such as Gierke and Rudolf Sohm. Yet Weber conceded his inability to arrive at novel overall conclusions. Already in the preparatory stage of the dissertation he commented in his ironic fashion:

> I had to learn Italian and Spanish well enough to work myself through books and to read hundreds of statutes . . . worst of all, statutes written in such ancient dreadful dialects that one can only be astonished by the ability of men at the time to understand such jargon. Well, I was kept busy, and if not much has come out of it, it is less my fault than that of the Italian and Spanish magistrates who failed to include in the statutes the very things I sought.[10]

Weber felt that he had not been able to answer a controversial question of the time: To what extent were the early forms of the capitalist partnership and firm shaped by Roman and Germanic legal influ-

9. *GAzSW*, 322.
10. Max Weber, *Jugendbriefe*, ed. Marianne Weber (Tübingen: Mohr, n.d.), 274.

ences? Conclusive answers to Gierke and Sohm appeared possible to him only after further comparative study, including also Germany. As it was, the dissertation limited itself to the differences among various forms of commercial institutions, in order to lay the groundwork for later research.

The dissertation shows that the exposition in *Economy and Society* of the open and closed relationships of household, family, kin-group and enterprise (esp. chs. II:2, III:1, and IV:2 of Part Two) rests on long-standing knowledge of historical specifics and early familiarity with the literature. The later treatment of the associations is a mere summary with a systematic place in a wider context, yet the illustrations, which at first sight seem to fill the "empty boxes" somewhat arbitrarily, are often based on careful consideration in those earlier studies.

Two years after the dissertation Weber completed a "Romanist" *Habilitation* on *The Roman Agrarian History in Its Bearing on Public and Private Law*,[11] which qualified him to read Roman, Germanic and commercial law. He became a law professor in Berlin in 1893 and almost immediately took over for the ailing Goldschmidt.

4. *Economic and Political Power in Ancient Germanic History*

Weber wrote his *Roman Agrarian History* with the encouragement of August Meitzen, who was then working on his monumental comparative study, *The Settlement and Agrarian Structure of the Western and Eastern Germanic Tribes, Celts, Romans, Finns and Slaves* (3 vols., 1895). For his analysis of property forms and social structure Meitzen ingeniously used the ancient survey maps of the villages. Weber proceeded from Meitzen's chapter on the Roman land surveys. This undertaking was far more difficult than the study of the medieval trading companies; the findings were bound to be much more hypothetical because of the paucity and ambiguity of the sources. Weber believed he had shown that Roman agriculture could be analyzed adequately with concepts derived from other Indo-Germanic agrarian structures. However, seventeen years later, in his second major work on Antiquity, he wrote that he was still defending the work, but that it had indeed been full of "youthful sins" and particularly mistaken in its attempt "to apply Meitzen's categories to heterogeneous conditions."[12] Thus, in his early years Weber too had been influenced by evolutionary analogues, but by

11. *Die römische Agrargeschichte in ihrer Bedeutung für das Staats- und Privatrecht* (Stuttgart: Enke, 1891).

12. Cf. *Agrargeschichte*, 2, and "Agrarverhältnisse . . . ," *GAzSW*, 287.

1904, when he intervened in the dispute about ancient Germanic social structure,[13] he combatted them energetically. Together with the critique of his contemporaries' methodology, Weber elaborated his view of the historic relationship between political and economic power, a view that became important for the typology of domination in *Economy and Society*. At issue was the origin of manorial domination (*Grundherrschaft*), for decades the center of scholarly debate. There was a tendency to explain the whole political and economic history of Germany in terms of the *Grundherrschaft* and its variants.

The thesis of the predominance of manorial domination as early as the period of Caesar and Tacitus was upheld by Georg Friedrich Knapp and his school, especially by Werner Wittich; they rejected the older view according to which manorial domination resulted from the transformation of the Frankish levy into a cavalry of feudal vassals. As against the thesis of the Knapp school, Meitzen asserted the free status of the Germanic peasantry of late Antiquity and pointed to the equal parcelling of land in the communes. Meitzen did leave an opening to his adversaries by acknowledging the nomadic way of life of Germanic tribes in Caesar's time, but he interpreted the transition from nomadic stock-breeding to husbandry as an emancipation of "labor from property," a phrase reminiscent of Karl Rodbertus' views. For Meitzen the Germanic settlement was the creation of the drive for economic independence inherent in the equalitarian spirit of the people. Knapp's school, however, insisted that the free Germanic man of Caesar's day had been a cattle-owner who despised agriculture and those who tilled the soil. The origin of *Grundherrschaft* was seen then to lie in the rule of cattle-owners over peasants. Wittich, for one, buttressed his view with Richard Hildebrand's scheme of cultural and legal development. "This theory," Weber commented, "is one of the attempts, recently so numerous, to comprehend cultural development in the manner of biological processes as a lawful sequence of universal stages."[14] Hence the assertion of a universal nomadic stage, at least in the Occident. The theory worked with analogies from the contemporary nomadic life of Bedouins and

13. "Der Streit um den Charakter der altgermanischen Sozialverfassung in der deutschen Literatur des letzten Jahrzehnts," in *GAzSW*, 508–556; first published in *Jahrbücher für Nationalökonomie und Statistik*, 3d series, vol. 28 (1904).

14. *GAzSW*, 513. Cf. Richard Hildebrand, *Recht und Sitte auf den primitiveren wirtschaftlichen Kulturstufen* (Jena: Fischer, 1896); for Hildebrand's counterattack, which rejects Weber's interpretation of Germanic agriculture in Caesar's time, see the second edition of 1907, pp. 55f., 64f.; see also Werner Wittich's review essay on Hildebrand, "Die wirtschaftliche Kultur der Deutschen zur Zeit Caesar's," *Historische Zeitschrift*, vol. 79, 1897, 45–67.

Kirghiz, applying them to elucidate Germanic prehistory. If these nomads scorned agricultural labor, by inference the Germanic nomads must
have done likewise. Weber objected:

> This procedure of a scholar whom I too hold in high esteem is a
> good example of the manner in which the concept of "cultural stages"
> should not be applied scientifically. Concepts such as "nomadic," "semi-
> nomadic," etc., are indispensable for descriptive purposes. For research,
> the continuous comparison of the developmental stages of peoples and
> the search for analogies are a heuristic means well suited, if cautiously
> used, to explain the causes of distinctiveness of each individual develop-
> ment. But it is a serious misunderstanding of the rationale of cultural
> history to consider the construction of stages as *more* than such a
> heuristic means, and the subsumption of historical events under such
> abstractions as the *purpose* of scholarly work—as Hildebrand does—;
> it is a violation of proper methodology to view a "cultural stage" as
> anything but a concept, to treat it as an entity in the manner of bio-
> logical organisms, or an Hegelian "idea," from which the individual
> components "emanate," and hence to use the "stage" for arriving at
> *conclusions* by analogy: If the historic phenomenon y usually follows
> x, or if both tend to be co-existent, y_1 must follow x_1, or be co-existent,
> since x and x_1 are conceptual components of "analogous" stages of
> culture.
>
> The mental construct of a cultural stage merely means, analyti-
> cally speaking, that the individual phenomena of which it is composed
> are "adequate" to one another, that they have—as we could say—a
> certain measure of inner "affinity," but not that they are related in any
> determinate way (*Gesetzmässigkeit*). . . .
>
> The belief in a universal "stage" of nomadic existence, through
> which all tribes passed and from which the settlement developed, can
> no longer be retained in view of our knowledge of the development of
> Asiatic peoples and after Hahn's investigations [*Die Haustiere*, 1896].
> At any rate, the knowledge of a by no means primitive form of agri-
> culture among the Indo-Germanic peoples goes back into the darkest
> past.[15]

In Weber's view the Germanic tribes of Caesar's day were not nomadic nor were the freemen a stratum of landlords (*Grundherren*) who
left most work to slaves and women; slaves were not a substantial part
of the workforce and the status differentiation between warrior and
peasant did not exist at the beginning of recorded history; rather, the
Germanic freemen were transformed very gradually into the politically
disenfranchised and economically harassed peasants of the Middle Ages.

Weber accepted Meitzen's view that the German village with its land
distribution was a product of legal autonomy, a monopolistic association
of relative equals, not a product of manorial decree. However, in contrast

15. GAzSW, 517, 524.

to Meitzen's assumption of an equalitarian folk spirit, Weber took an economically more realistic line and reasoned persuasively that the equal parcelling out of land by a closed association pointed to the narrowing of economic opportunities (land shortage), similar to the monopolistic policies of medieval guilds.[16]

In examining the Roman sources, Weber pointed out that Caesar's report about the Suevi was no proof for a nomadic way of life of the Germanic tribes. The Suevi, a frontier people, had developed into a group of professional warriors, engaging in periodic raids on adjacent areas and neglecting agriculture. This brought Weber to the phenomenon of warrior communism and his most general point: the historical primacy of political over economic factors:

> If one wants at all to search for distant analogies such as might be offered by the Kirghiz and Bedouins, the traits of an "autarkous state" [an allusion to Fichte's collectivist utopia] found among the Suevi will remind one much more of the robber communism that existed in Antiquity on the Liparian islands or—if the expression be permitted— the "officers' mess communism" of the ancient Spartans, or of the grandiose booty communism of a Caliph Omar. In one phrase, these traits are the outcome of "warrior communism." They can easily be explained as a result of purely military interests. . . . They would scarcely be in tune with the living conditions of a tribe stagnant at the nomadic stage and ruled by great cattle-owners in a patriarchal manner. . . .
>
> The oldest social differentiation of Germanic and Mediterranean prehistory is, as far as we can see, determined primarily politically, in part religiously, *not,* however, primarily economically. Economic differentiation must be considered more as a consequence and epiphenomenon or, if you want it in the most fashionable terms, as a "function" of the former, rather than vice versa. . . .
>
> If the term may be applied to prehistory at all, a "knightly" life style . . . often goes together with a manorial position; in fact, this is the rule once private hereditary landownership has fully developed. . . . However, it is by no means generally true that this life style leads to, or is related to, manorial superordination over other freemen—in the age of Homer and Hesiod as little as in that of the Germanic epics. It means a reversal of the usual causal relationship to view the later manorial constitution not as a consequence but as the original basis of the priviliged position of the high-ranking families. The historical primacy of manorial domination appears highly unlikely, first of all, because in an age of land surplus mere land ownership could not very well be the basis of economic power.[17]

16. This is again the phenomenon of closed economic relationships treated in Part Two, ch. II:2 below.

17. *GAzSW,* 523, 554f.

Weber concluded his essay with a reminder about the triviality inherent in correct scholarly results and anticipated that the older view would probably survive the recent challenges: "This may appear trivial. But unfortunately, trivial results, by their very quality, are often the correct ones."

It is from concrete historical issues such as these that Weber fashioned, in *Economy and Society*, his contrast between patrimonial domination and charismatic rule. The joining of these military with religious phenomena established the category of charismatic domination.[18]

5. *The Roman Empire and Imperial Germany*

Weber had an early interest in the comparison and comparability of Imperial Germany and Imperial Rome. On this score he was close to Theodor Mommsen, who described the Roman Republic in the terms of liberal political theory and polemicized against Imperial Germany with analogies from Antiquity. In the academic public Weber's comparative interest was at first not widely noticed. The *Roman Agrarian History* proved technically too difficult to be understood by more than a very small group of scholars. Alfred Heuss, today counted among the foremost Roman historians, has pointed out that Weber

> was the first to take the Roman agrarian writers (Cato, Varro, Columella) seriously, examining them in a matter-of-fact way . . . and uncovering the crass principles of Roman agrarian capitalism in its technical details. In this respect, the book, although generally neglected by the historians, became path-breaking, and subsequent research had to continue along its line of inquiry. . . . Who else among the historians of the time was capable of handling the legal sources and the technical language of land surveyors, both of which Weber combined in a virtuoso fashion? The book, hard to understand because of its dry and remote subject matter, is an ingenious work.[19]

Among the historians of the time the aged Mommsen was best qualified to judge Weber's work. He hailed its publication and welcomed its author onto his previously exclusive ground: the borderlines of Roman private and public law. As early as the occasion of Weber's doctoral defense Mommsen had said: "When the time comes for me to descend into the grave, there is no one to whom I would rather say: 'Son, here is my spear, it has become too heavy for my arm,' than Max

18. Specifically, booty and military communism is treated in Part Two, ch. XIV:6.
19. Alfred Heuss, "Max Webers Bedeutung für die Geschichte des griechisch-römischen Altertums," *Historische Zeitschrift*, vol. 201, 1965, 535.

Weber."[20] However, Weber did not become his successor and quickly moved beyond the confines of ancient history. In the early nineties he involved himself in a questionnaire study of the conditions of rural laborers conducted under the auspices of the *Verein für Sozialpolitik*, the most important association of professors, politicians and higher civil servants for the study of the Social Question in Imperial Germany. Between 1892 and 1894 Weber published extensively on farm labor, and, in contrast to the *Roman Agrarian History*, his new writings did attract considerable attention. Weber's turn of interest was acknowledged with the offer of an economics chair at the University of Freiburg, which he accepted in 1894; this was an extraordinary offer for a jurist—not even the usual "rehabilitation" (that is, the writing of a second *Habilitation* to qualify in a different academic field) was required.

In Freiburg Weber delivered a popular lecture on "The Social Causes of the Decay of Ancient Civilization" (1896).[21] The major political link between his studies of Antiquity and of East Elbia was the problem of the "rise and fall of empire." The common theme was the self-destruction of empire through the cleavage between the rich and the poor. In the *Roman Agrarian History* Weber had searched for the "social strata and economic interest groups" behind the expansionism of the Empire and the unparalleled capitalist exploitation: "It is likely that the political domination of a large polity has never been so lucrative."[22] The Roman state suffered from a "convulsive sickness of its social body." Weber freely stated his value judgment. The transition from the condition of the barrack slaves to that of hereditarily attached peasants, who were permitted families of their own and conditional land use, appeared to him a decisive change for the better:

> The moral significance of this development need scarcely be emphasized. One must remember that at the beginning of the Empire Bebel's ideal of legal marriage [i.e., freely contracted and dissoluble marriage] was realized *de facto* among the upper strata, *de jure* for citizens in general. The consequences are known. In this study it has not been possible to show the connection between the influence of the Christian ideal of marriage and this economic development, but it should be obvious that the separation of the slaves from the manorial household was an element of profound internal recovery (*Gesundung*), which

20. Marianne Weber, *Max Weber. Ein Lebensbild* (Tübingen: Mohr, 1926), 121—(henceforth cited as *Lebensbild*).

21. "Die sozialen Gründe des Untergangs der antiken Kultur," in GAzSW, 289–311; a translation by Christian Mackauer in *Journal of General Education*, V, 1950–51, 75–88.

22. *Agrargeschichte*, 6.

was by no means bought too dearly with the relapse of the "upper ten thousand" into centuries of barbarism.[23]

Weber saw the social developments in East Elbia against the background of Roman history. He observed with apprehension the proletarization of the peasants in the second half of the 19th century. The manorial *Junkers* gradually turned into capitalist entrepreneurs; they preferred cheap seasonal labor—little more than barrack slaves—from beyond the Russian frontier to a permanent and landowning German workforce. Weber foresaw grave dangers in the *Junkers'* labor and tariff policies and rejected their hollow claim to be the military pillars of the Empire even as they undermined it socially and economically. He warned his elders in the *Verein für Sozialpolitik* in 1893 that "the most horrible of all horrors is a landowning proletariat for whom the inherited land has become a curse."[24]

In his 1896 Freiburg address Weber repeated his judgments and cautioned his classically educated audience against its ready belief that the decline of the Roman Empire could provide lessons for the solution of modern social problems. He even went so far as to label the topic as "merely of historic interest." But this was primarily a didactic stricture. He did mean to teach his listeners something about the *relative* importance of the economic factor and of social changes in the lower strata. An intellectual and political culture should not be viewed in isolation from the economic and social structure, as the Humanists had done up to Jakob Burckhardt, and as the classical schools were still doing; basic shifts in the mode and division of labor, and especially economic and cultural changes within the lower strata, could be historically as significant as changes in the ruling groups and their culture. Imperial Germany faced such shifts with the growth of its industrial

23. *Ibid.*, 274f. Weber's view was later detailed by Marianne Weber, *Ehefrau und Mutter in der Rechtsentwicklung* (Tübingen: Mohr, 1907); on marriage in the Roman upper classes, 168–173, on slavery, marriage and Christianity, 177–187, on Bebel, 80. This voluminous comparative study, which Weber suggested to his wife and in which he took a hand, should be seen as the background for the cursory treatment of marriage and property rights in chs. III and IV of Part Two below.

The sudden ironic reference to August Bebel, after many highly technical pages, is to the most popular socialist book of the time, *Woman and Socialism* (1879), esp. ch. 28. In the 9th edition of 1891, Bebel popularized Friedrich Engels' *The Origin of the Family, Private Property and the State* (1884), the Marxist sequel to Lewis H. Morgan's *Ancient Society* (1877). Throughout his career Weber gave attention to the socialist theory of marriage and property. For the last statement (1919/20), see *Economic History*, 20.

24. "Die ländliche Arbeitsverfassung," *GAzSW*, 462.

and agrarian proletariat, although her specific troubles were largely the opposite of those that had brought down the Roman Empire.

Weber presented a simplified version of his explanation for the decline of the Roman Empire—later part of his economic theory of the ancient states: With the stabilization of the Empire the flow of new slaves, the chief capital good of ancient capitalism, began to dwindle. Commerce waned. Administering the vast conquered inland areas with the means of a maritime city state proved increasingly difficult. The latifundia established themselves as administrative units independent of the cities. Local troops replaced the standing army that had been largely self-perpetuating, up to one half of the recruits being the sons of soldiers. As economy and culture became rural, cosmopolitanism vanished. Thus the economic development of Antiquity, which had started out as a localized subsistence economy, came full circle. However, for Weber this circularity (*Kreislauf*) did not involve morphological assumptions in the mode of Oswald Spengler.

The disintegration of the Empire was a problem of super- and substructure: "In essence, the decline meant merely that the urban administrative apparatus disappeared, and with it the political superstructure dependent upon a money economy, since it was no longer adapted to the economic substructure with its natural economy."[25] What had been an urban substructure, the money economy and commerce, became a superstructure without sustaining basis as the shift occurred from a maritime to an inland economy. Thus Weber handled the relationship of super- and substructure in terms of geographical shift as well as time sequence.

Throughout the address, Weber used various comparative devices. He began with the similarities of the ancient and the medieval city in order to identify the causes for their difference; the more similarities he found, the more he could narrow down the area of crucial difference. In order to clarify the dissolution of the ancient municipalities, he resorted to a negative contemporary analogy, the resistance of the Prussian *Junkers* to the administrative incorporation of their estates into the rural "communes" (*Landgemeinden*),[26] and he contrasted the familiar medieval and modern flight from the land with the late Roman flight from the cities. He made the military discipline of the Roman slaves more understandable to his listeners by comparing it illustratively to an experience they knew: military service with its regimented barrack life

25. "Die sozialen Gründe . . . ," *GAzSW*, 308.
26. On the Prussian *Gutsbezirke*, the *Junker*-ruled "estate-districts," see below, ch. XVI:*v*, n. 9 (p. 1369).

for the unmarried recruits ("slaves"), who were drilled by married non-commissioned officers ("*villici*"). Comparing the slaves on the Roman latifundia with those on the Carolingian estates, Weber pointed to the decisive difference: the latter were permitted a family and the use of land upon their separation from the lord's *oikos*.

6. The Economic Theory of Antiquity

Weber's most comprehensive work on Antiquity was written shortly before *Economy and Society*. Behind the title "Agrarian Conditions in Antiquity"[27] was hidden nothing less than a comparative social and economic study of Mesopotamia, Egypt, Israel, Greece, the Hellenist realm, and Republican and Imperial Rome. Alfred Heuss called it "the most original, daring and persuasive analysis ever made of the economic and social development of Antiquity . . . the area in which Weber's judgment, especially in the details, was most sovereign and surefooted, . . . a claim that stands although he was even more 'original' in the sociology of religion."[28]

In contrast to *Economy and Society,* the study focussed on an economic and politico-military typology and did not yet include the categories of legitimate domination. It should be noted that in Weber's thinking the category of appropriation, both of economic and military resources, is older than that of legitimacy; furthermore, that differences in the mode of appropriation in both areas remained equally important to him:

> Whether a military constitution rests on the principle of self-equipment or that of provisioning by the warlord who supplies horses, arms and food, is as fundamental a distinction for social history as is

27. "Agrarverhältnisse im Altertum," GAzSW, 1–288; originally published in the *Handwörterbuch der Staatswissenschaften,* third ed. (1909), vol. I, 52–188. The restricted title was determined by the division of the handbook. The ten-page annotated bibliography should be consulted for *Economy and Society.* The book-length study was dashed off in four months in 1908, a feat made possible by the fact that Weber had done his thinking ahead of the period of writing and was thoroughly familiar with the literature.

Weber seems to have divided some of the subject matter with Rostovzeff, who contributed the handbook article on *coloni.* Rostovzeff, who in the United States became much better known than Weber as an ancient economic historian, was one of the few to utilize Weber's analysis. Other historians rediscovered some of Weber's results after the First World War—another instance of the discontinuity that plagues most scholarly disciplines. By and large, it still appears that Weber's ancient studies have not yet been followed through sufficiently.

28. Heuss, *loc. cit.,* 538.

another: whether the means of production are owned by the workers or appropriated by a capitalist entrepreneur.[29]

Given this perspective Weber set himself the task of relating the ancient economy to the major political structures. Almost incidentally, he further clarified his comparative approach. Two issues stood out: (1) If there are no universal evolutionary stages, at any rate, if they cannot be identified historically, what kind of typology is suitable for analysis? (2) If the categories of economic history appropriate for medieval and modern conditions are not applicable to Antiquity, which conceptual alternatives should be used?

As against evolutionary conceptions, Weber advanced a limited developmental scheme that left the actual historical sequences open and put in their stead logical "states" or "conditions"—a model-building device that became basic for *Economy and Society*. This was a "static" approach only in comparison with evolutionary sequences. Weber argued that ancient social history had no visible starting point, since most historical phenomena appeared to be secondary, militarily determined, developments, such as the phratries, phylae and *tribus*. Nothing reliable was known about the primeval rural structure. For Weber even the "plausible hypothesis" that the ruling families at least originated as nomadic conquerors was not generally acceptable, since the aristocratic polity developed at the Mediterranean coast and could be proven to have other origins; the starting points were lost in the darkness of prehistory. All that could be historically reconstructed were "certain organizational states, which apparently repeated themselves to some extent in all those ancient peoples, from the Seine to the Euphrates, that had at least some urban development."[30]

Weber began his analysis with a series of brief comparisons that linked up with his reasoning in "The Controversy About Ancient Germanic Social Structure." European and Asian agrarian history differed in a crucial category: land appropriation. Comparing the course of early settlement in Europe and Asia, Weber saw the former proceeding from initial nomadic livestock raising to mixed crop and livestock agriculture, the latter from nomadic crop raising to intensive agriculture of a gardening type. Hence the development in Europe, but relative absence in Asia, of communal property in grazing grounds.

Next, Weber compared ancient and medieval agriculture in the Occident. In both cases agriculture intensified with the narrowing of economic opportunities. Agricultural preoccupation made the majority

29. Cf. *Economic History*, 237, for a slightly different wording.
30. "Agrarverhältnisse . . . ," *GAzSW*, 35.

of men economically unavailable for military service. Thus arose the professional warriors who exploited the masses. Weber defined feudalism in a manner transcending the medieval case. This enabled him to point to the decisive difference between the ancient and the medieval conditions. Medieval feudalism dispersed the warriors over the countryside as manorial lords (*Grundherren*); ancient feudalism was urban: the warriors lived together in the polis.

In this development military technology was partly cause, partly epiphenomenon. Weber emphasized that in Antiquity, in contrast to the Middle Ages, both the diffusion of superior military techniques and the spread of commerce occurred by sea. Whereas central and western Europe became manorial and feudal at a time when trade by land had declined, "feudal" development in Antiquity led to the creation of the city state. This centralization had the consequence that citizenship was a much firmer bond than were the ties of personal loyalty typical of decentralized medieval feudalism.

At this point Weber cautioned again not to mistake analogy for identity:

> The relationship of ancient urban feudalism to the exchange economy is reminiscent of the rise of the free crafts in our medieval cities, the decline of patrician rule, the latent struggle between urban and manorial economy, and the distintegration of the feudal polity under the impact of the money economy. . . . But these ever present analogies with medieval and modern phenomena are frequently most unreliable and often outright detrimental to unbiassed comprehension. . . . Ancient civilization has specific characteristics that distinguish it sharply from the medieval and the modern.[31]

Weber listed a series of features: Ancient civilization centered on the coasts and the rivers; trade was widespread and highly profitable, but lacked the volume it had in the late Middle Ages; the great ancient empires were more mercantilist than the modern Mercantilist states; private trade was insufficiently developed to guarantee the politically crucial grain supply of the urban centers, which maintained a consumer proletariat of declassed citizens, not a working class; slavery was more important than in the Middle Ages.[32]

These comparisons led Weber to the issue, heatedly debated for many decades, whether the categories of modern and medieval economic history were appropriate for Antiquity. In the eighteen-sixties

31. *Ibid.*, 4.
32. Weber conceded that in earlier writings he had overestimated the importance of slavery relative to free labor, but insisted that in the classic period of the "free" polities slavery was especially important. Cf. *GAzSW*, 7–11, as against his older view, *ibid.*, 293.

Karl Rodbertus, himself a country squire, had investigated the master's extended household (the *oikos*) as the dominant unit of ancient economy; he also gave much attention to ancient capitalism. As a scholar of Antiquity, the conservative socialist Rodbertus surpassed Marx, who had labelled the agrarian developments the "secret history of the Romans." Karl Bücher, whose work proceeded from Rodbertus, Marx, Engels and Schmoller, accepted the *oikos* as one stage within his influential scheme of economic development—household, urban and national economy.[33] Bücher, who believed in the "lawful course of economic development" (Preface, *iii*), was criticized by Eduard Meyer, who denied the need for particular economic concepts in the study of Antiquity. Weber, in turn, warned of the futility of Meyer's approach: "Nothing could be more dangerous than to conceive of ancient conditions as 'modern.' Whoever does it underestimates, as so often happens, the structural differences. . . ."[34]

Weber recognized the importance of the *oikos,* but viewed it, within the Roman context, as the "developmental product" of the Imperial period and as the transition to medieval feudalism; by contrast, the Oriental *oikos* had existed from the beginning of history. As against Rodbertus, who saw the *oikos* developing directly out of the self-sufficient household, Weber pointed for the Orient to its origins in the irrigation economy and trade profit: The early military chieftains were also merchants.

Weber affirmed that Antiquity had a capitalist economy "to a degree relevant for cultural history." He opposed the view that there had been no capitalism because the large-scale enterprise with free and differentiated labor was absent. Such an approach focussed too narrowly, he thought, on the social problems of modern capitalism. Instead, he insisted on a purely economic concept of capitalism: "If the terminology is to have any classificatory value at all," capital must mean private acquisitive capital (*Erwerbskapital*) used for profit in an exchange economy.[35] In this sense the "greatest" periods of Antiquity did have capitalism. The ancient polis began with ground rents and tributes collected by the ruler and the patriciate; its economic prosperity was

33. Cf. Karl Rodbertus, "Zur Geschichte der römischen Tributsteuern seit Augustus," *Jahrbücher für Nationalökonomie und Statistik*, V, 1865, 241–315; "Zur Frage des Sachwerts des Geldes im Altertum," *loc. cit.*, XIV, 1870, 341–420; Karl Marx, *Das Kapital*, in *Werke*, vol. 23 (Berlin: Dietz, 1962), 96; Karl Bücher, *Die Entstehung der Volkswirtschaft* (14th ed.; Tübingen: Laupp, 1920), 83–160—first published in 1893 as a collection of older articles; an English edition s.t. *Industrial Evolution* (New York: Holt, 1901).

34. *GAzSW*, 10.

35. *Ibid.*, 13.

politically determined. However, the mere rendering of tributes to personal rulers lay outside the realm of capitalism and the exchange economy. In this case neither the rent-yielding land nor the retainers could be considered "capital," since domination had a traditional, not a market basis: it was manorial domination (*Grundherrschaft*). When the landowners leased land in an exchange economy, ownership became a capitalist rent fund. But the capitalist enterprise proper came into existence only when both land and slaves became transferrable on the market. The classic cities did not have large-scale private enterprise for any length of time. There was no qualitative division of labor; instead of machinery, debt serfs and purchased slaves were used; the crafts played a secondary role, and the guilds remained unimportant. Much of the ancient economy, then, was a "mixed economy," partly manorial, partly capitalist.

Weber considered the political and administrative structure of the ancient states decisive for the fate of capitalism. The state administration, especially public finance, constituted the biggest enterprise. Only in the city state, which lacked a bureaucratic apparatus for the administration of its territories, could public finances act as a pacemaker for private capital formation—because the polity was for its financing dependent upon the private tax farmer. Weber pointed to a major difference between monarchic and republican states: Ancient capitalism culminated in the Roman Republic, where the public lands became the object of the crassest form of private exploitation. The monarchies constricted capitalism; in the interest of dynastic continuity they were concerned with the subjects' loyalty. In the city republic the primary goal was capitalist exploitation, in the monarchy it was political stability. "In republics tax-farming is always at the ready to turn the state into an enterprise of the state creditors and tax-farmers in the manner of medieval Genoa." Whereas the city state allowed private capital accumulation of a highly unstable kind, the bureaucratic order of the monarchic state economy gradually destroyed the opportunities for private gain. "The monarchic order, so beneficial for the masses of the subjects, was the death of capitalist development and of everything dependent on it."[36]

7. *A Political Typology of Antiquity*

Beyond the contrast between republics and monarchies, well-known from ancient political theory, Weber elaborated a developmental scheme

36. *Ibid.,* 29 and 31.

with open historical direction. Apart from its classificatory uses, he hoped that it would remind the reader of the very different stages of development at which the polities entered the light of history—depending on the "accidental" availability of the sources. In contrast to Greece, Mesopotamia and Egypt had had some kind of urban culture many centuries before the first records were made.

Weber based his typology on the "military constitution" and distinguished:

I. the merely fortified location; II. the petty "castle kings"; III. the clan polity; IV. the bureaucratic urban principality; V. the liturgic monarchy; VI. the polis of privileged citizens; VII. the democratic polis; and outside the scheme, VIII. the military peasant confraternity.

I. The distant forerunner of the city is the walled settlement. Household and village constitute the organizational environment of the individual. Associations for blood revenge, cultic activities, and defense provide police, sacral and political protection, but nothing historically certain can be established about the functional division or overlap of these early associations which come out of prehistory. Free members share in the landed property; the extent of slavery seems to be moderate. Political chieftains, if they exist at all, have mainly arbitrational functions. "It depends on the political situation whether there are any joint political affairs."[37]

II. A closer forerunner of the city is the castle controlled by an owner of land, slaves, cattle and precious metals, that is, a ruler with a personal following. Almost nothing is known about the state of the countryside. The exploitation of the subjects seems to have varied greatly. Fertile land and trade profits led to the rise of these "castle kings"; their law was set against popular law. The separation of the followers from the rural population was important; according to tradition and fact, the following often consisted of bands of aliens and adventurers ("robber bands"). The ancient states originated in the victory of one "castle king" over others.

III. Another approximation to the classic polis is the clan polity (*Adelsstaat*). The nobility is made up of creditors who develop into a stratum of landed *rentiers*. The peasants become first debt serfs and then hereditary dependents. A group of noble families that have accumulated enough land and retainers to equip and train themselves as professional warriors rules the countryside from an acropolis. The "king" loses influence and becomes *primus inter pares* in a militarily organized urban community (in contrast to the feudal-manorial development of the

---

37. *Ibid.*, 36. Weber deals here with the relatively "universal groups" to which he returned again below, in Part Two, chs. III–VI and VIII.

continental Middle Ages). There is no bureaucracy; at most there are elected officials. The peasants may be legally separate from the status group of free men, but ancient trial and debt procedures as well as the manipulation of the courts by the ruling class are sufficient to maintain the social distance without formal barriers.

iv. From state ii (the "castle kingship") development may proceed in a direction contrary to state iii: The king may succeed in effectively subordinating his following and in establishing an officialdom through which he governs the "subjects." In this case the city is not autonomous (witness Egypt, Assur and Babylon). The economy may approach "state socialism" or an exchange economy, depending on the mode of want satisfaction of the royal household. Under condition iii and iv the extent of the direct utilization of the labor force by the rulers is inversely correlated with the development of the private exchange economy. Insofar as domination rests on taxation, free transfer of real estate may be tolerated. However, the bureaucratic king tends to oppose land accumulation by the aristocracy, whereas he may permit land fragmentation. Witness the Greek tyrants—and Napoleon I.

v. With the rationalization of royal want satisfaction the bureaucratic city or river kingdom may develop into the authoritarian liturgy state, which meets its demands through "an artful system of compulsory services and treats the subjects as mere objects."[38] Even in such a state there may be free trade and geographical mobility, as long as they produce revenue. In fact, the state may favor both, in the manner of the "enlightened despotism" of the 17th and 18th century—another illustrative analogy.

vi. This type emerges from state iii, but not without the most heterogeneous transitions. It is the "polis of hoplites," in which the citizens form a heavily armed infantry. The rule of the noble kinship groups over the city and of the city over the countryside is broken. The citizens' army of hoplites comprises all owners of land; hence military service is relatively democratized.

vii. The democratic polis proper is a further development of condition vi. Military service and even citizenship are emancipated from the requirement of landownership, and there is an inconsistent trend to formally qualify for office-holding everyone who has served in the navy, a military branch not requiring self-equipment.

viii. A major case outside this typology is the association of peasants organized as hoplites, which in some instances made history, from ancient Israel to the medieval Swiss confederation.

38. *Ibid.*, 40.

One important dimension cuts across this typology of military-political organization: "the manifest and latent struggle of the secular-political and the theocratic powers, a struggle that affects the whole structure of social life."[39] Functional specialization separated the primeval linkage of princely and priestly power. The priests became powerful through their control of economic resources, their hold over the religious anxieties of the masses, their possession of early "science" and, especially, their control of education in the bureaucratized states. This struggle led to the historical ups and downs of secularization and restoration in the "substantive development of culture," with usurpers ultimately striving for legitimacy and hence restoration.

Thus did Weber assemble the elements that went into the making of his Sociology of Domination in *Economy and Society*: patrimonialism, feudalism, charisma (as military communism), the city and hierocracy. In sum, Weber's ancient and medieval studies contain not only much of the historical substance of the later work, but also its gradual conceptualization.

8. *Weber's Vision of the Future and His Academic Politics*

Weber did not hesitate to draw political lessons from academic studies, but the relationship must be properly understood. He believed that scholars should unflinchingly face the arduous work of fact-finding and only then express political views. He insisted on detachment in order to gain a hearing for his views—the basic strategy in his academic politics. Sociology became for him a weapon in the struggle against the predominant views in the *Verein für Sozialpolitik* and the founding of the German Sociological Association a vehicle for the same purpose. The two great issues, closely related, were the social dynamics and future of German society and the feasibility and desirability of value-neutrality in social science.[40]

In warning of the political dangers he foresaw, Weber used historical parallels, although he rejected the use of analogies for historical explanation. Thus he appended one page of warnings to his 1908 study of Antiquity in order to impress his readers with vivid parallels. Without

39. *Ibid.*, 44.
40. On the tensions between politics and scholarship in the men of the *Verein für Sozialpolitik*, see Dieter Lindenlaub, *Richtungskämpfe im Verein für Sozialpolitik. Wissenschaft und Sozialpolitik im Kaiserreich* (Wiesbaden: Steiner, 1967). This massive study will be the standard work on the politics of German academic men during the period; the present introduction was still written independently of it.

implying any historical inevitability he upheld—at least didactically—the maxim: "If it has happened before, it may happen again." At issue were the effects of bureaucratization:

The paralysis of private economic initiative through bureaucracy is not limited to Antiquity. Every bureaucracy, including ours, has the same tendency by virtue of its expansionism. In Antiquity the policies of the city state paved the way for capitalism; today capitalism is the pacemaker for the bureaucratization of the economy. Let us imagine coal, iron and mining products, metallurgy, distilleries, sugar, tobacco, matches —in short, all mass products that are already highly cartellized—taken over by state-owned or state-controlled enterprises; let the crown domains, entailed estates, and state-controlled resettlement holdings (Rentengüter) proliferate and let the "Kanitz motion" be passed and executed with all its consequences;[41] let all military and civilian needs of the state administration be met by state-operated workshops and cooperatives; let shipping operations on inland waterways be compelled to use state tugs [as partly realized in 1913], put the merchant marine under state supervision, have all railroads etc. nationalized, and perhaps subject cotton imports to international agreements; let all these enterprises be managed in bureaucratic "order," introduce state-supervised syndicates, and let the rest of the economy be regulated on the guild principle with innumerable certificates of competency, academic and otherwise; let the citizenry in general be of the rentier paisible type—then, under a militarist-dynastic regime, the condition of the late Roman Empire will have been reached, albeit on a technologically more elaborate basis. After all, the German burgher of today has retained scarcely more of his ancestors' qualities from the medieval Town Leagues than the Athenean in Caesar's time had preserved those of the fighters at Marathon. "Order" is the motto of the German burgher—even, in most cases, if he calls himself a Social Democrat. It is very likely that the bureaucratization of society will one day subdue capitalism just as it did in Antiquity. Then the "anarchy of production" will be replaced by that "order" which, in a very similar way, characterized the late Roman Empire and, even more, the New Kingdom and the rule of the Ptolemies in Egypt. Let no one believe that the citizens' service in a barracked army, bureaucratically equipped, clothed, fed, drilled and commanded, can provide a countervailing force to such bureaucratization or, more generally, that

41. Rentengüter were small holdings, indivisible and inalienable except with government permission, created for the "inner colonization" (Germanisation) of the eastern part of the Reich, first under the Prussian resettlement act of 1886.— Count Kanitz, a Conservative Reichstag deputy, in 1894 demanded the institution of a state monopoly for grain imports in the interest of price supports for the output of the grain-producing Junker estates of eastern Germany. The so-called "Kanitz motion" failed, but was thereafter resubmitted year after year by the agrarian groups.

modern conscription in dynastic states has any inner affinity with the spirit of the citizenry-in-arms of the distant past. However, these perspectives do not belong here.[42]

It is, of course, significant that Weber added these perspectives in spite of his disclaimer. In the fall of 1909 the Weber brothers, Max and Alfred, clashed with an older generation of scholars at the Vienna meeting of the *Verein für Sozialpolitik*. Some younger members were critical of the state metaphysics of men like Gustav von Schmoller and were ready to go beyond their elders in matters of social reform, against them with regard to democratization. The two Webers attacked the belief of the older reform generation that strengthening the power of the state and extending the economic functions of its bureaucracy would lead to greater social harmony. Opposing the conservative State Socialism of the aged Adolf Wagner, they pointed to the dangers of bureaucratization. *Economy and Society* later demonstrated how the bureaucratic phenomenon could be studied comparatively in a non-ideological way. But at Vienna Weber expressed his sentiments and convictions, which should be seen not only as the counterpoint, but as one of the motives, for the Sociology of Domination. Weber granted to the older view of bureaucracy—perhaps in part as a tactical concession—that

> no machinery in the world functions so precisely as this apparatus of men and, moreover, so cheaply. . . . When the *Verein für Sozialpolitik* was founded [in 1872], the generation of Privy Councillor. Wagner called for more than purely technical yardsticks in economic affairs; at the time this group was just as small as we who think differently are today in relation to you. Gentlemen, you then had to fight the salvo of applause for the purely technological accomplishments of industrial mechanization emanating from the laissez-faire doctrine. It appears to me that today you are in danger of providing such cheap applause to mechanical efficiency as an administrative and political criterion. . . . Rational calculation . . . reduces every worker to a cog in this [bureaucratic] machine and, seeing himself in this light, he will merely ask how to transform himself from a little into a somewhat bigger cog, . . . an attitude you find, just as in the Egyptian *papyri*, increasingly among our civil servants and especially their successors, our students. The passion for bureaucratization at this meeting drives us to despair.[43]

Weber was not opposed to the *Verein für Sozialpolitik* as a propaganda association, as he called it, but its academic activities were unduly handicapped, he felt, by its ideological preoccupations. Hence, after the

42. *GAzSW*, 277f.
43. *GAzSS*, 413f.

Vienna meeting, he proposed the founding of the German Sociological Association—to be an instrument of collective empirical research and "purely scientific discussions." In the winter of 1909/10 he suggested team projects on the press, voluntary associations, and the relationship of technology and culture. Weber apparently sustained most of the organizing effort. It was soon clear that his colleagues resisted project cooperation and only hesitantly accepted organizational responsibilities. And some men whose academic careers had suffered because of their novel sociological interests, Weber noted with chagrin, viewed the association as compensation for status deprivation—he spoke of a *salon des refusés*. The Sociological Association first met in the fall of 1910. Weber summarized the intent of the statutes: "The association rejects, in principle and definitely, all propaganda for action-oriented ideas from its midst." He immediately added that this had nothing to do with general non-partisanship or the "popular middle-of-the-road line"; rather, it meant studying "what is, why something is the way it is, for what historical and social reasons."[44] Secondly, the association should not be an assembly of notables for whom membership in one or another committee was a matter of honor. Thirdly, the association should not engage in "empire-building" and arrogate to itself tasks better left to decentralized study.

Sociology, then, was to be disciplined discourse and information gathering, but sociologists should be politically articulate. Weber wanted to separate the organizational setting for research from political action. In the fall of 1912 he attempted to organize men from the left wing of the *Verein für Sozialpolitik;* a few met in Leipzig to arrange periodic meetings on the failures and the future of welfare legislation and social reform. Differences of opinion, however, proved too great and no further meetings took place.[45]

At the second annual gathering of the German Sociological Association Weber pleaded once more for the *raison d'être* of the association,

44. *Verhandlungen des Ersten Deutschen Soziologentages*, Frankfurt, 19.–22. Okt. 1910 (Tübingen: Mohr, 1911), 39f. On the contrast between scientific assessment and ideological judgment and the need for a technical terminology, see also Friedrich von Gottl-Ottlilienfeld, *Die Herrschaft des Wortes* (Jena: Fischer, 1901). Weber esteemed this neglected work and acknowledged it in the prefatory note to *Economy and Society*. Gottl was one of the first expositors and defenders of "jargon" in social science, that means, of terms removed from both common sense meanings and ideological preference. On the definition of value-neutrality (*Werturteilsfreiheit*) see Johannes Winckelmann's article in *Historisches Wörterbuch der Philosophie* (forthcoming).

45. See Weber's *post mortem* circular to the participants dated Nov. 15, 1912, in Bernhard Schäfer, ed., "Ein Rundschreiben Max Webers zur Sozialpolitik," *Soziale Welt*, XVIII, 1967, 261–271.

"somber discussion" and the study of "questions of fact," since the habit of value judgment persisted. As he later said: "Will the gentlemen, none of whom can manage to hold back his subjective 'valuations,' all infinitely uninteresting to me, please stay with their kind. I am absolutely tired of appearing time and again as the Don Quixote of an allegedly unworkable approach and of provoking embarrassing scenes."[46]

This aggressive stand for detachment must be seen in the institutional context of the time. Weber especially abhorred the misuse of the rostrum for the indoctrination of the students, who could neither answer nor argue. "The least tolerable of all prophecies is surely the professor's with its highly personal tinge."[47] However, many students indulged in "zoological nationalism." In that case Weber's postulate involved the attempt to face them with inconvenient facts. Weber also continued Mommsen's struggle for a "science without presuppositions"—Mommsen's war-cry against the repeated intrusion of religious criteria in academic appointments.

Weber's advocacy of field and survey research, a crucial part of his notion of "value-neutral" fact-finding,[48] put him ahead of most of his colleagues, but here he was also his own worst enemy. He was quite successful at raising funds and opening channels for the large-scale projects of the Sociological Association, yet he was not well-suited for the role of project or institute director who furthers research by diplomatically avoiding controversy with clients and colleagues. The press study did not materialize when Weber withdrew as director to avoid biassing the project: Early in 1911 he had begun a lawsuit to force a newspaper to reveal a slanderous source, a move that made him controversial in some press circles.[49] Weber was never content to be a mere student of law; in the nineties he had practiced law along with his teaching and writing. He considered the suit an honorable and pragmatic form of normatively controlled struggle—one of his major scholarly concerns.

46. Marianne Weber, *Lebensbild*, 430.

47. *Ibid.*, 335.

48. On the pioneering efforts of Weber and Tönnies, see Anthony R. Oberschall, *Empirical Social Research in Germany, 1848–1914* (The Hague: Mouton, 1965). Weber and Tönnies stood firmly together in their advocacy of field and survey research. Tönnies strongly backed Weber's notion of value-neutral sociology against Troeltsch. See Ferdinand Tönnies, "Troeltsch und die Philosophie der Geschichte," in his *Soziologische Studien und Kritiken* (Jena: Fischer, 1926), 419f.

49. For Weber's explanation see *Verhandlungen des Zweiten Deutschen Soziologentages*, Berlin, 20.–22. Okt. 1912 (Tübingen: Mohr, 1913), 75ff. On the background of the suit, see below, p. 354, n. 6.

His willingness to fight openly, and to sue if necessary, in academic and personal affairs made him a highly inconvenient man and tended to impair his effectiveness as an organizer of academic enterprises. Weber persistently criticized the corporate failings of the professorial estate. His articles and statements on academic improprieties, the general state of the universities and the need for university reform elicited the public counter-attack, at one time or another, of groups of professors and officials of the ministries of education.[50] In general, his intellectual, political and moral demands were beyond the capabilities of most of his colleagues.

At any rate, in 1912 Weber withdrew completely from his executive duties in the Sociological Association: "I must return now to my scientific work. Things can't go on this way; I am the only one to sacrifice personal scholarly interests, yet I have achieved no more than the bare running of a coasting machine."[51] The work to which he returned was *Economy and Society*.

9. *The Planning of* Economy and Society

Marianne Weber reminisced in her husband's biography that *Economy and Society* "unintendedly grew into the major work of his life."[52] The impetus came from Paul Siebeck, publisher of the famed *Archiv für Sozialwissenschaft und Sozialpolitik,* which Weber, Werner Sombart and Edgar Jaffé had taken over in 1904. In 1909 Siebeck proposed to replace the outdated *Handbuch der politischen Oekonomie* edited by Gustav Schönberg in the eighteen-eighties,[53] which among two dozen contributions contained Schönberg's theory of economic stages (2nd ed., I, 25–45; criticized below on p. 117) and August Meitzen's rationale for agrarian research from a liberal point of view (2nd ed., II, 149–224). Weber agreed to edit an entirely new series. However, the fact that this was a new venture did not prevent an acrimonious academic row, when a young professor who had failed to find contributors for a revised edition of the old handbook accused the publisher and, by implication, Weber of slighting the financial interests of Schönberg's impoverished heirs. Weber came to Siebeck's defense; the young man, in turn, mobilized a group of older professors and threatened a public

50. For an account, see Marianne Weber, *Lebensbild,* 413–17, 430–56.
51. *Ibid.,* 429.
52. *Ibid.,* 425.
53. Gustav Schönberg (ed.), *Handbuch der Politischen Oekonomie* (2 vols.; Tübingen: Laupp, 1882; 2nd revised and enlarged ed. in 3 vols., 1885–86).

scandal. In the ensuing morality play Weber's acute sense of honor and propriety was once again engaged.[54]

The old handbook was limited to the traditional topics of political economy. Weber titled his series *Outline of Social Economics* (*Grundriss der Sozialökonomik*); the term, wider than "institutional economics" and less inclusive than "sociology," enabled him to encompass all relationships of economy and society. He asked a number of men for contributions to be completed within two years. However, some failed in their promises, others produced disappointing manuscripts, still others were dismayed as their contributions were outdated by the resulting delays. The first volumes did not appear until 1914; then the war interrupted the venture. The series closed in 1930 with more than a dozen volumes published. Among contributors well-known in the United States were Robert Michels, Werner Sombart, Joseph Schumpeter, Emil Lederer, Karl Bücher and Alfred Weber. Some titles in the series were: *The Economy and the Science of Economics; Economic Theory; Economy and Nature; Modern Capitalist Economy; Social Stratification Under Capitalism; Welfare Politics Under Capitalism; Foreign Trade and Trade Policies;* there were also several volumes on primary, secondary and tertiary industries.

As the coordination troubles of the projected series mounted, Weber expanded his own contribution. Without this exigency, he might never have attempted a *summa* of his sociology, given his absorption in other interests and his conviction of the "futility of the idea . . . that it could be the goal of the cultural sciences, no matter how distant, to construct a closed system of concepts which can encompass and classify reality in some definitive manner and from which it can be deduced again."[55] Now, however, he was motivated to attempt his own historically open systematization: "Since it was impossible to find a substitute for some [promised but unwritten] contributions, I concluded that I should write a rather comprehensive sociological treatise for the section on *Economy and Society,* to provide an equivalent presentation and to improve the quality of the series. I had to sacrifice other projects much more important to me; in other circumstances I would never have taken on such a task." His wife saw through these complaints: "At last he was under the spell of a great unified task."[56]

In his 1914 introduction to the series Weber spelled out the rationale

54. Marianne Weber, *Lebensbild,* 446–453.
55. *GAzW,* 184; cf. Shils and Finch (eds.), *Methodology . . . ,* 84.
56. Marianne Weber, *Lebensbild,* 424.

of the project: "The basic idea was to study economic development particularly as part of the general rationalization of life. In view of the systematic character of the work the addition of a general economic history has not been planned for the time being."[57]

Tracing the historical lines of rationalization was certainly one of Weber's intentions in *Economy and Society*, as is also indicated by scattered remarks in the text (for example, below, 333). However, the work is not primarily a study in the rationalization and the "disenchantment" of the world.[58] In a letter of June 21, 1914, Weber explained to the redoubtable medievalist Georg von Below his specifically sociological intention:

> This winter I will probably begin with the printing of a fairly voluminous contribution to the *Outline of Social Economics*. I am dealing with the structure of the political organizations in a comparative and systematic manner, at the risk of falling under the anathema: "dilettantes compare." We are absolutely in accord that history should establish what is specific to, say, the medieval city; but this is possible only if we first find what is missing in other cities (ancient, Chinese, Islamic). And so it is with everything else. It is the subsequent task of history to find a causal explanation for these specific traits. I cannot believe that ultimately you think otherwise; some of your remarks speak more for than against my assumption. Sociology, as I understand it, can perform this very modest preparatory work. In this endeavor it is unfortunately almost inevitable to give offense to the researcher who *completely* masters *one* broad field, since it is, after all, impossible to be a specialist in *all* areas. But this does not convince me of the scientific futility of such work. Even my hastily written essay on ancient agrarian history (in the *Handwörterbuch der Staatswissenschaften*) has been useful, including those findings that have been superseded. This seems to me proven

57. In Karl Bücher et al., *Wirtschaft und Wirtschaftswissenschaft*, Section I, Vol. 1 of *Grundriss der Sozialökonomik* (2nd ed.; Tübingen: Mohr, 1924), vii. Upon the urging of students, Weber turned to the task of a general economic history in the winter of 1919/20. This was his last completed lecture course. After his death the lectures were reconstructed from student notes and published as *Wirtschaftsgeschichte. Abriss der universalen Sozial- und Wirtschaftsgeschichte* (3rd ed.; Berlin: Duncker & Humblot, 1958), translated by Frank H. Knight as *General Economic History* (New York: Greenberg, 1927). The *Economic History* suffers from various gaps; the English edition also omits the terminological introduction. The work makes easier reading than *Economy and Society* insofar as it treats phenomena such as the household, neighborhood, kin-group, village, and manor in greater historical continuity; it is inferior in terminological and systematic respects.

58. For an interpretation merely along this line, see Günter Abramowski, *Das Geschichtsbild Max Webers. Universalgeschichte am Leitfaden des okzidentalen Rationalisierungsprozesses* (Stuttgart: Klett, 1966).

by the dissertations of Wilcken's pupils in Leipzig. But the essay was certainly no masterpiece.[59]

In the same year—1914—Weber published a projected table of contents for the *Outline of Social Economics,* including a detailed plan for the manuscript (Part Two) he had written between 1910 and 1914 —Part One was written years later. The table of contents shows that Section III of the *Outline* was titled "Economy and Society" and was to contain two parts, "The Evolution of Systems and Ideals in Economic Policy and Social Reform" by Eugen von Philippovich[60] and "The Economy and the Normative and De Facto Powers" (*Die Wirtschaft und die gesellschaftlichen Ordnungen und Mächte*) by Weber. *Economy and Society* is not, then, the original title of Weber's work. The title now used for Part Two of the work is the "true" one, if more cumbersome in English. However, its meaning is not obvious. Weber does not proceed from the national economy and its relation to society; rather he begins with social action, of which economic action is that rational case concerned with want-satisfaction under conditions of resource scarcity and a limited number of possible actions. The basic "economy" is the "household" in the archaic English sense; in common German parlance *Wirtschaft* may refer to a farm or an inn as well as to the national economy.

The "normative and de facto powers" are the laws and conventions, on the one hand, and the groups that sustain them on the other. The relationship between the normative and the merely coercive, between legitimacy and force, is ever varying in the flux of ideal and material interests and the vicissitudes of power struggle. There are no historically effective ideas and ideals without social interests backing them, and force is rarely used without at least the semblance of a rationale before the staff and the subjects. The formulation of the title expresses these dual forces that impinge on the individual's social action.

Weber's projected table of contents (of Part Two) compares with the chapters of the English edition (in parentheses) as follows:[61]

59. The letter is reprinted in the second edition of Georg von Below, *Der deutsche Staat des Mittelalters* (Leipzig: Quelle und Meyer, 1925), xxiv. The dictum "dilettantes compare" was coined by Goethe and hurled by Heinrich Brunner against representatives of the comparative method (cf. *ibid.,* 333).— Weber certainly addressed himself *ad hominem,* but more in emphasis than content.

60. Published in Karl Bücher *et al., op. cit.,* 126–183.

61. The table of contents, which was included in the early volumes of the *Grundriss der Sozialökonomik,* is reprinted in Johannes Winckelmann, "Max Webers Opus Posthumum," *Zeitschrift für die gesamten Staatswissenschaften,* vol. 105, 1949, 370f. In this essay Winckelmann first proposed his reorganization

1. Categories of the Various Forms of Social Order (*partly contained in ch. I:1–2, but mostly in "On Some Categories of Interpretive Sociology"; cf. Appendix I, below*)
   The Most General Relationships Between Economy and Law (*ch. I:4*)
   The Economic Relationships of Organized Groups (*ch. II*)
2. Household, Oikos and Enterprise (*ch. IV*)
3. Neighborhood, Kin Group and Local Community (*ch. III*)
4. Ethnic Group Relationships (*ch. V*)
5. Religious Groups
   The Class Basis of the Religions; Complex Religions and Economic Orientation (*ch. VI*)
6. The Market (*ch. VII*)
7. The Political Association (*ch. IX*)
   The Social Determinants of Legal Development (*ch. VIII*)
   Status Groups, Classes, Parties (*ch. IX:6*)
   The Nation (*ch. IX:5*)
8. Domination
   a) The Three Types of Legitimate Domination (*ch. X–XIV*)
   b) Political and Hierocratic Domination (*ch. XV*)
   c) Non-Legitimate Domination. The Typology of Cities (*ch. XVI*)
   d) The Development of the Modern State
   e) The Modern Political Parties

Weber died in 1920 before finishing either Part Two or the later Part One. The last two sections on the modern state and the modern political parties remained unwritten. Weber's table of contents of Part Two was not followed in the two editions undertaken by Marianne Weber and Melchior Palyi (1922 and 1925) and the reprint of 1947 (third ed.). It was not until Johannes Winckelmann's edition of 1956 (fourth ed.) that the intended structure of the manuscript was largely restored.

10. *The Structure of* Economy and Society

The following remarks are not intended to summarize *Economy and Society*, but to elucidate some of Weber's underlying reasoning as well as

of *Wirtschaft und Gesellschaft*. See also his introduction to the 1956 edition (*WuG*, xi–xvii); the preface for the 1964 paperback edition (*WuG*-Studienausgabe, xv–xvi) indicates some further changes.

some of the systematic connections among the chapters, irrespective of their length. Particular attention will be given to the previously untranslated chapters and sections and their relationship with the other parts.

I. PART TWO: THE EARLIER PART

CH. I. THE ECONOMY AND SOCIAL NORMS: ON STAMMLER

Most books have a foil as well as a model. They are written to criticize some books and emulate others. One visible starting point of *Economy and Society* is the attempt at a positive statement of what Rudolf Stammler "should have meant," as Weber put it in the prefatory note to his essay "On Some Categories of Interpretive Sociology" (1913).[62] This essay was part of a longer methodological introduction to the work and corresponds to the first section in the 1914 outline, "Categories of the Various Forms of Social Order."

Like his friends Jellinek, Simmel and Sombart, Weber wrote a critique of Stammler's *Economy and Law According to the Materialist Interpretation of History*.[63] Weber bluntly denied its "right to scientific existence,"[64] but his critique was not identical with his objections to historical materialism. Stammler, a neo-Kantian philosopher, claimed to have systematically deduced the feasibility of objectively correct social action and laid a new epistemological foundation for social science by demonstrating the identity of social ideal and social law. He discussed at great length the relations between legal and economic order and denied their causal relationship in favor of their correspondence as form and content, a position diametrically opposed to Weber's, who repeated in *Economy and Society* (below, 325ff. and 32f.) that his critique was directed against (a) the confusion of the normative with the empirical validity of an order, (b) the confusion of regularities of action due to normative orientation with merely factual regularities, (c) the contrast between convention and law in terms of free will—as if conventions

62. "Über einige Kategorien der verstehenden Soziologie," *Logos*, IV, 1913, reprinted in *GAzW*, 427. See also below, p. 4.

63. Cf. Rudolf Stammler, *Wirtschaft und Recht nach der materialistischen Geschichtsauffassung. Eine sozialphilosophische Untersuchung* (2nd improved ed.; Leipzig: Veit, 1906). For Stammler's definition of the task of the social sciences and a summary of his theory, see 574ff. Weber spoke on the difference between Marx and Stammler at the 1910 meeting of the Sociological Association; cf. *Verhandlungen des Ersten Deutschen Soziologentages*, 96.

64. "R. Stammler's 'Überwindung' der materialistischen Geschichtsauffassung" (1907), reprinted in *GAzW*, 291.

were not coercive—, and (d) the identification of law and convention as the "forms" of conduct as against its "substance."

As a trained jurist and economist Weber was faced with both the normative orientation of jurisprudence and the ethical components of laissez-faire and state-socialist economics. He could develop a sociological approach only by insisting on the separation of the normative and the empirical, a separation accomplished with his theory of social action. In the essay on interpretive sociology and in Part Two of *Economy and Society* he defined social action just as he did later in Part One: subjectively meaningful action oriented to the behavior of others—it is called *Gemeinschaftshandeln* in the older part and *soziales Handeln* in the newer. Normatively regulated action is only one variant of social action. "Sociology, insofar as it is concerned with law, deals not with the logically correct 'objective' content of legal norms but with action for which, *among other considerations,* the ideas of men about the meaning and validity of certain regulations may play a significant role as both determinants and resultants."[65]

Weber elaborated a continuous typology of social action along the line of increasing rational control, persistence and legal compulsion. This typology—partly presented in Appendix I—ranges from mere consensual action (*Einverständnishandeln*) and *ad hoc* agreement (*Gelegenheitsvergesellschaftung*), through various kinds of regulated action and enduring association (*Vergesellschaftung*), to the organization (*Verband*) and compulsory institution (*Anstalt*). These kinds of action differ from behavior that is not social or borderline: *Massenhandeln,* which may be rendered "mass action," "statistically frequent action" or "collective behavior."

In this scheme only men act, neither society nor individual groups. However, men acting in concert form groups (*Gemeinschaften*), and these persist only if they have a "constitution" in the sociological sense, that is, if their order is consensually accepted by members (or outsiders) for whatever reasons. Belief in legitimacy need not be the primary reason. Therefore, Weber deals in the first chapter with the consequences of the factual impact of law on economic conduct.

The economic order is made up of the actual control over goods and services insofar as it is consensually recognized. Sociological economics, then, deals with the actions of men insofar as they are conditioned "by the necessity to take into account the facts of economic life." However, instrumentally rational action must also take into account the fact of law, defined empirically as "guaranteed law": A legal order exists whenever an association is ready to enforce it. Weber makes it immediately

65. *GAzW,* 440. Emphasis added.

clear that law is by no means in all cases "guaranteed" by violence (*Gewalt*), and he rejects the view that "a state exists only if the coercive means of the political community are superior to all other communities" (below, 316).

The two basic categories of an order—convention and law—Weber defines in close proximity to Sumner and in contrast to Stammler. Although conventions are not safeguarded by men (a staff or apparatus) specifically associated to uphold them, they can be enforced just as effectively as law by psychological, and even physical, coercion on the part of the group members. Compliance with a conventional or legal order is frequently determined by a person's self-interest in the continuation of consensual action. Unreflecting habit is another universal reason for regular and regulated behavior. The beginnings of convention and law in habit, usage and custom lie in the realm of inaccessible prehistory. Yet, in view of these powers of persistence, the historian must be able to account for the innovating capacity of men. Rejecting older views of imitation, Weber prefers Hellpach's theory of innovation through inspiration and empathy—an anticipation of the theory of charisma in chs. VI and XIV.

Throughout his analysis, Weber combines his effort at terminological precision with an insistently realistic approach to human affairs: Men are creatures of habit, but they are also strongly motivated by their material and ideal interests to circumvent conventional and legal rules; in all societies the economically powerful tend to have a strong influence on the enactment and interpretation of the law. However, the presence of law, with its various forms of coercion, makes a great deal of difference for social action. On a general level more cannot be said. Here as elsewhere Weber carefully points out the limits of generalization: "The extent of the law's factual impact on economic conduct cannot be determined generally, but must be calculated for each particular case."

CH. II: ON MARX, MICHELS AND SOMBART

Weber's emphasis on the limits of generalization has here a critical thrust directed against historical materialism and economic functionalism (below, 341). A work on economy and society must sooner or later take a stand on historical materialism—Weber took his stand at the first appropriate moment. It would be wrong, however, to say that the critique of historical materialism occupies the dominant place in the work, above and beyond Weber's other polemical and positive interests. What may appear at first sight as "reaction" to, or "reflection" of, historical materialism—such as Weber's interest in ancient capitalism—more often stands in a tradition of economic and legal history of which Marxism was an extreme offshoot. Weber recognized historical materialism as a political force but did not take its ultimate claims seriously. About the time this chapter was written, he told his peers at the first meeting of the Sociological Association:

> I would like to protest the statement by one of the speakers that some one factor, be it technology or economy, can be the "ultimate" or "true" cause of another. If we look at the causal lines, we see them run, at one time, from technical to economic and political matters, at another from political to religious and economic ones, etc. There is no resting point. In my opinion, the view of historical materialism, frequently espoused, that the economic is in some sense the ultimate point in the chain of causes is completely finished as a scientific proposition.[66]

Weber also rejects economic functionalism insofar as it postulated an unambiguous interdependence of economic and non-economic elements. Not all social action is economically influenced, and not all groups are economically relevant. Culturally important groups, however, have some kind of relationship with economic elements; all persistent groups must in some way meet their wants. Weber presents a simple typology of economically active groups, ranging from economic groups proper, through various economically active groups and those merely influenced by economic factors, to regulatory groups of a political, religious or other nature.[67] (In line with the reasoning in ch. I, regulatory groups belong into an economic typology of groups.)

Although Weber gave attention to the technological factor in history, he related want satisfaction primarily to modes of appropriation and expropriation, not to modes of production. The crucial importance of appropriation appears at first sight as a "quasi-Marxist" position, but in fact is another difference from Marx. Weber saw the Marxist concept of the mode of production blurring the technological and economic aspects. He explained before the Sociological Association:

> To my knowledge, Marx has not defined technology. There are many things in Marx that not only appear contradictory but actually are found contrary to fact if we undertake a thorough and pedantic analysis, as indeed we must. Among other things, there is an oft-quoted passage: The hand-mill results in feudalism, the steam-mill in capitalism. That is a technological, not an economic construction, and as an assertion it is simply false, as we can clearly prove. For the age of the hand-mill, which extended up to modern times, had cultural "super-structures" of all conceivable kinds in all fields.[68]

66. *Verhandlungen des Ersten Deutschen Soziologentages,* 101.
67. In Part Two the economically active groups are called *Gemeinschaften,* in Part One *Verbände* (organizations).
68. *Verhandlungen, op. cit.,* 95f. The point is repeated below, 1091.

Such superstructures are related to modes of appropriation, which emerge from the competition for livelihood but also depend on the nature of an object, material or immaterial. Weber does accept the historical generalization that free property and acquired rights grew out of the gradual appropriation by group members of their shares in the group's holdings. Private property became important with the disintegration of the old monopolist associations. It is a recurrent process in history that decreasing opportunities lead to monopolization; then legally privileged groups with privileged members (*Rechtsgenossen*) and organs come into being. Weber lists the stages of the appropriation of opportunities through external and internal closure. With fine nominalist irony he mixes contemporary examples from Imperial Germany with historically early illustrations (below, 342).

Once an organization has been established, the vested interests of the organs (functionaries, officials) tend to perpetuate or transform it beyond the original purpose. This phenomenon of institutionalization was a controversial point between Weber and his friend Robert Michels, who was just completing his *Political Parties* (1911).[69] Whereas Michels reified his observations into the "iron law of oligarchy" and thus stressed the sameness of the phenomena at issue, Weber pointed to the multiple, and often contradictory, consequences of institutionalization, which might lead to monopolization *or* expansionism (ch. II:3). For Weber the greatest historical example for the expansionist tendency was the age-old connection of capitalist interests with imperialism. The expansionist tendencies of an organization could, however, be restrained by monopolist interests. In voluntary organizations the rational primary purpose might be overshadowed by "communal" goals if social action involved personal elements (below, 346), thus promoting closure and establishing social legitimacy.

Irrespective of this dualism, most rationally organized groups must satisfy their wants in one or more of the following ways: (1) the *oikos;* (2) market-oriented assessments; (3) production for the market; (4) maecenatic support; (5) contributions and services linked to positive and negative privileges (ch. II:4).

With this typology Weber completes the economic framework for the substantive theme that runs through all of *Economy and Society:* the preconditions and the rise of modern capitalism. Subsequently, this

69. On the close intellectual relationship between Michels and Weber, see my *The Social Democrats in Imperial Germany* (Totowa, N.J.: Bedminster Press, 1963), 249–257; cf. also Juan Linz, "Michels e il suo contributo alla sociologia politica," introduction to Roberto Michels, *La Sociologia del Partito politico nella Democrazia moderna* (Bologna: Il Mulino, 1966), 7–119.

problem is treated from several vantage points: the household and other relatively universal groups (chs. III–V), religion (ch. VI), law (ch. VIII), political community (ch. IX), and the various kinds of rulership (chs. X–XVI). This underlying theme, however, does not determine the typological structure of the chapters; moreover, it is paralleled by the themes of rationalization in religion, law and politics. In view of the importance that Weber attributed to the political factor in his previous work, it is no surprise that his first historical explanation (ch. II:5) concerns the way in which the fiscal and monetary policies of the modern states made possible the rise and persistence of capitalism.

The issue of the origins of capitalism puts *Economy and Society* besides the work that apparently was both inspiration and foil: Werner Sombart's *Modern Capitalism.*⁷⁰ Its two massive volumes were published in 1902, shortly before Weber began writing "The Protestant Ethic and the Spirit of Capitalism." Sombart and Weber had been close allies since the mid-nineties. Weber unsuccessfully tried to have Sombart succeed him in Freiburg when he left for Heidelberg in 1897; in the reactionary nineties—the so-called Era Stumm—official resistance to Sombart was too strong. Both men shared a wide interest in the capitalist enterprise, the spirit of capitalism, social reform and the labor movement, and together they advocated the value-neutral approach in the *Archiv für Sozialwissenschaft.* Sombart was the more flamboyant of the two and proved to be more mercurial. On the one hand, he demanded "facts, facts, facts—this admonition rang in my ears all the time I was writing the book." On the other, he also tried to explain them from ultimate causes: "What separates me from Schmoller and his school is the constructive element in the ordering of the material, the radical postulate of a uniform explanation from last causes, the reconstruction of all historical phenomena as a social system, in short, what I call the specifically theoretical. I also might say: Karl Marx."⁷¹

This was not much more than a rhetorical declaration exaggerating the difference from his former teacher Schmoller. The work failed to link the many facts with its postulate and showed that Sombart was

70. Werner Sombart, *Der moderne Kapitalismus,* vol. I: *Die Genesis des Kapitalismus,* vol. II: *Die Theorie der kapitalistischen Entwicklung* (Leipzig: Duncker & Humblot, 1902). Vol. III appeared much later as *Das Wirtschaftsleben im Zeitalter des Hochkapitalismus* (Munich: Duncker & Humblot, 1927). For Talcott Parsons' interpretation of Sombart's relation to Marx, on the one hand, and to Weber on the other, see his *Structure of Social Action* (Glencoe, Ill.: The Free Press, 1949), 495–499, and "Capitalism in Recent German Literature: Sombart and Weber," *Journal of Political Economy,* vol. 36, 1928, 641–661, and vol. 37, 1929, 31–51. Parsons, however, does not deal with the question of the extent to which Weber's writings were a direct response to Sombart.

71. Sombart, *op. cit.,* I, xii and xxix.

already far removed from Marxism, if he ever was an orthodox Marxist. At any rate, Weber did not consider the postulate feasible, but he was interested in Sombart's facts and decided to approach them through systematic comparative study. Since this involved a methodological difference, it was more than a mere sensible division of labor.[72] Sombart contrasted the traditionalist orientation of craft production with the spirit of capitalism, which to both men appeared very different from the universal desire for wealth. This spirit was a peculiarly European phenomenon, but Sombart barely hinted at the comparative perspective: "A glance at other major civilizations, such as the Chinese, Indian, or ancient American, is enough to prove, in this regard too, the insufficiency of the view that the genesis of modern capitalism can be explained from a 'general law of development' of the human economy."[73] Where Sombart merely glanced, Weber proceeded to the comparisons of *Economy and Society* and, immediately afterwards, the studies of China, India and ancient Judaism.

CHS. III–V: THE RELATIVELY UNIVERSAL GROUPS

At the beginning of ch. III Weber limits his use of the term "society" to "the general kinds of human groups." He intends to deal with economy and society in this sense, not with economy and *Kultur*—literature, art, science. The first groups to be treated are relatively universal—household, neighborhood, kin group, ethnic group, religious group, political community—; in other words, they are found at various levels of historical development. The "developmental forms" of these groups are taken up in the Sociology of Domination. The treatment of the more basic forms is intentionally brief, in part because Weber is primarily interested in the more differentiated associations and their relationship to religion, law and politics, in part, presumably, because Marianne Weber had dealt with some of the subject matter at length in her work on *Wife and Mother in Legal Development* (1907). Weber limits himself to a series of points that either have polemical value or prepare the later exposition. His critical targets are evolutionary conceptions, especially the theory of matriarchy and the related socialist theory of family, property and the state (Engels and Bebel); the neighborhood sentimentalism of agrarian romantics; Gierke's notion of the kin group as the first political association; and racist and nationalist ideas. Against the Romanticist notions of those mourning the passing of Community, but also against the apostles of Progress, Weber endeavors to show that

72. Cf. Parsons, "Capitalism . . . ," *loc. cit.*, 31, 50.
73. Sombart, *op. cit.*, I, 379.

"communal" and rationalist, capitalist and communist, traditionalist and modernist elements appear in ever new combinations—in short, that history is not the progression from *Gemeinschaft* to *Gesellschaft*.

Positively, Weber points out: The household is the original locus of patriarchal rulership and the capitalist enterprise; the neighborhood is an unsentimental economic brotherhood; the kin group is the protective counter-force to the authoritarian household; ethnic groups are not groups, strictly speaking, but propensities for, or residues of, group formation. Weber particularly stresses the pluralism of group affiliation in relatively undeveloped societies before the emerging political community gradually monopolizes the use of force—contrary to the view that modern society is more pluralist than traditionalist society in this respect.

Weber sees no evidence for a universal stage of matriarchy. He explains maternal groupings as a result of military separation of the males from the household. This separation produces the men's house, which nowadays appears in residual form in army barracks and student dormitories—Weber likes to move back and forth, often with ironic undertones, between the ancient origin of a phenomenon and its survival into modern times. The patriarchal household emerges with the military dispersion of warriors in the countryside. In dealing with polygamy and monogamy Weber provides a specifically economic, non-romantic explanation. Monogamy suited the household of the emergent urban patriciate; only later did Christianity raise it to an ethical level. With the dowry the calculative spirit entered the domestic communism of the family. This spirit reached a high point with the rise of the capitalist family enterprise. The legal forms of early modern capitalism originated in part in the communistic household, as Weber had already shown in his dissertation. The enterprise was eventually separated from the household, but Weber points to an historical twist: a "later" economic stage, such as capitalism, may perpetuate or recreate an "earlier" (communistic) family structure in which the extended family remains a unit: "Beyond the balance sheet, those lucky enough to participate enter the realm of equality and brotherhood" (below, 360)—a reference to the communist slogan. Here Weber takes obvious pleasure in outdoing the dialectic of historical materialism. His general point is that the household and domestic authority are relatively independent of economic conditions; in fact, they often shape economic relationships because of their historically developed structure. Weber believed that the contractual regulation of household relations was a peculiarly Occidental phenomenon. Only in Europe did the household create out of itself the capitalist enterprise; elsewhere it developed into the *oikos*, the economic basis of patrimonial domination.

Households are related to one another through neighborliness in an unpathetic, economic sense. The neighbor is the typical helper in need. Thus, neighborliness is not restricted to social equals, but customary help rendered by social inferiors may gradually turn into manorial service. The neighborhood may become an economic group proper or an economically regulatory group, but even in the self-sufficient economy of early times there is no necessary identity between neighborhood and other associations. Only in the case of joint political action can the neighborhood develop into a local community.

The kin group is usually not an extension of the household but a protective group guaranteeing the security and legal protection of the individual. Collective self-help is the most typical means for the defense of its interests. The oldest trial procedures originate in compulsory arbitration within, and between, kin groups. Insofar as kin groups do not have a head with powers of command and a staff, they are not organizations in Weber's sense. Through their regulation of marriage and lineage relations kin groups may effectively curb domestic authority. Similarly, the property laws of the great empires steadily weaken unlimited patriarchal power, but because of the very predominance of patriarchalism—another dialectical feature of historical development. Kin groups may oppose political associations and cross the boundaries of political communities. They tend to become associations only when economic conditions make it desirable to erect monopolies against outsiders.

Race and ethnicity are familiar devices for the monopolist protection of interests. Weber doubts the sociological utility of both concepts if understood in a naturalistic way. He insists that, regardless of the outcome of genetic research, social behavior must be interpreted primarily in social terms. Ethnic membership derives from some consciousness of kind due to common customs, common language and common historical experiences. It may be the product of political association and may remain after the group has dissolved politically. The cultural and political importance of ethnicity rests on the fact that the sense of ethnic honor is a specific honor of the masses and, in the extreme, leads to the notion of the chosen people.

Weber's sketch of nationality and cultural prestige (ch. V:4) illuminates the political situation of Central Europe before the first World War. The section is closely linked to the chapter on the political communities (ch. IX). However, Weber had one more major universal group to deal with: the religious *Gemeinschaft*. In theoretical complexity, originality and sheer size the chapter on religious groups was bound to transcend the preceding chapters.

CH. VI: THE SOCIOLOGY OF RELIGION

In 1902 Sombart touched on the impact of Calvinism and Quakerism on capitalist development and noted that it was "too well-known a fact to require detailed explanation."[74] Weber, far from being deterred by this dismissal, proceeded to state more fully the case for the Protestant ethic's impact on the spirit of capitalism.[75] He may also have been prompted by Schmoller, who in a masterful review of Sombart, his most exasperating pupil, observed:

> Whatever Marx and the Social Democrats have against the capitalist— the "hunger for profit" and the untrammeled ruthlessness toward the worker's welfare—concerns primarily the manner in which the individualist drive for acquisition developed between 1500 and 1900 and cut itself loose from most earlier moral and social restraints. These phenomena must be investigated if one wants to understand today's economy.[76]

If it is unclear whether Schmoller's suggestion really was a major factor in Weber's decision to write the "Protestant Ethic and the Spirit of Capitalism," it can be stated affirmatively that the relationship between Calvinism and capitalism had been an "internal" academic issue for some time and that Weber wrote in response to other studies, and

74. Sombart, op. cit., I, 381.

75. Weber stated the major differences between Sombart's approach and his own in the 1920 re-issue of "Die Protestantische Ethik und der Geist des Kapitalismus," GAzRS, I (1920), 34; for other references to Sombart see ibid., 5, 21, 33, 38 et passim; these include his replies to Sombart's later critiques. Weber explained: "Although the essays go back, in all important respects, to much earlier studies of mine, I need scarcely emphasize how much their presentation owes to the mere existence of Sombart's substantial works, with their pointed formulations, even—and especially—where they diverge from them" (ibid., 42). In his last anti-critique Weber mentioned that he had presented some of his ideas on the Protestant ethic in his courses at the University of Heidelberg in 1897/98. See "Antikritisches zum 'Geist' des Kapitalismus," AfS, XXX, 1910, 177.

76. Gustav Schmoller on Sombart in his Jahrbuch für Gesetzgebung, Verwaltung und Volkswirtschaft, vol. 27, 1903, 298; cf. Lindenlaub, Richtungskämpfe . . . , op. cit., 287. It is true that Weber did not recognize Schmoller, the most powerful figure in the Verein für Sozialpolitik, as one of his teachers and openly disagreed with him in political matters, but this may have been more of an additional incentive than a hindrance to prove to him what could be done in this regard. In fact, Schmoller later worked Weber's findings into his Grundriss der allgemeinen Volkswirtschaftslehre (Leipzig: Duncker & Humblot, 1908). Marianne Weber believed that Weber had started the first essay on the Protestant ethic ". . . in 1903, probably in the second half, just after finishing the first part of his treatise on Roscher and Knies" (Lebensbild, 340). Schmoller published Weber's treatise on "Roscher and Knies and the Logical Problems of Historical Economics" in his Jahrbuch in the fourth issue of the 1903 volume, having reviewed Sombart in the first issue.

not just against historical materialism as has sometimes been suggested in spite of his own denial at the end of the work.[77] Weber acknowledged particularly the earlier work of three colleagues: Eberhard Gothein's monumental study modestly entitled *Economic History of the Black Forest*, Werner Wittich's "tremendously perceptive remarks" on religious differences between France and Germany, and Georg Jellinek's "proof of religious traces in the genesis of the Rights of Man . . . which gave me a crucial stimulus . . . to investigate the impact of religion in areas where one might not otherwise look."[78]

The publication of the two essays on the Protestant ethic in the *Archiv für Sozialwissenschaft* in 1904/5 was an instantaneous literary success and almost immediately led to the controversy that has since continued unabated. The exchange of critiques and anti-critiques between Weber and his adversaries lasted until 1910.[79] Weber considered the exchanges "pretty unrewarding" and decided on another positive statement, which became the present chapter. He left the historical treatment of Protestantism to his friend Ernst Troeltsch, who was then working on *The Social Teachings of the Christian Churches and Sects*,[80] and instead put the theme in a comparative perspective. Yet neither the "underlying" issue of the rise of capitalism nor that of rationalization and secularization over the ages determines the structure of the Sociology of Religion; it is built, rather, around the relation of *religions* to

77. For example, Parsons has written that "the essay was intended to be a refutation of the Marxian thesis in a particular historical case." However, Weber's general theoretical interest in the critique of historical materialism should not be equated with his reasons for writing the essays at that time. Cf. Parsons, "Capitalism . . . ," *loc. cit.*, 40.

78. Cf. Eberhard Gothein, *Wirtschaftsgeschichte des Schwarzwaldes* (Strassburg: Trübner, 1892), 674; Werner Wittich, *Deutsche und französische Kultur im Elsass* (Strassburg: Schlesier & Schweikhardt, 1900), 18–32 (the quote is from GAzRS, I, 25; cf. below, 396); Georg Jellinek, *Die Erklärung der Menschen- und Bürgerrechte* (Leipzig: Duncker & Humblot, 1895; 2nd ed., 1904), *passim* (cf. below, 1209)—the quote is from Weber's memorial address on Jellinek (René König and Johannes Winckelmann, eds., *Max Weber zum Gedächtnis* [Köln: Westdeutscher Verlag, 1963], 15).—On the general familiarity of the 18th and 19th-century literature with the relationship between religious dissent and economic motivation, Protestantism and capitalism, see Reinhard Bendix, "The Protestant Ethic—Revisited," in *Comparative Studies in Society and History*, IX:3, 1967, 266–273.

79. For an account, see Ephraim Fischoff, "The Protestant Ethic and the Spirit of Capitalism: The History of a Controversy," *Social Research*, XI, 1944, 52–77.

80. Ernst Troeltsch, *Die Soziallehren der christlichen Kirchen und Gruppen* (Tübingen: Mohr, 1912), in part published earlier in the form of articles in *AfS*, 1908–10; trsl. by O. Wyon (London: Allen & Unwin, 1931).

their organizational carriers (functionaries), to the status groups and classes supporting them, and to their inherent theological elaboration. Weber took the general functions of religion, whether in a Durkheimian or a Marxist sense, for granted. With his customary realism, he stressed the compensatory functions of religion and, even more, the political uses of religion for legitimation and pacification. In a limited way, it is possible to see his sociology of religion as a vast paraphrase of Marx's dictum that "religion is the sigh of a creature in distress, the heart of a heartless world, the spirit of times without spirit. It is the opiate of the people."[81] But there is an important difference: Weber had a much more profound sense than Marx for the meaning of ethical conduct. The religious polemics of Engels, August Bebel and Karl Kautsky appeared to him as shallow rationalism. Possibly, Weber was familiar with Engels' fleeting remarks on Calvinism: "Where Luther failed, Calvin triumphed. His dogma was adapted to the most daring of the bourgeois. His doctrine of predestination was the religious expression of the fact that in the commercial world of competition success or bankruptcy depend not on the enterprise or skill of the individual but on circumstances independent of him."[82] At any rate, the "Protestant Ethic and the Spirit of Capitalism" reversed this materialist interpretation without substituting a mere spiritualist one. Behind the divergent perspectives of Weber and the Marxists was a personal difference: The Marxists were psychologically unable to take religion seriously enough to undertake his kind of study. Weber called himself "unmusical" in matters religious—this gave him the necessary analytical distance—, but he lived in an extended family in which the women were devout and articulate believers. With his strong family sense, Weber could have disdained religion only at the price of offending those closest to him—this gave him the requisite empathy for the study of religion.[83]

For systematic reasons, ch. VI begins with a brief treatment of primitive religion and the original this-worldly orientation of magical and religious action (secs. i–ii).[84] Weber quickly sketches the rise of functional, local and, finally, universalist and monotheist conceptions of deity. As in the preceding chapters, his ethnographic examples are occasionally doubtful or erroneous, or a statement may suffer from the telescoping of historical events over millennia, or the love of paradox

81. Karl Marx, "Zur Kritik der Hegelschen Rechtsphilosophie," in *Die Frühschriften* (Stuttgart: Kröner, 1953), 208.

82. Friedrich Engels, English introduction to *Socialism Utopian and Scientific* (London 1892), published in German in *Neue Zeit*, XI:1–2, 1892/93; Marx/Engels, *Werke* (Berlin: Dietz, 1963), vol. 22, 300.

83. Cf. Marianne Weber, *Lebensbild*, 27, 84, 88, 91f, 351f.

84. For an explanation of Weber's intention, see below, 421, n. 1.

carries him to an extreme. When he comes to the rationalization of conduct through ethical and exemplary prophecy (secs. *iii–iv*), Weber strikes out on his own. Building on Harnack's typology, he isolates the features peculiar to the prophet through a comparison with magicians, lawgivers, teachers of ethics and mystagogues. Prophets and priests organize the permanent association of laymen: the congregation. Prophets develop preaching and pastoral care, priests the dogmata and the canonical writings.

After thus dealing with the religious leaders and the associations created by them Weber turns to an examination of all major social strata and their affinity to religion (secs. *v–vi*). This provides a comparative frame for assessing the Puritan bourgeoisie, but in the context of the present work it also prepares the treatment of aristocratic and bureaucratic rulership, the role of the intelligentsia, and the themes of bureaucratization and democratization. Aristocrats tend toward irreligion, unless they are warriors for the faith, an historically important, but transitional phenomenon. Bureaucrats are inclined toward a formalistic religion or philosophy, while permitting less complex magical beliefs among the masses for the sake of "mass domestication." The urban bourgeois, even though concerned with economic rationality, tends to be more religious than the aristocrat and bureaucrat. In fact, the rationalist piety of bourgeois believers is a step on the road that ultimately led to the Protestant ethic. Non-privileged strata have powerful needs for salvation, but they may find primarily passive or purely affective expression. Weber goes down the social ladder from the craftsmen's piety, so important in early Christianity, to the religious disinclinations of slaves, day laborers and the modern proletariat. Peasants are traditionally concerned not with salvation but with the practical, magical effects of religion, even though in modern times the rural population is a mainstay of Christian conservatism. Salvation religions, usually the creation of intellectuals of higher social rank, can devolve into the creed of non-privileged strata, changing their function from legitimation to compensation. Pariah peoples tend to develop an intense religious attachment —Judaism being the historically decisive case.

After this tour de force in the sociology of knowledge Weber balances his analysis of status tendencies with an investigation of religious intellectualism (secs. *vii–xi*). Intellectuals of *diverse* status elaborate religions on logical and theological grounds. Status differences may recede in the face of changing political fortunes; an important case is the escapism of intellectuals of politically declining strata or defeated communities. Conversely, nativist lower-class intellectuals may turn against the intellectualism of higher strata, as it happened in Judaism and early

Christianity vis-à-vis Hellenized intellectuals. Weber carries his analysis up to his own time, ending with secular salvation ideologies and some biting remarks on café-house intellectuals (sec. *vii*:8).

The last part (secs. *xii–xv*) examines the influence of religious ethics on the "world": the sphere of the economic, political, artistic, and sexual. The last extant section breaks off with yet another attempt to contrast Jewish rationalism, Puritan asceticism, Islamic this-worldliness, Buddhist other-worldliness and Jesus' indifference to the world—all with a look back toward "The Protestant Ethic," but also in anticipation of the subsequent large-scale studies of the great world religions, to which Weber turned without completing Part Two of *Economy and Society.*

CH. VII. THE MARKET: ITS IMPERSONALITY AND ETHIC

The chapter on the market—another group (*Gemeinschaft*) in Weber's terminology—logically follows the treatment of religion. The economically rationalized, hence ethically irrational, character of pure market relationships is basically irreconcilable with ethical religion—with the historic exception of Calvinism. Whereas Weber gave much attention to the chapter on religion, his market chapter is only a brief sketch. Unlike the sociology of religion, the market was a topic that could be handled by many other men. Perhaps Weber postponed writing the chapter because he waited for other contributions to the series, the better to coordinate the various expositions. In any case, the fragment he did write was sufficient to distinguish the market (*Marktgemeinschaft* or *Marktvergemeinschaftung*) from the more "natural" groups and the political community. The market is the *Gemeinschaft* based on the most rational kind of social action: association (*Vergesellschaftung*) through exchange. The association may last only for the duration of the exchange, or it may develop into a continuous relationship.

In early history the market was the only peaceful relationship of men who were not linked through household, kinship or tribal ties. The participants were strangers, "enemies" who did not expect action in accordance with an ethic of brotherhood. The "community" of the market is the most impersonal group, but not because it involves struggle (*Kampf*) between opposed interests—there is struggle also in the most intimate relationships; rather, the market is the more impersonal, the more the struggle of the participants is oriented merely to actual or potential exchanges. In this manner the market is the exact opposite of any association (*Vergesellschaftung*) based on a formal order, voluntary or imposed. Even so, neither the use of money nor the impersonality of exchange prevent the eventual rise of a market ethic binding on those who continually trade. Such exchange partners develop expectations of reciprocity which make them abide by the rules. Occasional traders are most likely to ignore the maxim that "honesty is the best policy"; Weber sarcastically cites aristocratic cavalry officers trading horses—a familiar current example is the private sale of automobiles. One aspect of the market ethic is the fixed price, a peculiarly European phenomenon that became one of the preconditions of modern capitalism.

The market proved destructive to many status monopolies of the past. Yet the very success of capitalist interests on the free market led to new monopolies based either on political alliances or sheer superiority over competitors. As markets increased in importance, religious and political associations moved to protect them for reasons of their own. This brings Weber to the organizations concerned with legal regulation.

CH. VIII. THE SOCIOLOGY OF LAW

The Sociology of Law gives historical depth to the introductory statement on convention and law (ch. I).[85] After the earlier methodological critique of Stammler's approach Weber now demonstrates what a sociology of law should be, in contrast to legal philosophy, jurisprudence, and mere legal history. The chapter provides a typological setting within which a given legal phenomenon can be located, not with regard to any systematically or dogmatically proper placement but for the sake of historical explanation. The impact of Roman law and common law on the rise of capitalism constitutes one link with the overall theme of *Economy and Society;* another is the varieties of rationalization, which may be mutually incompatible. The chapter is also constructed with a view to the frequently mentioned Sociology of Domination: Here Weber treats the creation and administration of law by political and other associations,

85. Chs. I and VIII are the only sections of *Wirtschaft und Gesellschaft* that could be compared with the original manuscript. Marianne Weber put these chapters in an envelope marked "Sociology of Law"—ch. VIII had no manuscript title—and presented them as a gift to Karl Loewenstein, whom they accompanied into exile, thus escaping the fate of the rest of the manuscript. On the basis of this original, now at the Max Weber Institute in Munich, Johannes Winckelmann prepared a definitive edition—although Weber's almost illegible handwriting leaves some passages doubtful—of the two chapters; see *Rechtssoziologie* (2nd ed.; Neuwied: Luchterhand, 1967). The text now differs considerably from that in the 1925 edition of *Wirtschaft und Gesellschaft,* on which the Rheinstein-Shils translation of the Sociology of Law was based. The changes involve not merely many printing errors, but also the sequence of sections and terminological clarifications. For example, the category of the "coercive contract" (*Zwangskontrakt*) turned out to be a misreading of *Zweckkontrakt,* which (in sec. *ii*) contrasts with *Statuskontrakt,* a distinction related to Henry Sumner Maine's *Ancient Law* (1861).

there the ruler's legitimation, organizational power and motives for imposing law.

If Weber was a self-made scholar in affairs religious, he was on
academic homeground in the Sociology of Law. Not only do legal topics
of his dissertation and *Habilitation* of two decades before appear, but so
does much of the later literature. Even as Weber broadened his intellectual concerns, he retained an active interest in legal studies. His ability
to write the Sociology of Law as a legal historian makes this the most
difficult chapter for the legal layman and mere sociologist, for whom it
may be helpful to perceive the broad structural parallels with the Sociology of Religion.[86] The substitution of legal for religious topics yields
the following rough outline: the basic categories of public and private
law; the development of contracts and of juristic personality; early forms
of law administered by non-political associations; an occupational typology of "specialists," ranging from charismatic law prophets to legal
honoratiores and university-trained judges; a typology of various forms of
legal training; the historical systems of theocratic and secular law; a
comparison of Indian, Islamic, Persian, Jewish, Canon and Roman law;
the great codifications; the revolutionary power of natural law; formal
and substantive rationalization and the ineradicable tension between
formal and substantive justice; finally, the irrationalist trends at the eve
of the first World War, with their "characteristic reaction" to formal rationality and the dominance of legal experts—paralleling the fashion of
surrogate religions in intellectual circles and the "romantic game of
syndicalism." Here Weber continues the sociology of intellectuals with
an examination of their propensity for substantive justice, on the one
hand, and skepticism on the other; he points to another historical
dialectic: 19th-century socialist intellectuals first advanced substantive
natural law against the formalist natural law of the bourgeoisie and then
undermined their own position through positivistic relativism and
Marxist evolutionism.

The gradual ascendancy of state law over the law of the other groups
is part of the larger theme of the rise of the political community. Weber
follows juridical usage when he makes the existence of a legal order
dependent on a staff ready to resort to physical or psychic coercion, and
when he defines the *modern* political community—the state—in terms
of its monopoly on the legal use of force. As a sociologist, however, he is

86. For interpretations of the Sociology of Law by jurists, see the introduc-
tions by Rheinstein (*Max Weber on Law in Economy and Society,* 1954, xxv–
lxxi) and Winckelmann (*Rechtssoziologie,* 1967, 15–49); also Karl Engisch,
"Max Weber als Rechtsphilosoph und als Rechtssoziologe," in K. Engisch, B.
Pfister and J. Winckelmann, eds., *Max Weber: Gedächtnisschrift der Ludwig-
Maximilians-Universität München* (Berlin: Duncker & Humblot, 1966), 67–88.

equally concerned with the extent to which this claim is *de facto* limited in the modern state, where conventional and religious sanctions continue to be powerful. Weber remembered as one of his youthful lessons the inability of the mighty Prussian state to triumph over the Catholic church in the *Kulturkampf* of the eighteen-seventies and again over the Social Democrats in the eighties, the period of the anti-socialist laws.

The chapter on political communities links the chapters on the more "universal" groups and the Sociology of Law with the Sociology of Domination; it describes the development of political community from rudimentary beginnings to complex differentiation.[87] For many centuries the political community differed only quantitatively from the other relatively "universal" groups that gradually lost their protective and coercive functions as the old political pluralism declined. Eventually a qualitative difference developed: a belief in the right of the state to define the legal order and the use of legitimate force. This belief in legitimacy resulted from gradual usurpation. Previously, the notion of legitimate force was part of the *consensual* action of kin members engaging in blood revenge; now it became part of the *organized* action (*Verbandshandeln*) of community members. In the modern state, the exercise of political powers (*Gewalt*) is a part of *institutional* action (*anstaltsmaessiges Handeln*).[88]

87. Until the fourth (1956) edition of *Wirtschaft und Gesellschaft*, the *Gemeinschaften* ranging from the household to the religious and legal associations and even the city were arranged into a separate part (Part Two, "Typen der Vergemeinschaftung und Vergesellschaftung") set off against the types of domination (Part Three, "Typen der Herrschaft") which included the political community. There is no warrant for this division in Weber's 1914 outline or in the logic of his exposition. The categories of social action and group formation (*Vergemeinschaftung, Vergesellschaftung, Herrschaft*) encompass all of the present Part Two, although the detailed treatment of *Herrschaft* is reserved for the last chapters. The definition of *Herrschaft* appears first, together with the other basic concepts, in "The Categories of Interpretive Sociology" (App. I, 1378 below) and in the first chapter of Part One.

88. In English, the use of "political power" for *politische Gewalt* can easily be misleading. Therefore the plural "powers" or the singular "authority" has been used. Linguistic habit and stylistic convenience make it difficult to render Weber's social action terms always in such ways as to avoid the impression that it is groups, rather than individuals, which act. "Organized action" is *organization-oriented* action and "institutional action" *institution-oriented* action; likewise, "class action" (below, 929) is *class-oriented* action and "party action" (below, 938) *party-oriented* action—four varieties of social action that contrast with "mass action." The juxtaposition of social and mass action was obscured in the Gerth and Mills translation of ch. IX:6, which interpolated the terminology of Part One (ch. I:9) into the text of Part Two (cf. Gerth and Mills, *From Max Weber* . . . , 183). In the different terminology of Part Two, *Gemeinschaftshandeln* means "social action," not "communal action," and *Vergesellschaftung* means

CH. IX. POLITICAL COMMUNITY AND STATE

The political community is a group ready to defend a given territory with force against outsiders. This minimum definition is designed to encompass all historical communities and thus does not even include the guarantee of internal security. Many communities actually did limit themselves to nothing more than the maintenance of territorial control. The Pennsylvanian commonwealth of the Quakers was exceptional in that it refused for a time to use external force. Between these two extremes social action may be oriented to any number of goals, and therefore a community may be robber state, welfare state, constitutional state or *Kulturstaat*. Communities united merely for defense may in peacetime relapse into a state of anarchy (in the strict sense)—the mere consensual recognition among the members of the given economic order. And external peacetime may also be a period of internal war. Thus the ascendancy of the political community over other groups becomes the history of internal pacification: of the peace edicts of kings, bishops and cities during their struggles with the feuding nobility. Old and new groups whose ideal and material interests were not adequately protected by the traditional arrangements demanded pacification and the "nationalization" of legal norms (treated in the Sociology of Law).

Weber clearly distinguishes between patriarchal powers, "non-authoritarian" consensual and arbitral powers, and political powers proper—autonomous military and judicial authority. The prototype for political powers is the *imperium* of the legitimate Roman officials (ch. VIII:*vi*), which later was usurped by military leaders who received *ex post facto* confirmation by the Senate. Political authority (*Gewalt*) involves the power over life and death which gives the political community its specific pathos. As the community develops, political coercion frequently becomes internal, since many demands of the political order are accepted by the members only under pressure. However, a political community is held together not only through coercion but also through common historical experiences: it is a "community of shared memory" (*Erinnerungsgemeinschaft*). Yet both the pathos of the supreme sacrifice and the shared memory of dangers persist also in other groups ranging from those practicing violence—the Camorra, nowadays the Mafia—to those suffering it, as in persecuted sects.

After an historical sketch of the development of political community

---

"association," not "societal action"—i.e., it is not a contrast in Toennies' sense (cf. below, 60, n. 24). Hence, terminological adjustments had to be made. For example, the seemingly illogical passage, "The communal actions of parties always mean a societalization" (Gerth and Mills, *op. cit.*, 194) now reads "party-oriented social action always involves association" (below, 938).

(sec. 2) Weber again takes up the European state of affairs on the eve of the first World War (cf. ch. V:4), comparing it with the capitalism and imperialism of Antiquity. The dynamics of international and national stratification is his dual theme: the relations of prestige and power among and within political communities. Here again was an issue previously raised by Sombart. His *Socialism and Social Movement in the 19th Century* (1896) opened with the dictum of the *Communist Manifesto* that "the history of all hitherto existing society has been a history of class struggles." Sombart considered this

> one of the greatest truths of the century . . . , but not the whole truth. For it is incorrect to say that all history of society is merely a history of class struggles. If it be worthwhile at all to subsume world history under one formula, we will have to say that social history has moved between two poles . . . which I will call the social and [inter-] national antagonisms (*Gegensätze*). . . . We find the same striving for wealth, power and prestige among communities as among individuals. . . . Today we are at the end of an historical epoch of national exaltation and in the midst of a period of great social cleavage; it seems to me that all the antagonistic viewpoints of the various groups can be reduced to the alternative: national or social.[89]

Sombart did not further pursue the topic of international stratification and instead focussed on the Marxist concept of class. Weber, however, carried the juxtaposition of the external and internal realm of honor to its logical conclusion and elaborated a scheme that also incorporated the Marxist approach as one segment. In the external sphere, he was concerned with power prestige, not just with national pride, which can also be found in non-expansionist Switzerland or Norway. Since power prestige derives from power over other political communities, it promotes expansionism and is thus a major component cause of war. The prestige pretensions of one country escalate those of others— Weber points to the deteriorating relations between France and Germany in the first decade of the century when, in contrast to the eighteen-nineties that Sombart had in mind, nationalist antagonisms prevailed again over internal cleavage. The carriers of power prestige are the "Great Powers," yet their ruling groups, fearing the seizure of power by their own victorious generals, are not always expansionist—witness ancient Rome and early 19th-century England. In both cases, however, capitalist interests enforced the resumption of political expansion.

Weber's theory of imperialism adds the economic element to the prestige factor. Building on his earlier writings, Weber constructs his

89. Werner Sombart, *Socialismus und sociale Bewegung im 19. Jahrhundert* (Jena: Fischer, 1896), 1f.

notion of imperialist capitalism from the first great historical case: ancient Rome with its tax-farmers and state purveyors. In modern times, as in Antiquity, it is the general structure of the economy, rather than trade interests, which is crucial for political expansionism. Imperialist capitalism may be restrained by the profitableness of "pacifist" capitalism, but for his own time Weber foresees the former's ascendancy, largely because of the state's role as the biggest customer of the defense contractors and similar enterprises. The economic-pacifist interests of the petty-bourgeois and proletarian strata are easily reduced by appeals to the emotive idea of "the nation."

Weber reviews the diverse cultural and social characteristics of individuals that may define membership in a nation. He emphasizes three elements: (1) the speed with which certain historical experiences can create the sense of nationhood, (2) the different meanings of the term from one country, and one stratum, to another, (3) the intellectuals' role in fashioning a sense of national identity. His unfinished analysis of the intellectuals—"those who usurp leadership in a *Kulturgemeinschaft*"—breaks off with a hint at the affinity of cultural prestige and power prestige, but not without the skeptical reminder that "art and literature of a specifically German character did *not* develop in the political center of Germany" (below, 926).

Weber's improvement on the Marxian class analysis lies in the detailed typology of the three phenomena of power distribution within the political community: class, status group, and party. Those powerful in the economic order need have neither political power nor social honor, but they often do have both. Apart from the economic order, the distribution of political power is codetermined by the legal order and the social or status order. Weber proposes to consider classes not as communities but as propensities for social action, similar to ethnic groups. Therefore, he speaks of "class situation," which is defined by market situation and has two basic categories: property and the lack of property. Property, in turn, differs according to whether it is used for rent income or profit-making. Although it does make a difference whether communities are based on labor, as in soil-tilling villages, or merely on property, as among cattle-breeders, the historical origin of class struggles lies not in the countryside but within the city: in the clash between creditors and debtors. At a later economic stage the class struggle was transformed into the struggle on the commodity market; in modern times it has come to center in wage disputes on the labor market. The contemporary bitterness of wage-earners is primarily directed against the entrepreneurs and managers, who are more visible than the "real" capitalists, the shareholders and bankers. This opaqueness is only one of the many social and cultural factors that influence the way in which class situation may (or may not) become the basis for class-oriented or party-oriented action.

The major polemical target of this exposition on class and class situation was "that kind of pseudo-scientific operation with the concepts of class and class interests which is so frequent these days and which has found its most classic expression in the assertion (*Behauptung*) of a talented author that the individual may be in error about his interests, but that the class is infallible" (below, 930)—a reference, it seems, to none other than the young Georg Lukács.[90] As against this class reification by a new breed of Marxian metaphysicians Weber insisted on his own empirical dialectic of class and status. Status groups are real, if often amorphous, groups limiting the sheer market principle with its opposition of class interests. Positive or negative social honor is the basis of status groups. Status differences express themselves in the style of life: a phenomenon extensively treated in the Sociology of Domination. In the extreme, status differentiation leads to caste formation: a link with the earlier exposition of ethnic and religious groups. Status groups are the bearers of all conventions: a structural explanation for the coercive character of conventions that Weber upheld against Stammler. In sum, classes are part of the economic order, status groups, of the social order; put in another way, classes are rooted in the sphere of production and acquisition, status groups in the realm of consumption.

Class interests as well as status interests may be represented by parties. In contrast to classes and status groups, parties are always purpose-rational associations, since their goal is the acquisition of power in larger associations. Thus parties are frequently authoritarian organizations—an issue of paramount concern for the sociology of political parties in modern democracy. However, adequately to understand the structure

90. When Weber wrote this passage, Georg Lukács was one of his close young friends. He had attracted public attention through his first German book, *Die Seele und die Formen* (1911). At the time he was preparing himself for an academic career, a plan destroyed by the onset of the war. In Weber's Heidelberg circle Lukács and Ernst Bloch represented a new generation of Marxians who were highly critical of "vulgar" Marxism. If the identification is correct, Weber refers to conversations rather than publications, as he also does elsewhere in the text. An early formulation of Lukács' theory that the proletariat as a whole is infallible about its interests is found in an Hungarian essay of 1919, "Tactics and Ethics"; see his *Schriften zur Ideologie und Politik*, ed. Peter Ludz (Neuwied: Luchterhand, 1967), esp. 9, 18f., 31. Lukács later adapted Weber's class terminology in his famous work on *History and Class Consciousness* (1923). On the relation of Weber and Lukács, see Marianne Weber, *Lebensbild*, 473–76, and Paul Honigsheim, "Erinnerungen an Max Weber," in R. König and J. Winckelmann, eds., *Max Weber zum Gedächtnis*, 184–88.

of parties one must first examine the larger associations within which they operate.

Herewith Weber has reached the Sociology of Domination. Parties vary not only according to class and status structure but also according to the larger group's structure of domination. In line with his comparative interests in earlier studies, Weber now proceeds to a broad typology comprising parties and polities of Antiquity as well as of the Middle Ages and of some non-European areas.

CHS. X–XVI. THE SOCIOLOGY OF DOMINATION

The Sociology of Domination is the core of *Economy and Society*.[91] The major purpose of the work was the construction of a typology of associations, with most prominence given to the types of domination and their relation to want-satisfaction through appropriation. To be sure, religion and law were constituent parts of the work, irrespective of whether Weber planned the chapters to be as comprehensive as they finally came to be, but the 1914 outline and the proportions of the manuscript show the Sociology of Domination to be the central theme. In the reception of the piecemeal translation of *Economy and Society*, the Sociology of Domination has been obscured as a whole. Until now, nearly half of it was untranslated; the other half was divided among three different translations.[92] In the theoretical discussions the three types of legitimate domination have usually been treated in isolation, and in research the complex typology of domination has all too frequently been reduced to the simple dichotomy of charisma and bureaucracy, if not just to the so-called Weberian "formal model of bureaucracy." Too

91. Weber was in the habit of speaking, respectively, of his Sociology of Law, Religion, Domination, and State, and he employed these terms in cross-references. However, since the 1914 outline does not contain the terms and the manuscript of ch. VIII was untitled, it appears likely that he did not want to use the phrase "sociology of" in a chapter title. At any rate, in view of the great overall length of chs. X–XVI, no summary title was chosen in the text for the Sociology of Domination. Even in its incomplete state this section is twice as long as the chapters on religion and law—a quantitative indicator of their importance for the work as a whole.

92. If ch. III of Part One is included, there are four different translations. The incomplete terminological summary of Part One further telescopes the historical dimension. It does not parallel the structure of the Sociology of Domination in Part Two, especially in the chapters on secular and hierocratic rulership and the city; the contrast of secular and hierocratic domination appears in Part One in ch. I:17, and the forms of legitimate rulership peculiar to the city are found mostly under rule by notables (ch. III:15–20). Moreover, feudalism is in Part Two a variant of patrimonialism, in Part One a variant of charisma—equally feasible classifications.

often a rulership has been measured only against the formal features of bureaucracy or of charismatic domination. In this manner the technical sense of the typology (see below, 263) has been disregarded: More than one type should be compared to any given case, rather than just one "ideal type" with one "natural system."

The Sociology of Domination is the mold in which some of Weber's most substantive interests, and the influences arousing them, were fused into a conceptual unity. As a basic influence Weber acknowledged the work of his friend Georg Jellinek: "From his great studies I received decisive impulses for whatever fate has permitted me to accomplish. . . . [Among these was] his coinage of the concept of the 'social theory of the state,' clarifying the blurred tasks of sociology."[93] In his *Allgemeine Staatslehre* Jellinek defined as the ultimate objective elements of the state the social relations of men, as against metaphysical notions of its corporeality:

> More precisely, the state exists in relations of will among a plurality of persons. Men who command and others who obey form the basis of the state. . . . In the state the relations of will, concentrated in an organizational unit, are essentially relations of domination. The quality of domination does not exhaust the essence of the state. But relations of domination are so necessary to the state that it cannot be conceived without them. The state has the powers of rulership (*Herrschergewalt*). To rule (*herrschen*) means the ability to impose one's own will upon others unconditionally. . . . Only the state has this power to enforce its will unconditionally against other wills. It is the only organization that rules by virtue of its inherently autonomous powers. . . . The state, then, is that organizational unit equipped with underived powers of command.[94]

Weber differentiated Jellinek's notion of rule. What Jellinek called *Herrschen,* he called "power" (*Macht*); this left the term *Herrschaft* (domination) free for an adaptation of the Kantian categorical imperative: "The situation in which the manifested will (command) of the ruler or rulers is meant to influence the conduct of one or more others (the ruled) and actually does influence it in such a way that their conduct, to a socially relevant degree, occurs as if the ruled had made the content of the command the maxim of their conduct for its very own sake" (below, 946). Domination transforms amorphous and intermittent social action into persistent association. Weber exemplifies the difference of domination from mere power with the case of monopolistic control in the market. In their own rational interest, the unorganized

93. R. König and J. Winckelmann, eds., *Max Weber zum Gedächtnis,* 15.
94. Georg Jellinek, *Allgemeine Staatslehre,* 2nd ed. (Berlin: Häring, 1905; 1st ed., 1900), 169, 172.

customers of a monopolistic enterprise may comply with its market dictate: this is domination by virtue of interest constellation. Through many gradual transitions, this relationship may be transformed into domination proper, that means, by virtue of the authoritarian power of command, as it prevails in the large-scale industrial enterprise and on the manor—the two most important economic structures of domination. Domination exists insofar as there is obedience to a command; in general, obedience is due to a mixture of habit, expediency and belief in legitimacy. The subjects' willingness to comply with a command is enhanced by the existence of a staff, which again acts on the basis of habit, legitimacy and self-interest. Sociologically, then, a *Herrschaft* is a structure of superordination and subordination sustained by a variety of motives and means of enforcement.[95] For the historical persistence of structures of domination, staff enforcement on whatever grounds is no less important than belief in legitimacy. In fact, explains Weber, he is "primarily interested in domination insofar as it is administration" (below, 948). Only after defining domination in terms of rule by a master and his apparatus does Weber add the ultimate grounds for its validity. He turns to legitimacy because of its inherent historical importance—the need of those who have power, wealth and honor to justify their good fortune.

The resulting typology of domination goes far beyond the three familiar types of authority. The substance of the Sociology of Domination consists in the general historical models of rulership. Weber does not wish to work out a "political system" applicable to all political groups irrespective of time and place; rather, he aims at a "systems analysis" of these models. Here he takes up the postulate of a "social theory of the state," but whereas Jellinek's typology of states remains largely on the level of constitutional theory and political philosophy, Weber "descends" to a level of greater historical descriptiveness. With the nature of the modern state and of industrial capitalism as underlying themes, Weber puts together a comparative scheme within which he integrates the major topics and results of his earlier studies:

i. the ancient and medieval city state as an autonomous polity, ranging from the patrimonial-bureaucratic kingdom to the confraternity of equals (cf. above, secs. 6 and 7);

ii. manorial domination (*Grundherrschaft*) in Germanic Antiquity and the Middle Ages, involving the issues of patriarchalism, feudalism, and military communism (cf. above, sec. 4);

95. For the terminological resolution of the translation of *Herrschaft* as domination or authority, see below, 61, n. 31.

III. the rise of modern public and private bureaucracy and the organizational realities of modern democracy (cf. above, sec. 8);

IV. the perennial tension between usurpation and legitimation (cf. above, sec. 7, p. li).

In the Sociology of Domination, theme I is treated mostly under patrimonialism (ch. XII) and the city (ch. XVI); theme II under feudalism (ch. XIII) and charismatic rulership (ch. XIV); theme III under bureaucracy (ch. XI) and again under charisma (ch. XIV); theme IV under caesaropapism and hierocracy (ch. XV) and under the special aspect of non-legitimate domination (again ch. XVI). However, Weber puts at the beginning of the Sociology of Domination (ch. X) what was politically most important to him: the meaning of democracy in an industrialized and bureaucratized society.

(A) THE THEORY OF MODERN DEMOCRACY. Since domination and administration are interdependent, domination is an irreducible component of democratic administration. So-called direct democracy is nothing primeval, but a product of historical development. Its aim is the minimization of domination; its precondition is the relative equality of the participants. Here is another historical twist: Direct democracy is most feasible in an aristocracy, whether it be Venetian noblemen or the vaunted German "aristocracy of the spirit"—the university professors. Direct democracy, however, is inherently unstable, and wherever there is economic differentiation in the group, domination tends to fall into the hands of those who have the economic requisites for performing administrative and political tasks. This is, first of all, a matter of "economic availability," not necessarily of high status; thus, managers of large-scale enterprises, teachers and medical doctors are less available than lawyers, country squires and urban *rentiers*. In general, the available groups also have social honor, and then they are *honoratiores* (notables). If direct democracy turns into rule by *honoratiores*, the demand for democracy easily becomes the battle cry of those lacking in wealth or honor. In that case both sides may form parties, which tend to be tightly organized because their object is, after all, the struggle for power. If this happens, and if the community grows beyond a certain size, "the meaning of democracy changes so radically that it no longer makes sense for the sociologist to ascribe to the term the same meaning as in the case discussed so far" (below, 951).

Weber's own theory of modern democracy was directed against the many intellectuals ("*literati*") to his right and left who failed to understand the *facts* of parliamentary government and democratic party organization and were thus unable to weigh them against the prevalent monarchic constitutionalism or against panaceas such as the "corporate" state, just as they failed to comprehend the *technical* imperatives of a private capitalist economy in contrast to state socialism and capitalism. Weber stressed the formal similarity of the democratic party and the capitalist enterprise: If parties are legal and party affiliation is voluntary, the business of politics is the pursuit of ideal and material interests, which is as inevitable as the activism of the few against the passivity of the many. Under the conditions of mass suffrage, the leadership of the few rests on mass mobilization, and this in turn requires an effective party apparatus. The party bureaucracies parallel those of state and economy. However, the bureaucratization of the parties does not necessarily spell the end of meaningful political democratization or of charismatic leadership. Here Weber's disagreements with Robert Michels reappear.[96] Michels' "iron law of oligarchy" became for a time very influential in the American literature on democracy and party organization, but eventually Weber's conception gained ground through its popularization in Joseph Schumpeter's *Capitalism, Socialism and Democracy*.[97]

The chapter on bureaucracy (ch. XI) elaborates the partly supportive and partly antagonistic relations between bureaucracy and modern democracy, and between passive and active democratization. The chapter on charisma (ch. XIV) adds the transition to democratic suffrage and the selection of democratic leadership. It contains the important recogni-

96. Traces of Weber's objections to Michels' arguments are found in chs. XI and XIV (cf. below, 991 and 1003, n. 8), apart from ch. II. Weber did not publicly state his disagreement with Michels, whose academic career in Germany had been forestalled by official disapproval of his political activities and in whose behalf he had protested vociferously in an article on "The So-Called Freedom of Teaching" (*Frankfurter Zeitung*, Sept. 20, 1908; cf. Marianne Weber, *Lebensbild*, 361). In 1913 Michels became co-editor of the *Archiv für Sozialwissenschaft und Sozialpolitik*. The two men corresponded extensively; Michels mentioned in the second edition of his *Political Parties* that he took into consideration a lengthy critique by Weber, to whom he had dedicated the first edition. The difficulties of reconstructing Weber's critical thrusts are similar in the case of Georg Simmel, whose career he tried to further against strong (in part anti-Semitic) resistance. In order to protect him, Weber terminated a projected severe critique after writing a few pages of personal testimonial to Simmel and a bitter denunciation of his academic and bureaucratic detractors.

97. Schumpeter, *Capitalism, Socialism, and Democracy* (3rd ed.; New York: Harper & Brothers, 1950), ch. XXII. Schumpeter, one of the earliest contributors to the *Outline of Social Economics* (1914), did not here mention Weber's name, but there is a point-by-point correspondence of his description with passages in both parts of *Economy and Society*. For Schumpeter's account of his relationship to Weber, see his *History of Economic Analysis*, ed. Elizabeth Boody Schumpeter (New York: Oxford University Press, 1954), 815–820, and his 1920 necrologue on Weber, reprinted in R. König and J. Winckelmann, eds., *Max Weber zum Gedächtnis*, 64–71.

tion that, far from being irreconcilable, charisma and bureaucracy may be interdependent. The adjustment of the Catholic church to bourgeois democracy, especially in the United States, appears in the chapter on political and hierocratic domination (ch. XV). The chapter on the city (ch. XVI) deals with the theory of ancient and medieval democracy, providing the historical contrast to modern democracy.[98]

(B) THE DIMENSIONS OF RULERSHIP. From the beginning, Weber deals with bureaucracy not only in its formal aspects but as a status group with vested interests. At the core of his approach to rulership is the three-way struggle between ruler, staff, and subjects. The types of rulership are distinguished by differing forms of appropriation—Weber speaks of appropriation because the legal concept of property is too narrow for many historical cases. Appropriation involves the means and positions of administration, ranging from economic resources and weaponry to managerial and political functions. The seizure of goods and the extraction of services often originate in usurpation. Normally, appropriation is carried through by a group rather than individuals. Legitimacy is used to defend appropriation. Weber suggests, for example, that European feudalism, although in many ways an "impossible" structure of domination, survived as long as it did because the vassals needed the shield of legitimacy. This "functional" emphasis on legitimacy pervades the whole exposition.

From the viewpoint of legitimation, the structure of the Sociology of Domination is the following:

(1) The historical models of bureaucracy, patriarchalism, patrimonialism, feudalism, *Ständestaat,* and military (and monastic) communism are subsumed under the three types of legitimate domination (chs. XI–XIV);

(2) As the greatest force of legitimation in history, the priesthood is ceaselessly struggling for power with secular rulership (ch. XV); their relationship is one of mutual antagonism as well as dependence;

(3) The city is the locus of specifically non-legitimate domination in history (ch. XVI).

However, the bulk of each chapter is concerned not with legitimacy, but with the various strategies and resources of domination on the part of ruler and staff. In each chapter, the military constituency, which was basic to the analysis of the ancient states in the "Agrarian Conditions of Antiquity," is treated next to the civilian administration. Each chapter also contains a section on the ethos and education of the status groups.

98. In Part One, the theory of democracy is treated especially in ch. III:*vii* and x.

Finally, the relation between each form of domination and economic development is examined. Weber finds that it is easier to state the impact of domination on the economy than vice versa. There are, for instance, striking similarities between the class struggle in the Italian cities of the Middle Ages and in the Roman Republic, although the economic conditions were quite different. The reason lies in the limited number of administrative techniques available for effecting compromises among the status groups of a polity. Therefore, similarities of political administration must not be interpreted as identical superstructures rising over identical economic foundations: "These things obey their own law" (below, 1309).

(c) THE TERMINOLOGY OF DOMINATION. The terminological integration of the Sociology of Domination was a remarkable achievement. By drawing on concepts from ancient, medieval and modern history Weber succeeded in fashioning a terminology applicable to all three eras. It should be remembered that this did not involve any assumptions about historical sameness, but an insistence on typological gradation. Weber addressed his comparative terminology to medievalists like Below and Gierke, who wrote on both manorial domination (*Grundherrschaft*) and the city, to ancient historians like Eduard Meyer, and to church and legal historians like Rudolf Sohm. He demonstrated some of the typological implications of their terminology.

The term *Herrschaft* has a very concrete and a very abstract meaning. In historiography a *Herrschaft* is a noble estate, corresponding to the French *seigneurie* and the English manor. In the philosophy of history, *Herrschaft* is the basic category of superordination, and in this sense it loomed large in the work of the young Marx. Weber uses the term frequently in the historical sense and occasionally in the philosophical meaning. Sometimes he refers to the "domination of man over man." However, this is not technically relevant to his typology. The *Herrschaftsverband* (authoritarian association)[99] was a term widely used after the late eighteen-sixties when Gierke made it the standard contrast to the *Genossenschaft* (equalitarian association). The term "patrimonial state" was older still; it was introduced early in the nineteenth century by Carl Ludwig von Haller.[100] Haller fought against the liberal doctrines

99. Since Weber did not use the term *Herrschaftsverband* as a contrast to *Genossenschaft,* the translation "ruling organization" was chosen for the most general formulation in the basic definitions (cf. below, 53) in order to exclude the colloquial connotations of "authoritarianism." In Weber's terminology even the most democratic organization is a *Herrschaftsverband.*

100. Carl Ludwig von Haller, *Restauration der Staats-Wissenschaft, oder Theorie des natürlich-geselligen Zustands der Chimäre des künstlich-bürgerlichen entgegengesetzt* (Winterthur: Steiner, 1817/18), vols. II and III.

of the social contract and for the thesis that all governmental authority was the private property of the ruler. He also elaborated the early ideal type of patrimonial bureaucracy. Whereas Haller equated patriarchalism and patrimonialism, Weber contrasted the two concepts and defined the latter as the *political* domination of a ruler with the help of his *personal* apparatus (consisting of slaves, retainers, *ministeriales*). This change reflected the controversy over the importance of *Grundherrschaft* (manorial domination) in Germanic history, which Weber downgraded in favor of the charismatic origin of political rulership. His 1914 letter to Georg von Below stressed the distinction between patriarchal and patrimonial domination:

> Although I have good reason to think very modestly of my own expertise, I have no doubt that you are right [about the existence of genuine political authority, not just private powers, in European feudalism]. It is astonishing that the old contrary theory—to which, admittedly, I too once adhered—is still so persistently defended. . . . Terminologically, I must limit the concept of patrimonialism to certain kinds of *political* domination. I hope you will find that I have sufficiently emphasized the absolute distinction between domestic, personal and manorial authority, on the one hand, and political *Herrschaft* on the other, which is none of these but rather military and judicial authority. This main thesis of your book will find no objection from my side. I will only show that this difference is as old as history.[101]

Weber demonstrated his point by drawing on examples from Antiquity and the Chinese empire. Patrimonialism was the most important kind of administration before the emergence of modern bureaucracy. In the most centralized case, it constituted a patrimonial-bureaucratic administration with a "state-socialist" *oikos* economy—Rodbertus' concept—; European feudalism was its most fragmented case, with its sole and limited analogy in Japan. Only European feudalism developed the *Ständestaat,* the consociation of ruler, nobility and *honoratiores* under a quasi-constitutional division of powers. Feudalism was for Weber a marginal case of patrimonialism, because the feudal vassal was a patrimonial lord in relation to his own retainers and because the feudal principle did not completely replace the patrimonial administration of the realm. Feudalism had charismatic features as well; the status group of warriors was first distinguished by personal military prowess and later by "noble" descent.

Precisely because feudalism was a unique medieval phenomenon, Weber's distinction between feudalism and patrimonialism has consider-

---

101. Weber's letter of June 21, 1914, printed in G. von Below, *Der deutsche Staat des Mittelalters,* 2nd ed. (1925), xxiv f.

able terminological utility today when "feudalism" is all too often an indiscriminate pejorative term referring to sundry situations in all countries where large-scale landownership and political power are still closely related. The concepts of patrimonialism and personal rulership—divested of traditionalist legitimation—are frequently more applicable to the New States than feudalism, bureaucracy or charismatic rulership.[102]

If patrimonialism has been conceptually underemployed, charisma has been used indiscriminately to label almost all non-bureaucratic forms of leadership.[103] Weber chose the term to characterize, first of all, the relationship between the military chieftain and his free following, the subject of his 1905 essay (sec. 4 above). He secularized Rudolf Sohm's notion of the charisma of the Christian church. In his major work on *Church Law* (1892), Sohm, a devout believer and conservative columnist, had described the church not as a "legal" but a "charismatic" organization—i.e., an organization established by virtue of divine inspiration, not man-made law. After using the concept of charisma in its religious connotations in the Sociology of Religion, Weber apparently decided that it could also denote the self-legitimation of political leadership, a usurpatory challenge from the viewpoint of patriarchal, patrimonial and bureaucratic legitimacy.

Throughout history political and religious charisma have warred and cooperated with one another. The secular rulers had to face, in one way or another, the institutionalized charisma of the priesthood—theocracy. Since Weber concerned himself with the charisma of both powers, he differentiated the traditional notion of theocracy—still his terminology in the "Agrarian Conditions in Antiquity"—into a typology of hierocracy contrasting with caesaropapism.[104] The latter term denoted the complete control of the secular ruler over the church, and since this was true of both the Anglican and Lutheran rulers, the phrase also suited Weber's penchant for nominalist irony.[105] Successful political usurpers or their successors often endeavored to fortify their rule through religious

102. For a proposal along these lines, see my "Personal Rulership, Patrimonialism and Empire-Building in the New States," *World Politics*, XX, 1968, 194–206.

103. On the indiscriminate application of the concept of charisma, cf. Reinhard Bendix, "Reflections on Charismatic Leadership," *Asian Survey*, VII, 1967, 341–352.

104. In this he followed the terminology of Byzantine studies; cf. *Religion in Geschichte und Gegenwart*, I (Tübingen: Mohr, 1909), cols. 1527–31.

105. The analytical advance made by Weber can be seen by comparing, for example, Wilhelm Roscher's treatment of "priestly aristocracy" in his *Politik: Geschichtliche Naturlehre der Monarchie, Aristokratie und Demokratie* (Stuttgart: Cotta, 1892), 87–117.

legitimation: the foremost European examples were Charlemagne and Napoleon I. Whereas these two rulers controlled the church, others were more dependent. European history was profoundly influenced by the great clash and subsequent stalemate between emperor and pope—a subject about which Weber wrote his first major essay at the age of thirteen.[106] This gave the Italian cities their historic opportunity to gain autonomy for a time from the patrimonial and hierocratic powers and to usher in the Renaissance with its unbridled individualism: an age of illegitimacy.

(D) THE CITY: USURPATION AND REVOLUTION.[107] It has been asserted occasionally that the Sociology of Domination, with its "static" ideal types, cannot explain revolutionary change. Were this true, Marxism as well could not have advanced a theory of revolution, since its "laws" and developmental constructs are nothing if not ideal types—as Weber pointed out in 1904.[108] The fact is that his own theory of revolution appears in the guise of usurpation and non-legitimate domination because of its attention to administration and legitimacy, marginal concerns to Marxism. Weber looked more closely at the consequences of the seizure of power than did Marx in spite of the "dictatorship of the proletariat"; he saw that revolutionary domination can survive only when an efficient administration suppresses the expropriated former holders of legitimate power.

The city as an autonomous, oath-bound commune of armed men existed only in the Occident, and then only in Antiquity and the Middle Ages. It was the specific locus of revolutionary domination in two respects: It was a "state within a state" erected by the patricians against the patrimonial rulerships with their traditionalist legitimation; it also was the scene of the uprising of the "people" against the patricians who had in turn assumed the mantle of legitimacy. The people's leaders created another "state within a state." Weber maintained that the oldest

106. In the same year, 1877, Weber wrote an essay on "The Roman Empire from Constantine to the Teutonic Migrations"; at the age of fifteen he wrote "Reflections on the Character, Development and History of the Indo-Germanic Peoples." These were standard topics in the classical schools, but the essays also indicate the early origins and the continuity of some of Weber's basic interests.

107. The chapter on the city was the fulfilment of a project that Weber had declared to be worthwhile in 1908/9 (cf. above, p. xxxi); he took himself by his own words and demonstrated how the ancient polis and medieval city could be compared to explain their differences and how an indirect contribution could be made to the study of modern democracy.

108. Cf. Shils and Finch, eds., *Methodology* . . . , 103. For a comparison of the ideal-typical constructs of Marx and Weber, see Judith Janoska-Bendl, *Methodologische Aspekte des Idealtypus. Max Weber und die Soziologie der Geschichte* (Berlin: Duncker & Humblot, 1965), 89–114.

historical records of the city as a commune proved its revolutionary character, but that this was often obscured in documents which purposively hid usurpations of political power.[109]

The first great usurpation of the early Middle Ages was the "revolutionary movement of 726 that led to the defection of Italy from Byzantine domination and centered around Venice. It was called forth especially by opposition to the icon destruction ordered by the emperor who was under the pressure of [the Islamic sympathies of] his own army. Thus the religious element, although not the only factor, triggered the revolution."[110] After a period of patrician rule, the Italian *popolo* rose under its leaders and established "the first deliberately nonlegitimate and revolutionary political association" (below, 1302).

Weber contrasted the patrician city with the plebeian city of the Middle Ages and of Antiquity, exploring the different forms of class struggle in each type and era. He stressed the remarkable parallels between the Italian *popolo* with its *capitano* and the ancient Roman plebs with its tribune. In the absence of traditional legitimation, the tribune was sustained by armed popular support. He checked the power of the senate and instigated the *plebiscita*.

Democratization means the political expropriation of the upper strata, which in these historical cases were as "closely policed, disenfranchized and outlawed as is the Russian bourgeoisie by Lenin. The basis of democratization is everywhere of a military nature; it lies in the emergence of a disciplined infantry. . . . Military discipline signified the victory of democracy, for the wish and the need to call on the nonknightly masses gave them arms and thereby political power. The parallels to the German revolution of 1918 are obvious."[111] However, democratization by no means leads to the waning of domination. Ancient and medieval democracy passed through the state of the *tyrannis* and the *signoria* before the city state disappeared, reverting to patrimonial rulership through internal transformation or external defeat. But this his-

---

109. Weber rejected Sombart's theory that "ground rent is the mother of the city" (cf. *Economic History*, 239). The two men differed in their interest and interpretation of the city. Sombart was primarily concerned with the economic aspects; cf. *Der moderne Kapitalismus*, II, 176–249, and his "Der Begriff der Stadt und das Wesen der Städtebildung," *AfS*, XXV, 1907, 1–9. In dealing with the city as a political phenomenon, Weber followed the tradition of ancient and medieval history. However, he reversed the standard political definition of the German medieval city as a self-governing body with a town council subject to confirmation by the legitimate overlord, and instead emphasized the aspect of usurpation. For the older definition, see Freiherr Roth von Schreckenstein, *Das Patriziat in den deutschen Städten* (Tübingen: Mohr, 1856), 28.

110. *Wirtschaftsgeschichte*, 274; cf. *Economic History*, 236.

111. *Wirtschaftsgeschichte*, 278f.; cf. *Economic History*, 240.

torical "cycle" had very different results in the two eras: In Antiquity a universal empire came into being, suppressing private capitalism; at the beginning of modern history, the competing patrimonial-bureaucratic states created the European balance of power, one of the preconditions of modern capitalism. They further developed the rational administration first promoted by the non-legitimate dictatorship of the Italian *signoria*. Thus the modern state and modern democracy were not the direct successors of the medieval city. Their rise was prepared by the struggle for representation in the *Ständestaat* and the absolutist state, which preceded their violent establishment in the American and French revolutions.

From the viewpoint of legitimacy and administrative control there is no basic difference between *coups d'état* and mass uprisings. Weber's reference to the Russian and German "revolutions" was more than a mere illustrative analogy. Structurally, the modern state, whether parliamentary, plebiscitary or a "people's democracy," is one city. Non-legitimate domination is at the root of modern democracies, whether they are more libertarian or more authoritarian. The United States, the "first new nation" in Seymour Martin Lipset's phrase, came into being in rejection of monarchic legitimacy and instead created a polity that, in analogous terms, resembles the Roman Republic: its President (tribune) and the plebeian House of Representatives contrast with the Senate, an imitation of the House of Lords, as the most traditionalist and aristocratic element.

It is a moot point which contemporary state should be considered less similar to a city and closer to patrimonial rulership. Hierocracy and caesaropapism continue to exist in some of their traditional ways, but more frequently in a new secularized form. Secular intellectuals have replaced priests as the new legitimizers, especially in the New States. Weber did not foresee how quickly and terribly totalitarianism would seize and exercise power, although he described it as an "objective possibility" (below, 644, 661, n.4). Toward the end of his life he considered it more likely that a Bonapartist *coup d'état* might occur in Bolshevist Russia or in Weimar Germany, a reasonable guess on the basis of historical precedent. But Weber had no deterministic view of history: "The continuum of cultural development in the Mediterranean-European realm has up to now shown neither completed 'cycles' nor an unambiguous unilinear development."[112] Despite his fulminations, he did not consider the oppressive dominance of bureaucracy politically inescapable (cf. below, 991). In his showdown with Oswald Spengler in

112. "Agrarverhältnisse . . . ," *GAzSW,* 278.

February of 1920, Weber extracted the admission from the author of the *Decline of the West* that his morphology was historical poetry. Domination in large-scale communities was for Weber the only historic inevitability—a point directed at the same occasion against a young communist who was dreaming of the perfect commune of intellectuals and proletarians in Siberia.[113]

If the course of history is not predetermined but domination inescapable at the same time that its forms are limited, a historically saturated typology is the best analytical tool for the researcher. This is the ultimate rationale for the typologies of *Economy and Society*.

II. PART ONE: THE LATER PART

Between 1918 and 1920, during and after the Empire's collapse, Weber turned to the terminological summary. In contrast to Part Two, where after 1918 he revised only the chapter on bureaucracy, he rewrote the definitions many times. Weber spent so much energy on the categories because he recognized that the discursive exposition of his complex and novel terminology made retention difficult. Several colleagues, among them the philosopher Heinrich Rickert, had told him that the Stammler critique and the essay on "Some Categories of Interpretive Sociology" were excessively hard to read. Weber heeded their advice and simplified the terminology. He divided the text into numbered main definitions and small-print comments, a device frequently employed in the older literature, as in Schönberg's *Handbook of Political Economy*.

In the first edition of *Wirtschaft und Gesellschaft*, Part One was published under the title now carried by Part Two, but Weber liked to call it his *Kategorienlehre* or casuistry. In those last months of his life he seems to have expressed some satisfaction with his progress—with the feeling, however: "People will shake their heads." He expected resistance to his redefining of well-known historical, economic, legal and theological terms for his sociological purposes. Thus, he wanted it clearly understood that his definitions were nothing more than a clarification of his own terms to be tested by their scholarly yield; they were not an attempt to impose a new terminology on his colleagues. Hundreds of students attended his courses at this time—in Vienna in 1918 and in Munich in 1919/20—but the course on the categories drove them away *en masse*.[114] Upon their urging, Weber compensated the students for

113. Cf. Marianne Weber, *Lebensbild*, 685ff., and Eduard Baumgarten, ed., *Max Weber: Werk und Person* (Tübingen: Mohr, 1964), 554f.

114. In a period when political agitation is again an issue at American universities, it may be worthwhile to recount that Weber opened the course on the most general categories of sociology with a statement showing that he was for

his definitions with his lectures on economic history. It is certainly true that the definitions are not "readable." Part One is really a reference text, and it would indeed have greatly facilitated the reading of Part Two had Weber lived to revise the old terminology in the light of the new. The discrepancy as it now exists makes additional demands upon the reader of both parts, but it also offers researchers the opportunity to work with Weber's alternative terminology.

When Schmoller wrote his critique of Sombart's *Modern Capitalism* he advanced a complaint that might have applied also to Weber: "Every few pages we find the sentence: 'I call this such and such,' and the reader is overwhelmed by a flood of new names, new etiquettes and pigeonholes."[115] Sombart considered his own terminological introduction a "considerable esthetic impairment" but an inevitable nuisance since he wanted to introduce a personal terminology; similarly, Weber acknowledged the stylistic awkwardness of his precise definitions. Sombart called for an esthetic science: "The guilt toward all living things that every science brings upon itself [by its deadening generalities] can be expiated only if scholarship produces new life through its creations, shaping them into works of art . . . It seems to me that we should strive to make a scientific scheme *beautiful* in itself."[116] Weber never advanced such an exuberant demand, but the casuistry of Part One, which is so much indebted to his legal training, does indeed have an esthetic quality, which will be revealed especially to the reader who works his way first through Part Two with its descriptive richness.

Weber finished three chapters of Part One and the beginning of chapter IV. These are the only chapters he could rework in the proofs.[117] Both parts of the work begin with basic definitions of social action and then take up economic action. In Part One, however, the typology of

---

"profession" even as he was against "indoctrination." In Marianne Weber's phrasing (*Lebensbild*, 673f.), he wanted to say a "first and last word on politics, which has no place in the lecture hall and in science, but rather belongs in an arena where the free airing of opposing judgements is possible. . . . We can have only *one* common goal: To turn the Versailles treaty into a scrap of paper. At the moment this is not possible, but the right of rebellion against foreign domination cannot be foresworn. Now we must practice the art of silence and return to the sober tasks of everyday life." Cf. Baumgarten, ed., *op. cit.*, 553, 716.

115. Schmoller, *loc. cit.*, 297.

116. Sombart, *op. cit.*, I, xxx.

117. The translation of chs. I–II of Part One was drafted by Henderson and reworked by Parsons, who did the subsequent chapters on his own. Terminologically, the original translation diverged from the German text by using "type" and "system" much more freely than did Weber, who in general spoke of "type" only when he really meant "ideal type" and for the rest employed terms such as "kind" or "phenomenon"; the term "system" was rarely used by Weber.

domination appears already in ch. III; classes and status groups (ch. IV) follow rather than precede it. Notes found with the manuscript indicate that Weber intended to go on to status groups of warriors. At least two chapters anticipated in the text of Part One are missing altogether: One on the more "universal" groups (household, kin group, etc.) treated early in Part Two, and another one on the theory of revolution (cf. the anticipatory reference below, 266), corresponding in Part Two to the chapter on the city as non-legitimate domination (ch. XVI). This chapter would have dealt with the German and Russian revolutions within a typology designed to give a more precise description than that afforded by the mere label "revolution."

Almost half of the first chapter of Part One is given over to a simplified presentation of the meaning of "interpretive sociology" and the concept of "social action."[118] This is Weber's easiest methodological statement, but because of its very conciseness the reader cannot afford to disregard the other methodological writings. In the second half of the chapter, the basic definitions of social action and association, Weber abandoned the older, more differentiated typology of Part Two (cf. below, Appendix I). He changed *Gemeinschaftshandeln* into *soziales Handeln* (social action) and *Gemeinschaft* mostly into *Verband* (organization). This made it possible to contrast *Vergemeinschaftung* and *Vergesellschaftung* (communal and associative relationships) in sec. 9 and to come closer to Tönnies' terminology without accepting his basic dichotomy. Tönnies' distinction had gained wide currency after the turn of the century, especially after the second edition of his work (1912). Apparently Weber felt that he should not insist on a quite different terminology. Weber treated Tönnies considerately as a comrade-in-arms in the struggle for social research and expressed himself with somewhat distant politeness about *Gemeinschaft und Gesellschaft* (1887), but there is no indication that the work was a major influence on his intellectual development, and *Economy and Society* appears partly conceived in opposition to it.[119]

118. For recent additions to the large literature on social action, see Helmut Girndt, *Das soziale Handeln als Grundkategorie erfahrungswissenschaftlicher Soziologie* ("Veröffentlichungen des Max Weber Instituts der Universität München"; Tübingen: Mohr, 1967); on the origin of the terminology of social action, see Johannes Winckelmann's introduction to Girndt, *ibid.*, 1–20; for an interpretation of Weber's theory of science in the light of subsequent developments in the natural and social sciences, see Winckelmann, "Max Webers Verständnis von Mensch und Gesellschaft," in K. Engisch *et al.*, eds., *Max Weber: Gedächtnisschrift der Ludwig-Maximilians-Universität München*, 195–243.

119. On the theoretical differences between Tönnies and Weber, see the definitive critique of Tönnies by René König, "Die Begriffe Gemeinschaft und

In communal as well as associative relationships conflict is normal (sec. 8). As in the case of power and domination, the definition of conflict has been wrenched out of context in discussions of Weber's orientation to power. He certainly was a political realist, but the purpose of the section is the definition of peaceful and regulated conflict ("competition") as against social selection and the free-for-all. The target of the section is Social Darwinism. Unrestrained struggle and social selection are marginal to Weber's analytical interest. Up to now the reversal of a key sentence has confused both German and English readers. Instead of the sentence: "The treatment of conflict involving the use of physical violence as a separate type is justified by the special characteristics of the employment of this means and the corresponding peculiarities of the sociological consequences of its use" (Parsons, ed., *Theory*, 133), it must read: "The conceptual separation (*Absonderung*) of peaceful [from violent] conflict is justified by the quality of the means normal to it and the peculiar sociological consequences of its occurrence" (below, 38). Weber goes on to emphasize the importance of the rules of the game as against inherent personal qualities (whether social or biological) and states that "we want to speak of conflict only when there really is competition" (cf. below, 39). He refers ahead to ch. II, where economic action is defined "as a peaceful use of the actor's control over resources" (below, 63).

The chapter on the sociological categories of economic action is remarkable for its length, the same as chs. I and III together. It is likely that Weber wanted to compensate for the relatively brief economic casuistry of Part Two. However, the many pages of seemingly dry definitions and comments owe some of their length—and hidden fervor—to Weber's political involvement with the problems of postwar economic and political reconstruction in the wake of the Empire's collapse and in the face of the victor's harsh demands at Versailles. The chapter also reflects the phenomenon of the wartime "state-socialist" economy and the syndicalist and socialist proposals for economic reconstruction. Some of Weber's comments on the much-debated question of the economic feasibility of socialism are definitely time-bound; other passages in this

Gesellschaft bei Ferdinand Tönnies," *Kölner Zeitschrift für Soziologie*, VII, 1955, 348–420. In the American literature the relationship apparently was misperceived for two reasons: (1) the early date (1887) of Tönnies work, which for a long time received little attention, and the fact that the *Gemeinschaft—Gesellschaft* dichotomy became well-known so much earlier than *Economy and Society*. For illustrations, see Robert Nisbet, *The Sociological Tradition* (New York: Basic Books, 1966), 79 and 326; Robert Presthus, *Men at the Top. A Study in Community Power* (New York: Oxford University Press, 1964), 9.

chapter show him years ahead of the critique that welfare economists later were to direct against classical economics, even though he did not use their technical apparatus.

While he was working intermittently on the economic categories, Weber in speeches and statements strenuously opposed the nationalization of the major industries. He considered neither the remaining state bureaucracy nor the inexperienced functionaries of the socialist labor movement capable of running the economy. In April, 1920, when the Democratic Party he had helped to establish in November, 1918, asked him to serve on the Nationalization Commission, he resigned, explaining that "the politician *must* make compromises—the scholar must not whitewash them."[120] A few weeks later he died.

11. Political Writings

"Parliament and Government in a Reconstructed Germany" (Appendix II) is offered for three reasons: (1) to compensate for the unwritten part on the sociology of the state; (2) to provide a corrective to the one-sided reception of the chapter on bureaucracy (ch. XI)—as if Weber had somehow missed the facts of bureaucracy as a vested interest group or a network of informal cliques; (3) to introduce to the English reader one of his major political writings, almost all of which are untranslated.[121]

The essay is a revision of newspaper articles originally written for

120. E. Baumgarten, ed., *Max Weber: Werk und Person,* 530; cf. also *ibid.,* 608 and Wolfgang Mommsen, *Max Weber und die deutsche Politik 1890–1920* (Tübingen: Mohr, 1959), 303f.

121. In the fourth edition of *Wirtschaft und Gesellschaft,* as a substitute for the chapters on the modern state and its parties that Weber did not live to write, Johannes Winckelmann provides a Sociology of the State constructed out of passages from *Economic History,* "Politics as a Vocation," and "Parliament and Government" with the omission of the more polemical and time-bound sections (for a separate edition, see Max Weber, *Staatssoziologie,* ed. Johannes Winckelmann; 2nd rev. ed., Berlin: Duncker & Humblot, 1966). In the English edition this imaginative didactic effort has been replaced by a continuous translation of the last essay. This appeared desirable because of the English reader's lack of familiarity with the political writings; by contrast, the *Economic History* was the first Weber translation (1927) and "Politics as a Vocation," a philosophical statement rather than a polemical article, is already well-known in the Gerth and Mills translation (*From Max Weber . . . ,* 77–128).—The list of Weber's political newspaper articles and journal essays is lengthy; it includes two essays on the 1905 Russian revolution, "On the Conditions of Bourgeois Democracy in Russia" and "Russia's Transition to Pseudo-Constitutionalism" (both 1906). The *Gesammelte Politische Schriften* comprise only part of the political writings. The Gerth and Mills volume contains somewhat more than one quarter of

the leftwing-liberal *Frankfurter Zeitung*, one of the best-known European newspapers until its suppression by the Nazis. The articles appeared in the summer of 1917, after Woodrow Wilson entered the war. They launched a sensational attack on the political incompetency of the Imperial and Prussian bureaucracy; the paper was subsequently put under pre-publication censorship, but the very publication of the articles is enough to show that even in wartime Imperial Germany was far less oppressive than Nazi Germany.

Weber made his impassioned plea for political democratization at a time when reform seemed highly uncertain and revolution only a slight possibility. His siding with parliamentarism was by no means a sudden conversion under the shadow of military disaster, as it was for Ludendorff and the general staff in September 1918. Weber had for many years advocated parliamentary government. He considered himself part of a vigorous but loyal opposition to the monarchy. He argued from premises of national interest, partly out of deep conviction, partly for tactical reasons, hoping that parliamentary government would make possible a more rational politics in the international no less than the national interest. He wanted Germany to play a major part in the rather discordant concert of European powers, but he never advocated her hegemony over Europe. In domestic politics he wanted to be recognized as a "class-conscious bourgeois" who opposed the entrenched Junkers and the rightwing romantics no less than the petty-bourgeois labor movement and the utopian leftwing intellectuals. He positively scorned the *litterateurs* of the right and left—witness his outbursts in "Parliament and Government." Weber took a humanitarian commitment for granted but was convinced that it would suffer from noisy display and moralistic sermonizing. He saluted pacifists as well as revolutionaries with a pure "ethic of ultimate ends" (*Gesinnungsethik*). But he believed in politics as the art of the possible—the morally imperative compromise in a world of irreconcilable ideologies and raw interests.

These few remarks cannot do justice to Weber's politics or to his political critics.[122] The reader of "Parliament and Government" should bear in mind that it represents only one phase of Weber's politics, neither the early period when the very young professor intentionally shocked his father's liberal generation with tough nationalist rhetoric in his Frei-

---

"Suffrage and Democracy in Germany" (1917) under the heading "National Character and the Junkers" (*op. cit.,* 386–95). Weber's political writings are, of course, partly dated; however, in part they can also be read as discussions of democratization, especially the issue of political development in "new" states.

122. For a review of the critics, see my "Political Critiques of Max Weber: Some Implications for Political Sociology," *American Sociological Review*, vol. 30, 1965, 213–23.

burg inaugural address of 1895—only to regret it later—nor the last phase when the despairing democrat returned from the Versailles treaty meetings with grave forbodings, just like John Maynard Keynes. Weber foresaw Wilson's failure at Versailles. In an unsigned editorial statement in the *Frankfurter Zeitung* (October 27, 1918) he lectured his colleague-in-politics on the hard facts of the power balance and the art of peacemaking:

> Men of good will and understanding do not question President Wilson's sincerity. However, it appears that he does not sufficiently grasp the following: If the German government accepts his armistice conditions, which make any further military resistance impossible, not only Germany *but he too* would be eliminated as a major factor in the peace settlement. His own position as arbiter for the world rests on the fact that the German army is at least strong enough to avoid defeat without the help of American troops on the Allied side. Were this to become different, the absolutely intransigent elements, which no doubt exist in other enemy countries, would gain the upper hand and simply push the President aside with polite thanks for his previous support. *His role would be over,* unless he went to war against his present allies. The German government, too, should have considered this state of affairs. Even though an armistice is desirable to avoid unnecessary bloodshed, it would certainly have been better not to focus deliberations so exclusively on the armistice offer as has been done. Peace negotiations could take place without an armistice if the enemies insist on continuation of the slaughter.[123]

In extremis, Weber was not averse to a *levée en masse* and guerrilla warfare ("national wars of liberation"), as he demonstrated in his speech at an anti-Versailles meeting of the University of Heidelberg in March, 1919; he protested against what appeared to him a flagrant violation of Wilson's promise of self-determination for all peoples. Such national pride, however, did not prevent rightwing students from picketing his house and disrupting his lectures. Emotional appeals aside, he devoted much constructive energy to the drafting of the Weimar constitution, through his writings and as member of the revolutionary government's planning committee.[124]

123. *GPS,* 435.
124. In the past, Weber's contribution to the presidential features of the Weimar constitution was exaggerated by friend and foe. For a correction, see Gerhard Schulz, *Zwischen Demokratie und Diktatur: Verfassungspolitik und Reichsreform in der Weimarer Republik* (Berlin: de Gruyter, 1963), I, 114–42. Schulz points out that far from taking a blunt position in favor of a "Caesarist" leader, Weber gradually shifted his opinions in response to the changing political situation and the diversity of opinion in committee meetings. Eventually he came to favor a popularly elected President as a mediator between the *Reichstag* and the States. Cf. also Weber, *GPS,* 394–471, 486–89.

In essence, Weber stood for the rational support of a political order that can be affirmed in most essentials. His sociology can serve the self-clarification of critical-minded organization men in industrialized and democratized society. This was the ultimate dialectic in Weber's position: he was a sharp critic of human and institutional failures, but basically a moralist with reformist convictions, not a revolutionary temper.[125]

12. *On Editing and Translating* Economy and Society

There are some misunderstandings abroad about the readability of *Economy and Society*. They relate in part to the original, in part to the translations. To begin with, it must be pointed out that Weber wrote lucidly and subtly. He wrote more clearly than did most of his colleagues, including Sombart, Tönnies, Troeltsch and his own brother Alfred, not to mention the legion of "ordinary" professors of his time. Weber does not stand in the tradition of German philosophical prose with its murky profundity that has usually suggested dangerous obscurantism to Anglo-Saxon readers. Considering that most of *Economy and Society* is a first draft, Weber's power of formulation proves extraordinary. Yet there are difficulties:

(1) Since Part Two was written with great speed, stylistic editing and judicious cutting would have been helpful to the reader, but this would also have been incompatible with the requirements of a complete edition.

(2) Weber never wrote a well-wrought book. His larger works are longish problem-centered research papers. *Economy and Society* is the only work conceived for a wider audience, but it never reached the stage of final literary form; moreover, it was simply not meant as a trot for introductory courses, or as the kind of polished study in cultural pessimism so popular in the nineteen-twenties.

(3) Weber uses a profusion of quotation marks as an alienating device to indicate that he employs familiar terms with reservations, with a new meaning, or in an ironic sense. This habit was the counterpoint to his concern with terminological precision and at times is a drawback. In the translation, the quotation marks were used more sparingly.

(4) Weber tended to overqualify his sentences, using terms such as

125. For a sketch of this dialectic, see Guenther Roth and Bennett M. Berger, "Max Weber and the Organized Society," *New York Times Book Review*, April 3, 1966, 6 and 44f.

"perhaps," "more or less," "in general," "as a rule," "frequently but not always," etc. This reflected the difficulty both of formulating historical generalizations and of identifying a specific cause. Weber's sense of caution became a stylistic mannerism.

Similar to the second and third volume of *Das Kapital*, Weber's work was edited from literary remains written in a scarcely legible handwriting. The early editions of *Wirtschaft und Gesellschaft* contained hundreds of reading and identification errors. For thirty-five years this distorted, or outright destroyed, the meaning of many passages and obviously affected the translations. In 1956, after many years of painstaking labor, Johannes Winckelmann published his critically revised (fourth) edition. In close cooperation, Winckelmann and the English editors have decided on a large number of further changes in wording, clauses, names and dates; some of these have been incorporated in the 1964 German paperback edition. The projected fifth edition will identify all these changes; listing them in the English edition would have been too cumbersome. The definitive German edition will be almost identical with the present English text, with the exception of Winckelmann's compilation of the Sociology of the State.[126] However, the German and English edition differ in the subheadings of the chapters. The manuscript had no subheadings, it seems, excepting the Sociology of Law, which in turn had no title. The early editions summarized the chapter contents, often inadequately, below the chapter headings. Winckelmann extensively revised them. The English editors proceeded at their own discretion and used subheadings in the text to improve its readability.

The systematic checking of the text required considerable library research, invisible where there are no corrections and annotations. The revision of the extant translations proved almost as time-consuming and difficult as the new translation since every sentence had to be compared to the German text and changed if it appeared necessary for textual, terminological and, more rarely, stylistic reasons. Weber's skilful use of German syntax permits more complex construction than is feasible in English. Thus, Weber is not really improved by "streamlining," by breaking up his carefully balanced and qualified sentences into a series of linear constructs. A more linear rendering was inevitable in the English version, but our inclination was to retain, and in some cases to restore, Weber's architecture. However, in most cases pragmatic pre-

126. Like the German paperback edition of 1964, the English edition omits Weber's essay on "The Rational and Social Foundations of Music," which was not part of the original but was appended to the second German edition. For an English version, see the translation by Don Martindale, Johannes Riedel and Gertrude Neuwirth (Carbondale: Southern Illinois University Press, 1958).

vailed over stylistic considerations, whether the revision of previous translations or our own formulations were involved.

In most academic translations, the task involves prosaic accuracy, not an esthetic recreation. Academic translation should properly be team-work. Individual "heroism" is bound to be affected by the limitations of any single translator, as was proven by Parsons, Fischoff and Kolegar. Some of the English translations have been undertaken by two men, one familiar with each language. This arrangement could not, however, lighten the burden of the primary translator. Our translation was aided by two-fold familiarity with the original language, which permitted collateral reading and prevented premature closure by either one of us. Our revision of the extant translations has also been in the nature of collateral reading, backed by the wisdom of hindsight. The ideal translation, however, requires a third man: the stylist in the language of translation. Our third man was missing.

Everett C. Hughes once remarked that, as a matter of principle, a work should only be translated as a whole. Each piecemeal translation tends to reduce the incentive for publishing the whole. This leads to unanticipated and fortuitous intellectual consequences. Theoretical developments in American sociology have been considerably influenced by the vagaries of the Weber translations. Thus, the Gerth and Mills edition created the impression that the Sociology of Domination centers about the contrast of bureaucracy and charisma. Parsons' translation of only Part One perforce attenuated the historical dimension of the work and led some writers to believe that Weber did not follow up on his categories.[127] Weber's case is far from exceptional. In recent years it has become clear that the translations of Durkheim and Nietzsche have had similar distorting consequences.

Without sustained support by foundations and institutes the desiderata of academic translation cannot be fulfilled in most cases. This support has been lacking largely because translation and editing are the most underestimated kind of work in the social sciences. But as long as sociologists continue to lean on the Sociological Tradition, the need for translation will persist. Moreover, in an era of world-wide comparative research the linguistic problem will be perpetual without adequate translation facilities and better linguistic training for social scientists.

127. Since David Easton explicitly aimed at a forceful and incisive improvement of Weber, it appears legitimate to observe that his *A Systems Analysis of Political Life* (New York: Wiley, 1965) is a major example for some unintended consequences of the partial translations by Gerth and Mills and by Parsons. The Rheinstein-Shils translation, which would have corrected part of his interpretation, was not consulted. This may be indicative of the difficulty to see partial translations as part of a whole. (See Easton, *op. cit.*, 183, 281, 283, 301 ff.)

13. *Acknowledgements*

I owe thanks to many persons, foremost to the following:

Reinhard Bendix, who has carried on the tradition of comparative study in creative adaptation to the American setting. In the late nineteen-fifties he gave me an opportunity, without insistence, to feel my way into Weber's work, to overcome some early preconceptions, and to watch the writing of his *Max Weber: An Intellectual Portrait* (1960);

Juan Linz, a scholar of Weberian breadth, who insisted for a long time on the necessity of a complete edition and kept wondering skeptically who would take on the task;

Benjamin Nelson, a critic with a Weberian temper, who suggested "rulership" as one translation of *Herrschaft* and insisted on standards to which mortals have difficulty measuring up;

My wife, who accommodated my abstract preoccupation with the "oct-opus" in her sensuous household of flora and fauna and took out time to improve the style of the introduction.

I greatly appreciate the support of the Research Foundation of the State University of New York (Stony Brook), which granted me fellowships in the summers of 1963 and 1964; the assistance of the Department of Sociology, University of California at Davis; the typing of Jeannette Freeman, who claims that she gained an education through it.

It was a great pleasure to share the task with Claus Wittich, native of my hometown and fellow graduate of its classical school where we learned our basic linguistic and historical skills.

VOLUME ONE

ECONOMY
AND
SOCIETY

Part One and Part Two, chapters I to VII

Conceptual Exposition

CHAPTER I

BASIC SOCIOLOGICAL TERMS

Prefatory Note

An introductory discussion of concepts can hardly be dispensed with, in spite of the fact that it is unavoidably abstract and hence gives the impression of remoteness from reality. The method employed makes no claim to any kind of novelty. On the contrary it attempts only to formulate what all empirical sociology really means when it deals with the same problems, in what it is hoped is a more convenient and somewhat more exact terminology, even though on that account it may seem pedantic. This is true even where terms are used which are apparently new or unfamiliar. As compared to the author's essay in *Logos*,[1] the terminology has been simplified as far as possible and hence considerably changed in order to render it more easily understandable. The most precise formulation cannot always be reconciled with a form which can readily be popularized. In such cases the latter aim has had to be sacrificed.

On the concept of "understanding"[2] compare the *Allgemeine Psychopathologie* of Karl Jaspers, also a few observations by Heinrich Rickert in the second edition of the *Grenzen der naturwissenschaftlichen Begriffsbildung* and particularly some of Simmel's discussions in the *Probleme der Geschichtsphilosophie*. For certain methodological considerations the reader may here be referred, as often before in the author's writings, to the procedure of Friedrich Gottl in his work *Die Herrschaft des Wortes*; this book, to be sure, is written in a somewhat difficult style and its argument does not appear everywhere to have been thoroughly thought through. As regards content, reference may be made especially to the fine work of Ferdinand Tönnies, *Gemeinschaft und Gesellschaft,* and also to the gravely misleading book of Rudolf Stamm-ler, *Wirtschaft und Recht nach der materialistischen Geschichtsauffas-sung,* which may be compared with my criticism in the *Archiv für Sozialwissenschaft* (vol. 14, 1907, [GAzW, 291-359]). This critical essay contains many of the fundamental ideas of the following exposi-tion. The present work departs from Simmel's method (in his *Soziologie* and his *Philosophie des Geldes*) in drawing a sharp distinction between subjectively intended and objectively valid "meanings"; two different things which Simmel not only fails to distinguish but often deliberately treats as belonging together.

1 . *The Definition of Sociology and of Social Action*

Sociology (in the sense in which this highly ambiguous word is used here) is a science concerning itself with the interpretive understanding of social action and thereby with a causal explanation of its course and consequences. We shall speak of "action" insofar as the acting individual attaches a subjective meaning to his behavior—be it overt or covert, omission or acquiescence. Action is "social"insofar as its subjective mean-ing takes account of the behavior of others and is thereby oriented in its course.[3]

A. METHODOLOGICAL FOUNDATIONS[4]

1. "Meaning" may be of two kinds. The term may refer first to the actual existing meaning in the given concrete case of a particular actor, or to the average or approximate meaning attributable to a given plurality of actors; or secondly to the theoretically conceived *pure type*[5] of subjec-tive meaning attributed to the hypothetical actor or actors in a given type of action. In no case does it refer to an objectively "correct" mean-ing or one which is "true" in some metaphysical sense. It is this which distinguishes the empirical sciences of action, such as sociology and history, from the dogmatic disciplines in that area, such as jurisprudence, logic, ethics, and esthetics, which seek to ascertain the "true" and "valid" meanings associated with the objects of their investigation.

2. The line between meaningful action and merely reactive behavior to which no subjective meaning is attached, cannot be sharply drawn empirically. A very considerable part of all sociologically relevant be-havior, especially purely traditional behavior, is marginal between the

two. In the case of some psychophysical processes, meaningful, i.e., subjectively understandable, action is not to be found at all; in others it is discernible only by the psychologist. Many mystical experiences which cannot be adequately communicated in words are, for a person who is not susceptible to such experiences, not fully understandable. At the same time the ability to perform a similar action is not a necessary prerequisite to understanding; "one need not have been Caesar in order to understand Caesar." "Recapturing an experience" is important for accurate understanding, but not an absolute precondition for its interpretation. Understandable and non-understandable components of a process are often intermingled and bound up together.

3. All interpretation of meaning, like all scientific observations, strives for clarity and verifiable accuracy of insight and comprehension (*Evidenz*).[6] The basis for certainty in understanding can be either rational, which can be further subdivided into logical and mathematical, or it can be of an emotionally empathic or artistically appreciative quality. Action is rationally evident chiefly when we attain a completely clear intellectual grasp of the action-elements in their intended context of meaning. Empathic or appreciative accuracy is attained when, through sympathetic participation, we can adequately grasp the emotional context in which the action took place. The highest degree of rational understanding is attained in cases involving the meanings of logically or mathematically related propositions; their meaning may be immediately and unambiguously intelligible. We have a perfectly clear understanding of what it means when somebody employs the proposition $2 \times 2 = 4$ or the Pythagorean theorem in reasoning or argument, or when someone correctly carries out a logical train of reasoning according to our accepted modes of thinking. In the same way we also understand what a person is doing when he tries to achieve certain ends by choosing appropriate means on the basis of the facts of the situation, as experience has accustomed us to interpret them. The interpretation of such rationally purposeful action possesses, for the understanding of the choice of means, the highest degree of verifiable certainty. With a lower degree of certainty, which is, however, adequate for most purposes of explanation, we are able to understand errors, including confusion of problems of the sort that we ourselves are liable to, or the origin of which we can detect by sympathetic self-analysis.

On the other hand, many ultimate ends or values toward which experience shows that human action may be oriented, often cannot be understood completely, though sometimes we are able to grasp them intellectually. The more radically they differ from our own ultimate values, however, the more difficult it is for us to understand them empathically. Depending upon the circumstances of the particular case we must be content either with a purely intellectual understanding of such values or when even that fails, sometimes we must simply accept them as given data. Then we can try to understand the action motivated by them on the basis of whatever opportunities for approximate emotional and intellectual interpretation seem to be available at different points in its course. These difficulties confront, for instance, people not susceptible to unusual acts of religious and charitable zeal, or persons who abhor extreme rationalist fanaticism (such as the fanatic advocacy of the "rights of man").

The more we ourselves are susceptible to such emotional reactions as anxiety, anger, ambition, envy, jealousy, love, enthusiasm, pride, vengefulness, loyalty, devotion, and appetites of all sorts, and to the "irrational" conduct which grows out of them, the more readily can we empathize with them. Even when such emotions are found in a degree of intensity of which the observer himself is completely incapable, he can still have a significant degree of emotional understanding of their meaning and can interpret intellectually their influence on the course of action and the selection of means.

For the purposes of a typological scientific analysis it is convenient to treat all irrational, affectually determined elements of behavior as factors of deviation from a conceptually pure type of rational action. For example a panic on the stock exchange can be most conveniently analysed by attempting to determine first what the course of action would have been if it had not been influenced by irrational affects; it is then possible to introduce the irrational components as accounting for the observed deviations from this hypothetical course. Similarly, in analysing a political or military campaign it is convenient to determine in the first place what would have been a rational course, given the ends of the participants and adequate knowledge of all the circumstances. Only in this way is it possible to assess the causal significance of irrational factors as accounting for the deviations from this type. The construction of a purely rational course of action in such cases serves the sociologist as a type (ideal type) which has the merit of clear understandability and lack of ambiguity. By comparison with this it is possible to understand the ways in which actual action is influenced by irrational factors of all sorts, such as affects and errors, in that they account for the deviation from the line of conduct which would be expected on the hypothesis that the action were purely rational.

Only in this respect and for these reasons of methodological convenience is the method of sociology "rationalistic." It is naturally not legitimate to interpret this procedure as involving a rationalistic bias of sociology, but only as a methodological device. It certainly does not involve a belief in the actual predominance of rational elements in human life, for on the question of how far this predominance does or does not exist, nothing whatever has been said. That there is, however, a danger of rationalistic interpretations where they are out of place cannot be denied. All experience unfortunately confirms the existence of this danger.

4. In all the sciences of human action, account must be taken of processes and phenomena which are devoid of subjective meaning, in the role of stimuli, results, favoring or hindering circumstances. To be devoid of meaning is not identical with being lifeless or non-human; every artifact, such as for example a machine, can be understood only in terms of the meaning which its production and use have had or were intended to have; a meaning which may derive from a relation to exceedingly various purposes. Without reference to this meaning such an object remains wholly unintelligible. That which is intelligible or understandable about it is thus its relation to human action in the role either of means or of end; a relation of which the actor or actors can be said to have been aware and to which their action has been oriented. Only in terms of such categories is it possible to "understand" objects of this kind. On the other hand processes or conditions, whether they are animate or inanimate, human or non-human, are in the present sense devoid of meaning in so far as they cannot be related to an intended purpose. That is to say they are devoid of meaning if they cannot be related to action in the role of means or ends but constitute only the stimulus, the favoring or hindering circumstances. It may be that the flooding of the Dollart [at the mouth of the Ems river near the Dutch-German border] in 1277 had historical significance as a stimulus to the beginning of certain migrations of considerable importance. Human mortality, indeed the organic life cycle from the helplessness of infancy to that of old age, is naturally of the very greatest sociological importance through the various ways in which human action has been oriented to these facts. To still another category of facts devoid of meaning belong certain psychic or psychophysical phenomena such as fatigue, habituation, memory, etc.; also certain typical states of euphoria under some conditions of ascetic mortification; finally, typical variations in the reactions of individuals according to reaction-time, precision, and other modes. But in the last analysis the same principle applies to these as to other phenomena which are devoid of meaning. Both the actor and the sociologist must accept them as data to be taken into account.

It is possible that future research may be able to discover non-interpretable uniformities underlying what has appeared to be specifically meaningful action, though little has been accomplished in this direction thus far. Thus, for example, differences in hereditary biological constitution, as of "races," would have to be treated by sociology as given data in the same way as the physiological facts of the need of nutrition or the effect of senescence on action. This would be the case if, and insofar as, we had statistically conclusive proof of their influence on sociologically relevant behavior. The recognition of the causal significance of such factors would not in the least alter the specific task of sociological analysis or of that of the other sciences of action, which is the interpretation of action in terms of its subjective meaning. The effect would be only to introduce certain non-interpretable data of the same order as others which are already present, into the complex of subjectively understandable motivation at certain points. (Thus it may come to be known that there are typical relations between the frequency of certain types of teleological orientation of action or of the degree of certain kinds of rationality and the cephalic index or skin color or any other biologically inherited characteristic.)

5. Understanding may be of two kinds: the first is the direct observational understanding[7] of the subjective meaning of a given act as such, including verbal utterances. We thus understand by direct observation, in this case, the meaning of the proposition $2 \times 2 = 4$ when we hear or read it. This is a case of the direct rational understanding of ideas. We also understand an outbreak of anger as manifested by facial expression, exclamations or irrational movements. This is direct observational understanding of irrational emotional reactions. We can understand in a similar observational way the action of a woodcutter or of somebody who reaches for the knob to shut a door or who aims a gun at an animal. This is rational observational understanding of actions.

Understanding may, however, be of another sort, namely explanatory understanding. Thus we understand in terms of *motive* the meaning an actor attaches to the proposition twice two equals four, when he states it or writes it down, in that we understand what makes him do this at precisely this moment and in these circumstances. Understanding in this sense is attained if we know that he is engaged in balancing a ledger or in making a scientific demonstration, or is engaged in some other task of which this particular act would be an appropriate part. This is rational understanding of motivation, which consists in placing the act in an intelligible and more inclusive context of meaning.[8] Thus we understand the chopping of wood or aiming of a gun in terms of motive in addition to direct observation if we know that the woodchopper is working for a wage or is chopping a supply of firewood for his own use or possibly is doing it for recreation. But he might also be working off a fit of rage, an irrational case. Similarly we understand the motive of a person aiming a gun if we know that he has been commanded to shoot as a member of a firing squad, that he is fighting against an enemy, or that he is doing it for revenge. The last is affectually determined and thus in a certain sense irrational. Finally we have a motivational understanding of the outburst of anger if we know that it has been provoked by jealousy, injured pride, or an insult. The last examples are all affectually determined and hence derived from irrational motives. In all the above cases the particular act has been placed in an understandable sequence of motivation, the understanding of which can be treated as an explanation of the actual course of behavior. Thus for a science which is concerned with the subjective meaning of action, explanation requires a grasp of the complex of meaning in which an actual course of understandable action thus interpreted belongs. In all such cases, even where the processes are largely affectual, the subjective meaning of the action, including that also of the relevant meaning complexes, will be called the intended meaning.[9] (This involves a departure from ordinary usage, which speaks of intention in this sense only in the case of rationally purposive action.)

6. In all these cases understanding involves the interpretive grasp of the meaning present in one of the following contexts: (a) as in the historical approach, the actually intended meaning for concrete individual action; or (b) as in cases of sociological mass phenomena, the average of, or an approximation to, the actually intended meaning; or (c) the meaning appropriate to a scientifically formulated pure type (an ideal type) of a common phenomenon. The concepts and "laws" of pure economic theory are examples of this kind of ideal type. They state what course a given type of human action would take if it were strictly rational, unaffected by errors or emotional factors and if, furthermore, it were completely and unequivocally directed to a single end, the maximization of economic advantage. In reality, action takes exactly this course only in unusual cases, as sometimes on the stock exchange; and even then there is usually only an approximation to the ideal type. (On the purpose of such constructions, see my essay in *AfS*, 19 [cf. n. 5] and point 11 below.)

Every interpretation attempts to attain clarity and certainty, but no matter how clear an interpretation as such appears to be from the point of view of meaning, it cannot on this account claim to be the causally valid interpretation. On this level it must remain only a peculiarly plausible hypothesis. In the first place the "conscious motives" may well, even to the actor himself, conceal the various "motives" and "repressions" which constitute the real driving force of his action. Thus in such cases even subjectively honest self-analysis has only a relative value. Then it

is the task of the sociologist to be aware of this motivational situation
and to describe and analyse it, even though it has not actually been concretely part of the conscious intention of the actor; possibly not at all,
at least not fully. This is a borderline case of the interpretation of meaning. Secondly, processes of action which seem to an observer to be the
same or similar may fit into exceedingly various complexes of motive in
the case of the actual actor. Then even though the situations appear
superficially to be very similar we must actually understand them or
interpret them as very different, perhaps, in terms of meaning, directly
opposed. (Simmel, in his *Probleme der Geschichtsphilosophie*, gives a
number of examples.) Third, the actors in any given situation are often
subject to opposing and conflicting impulses, all of which we are able to
understand. In a large number of cases we know from experience it is
not possible to arrive at even an approximate estimate of the relative
strength of conflicting motives and very often we cannot be certain of
our interpretation. Only the actual outcome of the conflict gives a solid
basis of judgment.

More generally, verification of subjective interpretation by comparison with the concrete course of events is, as in the case of all hypotheses,
indispensable. Unfortunately this type of verification is feasible with
relative accuracy only in the few very special cases susceptible of
psychological experimentation. In very different degrees of approximation,
such verification is also feasible in the limited number of cases of mass
phenomena which can be statistically described and unambiguously
interpreted. For the rest there remains only the possibility of comparing
the largest possible number of historical or contemporary processes
which, while otherwise similar, differ in the one decisive point of their
relation to the particular motive or factor the role of which is being
investigated. This is a fundamental task of comparative sociology.
Often, unfortunately, there is available only the uncertain procedure
of the "imaginary experiment" which consists in thinking away certain
elements of a chain of motivation and working out the course of action
which would then probably ensue, thus arriving at a causal judgment.[10]

For example, the generalization called Gresham's Law is a rationally
clear interpretation of human action under certain conditions and under
the assumption that it will follow a purely rational course. How far any
actual course of action corresponds to this can be verified only by the
available statistical evidence for the actual disappearance of under-valued
monetary units from circulation. In this case our information serves to
demonstrate a high degree of accuracy. The facts of experience were
known before the generalization, which was formulated afterwards;
but without this successful interpretation our need for causal understand-

ing would evidently be left unsatisfied. On the other hand, without the demonstration that what can here be assumed to be a theoretically adequate interpretation also is in some degree relevant to an actual course of action, a "law," no matter how fully demonstrated theoretically, would be worthless for the understanding of action in the real world. In this case the correspondence between the theoretical interpretation of motivation and its empirical verification is entirely satisfactory and the cases are numerous enough so that verification can be considered established. But to take another example, Eduard Meyer has advanced an ingenious theory of the causal significance of the battles of Marathon, Salamis, and Platea for the development of the cultural peculiarities of Greek, and hence, more generally, Western, civilization.[11] This is derived from a meaningful interpretation of certain symptomatic facts having to do with the attitudes of the Greek oracles and prophets towards the Persians. It can only be directly verified by reference to the examples of the conduct of the Persians in cases where they were victorious, as in Jerusalem, Egypt, and Asia Minor, and even this verification must necessarily remain unsatisfactory in certain respects. The striking rational plausibility of the hypothesis must here necessarily be relied on as a support. In very many cases of historical interpretation which seem highly plausible, however, there is not even a possibility of the order of verification which was feasible in this case. Where this is true the interpretation must necessarily remain a hypothesis.

7. A motive is a complex of subjective meaning which seems to the actor himself or to the observer an adequate ground for the conduct in question. The interpretation of a coherent course of conduct is "subjectively adequate" (or "adequate on the level of meaning"), insofar as, according to our habitual modes of thought and feeling, its component parts taken in their mutual relation are recognized to constitute a "typical" complex of meaning.[12] It is more common to say "correct." The interpretation of a sequence of events will on the other hand be called *causally* adequate insofar as, according to established generalizations from experience, there is a probability that it will always actually occur in the same way. An example of adequacy on the level of meaning in this sense is what is, according to our current norms of calculation or thinking, the correct solution of an arithmetical problem. On the other hand, a causally adequate interpretation of the same phenomenon would concern the statistical probability that, according to verified generalizations from experience, there would be a correct or an erroneous solution of the same problem. This also refers to currently accepted norms but includes taking account of typical errors or of typical confusions. Thus causal explanation depends on being able to determine that there is a

probability, which in the rare ideal case can be numerically stated, but is always in some sense calculable, that a given observable event (overt or subjective) will be followed or accompanied by another event.

A correct causal interpretation of a concrete course of action is arrived at when the overt action and the motives have both been correctly apprehended and at the same time their relation has become meaningfully comprehensible. A correct causal interpretation of typical action means that the process which is claimed to be typical is shown to be both adequately grasped on the level of meaning and at the same time the interpretation is to some degree causally adequate. If adequacy in respect to meaning is lacking, then no matter how high the degree of uniformity and how precisely its probability can be numerically determined, it is still an incomprehensible statistical probability, whether we deal with overt or subjective processes. On the other hand, even the most perfect adequacy on the level of meaning has causal significance from a sociological point of view only insofar as there is some kind of proof for the existence of a probability[13] that action in fact normally takes the course which has been held to be meaningful. For this there must be some degree of determinable frequency of approximation to an average or a pure type.

Statistical uniformities constitute understandable types of action, and thus constitute sociological generalizations, only when they can be regarded as manifestations of the understandable subjective meaning of a course of social action. Conversely, formulations of a rational course of subjectively understandable action constitute sociological types of empirical process only when they can be empirically observed with a significant degree of approximation. By no means is the actual likelihood of the occurrence of a given course of overt action always directly proportional to the clarity of subjective interpretation. Only actual experience can prove whether this is so in a given case. There are statistics of processes devoid of subjective meaning, such as death rates, phenomena of fatigue, the production rate of machines, the amount of rainfall, in exactly the same sense as there are statistics of meaningful phenomena. But only when the phenomena are meaningful do we speak of sociological statistics. Examples are such cases as crime rates, occupational distributions, price statistics, and statistics of crop acreage. Naturally there are many cases where both components are involved, as in crop statistics.

8. Processes and uniformities which it has here seemed convenient not to designate as sociological phenomena or uniformities because they are not "understandable," are naturally not on that account any the less important. This is true even for sociology in our sense which is restricted

to subjectively understandable phenomena—a usage which there is no intention of attempting to impose on anyone else. Such phenomena, however important, are simply treated by a different method from the others; they become conditions, stimuli, furthering or hindering circumstances of action.

9. Action in the sense of subjectively understandable orientation of behavior exists only as the behavior of one or more *individual* human beings. For other cognitive purposes it may be useful or necessary to consider the individual, for instance, as a collection of cells, as a complex of bio-chemical reactions, or to conceive his psychic life as made up of a variety of different elements, however these may be defined. Undoubtedly such procedures yield valuable knowledge of causal relationships. But the behavior of these elements, as expressed in such uniformities, is not subjectively understandable. This is true even of psychic elements because the more precisely they are formulated from a point of view of natural science, the less they are accessible to subjective understanding. This is never the road to interpretation in terms of subjective meaning. On the contrary, both for sociology in the present sense, and for history, the object of cognition is the subjective meaning-complex of action. The behavior of physiological entities such as cells, or of any sort of psychic elements, may at least in principle be observed and an attempt made to derive uniformities from such observations. It is further possible to attempt, with their help, to obtain a causal explanation of individual phenomena, that is, to subsume them under uniformities. But the subjective understanding of action takes the same account of this type of fact and uniformity as of any others not capable of subjective interpretation. (This is true, for example, of physical, astronomical, geological, meteorological, geographical, botanical, zoological, and anatomical facts, of those aspects of psycho-pathology which are devoid of subjective meaning, or of the natural conditions of technological processes.)

For still other cognitive purposes—for instance, juristic ones—or for practical ends, it may on the other hand be convenient or even indispensable to treat social collectivities, such as states, associations, business corporations, foundations, as if they were individual persons. Thus they may be treated as the subjects of rights and duties or as the performers of legally significant actions. But for the subjective interpretation of action in sociological work these collectivities must be treated as *solely* the resultants and modes of organization of the particular acts of individual persons, since these alone can be treated as agents in a course of subjectively understandable action. Nevertheless, the sociologist cannot for his purposes afford to ignore these collective concepts derived from other disciplines. For the subjective interpretation of action has at least three important relations to these concepts. In the first place it is often necessary to employ very similar collective concepts, indeed often using the same terms, in order to obtain an intelligible terminology. Thus both in legal terminology and in everyday speech the term "state" is used both for the legal concept of the state and for the phenomena of social action to which its legal rules are relevant. For sociological purposes, however, the phenomenon "the state" does not consist necessarily or even primarily of the elements which are relevant to legal analysis; and for sociological purposes there is no such thing as a collective personality which "acts." When reference is made in a sociological context to a state, a nation, a corporation, a family, or an army corps, or to similar collectivities, what is meant is, on the contrary, *only* a certain kind of development of actual or possible social actions of individual persons. Both because of its precision and because it is established in general usage the juristic concept is taken over, but is used in an entirely different meaning.

Secondly, the subjective interpretation of action must take account of a fundamentally important fact. These concepts of collective entities which are found both in common sense and in juristic and other technical forms of thought, have a meaning in the minds of individual persons, partly as of something actually existing, partly as something with normative authority. This is true not only of judges and officials, but of ordinary private individuals as well. Actors thus in part orient their action to them, and in this role such ideas have a powerful, often a decisive, causal influence on the course of action of real individuals. This is above all true where the ideas involve normative prescription or prohibition. Thus, for instance, one of the important aspects of the existence of a modern state, precisely as a complex of social interaction of individual persons, consists in the fact that the action of various individuals is oriented to the belief that it exists or should exist, thus that its acts and laws are valid in the legal sense. This will be further discussed below. Though extremely pedantic and cumbersome, it would be possible, if purposes of sociological terminology alone were involved, to eliminate such terms entirely, and substitute newly-coined words. This would be possible even though the word "state" is used ordinarily not only to designate the legal concept but also the real process of action. But in the above important connexion, at least, this would naturally be impossible.

Thirdly, it is the method of the so-called "organic" school of sociology —classical example: Schäffle's brilliant work, *Bau und Leben des sozialen Körpers*—to attempt to understand social interaction by using as a point of departure the "whole" within which the individual acts. His action and behavior are then interpreted somewhat in the way that a physiologist would treat the role of an organ of the body in the "economy" of the organism, that is from the point of view of the survival of the latter. (Compare the famous dictum of a well-known physiologist: "Sec. 10. The spleen. Of the spleen, gentlemen, we know nothing. So much for the spleen." Actually, of course, he knew a good deal about the spleen—its position, size, shape, etc.; but he could say nothing about its function, and it was his inability to do this that he called "ignorance.") How far in other disciplines this type of functional analysis of the relation of "parts" to a "whole" can be regarded as definitive, cannot be discussed here; but it is well known that the bio-chemical and bio-physical modes of analysis of the organism are on principle opposed to stopping there. For purposes of sociological analysis two things can be said. First this functional frame of reference is convenient for purposes of practical illustration and for provisional orientation. In these respects it is not only useful but indispensable. But at the same time if its cognitive value is overestimated and its concepts illegitimately "reified,"[14] it can be highly dangerous. Secondly, in certain circumstances this is the only available way of determining just what processes of social action it is important to understand in order to explain a given phenomenon. But this is only the beginning of sociological analysis as here understood. In the case of social collectivities, precisely as distinguished from organisms, we are in a position to go beyond merely demonstrating functional relationships and uniformities. We can accomplish something which is never attainable in the natural sciences, namely the subjective understanding of the action of the component individuals. The natural sciences on the other hand cannot do this, being limited to the formulation of causal uniformities in objects and events and the explanation of individual facts by applying them. We do not "understand" the behavior of cells, but can only observe the relevant functional relationships and generalize on the basis of these observations. This additional achievement of explanation by interpretive understanding, as distinguished from external observation, is of course attained only at a price—the more hypothetical and fragmentary character of its results. Nevertheless, subjective understanding is the specific characteristic of sociological knowledge.

It would lead too far afield even to attempt to discuss how far the behavior of animals is subjectively understandable to us and vice versa; in both cases the meaning of the term understanding and its extent of application would be highly problematical. But in so far as such understanding existed it would be theoretically possible to formulate a sociology of the relations of men to animals, both domestic and wild. Thus many animals "understand" commands, anger, love, hostility, and react to them in ways which are evidently often by no means purely instinctive and mechanical and in some sense both consciously meaningful and affected by experience. In a way, our ability to share the feelings of primitive men is not very much greater. We either do not have any reliable means of determining the subjective state of mind of an animal or what we have is at best very unsatisfactory. It is well known that the problems of animal psychology, however interesting, are very thorny ones. There are in particular various forms of social organization among animals: monogamous and polygamous "families," herds, flocks, and finally "states," with a functional division of labour. (The extent of functional differentiation found in these animal societies is by no means, however, entirely a matter of the degree of organic or morphological differentiation of the individual members of the species. Thus, the functional differentiation found among the termites, and in consequence that of the products of their social activities, is much more advanced than in the case of the bees and ants.) In this field it goes without saying that a purely functional point of view is often the best that can, at least for the present, be attained, and the investigator must be content with it. Thus it is possible to study the ways in which the species provides for its survival; that is, for nutrition, defence, reproduction, and reconstruction of the social units. As the principal bearers of these functions, differentiated types of individuals can be identified: "kings," "queens," "workers," "soldiers," "drones," "propagators," "queen's substitutes," and so on. Anything more than that was for a long time merely a matter of speculation or of an attempt to determine the extent to which heredity on the one hand and environment on the other would be involved in the development of these "social" proclivities. This was particularly true of the controversies between Götte and Weismann.[15] The latter's conception in *Die Allmacht der Naturzüchtung* was largely based on wholly non-empirical deductions. But all serious authorities are naturally fully agreed that the limitation of analysis to the functional level is only a necessity imposed by our present ignorance, which it is hoped will only be temporary. (For an account of the state of knowledge of the termites, for example, see the study by Karl Escherich, *Die Termiten oder weissen Ameisen*, 1909.)

The researchers would like to understand not only the relatively obvious survival functions of these various differentiated types, but also the bearing of different variants of the theory of heredity or its reverse on the problem of explaining how these differentiations have come about. Moreover, they would like to know first what factors account for the original differentiation of specialized types from the still neutral undifferentiated species-type. Secondly, it would be important to know what leads the differentiated individual in the typical case to behave in a way which actually serves the survival value of the organized group. Wherever research has made any progress in the solution of these problems it has been through the experimental demonstration of the probability or possibility of the role of chemical stimuli or physiological processes, such as nutritional states, the effects of parasitic castration, etc., in the case of the individual organism. How far there is even a hope that the existence of "subjective" or "meaningful" orientation could be made experimentally probable, even the specialist today would hardly be in a position to say. A verifiable conception of the state of mind of these social animals accessible to meaningful understanding, would seem to be attainable even as an ideal goal only within narrow limits. However that may be, a contribution to the understanding of human social action is hardly to be expected from this quarter. On the contrary, in the field of animal psychology, human analogies are and must be continually employed. The most that can be hoped for is, then, that these biological analogies may some day be useful in suggesting significant problems. For instance they may throw light on the question of the relative role in the early stages of human social differentiation of mechanical and instinctive factors, as compared with that of the factors which are accessible to subjective interpretation generally, and more particularly to the role of consciously rational action. It is necessary for the sociologist to be thoroughly aware of the fact that in the early stages even of human development, the first set of factors is completely predominant. Even in the later stages he must take account of their continual interaction with the others in a role which is often of decisive importance. This is particularly true of all "traditional" action and of many aspects of charisma, which contain the seeds of certain types of psychic "contagion" and thus give rise to new social developments. These types of action are very closely related to phenomena which are understandable either only in biological terms or can be interpreted in terms of subjective motives only in fragments. But all these facts do not discharge sociology from the obligation, in full awareness of the narrow limits to which it is confined, to accomplish what it alone can do.

The various works of Othmar Spann [1878–1950] are often full of suggestive ideas though at the same time he is guilty of occasional misunderstandings and above all of arguing on the basis of pure value judgments which have no place in an empirical investigation. But he is undoubtedly correct in doing something to which, however, no one seriously objects, namely, emphasizing the sociological significance of the functional point of view for preliminary orientation to problems. This is what he calls the "universalistic method." It is true that we must know what kind of action is functionally necessary for "survival," but even more so for the maintenance of a cultural type and the continuity of the corresponding modes of social action, before it is possible even to inquire how this action has come about and what motives determine it. It is necessary to know what a "king," an "official," an "entrepreneur," a "procurer," or a "magician" does, that is, what kind of typical action, which justifies classifying an individual in one of these categories, is important and relevant for an analysis, before it is possible to undertake the analysis itself. (This is what Rickert means by *Wertbezogenheit*.) But it is only this analysis itself which can achieve the sociological understanding of the actions of typically differentiated human (and only human) individuals, and which hence constitutes the specific function of sociology. It is a tremendous misunderstanding to think that an "individualistic" *method* should involve what is in any conceivable sense an individualistic system of *values*. It is as important to avoid this error as the related one which confuses the unavoidable tendency of sociological concepts to assume a rationalistic character with a belief in the predominance of rational motives, or even a positive valuation of rationalism. Even a socialistic economy would have to be understood sociologically in exactly the same kind of "individualistic" terms; that is, in terms of the action of individuals, the types of officials found in it, as would be the case with a system of free exchange analysed in terms of the theory of marginal utility or a "better," but in this respect similar theory). The real empirical sociological investigation begins with the question: What motives determine and lead the individual members and participants in this socialistic community to behave in such a way that the community came into being in the first place and that it continues to exist? Any form of functional analysis which proceeds from the whole to the parts can accomplish only a preliminary preparation for this investigation— a preparation, the utility and indispensability of which, if properly carried out, is naturally beyond question.

10. It is customary to designate various sociological generalizations, as for example "Gresham's Law," as "laws." These are in fact typical probabilities confirmed by observation to the effect that under certain given conditions an expected course of social action will occur, which is understandable in terms of the typical motives and typical subjective intentions of the actors. These generalizations are both understandable and definite in the highest degree insofar as the typically observed course of action can be understood in terms of the purely rational pursuit of an end, or where for reasons of methodological convenience such a theoretical type can be heuristically employed. In such cases the relations of means and end will be clearly understandable on grounds of experience, particularly where the choice of means was "inevitable." In such

cases it is legitimate to assert that insofar as the action was rigorously rational it could not have taken any other course because for technical reasons, given their clearly defined ends, no other means were available to the actors. This very case demonstrates how erroneous it is to regard any kind of psychology as the ultimate foundation of the sociological interpretation of action. The term psychology, to be sure, is today understood in a wide variety of senses. For certain quite specific methodological purposes the type of treatment which attempts to follow the procedures of the natural sciences employs a distinction between "physical" and "psychic" phenomena which is entirely foreign to the disciplines concerned with human action, at least in the present sense. The results of a type of psychological investigation which employs the methods of the natural sciences in any one of various possible ways may naturally, like the results of any other science, have outstanding significance for sociological problems; indeed this has often happened. But this use of the results of psychology is something quite different from the investigation of human behavior in terms of its subjective meaning. Hence sociology has no closer relationship on a general analytical level to this type of psychology than to any other science. The source of error lies in the concept of the "psychic." It is held that everything which is not physical is *ipso facto* psychic. However, the *meaning* of a train of mathematical reasoning which a person carries out is not in the relevant sense "psychic." Similarly the rational deliberation of an actor as to whether the results of a given proposed course of action will or will not promote certain specific interests, and the corresponding decision, do not become one bit more understandable by taking "psychological" considerations into account. But it is precisely on the basis of such rational assumptions that most of the laws of sociology, including those of economics, are built up. On the other hand, in explaining the irrationalities of action sociologically, that form of psychology which employs the method of subjective understanding undoubtedly can make decisively important contributions. But this does not alter the fundamental methodological situation.

11. We have taken for granted that sociology seeks to formulate type concepts and generalized uniformities of empirical process. This distinguishes it from history, which is oriented to the causal analysis and explanation of individual actions, structures, and personalities possessing cultural significance. The empirical material which underlies the concepts of sociology consists to a very large extent, though by no means exclusively, of the same concrete processes of action which are dealt with by historians. An important consideration in the formulation of sociological concepts and generalizations is the contribution that sociology

can make toward the causal explanation of some historically and culturally important phenomenon. As in the case of every generalizing science the abstract character of the concepts of sociology is responsible for the fact that, compared with actual historical reality, they are relatively lacking in fullness of concrete content. To compensate for this disadvantage, sociological analysis can offer a greater precision of concepts. This precision is obtained by striving for the highest possible degree of adequacy on the level of meaning. It has already been repeatedly stressed that this aim can be realized in a particularly high degree in the case of concepts and generalizations which formulate rational processes. But sociological investigation attempts to include in its scope various irrational phenomena, such as prophetic, mystic, and affectual modes of action, formulated in terms of theoretical concepts which are adequate on the level of meaning. In *all* cases, rational or irrational, sociological analysis both abstracts from reality and at the same time helps us to understand it, in that it shows with what degree of approximation a concrete historical phenomenon can be subsumed under one or more of these concepts. For example, the same historical phenomenon may be in one aspect feudal, in another patrimonial, in another bureaucratic, and in still another charismatic. In order to give a precise meaning to these terms, it is necessary for the sociologist to formulate pure ideal types of the corresponding forms of action which in each case involve the highest possible degree of logical integration by virtue of their complete adequacy on the level of meaning. But precisely because this is true, it is probably seldom if ever that a real phenomenon can be found which corresponds exactly to one of these ideally constructed pure types. The case is similar to a physical reaction which has been calculated on the assumption of an absolute vacuum. Theoretical differentiation (*Kasuistik*) is possible in sociology only in terms of ideal or pure types. It goes without saying that in addition it is convenient for the sociologist from time to time to employ average types of an empirical statistical character, concepts which do not require methodological discussion. But when reference is made to "typical" cases, the term should always be understood, unless otherwise stated, as meaning *ideal* types, which may in turn be rational or irrational as the case may be (thus in economic theory they are always rational), but in any case are always constructed with a view to adequacy on the level of meaning.

It is important to realize that in the sociological field as elsewhere, averages, and hence average types, can be formulated with a relative degree of precision only where they are concerned with differences of degree in respect to action which remains qualitatively the same. Such cases do occur, but in the majority of cases of action important to history or sociology the motives which determine it are qualitatively heterogeneous. Then it is quite impossible to speak of an "average" in the true sense. The ideal types of social action which for instance are used in economic theory are thus unrealistic or abstract in that they always ask what course of action would take place if it were purely rational and oriented to economic ends alone. This construction can be used to aid in the understanding of action not purely economically determined but which involves deviations arising from traditional restraints, affects, errors, and the intrusion of other than economic purposes or considerations. This can take place in two ways. First, in analysing the extent to which in the concrete case, or on the average for a class of cases, the action was in part economically determined along with the other factors. Secondly, by throwing the discrepancy between the actual course of events and the ideal type into relief, the analysis of the non-economic motives actually involved is facilitated. The procedure would be very similar in employing an ideal type of mystical orientation, with its appropriate attitude of indifference to worldly things, as a tool for analysing its consequences for the actor's relation to ordinary life—for instance, to political or economic affairs. The more sharply and precisely the ideal type has been constructed, thus the more abstract and unrealistic in this sense it is, the better it is able to perform its functions in formulating terminology, classifications, and hypotheses. In working out a concrete causal explanation of individual events, the procedure of the historian is essentially the same. Thus in attempting to explain the campaign of 1866, it is indispensable both in the case of Moltke and of Benedek to attempt to construct imaginatively how each, given fully adequate knowledge both of his own situation and of that of his opponent, would have acted. Then it is possible to compare with this the actual course of action and to arrive at a causal explanation of the observed deviations, which will be attributed to such factors as misinformation, strategical errors, logical fallacies, personal temperament, or considerations outside the realm of strategy. Here, too, an ideal-typical construction of rational action is actually employed even though it is not made explicit.

The theoretical concepts of sociology are ideal types not only from the objective point of view, but also in their application to subjective processes. In the great majority of cases actual action goes on in a state of inarticulate half-consciousness or actual unconsciousness of its subjective meaning. The actor is more likely to "be aware" of it in a vague sense than he is to "know" what he is doing or be explicitly self-conscious about it. In most cases his action is governed by impulse or habit. Only occasionally and, in the uniform action of large numbers, often only in the case of a few individuals, is the subjective meaning of the action, whether rational or irrational, brought clearly into consciousness. The ideal type of meaningful action where the meaning is fully conscious and explicit is a marginal case. Every sociological or historical investigation, in applying its analysis to the empirical facts, must take this fact into account. But the difficulty need not prevent the sociologist from systematizing his concepts by the classification of possible types of subjective meaning. That is, he may reason as if action actually proceeded on the basis of clearly self-conscious meaning. The resulting deviation from the concrete facts must continually be kept in mind whenever it is a question of this level of concreteness, and must be carefully studied with reference both to degree and kind. It is often necessary to choose between terms which are either clear or unclear. Those which are clear will, to be sure, have the abstractness of ideal types, but they are none the less preferable for scientific purposes. (On all these questions see " 'Objectivity' in Social Science and Social Policy.")

B. SOCIAL ACTION

1. Social action, which includes both failure to act and passive acquiescence, may be oriented to the past, present, or expected future behavior of others. Thus it may be motivated by revenge for a past attack, defence against present, or measures of defence against future aggression. The "others" may be individual persons, and may be known to the actor as such, or may constitute an indefinite plurality and may be entirely unknown as individuals. (Thus, money is a means of exchange which the actor accepts in payment because he orients his action to the expectation that a large but unknown number of individuals he is personally unacquainted with will be ready to accept it in exchange on some future occasion.)

2. Not every kind of action, even of overt action, is "social" in the sense of the present discussion. Overt action is non-social if it is oriented solely to the behavior of inanimate objects. Subjective attitudes constitute social action only so far as they are oriented to the behavior of others. For example, religious behavior is not social if it is simply a matter of contemplation or of solitary prayer. The economic activity of an individual is social only if it takes account of the behavior of someone else. Thus very generally it becomes social insofar as the actor assumes that others will respect his actual control over economic goods. Concretely it is social, for instance, if in relation to the actor's own consumption the future wants of others are taken into account and this becomes one consideration affecting the actor's own saving. Or, in another connexion, production may be oriented to the future wants of other people.

3. Not every type of contact of human beings has a social character; this is rather confined to cases where the actor's behavior is meaningfully oriented to that of others. For example, a mere collision of two cyclists may be compared to a natural event. On the other hand, their attempt to avoid hitting each other, or whatever insults, blows, or friendly discussion might follow the collision, would constitute "social action."

4. Social action is not identical either with the similar actions of many persons or with every action influenced by other persons. Thus, if at the beginning of a shower a number of people on the street put up their umbrellas at the same time, this would not ordinarily be a case of action mutually oriented to that of each other, but rather of all reacting in the same way to the like need of protection from the rain. It is well known that the actions of the individual are strongly influenced by the mere fact that he is a member of a crowd confined within a limited space. Thus, the subject matter of studies of "crowd psychology," such as those of Le Bon, will be called "action conditioned by crowds." It is also possible for large numbers, though dispersed, to be influenced simultaneously or successively by a source of influence operating similarly on all the individuals, as by means of the press. Here also the behavior of an individual is influenced by his membership in a "mass" and by the fact that he is aware of being a member. Some types of reaction are only made possible by the mere fact that the individual acts as part of a crowd. Others become more difficult under these conditions. Hence it is possible that a particular event or mode of human behavior can give rise to the most diverse kinds of feeling—gaiety, anger, enthusiasm, despair, and passions of all sorts—in a crowd situation which would not occur at all or not nearly so readily if the individual were alone. But for this to happen there need not, at least in many cases, be any meaningful relation between the behavior of the individual and the fact that he is a member of a crowd. It is not proposed in the present sense to call action "social" when it is merely a result of the effect on the individual of the existence of a crowd as such and the action is not oriented to that fact on the level of meaning. At the same time the borderline is naturally highly indefinite. In such cases as that of the influence of the demagogue, there may be a wide variation in the extent to which his mass clientele is affected by a meaningful reaction to the fact of its large numbers; and whatever this relation may be, it is open to varying interpretations.

But furthermore, mere "imitation" of the action of others, such as that on which Tarde has rightly laid emphasis, will not be considered a case of specifically social action if it is purely reactive so that there is no meaningful orientation to the actor imitated. The borderline is, however, so indefinite that it is often hardly possible to discriminate. The mere fact that a person is found to employ some apparently useful procedure which he learned from someone else does not, however, constitute, in the present sense, social action. Action such as this is not oriented to the action of the other person, but the actor has, through observing the other, become acquainted with certain objective facts; and it is these to which his action is oriented. His action is then *causally* determined by the action of others, but not meaningfully. On the other hand, if the action of others is imitated because it is fashionable or traditional or exemplary, or lends social distinction, or on similar grounds, it is meaningfully oriented either to the behavior of the source of imitation or of third persons or of both. There are of course all manner of transitional cases between the two types of imitation. Both the phenomena discussed above, the behavior of crowds and imitation, stand on the indefinite borderline of social action. The same is true, as will often appear, of traditionalism and charisma. The reason for the indefiniteness of the line in these and other cases lies in the fact that both the orientation to the behavior of others and the meaning which can be imputed by the actor himself, are by no means always capable of clear determination and are often altogether unconscious and seldom fully self-conscious. Mere "influence" and meaningful orientation cannot therefore always be clearly differentiated on the empirical level. But conceptually it is essential to distinguish them, even though merely reactive imitation may well have a degree of sociological importance at least equal to that of the type which can be called social action in the strict sense. Sociology, it goes without saying, is by no means confined to the study of social action; this is only, at least for the kind of sociology being developed here, its central subject matter, that which may be said to be decisive for its status as a science. But this does not imply any judgment on the comparative importance of this and other factors.

2. *Types of Social Action*

Social action, like all action, may be oriented in four ways. It may be:

(1) *instrumentally rational (zweckrational)*, that is, determined by expectations as to the behavior of objects in the environment and of other human beings; these expectations are used as "conditions" or "means" for the attainment of the actor's own rationally pursued and calculated ends;

(2) *value-rational (wertrational)*, that is, determined by a conscious

belief in the value for its own sake of some ethical, aesthetic, religious, or other form of behavior, independently of its prospects of success;
(3) *affectual* (especially emotional), that is, determined by the actor's specific affects and feeling states;
(4) *traditional*, that is, determined by ingrained habituation.

1. Strictly traditional behavior, like the reactive type of imitation discussed above, lies very close to the borderline of what can justifiably be called meaningfully oriented action, and indeed often on the other side. For it is very often a matter of almost automatic reaction to habitual stimuli which guide behavior in a course which has been repeatedly followed. The great bulk of all everyday action to which people have become habitually accustomed approaches this type. Hence, its place in a systematic classification is not merely that of a limiting case because, as will be shown later, attachment to habitual forms can be upheld with varying degrees of self-consciousness and in a variety of senses. In this case the type may shade over into value rationality (*Wertrationalität*).

2. Purely affectual behavior also stands on the borderline of what can be considered "meaningfully" oriented, and often it, too, goes over the line. It may, for instance, consist in an uncontrolled reaction to some exceptional stimulus. It is a case of sublimation when affectually determined action occurs in the form of conscious release of emotional tension. When this happens it is usually well on the road to rationalization in one or the other or both of the above senses.

3. The orientation of value-rational action is distinguished from the affectual type by its clearly self-conscious formulation of the ultimate values governing the action and the consistently planned orientation of its detailed course to these values. At the same time the two types have a common element, namely that the meaning of the action does not lie in the achievement of a result ulterior to it, but in carrying out the specific type of action for its own sake. Action is affectual if it satisfies a need for revenge, sensual gratification, devotion, contemplative bliss, or for working off emotional tensions (irrespective of the level of sublimation).

Examples of pure value-rational orientation would be the actions of persons who, regardless of possible cost to themselves, act to put into practice their convictions of what seems to them to be required by duty, honor, the pursuit of beauty, a religious call, personal loyalty, or the importance of some "cause" no matter in what it consists. In our terminology, value-rational action always involves "commands" or "demands" which, in the actor's opinion, are binding on him. It is only in cases where human action is motivated by the fulfillment of such unconditional demands that it will be called value-rational. This is the case in widely varying degrees, but for the most part only to a relatively slight extent. Nevertheless, it will be shown that the occurrence of this mode of action is important enough to justify its formulation as a distinct type;

though it may be remarked that there is no intention here of attempting to formulate in any sense an exhaustive classification of types of action.

4. Action is instrumentally rational (*zweckrational*) when the end, the means, and the secondary results are all rationally taken into account and weighed. This involves rational consideration of alternative means to the end, of the relations of the end to the secondary consequences, and finally of the relative importance of different possible ends. Determination of action either in affectual or in traditional terms is thus incompatible with this type. Choice between alternative and conflicting ends and results may well be determined in a value-rational manner. In that case, action is instrumentally rational only in respect to the choice of means. On the other hand, the actor may, instead of deciding between alternative and conflicting ends in terms of a rational orientation to a system of values, simply take them as given subjective wants and arrange them in a scale of consciously assessed relative urgency. He may then orient his action to this scale in such a way that they are satisfied as far as possible in order of urgency, as formulated in the principle of "marginal utility." Value-rational action may thus have various different relations to the instrumentally rational action. From the latter point of view, however, value-rationality is always irrational. Indeed, the more the value to which action is oriented is elevated to the status of an absolute value, the more "irrational" in this sense the corresponding action is. For, the more unconditionally the actor devotes himself to this value for its own sake, to pure sentiment or beauty, to absolute goodness or devotion to duty, the less is he influenced by considerations of the consequences of his action. The orientation of action wholly to the rational achievement of ends without relation to fundamental values is, to be sure, essentially only a limiting case.

5. It would be very unusual to find concrete cases of action, especially of social action, which were oriented *only* in one or another of these ways. Furthermore, this classification of the modes of orientation of action is in no sense meant to exhaust the possibilities of the field, but only to formulate in conceptually pure form certain sociologically important types to which actual action is more or less closely approximated or, in much the more common case, which constitute its elements. The usefulness of the classification for the purposes of this investigation can only be judged in terms of its results.

3. *The Concept of Social Relationship*

The term "social relationship" will be used to denote the behavior of a plurality of actors insofar as, in its meaningful content, the action of each takes account of that of the others and is oriented in these terms. The social relationship thus consists entirely and exclusively in the exist-

ence of a probability that there will be a meaningful course of social action
—irrespective, for the time being, of the basis for this probability.

1. Thus, as a defining criterion, it is essential that there should be
at least a minimum of mutual orientation of the action of each to that
of the others. Its content may be of the most varied nature: conflict,
hostility, sexual attraction, friendship, loyalty, or economic exchange. It
may involve the fulfillment, the evasion, or the violation of the terms
of an agreement; economic, erotic, or some other form of "competition";
common membership in status, national or class groups (provided it
leads to social action). Hence, the definition does not specify whether
the relation of the actors is co-operative or the opposite.

2. The "meaning" relevant in this context is always a case of the
meaning imputed to the parties in a given concrete case, on the average,
or in a theoretically formulated pure type—it is never a normatively
"correct" or a metaphysically "true" meaning. Even in cases of such
forms of social organization as a state, church, association, or marriage,
the social relationship consists exclusively in the fact that there has existed, exists, or will exist a probability of action in some definite way
appropriate to this meaning. It is vital to be continually clear about this
in order to avoid the "reification" of those concepts. A "state," for example, ceases to exist in a sociologically relevant sense whenever there
is no longer a probability that certain kinds of meaningfully oriented
social action will take place. This probability may be very high or it may
be negligibly low. But in any case it is only in the sense and degree in
which it does exist that the corresponding social relationship exists. It is
impossible to find any other clear meaning for the statement that, for
instance, a given "state" exists or has ceased to exist.

3. The subjective meaning need not necessarily be the same for all
the parties who are mutually oriented in a given social relationship;
there need not in this sense be "reciprocity." "Friendship," "love,"
"loyalty," "fidelity to contracts," "patriotism," on one side, may well be
faced with an entirely different attitude on the other. In such cases the
parties associate different meanings with their actions, and the social
relationship is insofar objectively "asymmetrical" from the points of view
of the two parties. It may nevertheless be a case of mutual orientation
insofar as, even though partly or wholly erroneously, one party pre-
sumes a particular attitude toward him on the part of the other and
orients his action to this expectation. This can, and usually will, have
consequences for the course of action and the form of the relationship.
A relationship is objectively symmetrical only as, according to the typical expectations of the parties, the meaning for one party is the same as
that for the other. Thus the actual attitude of a child to its father may be
a least approximately that which the father, in the individual case, on
the average or typically, has come to expect. A social relationship in
which the attitudes are completely and fully corresponding is in reality
a limiting case. But the absence of reciprocity will, for terminological

purposes, be held to exclude the existence of a social relationship only if it actually results in the absence of a mutual orientation of the action of the parties. Here as elsewhere all sorts of transitional cases are the rule rather than the exception.

4. A social relationship can be of a very fleeting character or of varying degrees of permanence. In the latter case there is a probability of the repeated recurrence of the behavior which corresponds to its subjective meaning and hence is expected. In order to avoid fallacious impressions, let it be repeated that it is *only* the existence of the probability that, corresponding to a given subjective meaning, a certain type of action will take place which constitutes the "existence" of the social relationship. Thus that a "friendship" or a "state" exists or has existed means this and only this: that we, the observers, judge that there is or has been a probability that on the basis of certain kinds of known subjective attitude of certain individuals there will result in the average sense a certain specific type of action. For the purposes of legal reasoning it is essential to be able to decide whether a rule of law does or does not carry legal authority, hence whether a legal relationship does or does not "exist." This type of question is not, however, relevant to sociological problems.

5. The subjective meaning of a social relationship may change, thus a political relationship once based on solidarity may develop into a conflict of interests. In that case it is only a matter of terminological convenience and of the degree of continuity of the change whether we say that a new relationship has come into existence or that the old one continues but has acquired a new meaning. It is also possible for the meaning to be partly constant, partly changing.

6. The meaningful content which remains relatively constant in a social relationship is capable of formulation in terms of maxims which the parties concerned expect to be adhered to by their partners on the average and approximately. The more rational in relation to values or to given ends the action is, the more is this likely to be the case. There is far less possibility of a rational formulation of subjective meaning in the case of a relation of erotic attraction or of personal loyalty or any other affectual type than, for example, in the case of a business contract.

7. The meaning of a social relationship may be agreed upon by mutual consent. This implies that the parties make promises covering their future behavior, whether toward each other or toward third persons. In such cases each party then normally counts, so far as he acts rationally, in some degree on the fact that the other will orient his action to the meaning of the agreement as he (the first actor) understands it. In part he orients his action rationally (*zweckrational*) to these expectations as given facts with, to be sure, varying degrees of subjectively "loyal" intention of doing his part. But in part also he is motivated value-rationally by a sense of duty, which makes him adhere to the agreement as he understands it. This much may be anticipated. (For a further elaboration, see secs. 9 and 13 below.)

4. *Types of Action Orientation: Usage, Custom, Self-Interest*

Within the realm of social action certain empirical uniformities can be observed, that is, courses of action that are repeated by the actor or (simultaneously) occur among numerous actors since the subjective meaning is meant to be the same. Sociological investigation is concerned with these typical modes of action. Thereby it differs from history, the subject of which is rather the causal explanation of important individual events; important, that is, in having an influence on human destiny.

If an orientation toward social action occurs regularly, it will be called "usage" (*Brauch*) insofar as the probability of its existence within a group is based on nothing but actual practice. A usage will be called a "custom" (*Sitte*) if the practice is based upon long standing. On the other hand, a uniformity of orientation may be said to be "determined by self-interest," if and insofar as the actors' conduct is instrumentally (*zweckrational*) oriented toward identical expectations.[16]

1. Usage also includes "fashion" (*Mode*). As distinguished from custom and in direct contrast to it, usage will be called fashion so far as the mere fact of the *novelty* of the corresponding behavior is the basis of the orientation of action. Its locus is in the neighborhood of "convention,"[17] since both of them usually spring from a desire for social prestige. Fashion, however, will not be further discussed here.

2. As distinguished from both "convention" and "law," "custom" refers to rules devoid of any external sanction. The actor conforms with them of his own free will, whether his motivation lies in the fact that he merely fails to think about it, that it is more comfortable to conform, or whatever else the reason may be. For the same reasons he can consider it likely that other members of the group will adhere to a custom.

Thus custom is not "valid" in anything like the legal sense; conformity with it is not "demanded" by anybody. Naturally, the transition from this to validly enforced convention and to law is gradual. Everywhere what has been traditionally handed down has been an important source of what has come to be enforced. Today it is customary every morning to eat a breakfast which, within limits, conforms to a certain pattern. But there is no obligation to do so, except possibly for hotel guests, and it has not always been customary. On the other hand, the current mode of dress, even though it has partly originated in custom, is today very largely no longer customary alone, but conventional.

(On the concepts of usage and custom, the relevant parts of vol. II of R. von Jhering's *Zweck im Recht* are still worth reading. Compare also, P. Oertmann, *Rechtsordnung und Verkehrssitte* (1914); and more recently E. Weigelin, *Sitte, Recht und Moral* (1919), which agrees with the author's position as opposed to that of Stammler.)

3. Many of the especially notable uniformities in the course of social action are not determined by orientation to any sort of norm which is held to be valid, nor do they rest on custom, but entirely on the fact that the corresponding type of social action is in the nature of the case best adapted to the normal interests of the actors as they themselves are aware of them. This is above all true of economic action, for example, the uniformities of price determination in a "free" market, but is by no means confined to such cases. The dealers in a market thus treat their own actions as means for obtaining the satisfaction of the ends defined by what they realize to be their own typical economic interests, and similarly treat as conditions the corresponding typical expectations as to the prospective behavior of others. The more strictly rational (*zweckrational*) their action is, the more will they tend to react similarly to the same situation. In this way there arise similarities, uniformities, and continuities in their attitudes and actions which are often far more stable than they would be if action were oriented to a system of norms and duties which were considered binding on the members of a group. This phenomenon—the fact that orientation to the situation in terms of the pure self-interest of the individual and of the others to whom he is related can bring about results comparable to those which imposed norms prescribe, very often in vain—has aroused a lively interest, especially in economic affairs. Observation of this has, in fact, been one of the important sources of economics as a science. But it is true in all other spheres of action as well. This type, with its clarity of self-consciousness and freedom from subjective scruples, is the polar antithesis of every sort of unthinking acquiescence in customary ways as well as of devotion to norms consciously accepted as absolute values. One of the most important aspects of the process of "rationalization" of action is the substitution for the unthinking acceptance of ancient custom, of deliberate adaptation to situations in terms of self-interest. To be sure, this process by no means exhausts the concept of rationalization of action. For in addition this can proceed in a variety of other directions; positively in that of a deliberate formulation of ultimate values (*Wertrationalisierung*); or negatively, at the expense not only of custom, but of emotional values; and, finally, in favor of a morally sceptical type of rationality, at the expense of any belief in absolute values. The many possible meanings of the concept of rationalization will often enter into the discussion.[18] (Further remarks on the analytial problem will be found at the end.)[19]

4. The stability of merely customary action rests essentially on the fact that the person who does not adapt himself to it is subjected to both petty and major inconveniences and annoyances as long as the majority of the people he comes in contact with continue to uphold the custom and conform with it.

Similarly, the stability of action in terms of self-interest rests on the fact that the person who does not orient his action to the interests of others, does not "take account" of them, arouses their antagonism

or may end up in a situation different from that which he had foreseen or wished to bring about. He thus runs the risk of damaging
his own interests.

5. *Legitimate Order*

Action, especially social action which involves a social relationship,
may be guided by the belief in the existence of a legitimate order. The
probability that action will actually be so governed will be called the
"validity" (*Geltung*) of the order in question.

1. Thus, the validity of an order means more than the mere
existence of a uniformity of social action determined by custom or
self-interest. If furniture movers regularly advertise at the time many
leases expire, this uniformity is determined by self-interest. If a
salesman visits certain customers on particular days of the month or
the week, it is either a case of customary behavior or a product of self-
interested orientation. However, when a civil servant appears in his
office daily at a fixed time, he does not act only on the basis of
custom or self-interest which he could disregard if he wanted to; as
a rule, his action is also determined by the validity of an order (viz.,
the civil service rules), which he fulfills partly because disobedience
would be disadvantageous to him but also because its violation would
be abhorrent to his sense of duty (of course, in varying degrees).

2. Only then will the content of a social relationship be called
an order if the conduct is, approximately or on the average, oriented
toward determinable "maxims." Only then will an order be called
"valid" if the orientation toward these maxims occurs, among other
reasons, also because it is in some appreciable way regarded by the
actor as in some way obligatory or exemplary for him. Naturally, in
concrete cases, the orientation of action to an order involves a wide
variety of motives. But the circumstance that, along with the other
sources of conformity, the order is also held by at least part of the
actors to define a model or to be binding, naturally increases the
probability that action will in fact conform to it, often to a very
considerable degree. An order which is adhered to from motives of
pure expediency is generally much less stable than one upheld on a
purely customary basis through the fact that the corresponding behavior
has become habitual. The latter is much the most common type of
subjective attitude. But even this type of order is in turn much less
stable than an order which enjoys the prestige of being considered
binding, or, as it may be expressed, of "legitimacy." The transitions
between orientation to an order from motives of tradition or of expediency to the case where a belief in its legitimacy is involved are
empirically gradual.

3. It is possible for action to be oriented to an order in other ways than through conformity with its prescriptions, as they are generally understood by the actors. Even in the case of evasion or disobedience, the probability of their being recognized as valid norms may have an effect on action. This may, in the first place, be true from the point of view of sheer expediency. A thief orients his action to the validity of the criminal law in that he acts surreptitiously. The fact that the order is recognized as valid in his society is made evident by the fact that he cannot violate it openly without punishment. But apart from this limiting case, it is very common for violation of an order to be confined to more or less numerous partial deviations from it, or for the attempt to be made, with varying degrees of good faith, to justify the deviation as legitimate. Furthermore, there may exist at the same time different interpretations of the meaning of the order. In such cases, for sociological purposes, each can be said to be valid insofar as it actually determines the course of action. The fact that, in the same social group, a plurality of contradictory systems of order may all be recognized as valid, is not a source of difficulty for the sociological approach. Indeed, it is even possible for the same individual to orient his action to contradictory systems of order. This can take place not only at different times, as is an everyday occurrence, but even in the case of the same concrete act. A person who fights a duel follows the code of honor; but at the same time, insofar as he either keeps it secret or conversely gives himself up to the police, he takes account of the criminal law. To be sure, when evasion or contravention of the generally understood meaning of an order has become the rule, the order can be said to be "valid" only in a limited degree and, in the extreme case, not at all. Thus for sociological purposes there does not exist, as there does for the law, a rigid alternative between the validity and lack of validity of a given order. On the contrary, there is a gradual transition between the two extremes; and also it is possible, as it has been pointed out, for contradictory systems of order to exist at the same time. In that case each is "valid" precisely to the extent that there is a probability that action will in fact be oriented to it.

[Excursus:] Those familiar with the literature of this subject will recall the part played by the concept of "order" in the brilliant book of Rudolf Stammler, which was cited in the prefatory note, a book which, though like all his works it is very able, is nevertheless fundamentally misleading and confuses the issues in a catastrophic fashion. (The reader may compare the author's critical discussion of it, which was also cited in the same place, a discussion which, because of the author's annoyance at Stammler's confusion, was unfortunately written in somewhat too acrimonious a tone.) Stammler fails to distinguish the normative meaning of "validity" from the empirical. He further fails to recognize that social action is oriented to other things beside systems of order. Above all, however, in a way which is wholly indefensible from a logical point of view, he treats order as a "form" of social action and then attempts to bring it into a type of relation to "content," which is analogous to that of form and content in the theory of knowledge. Other errors in his argument will be left aside. But economic action, for instance, is oriented to knowledge of the relative scarcity of certain available means to want satisfaction, in relation to the actor's state of needs and to the present and probable action of others, insofar as the latter affects the same resources. But at the same time, of course, the actor in his choice of economic procedures naturally orients himself *in addition* to the conventional and legal rules which he recognizes as valid, that is, of which he knows that a violation on his part would call forth a given reaction of other persons. Stammler succeeds in introducing a state of hopeless confusion into this very simple empirical situation, particularly in that he maintains that a causal relationship between an order and actual empirical action involves a contradiction in terms. It is true, of course, that there is no causal relationship between the *normative* validity of an order in the legal sense and any empirical process. In that context there is only the question of whether the order as correctly interpreted in the legal sense "applies" to the empirical situation. The question is whether in a *normative* sense it *should* be treated as valid and, if so, what the content of its normative prescriptions for this situation should be. But for sociological purposes, as distinguished from legal, it is only the probability of orientation to the subjective *belief* in the validity of an order which constitutes the valid order itself. It is undeniable that, in the ordinary sense of the word "causal," there is a causal relationship between this probability and the relevant course of economic action.

6. *Types of Legitimate Order: Convention and Law*

The legitimacy of an order may be guaranteed in two principal ways:[20]

I. The guarantee may be purely subjective, being either

  1. affectual: resulting from emotional surrender; or
  2. value-rational: determined by the belief in the absolute validity of the order as the expression of ultimate values of an ethical, esthetic or of any other type; or
  3. religious: determined by the belief that salvation depends upon obedience to the order.

II. The legitimacy of an order may, however, be guaranteed also (or merely) by the expectation of specific external effects, that is, by interest situations.

An order will be called

(a) *convention* so far as its validity is externally guaranteed by the probability that deviation from it within a given social group will result in a relatively general and practically significant reaction of disapproval;

(b) *law* if it is externally guaranteed by the probability that physical or psychological coercion will be applied by a *staff* of people in order to bring about compliance or avenge violation.

(On the concept of convention see Weigelin, *op. cit.*, and F. Tönnies, *Die Sitte* [1909], besides Jhering, *op. cit.*)

1. The term convention will be employed to designate that part of the custom followed within a given social group which is recognized as "binding" and protected against violation by sanctions of disapproval. As distinguished from "law" in the sense of the present discussion, it is not enforced by a staff. Stammler distinguishes convention from law in terms of the entirely voluntary character of conformity. This is not, however, in accord with everyday usage and does not even fit the examples he gives. Conformity with convention in such matters as the usual forms of greeting, the mode of dress recognized as appropriate or respectable, and various of the rules governing the restrictions on social intercourse, both in form and in content, is very definitely expected of the individual and regarded as binding on him. It is not, as in the case of certain ways of preparing food, a mere usage, which he is free to conform to or not as he sees fit. A violation of conventional rules—such as standards of "respectability" (*Standessitte*)—often leads to the extremely severe and effective sanction of an informal boycott on the part of members of one's status group. This may actually be a more severe punishment than any legal penalty. The only thing lacking is a staff with the specialized function of maintaining enforcement of the order, such as judges, prosecuting attorneys, administrative officials, or sheriffs. The transition, however, is gradual. The case of conventional guarantee of an order which most closely approaches the legal is the application of a formally threatened and organized boycott. For terminological purposes, this is best considered a form of legal coercion. Conventional rules may, in addition to mere disapproval, also be upheld by other means; thus domestic authority may be employed to expel a visitor who defies convention. This fact is not, however, important in the present context. The decisive point is that the individual, by virtue of the existence of conventional disapproval, applies these sanctions, however drastic, on his own authority, not as a member of a staff endowed with a specific authority for this purpose.

2. For the purposes of this discussion the concept "law" will be made to turn on the presence of a staff engaged in enforcement, however useful it might be to define it differently for other purposes. The

character of this agency naturally need not be at all similar to what is at present familiar. In particular it is not necessary that there should be any specifically "judicial" authority. The clan, as an agency of blood revenge and of the prosecution of feuds, is such an enforcing agency if there exist any sort of rules which governs its behavior in such situations. But this is on the extreme borderline of what can be called legal enforcement. As is well known, it has often been denied that international law could be called law, precisely because there is no legal authority above the state capable of enforcing it. In terms of the present terminology this would be correct, for we could not call "law" a system the sanctions of which consisted wholly in expectations of disapproval and of the reprisals of injured parties, which is thus guaranteed entirely by convention and self-interest without the help of a specialized enforcement agency. But for purposes of legal terminology exactly the opposite might well be acceptable.

In any case the means of coercion are irrelevant. Even a "brotherly admonition," such as has been used in various religious sects as the first degree of mild coercion of the sinner, is "law" provided it is regulated by some order and applied by a staff. The same is to be said about the [Roman] censorial reprimand as a means to guarantee the observance of ethical duties and, even more so, about psychological coercion through ecclesiastic discipline. Hence "law" may be guaranteed by hierocratic as well as political authority, by the statutes of a voluntary association or domestic authority or through a sodality or some other association. The rules of [German students' fraternities known as] the *Komment* [and regulating such matters as convivial drinking or singing] are also law in our sense, just as the case of those [legally regulated but unenforceable] duties which are mentioned in Section 888, paragraph 2 of the German Code of Civil Procedure [for instance, the duty arising from an engagement to marry].[21] The *leges imperfectae* and the category of "natural obligations" are forms of legal terminology which express indirectly limits or conditions of the application of compulsion. In the same sense a trade practice which is compulsorily enforced is also law. See secs. 157 and 242 of the German Civil Code. On the concept of "fair practice" (*gute Sitte*), that is, desirable custom which is worthy of legal sanction, see Max Rümelin's essay in the *Schwäbische Heimatgabe für Theodor Häring* (1918).

3. It is not necessary for a valid order to be of a general and abstract character. The distinction between a legal norm and the judicial decision in a concrete case, for instance, has not always and everywhere been as clearly made as we have today come to expect. An "order" may thus occur simply as the order governing a single concrete situation. The details of this subject belong in the Sociology of Law. But for present purposes, unless otherwise specified, the modern distinction between a norm and a specific decision will be taken for granted.

4. A system of order which is guaranteed by external sanctions may at the same time be guaranteed by disinterested subjective attitudes.

The relations of law, convention, and "ethics" do not constitute a problem for sociology. From a sociological point of view an "ethical" standard is one to which men attribute a certain type of value and which, by virtue of this belief, they treat as a valid norm governing their action. In this sense it can be spoken of as defining what is ethically good in the same way that action which is called beautiful is measured by esthetic standards. It is possible for ethically normative beliefs of this kind to have a profound influence on action in the absence of any sort of external guarantee. This is often the case when the interests of others would be little affected by their violation.

Such ethical beliefs are also often guaranteed by religious motives, but they may at the same time, in the present terminology, be upheld to an important extent by disapproval of violations and the consequent boycott, or even legally with the corresponding sanctions of criminal or private law or of police measures. Every system of ethics which has in a sociological sense become validly established is likely to be upheld to a large extent by the probability that disapproval will result from its violation, that is, by convention. On the other hand, it is by no means necessary that all conventionally or legally guaranteed forms of order should claim the authority of ethical norms. Legal rules, much more often than conventional ones, may have been established entirely on grounds of expediency. Whether a belief in the validity of an order as such, which is current in a social group, is to be regarded as belonging to the realm of "ethics" or is a mere convention or a mere legal norm, cannot, for sociological purposes, be decided in general terms. It must be treated as relative to the conception of what values are treated as "ethical" in the social group in question.

7. Bases of Legitimacy: Tradition, Faith, Enactment

The actors may ascribe legitimacy to a social order by virtue of:

(a) *tradition:* valid is that which has always been;

(b) *affectual*, especially emotional, *faith:* valid is that which is newly revealed or exemplary;

(c) *value-rational* faith: valid is that which has been deduced as an absolute;

(d) positive enactment which is believed to be *legal.*

Such legality may be treated as legitimate because:

(α) it derives from a voluntary agreement of the interested parties;

(β) it is imposed by an authority which is held to be legitimate and therefore meets with compliance.

All further details, except for a few other concepts to be defined below, belong in the Sociology of Law and the Sociology of Domination. For the present, only a few remarks are necessary.

1. The validity of a social order by virtue of the sacredness of tradition is the oldest and most universal type of legitimacy. The fear of magical evils reinforces the general psychological inhibitions against any sort of change in customary modes of action. At the same time the manifold vested interests which tend to favor conformity with an established order help to perpetuate it. (More in ch. III.)

2. Conscious departures from tradition in the establishment of a new order were originally almost entirely due to prophetic oracles or at least to pronouncements which were sanctioned as prophetic and thus were considered sacred. This was true as late as the statutes of the Greek *aisymnetai.* Conformity thus depended on belief in the legitimacy of the prophet. In times of strict traditionalism a new order—one actually regarded as new—was not possible without revelation unless it was claimed that it had always been valid though not yet rightly known, or that it had been obscured for a time and was now being restored to its rightful place.

3. The purest type of legitimacy based on value-rationality is *natural law.* The influence of its logically deduced propositions upon actual conduct has lagged far behind its ideal claims; that they have had some influence cannot be denied, however. Its propositions must be distinguished from those of revealed, enacted, and traditional law.

4. Today the most common form of legitimacy is the belief in legality, the compliance with enactments which are *formally* correct and which have been made in the accustomed manner. In this respect, the distinction between an order derived from voluntary agreement and one which has been imposed is only relative. For so far as the agreement underlying the order is not unanimous, as in the past has often been held necessary for complete legitimacy, the order is actually imposed upon the minority; in this frequent case the order in a given group depends upon the acquiescence of those who hold different opinions. On the other hand, it is very common for minorities, by force or by the use of more ruthless and far-sighted methods, to impose an order which in the course of time comes to be regarded as legitimate by those who originally resisted it. Insofar as the ballot is used as a legal means of altering an order, it is very common for the will of a minority to attain a formal majority and for the majority to submit. In this case majority rule is a mere illusion. The belief in the legality of an order as established by voluntary agreement is relatively ancient and is occasionally found among so-called primitive people; but in these cases it is almost always supplemented by the authority of oracles.

5. So far as it is not derived merely from fear or from motives of expediency, a willingness to submit to an order imposed by one man or a small group, always implies a belief in the legitimate authority (*Herrschaftsgewalt*) of the source imposing it. This subject will be dealt with separately below: see sections 13 and 16 and ch. III.

6. Submission to an order is almost always determined by a variety of interests and by a mixture of adherence to tradition and belief in

legality, unless it is a case of entirely new regulations. In a very large proportion of cases, the actors subject to the order are of course not even aware how far it is a matter of custom, of convention, or of law. In such cases the sociologist must attempt to formulate the typical basis of validity.

8. Conflict, Competition, Selection

A social relationship will be referred to as "conflict" (*Kampf*) insofar as action is oriented intentionally to carrying out the actor's own will against the resistance of the other party or parties. The term "peaceful" conflict will be applied to cases in which actual physical violence is not employed. A peaceful conflict is "competition" insofar as it consists in a formally peaceful attempt to attain control over opportunities and advantages which are also desired by others. A competitive process is "regulated" competition to the extent that its ends and means are oriented to an order. The struggle, often latent, which takes place between human individuals or social types, for advantages and for survival, but without a meaningful mutual orientation in terms of conflict, will be called "selection." Insofar as it is a matter of the relative opportunities of individuals during their own lifetime, it is "social selection"; insofar as it concerns differential chances for the survival of hereditary characteristics, "biological selection."

1. There are all manner of continuous transitions ranging from the bloody type of conflict which, setting aside all rules, aims at the destruction of the adversary, to the case of the battles of medieval chivalry, bound as they were to the strictest conventions, and to the strict regulations imposed on sport by the rules of the game. A classic example of conventional regulation in war is the herald's call before the battle of Fontenoy: "Messieurs les Anglais, tirez les premiers."[22] There are transitions such as that from unregulated competition of, let us say, suitors for the favor of a woman to the competition for economic advantages in exchange relationships, bound as that is by the order governing the market, or to strictly regulated competitions for artistic awards or, finally, to the struggle for victory in election campaigns. The conceptual separation of peaceful [from violent] conflict is justified by the quality of the means normal to it and the peculiar sociological consequences of its occurrence (see ch. II and later).

2. All typical struggles and modes of competition which take place on a large scale will lead, in the long run, despite the decisive importance in many individual cases of accidental factors and luck, to a selection of those who have in the higher degree, on the average, possessed the personal qualities important to success. What qualities are

important depends on the conditions in which the conflict or competition takes place. It may be a matter of physical strength or of unscrupulous cunning, of the level of mental ability or mere lung power and skill in the technique of demagoguery, of loyalty to superiors or of ability to flatter the masses, of creative originality, or of adaptability, of qualities which are unusual, or of those which are possessed by the mediocre majority. *Among* the decisive conditions, it must not be forgotten, belong the systems of order to which the behavior of the parties is oriented, whether traditionally, as a matter of rationally disinterested loyalty (*wertrational*), or of expediency. Each type of order influences opportunities in the process of social selection differently.

Not every process of social selection is, in the present sense, a case of conflict. Social selection, on the contrary, means only in the first instance that certain types of behavior, and possibly of the corresponding personal qualities, lead more easily to success in the role of "lover," "husband," "member of parliament," "official," "contractor," "managing director," "successful business man," and so on. But the concept does not specify whether this differential advantage in selection for social success is brought to bear through conflict or not, neither does it specify whether the biological chances of survival of the type are affected one way or the other.

It is only where there is a genuine competitive process that the term conflict will be used [i.e., where regulation is, in principle, possible].[23] It is only in the sense of "selection" that it seems, according to our experience, that conflict is empirically inevitable, and it is furthermore only in the sense of *biological* selection that it is inevitable in principle. Selection is inevitable because apparently no way can be worked out of eliminating it completely. Even the most strictly pacific order can eliminate means of conflict and the objects of and impulses to conflict only partially. Other modes of conflict would come to the fore, possibly in processes of open competition. But even on the utopian assumption that all competition were completely eliminated, conditions would still lead to a latent process of selection, biological or social, which would favor the types best adapted to the conditions, whether their relevant qualities were mainly determined by heredity or by environment. On an empirical level the elimination of conflict cannot go beyond a point which leaves room for some social selection, and in principle a process of biological selection necessarily remains.

3. From the struggle of individuals for personal advantages and survival, it is naturally necessary to distinguish the "conflict" and the "selection" of social relationships. It is only in a metaphorical sense that these concepts can be applied to the latter. For relationships exist only as individual actions with particular subjective meanings. Thus a process of selection or a conflict between them means only that one type of action has in the course of time been displaced by another, whether it is action by the same persons or by others. This may occur in various ways. Human action may in the first place be consciously aimed to alter cer-

tain social relationships—that is, to alter the corresponding action—or it may be directed to the prevention of their development or continuance. Thus a "state" may be destroyed by war or revolution, or a conspiracy may be broken up by savage suppression; prostitution may be suppressed by police action; "usurious" business practices, by denial of legal protection or by penalties. Furthermore, social relationships may be influenced by the creation of differential advantages which favor one type over another. It is possible either for individuals or for organized groups to pursue such ends. Secondly, it may, in various ways, be an unanticipated consequence of a course of social action and its relevant conditions that certain types of social relationships (meaning, of course, the corresponding actions) will be adversely affected in their opportunities to maintain themselves or to arise. All changes of natural and social conditions have some sort of effect on the differential probabilities of survival of social relationships. Anyone is at liberty to speak in such cases of a process of "selection" of social relationships. For instance, he may say that among several states the "strongest," in the sense of the best "adapted," is victorious. It must, however, be kept in mind that this so-called "selection" has nothing to do with the selection of types of human individuals in either the social or the biological sense. In every case it is necessary to inquire into the reasons which have led to a change in the chances of survival of one or another form of social action or social relationship, which have broken up a social relationship or permitted it to continue at the expense of other competing forms. The explanation of these processes involves so many factors that it does not seem expedient to employ a single term for them. When this is done, there is always a danger of introducing uncritical value-judgments into empirical investigation. There is, above all, a danger of being primarily concerned with justifying the success of an individual case. Since individual cases are often dependent on highly exceptional circumstances, they may be in a certain sense "fortuitous." In recent years there has been more than enough of this kind of argument. The fact that a given specific social relationship has been eliminated for reasons peculiar to a particular situation, proves nothing whatever about its "fitness to survive" in general terms.

9. *Communal and Associative Relationships*

A social relationship will be called "communal" (*Vergemeinschaftung*) if and so far as the orientation of social action—whether in the individual case, on the average, or in the pure type—is based on a subjective feeling of the parties, whether affectual or traditional, that they belong together.

A social relationship will be called "associative" (*Vergesellschaftung*) if and insofar as the orientation of social action within it rests on a rationally motivated adjustment of interests or a similarly motivated agreement, whether the basis of rational judgment be absolute values or reasons of expediency. It is especially common, though by no means inevitable, for the associative type of relationship to rest on a rational agreement by mutual consent. In that case the corresponding action is, at the pole of rationality, oriented either to a value-rational belief in one's own obligation, or to a rational (*zweckrationale*) expectation that the other party will live up to it.

This terminology is similar to the distinction made by Ferdinand Tönnies in his pioneering work, *Gemeinschaft und Gesellschaft;* but for his purposes, Tönnies has given this distinction a rather more specific meaning than would be convenient for purposes of the present discussion.[24] The purest cases of associative relationships are: (a) rational free market exchange, which constitutes a compromise of opposed but complementary interests; (b) the pure voluntary association based on self-interest (*Zweckverein*), a case of agreement as to a long-run course of action oriented purely to the promotion of specific ulterior interests, economic or other, of its members; (c) the voluntary association of individuals motivated by an adherence to a set of common absolute values (*Gesinnungsverein*), for example, the rational sect, insofar as it does not cultivate emotional and affective interests, but seeks only to serve a "cause." This last case, to be sure, seldom occurs in anything approaching the pure type.

2. Communal relationships may rest on various types of affectual, emotional, or traditional bases. Examples are a religious brotherhood, an erotic relationship, a relation of personal loyalty, a national community, the *esprit de corps* of a military unit. The type case is most conveniently illustrated by the family. But the great majority of social relationships has this characteristic to some degree, while being at the same time to some degree determined by associative factors. No matter how calculating and hard-headed the ruling considerations in such a social relationship—as that of a merchant to his customers—may be, it is quite possible for it to involve emotional values which transcend its utilitarian significance. Every social relationship which goes beyond the pursuit of immediate common ends, which hence lasts for long periods, involves relatively permanent social relationships between the same persons, and these cannot be exclusively confined to the technically necessary activities. Hence in such cases as association in the same military unit, in the same school class, in the same workshop or office, there is always some tendency in this direction, although the degree, to be sure, varies enormously. Conversely, a social relationship which is normally considered primarily communal may involve action on the part of some or even all of the participants which is to an important degree oriented to considerations of expediency. There is, for instance, a wide variation in the extent to which the members of a family group feel a genuine community of interests or, on the other hand, exploit the relationship for

their own ends. The concept of communal relationship has been intentionally defined in very general terms and hence includes a very heterogeneous group of phenomena.

3. The communal type of relationship is, according to the usual interpretation of its subjective meaning, the most radical antithesis of conflict. This should not, however, be allowed to obscure the fact that coercion of all sorts is a very common thing in even the most intimate of such communal relationships if one party is weaker in character than the other. Furthermore, a process of the selection of types leading to differences in opportunity and survival, goes on within these relationships just the same as anywhere else. Associative relationships, on the other hand, very often consist only in compromises between rival interests, where only a part of the occasion or means of conflict has been eliminated, or even an attempt has been made to do so. Hence, outside the area of compromise, the conflict of interests, with its attendant competition for supremacy, remains unchanged. Conflict and communal relationships are relative concepts. Conflict varies enormously according to the means employed, especially whether they are violent or peaceful, and to the ruthlessness with which they are used. It has already been pointed out that any type of order governing social action in some way leaves room for a process of selection among various rival human types.

4. It is by no means true that the existence of common qualities, a common situation, or common modes of behavior imply the existence of a communal social relationship. Thus, for instance, the possession of a common biological inheritance by virtue of which persons are classified as belonging to the same "race," naturally implies no sort of communal social relationship between them. By restrictions on social intercourse and on marriage persons may find themselves in a similar situation, a situation of isolation from the environment which imposes these distinctions. But even if they all react to this situation in the same way, this does not constitute a communal relationship. The latter does not even exist if they have a common "feeling" about this situation and its consequences. It is only when this feeling leads to a mutual orientation of their behavior to each other that a social relationship arises between them rather than of each to the environment. Furthermore, it is only so far as this relationship involves feelings of belonging together that it is a "communal" relationship. In the case of the Jews, for instance, except for Zionist circles and the action of certain associations promoting specifically Jewish interests, there thus exist communal relationships only to a relatively small extent; indeed, Jews often repudiate the existence of a Jewish "community."

A common language, which arises from a similarity of tradition through the family and the surrounding social environment, facilitates mutual understanding, and thus the formation of all types of social relationships, in the highest degree. But taken by itself it is not sufficient to constitute a communal relationship, rather, it facilitates intercourse within the groups concerned, hence the development of associate relationships. This takes place between *individuals,* not because they speak the same language, but because they have other types of interests. Orientation to the rules of a common language is thus primarily important as a means of communication, not as the content of a social relationship. It is only with the emergence of a consciousness of difference from third persons who speak a different language that the fact that two persons speak the same language, and in that respect share a common situation, can lead them to a feeling of community and to modes of social organization consciously based on the sharing of the common language.

Participation in a "market" is of still another kind. It encourages association between the exchanging parties and a social relationship, above all that of competition, between the individual participants who must mutually orient their action to each other. But no further modes of association develop except in cases where certain participants enter into agreements in order to better their competitive situations, or where they all agree on rules for the purpose of regulating transactions and of securing favorable general conditions for all. (It may further be remarked that the market and the competitive economy resting on it form the most important type of the reciprocal determination of action in terms of pure self-interest, a type which is characteristic of modern economic life.)

1 0. *Open and Closed Relationships*

A social relationship, regardless of whether it is communal or associative in character, will be spoken of as "open" to outsiders if and insofar as its system of order does not deny participation to anyone who wishes to join and is actually in a position to do so. A relationship will, on the other hand, bes called "closed" against outsiders so far as, according to its subjective meaning and its binding rules, participation of certain persons is excluded, limited, or subjected to conditions. Whether a relationship is open or closed may be determined traditionally, affectually, or rationally in terms of values or of expediency. It is especially likely to be closed, for rational reasons, in the following type of situation: a social relationship may provide the parties to it with opportunities for the satisfaction of spiritual or material interests, whether absolutely or instrumentally, or whether it is achieved through co-operative action or by a compromise of interests. If the participants expect that the admission of others will lead to an improvement of their situation, an improvement in degree, in kind, in the security or the value of the satisfaction, their interest will be in keeping the relationship open. If, on the other hand, their expectations are of improving their position by monopolistic tactics, their interest is in a closed relationship.

There are various ways in which it is possible for a closed social relationship to guarantee its monopolized advantages to the parties. (a) Such advantages may be left free to competitive struggle within the group; (b) they may be regulated or rationed in amount and kind, or (c) they may be appropriated by individuals or sub-groups on a permanent basis and become more or less inalienable. The last is a case of closure within, as well as against outsiders. Appropriated advantages will be called "rights." **As determined by the relevant order, appropriation may be (1) for the benefit of the members of particular communal or associative groups (for** instance, household groups), or (2) for the benefit of individuals. In the latter case, the individual may enjoy his rights on a purely personal basis or in such a way that in case of his death one or more other persons related to the holder of the right by birth (kinship), or by some other social relationship, may inherit the rights in question. Or the rights may pass to one or more individuals specifically designated by the holder. These are cases of hereditary appropriation. Finally, (3) it may be that the holder is more or less fully empowered to alienate his rights by voluntary agreement, either to other specific persons or to anyone he chooses. This is alienable appropriation. A party to a closed social relationship will be called a "member"; in case his participation is regulated in such a way as to guarantee him appropriated advantages, a privileged member (*Rechtsgenosse*). Appropriated rights which are enjoyed by individuals through inheritance or by hereditary groups, whether communal or associative, will be called the "property" of the individual or of groups in question; and, insofar as they are alienable, "free" property.

The apparently gratuitous tediousness involved in the elaborate definition of the above concepts is an example of the fact that we often neglect to think out clearly what seems to be obvious, because it is intuitively familiar.

1. (a) Examples of communal relationships, which tend to be closed on a traditional basis, are those in which membership is determined by family relationship.

(b) Personal emotional relationships are usually affectually closed. Examples are erotic relationships and, very commonly, relations of personal loyalty.

(c) Closure on the basis of value-rational commitment to values is usual in groups sharing a common system of explicit religious belief.

(d) Typical cases of rational closure on grounds of expediency are economic associations of a monopolistic or a plutocratic character.

A few examples may be taken at random. Whether a group of people engaged in conversation is open or closed depends on its content. General conversation is apt to be open, as contrasted with intimate conversation or the imparting of official information. Market relationships are in most, or at least in many, cases essentially open. In the case of many relationships, both communal and associative, there is a tendency to shift from a phase of expansion to one of exclusiveness. Examples are the guilds and the democratic city-states of Antiquity and the Middle Ages. At times these groups sought to increase their membership in the interest of improving the security of their position of power by adequate numbers. At other times they restricted their membership to protect the value of their monopolistic position. The same phenomenon is not uncommon in monastic orders and religious sects which have passed from a stage of religious proselytizing to one of restriction in the interest of the maintenance of an ethical standard or for the protection of material interests. There is a similar close relationship between the extension of market relationships in the interest of increased turnover on the one hand, their monopolistic restriction on the other. The promotion of linguistic uniformity is today a natural result of the interests of publishers and writers, as opposed to the earlier, not uncommon, tendency for status groups to maintain linguistic peculiarities or even for secret languages to emerge.

2. Both the extent and the methods of regulation and exclusion in relation to outsiders may vary widely, so that the transition from a state of openness to one of regulation and closure is gradual. Various conditions of participation may be laid down; qualifying tests, a period of probation, requirement of possession of a share which can be purchased under certain conditions, election of new members by ballot, membership or eligibility by birth or by virtue of achievements open to anyone. Finally, in case of closure and the appropriation of rights within the group, participation may be dependent on the acquisition of an appropriated right. There is a wide variety of different degrees of closure and of conditions of participation. Thus regulation and closure are relative concepts. There are all manner of gradual shadings as between an exclusive club, a theatrical audience the members of which have purchased tickets, and a party rally to which the largest possible number has been urged to come; similarly, from a church service open to the general public through the rituals of a limited sect to the mysteries of a secret cult.

3. Similarly, closure within the group may also assume the most varied forms. Thus a caste, a guild, or a group of stock exchange brokers, which is closed to outsiders, may allow to its members a perfectly free competition for all the advantages which the group as a whole monopolizes for itself. Or it may assign every member strictly to the enjoyment of certain advantages, such as claims over customers or particular business opportunities, for life or even on a hereditary basis. This is particularly characteristic of India. Similarly, a closed group of settlers (*Markgenossenschaft*) may allow its members free use of the resources of its area or may restrict them rigidly to a plot assigned to each individual household. A closed group of colonists may allow free use of the land or sanction and guarantee permanent appropriation of

separate holdings. In such cases all conceivable transitional and intermediate forms can be found. Historically, the closure of eligibility to
fiefs, benefices, and offices within the group, and the appropriation on
the part of those enjoying them, have occurred in the most varied forms.
Similarly, the establishment of rights to and possession of particular
jobs on the part of workers may develop all the way from the "closed
shop" to a right to a particular job. The first step in this development
may be to prohibit the dismissal of a worker without the consent of the
workers' representatives. The development of the "works councils" [in
Germany after 1918] might be a first step in this direction, though it
need not be.[25]

All the details must be reserved for the later analysis. The most
extreme form of permanent appropriation is found in cases where particular rights are guaranteed to an individual or to certain groups of
them, such as households, clans, families, in such a way that it is specified in the order either that, in case of death, the rights descend to specific
heirs, or that the possessor is free to transfer them to any other person
at will. Such a person thereby becomes a party to the social relationship so that, when appropriation has reached this extreme within the
group, it becomes to that extent an open group in relation to outsiders.
This is true so long as acquisition of membership is not subject to the
ratification of the other, prior members.

4. The principal motives for closure of a relationship are: (a) The
maintenance of quality, which is often combined with the interest in
prestige and the consequent opportunities to enjoy honor, and even
profit; examples are communities of ascetics, monastic orders, especially,
for instance, the Indian mendicant orders, religious sects like the Puritans, organized groups of warriors, of *ministeriales* and other functionaries, organized citizen bodies as in the Greek states, craft guilds;
(b) the contraction of advantages in relation to consumption needs
(*Nahrungsspielraum*);[26] examples are monopolies of consumption, the
most developed form of which is a self-subsistent village community;
(c) the growing scarcity of opportunities for acquisition (*Erwerbsspielraum*). This is found in trade monopolies such as guilds, the ancient monopolies of fishing rights, and so on. Usually motive (a) is
combined with (b) or (c).

11. *The Imputation of Social Action: Representation and Mutual Responsibility*

Within a social relationship, whether it is traditional or enacted, certain kinds of action of *each* participant may be imputed to *all* others, in
which case we speak of "mutually responsible members"; or the action
of certain members (the "representatives") may be attributed to the

others (the "represented"). In both cases, the members will share the resulting advantages as well as the disadvantages.

In accordance with the prevailing order, the power of representation may be (a) completely appropriated in all its forms—the case of self-appointed authority (*Eigenvollmacht*); (b) conferred in accordance with particular *characteristics,* permanently or for a limited term; (c) conferred by specific *acts* of the members or of outside persons, again permanently or for a limited term—the cases of "derived" or "delegated" powers.

There are many different conditions which determine the ways in which social relationships, communal or associative, develop relations of mutual responsibility or of representation. In general terms, it is possible only to say that one of the most decisive is the extent to which the action of the group is oriented to violent conflict or to peaceful exchange as its end. Besides these, many special circumstances, which can only be discussed in the detailed analysis, may be of crucial importance. It is not surprising that this development is least conspicuous in groups which pursue purely ideal ends by peaceful means. Often the degree of closure against outsiders is closely related to the development of mutual responsibility or of representation. But this is by no means always the case.

1. Imputation may in practice involve both active and passive mutual responsibility. All participants may be held responsible for the action of any one just as he himself is, and similarly may be entitled to enjoy any benefits resulting from this action. This responsibility may be owed to spirits or gods, that is, involve a religious orientation; or it may be responsibility to other human beings, as regulated by convention or by law. Examples of regulation by convention are blood revenge carried out against or with the help of members of the kin group, and reprisals against the inhabitants of the town or the country of the offender; of the legal type, formal punishment of relatives and members of the household or community, and personal liability of members of a household or of a commercial partnership for each other's debts. Mutual responsibility in relation to gods has also had very significant historical results. For instance, in the covenant of Israel with Jahveh, in early Christianity, and in the early Puritan community.

On the other hand, the imputation may mean no more than that the participants in a closed social relationship, by virtue of the traditional or legal order, accept as legally binding a representative's decisions, especially over economic resources. (Examples are the "validity" of decisions by the executive committee of a voluntary association or by the responsible agent of a political or economic organization over resources which, as specified in the statutes, are meant to serve the group's purposes.)

2. Mutual responsibility is typically found in the following cases: (a) In traditional, communal groups based on birth or the sharing of a

common life; for example, the household and the kinship unit; (b) in closed relationships which maintain by force a monopolized position and control over the corresponding benefits; the typical case is the political association, especially in the past, but also today, most strikingly in time of war; (c) in profit-oriented enterprises whose participants personally conduct the business; the type case is the business partnership; (d) in some cases, in labor associations; e.g., the [Russian] *artel*.

Representation is most frequently found in associations devoted to specific purposes and in legally organized groups, especially when funds have been collected and must be administered in the interests of the group. This will be further discussed in the Sociology of Law.

3. The power of representation is conferred according to characteristics when it goes by seniority or some other such rule.

4. It is not possible to carry the analysis of this subject further in general terms; its elaboration must be reserved to the detailed investigation. The most ancient and most universal phenomenon in this field is that of reprisal, meant either as revenge or as a means of gaining control of hostages, or some other kind of security against future injury.

12. *The Organization*

A social relationship which is either closed or limits the admission of outsiders will be called an organization (*Verband*) when its regulations are enforced by specific individuals: a chief and, possibly, an administrative staff, which normally also has representative powers. The incumbency of a policy-making position or participation in the functions of the staff constitute "executive powers" (*Regierungsgewalten*). These may be appropriated, or they may be assigned, in accordance with the regulations of the organization, to specific persons or to individuals selected on the basis of specific characteristics or procedures. "Organized action" is (a) either the staff's action, which is legitimated by its executive or representative powers and oriented to realizing the organization's order, or (b) the members' action as directed by the staff.[27]

1. It is terminologically indifferent whether the relationship is of a communal or associative character. It is sufficient for there to be a person or persons in authority—the head of a family, the executive committee of an association, a managing director, a prince, a president, the head of a church—whose action is concerned with carrying into effect the order governing the organization. This criterion is decisive because it is not merely a matter of action which is *oriented* to an order, but which is specifically directed to its *enforcement*. Sociologically, this adds to the concept of a closed social relationship a further element, which is of far-reaching empirical importance. For by no means every closed communal or associative relationship is an organization. For instance, this is

not true of an erotic relationship or of a kinship group without a head.

2. Whether or not an organization exists is entirely a matter of the presence of a person in authority, with or without an administrative staff. More precisely, it exists so far as there is a probability that certain persons will act in such a way as to carry out the order governing the organization; that is, that persons are present who can be counted on to act in this way whenever the occasion arises. For purposes of definition, it is indifferent what is the basis of the relevant expectation, whether it is a case of traditional, affectual or value-rational devotion (such as feudal fealty, loyalty to an officer or to a service). It may, on the other hand, be a matter of expediency, as, for instance, a pecuniary interest in the attached salary. Thus, for our purposes, the organization does not exist apart from the probability that a course of action oriented in this way will take place. If there is no probability of this type of action on the part of a particular group of persons or of a given individual, there is in these terms only a social relationship. On the other hand, so long as there is a probability of such action, the organization as a sociological phenomenon continues to exist, in spite of the fact that the specific individuals whose action is oriented to the order in question, may have been completely changed. The concept has been defined intentionally to include precisely this phenomenon.

3. It is possible (a) that, in addition to the action of the administrative staff itself or that which takes place under its direction, there may be other cases where action of the participants is intended to uphold the authority of the order; for instance, contributions or "liturgies," that is, certain types of personal services, such as jury service or military service. It is also possible (b) for the order to include norms to which it is expected that the action of the members of an organization will be oriented in respects other than those pertaining to the affairs of the organization as a unit. For instance, the law of the state includes rules governing private economic relations which are not concerned with the enforcement of the state's legal order as such, but with action in the service of private interests. This is true of most of the "civil" law. In the first case (a) one may speak of action oriented to organizational affairs (*verbandsbezogenes Handeln*); in the second (b) of action subject to the organization's regulation (*verbandsgeregeltes Handeln*). It is only in the cases of the action of the administrative staff itself and of that deliberately directed by it that the term "organized action" (*Verbandshandeln*) will be used. Examples of such action would be participation in any capacity in a war fought by a state, or a motion which is passed by the members at the behest of its executive committee, or a contract entered into by the person in authority, the validity of which is imposed on all members and for which they are held responsible (cf. section 11). Further, all administration of justice and administrative procedure belongs in this category (cf. section 14).

An organization may be (a) autonomous or heteronomous, (b) autocephalous or heterocephalous. Autonomy means that the order governing the organization has been established by its own members on their own authority, regardless of how this has taken place in other respects. In the case of heteronomy, it has been imposed by an outside agency. Auto-cephaly means that the chief and his staff are selected according to the autonomous order of the organization itself, not, as in the case of hetero-cephaly, that they are appointed by outsiders. Again, this is regardless of any other aspects of the relationship.

A case of heterocephaly is the appointment of the governors of the Canadian provinces by the central government of the Dominion. It is possible for a heterocephalous group to be autonomous and an auto-cephalous group to be heteronomous. It is also possible in both respects for an organization to have both characters at the same time in different spheres. The member-states of the German Empire, a federal state, were autocephalous. But in spite of this, within the sphere of authority of the Reich, they were heteronomous; whereas, within their own sphere, in such matters as religion and education, they were autonomous. Alsace-Lorraine was, under German jurisdiction, in a limited degree autono-mous, but at the same time heterocephalous in that the governor was appointed by the Kaiser. All those elements may be present in the same situation to some degree. An organization which is at the same time completely heteronomous and completely heterocephalous is usually best treated as a "part" of the more extensive group, as would ordinarily be done with a "regiment" as part of an army. But whether this is the case depends on the actual extent of independence in the orientation of action in the particular case. For terminological purposes, it is entirely a question of convenience.

13. Consensual and Imposed Order in Organizations

An association's enacted order may be established in one of two ways: by voluntary agreement, or by being imposed and acquiesced in. The leadership in an organization may claim a legitimate right to impose new rules. The "constitution" of an organization is the empirically existing porbability, varying in extent, kind and conditions, that rules imposed by the leadership will be acceded to. The existing rules may specify that certain groups or sections of the members must consent, or at least have been heard. Besides this, there may be any number of other conditions.

An organization's order may be imposed not only on its members but also on certain non-members. This is especially true of persons who are linked to a given territorial area by virtue of residence, birth, or the per-formance of certain actions. In this case the order possesses "territorial validity" (Gebietsgeltung). An organization which imposes its order in principle on a territory will be called a "territorial organization" (Gebiets-

verband). This usage will be employed regardless of how far the claim to the validity of its order over its own members is also confined to matters pertaining to the area. (Such a limitation is possible[28] and indeed occurs to some extent.)

1. In our terminology, an order is always "imposed" to the extent that it does not originate from a voluntary personal agreement of all the individuals concerned. The concept of imposition hence includes "majority rule," in that the minority must submit. For that reason there have been long periods when the legitimacy of majority rule has either not been recognized at all, or been held doubtful. This was true in the case of the Estates of the Middle Ages, and in very recent times, in the Russian *obshchina*. (This will be further discussed in the Sociology of Law and of Domination.)

2. Even in cases where there is formally voluntary agreement, it is very common, as is generally known, for there to be a large measure of imposition. (This is true of the *obshchina*.) In that case, it is the actual state of affairs which is decisive for sociological purposes.

3. The concept of constitution made use of here is that also used by Lassalle. It is not the same as what is meant by a "written" constitution, or indeed by "constitution" in any sort of legal meaning.[29] The only relevant question for sociological purposes is when, for what purposes, and *within what limits,* or possibly under what special conditions (such as the approval of gods or priests or the consent of electors), the members of the organization will submit to the leadership. Furthermore, under what circumstances the administrative staff and the organized actions of the group will be at the leadership's disposal when it issues orders, in particular, new rules.

4. The major cases of the territorial imposition of an order are criminal law and various other legal rules the applicability of which depends on whether the actor was resident, born, performed or completed the action within the area controlled by a political organization. (Compare the concept of the "territorial corporate organization"—*Gebietskörperschaft*—as used by Gierke and Preuss.)[30]

14. *Administrative and Regulative Order*

Rules which govern organized action constitute an administrative order (*Verwaltungsordnung*). Rules which govern other kinds of social action and thereby protect the actors' enjoyment of the resulting benefits will be called a regulative order (*Regulierungsordnung*). So far as an organization is solely oriented to the first type, it will be called an administrative organization; so far as it is oriented to the second type, a regulative organization.

1. It goes without saying that the majority of actual organizations partake of both characteristics. An example of a merely regulative organization would be a theoretically conceivable state based purely on the upholding of public order (*Rechtsstaat*) and committed to absolute laissez-faire. (This would imply that even the control of the monetary system was left to private enterprise.)

2. On the concept of organized action see above, sec. 12:3. Under the concept of administrative order would be included all the rules which govern not only the action of the administrative staff, but also that of the members in their direct relation to the organization; hence these rules pertain to those goals the pursuit of which the administrative order seeks to facilitate through prescribed and coordinated action on the part of the administrative staff and the members. In a completely communist economy almost all social action would be of this character. In an absolute laissez-faire state (*Rechtsstaat*) only the functions of judges, police authorities, jurors and soldiers, and activity as legislator and voter would be included. The distinction between administrative and regulative order coincides in its broad lines, though not always in detail, with the distinction between public and private law. (All further details are treated in the Sociology of Law.)

15. *Enterprise, Formal Organization, Voluntary and Compulsory Association*

Continuous rational activity of a specified kind will be called an *enterprise;* an association with a continuously and rationally operating staff will be called a *formal organization.*

An organization which claims authority only over voluntary members will be called a *voluntary association* (*Verein*); an organization which imposes, within a specifiable sphere of operations, its order (with relative success) on all action conforming with certain criteria will be called a *compulsory organization* or *association* (*Anstalt*).

1. The concept of the enterprise covers business conducted by political and ecclesiastic organizations as well as by voluntary associations insofar as it has rational continuity.

2. Voluntary as well as compulsory associations are organizations with rationally established rules. More correctly, insofar as an organization has rationaly established rules, it is either a voluntary or a compulsory association. Compulsory organizations are, above all, the state with its subsidiary heterocephalous organizations, and the church insofar as its order is rationally established. The order governing a compulsory association claims to be binding on all persons to whom the particular relevant criteria apply—such as birth, residence, or the use of certain facilities. It makes no difference whether the individual joined volun-

tarily; nor does it matter whether he has taken any part in establishing the order. It is thus a case of imposed order in the most definite sense. Compulsory associations are frequently territorial organizations.

3. The distinction between voluntary and compulsory associations is relative in its empirical application. The rules of a voluntary association may affect the interests of non-members, and recognition of the validity of these rules may be imposed upon them by usurpation and the exercize of naked power, but also by legal regulation, as in the case of the law governing corporate securities.

4. It is hardly necessary to emphasize that the concepts of voluntary and compulsory associations are by no means exhaustive of all conceivable types of organizations. Furthermore, they are to be thought of as polar types, as are sect and church in the religious sphere.

16. Power and Domination

A. "Power" (*Macht*) is the probability that one actor within a social relationship will be in a position to carry out his own will despite resistance, regardless of the basis on which this probability rests.

B. "Domination" (*Herrschaft*)[31] is the probability that a command with a given specific content will be obeyed by a given group of persons. "Discipline" is the probability that by virtue of habituation a command will receive prompt and automatic obedience in stereotyped forms, on the part of a given group of persons.[32]

1. The concept of power is sociologically amorphous. All conceivable qualities of a person and all conceivable combinations of circumstances may put him in a position to impose his will in a given situation. The sociological concept of domination must hence be more precise and can only mean the probability that a *command* will be obeyed.

2. The concept of discipline includes the habituation characteristic of uncritical and unresisting mass obedience.

C. The existence of domination turns only on the actual presence of one person successfully issuing orders to others; it does not necessarily imply either the existence of an administrative staff or, for that matter, of an organization. It is, however, uncommon to find it unrelated to at least one of these. A "ruling organization" (*Herrschaftsverband*) exists insofar as its members are subject to domination by virtue of the established order.

1. The head of a household rules without an administrative staff. A Bedouin chief, who levies contributions from the caravans, persons and shipments which pass his stronghold, controls this group of changing individuals, who do not belong to the same organization, as soon and as

long as they face the same situation; but to do this, he needs a following which, on the appropriate occasions, serves as his administrative staff
in exercising the necessary compulsion. (However, it is theoretically
conceivable that this type of control is exercised by a single individual.)

2. If it possesses an administrative staff, an organization is always to
some degree based on domination. But the concept is relative. In general, an effectively ruling organization is also an administrative one. The
character of the organization is determined by a variety of factors: the
mode in which the administration is carried out, the character of the
personnel, the objects over which it exercises control, and the extent of
effective jurisdiction. The first two factors in particular are dependent in
the highest degree on the way in which domination is legitimized (see
ch. III).

17. Political and Hierocratic Organizations

A "ruling organization" will be called "political" insofar as its existence and order is continuously safeguarded within a given *territorial* area
by the threat and application of physical force on the part of the administrative staff. A compulsory political organization with continuous operations (*politischer Anstaltsbetrieb*) will be called a "state" insofar as its
administrative staff successfully upholds the claim to the *monopoly* of
the *legitimate* use of physical force in the enforcement of its order. Social
action, especially organized action, will be spoken of as "politically
oriented" if it aims at exerting influence on the government of a political
organization; especially at the appropriation, expropriation, redistribution
or allocation of the powers of government.

A "hierocratic organization" is an organization which enforces its
order through psychic coercion by distributing or denying religious
benefits ("hierocratic coercion"). A compulsory hierocratic organization
will be called a "church" insofar as its administrative staff claims a
monopoly of the legitimate use of hierocratic coercion.

1. It goes without saying that the use of physical force (*Gewaltsam-
keit*) is neither the sole, nor even the most usual, method of administration of political organizations. On the contrary, their heads have employed all conceivable means to bring about their ends. But, at the same
time, the threat of force, and in the case of need its actual use, is the
method which is specific to political organizations and is always the last
resort when others have failed. Conversely, physical force is by no means
limited to political groups even as a legitimate method of enforcement.
It has been freely used by kinship groups, household groups, consociations and, in the Middle Ages, under certain circumstances by all those
entitled to bear arms. In addition to the fact that it uses, among other

means, physical force to enforce its system of order, the political organization is further characterized by the fact that the authority of its administrative staff is claimed as binding within a territorial area and this claim is upheld by force. Whenever organizations which make use of force are also characterized by the claim to territorial jurisdiction, such as village communities or even some household groups, federations of guilds or of workers' associations ("soviets"), they are by definition to that extent political organizations.

2. It is not possible to define a political organization, including the state, in terms of the end to which its action is devoted. All the way from provision for subsistence to the patronage of art, there is no conceivable end which *some* political association has not at some time pursued. And from the protection of personal security to the administration of justice, there is none which *all* have recognized. Thus it is possible to define the "political" character of an organization only in terms of the *means* peculiar to it, the use of force. This means is, however, in the above sense specific, and is indispensable to its character. It is even, under certain circumstances, elevated into an end in itself.

This usage does not exactly conform to everyday speech. But the latter is too inconsistent to be used for technical purposes. We speak of the foreign currency *policy*[33] of a central bank, the financial *policy* of an association, or the educational *policy* of a local authority, and mean the systematic treatment and conduct of particular affairs. It comes considerably closer to the present meaning when we distinguish the "political" aspect or implication of a question. Thus there is the "political" official, the "political" newspaper, the "political" revolution, the "political" club, the "political" party, and the "political" consequences of an action, as distinguished from others such as the economic, cultural, or religious aspect of the persons, affairs or processes in question. In this usage we generally mean by "political," things that have to do with relations of authority within what is, in the present terminology, a political organization, the state. The reference is to things which are likely to uphold, to change or overthrow, to hinder or promote, these authority relations as distinguished from persons, things, and processes which have nothing to do with it. This usage thus seeks to bring out the common features of domination, the way it is exercised by the state, irrespective of the ends involved. Hence it is legitimate to claim that the definition put forward here is only a more precise formulation of what is meant in everyday usage in that it gives sharp emphasis to what is most characteristic of this *means*: the actual or threatened use of force. It is, of course, true that everyday usage applies the term "political," not only to groups which are the direct agents of the legitimate use of force itself, but also to other, often wholly peaceful groups, which attempt to influence the activities of the political organization. It seems best for present purposes to distinguish this type of social action, "politically oriented" action, from political action as such, the actual organized action of political groups.

3. Since the concept of the state has only in modern times reached its full development, it is best to define it in terms appropriate to the modern type of state, but at the same time, in terms which abstract from the values of the present day, since these are particularly subject to change. The primary formal characteristics of the modern state are as follows: It possesses an administrative and legal order subject to change by legislation, to which the organized activities of the administrative staff, which are also controlled by regulations, are oriented. This system of order claims binding authority, not only over the members of the state, the citizens, most of whom have obtained membership by birth, but also to a very large extent over all action taking place in the area of its jurisdiction. It is thus a compulsory organization with a territorial basis. Furthermore, today, the use of force is regarded as legitimate only so far as it is either permitted by the state or prescribed by it. Thus the right of a father to discipline his children is recognized—a survival of the former independent authority of the head of a household, which in the right to use force has sometimes extended to a power of life and death over children and slaves. The claim of the modern state to monopolize the use of force is as essential to it as its character of compulsory jurisdiction and of continuous operation.

4. In formulating the concept of a hierocratic organization, it is not possible to use the character of the religious benefits it offers, whether worldly or other-worldly, material or spiritual, as the decisive criterion. What is important is rather the fact that its control over these values can form the basis of a system of spiritual domination over human beings. What is most characteristic of the church, even in the common usage of the term, is the fact that it is a rational, compulsory association with continuous operation and that it claims a monopolistic authority. It is normal for a church to strive for complete control on a territorial basis and to attempt to set up the corresponding territorial or parochial organization. So far as this takes place, the means by which this claim to monopoly is upheld will vary from case to case. But historically, its control over territorial areas has not been nearly so essential to the church as to political associations; and this is particularly true today. It is its character as a compulsory association, particularly the fact that one beomes a member of the church by birth, which distinguishes the church from a "sect." It is characteristic of the latter that it is a voluntary association and admits only persons with specific religious qualifications. (This subject will be further discussed in the Sociology of Religion.)

NOTES

Unless otherwise noted, all notes in this chapter are by Talcott Parsons. For Parsons' exposition and critique of Weber's methodology, see his introduction to *The Theory of Social and Economic Organization* and his *Structure of Social Action*.

1. "Über einige Kategorien der verstehenden Soziologie," originally in *Logos,* IV, 1913, 253ff; reprinted in *GAzW,* 427–74. However, the reader should be aware from the very beginning that Part Two below, the older and major body of the manuscript, follows the terminology of this essay. For some of the relevant terminology, see Appendix I. (R)

2. It has not seemed advisable to attempt a rigorous use of a single English term whenever Weber employs *Verstehen.* "Understanding" has been most commonly used. Other expressions such as "subjectively understandable," "interpretation in subjective terms," "comprehension," etc., have been used from time to time as the context seemed to demand.

3. In this series of definitions Weber employs several important terms which need discussion. In addition to *Verstehen,* which has already been commented upon, there are four important ones: *Deuten, Sinn, Handeln,* and *Verhalten. Deuten* has generally been translated as "interpret." As used by Weber in this context it refers to the interpretation of subjective states of mind and the meanings which can be imputed as intended by an actor. Any other meaning of the word "interpretation" is irrelevant to Weber's discussion. The term *Sinn* has generally been translated as "meaning"; and its variations, particularly the corresponding adjectives, *sinnhaft, sinnvoll, sinnfremd,* have been dealt with by appropriately modifying the term *meaning.* The reference here again is always to features of the content of subjective states of mind or of symbolic systems which are ultimately referable to such states of mind.

The terms *Handeln* and *Verhalten* are directly related. *Verhalten* is the broader term referring to any mode of behavior of human individuals, regardless of the frame of reference in terms of which it is analysed. "Behavior" has seemed to be the most appropriate English equivalent. *Handeln,* on the other hand, refers to the concrete phenomenon of human behavior only insofar as it is capable of "understanding," in Weber's technical sense, in terms of subjective categories. The most appropriate English equivalent has seemed to be "action." This corresponds to [Parsons'] usage in *The Structure of Social Action* and would seem to be fairly well established. "Conduct" is also similar and has sometimes been used. *Deuten, Verstehen,* and *Sinn* are thus applicable to human behavior only insofar as it constitutes action or conduct in this specific sense.

4. Weber's text in Part One is organized in a manner frequently found in the German academic literature of his day, in that he first lays down certain fundamental definitions and then proceeds to comment on them. These comments, which apparently were not intended to be "read" in the ordinary sense, but rather serve as reference material for the clarification and systematization of the theoretical concepts and their implications, are in the German edition printed in a smaller type, a convention which we have followed in the rest of Part One. However, while in most cases the comments are relatively brief, under the definitions of "sociology" and "social action" Weber wrote what are essentially methodological essays (sec. 1:A–B), which because of their length we have printed in the ordinary type. (R)

5. Weber means by "pure type" what he himself generally called and what has come to be known in the literature about his methodology as the "ideal type." The reader may be referred for general orientation to Weber's own essay (to which he himself refers below), "Die 'Objektivität' sozialwissenschaftlicher Erkenntnis" ("'Objectivity' in Social Science and Social Policy," in *Max Weber: The Methodology of the Social Sciences.* Edward Shils and Henry Finch, trans. and eds. (Glencoe: The Free Press, 1949), 50–113; originally published in *AfS,* vol. 19, 1904, reprinted in *GAzW,* 146–214); to two works of Alexander von Schelting, "Die logische Theorie der historischen Kulturwissenschaften von Max

Weber," *AfS*, vol. 49, 1922, 623ff and *Max Webers Wissenschaftslehre*, 1934; Talcott Parsons, *The Structure of Social Action* (New York: McGraw-Hill, 1937), ch. 16; Theodore Abel, *Systematic Sociology in Germany*, (New York: Columbia University Press, 1929). [See now also Raymond Aron, *German Sociology*, trans. by M. and T. Bottomore (New York: The Free Press of Glencoe, 1964), based on 2nd French ed. of 1950.]

6. This is an imperfect rendering of the German term *Evidenz*, for which, unfortunately, there is no good English equivalent. It has hence been rendered in a number of different ways, varying with the particular context in which it occurs. The primary meaning refers to the basis on which a scientist or thinker becomes satisfied of the certainty or acceptability of a proposition. As Weber himself points out, there are two primary aspects of this. On the one hand a conclusion can be "seen" to follow from given premises by virtue of logical, mathematical, or possibly other modes of meaningful relation. In this sense one "sees" the solution of an arithmetical problem or the correctness of the proof of a geometrical theorem. The other aspect is concerned with empirical observation. If an act of observation is competently performed, in a similar sense one "sees" the truth of the relevant descriptive proposition. The term *Evidenz* does not refer to the process of observing, but to the quality of its result, by virtue of which the observer feels justified in affirming a given statement. Hence "certainty" has seemed a suitable translation in some contexts, "clarity" in others, "accuracy" in still others. The term "intuition" is not usable because it refers to the process rather than to he result.

7. Weber here uses the term *aktuelles Verstehen*, which he contrasts with *erklärendes Verstehen*. The latter he also refers to as *motivationsmässig*. "*Aktuell*" in this context has been translated as "observational." It is clear from Weber's discussion that the primary criterion is the possibility of deriving the meaning of an act or symbolic expression from immediate observation without reference to any broader context. In *erklärendes Verstehen*, on the other hand, the particular act must be placed in a broader context of meaning involving facts which cannot be derived from immediate observation of a particular act or expression.

8. The German term is *Sinnzusammenhang*. It refers to a plurality of elements which form a coherent whole on the level of meaning. There are several possible modes of meaningful relation between such elements, such as logical consistency, the esthetic harmony of a style, or the appropriateness of means to an end. In any case, however, a *Sinnzusammenhang* must be distinguished from a system of elements which are causally interdependent. There seems to be no single English term or phrase which is always adequate. According to variations in context, "context of meaning," "complex of meaning," and sometimes "meaningful system" have been employed.

9. The German is *gemeinter Sinn*. Weber departs from ordinary usage not only in broadening the meaning of this conception. As he states at the end of the present methodological discussion, he does not restrict the use of this concept to cases where a clear self-conscious awareness of such meaning can be reasonably attributed to every individual actor. Essentially, what Weber is doing is to formulate an operational concept. The question is not whether in a sense obvious to the ordinary person such an intended meaning "really exists," but whether the concept is capable of providing a logical framework within which scientifically important observations can be made. The test of validity of the observations is not whether their object is immediately clear to common sense, but whether the results of these technical observations can be satisfactorily organized and related to those of others in a systematic body of knowledge.

10. The above passage is an exceedingly compact statement of Weber's theory of the logical conditions of proof of causal relationship. He developed this most fully in his essay on " 'Objectivity' in Social Science . . . ," *op. cit.* It is also discussed in other parts of *GAzW*. The best and fullest secondary discussion is to be found in Schelting's book, *Max Webers Wissenschaftslehre*. There is a briefer discussion in Parsons' *Structure of Social Action*, ch. 16.

11. See Eduard Meyer, *Geschichte des Altertums*, 1901, vol. III, 420, 444ff, and Weber's essay on "Critical Studies in the Logic of the Cultural Sciences," in Shils and Finch, eds., *op. cit.*, 113–188; also in *GAzW*, 215–90. (R)

12. The expression *sinnhafte Adäquanz* is one of the most difficult of Weber's technical terms to translate. In most places the cumbrous phrase "adequacy on the level of meaning" has had to be employed. It should be clear from the progress of the discussion that what Weber refers to is a satisfying level of knowledge for the particular purposes of the subjective state of mind of the actor or actors. He is, however, careful to point out that *causal* adequacy involves in addition to this a satisfactory correspondence between the results of observations from the subjective point of view and from the objective; that is, observations of the overt course of action which can be described without reference to the state of mind of the actor. For a discussion of the methodological problem involved here, see *Structure of Social Action*, chaps. II and V.

13. This is the first occurrence in Weber's text of the term *Chance* which he uses very frequently. It is here translated by "probability," because he uses it as interchangeable with *Wahrscheinlichkeit*. As the term "probability" is used in a technical mathematical and statistical sense, however, it implies the possibility of numerical statement. In most of the cases where Weber uses *Chance* this is out of the question. It is, however, possible to speak in terms of higher and lower degrees of probability. To avoid confusion with the technical mathematical concept, the term "likelihood" will often be used in the translation. It is by means of this concept that Weber, in a highly ingenious way, has bridged the gap between the interpretation of meaning and the inevitably more complex facts of overt action.

14. The term "reification" as used by Professor Morris Cohen in his book, *Reason and Nature*, seems to fit Weber's meaning exactly. A concept or system of concepts, which critical analysis can show to be abstract, is "reified" when it is used naively as though it provided an adequate total description of the concrete phenomenon in question. The fallacy of "reification" is virtually another name for what Professor Whitehead has called "the fallacy of misplaced concreteness." See his *Science and the Modern World*.

15. See August Weismann, *Die Allmacht der Naturzüchtung* (Jena: Fischer, 1893); his opponent was probably Alexander Götte (1840–1922), author of *Lehrbuch der Zoologie* (Leipzig: Engelmann, 1902) and of *Tierkunde* (Strasbourg: Trübner, 1904). (R)

16. In the above classification as well as in some of those which follow, the terminology is not standardized either in German or in English. Hence, just as there is a certain arbitrariness in Weber's definitions, the same is true of any corresponding set of definitions in English. It should be kept in mind that all of them are modes of orientation of action to patterns which contain a normative element. "Usage" has seemed to be the most appropriate translation of *Brauch* since, according to Weber's own definition, the principal criterion is that "it is done to conform with the pattern." There would also seem to be good precedent for the translation of *Sitte* by "custom." The contrast with fashion, which Weber takes up in his first comment, is essentially the same in both languages. The term *Interessenlage* presents greater difficulty. It involves

two components: the motivation in terms of self-interest and orientation to the opportunities presented by the situation. It has not seemed possible to use any single term to convey this meaning in English and hence, a more roundabout expression has had to be resorted to.

17. The term "convention" in Weber's usage is narrower than *Brauch*. The difference consists in the fact that a normative pattern to which action is oriented is conventional only insofar as it is regarded as part of a legitimate order, whereas the question of moral obligation to conformity which legitimacy implies is not involved in "usage." The distinction is closely related to that of W. G. Sumner between "mores" and "folkways." It has seemed best to retain the English term closest to Weber's own.

18. It is, in a sense, the empirical reference of this statement which constitutes the central theme of Weber's series of studies in the Sociology of Religion. Insofar as he finds it possible to attribute importance to "ideas" in the determination of action, the most important differences between systems of ideas are not so much those in the degree of rationalization as in the direction which the process of rationalization in each case has taken. This series of studies was left uncompleted at his death, but all the material which was in a condition fit for publication has been assembled in the three volumes of the *Gesammelte Aufsätze zur Religionssoziologie* (*GAzRS*).

19. It has not been possible to identify this reference of Weber's. It refers most probably to a projected conclusion which was never written.

20. The reader may readily become confused as to the basis of the following classification, as compared with that presented in sec. 7. The first classification is one of motives for maintaining a legitimate order in force, whereas the second is one of motives for attributing legitimacy to the order. This explains the inclusion of self-interested motives in the first classification, but not in the second. It is quite possible, for instance, for irreligious persons to support the doctrine of the divine right of kings, because they feel that the breakdown of an order which depends on this would have undesirable consequences. This is not, however, a possible motive on which to base a direct sense of personal moral obligation to conform with the order.

21. Rheinstein's emendation, see his edition, *op. cit.*, 7. (R)

22. In 1745, Maurice de Saxe defeated the British under the Duke of Cumberland even though he sustained heavy losses in the one-sided opening round. (R)

23. A cautionary note is in order here: The definitions of conflict or struggle (*Kampf*) and of power (section 16) have often been wrenched out of context in discussions of Weber as a "power politician." The present section, however, defines the *varieties* of conflict, from the extreme case of violent, unlimited and unregulated struggle to peaceful and regulated competition. In fact, mere conflict and power are not Weber's major concern, which is rather with variously regulated and legitimated actions and their group context. (R)

24. As Weber goes on to explain, he uses *Vergemeinschaftung* and *Vergesellschaftung* in a continuous rather than a dichotomous sense, and thus maintains his critical distance from Tönnies' paired contrast of *Gemeinschaft* and *Gesellschaft*. Similarly, Weber rejected Gierke's invidious contrast between "cold-blooded" Roman law and "communal" Germanic law, even though he started his career as a Germanist rather than a Romanist. (R)

25. This is a reference to the *Betriebsräte* which were formed in German industrial plants during the Revolution of 1918–19 and were recognized in the Weimar Constitution as entitled to representation in the Federal Economic

Council. The standard work in English is W. C. Guillebaud, *The Works Council. A German Experiment in Industrial Democracy* (Cambridge University Press, 1928).

26. Weber's term here is *Nahrungsspielraum.* The concept refers to the scope of economic resources and opportunities on which the standard of living of an individual or a group is dependent. By contrast with this, *Erwerbsspielraum* is a similar scope of resources and economic opportunities seen from the point of view of their possible role as sources of profit. The basic distinction implied in this contrast is of central importance to Weber's analysis later on (see chapter II, sec. 10ff.).

27. The term "corporate group" for *Verband,* as used by Parsons, is open to misunderstandings on both the common-sense and the historical level since Weber's term includes more than either economic groups or self-governing, often professional bodies. Parsons' alternative term, "organized group," has been retained. The term "organization" should be understood literally in the sense of a group with an "organ," but not necessarily of a rationalized kind; the latter would make it an "enterprise" or a "formal organization" (see sec. 15). —For Weber's older definition of *Verband* and *Verbandshandeln* see Appendix I. (R)

28. The concept "objective possibility" (*objektive Möglichkeit*) plays an important technical role in Weber's methodological studies. According to his usage, a thing is "objectively possible" if it "makes sense" to conceive it as an empirically existing entity. It is a question of conforming with the formal, logical conditions. The question whether a phenomenon which is in this sense "objectively possible" will actually be found with any significant degree of probability or approximation, is a logically distinct question.

29. See Ferdinand Lassalle, "Über Verfassungswesen" (1862), in *Gesammelte Reden und Schriften,* Eduard Bernstein, ed. (Berlin: Cassirer, 1919), 7–62. (R)

30. See Otto Gierke, *Geschichte des deutschen Körperschaftsbegriffs* (Berlin: Weidmann, 1873), 829; Hugo Preuss, *Gemeinde, Staat, Reich als Gebietskörperschaft* (1889). Preuss, one of Gierke's pupils, exerted decisive influence on the making of the Weimar constitution, to which Weber also contributed at about the same time that he worked intermittently on these definitions. (W and R)

31. In his translation Parsons pointed out that "the term *Herrschaft* has no satisfactory English equivalent. The term "imperative control," however, as used by N. S. Timasheff in his *Introduction to the Sociology of Law* is close to Weber's meaning" (Parsons, ed., *op. cit.,* 152). Therefore, he borrowed this term "for the most general purposes." At a later time, Parsons indicated that he now preferred the term "leadership." For more specific purposes, however, he used the term "authority." In objecting to "domination" (as used by Bendix and Rheinstein/Shils) Parsons noted: "It is true to be sure that the term *Herrschaft,* which in its most general meaning I should now translate as "leadership," implies that a leader has power *over* his followers. But "domination" suggests that this fact, rather than the integration of the collectivity, in the interest of effective functioning (especially the integration of the crucial *Verband* or corporate group), is the critical factor from Weber's point of view. I do not believe that the former interpretation represents the main trend of Weber's thought, although he was in certain respects a "realist" in the analysis of power. The preferable interpretation, as I see it, is represented especially by his tremendous emphasis on the importance of legitimation. I should therefore wish to stick to my own decision to translate *legitime Herrschaft,* which for Weber was overwhelmingly the most significant case for general structural analysis, as authority." (See T. Parsons' review article

of Reinhard Bendix, *Max Weber: An Intellectual Portrait,* in *American Socio-logical Review,* 25:5, 1960, 752.)

I prefer the term domination in this section because Weber stresses the fact of mere compliance with a command, which may be due to habit, a belief in legitimacy, or to considerations of expediency. However, Weber emphasizes here as later that, in addition to the willingness of subjects to comply with a command, there is usually a staff, which again may act on the basis of habit, legitimacy or self-interest. Sociologically, a *Herrschaft* is a structure of superordination and subordination, of leaders and led, rulers and ruled; it is based on a variety of motives and of means of enforcement. In ch. III, Weber presents a typology of legitimate *Herrschaft* where the term "authority" is indeed feasible. However, in ch. X, he deals extensively with both faces of *Herrschaft:* legitimacy and force. It should be clear to the reader that both "domination" and "authority" are "cor-rect" although each stresses a different component of *Herrschaft.* Moreover, in Part Two a *Herrschaft* is quite specifically the medieval *seigneurie* or manor or simi-lar structures in patrimonial regimes. This is also the historical derivation of the term. For a major, and sociologically valuable, study see Otto Brunner, *Land und Herrschaft: Grundfragen der territorialen Verfassungsgeschichte Österreichs im Mittelalter* (Vienna, 1959). (R)

32. For the earlier discussion of discipline, see Part Two, ch. XIV:*iii*:1, "The Meaning of Discipline."

33. The German is *Devisenpolitik.* Translation in this context is made more difficult by the fact that the German language does not distinguish between "politics" and "policy," *Politik* having both meanings. The remarks which Weber makes about various kinds of policy would have been unnecessary, had he written originally in English.

CHAPTER II

SOCIOLOGICAL CATEGORIES
OF ECONOMIC ACTION

Prefatory Note

What follows is not intended in any sense to be "economic theory." Rather, it consists only in an attempt to define certain concepts which are frequently used and to analyze certain of the simplest sociological relationships in the economic sphere. As in the first chapter, the procedure here has been determined entirely by considerations of convenience. It has proved possible entirely to avoid the controversial concept of "value."[1] The usage here, in the relevant sections on the division of labor [see sec. 15ff.], has deviated from the terminology of Karl Bücher only so far as seemed necessary for the purposes of the present undertaking. For the present all questions of dynamic process will be left out of account.

1. The Concept of Economic Action

Action will be said to be "economically oriented" so far as, according to its subjective meaning, it is concerned with the satisfaction of a desire for "utilities" (*Nutzleistungen*). "Economic action" (*Wirtschaften*) is any peaceful exercise of an actor's control over resources which is in its main impulse oriented towards economic ends. "Rational economic action" requires instrumental rationality in this orientation, that is, deliberate planning. We will call autocephalous economic action an "economy" (*Wirtschaft*), and an organized system of continuous economic action an "economic establishment" (*Wirtschaftsbetrieb*).

    1. It was pointed out above (ch. I, sec. 1:B) that economic action as such need not be social action.

[63]

2. The definition of economic action must be as general as possible and must bring out the fact that all "economic" processes and objects are characterized as such entirely by the *meaning* they have for human action in such roles as ends, means, obstacles, and by-products. It is not, however, permissible to express this by saying, as is sometimes done, that economic action is a "psychic" phenomenon. The production of goods, prices, or even the "subjective valuation" of goods, if they are empirical processes, are far from being merely psychic phenomena. But underlying this misleading phrase is a correct insight. It is a fact that these phenomena have a peculiar type of subjective *meaning*. This alone defines the unity of the corresponding processes, and this alone makes them accessible to subjective interpretation.

The definition of "economic action" must, furthermore, be formulated in such a way as to include the operation of a modern business enterprise run for profit. Hence the definition cannot be based directly on "consumption needs" and the "satisfaction" of these needs, but must, rather, start out on the one hand from the fact that there is a *desire* (demand) for utilities (which is true even in the case of orientation to purely monetary gains), and on the other hand from the fact that *provision* is being made to furnish the supplies to meet this demand (which is true even in the most primitive economy merely "satisfying needs," and regardless of how primitive and frozen in tradition the methods of this provision are).

3. As distinguished from "economic action" as such, the term "economically oriented action" will be applied to two types: (a) every action which, though primarily oriented to other ends, takes account, in the pursuit of them, of economic considerations; that is, of the consciously recognized necessity for economic prudence. Or (b) that which, though primarily oriented to economic ends, makes use of physical force as a means. It thus includes all primarily non-economic action and all non-peaceful action which is influenced by economic considerations. "Economic action" thus is a *conscious, primary* orientation to economic considerations. It must be conscious, for what matters is not the objective necessity of making economic provision, but the belief that is is necessary. Robert Liefmann has rightly laid emphasis on the subjective understandable orientation of action which makes it economic action. He is not, however, correct in attributing the contrary view to all other authors.[2]

4. Every type of action, including the use of violence, may be economically *oriented*. This is true, for instance, of war-like action, such as marauding expeditions and trade wars. Franz Oppenheimer, in particular, has rightly distinguished "economic" means from "political" means.[3] It is essential to distinguish the latter from economic action. The use of force is unquestionably very strongly opposed to the spirit of economic acquisition in the usual sense. Hence the term "economic action" will not be applied to the direct appropriation of goods by force and the direct coercion of the other party by threats of force. It goes without saying, at

the same time, that exchange is not the *only* economic means, though it is one of the most important. Furthermore, the formally peaceful provision for the means and the success of a projected exercise of force, as in the case of armament production and economic organization for war, is just as much economic action as any other.

Every rational course of political action is economically oriented with respect to provision for the necessary means, and it is always possible for political action to serve the interest of economic ends. Similarly, though it is not necessarily true of every economic system, certainly the modern economic order under modern conditions could not continue if its control of resources were not upheld by the legal compulsion of the state; that is, if its formally "legal" rights were not upheld by the threat of force. But the fact that an economic system is thus dependent on protection by force, does not mean that it is itself an example of the use of force.

How entirely untenable it is to maintain that the economy, however defined, is only a *means,* by contrast, for instance, with the state, becomes evident from the fact that it is possible to define the state itself only in terms of the means which it today monopolizes, namely, the use of force. If anything, the most essential aspect of economic action for practical purposes is the prudent choice *between ends.* This choice is, however, oriented to the scarcity of the means which are available or could be procured for these various ends.

5. Not every type of action which is rational in its choice of means will be called "rational economic action," or even "economic action" in any sense; in particular, the term "economy" will be distinguished from that of "technology."[4] The "technique" of an action refers to the means employed as opposed to the meaning or end to which the action is, in the last analysis, oriented. "Rational" technique is a choice of means which is consciously and systematically oriented to the experience and reflection of the actor, which consists, at the highest level of rationality, in scientific knowledge. What is concretely to be treated as a "technique" is thus variable. The ultimate meaning of a concrete act may, seen in the total context of action, be of a "technical" order; that is, it may be significant only as a means in this broader context. Then the "meaning" of the concrete act (viewed from the larger context) lies in its technical function; and, conversely, the means which are applied in order to accomplish this are its "techniques." In this sense there are techniques of every conceivable type of action, techniques of prayer, of asceticism, of thought and research, of memorizing, of education, of exercising political or hierocratic domination, of administration, of making love, of making war, of musical performances, of sculpture and painting, of arriving at legal decisions. All these are capable of the widest variation in degree of rationality. The presence of a "technical question" always means that there is some doubt over the choice of the most rational *means* to an end. Among others, the standard of rationality for a technique may be the famous principle of "least effort," the achievement of

an optimum *in the relation* between the result and the means to be expended on it (and not the attainment of a result with the *absolute* minimum of means). Seemingly the same principle, of course, applies to
economic action—or to any type of rational action. But there it has a
different *meaning*. As long as the action is purely "technical" in the present sense, it is oriented only to the selection of the means which, with
equal quality, certainty, and permanence of the result, are comparatively
most "economical" of effort in the attainment of a *given* end; comparatively, that is, insofar as there are at all directly comparable expenditures
of means in different methods of achieving the end. The end itself is
accepted as beyond question, and a purely technical consideration ignores other wants. Thus, in a question of whether to make a technically
necessary part of a machine out of iron or platinum, a decision on technical grounds alone would, so long as the requisite quantities of both
metals for their particular purpose were available, consider only which
of the two would in this case best bring about the given result and
would at the same time minimize the other comparable expenditure of
resources, such as labor. But once consideration is extended to take account of the relative scarcity of iron and platinum in relation to their
potential uses, as today every technician is accustomed to do even in the
chemical laboratory, the action is no longer in the present sense purely
technical, but *also* economic. From the economic point of view, "technical" questions always involve the consideration of "costs." This is a
question of crucial importance for economic purposes and in this context always takes the form of asking what would be the effect on the
satisfaction of other wants if this particular means were not used for
satisfaction of one given want. The "other wants" may be qualitatively
different present wants or qualitatively identical future wants. (A similar position is taken by Friedrich von Gottl-Ottlilienfeld in *Grundriss
der Sozialökonomik*, Part II, 2; an extensive and very good discussion of
this issue in R. Liefmann, *Grundsätze der Volkswirtschaftslehre*, vol. I
(3rd ed.), p. 322ff. Any attempt to reduce all means to "ultimate expenditures of labor" is erroneous.)

For the answer to the question, what is, in comparative terms, the
"cost" of using various means for a given technical end, depends in the
last analysis on their potential usefulness as means to other ends. This is
particularly true of labor. A *technical* problem in the present sense is,
for instance, that of what equipment is necessary in order to move loads
of a particular kind or in order to raise mineral products from a given
depth in a mine, and which of the alternatives is the most "suited," that
is, among other things, which achieves a given degree of success with
the least expenditure of effort. It is, on the other hand, an *economic*
problem whether, on the assumption of a market economy, these expenditures will pay off in terms of money obtained through the sale of the
goods; or, on the assumption of a planned economy, whether the necessary labor and other means of production can be provided without
damage to the satisfaction of other wants held to be more urgent. In
both cases, it is a problem of the comparison of *ends*. Economic action

is primarily oriented to the problem of choosing the *end* to which a thing shall be applied; technology, to the problem, given the end, of choosing the appropriate *means*. For purposes of the theoretical (not, of course, the practical) definition of technical rationality it is wholly indifferent whether the product of a technical process is in any sense useful. In the present terminology we can conceive of a rational technique for achieving ends which no one desires. It would, for instance, be possible, as a kind of technical amusement, to apply all the most modern methods to the production of atmospheric air. And no one could take the slightest exception to the purely technical rationality of the action. Economically, on the other hand, the procedure would under normal circumstances be clearly irrational because there would be no demand for the product. (On all this, compare v. Gottl-Ottlilienfeld, *op. cit.*)

The fact that what is called the technological development of modern times has been so largely oriented economically to profit-making is one of the fundamental facts of the history of technology. But however fundamental it has been, this economic orientation has by no means stood alone in shaping the development of technology. In addition, a part has been played by the games and cogitations of impractical ideologists, a part by other-worldly interests and all sorts of fantasies, a part by preoccupation with artistic problems, and by various other non-economic motives. None the less, the main emphasis at all times, and especially the present, has lain in the economic determination of technological development. Had not rational calculation formed the basis of economic activity, had there not been certain very particular conditions in its economic background, rational technology could never have come into existence.

The fact that the aspects of economic orientation which distinguish it from technology were not explicitly brought into the initial definition, is a consequence of the sociological starting point. From a sociological point of view, the weighing of alternative ends in relation to each other and to costs is a consequence of "continuity." This is true at least so far as costs mean something other than altogether giving up one end in favor of more urgent ones. An economic theory, on the other hand, would do well to emphasize this criterion from the start.

6. It is essential to include the criterion of power of control and disposal (*Verfügungsgewalt*)[5] in the sociological concept of economic action, if for no other reason than that at least a modern market economy (*Erwerbswirtschaft*) essentially consists in a complete network of exchange contracts, that is, in deliberate planned acquisitions of powers of control and disposal. This, in such an economy, is the principal source of the relation of economic action to the law. But any other type of organization of economic activities would involve some kind of *de facto* distribution of powers of control and disposal, however different its underlying principles might be from those of the modern private enterprise economy with its legal protection of such powers held by autonomous and autocephalous economic units. Either the central authority, as in the case of socialism, or the subsidiary parts, as in anarchism, must be able

to count on having some kind of control over the necessary services of labor and of the means of production. It is possible to obscure this fact by verbal devices, but it cannot be interpreted out of existence. For purposes of definition it is a matter of indifference in what way this control is guaranteed; whether by convention or by law, or whether it does not even enjoy the protection of any external sanctions at all, but its security rests only on actual expectations in terms of custom or self-interest. These possibilities must be taken into account, however essential legal compulsion may be for the modern economic order. The indispensability of powers of control for the concept of social action in its economic aspects thus does not imply that *legal* order is part of that concept by definition, however important it may be held to be on empirical grounds.

7. The concept of powers of control and disposal will here be taken to include the possibility of control over the actor's own labor power, whether this is in some way enforced or merely exists in fact. That this is not to be taken for granted is shown by its absence in the case of slaves.

8. It is necessary for the purposes of a sociological theory of economic action to introduce the concept of "goods" at an early stage, as is done in sec. 2. For this theory is concerned with a type of action which is given its specific *meaning* by the *results* of the actors' deliberations, which themselves can be isolated only in theory [but cannot be observed empirically]. Economic theory, the theoretical insights of which provide the basis for the sociology of economic action, might (perhaps) be able to proceed differently; the latter may find it necessary to create its own theoretical constructs.

2. *The Concept of Utility*

By "utilities" (*Nutzleistungen*) will always be meant the specific and concrete, real or imagined, advantages (*Chancen*) of opportunities for present or future use as they are estimated and made an object of specific provision by one or more economically acting individuals. The action of these individuals is oriented to the estimated importance of such utilities as means for the ends of their economic action.

Utilities may be the services of non-human or inanimate objects or of human beings. Non-human objects which are the sources of potential utilities of whatever sort will be called "goods." Utilities derived from a human source, so far as this source consists in active conduct, will be called "services" (*Leistungen*). Social relationships which are valued as a potential source of present or future disposal over utilities are, however, also objects of economic provision. The opportunities of economic advantage, which are made available by custom, by the constellation of interest, or by a conventional or legal order for the purposes of an economic unit, will be called "economic advantages."

On the following comments, compare E. von Böhm-Bawerk, *Rechte und Verhältnisse vom Standpunkt der volkswirtschaftlichen Güterlehre* (Innsbruck 1881).

1. The categories of goods and services do not exhaust those aspects of the environment which may be important to an individual for economic purposes and which may hence be an object of economic concern. Such things as "good will," or the tolerance of economic measures on the part of individuals in a position to interfere with them, and numerous other forms of behavior, may have the same kind of economic importance and may be the object of economic provision and, for instance, of contracts. It would, however, result in a confusion of concepts to try to bring such things under either of these two categories. This choice of concepts is thus entirely determined by consideration of convenience.

2. As Böhm-Bawerk has correctly pointed out, it would be equally imprecise if all *concrete* objects of life and of everyday speech were without distinction designated as "goods," and the concept of a good were then equated to that of a material utility. In the strict sense of utility, it is not a "horse" or a "bar of iron" which is an economic "good," but the specific ways in which they can be put to desirable and practical uses; for instance the power to haul loads or to carry weights, or something of the sort. Nor can we, in the present terminology, call *goods* such potential future advantages (*Chancen*) which appear as objects of exchange in economic transactions, as "good will," "mortgage," "property." Instead, for simplicity's sake, we shall call the services of such potential powers of control and disposal over the utilities of goods and services, promised or guaranteed by the traditional or legal order, "economic advantages" (*Chancen*) or simply "advantages" wherever this is not likely to be misunderstood.

3. The fact that only active conduct, and not mere acquiescence, permission, or omission, are treated as "services" is a matter of convenience. But it must be remembered that it follows from this that goods and services do not constitute an exhaustive classification of all economically significant utilities.

On the concept of "labor," see below, sec. 15.

3. *Modes of the Economic Orientation of Action*

Economic orientation may be a matter of tradition or of goal-oriented rationality. Even in cases where there is a high degree of rationalization of action, the element of traditional orientation remains considerable. For the most part, rational orientation is primarily significant for "managerial" action, no matter under what form of organization. (See below,

sec. 15.) The development of rational economic action from the instinc-
tively reactive search for food or traditional acceptance of inherited
techniques and customary social relationships has been to a large extent
determined by non-economic events and actions, including those outside
everyday routine,[6] and also by the pressure of necessity in cases of increasing absolute or relative limitations on subsistence.

1. Naturally there cannot in principle be any scientific standard for
any such concept as that of an "original economic state." It would be
possible to agree arbitrarily to take the economic state on a given technological level, as, for instance, that characterized by the lowest development of tools and equipment known to us, and to treat it and analyze
it as the most primitive. But there is no scientific justification for concluding from observations of living primitive peoples on a low technological level that the economic organization of all peoples of the past
with similar technological standing has been the same as, for instance,
that of the Vedda or of certain tribes of the Amazon region. For, from
a purely economic point of view, this level of technology has been just
as compatible with large-scale organization of labor as with extreme
dispersal in small groups (see below, sec. 16). It is impossible to infer
from the economic aspects of the natural environment alone, which of
these would be more nearly approached. Various non-economic factors,
for instance, military, could make a substantial difference.

2. War and migration are not in themselves economic processes,
though particularly in early times they have been largely oriented to
economic considerations. At all times, however, indeed up to the present, they have often been responsible for radical changes in the economic system. In cases where, through such factors as climatic changes,
inroads of sand, or deforestation, there has been an absolute decrease in
the means of subsistence, human groups have adapted themselves in
widely differing ways, depending on the structure of interests and on
the manner in which non-economic factors have played a role. The typical reactions, however, have been a fall in the standard of living and
an absolute decrease in population. Similarly, in cases of relative impov-
erishment in means of subsistence, as determined by a given standard of
living and of the distribution of chances of acquisition, there have also
been wide variations. But on the whole, this type of situation has, more
frequently than the other, been met by the increasing rationalization of
economic activities. Even in this case, however, it is not possible to make
general statements. So far as the "statistical" information can be relied
upon, there was a tremendous increase of population in China after the
beginning of the eighteenth century, but it had exactly the opposite
effect from the similar phenomenon of about the same time in Europe.
It is, however, possible to say at least something about the reasons for
this (see below, sec. 11.). The chronic scarcity of the means of subsistence in the Arabian desert has only at certain times resulted in a change
in the economic and political structure, and these changes have been

most prominent when non-economic (religious) developments have played a part.

3. A high degree of traditionalism in habits of life, such as characterized the laboring classes in early modern times, has not prevented a great increase in the rationalization of economic enterprise under capitalistic direction. But it was also compatible with, for instance, the rationalization of public finances in Egypt on a state-socialistic model. Nevertheless, this traditionalistic attitude had to be at least partly overcome in the Western World before the further development to the specifically modern type of rational capitalistic economy could take place.

4. *Typical Measures of Rational Economic Action*

The following are typical measures of rational economic action:

(1) The systematic allocation as between present and future of utilities, on the control of which the actor for whatever reason feels able to count. (These are the essential features of saving.)

(2) The systematic allocation of available utilities to various potential uses in the order of their estimated relative urgency, ranked according to the principle of marginal utility.

These two cases, the most definitely "static," have been most highly developed in times of peace. Today, for the most part, they take the form of the allocation of money incomes.

(3) The systematic procurement[7] through production or transportation of such utilities for which all the necessary means of production are controlled by the actor himself. Where action is rational, this type of action will take place so far as, according to the actor's estimate, the urgency of his demand for the expected result of the action exceeds the necessary expenditure, which may consist in (a) the irksomeness of the requisite labor services, and (b) the other potential uses to which the requisite goods could be put; including, that is, the utility of the potential alternative products and their uses. This is "production" in the broader sense, which includes transportation.

(4) The systematic acquisition, by agreement (*Vergesellschaftung*) with the present possessors or with competing bidders, of assured powers of control and disposal over utilities. The powers of control may or may not be shared with others. The occasion may lie in the fact that utilities themselves are in the control of others, that their means of procurement are in such control, or that third persons desire to acquire them in such a way as to endanger the actor's own supply.

The relevant rational association (*Vergesellschaftung*) with the present possessor of a power of control or disposal may consist in (a) the establishment of an organization with an order to which the procurement and use of utilities is to be oriented, or (b) in exchange. In the first case the purpose of the organization may be to ration the procurement, use, or consumption, in order to limit competition of procuring actors. Then it is a "regulative organization." Or, secondly, its purpose may be to set up a unified authority for the systematic administration of the utilities which had hitherto been subject to a dispersed control. In this case there is an "administrative organization."

"Exchange" is a compromise of interests on the part of the parties in the course of which goods or other advantages are passed as reciprocal compensation. The exchange may be traditional or conventional,[8] and hence, especially in the latter case, not economically rational. Or, secondly, it may be economically rational both in intention and in result. Every case of a rationally oriented exchange is the resolution of a previously open or latent conflict of interests by means of a compromise. The opposition of interests which is resolved in the compromise involves the actor potentially in two different conflicts. On the one hand, there is the conflict over the price to be agreed upon with the partner in exchange; the typical method is bargaining. On the other hand, there may also be competition with actual or potential rivals, either in the present or in the future, who are competitors in the same market. Here, the typical method is competitive bidding and offering.

1. Utilities, and the goods or labor which are their sources, are under the control (*Eigenverfügung*) of an economically acting individual if he is in a position to be able in fact to make use of them at his convenience (at least, up to a point) without interference from other persons, regardless of whether this ability rests on the legal order, on convention, on custom or on a complex of interests. It is by no means true that only the legal assurance of powers of disposal is decisive, either for the concept or in fact. It is, however, today empirically an indispensable basis for economic activitiy with the *material* means of production.

2. The fact that goods are not as yet consumable may be a result of the fact that while they are, as such, finished, they are not yet in a suitable place for consumption; hence the transportation of goods, which is naturally to be distinguished from trade, a change in the control over the goods, may here be treated as part of the process of production.

3. When there is a lack of control (*Eigenverfügung*) over desired utilities, it is in principle indifferent whether the individual is typically prevented from forcibly interfering with the control of others by a legal order, convention, custom, his own self-interest, or his consciously-held moral standards.

4. Competition in procurement may exist under the most various conditions. It is particularly important when supplies are obtained by seizure, as in hunting, fishing, lumbering, pasturage, and clearing new

land. It may also, and most frequently does, exist within an organization which is closed to outsiders. An order which seeks to restrain such competition then always consists in the rationing of supplies, usually combined with the appropriation of the procurement possibilities thus guaranteed for the benefit of a limited number of individuals or, more often, households. All medieval *Mark-* and fishing associations, the regulation of forest clearing, pasturage and wood gathering rights in the common fields and wastes, the grazing rights on Alpine meadows, and so on, have this character. Various types of hereditary property-rights in land owe their development to this type of regulation.

5. Anything which may in any way be transferred from the control of one person to that of another and for which another is willing to give compensation, may be an object of exchange. It is not restricted to goods and services, but includes all kinds of potential economic advantages; for instance, "good will," which exists only by custom or self-interest and cannot be enforced; in particular, however, it includes all manner of advantages, claims to which are enforceable under some kind of order. Thus objects of exchange are not necessarily presently existing utilities.

For present purposes, by "exchange" in the broadest sense will be meant every case of a formally voluntary agreement involving the offer of any sort of present, continuing, or future utility in exchange for utilities of any sort offered in return. Thus it includes the turning over of the utility of goods or money in exchange for the future return of the same kind of goods. It also includes any sort of permission for, or tolerance of, the use of an object in return for "rent" or "hire," or the hiring of any kind of services for wages or salary. The fact that the last example today involves, from a sociological point of view, the subjection of the "worker," as defined in sec. 15 below, under a form of domination will, for preliminary purposes, be neglected, as will the distinction between loan and purchase.

6. The conditions of exchange may be traditional, partly traditional though enforced by convention, or rational. Examples of conventional exchanges are exchanges of gifts between friends, heroes, chiefs, princes; as, for instance, the exchange of armor between Diomedes and Glaucos. It is not uncommon for these to be rationally oriented and controlled to a high degree, as can be seen in the Tell-el-Amarna documents. Rational exchange is only possible when both parties expect to profit from it, or when one is under compulsion because of his own need or the other's economic power. Exchange may serve either purposes of consumption or of acquisition (see below, sec. 11). It may thus be oriented to provision for the personal use of the actor or to opportunities for profit. In the first case, its conditions are to a large extent differentiated from case to case, and it is in *this* sense irrational. Thus, for instance, household surpluses will be valued according to the individual marginal utilities of the particular household economy and may on occasion be sold very cheaply, and the fortuitous desires of the moment may establish the marginal utility of goods which are sought in ex-

change at a very high level. Thus the exchange ratios, as determined by marginal utility, will fluctuate widely. Rational competition develops only in the case of "marketable goods" (see sec. 8) and, to the highest degree, when goods are used and sold in a profit system (see sec. 11).

7. The modes of intervention of a regulatory system mentioned above under point (4) are not the only possible ones, but merely those which are relevant here because they are the most immediate consequences of a tightening of the supply basis. The regulation of marketing processes will be discussed below.

5. *Types of Economic Organizations*

According to its relation to the economic system, an economically oriented organization may be: (a) an "economically active organization" (*wirtschaftender Verband*) if the primarily non-economic organized action oriented to its order includes economic action; (b) an "economic organization" (*Wirtschaftsverband*) if its organized action, as governed by the order, is *primarily* autocephalous economic action of a given kind; (c) an "economically regulative organization" (*wirtschaftsregulierender Verband*) if the autocephalous economic activity of the members is directly oriented to the order governing the group; that is, if economic action is heteronomous in that respect; (d) an "organization enforcing a formal order" (*Ordnungsverband*)[9] if its order merely guarantees, by means of formal rules, the autocephalous and autonomous economic activities of its members and the corresponding economic advantages thus acquired.

1. The state, except for the socialistic or communist type, and all other organizations like churches and voluntary associations are economically active groups if they manage their own financial affairs. This is also true of educational institutions and all other organizations which are not primarily economic.

2. In the category of "economic organizations" in the present sense are included not only business corporations, co-operative associations, cartels, partnerships, and so on, but all permanent economic establishments (*Betriebe*) which involve the activities of a plurality of persons, all the way from a workshop run by two artisans to a conceivable communistic organization of the whole world.

3. "Economically regulative organizations" are the following: medieval village associations, guilds, trade unions, employers' associations, cartels, and all other groups, the directing authorities of which carry on an "economic policy" which seeks to regulate both the ends and the procedures of economic activity. It thus includes the villages and towns of the Middle Ages, just as much as a modern state which follows such a policy.

4. An example of a group confined to the "enforcement of a formal order" is the pure laissez-faire state, which would leave the economic activity of individual households and enterprises entirely free and confine its regulation to the formal function of settling disputes connected with the fulfillment of free contractual obligations.

5. The existence of organizations "regulating economic activity" or merely "enforcing a formal order" presupposes in principle a certain amount of autonomy in the field of economic activity. Thus there is in principle a sphere of free disposal over economic resources, though it may be limited in varying degrees by means of rules to which the actors are oriented. This implies, further, the (at least relative) appropriation of economic advantages, over which the actors then have autonomous control. The purest type of a group "enforcing a formal order" is thus present when all *human* action is autonomous with respect to content, and oriented to regulation only with respect to form, and when all *non-human* sources of utility are completely appropriated so that individuals can have free disposal of them, in particular by exchange, as is the case in a modern property system. Any other kind of limitation on appropriation and autonomy implies "regulation of economic activity," because it restricts the orientation of human activities.

6. The dividing line between "regulation of economic activity" and mere "enforcement of a formal order" is vague. For, naturally, the type of "formal" order not only may, but must, in some way also exert a material influence on action; in some cases, a fundamental influence. Numerous modern legal ordinances, which claim to do no more than set up formal rules, are so drawn up that they actually exert a material influence (see "Soc. of Law," Part Two, ch. VIII). Indeed, a really strict limitation to purely formal rules is possible only in theory. Many of the recognized "overriding" principles of law, of a kind which cannot be dispensed with, imply to an appreciable degree important limitations on the content of economic activity. Especially "enabling provisions" can under certain circumstances, as in corporation law, involve quite appreciable limitations on economic autonomy.

7. The limits of the material regulation of economic activity may be reached when it results in (a) the abandonment of certain kinds of economic activity, as when a tax on turnover leads to the cultivation of land only for consumption; or (b) in evasion, in such cases as smuggling, bootlegging, etc.

6. *Media of Exchange, Means of Payment, Money*

A material object offered in exchange will be called a "medium of exchange" so far as it is typically accepted primarily by virtue of the fact that the recipients estimate that they will, within the relevant time horizon, be able to utilize it in another exchange to procure other goods at an acceptable exchange ratio, regardless of whether it is exchangable for *all* other goods or only for certain specific goods. The probability that the medium of exchange will be accepted at a given rate for specific other goods will be called its "substantive validity" (*materiale Geltung*) in relation to these. The use itself will be called the "formal validity" (*formale Geltung*).

An object will be called a "means of payment" so far as its acceptance in payment of specific agreed or imposed obligations is *guaranteed* by convention or by law. This is the "formal validity" of the means of payment, which may also signify its formal validity as a means of exchange. Means of exchange or of payment will be called "chartal" (*chartal*)[10] when they are artifacts which, by virtue of their specific form, enjoy a definite quantum, conventional or legal, agreed or imposed, of formal validity within the membership of a group of persons or within a territorial area; and when (b) they are divisible in such a way that they represent a particular unit of nominal value or a multiple or a fraction of it, so that it is possible to use them in arithmetical calculations.

"Money" we call a chartal means of payment which is also a means of exchange.

An organization will be called a "means of exchange," "means of payment," or "money" group insofar as it effectively imposes within the sphere of authority of its orders the conventional or legal (formal) validity of a means of exchange, of payment, or money; these will be termed "internal" means of exchange, etc. Means used in transactions with non-members will be called "external" means of exchange.

Means of exchange or of payment which are not chartal are "natural" means. They may be differentiated (a) in technical terms, according to their physical characteristic—they may be ornaments, clothing, useful objects of various sorts—or according to whether their utilization occurs in terms of weight or not. They may also (b) be distinguished economically according to whether they are used primarily as means of exchange or for purposes of social prestige, the prestige of possession. They may also be distinguished according to whether they are used as means of exchange and payment in internal or in external transactions.

Money, means of exchange or of payment are "tokens" so far as they do not or no longer possess a value independent of their use as means of exchange and of payment. They are, on the other hand, "material" means so far as their value as such is influenced by their possible use for other purposes, or may be so influenced.

Money may consist either of coined or of note (document) money. Notes are usually adapted to a system of coinage or have a name which is historically derived from it.

(1) Coined money will be called "free" money or "market" money so far as the monetary metal will be coined by the mint on the initiative

of any possessor of it without limit of amount. This means that in effect the amount issued is determined by the demand of parties to market transactions.

(2) It will be called "limited" money or "administrative" money if the transformation of the metal into its chartal form (coinage) is subject to the formally quite arbitrary decisions of the governing authority of an organization and is in effect primarily oriented to its fiscal needs.

(3) It will be called "regulated" money if, though its issue is limited, the kind and amount of coinage is effectively subject to rules.

The term "means of circulation" will be applied to a document which functions as "note" money, if it is accepted in normal transactions as "provisional" money with the expectation that it can, at any time, be converted into "definitive" money, that is into coins, or a given weight of monetary metal. It is a "certificate" if this is assured by regulations which require maintenance of stocks providing full coverage in coin or bullion.

We call "conversion scales" the conventional or legally imposed exchange ratios valid within an organization for the different "natural" means of exchange or payment.

"Currency money" is the money which by the effective arrangements within an organization has validity as a means of payment without limitation on the amount that need be accepted. "Monetary material" is the material from which money is made; "monetary metal" is this material in the case of market money. "Monetary value scale" we call the relative valuation of the various subdivisions and denominations, consisting of different material substances, of "note" or "administrative" money; the same ratios in the case of types of market money made of different metals we call "exchange ratios."

"International" means of payment are those means of payment which serve to balance accounts between different monetary systems, that is, so far as payments are not postponed by funding operations.

Every reform of the monetary system by an organization must necessarily take account of the fact that certain means of payment have previously been used for the liquidation of debts. It must either accept as legal their continued use as a means of payment, or impose new ones. In the latter case an exchange ratio must be established between the old units, whether natural, by weight, or chartal, and the new ones. This is the principle of the so-called "historical" definition of money as a means of payment. It is impossible here to discuss how far this reacts upon the exchange relation between money as a means of exchange and goods.

It should be strongly emphasized that the present discussion is not an essay in monetary theory, but only an attempt to work out the simplest possible formulations of a set of concepts which will have to be frequently employed later on. In addition, this discussion is concerned primarily with certain very elementary *sociological* consequences of the use of money. The formulation of monetary theory, which has been most acceptable to the author, is that of von Mises.[11] The *Staatliche Theorie des Geldes* by G. F. Knapp[12] is the most imposing work in the field and in its way solves the formal problem brilliantly. It is, however, as will be seen below, incomplete for substantive monetary problems. Its able and valuable attempt to systematize terminology and concepts will be left out of account at this point.

1. Means of exchange and means of payment very often, though by no means always, coincide empirically. They are, however, particularly likely not to do so in primitive conditions. The means of payment for dowries, tribute, obligatory gifts, fines, wergild, etc., are often specified in convention or by law without regard to any relation to the means of exchange actually in circulation. It is only when the economic affairs of the organization are administered in money terms that von Mises' contention that even the state seeks means of payment only as a means of exchange becomes tenable. This has not been true of cases where the possession of certain means of payment has been primarily significant as a mark of social status. (See Heinrich Schurtz, *Grundriss einer Entstehungsgeschichte des Geldes*, 1898). With the introduction of regulation of money by the state, means of payment becomes the legal concept and means of exchange the economic concept.

2. There seems at first sight to be an indistinct line between a "good" which is purchased solely with a view to its future resale and a medium of exchange. In fact, however, even under conditions which are otherwise primitive there is a strong tendency for particular objects to monopolize the function of medium of exchange so completely that there is no doubt about their status. Wheat futures are traded in terms which imply that there will be a final buyer. Therefore they cannot be treated as means of payment or medium of exchange, let alone money.

3. So long as there is no officially sanctioned money, what is used as means of exchange is primarily determined by the customs, interests, and conventions to which the agreements between the parties to transactions are oriented. The reasons why specific things have become accepted as means of exchange cannot be gone into here. They have, however, been exceedingly various and tend to be determined by the type of exchange which has been of the greatest importance. By no means every medium of exchange, even within the social group where it has been employed, has been universally acceptable for every type of exchange. For instance, cowry shells, though used for other things, have not been acceptable in payment for wives or cattle.

4. Sometimes means of payment which were not the usual means of exchange have played an important part in the development of money to its special status. As G. F. Knapp has pointed out, the fact that various types of debt have existed, such as obligations stemming from tributes, dowries, payments for bride purchase, conventional gifts to kings

or by kings to each other, wergild, etc., and the fact that these have often been payable in certain specific media, has created for these media, by convention or by law, a special position. Very often they have been specific types of artifacts.

5. Money in the meaning of the present terminology may have been the one-fifth shekel pieces bearing the stamp of merchant firms which are mentioned in the Babylonian records, on the assumption, that is, that they were actually used as means of exchange. On the other hand, bars of bullion which were not coined, but weighed, will here not be treated as money, but only as means of payment and exchange. The fact, however, that they were weighed has been enormously important for the development of the habit of economic calculations. There are, naturally, many transitional forms, such as the acceptance of coins by weight rather than by denomination.

6. "Chartal" is a term introduced by Knapp in his *Staatliche Theorie des Geldes*. All types of money which have been stamped or coined, endowed with validity by law or by agreement, belong in this category, whether they were metal or not. It does not, however, seem reasonable to confine the concept to regulations by the state and not to include cases where acceptance is made compulsory by convention or by some agreement. There seems, furthermore, to be no reason why actual minting by the state or under the control of the political authorities should be a decisive criterion. For long periods this did not exist in China at all and was very much limited in the European Middle Ages. As Knapp would agree, it is only the existence of norms regulating the monetary form which is decisive. As will be noted below, validity as a means of payment and formal acceptability as means of exchange in private transactions may be made compulsory by law within the jurisdiction of the political authority.

7. Natural means of exchange and of payment may sometimes be used more for internal transactions, sometimes more for external. The details need not be considered here. The question of the substantive validity of money will be taken up later.

8. This is, furthermore, not the place to take up the substantive theory of money in its relation to prices so far as this subject belongs in the field of economic sociology at all. For present purposes it will suffice to state the fact that money, in its most important forms, is used, and then to proceed to develop some of the most general sociological consequences of this fact, which is merely a formal matter when seen from an economic point of view. It must, however, be emphasized that money can *never* be merely a harmless "voucher" or a purely nominal unit of accounting so long as it *is* money. Its valuation is always in very complex ways dependent also on its scarcity or, in case of inflation, on its overabundance. This has been particularly evident in recent times, but is equally true for all times.

A socialistic regime might issue vouchers, in payment for a given quantity of socially useful "labor," valid for the purchase of certain types of goods. These might be saved or used in exchange, but their behavior would follow the rules of barter exchange, not of money, though the exchange might be indirect.

9. Perhaps the most instructive case of the far-reaching economic consequences of the relations between the monetary and non-monetary uses of a monetary metal is that of Chinese monetary history, because copper money, with high costs of production and wide fluctuations in output of the monetary metal, permits an especially clear view of the phenomena involved.

7. *The Primary Consequences of the Use of Money. Credit*

The primary consequences of the widespread use of money are:

(1) The so-called "indirect exchange" as a means of satisfying consumers' wants. The use of money makes it possible to obtain goods which are separated from those offered in exchange for them in space, in time, in respect to the persons involved, and, what is very important, in respect to the quantity on each side of the transaction. This results in a tremendous extension of the area of possible exchange relationships.

(2) The valuation in terms of money of delayed obligations, especially of compensatory obligations arising out of an exchange (that is, debts). This is, of course, closely related to the first point.

(3) The so-called "storage of value"; that is, the accumulation of money in specie or in the form of claims to payment collectable at any time as a means of insuring future control over opportunities of advantageous economic exchange.

(4) The increasing transformation of all economic advantages into the ability to control sums of money.

(5) The qualitative individuation of consumption and, indirectly, its expansion for those who have control of money, of claims to money payment, or of opportunities to acquire money. This means the ability to offer money as a means of obtaining goods and services of all kinds.

(6) The orientation of the procurement of utilities, as it has become widespread today, to their bearing on the marginal utility of the sums of money which the directing authorities of an economic unit expect to be able to control in the relevant future.

(7) With this goes the orientation of acquisitive activities to all the opportunities which are made available by the extension of the area of possible exchanges, in time, in place, and with respect to personal agents, as noted above.

(8) All of these consequences are dependent on what is, in principle, the most important fact of all, the possibility of monetary *calculation;* that is, the possibility of assigning money values to all goods and services which in any way might enter into transactions of purchase and sale.

In substantive as distinguished from formal terms, monetary calculation means that goods are not evaluated merely in terms of their immediate importance as utilities at the given time and place and for the given person only. Rather, goods are more or less systematically compared, whether for consumption or for production, with all potential future opportunities of utilization or of gaining a return, including their possible utility to an indefinite number of other persons who can be brought into the comparison insofar as they are potential buyers of the powers of control and disposal of the present owner. Where money calculations have become typical, this defines the "market situation" of the good in question. (The above statement formulates only the simplest and best-known elements of any discussion of "money" and does not need to be further commented upon. The sociology of the "market" will not yet be developed here. On the formal concepts, see secs. 8 and 10.)

The term "credit" in the most general sense will be used to designate any exchange of goods presently possessed against the promise of a future transfer of disposal over utilities, no matter what they may be. The granting of credit means in the first instance that action is oriented to the probability that this future transfer of disposal will actually take place. In this sense the primary significance of credit lies in the fact that it makes it possible for an economic unit to exchange an expected future surplus of control over goods or money against the present control of some other unit over goods which the latter does not now intend to use. Where the action is rational, both parties expect an improvement in their position, regardless of what it consists in, over what it would be under the present distribution of resources without the exchange.

1. It is by no means necessary for the advantages in question to be economic. Credit may be granted and accepted for all conceivable purposes; for instance, charitable and military.

2. Credit may be granted and accepted in kind or in money, and in both cases the promises may be of concrete goods or services or of money payments. Carrying out credit transactions in terms of money, however, means that they become the subject of monetary calculations with all the attendant consequences, which will be discussed below.

3. This definition (of credit) for the most part corresponds to the usual one. It is clear that credit relationships may exist between organizations of all sorts, especially socialist or communist organizations. If there exist side by side several such groups, which are not economically autarkic, credit relationships are unavoidable. When the use of money

is completely absent,[13] there is a difficult problem of finding a rational basis of calculation. For the mere fact of the possibility of transactions involving compensation in the future does not tell us anything about the degree of rationality with which the parties agree on the conditions, especially in the case of long-term credit. Such parties would be in somewhat the same situation as the household economic units (*oikos*) of ancient times which exchanged their surpluses for things they had need of. But there is this difference, that in the present situation the interests of huge masses on a long-term basis would be at stake; and for the great masses of the low-income groups, the marginal utility of present consumption is particularly high. Thus there would be a probability that goods urgently needed could only be obtained on unfavorable terms.

4. Credit may be obtained and used for the purpose of satisfying present consumption needs which are inadequately provided for. Even in that case it will, so far as the action is economically rational, only be granted in exchange for advantages. This is not, however, historically usual for the earliest type of consumption credit and especially for emergency credit, the motives for which more frequently stemmed from an appeal to ethical obligations. This will be discussed in Part Two, chap. III:2.

5. What is the most common basis of credit, in money or in kind, when it is granted for profit, is very obvious. It is the fact that, because the lender is usually in a better economic situation, the marginal utility of future expectations, as compared with present ones, is higher than it is for the borrower. It should, however, be noted that what constitutes a "better" situation is highly relative.

8. *The Market*

By the "market situation" (*Marktlage*) for any object of exchange is meant all the opportunities of exchanging it for money which are known to the participants in exchange relationships and aid their orientation in the competitive price struggle.

"Marketability" (*Marktgängigkeit*) is the degree of regularity with which an object tends to be an object of exchange on the market.

"Market freedom" is the degree of autonomy enjoyed by the parties to market relationships in the price struggle and in competition.

"Regulation of the market," on the contrary, is the state of affairs where there is a substantive restriction, effectively enforced by the provisions of an order, on the marketability of certain potential objects of exchange or on the market freedom of certain participants. Regulation of the market may be determined (1) traditionally, by the actors' becoming accustomed to traditionally accepted limitations on exchange or to traditional conditions; (2) by convention, through social disapproval of treating certain utilities as marketable or of subjecting certain objects of exchange to free competition and free price determination, in general or when undertaken by certain groups of persons; (3) by law, through legal restrictions on exchange or on the freedom of competition, in general or for particular groups of persons or for particular objects of exchange. Legal regulations may take the form of influencing the market situation of objects of exchange by price regulation, or of limiting the possession, acquisition, or exchange of rights of control and disposal over certain goods to certain specific groups of persons, as in the case of legally guaranteed monopolies or of legal limitations on economic action. (4) By voluntary action arising from the structure of interests. In this case there is substantive regulation of the market, though the market remains formally free. This type of regulation tends to develop when certain participants in the market are, by virtue of their totally or approximately exclusive control of the possession of or opportunities to acquire certain utilities—that is, of their monopolistic powers—in a position to influence the market situation in such a way as actually to abolish the market freedom of others. In particular, they may make agreements with each other and with typical exchange partners for regulating market conditions. Typical examples are market quota agreements and price cartels.

  1. It is convenient, though not necessary, to confine the term "market situation" to cases of exchange for money, because it is only then that uniform numerical statements of relationships become possible. Opportunities for exchange *in kind* are best described simply as "exchange opportunities." Different kinds of goods are and have been marketable in widely different and variable degrees, even where a money economy was well developed. The details cannot be gone into here. In general, articles produced in standardized form in large quantities and widely consumed have been the most marketable; unusual goods, only occasionally in demand, the least. Durable consumption goods which can be used up over long periods and means of production with a long or indefinite life, above all, agricultural and forest land, have been marketable to a much less degree than finished goods of everyday use or means of production which are quickly used up, which can be used only once, or which give quick returns.

  2. Rationality of the regulation of markets has been historically associated with the growth of formal market freedom and the extension of marketability of goods. The original modes of market regulation have been various, partly traditional and magical, partly dictated by kinship relations, by status privileges, by military needs, by welfare policies, and not least by the interests and requirements of the governing authorities of organizations. But in each of these cases the dominant interests have not been primarily concerned with maximizing the opportunities of acquisition and economic provision of the participants in the market

themselves; have, indeed, often been in conflict with them. (1) Sometimes the effect has been to exclude certain objects from market dealings, either permanently or for a time. This has happened in the magical case, by taboo; in that of kinship, by the entailing of landed property; on the basis of social status, as with knightly fiefs. In times of famine the sale of grain has been temporarily prohibited. In other cases permission to sell has been made conditional on a prior offer of the good to certain persons, such as kinsmen, co-members of the status group, of the guild, or of the town association; or the sale has been limited by maximum prices, as is common in war time, or by minimum prices. Thus, in the interests of their status dignity magicians, lawyers, or physicians may not be allowed to accept fees below a certain minimum. (2) Sometimes certain categories of persons, such as members of the nobility, peasants, or sometimes even artisans, have been excluded from market trade in general or with respect to certain commodities. (3) Sometimes the market freedom of consumers has been restricted by regulations, as by the sumptuary laws regulating the consumption of different status groups, or by rationing in case of war or famine. (4) Another type is the restriction of the market freedom of potential competitors in the interest of the market position of certain groups, such as the professions or the guilds. Finally, (5) certain economic opportunities have been reserved to the political authorities (royal monopolies) or to those holding a charter from such authorities. This was typical for the early capitalistic monopolies.

Of all these, the fifth type of market regulation had the highest "market-rationality," and the first the lowest. By "rationality" we here mean a force which promotes the orientation of the economic activity of strata interested in purchase and sale of goods on the market to the market situations. The other types of regulation fit in between these two with respect to their rationality-impeding effect. The groups which, relative to these forms of regulation, have been most interested in the freedom of the market, have been those whose interests lay in the greatest possible extension of the marketability of goods, whether from the point of view of availability for consumption, or of ready opportunities for sale. Voluntary market regulation first appeared extensively and permanently only on behalf of highly developed profit-making interests. With a view to the securing of monopolistic advantages, this could take several forms: (1) the pure regulation of opportunities for purchase and sale, which is typical of the widespread phenomena of trading monopolies: (2) the regulation of transportation facilities, as in shipping and railway monopolies; (3) the monopolization of the production of certain goods; and (4) that of the extension of credit and of financing. The last two types generally are accompanied by an increase in the regulation of economic activity by organizations. But unlike the primitive, irrational forms of regulation, this is apt to be oriented in a methodical manner to the market situation. The starting point of voluntary market regulation has in general been the fact that certain groups with a far-reaching degree of actual control over economic resources have been in a position to take advantage of the formal freedom of the market to establish monopolies. Voluntary associations of consumers, such as consumers' co-operatives, have, on the other hand, tended to originate among those who were in an economically weak position. They have hence often been able to accomplish savings for their members, but only occasionally and limited to particular localities have they been able to establish an effective system of market regulation.

9. *Formal and Substantive Rationality of Economic Action*

The term "formal rationality of economic action" will be used to designate the extent of quantitative calculation or accounting which is technically possible and which is actually applied. The "substantive rationality," on the other hand, is the degree to which the provisioning of given groups of persons (no matter how delimited) with goods is shaped by economically oriented social action under some criterion (past, present, or potential) of ultimate values (*wertende Postulate*), regardless of the nature of these ends. These may be of a great variety.

1. The terminology suggested above is thought of merely as a means of securing greater consistency in the use of the word "rational" in this field. It is actually only a more precise form of the meanings which are continually recurring in the discussion of "nationalization" and of the economic calculus in money and in kind.

2. A system of economic activity will be called "formally" rational according to the degree in which the provision for needs, which is essential to every rational economy, is capable of being expressed in numerical, calculable terms, and is so expressed. In the first instance, it is quite independent of the technical form these calculations take, particularly whether estimates are expressed in money or in kind. The concept is thus unambiguous, at least in the sense that expression in money term yields the highest degree of formal calculability. Naturally, even this is true only relatively, so long as other things are equal.

3. The concept of "substantive rationality," on the other hand, is full of ambiguities. It conveys only one element common to all "substantive" analyses: namely, that they do not restrict themselves to note the purely formal and (relatively) unambiguous fact that action is based on "goal-oriented" rational calculation with the technically most adequate available methods, but apply certain criteria of ultimate ends, whether they be ethical, political, utilitarian, hedonistic, feudal (*ständisch*), egalitarian, or whatever, and measure the results of the economic action, however formally "rational" in the sense of correct calculation they may be, against these scales of "value rationality" or "*substantive* goal ration-

ality." There is an infinite number of possible value scales for this type of rationality, of which the socialist and communist standards constitute only one group. The latter, although by no means unambiguous in themselves, always involve elements of social justice and equality. Others are criteria of status distinctions, or of the capacity for power, especially of the war capacity, of a political unit; all these and many others are of potential "substantive" significance. These points of view are, however, significant only as bases from which to judge the *outcome* of economic action. In addition and quite independently, it is possible to judge from an ethical, ascetic, or esthetic point of view the *spirit* of economic activity (*Wirtschaftsgesinnung*) as well as the *instruments* of economic activity. All of these approaches may consider the "purely formal" rationality of calculation in monetary terms as of quite secondary importance or even as fundamentally inimical to their respective ultimate ends, even before anything has been said about the consequences of the specifically modern calculating attitude. There is no question in this discussion of attempting value judgments in this field, but only of determining and delimiting what is to be called "formal." In this context the concept "substantive" is itself in a certain sense "formal;" that is, it is an abstract, generic concept.

10. *The Rationality of Monetary Accounting. Management and Budgeting*

From a purely technical point of view, money is the most "perfect" means of economic calculation. That is, it is formally the most rational means of orienting economic activity. Calculation in terms of money, and not its actual use, is thus the specific means of rational, economic provision. So far as it is completely rational, money accounting has the following primary consequences:

(1) The valuation of all the means of achieving a productive purpose in terms of the present or expected market situation. This includes everything which is needed at present or is expected to be needed in the future; everything actually in the actor's control, which he may come to control or may acquire by exchange from the control of others; everything lost, or in danger of damage or destruction; all types of utilities, of means of production, or any other sort of economic advantage.

(2) The quantitative statement of (a) the expected advantages of every projected course of economic action and (b) the actual results of every completed action, in the form of an account comparing money costs and money returns and the estimated net profit to be gained from alternatives of action.

(3) A periodical comparison of all the goods and other assets con-

trolled by an economic unit at a given time with those controlled at the beginning of a period, both in terms of money.

(4) An *ex-ante* estimate and an *ex-post* verification of receipts and expenditures, either those in money itself, or those which can be valued in money, which the economic unit is likely to have available for its use during a period if it maintains the money value of the means at its disposal intact.

(5) The orientation of consumption to these data by the utilization of the money available (on the basis of point 4) during the accounting period for the acquisition of the requisite utilities in accordance with the principle of marginal utility.

The continual utilization and procurement of goods, whether through production or exchange, by an economic unit for purposes of its own *consumption* or to procure other goods for *consumption* will be called "budgetary management" (*Haushalt*).[14] Where rationality exists, its basis for an individual or for a group economically oriented in this way is the "budget" (*Haushaltsplan*), which states systematically in what way the needs expected for an accounting period—needs for utilities or for means of procurement to obtain them—can be covered by the anticipated income.

The "income" of a "budgetary unit" is the total of goods valued in money, which, as estimated according to the principle stated above in point (4), has been available during a previous period or on the availability of which the unit is likely to be able to count on the basis of a rational estimate for the present or for a future period. The total estimated value of the goods at the disposal of a budgetary unit which are normally utilized over a longer period, either directly or as a source of income, will be called its "wealth" (*Vermögen*).[15] The possibility of complete monetary budgeting for the budgetary unit is dependent on the possibility that its income and wealth consist either in money or in goods which are at any time subject to exchange for money; that is, which are in the highest degree marketable.

A rational type of management and budgeting of a budgetary unit is possible also where calculation is carried out in terms of physical units, as will be further discussed below. It is true that in that case there is no such thing as "wealth" capable of being expressed in a single sum of money, nor is there a single "income" in the same sense. Calculation is in terms of "holdings" of concrete goods and, where acquisition is limited to peaceful means, of concrete "receipts" from the expenditure of available real goods and services, which will be administered with a view to attaining the optimum provision for the satisfaction of wants. If the wants are strictly given, this involves a comparatively simple problem from the technical point of view so long as the situation does not require a very precise estimate of the comparative utility to be gained from the allocation of the available resources to each of a large number of very heterogeneous modes of use. If the situation is markedly different, even the simple self-sufficient household is faced with problems which are only to a very limited degree subject to a formally exact solution by calculation. The actual solution is usually found partly by the application of purely traditional standards, partly by making very rough estimates, which, however, may be quite adequate where both the wants concerned and the conditions of provision for them are well known and readily comparable. When the "holdings" consist in heterogeneous goods, as must be the case in the absence of exchange, a formally exact calculable comparison of the state of holdings at the beginning and the end of a period, or of the comparison of different possible ways of securing receipts, is possible only for categories of goods which are qualitatively identical. The typical result is that all available goods are treated as forming a totality of physical holdings, and certain quantities of goods are treated as available for consumption, so long as it appears that this will not in the long run diminish the available resources. But every change in the conditions of production—as, for instance, through a bad harvest —or any change in wants necessitates a new allocation, since it alters the scale of relative marginal utilities. Under conditions which are simple and adequately understood, this adaptation may be carried out without much difficulty. Otherwise, it is technically more difficult than if money terms could be used, in which case any change in the price situation in principle influences the satisfaction only of the wants which are marginal on the scale of relative urgency and are met with the last increments of money income.

As accounting in kind becomes completely rational and is emancipated from tradition, the estimation of marginal utilities in terms of the relative urgency of wants encounters grave complications; whereas, if it were carried out in terms of monetary wealth and income, it would be relatively simple. In the latter case the question is merely a "marginal" one, namely whether to apply *more* labor or whether to satisfy or sacrifice, as the case may be, one or more wants, rather than others. For when the problems of budgetary management are expressed in money terms, this is the form the "costs" take [opportunity cost]. But if calculations are in physical terms, it becomes necessary to take into account, besides the scale of urgency of the wants, also (1) the alternative modes of utilization of *all* means of production, including the *entire* amount of labor hitherto expended, which means different (according to the mode of utilization) and variable ratios between want satisfaction and the expenditure of resources, and therefore, (2), requires a consideration of the volume and type of *additional* labor which the householder would have to expend to secure additional receipts and, (3), of the mode of utilization of the material expenditures if the goods to be procured can be of various types. It is one of the most important tasks of economic theory to analyse the various possible ways in which these evaluations can be rationally carried out. It is, on the other hand, a task for economic history to pursue the ways in which the budgetary management in physical terms has been actually worked out in the course of various historical epochs. In general, the following may be said: (1) that the degree of formal rationality has, generally speaking, fallen short of the level which was even empirically possible, to say nothing of the theoretical maximum. As a matter of necessity, the calculations of money-less budgetary management have in the great majority of cases remained strongly bound to tradition. (2) In the larger units of this type, precisely because an expansion and refinement of everyday wants has not taken place, there has been a tendency to employ surpluses for uses of a non-routine nature—above all, for artistic purposes. This is an important basis for the artistic, strongly stylized cultures of epochs with a "natural economy."

1. The category of "wealth" includes more than physical goods. Rather, it covers *all* economic advantages over which the budgetary unit has an assured control, whether that control is due to custom, to the play of interests, to convention, or to law. The "good will" of a profit-making organization, whether it be a medical or legal practice, or a retail shop, belongs to the "wealth" of the owner if it is, for whatever reason, relatively stable since, if it is legally appropriated, it can constitute "property" in the terms of the definition in ch. I:10 above.

2. Monetary calculation can be found without the actual use of money or with its use limited to the settlement of balances which cannot be paid in kind in the goods being exchanged on both sides. Evidence of this is common in the Egyptian and Babylonian records. The use of money accounting as a measure for payments in kind is found in the permission in Hammurabi's Code and in provincial Roman and early Medieval law that a debtor may pay an amount due expressed in money "in whatever form he will be able" (*in quo potuerit*). The establishment of equivalents must in such cases have been carried out on the basis of traditional prices or of prices laid down by decree.

3. Apart from this, the above discussion contains only commonplaces, which are introduced to facilitate the formulation of a precise concept of the rational budgetary unit as distinguished from that of a rational profit-making enterprise—the latter will be discussed presently. It is important to state explicitly that both can take rational forms. The satisfaction of needs is not something more "primitive" than profit-seeking; "wealth" is not necessarily a more primitive category

than capital; "income," than profit. It is, however, true that historically the budgetary unit has been prior and has been the dominant form in most periods of the past.

4. It is indifferent what unit is the bearer of a budgetary management economy. Both the budget of a state and the family budget of a worker fall under the same category.

5. Empirically the administration of budgetary units and profit-making are not mutually exclusive alternatives. The business of a consumers' cooperative, for instance, is normally oriented to the economical provision for wants; but in the form of its activity, it is a "profit-making organization" without being oriented to profit as a substantive end. In the action of an individual, the two elements may be so intimately intertwined, and in the past have typically been so, that only the concluding act—namely, the sale or the consumption of the product—can serve as a basis for interpreting the meaning of the action. This has been particularly true of small peasants. Exchange may well be a part of the process of budgetary management where it is a matter of acquiring consumption goods by exchange and of disposing of surpluses. On the other hand, the budgetary economy of a prince or a landed lord may include profit-making enterprises in the sense of the following discussion. This has been true on a large scale in earlier times. Whole industries have developed out of the heterocephalous and heteronomous auxiliary enterprises which seigneurial landowners, monasteries, princes, etc., have established to exploit the products of their lands and forests. All sorts of profit-making enterprises today are part of the economy of such budgetary units as local authorities or even states. In these cases it is legitimate to include in the "income" of the budgetary units, if they are rationally administered, only the net profits of these enterprises. Conversely, it is possible for profit-making enterprises to establish various types of heteronomous budgetary units under their direction for such purposes as providing subsistence for slaves or wage workers—among them are "welfare" organizations, housing and eating facilities. Net profits in the sense of point (2) of this section are money surpluses after the deduction of all money costs.

6. It has been possible here to give only the most elementary starting points for analysing the significance of economic calculations in kind for general social development.

11. *The Concept and Types of Profit-Making. The Role of Capital*

"Profit-making" (*Erwerben*)[16] is activity which is oriented to opportunities for seeking new powers of control over goods on a single occasion, repeatedly, or continuously. "Profit-making activity" is activity which is oriented at least in part to opportunities of profit-making. Profit-making is "economic" if it is oriented to acquisition by peaceful methods. It may be oriented to the exploitation of market situations. "Means of profit-making" (*Erwerbsmittel*) are those goods and other economic advantages which are used in the interests of economic profit-making. "Exchange for profit" is that which is oriented to market situations in order to increase control over goods rather than to secure means for consumption (budgetary exchange). "Business credit" is that credit which is extended or taken up as a means of increasing control over the requisites of profit-making activity.

There is a form of monetary accounting which is peculiar to rational economic profit-making; namely, "capital accounting." Capital accounting is the valuation and verification of opportunities for profit and of the success of profit-making activity by means of a valuation of the total assets (goods and money) of the enterprise at the beginning of a profit-making venture, and the comparison of this with a similar valuation of the assets still present and newly acquired, at the end of the process; in the case of a profit-making organization operating continuously, the same is done for an accounting period. In either case a balance is drawn between the initial and final states of the assets. "Capital" is the money value of the means of profit-making available to the enterprise at the balancing of the books; "profit" and correspondingly "loss," the difference between the initial balance and that drawn at the conclusion of the period. "Capital risk" is the estimated probability of a loss in this balance. An economic "enterprise" (*Unternehmen*) is autonomous action capable of orientation to capital accounting. This orientation takes place by means of "calculation": ex-ante calculation of the probable risks and chances of profit, ex-post calculation for the verification of the actual profit or loss resulting. "Profitability" means, in the rational case, one of two things: (1) the profit estimated as possible by ex-ante calculations, the attainment of which is made an objective of the entrepreneur's activity; or (2) that which the ex-post calculation shows actually to have been earned in a given period, and which is available for the consumption uses of the entrepreneur without prejudice to his chances of future profitability. In both cases it is usually expressed in ratios—today, percentages—in relation to the capital of the initial balance.

Enterprises based on capital accounting may be oriented to the exploitation of opportunities of acquisition afforded by the market, or they may be oriented toward other chances of acquisition, such as those based on power relations, as in the case of tax farming or the sale of offices.

Each individual operation undertaken by a rational profit-making enterprise is oriented to estimated profitability by means of calculation. In the case of profit-making activities on the market, capital accounting requires: (1) that there exist, subject to estimate beforehand, adequately extensive and assured opportunities for sale of the goods which the enterprise procures; that is, normally, a high degree of marketability; (2) that the means of carrying on the enterprise, such as the potential means of production and the services of labor, are also available in the market at costs which can be estimated with an adequate degree of certainty; and finally, (3) that the technical and legal conditions, to which the process from the acquisition of the means of production to final sale, including transport, manufacturing operations, storage, etc., is subjected, give rise to money costs which in principle are calculable.

The extraordinary importance of the highest possible degree of calculability as the basis for efficient capital accounting will be noted time and again throughout the discussion of the sociological conditions of economic activity. It is far from the case that only economic factors are important to it. On the contrary, it will be shown that the most varied sorts of external and subjective barriers account for the fact that capital accounting has arisen as a basic form of economic calculation only in the Western World.

As distinguished from the calculations appropriate to a budgetary unit, the capital accounting and calculations of the market entrepreneur are oriented not to marginal utility, but to profitability. To be sure, the probabilities of profit are in the last analysis dependent on the income of consumption units and, through this, on the marginal utility structure of the disposable money incomes of the final consumers of consumption goods. As it is usually put, it depends on their "purchasing power" for the relevant commodities. But from a technical point of view, the accounting calculations of a profit-making enterprise and of a consumption unit differ as fundamentally as do the ends of want satisfaction and of profit-making which they serve. For purposes of economic theory, it is the marginal *consumer* who determines the direction of production. In actual fact, given the actual distribution of power, this is only true in a limited sense for the modern situation. To a large degree, even though the consumer has to be in a position to buy, his wants are "awakened" and "directed" by the entrepreneur.

In a market economy every form of rational calculation, especially of capital accounting, is oriented to expectations of prices and their changes as they are determined by the conflicts of interests in bargaining and competition and the resolution of these conflicts. In profitability-accounting this is made particularly clear in that system of bookkeeping which is (up to now) the most highly developed one from a technical point of view, in the so-called double-entry bookkeeping. Through a system of individual accounts the fiction is here created that different depart-ments within an enterprise, or individual accounts, conduct exchange operations with each other, thus permitting a check in the technically most perfect manner on the profitability of each individual step or measure.

Capital accounting in its formally most rational shape thus presupposes the *battle of man with man*. And this in turn involves a further very specific condition. No economic system can directly translate subjective "feelings of need" into effective demand, that is, into demand which needs to be taken into account and satisfied through the production of goods. For whether or not a subjective want can be satisfied depends, on the one hand, on its place in the scale of relative urgency; on the other hand, on the goods which are estimated to be actually or potentially available for its satisfaction. Satisfaction does not take place if the utilities needed for it are applied to other more urgent uses, or if they either cannot be procured at all, or only by such sacrifices of labor and goods that future wants, which are still, from a present point of view, adjudged more urgent, could not be satisfied. This is true of consumption in every kind of economic system, including a communist one.

In an economy which makes use of capital accounting and which is thus characterized by the appropriation of the means of production by individual units, that is by "property" (see ch. I, sec. 10), profitability depends on the prices which the "consumers," according to the marginal utility of money in relation to their income, can and will pay. It is possible to produce profitably only for those consumers who, in these terms, have sufficient income. A need may fail to be satisfied not only when an individual's own demand for other goods takes precedence, but also when the greater purchasing power of others for *all* types of goods prevails. Thus the fact that the battle of man against man on the market is an essential condition for the existence of rational money–accounting further implies that the outcome of the economic process is decisively influenced by the ability of persons who are more plentifully supplied with money to outbid the others, and of those more favorably situated for production to underbid their rivals on the selling side. The latter are particularly those well supplied with goods essential to production or with money. In particular, rational money–accounting presupposes the existence of effective prices and not merely of fictitious prices conventionally employed for technical accounting purposes. This, in turn, presupposes money functioning as an effective medium of exchange, which is in demand as such, not mere tokens used as purely technical accounting units.[17] Thus the orientation of action to money prices and to profit has the following consequences: (1) that the differences in the distribution of money or marketable goods between the individual parties in the market is decisive in determining the direction taken by the production of goods, so far as it is carried on by profit-making enterprises, in that it is only demand made effective through the possession of purchasing power which is and can be satisfied. Further, (2) the question, what type of demand is to be satisfied by the production of goods, becomes in turn dependent on the profitability of production itself. Profitability is indeed *formally* a rational category, but for that very reason it is indifferent with respect to *substantive* postulates unless these can make themselves felt in the market in the form of sufficient purchasing power.

"Capital goods," as distinguished from mere possessions or parts of wealth of a budgetary unit, are all such goods as are administered on the basis of capital accounting. "Capital interest," as distinct from various other possible kinds of interest on loans, is: (1) what is estimated to be the minimum normal profitability of the use of material means of profit-making; (2) the rate of interest at which profit-making enterprises can obtain money or capital goods.

This exposition only repeats generally known things in a somewhat more precise form. For the technical aspects of capital accounting, compare the standard textbooks of accountancy, which are, in part, excellent. E.g. those of Leitner, Schär, etc.

1. The concept of capital has been defined strictly with reference to the individual private enterprise and in accordance with private business-accounting practice, which was, indeed, the most convenient method for present purposes. This usage is much less in conflict with everyday speech than with the usage which in the past was frequently found in the social sciences and which has by no means been consistent. In order to test the usefulness of the present business-accounting term, which is now being increasingly employed in scientific writings again, it is necessary only to ask the following questions: (1) What does it mean when we say that a corporation has a "basic capital" (net worth) of one million pounds? And (2), what when we say that capital is "written down"? What, (3), when corporation law prescribes what objects may be "brought in" as capital and in what manner? The first statement means that only that part of a surplus of assets over liabilities, as shown on the balance-sheet after proper inventory control and verification, which *exceeds* one million pounds can be accounted as "profit" and distributed to the share-holders to do with as they please (or, in the case of a one-man enterprise, that only this excess can be consumed in the household). The second statement concerns a situation where there have been heavy business losses, and means that the distribution of profit need not be postponed until perhaps after many years a surplus exceeding one million pounds has again been accumulated, but that the distribution of "profits" may begin at a lower surplus. But in order to do this, it is necessary to "write down" the capital, and this is the purpose of the operation. Finally, the purpose

of prescriptions as to how basic capital (net worth, or ownership) can be "covered" through the bringing into the company of material assets, and how it may be "written up" or "written down," is to give creditors and purchasers of shares the guarantee that the distribution of profits will be carried out "correctly" in accordance with the rules of rational business accounting, i.e., in such a way that (a) long-run profitability is maintained and, (b), that the security of creditors is not impaired. The rules about "bringing in" are all concerned with the admissability and valuation of objects as paid-in capital. (4) What does it mean when we say that as a result of unprofitability capital "seeks different investments"? Either we are talking about "wealth," for "investment" (*Anlegen*) is a category of the administration of wealth, not of profit-making enterprise. Or else, more rarely, it may mean that real capital *goods* on the one hand have ceased to be such by being sold, for instance as scrap or junk, and on the other have regained that quality in other uses. (5) What is meant when we speak of the "power of capital"? We mean that the possessors of control over the means of production and over economic advantages which can be used as capital *goods* in a profit-making enterprise enjoy, by virtue of this control and of the orientation of economic action to the principles of capitalistic business calculation, a specific position of power in relation to others.

In the earliest beginnings of rational profit-making activity capital appears, though not under this name, and only as a sum of money used in accounting. Thus in the *commenda* relationship various types of goods were entrusted to a travelling merchant to sell in a foreign market and at times for the purchase of other goods wanted for sale at home. The profit or loss was then divided in a particular proportion between the travelling merchant and the entrepreneur who had advanced the capital. For for this to take place it was necessary to value the goods in money; that is, to strike balances at the beginning and the conclusion of the venture. The "capital" of the *commenda* or the *societas maris* was simply this money valuation, which served only the purpose of settling accounts between the parties and no other.

What do we mean by the term "capital market"? We mean that certain "goods," including in particular money, are in demand in order to be used as capital goods, and that there exist profit-making enterprises, especially certain types of "banks," which derive their profit from the business of providing these goods. In the case of so-called "loan capital," which consists in handing over money against a promise to return the same amount at a later time with or without the addition of interest, the term "capital" will be used only if lending is the object of a profit-making enterprise. Otherwise, the term "money loans" will be used. Everyday speech tends to talk about "capital" whenever "interest" is paid, because the latter is usually expressed as a percentage of the basic sum; only because of this calculatory function is the amount of a loan or a deposit called a "capital." It is true, of course, that this was the origin of the term: *capitale* was the principal sum of a loan; the term is said, though it cannot be proved, to derive from the heads counted in a loan of cattle. But this is irrelevant. Even in very early times a loan of real goods was reckoned in money terms, on which basic interest was then calculated, so that already here capital goods and capital accounting are typically related, as has been true in later times. In the case of an ordinary loan, which is made simply as a phase in the administration of budgetary wealth and so far as it is employed for the needs of a budgetary unit, the term "loan capital" will not be used. The same, of course, applies to the recipient of the loan.

The concept of an "enterprise" is in accord with the ordinary usage, except for the fact that the orientation to capital accounting, which is usually taken for granted, is made explicit. This is done in order to emphasize that not every case of search for profit as such constitutes an "enterprise," but only when it is capable of orientation to capital accounting, regardless of whether it is on a large or a small scale. At the same time it is indifferent whether this capital accounting is in fact rationally carried out according to rational principles. Similarly the terms "profit" and "loss" will be used only as applying to enterprises oriented to capital accounting. The money earned without the use of capital by such persons as authors, physicians, lawyers, civil servants, professors, clerks, technicians, or workers, naturally is also "acquisition" (*Erwerb*), but shall here not be called "profit." Even everyday usage would not call it profit. "Profitability" is a concept which is applicable to every discrete act which can be individually evaluated in terms of business accounting technique with respect to profit and loss, such as the employment of a particular worker, the purchase of a new machine, the determination of rest periods in the working day, etc.

It is not expedient in defining the concept of interest on capital to start with contracted interest returns on any type of loan. If somebody helps out a peasant by giving him seed and demands an increment on its return, or if the same is done in the case of money loaned to a household to be returned with interest, we would hardly want to call this a "capitalistic" process. It is possible, where action is rational, for the lender to secure an additional amount because his creditor is in a position to expect benefits from the use of the loan greater than the amount of the interest he pays; when, that is, the situation is seen in terms of what it would be if he had to do without the loan. Similarly, the lender, being aware of the situation, is in a position to exploit it, in that for him the marginal utility of his present control over the goods he lends is exceeded by the marginal utility at the relevant future time of the repayment with the addition of the interest. These are essentially categories of the administration of budgetary units and their wealth, not of capital accounting. Even a person who secures an emergency loan for his urgent personal needs from a "Shylock" is not for purposes of the present discussion said to be paying interest on capital, nor does the lender receive such interest. It is rather a case of return for the loan. The person who makes a business of lending charges *himself* interest on his business capital if he acts rationally, and must consider that he has suffered a "loss" if the returns from loans do not cover this rate of profitability. *This* interest we will consider "interest on capital"; the former is simply "interest." Thus for the present terminological purposes, interest on capital is always that which is calculated *on* capital, not that which is a payment *for* capital. It is always oriented to money valuations, and thus to the sociological fact that disposal over profit-making means, whether through the market or not, is in private hands; that is, appropriated. Without this, capital accounting, and thus calculation of interest, would be unthinkable.

In a rational profit-making enterprise, the interest, which is charged on the books to a capital sum, is the minimum of profitability. It is in terms of whether or not this minimum is reached that a judgment of the advisability of this particular mode of use of capital goods is arrived at. Advisability in this context is naturally conceived from the point of view of profitability. The rate for this minimum profitability is, it is well known, only approximately that which it is possible to obtain by giving credit on the capital market at the time. But nevertheless, the existence of the capital market is the reason why calculations are made on this basis, just as the existence of market exchange is the basis for making entries against the different accounts. It is one of the fundamental phenomena of a capitalistic economy that entrepreneurs are permanently willing to pay interest for loan capital. This phenomenon can only be explained by understanding how it is that the average entrepreneur may hope in the long run to earn a profit, or that entrepreneurs on the average in fact do earn it, over and above what they have to pay as interest on loan capital—that is, under what conditions it is, on the average, rational to exchange 100 at the present against 100 *plus* X in the future.

Economic theory approaches this problem in terms of the relative marginal utilities of goods under present and under future control. So far, so good. But the sociologist would then like to know in what human *actions* this supposed relation is reflected in such a manner that the actors can take the consequences of this differential valuation [of present and future goods], in the form of an "interest rate," as a criterion for their own operations. For it is by no means obvious that this should happen at all times and places. It does indeed happen, as we know, in profit-making economic units. But here the primary cause is the economic power distribution (*Machtlage*) between profit-making enterprises and budgetary units (households), both those consuming the goods offered and those offering certain means of production (mainly labor). Profit-making enterprises will be founded and operated continuously (capitalistically) *only if* it is expected that the minimum rate of interest on capital can be earned. Economic theory—which could, however, also be developed along very different lines—might then very well say that this exploitation of the power distribution (which itself is a consequence of the institution of private property in goods and the means of production) permits it only to this particular class of economic actors to conduct their operations in accordance with the "interest" criterion.

2. The administration of budgetary "wealth" and profit-making enterprises may be outwardly so similar as to appear identical. They are in fact in the analysis only distinguishable in terms of the difference in *meaningful* orientation of the corresponding economic activities. In the one case, it is oriented to maintaining and improving profitability and the market position of the enterprise; in the other, to the security and increase of wealth and income. It is, however, by no means necessary that this fundamental orientation should always, in a concrete case, be turned exclusively in one direction or the other; sometimes, indeed, this is impossible. In cases where the private wealth of an entrepreneur is identical with this business control over the means of production of his firm and his private income is identical with the profit of the business, the two things seem to go entirely hand in hand. But all manner of personal considerations may in such a case cause the entrepreneur to enter upon business policies which, in terms of the rationality of the conduct of enterprise, are irrational. Yet very generally private wealth and control of the business are not identical. Furthermore, such factors as personal indebtedness of the proprietor, his personal demand for a higher present income, division of an inheritance, and the like, often exert what is, in terms of business considerations, a highly irrational influence on the business. Such situations often lead to measures intended to eliminate these influences altogether, as in the incorporation of family businesses.

The tendency to separate the sphere of private affairs from the business is thus not fortuitous. It is a consequence of the fact that, from the point of view of business interest, the interest in maintaining the private wealth of the owner is often irrational, as is his interest in income receipts at any given time from the point of view of the profitability of the enterprise. Considerations relevant to the profitability of a business are also not identical with those governing the private interests of persons who are related to it as workers or as consumers. Conversely, the interests growing out of the private fortunes and income of persons or organizations having powers of control over an enterprise do not necessarily lie in the same direction as the long-run considerations of optimizing its profitability and its market power position. This is definitely, even especially, also true when a profit-making enterprise is controlled by a producers' co-operative association. The objective interests of rational management of a business enterprise and the personal interest of the individuals who control it are by no means identical and are often opposed. This fact implies the separation as a matter of principle of the budgetary unit and the enterprise, even where both, with respect to powers of control and the objects controlled, are identical.

The sharp distinction between the budgetary unit and the profit-making enterprise should also be clearly brought out in the terminology. The purchase of securities on the part of a private investor who wishes to consume the proceeds is not a "*capital*-investment," but a "*wealth*-investment." A money loan made by a private individual for obtaining the interest is, when regarded from the standpoint of the lender, entirely different from one made by a bank to the same borrower. On the other hand, a loan made to a consumer and one to an entrepreneur for business purposes are quite different from the point of view of the borrower. The bank is investing *capital* and the entrepreneur is borrowing *capital*; but in the first case, it may be for the borrower a matter simply of borrowing for purposes of budgetary management; in the second it may be, for the lender, a case of investment of private *wealth*. This distinction between private wealth and capital, between the budgetary unit and the profit-making enterprise, is of far-reaching importance. In particular, without it it is impossible to understand the economic development of the ancient world and the limitations on the development of the capitalism of those times. (The well-known articles of Rodbertus are, in spite of their errors and incompleteness, still important in this context, but should be supplemented by the excellent discussion of Karl Bücher.)[18]

3. By no means all profit-making enterprises with capital accounting are doubly oriented to the market in that they both purchase means of production on the market and sell their product or final services there. Tax farming and all sorts of financial operations have been carried on with capital accounting, but without selling any products. The very important consequences of this will be discussed later. It is a case of capitalistic profit-making which is not oriented to the market.

4. For reasons of·convenience, acquisitive activity (*Erwerbstätigkeit*) and profit-making enterprise (*Erwerbsbetrieb*) have been distinguished. Anyone is engaged in acquisitive activity so far as he seeks, among other things, in given ways to acquire goods—money or others—which he does not yet possess. This includes the civil servant and the worker, no less than the entrepreneur. But the term "profit-making enterprise" will be confined to those types of acquisitive activity which are continually oriented to market advantages, using goods as means to secure profit, either (a) through the production and sale of goods in demand, or (b) through the offer of services in demand in exchange for money, be it through free exchange or through the exploitation of appropriated advantages, as has been pointed out above under (3). The person who is a mere rentier or investor of private wealth is, in the present terminology, not engaged in profit-making, no matter how rationally he administers his resources.

5. It goes without saying that in terms of *economic* theory the direction in which goods can be profitably produced by profit-making enterprises is determined by the marginal utilities for the last consumers in conjunction with the latter's incomes. But from a *sociological* point of view it should not be forgotten that, to a large extent, in a capitalistic economy (a) new wants are created and others allowed to disappear and (b) capitalistic enterprises, through their aggressive advertising policies,

exercise an important influence on the demand functions of consumers. Indeed, these are essential traits of a capitalistic economy. It is true that this applies primarily to wants which are not of the highest degree of necessity, but even types of food provision and housing are importantly determined by the producers in a capitalistic economy.

12. *Calculations in Kind*

Calculations in kind can occur in the most varied form. We speak of a "money economy," meaning an economy where the use of money is typical and where action is typically oriented to market situations in terms of money prices. The term "natural economy" (*Naturalwirtschaft*), on the other hand, means an economy where money is not used. The different economic systems known to history can be classified according to the degree to which they approximate the one or the other.

The concept "natural economy" is not, however, very definite, since it can cover systems with widely varying structures. It may mean (a) an economy where no exchange at all takes place or (b) one where exchange is only by barter, and thus money is not used as a medium of exchange. The first type may be an individual economic unit organized on a completely communistic basis, or with some determinate distribution of rights of participation. In both cases, there would be a complete lack of autonomy or autocephaly of the component parts. This may be called a "closed household economy." Or, secondly, it may be a combination of otherwise autonomous and autocephalous individual units, all of which, however, are obligated to make contributions in kind to a central organization which exists for the exercise of authority or as a communal institution. This is an "economy based on payments in kind" (*oikos* economy, "liturgically" organized political group). In both cases, so far as the pure type is conformed to, there is only calculation in kind.

In the second case, type (b), where exchange is involved, there may be natural economies where exchange is only by barter without either the use of money or calculation in money terms. Or there may be economies where there is exchange in kind, but where calculation is occasionally or even typically carried out in money terms. This was typical of the Orient in ancient times and has been common everywhere.

For the purposes of analysing calculation in kind, it is only the cases of type (a) which are of interest, where the unit is either completely self-sufficient, or the liturgies are produced in rationally organized permanent units, such as would be inevitable in attempting to employ modern technology in a completely "socialized" economy.

Calculation in kind is in its essence oriented to consumption, the satisfaction of wants. It is, of course, quite possible to have something analogous to profit-making on this basis. This may occur (a) in that, without resort to exchange, available material means of production and labor are systematically applied to the production and transportation of goods on the basis of calculations, according to which the state of want satisfaction thus attained is compared with the state which would exist without these measures or if the resources were used in another way, and thus a judgment as to the most advantageous procedure is arrived at. Or (b) in a barter economy, goods may be disposed of and acquired by exchange, perhaps in systematically repeated barters, though strictly without the use of money. Such action would be systematically oriented to securing a supply of goods which, as compared with the state which would exist without these measures, is judged to establish a more adequate provision for the needs of the unit. It is, in such cases, only when quantities of goods which are qualitatively similar are compared that it is possible to use numerical terms unambiguously and without a wholly subjective valuation. It is possible, of course, to set up a system of in-kind wages consisting of typical bundles of consumer goods (*Konsum-Deputate*), such as were the in-kind salaries and benefices particularly of the ancient Orient (where they even became objects of exchange transactions, similar to our government bonds). In the case of certain very homogenous commodities, such as the grain of the Nile valley, a system of storage and trade purely in terms of paper claims to certain quantities of the commodity was of course technically just as possible as it is with silver bars under the conditions of *banco*-currencies.[19] What is more important, it is in that case also possible to express the technical efficiency of a process of production in numerical terms and thereby compare it with other types of technical processes. This may be done, if the final product is the same, by comparing the relative requirements of different processes in both the quantity and the type of means of production. Or, where the means of production are the same, the different products which result from different production processes may be compared. It is often, though by no means always, possible in this way to secure numerical comparisons for the purposes of important, though sectorally restricted, problems. But the more difficult problems of calculation begin when it becomes a question of comparing different *kinds* of means of production, their different possible modes of use, and qualitatively different final products.

Every capitalistic enterprise is, to be sure, continually concerned with calculations in kind. For instance, given a certain type of loom and a certain quality of yarn, it is a question of ascertaining, given certain other relevant data such as the efficiency of machines, the humidity of the air, the rate of consumption of coal, lubricating oil, etc., what will be the product per hour per worker and thus the amount of the product which is attributable to any individual worker for each unit of time. For industries with typical waste products or by-products, this can be determined without any use of money accounting and is in fact so determined. Similarly, under given conditions, it is possible to work out, in technical terms without the use of money, the normally expected annual consumption of raw materials by the enterprise according to its technical production capacity, the depreciation period for buildings and machinery, the typical loss by spoiling or other forms of waste. But the comparison of different kinds of processes of production, with the use of different kinds of raw materials and different ways of treating them, is carried out today by making a calculation of comparative profitability in terms of money costs. For accounting in kind, on the other hand, there are formidable problems involved here which are incapable of objective solution. Though it does not at first sight seem to be necessary, a modern enterprise tends to employ money terms in its capital calculations even where such difficulties do not arise. But this is not entirely fortuitous. In the case of depreciation write-offs, for example, money accounting is used because this is the method of assuring the conditions of future productivity of the business which combines the greatest degree of certainty with the greatest flexibility in relation to changing circumstances; with any storing of real stocks of materials or any other mode of provision in kind such flexibility would be irrationally and severely impeded. It is difficult to see, without money accounting, how "reserves" could be built up without being specified in detail. Further, an enterprise is always faced with the question as to whether any of its parts is operating irrationally: that is, unprofitably, and if so, why. It is a question of determining which components of its real physical expenditures (that is, of the "costs" in terms of capital accounting) could be saved and, above all, could more rationally be used elsewhere. This can be determined with relative ease in an ex-post calculation of the relation between accounting "costs" and "receipts" in money terms, the former including in particular the interest charge allocated to that account. But it is exceedingly difficult to do this entirely in terms of an in-kind calculation, and indeed it can be accomplished at all only in very simple cases. This, one may believe, is not a matter of circumstances which could be overcome by technical improvements in the methods of calculation, but of fundamental limitations, which make really exact accounting in terms of calculations in kind impossible in principle.

It is true this might be disputed, though naturally not with arguments drawn from the Taylor system and from the possibility of achieving improvements in efficiency by employing a system of bonus points without the use of money. The essential question is that of how it is possible to discover *at what point* in the organization it would be profitable to employ such measures because there existed at that point certain elements of irrationality. It is in finding out these points that accounting in kind encounters difficulties which an ex-post calculation in money terms does not have to contend with. The fundamental limitations of accounting in kind as the *basis* of calculation in enterprises—of a type which would include the heterocephalous and heteronomous units of production in a planned economy—are to be found in the problem of imputation, which in such a system cannot take the simple form of an ex-post calculation of profit or loss on the books, but rather that very controversial form which it has in the theory of marginal utility. In order to make possible a rational utilization of the means of production, a system of in-kind accounting would have to determine "value"-indicators of some kind for the individual capital goods which could take over the role of the "prices" used in book valuation in modern business accounting. But it is not at all clear how such indicators could be established and, in particular, verified; whether, for instance, they should vary from one production unit to the next (on the basis of economic location), or whether they should be uniform for the entire economy, on the basis of "social utility," that is, of (present *and future*) consumption requirements?

Nothing is gained by assuming that, if only the problem of a non-monetary economy were seriously enough attacked, a suitable accounting method would be discovered or invented. The problem is fundamental to any kind of complete socialization. We cannot speak of a *rational* "planned economy" so long as in this decisive respect we have no instrument for elaborating a rational "plan."

The difficulties of accounting in kind become more marked when the question is considered of whether, from the point of view of efficiently satisfying the wants of a given group of persons, it is rational to locate a certain enterprise with a given productive function at one or an alternative site. The same difficulties arise if we want to determine whether a given economic unit, from the point of view of the most rational use of the labor and raw materials available to it, would do better to obtain certain products by exchange with other units or by producing them itself. It is true that the criteria for the location of industries consist of "natural" considerations and its simplest data are capable of formulation in non-monetary terms. (On this point, see Alfred Weber in the *Grundriss der Sozialökonomik*, Part IV [English ed.: *The Theory of Location*, trsl. C. J. Friedrich, Chicago 1929]). Nevertheless, the concrete determina-

tion of whether, according to the relevant circumstances of its particular
location, a production unit with a given set of output possibilities or one
with a different set would be rational, is in terms of calculation in kind
capable of solution only in terms of very crude estimates, apart from the
few cases where the solution is given by some natural peculiarity, such
as a unique source of a raw material. But in spite of the numerous un-
knowns which may be present, the problem in money terms is always
capable of a determinate solution in principle.

Finally, there is the independent problem of the comparative importance of the satisfaction of different wants, provision for which is,
under the given conditions, equally feasible. In the last analysis, this
problem is, in at least some of its implications, involved in every particular case of the calculations of a productive unit. Under conditions of
money accounting, it has a decisive influence on profitability and thereby
on the direction of production of profit-making enterprises. But where
calculation is only in kind, it is in principle soluble only in one of two
ways: by adherence to tradition or by an arbitary dictatorial regulation
which, on whatever basis, lays down the pattern of consumption *and*
enforces obedience. Even when that is resorted to, it still remains a fact
that the problem of imputation of the part contributed to the total output
of an economic unit by the different factors of production and by different executive decisions is not capable of the kind of solution which is
at present attained by calculations of profitability in terms of money. It
is precisely the process of provision for mass demand by mass production
so typical of the present day which would encounter the greatest difficulties.

     1. The problems of accounting in kind have been raised in a par-
ticularly penetrating form by Dr. Otto Neurath in his numerous works[20]
apropos of the tendencies to "socialization" in recent years. The problem
is a central one in any discussion of *complete* socialization; that is, that
which would lead to the disappearance of effective prices. It may, however, be explicitly noted that the fact that it is incapable of rational solution serves only to point out some of the "costs," including economic
ones, which would have to be incurred for the sake of enacting this type
of socialism; however, this does not touch the question of the justification of such a program, so far as it does not rest on *technical* considerations, but, like most such movements, on *ethical* postulates or other forms
of absolute value. A "refutation" of these is beyond the scope of any
science. From a purely technical point of view, however, the possibility
must be considered that the maintenance of a certain density of population within a given area may be possible only on the basis of accurate
calculation. Insofar as this is true, a limit to the possible degree of socialization would be set by the necessity of maintaining a system of
effective prices. That cannot, however, be considered here. It may be

noted, though, that the distinction between "socialism" and "social re-form," if there is any such, should be made in these terms.

2. It is naturally entirely correct that mere money accounts, whether they refer to single enterprises, to any number of them, or to all enterprises—indeed, even the most complete statistical information about the movement of goods in money terms—tell us nothing whatever about the nature of the real provision of a given group with what it needs; namely, real articles of consumption. Furthermore, the much discussed estimates of "national wealth" in money terms are only to be taken seriously so far as they serve fiscal ends; that is, as they determine taxable wealth. This stricture does not apply, of course, in any similar degree to income statistics in money terms, provided the prices of goods in money are known. But even then there is no possibility of checking real welfare in terms of substantive rationality. It is further true, as has been convincingly shown for the case of extensive farming in the Roman *campagna* by Sismondi and Sombart,[21] that satisfactory profitability, which in the *campagna* existed for all participants, in numerous cases has nothing to do with an optimum use of the available productive resources for the provision of consumers' goods for a given population. The mode of appropriation, especially that of land (this much must be conceded to Franz Oppenheimer),[22] leads to a system of claims to rent and earnings of various kinds which may well obstruct permanently the development of a technical optimum in the exploitation of productive resources. This is, however, very far from being a peculiarity of capitalistic economies. In particular, the much-discussed limitation of production in the interest of profitability was very highly developed in the economy of the Middle Ages, and the modern labor movement is acquiring a position of power which may lead to similar consequences. But there is no doubt that this phenomenon exists in the modern capitalistic economy.

The existence of statistics (or estimates) of money flows has not, as some writers have tended to give the impression, hindered the development of statistics of physical quantities. This is true, however much fault we may find with the available statistics when measured by ideal standards. Probably more than nine-tenths of economic statistics are not in terms of money, but of physical quantities.

The work of a whole generation of economists has been concentrated almost entirely on a critique of the orientation of economic action to profitability with respect to its effects on the provision of the population with real goods. All the work of the so-called "socialists of the lectern" (*Kathedersozialisten*) was, in the last analysis, quite consciously concerned with this. They have, however, employed as a standard of judgment a mode of social reform oriented to social welfare, implying (in contrast to a moneyless economy) the continued existence of effective prices, rather than full socialization, as the only solution possible either at the present or at any time in an economy at the stage of mass production. It is, of course, quite possible to consider this merely a half-measure, but it is not in itself a nonsensical attitude. It is true that the problems of a non-monetary economy, and especially of the possibility of rational action in terms of calculations in kind, have not received much attention. Indeed most of the attention they have received has been historical and not concerned with present problems. But the World War, like every war in history, has brought these problems emphatically to the fore in the form of the problems of war economy and the post-war adjustment. It is, indeed, one of the merits of Otto Neurath to have produced an analysis of just these problems, which, however much it is open to criticism both in principle and in detail, was one of the first and was very penetrating. That "the profession" has taken little notice of his work is not surprising because until now he has given us only stimulating suggestions, which are, however, so very broad that it is difficult to use them as a basis of intensive analysis. The problem only begins at the point where his public pronouncements up to date have left off.

3. It is only with the greatest caution that the results and methods of war economy can be used as a basis for criticizing the substantive rationality of forms of economic organization. In wartime the whole economy is oriented to what is in principle a single clear goal, and the authorities are in a position to make use of powers which would generally not be tolerated in peace except in cases where the subjects are "slaves" of an authoritarian state. Furthermore, it is an economy with an inherent attitude of "going for broke": the overwhelming urgency of the immediate end overshadows almost all concern for the post-war economy. Only on the engineering level does preciseness of calculations exist, but economic constraints on the consumption, especially of labor and of all materials not directly threatened with exhaustion, are only of the roughest nature. Hence calculation has predominantly, though not exclusively, a technical character. So far as it has a genuinely economic character—that is, so far as it takes account of alternative ends and not only of means for a given end—it is restricted to what is, from the standpoint of careful monetary calculation, a relatively primitive level of calculation on the marginal utility principle. In type this belongs to the class of budgetary calculations, and it is not meant to guarantee long-run rationality for the chosen allocation of labor and the means of production. Hence, however illuminating the experience of war-time and post-war adjustments is for the analysis of the possible range of variation of economic forms, it is unwise to draw conclusions from the type of in-kind accounting associated with it for its suitability in a peacetime economy with its long-run concerns.

It may be freely conceded: (1) That it is necessary also in money accounting to make arbitrary assumptions in connection with means of production which have no market price. This is particularly common in the case of agricultural accounting; (2) that to a less extent something similar is true of the allocation of overhead costs among the different branches of a complicated enterprise; (3) that the formation of cartel agreements, no matter how rational their basis in relation to the market situation may be, immediately diminishes the stimulus to accurate calculation on the basis of capital accounting, because calculation declines in the absence of an enforced objective need for it. If calculation were in kind, however, the situation described under (1) would be universal;

any type of accurate allocation of overhead costs, which, however roughly, is now somehow achieved in money terms, would become impossible; and, finally, every stimulus to exact calculation would be eliminated and would have to be created anew by artificial means, the effectiveness of which would be questionable.

It has been suggested that the huge clerical staff of the private sector of the economy, which is actually to a large extent concerned with calculations, should be turned into a universal Statistical Office which would have the function of replacing the monetary business accounting of the present system with a statistical accounting in kind. This idea not only fails to take account of the fundamentally different motives underlying "statistics" and "business accounting," it also fails to distinguish their fundamentally different functions. They differ just like the bureaucrat differs from the entrepreneur.

4. Both calculation in kind and in money are rational techniques. They do not, however, by any means exhaust the totality of economic action. There also exist types of action which, though actually oriented to economic considerations, do not know calculation. Economic action may be traditionally oriented or may be affectually determined. In its more primitive aspects, the search for food on the part of human beings is closely related to that of animals, dominated as the latter is by instinct. Economically oriented action dominated by a religious faith, by war-like passions, or by attitudes of personal loyalty and similar modes of orientation, is likely to have a very low level of rational calculation, even though the motives are fully self-conscious. Haggling is excluded "between brothers," whether they be brothers in kinship, in a guild, or in a religious group. It is not usual to be calculating within a family, a group of comrades, or of disciples. At most, in cases of necessity, a rough sort of rationing is resorted to, which is a very modest beginning of calculation. In Part Two, ch. IV, the process by which calculation gradually penetrates into the earlier form of family communism will be taken up. Everywhere it has been money which was the propagator of calculation. This explains the fact that calculation in kind has remained on an even lower technical level than the actual nature of its problems might have necessitated; hence in this respect Otto Neurath appears to be right.

During the printing of this work an essay by Ludwig von Mises dealing with these problems came out. See his "Die Wirtschaftsrechnung im sozialistischen Gemeinwesen," *Archiv für Sozialwissenschaft*, vol. 47 (1920).[23]

1 3. Substantive Conditions of Formal Rationality in a Money Economy

It is thus clear that the formal rationality of money calculation is dependent on certain quite specific substantive conditions. Those which are of a particular sociological importance for present purposes are the

following: (1) Market struggle of economic units which are at least relatively autonomous. Money prices are the product of conflicts of interest
and of compromises; they thus result from power constellations. Money
is not a mere "voucher for unspecified utilities," which could be altered
at will without any fundamental effect on the character of the price system as a struggle of man against man. "Money" is, rather, primarily a
weapon in this struggle, and prices are expressions of the struggle; they
are instruments of calculation only as estimated quantifications of relative
chances in this struggle of interests. (2) Money accounting attains the
highest level of rationality, as an instrument of calculatory orientation of
economic action, when it is applied in the form of capital accounting.
The substantive precondition here is a thorough market freedom, that is,
the absence of monopolies, both of the imposed and economically irrational and of the voluntary and economically rational (i.e., market-
oriented) varieties. The competitive struggle for customers, which is
associated with this state, gives rise to a great volume of expenditures,
especially with regard to the organization of sales and advertising, which
in the absence of competition—in a planned economy or under complete
monopolization—would not have to be incurred. Strict capital accounting is further associated with the social phenomena of "shop discipline"
and appropriation of the means of production, and that means: with the
existence of a "system of domination" (*Herrschaftsverhältniss*). (3) It is
not "demand" (wants) as such, but "effective demand" for utilities which,
in a substantive respect, regulates the production of goods by profit-
making enterprises through the intermediary of capital accounting.
What is to be produced is thus determined, given the distribution of
wealth, by the structure of marginal utilities in the income group which
has both the inclination and the resources to purchase a given utility.
In combination with the complete indifference of even the formally
most perfect rationality of capital accounting towards all substantive
postulates, an indifference which is absolute if the market is perfectly
free, the above statement permits us to see the ultimate limitation, inherent in its very structure, of the rationality of monetary economic
calculation. It is, after all, of a purely formal character. Formal and
substantive rationality, no matter by what standard the latter is measured,
are always in principle separate things, no matter that in many (and
under certain very artificial assumptions even in all) cases they may
coincide empirically. For the formal rationality of money accounting does
not reveal anything about the actual distribution of goods. This must
always be considered separately. Yet, if the standard used is that of the
provision of a certain minimum of subsistence for the maximum size of
population, the experience of the last few decades would seem to show

that formal and substantive rationality coincide to a relatively high degree. The reasons lie in the nature of the incentives which are set into motion by the type of economically oriented social action which alone is adequate to money calculations. But it nevertheless holds true under all circumstances that formal rationality itself does not tell us anything about real want satisfaction unless it is combined with an analysis of the distribution of income.[24]

14. Market Economies and Planned Economies

Want satisfaction will be said to take place through a "market economy" so far as it results from action oriented to advantages in exchange on the basis of self-interest and where co-operation takes place only through the exchange process. It results, on the other hand, from a "planned economy" so far as economic action is oriented systematically to an established substantive order, whether agreed or imposed, which is valid within an organization.

Want satisfaction through a market economy normally, and in proportion to the degree of rationality, presupposes money calculation. Where capital accounting is used it presupposes the economic separation of the budgetary unit (household) and the enterprise. Want satisfaction by means of a planned economy is dependent, in ways which vary in kind and degree according to its extensiveness, on calculation in kind as the ultimate basis of the *substantive* orientation of economic action. Formally, however, the action of the producing individual is oriented to the instructions of an administrative staff, the existence of which is indispensable. In a market economy the individual units are autocephalous and their action is autonomously oriented. In the administration of budgetary units (households), the basis of orientation is the marginal utility of money holdings and of anticipated money income; in the case of intermittent entrepreneurship (*Gelegenheitserwerben*), the probabilities of market gain, and in the case of profit-making enterprises, capital accounting are the basis of orientation. In a planned economy, all economic action, so far as "planning" is really carried through, is oriented heteronomously and in a strictly "budgetary" manner, to rules which enjoin certain modes of action and forbid others, and which establish a system of rewards and punishments. When, in a planned economy, the prospect of additional individual income is used as a means of stimulating self-interest, the type and direction of the action thus rewarded is substantively heteronomously determined. It is possible for the same thing to be true of a market economy, though in a formally voluntary way. This is true wherever the unequal distribution of wealth, and particularly of capital goods, forces the non-owning group to comply with the authority of others in order to obtain any return at all for the utilities they can offer on the market—either with the authority of a wealthy householder, or with the decisions, oriented to capital accounting, of the owners of capital or of their agents. In a purely capitalistic organization of production, this is the fate of the entire working class.

The following are decisive as elements of the motivation of economic activity under the conditions of a market economy: (1) For those without substantial property: (a) the fact that they run the risk of going entirely without provisions, both for themselves and for those personal dependents, such as children, wives, sometimes parents, whom the individual typically maintains on his own account; (b) that, in varying degrees subjectively they value economically productive work as a mode of life. (2) For those who enjoy a privileged position by virtue of wealth or the education which is usually in turn dependent on wealth: (a) opportunities for large income from profitable undertakings; (b) ambition; (c) the valuation as a "calling" of types of work enjoying high prestige, such as intellectual work, artistic performance, and work involving high technical competence. (3) For those sharing in the fortunes of profit-making enterprises: (a) the risk to the individual's own capital, and his own opportunities for profit, combined with (b) the valuation of rational acquisitive activity as a "calling." The latter may be significant as a proof of the individual's own achievement or as a symbol and a means of autonomous control over the individuals subject to his authority, or of control over economic advantages which are culturally or materially important to an indefinite plurality of persons—in a word, power.

A planned economy oriented to want satisfaction must, in proportion as it is radically carried through, weaken the incentive to labor so far as the risk of lack of support is involved. For it would, at least so far as there is a rational system of provision for wants, be impossible to allow a worker's dependents to suffer the full consequences of his lack of efficiency in production. Furthermore, autonomy in the direction of organized productive units would have to be greatly reduced or, in the extreme case, eliminated. Hence it would be impossible to retain capital risk and proof of merit by a formally autonomous achievement. The same would be true of autonomous power over other individuals and important features of their economic situation. Along with opportunities for special material rewards, a planned economy may have command over certain ideal motives of what is in the broadest sense an altruistic type, which can be used to stimulate a level of achievement in economic production comparable to that which autonomous orientation to opportunities for profit, by producing for the satisfaction of effective demand, has empirically been able to achieve in a market economy. Where a planned economy is radically carried out, it must further accept the inevitable reduction in formal, calculatory rationality which would result from the elimination of money and capital accounting. Substantive and formal (in the sense of exact *calculation*) rationality are, it should be stated again, after all largely distinct problems. This fundamental and, in the last analysis, unavoidable element of irrationality in economic systems is one of the important sources of all "social" problems, and above all, of the problems of socialism.

The following remarks apply to both secs. 13 and 14.

1. The above exposition obviously formulates only things which are generally known, in a somewhat more precise form. The market economy is by far the most important case of typical widespread social action predominantly oriented to "self-interest." The process by which this type of action results in the satisfaction of wants is the subject matter of economic theory, knowledge of which in general terms is here presupposed. The use of the term "planned economy" (*Planwirtschaft*) naturally does not imply acceptance of the well-known proposals of the former German Minister of Economic Affairs.[25] The term has been chosen because, while it does not do violence to general usage, it has, since it was used officially, been widely accepted. This fact makes it preferable to the term used by Otto Neurath, "administered economy" (*Verwaltungswirtschaft*), which would otherwise be suitable.

2. So far as it is oriented to profit-making, the economic activity of organizations, or that regulated by organizations, is not included in the concept of "planned economy," whether the organization be a guild, a cartel, or a trust. "Planned economy" includes the economic activity of organizations only so far as it is oriented to the provision for needs. Any system of economic activity oriented to profit-making, no matter how strictly it is regulated or how stringently controlled by an administrative staff, presupposes effective prices, and thus capital accounting as a basis of action; this includes the limiting case of total cartellization, in which prices would be determined by negotiation between the cartel groups and by negotiated wage agreements with labor organizations. In spite of the identity of their objectives, *complete* socialization in the sense of a planned economy administered purely as a budgetary unit and *partial* socialization of various branches of production with the retention of capital accounting are technically examples of quite different types. A preliminary step in the direction of the budgetary planned economy is to be found wherever consumption is rationed or wherever measures are taken to effect the direct "in-kind" distribution of goods. A planned direction of *production*, whether it is undertaken by voluntary or authoritatively imposed cartels, or by agencies of the government, is primarily concerned with a rational organization of the use of means of production and labor resources and cannot, on its own terms, do without prices—

or at least, not yet. It is thus by no means fortuitous that the "rationing-type" of socialism gets along quite well with the "works councils" (*Betriebsräte*) type of socialism which, against the will of its leading personalities (who are in favor of a rationalistic solution), must pursue the income interests of the workers.

3. It will not be possible to enter at this point into a detailed discussion of the formation of such economic organizations as cartels, corporations or guilds. Their general tendency is orientation to the regulation or monopolistic exploitation of opportunities for profit. They may arise by voluntary agreement, but are more generally imposed even where formally voluntary. Compare in the most general terms, chap. I, sec. 10, and also the discussion of the appropriation of economic advantages, sec. 19ff. of the present chapter.

The conflict between two rival forms of socialism has not died down since the publication of Marx's *Misère de la Philosophie*. On the one hand, there is the type, which includes especially the Marxists, which is evolutionary and oriented to the problem of production; on the other, the type which takes the problem of distribution as its starting point and advocates a rational planned economy. The latter is again today coming to be called "communism." The conflict within the Russian socialist movement, especially as exemplified in the passionate disputes between Plekhanov and Lenin, was, after all, also concerned with this issue. While the internal divisions of present-day socialism are very largely concerned with competition for leadership and for "benefices," along with these issues goes the same set of problems. In particular, the economic experience of the War has given impetus to the idea of a planned economy, but at the same time to the development of interests in appropriation.

The question of whether a planned economy, in whatever meaning or extent, *should* be introduced, is naturally not in this form a scientific problem. On scientific grounds it is possible only to inquire, what would be the probable results of any given specific proposal, and thus what consequences would have to be accepted if the attempt were made. Honesty requires that all parties should admit that, while some of the factors are known, many of those which would be important are only very partially understood. In the present discussion, it is not possible to enter into the details of the problem in such a way as to arrive at concretely conclusive results. The points which will be taken up can be dealt with only in a fragmentary way in connection with forms of organizations, particularly the state. It was possible above only to introduce an unavoidably brief discussion of the most elementary aspects of the technical problem. The phenomenon of a *regulated* market economy has, for the reasons noted above, not yet been taken up.

4. The organization of economic activity on the basis of a market economy presupposes the appropriation of the material sources of utilities on the one hand, and market freedom on the other. The effectiveness of market freedom increases with the degree to which these sources of utility, particularly the means of transport and production, are ap-

propriated. For, the higher the degree of marketability, the more will economic action be oriented to market situations. But the effectiveness of market freedom also increases with the degree to which appropriation is limited to *material* sources of utility. Every case of the appropriation of human beings through slavery or serfdom, or of economic advantages through market monopolies, restricts the range of human action which can be market-oriented. Fichte, in his *Der geschlossene Handelsstaat* (Tübingen, 1800), was right in treating this limitation of the concept of "property" to material goods, along with the increased autonomy of control over the objects which do fall under this concept, as characteristic of the modern market-oriented system. All parties to market relations have had an interest in this expansion of property rights because it increased the area within which they could orient their action to the opportunities of profit offered by the market situation. The development of this type of property is hence attributable to their influence.

5. For reasons of accuracy of expression, we have avoided the term "communal economy" (*Gemeinwirtschaft*), which others have frequently used [in the German discussions of 1918–1920], because it pretends the existence of a "common interest" or of a "feeling of community" (*Gemeinschaftsgefühl*) as the normal thing, which conceptually is not required: the economic organization of a feudal lord exacting *corvée* labor or that of rulers like the Pharaohs of the New Kingdom belongs to the same category as a family household. Both are equally to be distinguished from a market economy.

6. For the purposes of the definition of a "market economy," it is indifferent whether or to what extent economic action is "capitalistic," that is, is oriented to capital accounting. This applies also to the normal case of a market economy, that in which the satisfaction of wants is effected in a monetary economy. It would be a mistake to assume that the development of capitalistic enterprises must occur proportionally to the growth of want satisfaction in the monetary economy, and an even larger mistake to believe that this development must take the form it has assumed in the Western world. In fact, the contrary is true. The extension of money economy might well go hand in hand with the increasing monopolization of the larger sources of profit by the *oikos* economy of a prince. Ptolemaic Egypt is an outstanding example. According to the evidence of the accounts which have survived, it was a highly developed money economy, but its accounting remained budgetary accounting and did not develop into capital accounting. It is also possible that with the extension of a money economy could go a process of "feudalization" (*Verpfründung*) of fiscal advantages resulting in a traditionalistic stabilization of the economic system. This happened in China, as will have to be shown elsewhere. Finally, the capitalistic utilization of money resources could take place through investment in sources of potential profit which were not oriented to opportunities of exchange in a free commodity market and thus not to the production of goods. For reasons which will be discussed below, this has been almost universally true outside the area of the modern Western economic order.

15. Types of Economic Division of Labor

Every type of social action in a group which is oriented to economic considerations and every associative relationship of economic significance involves to some degree a particular mode of division and organization of human services in the interest of production. A mere glance at the facts of economic action reveals that different persons perform different types of work and that these are combined in the service of common ends, with each other and with the non-human means of production, in the most varied ways. The complexity of these phenomena is extreme, but yet it is possible to distinguish a few types.

Human services for economic purposes may be distinguished as (a) "managerial," or (b) oriented to the instructions of a managerial agency. The latter type will be called "labor" for purposes of the following discussion.

> It goes without saying that managerial activity constitutes "labor" in the most definite sense if labor is taken to mean the expenditure of time and effort as such. The use of the term "labor" in the sense defined above, as something distinct from managerial activity, has, however, come to be generally accepted for social reasons, and this usage will be followed in the present discussion. For more general purposes, the terms "services" or "work" (*Leistungen*) will be used.

Within a social group the ways in which labor or other work may be carried on may be classified in the following way: (1) *technically,* according to the way in which the services of a plurality of co-operating individuals are divided up and combined, with each other and with the non-human means of production, to carry out the technical procedures of production; (2) *socially.* In the first place, classification may be according to whether particular services do or do not fall within the jurisdiction of autocephalous and autonomous economic units, and according to the economic character of these units. Closely connected with this is classification according to the modes and extent to which the various services, the material means of production, and the opportunities for economic profit used as sources of profit or as means of acquisition, are or are not appropriated. These factors determine the mode of occupational differentiation, a social phenomenon, and the organization of the market, an economic phenomenon; (3) finally, an *economic* criterion: for every case of combination of services with each other and with material means of production, of division among different types of economic units, and of mode of appropriation, one must ask separately whether they are used in a context of budgetary administration or of profit-making enterprise.

> For this and the following section, compare the authoritative discussion by Karl Bücher in his article "Gewerbe" in the *Handwörterbuch*

der Staatwissenschaften and in his book, *Die Entstehung der Volkswirt-schaft.*[26] These are fundamentally important works. Both the terminology and the classification here presented have departed from Bücher's only where it seemed necessary for reasons of convenience. There is little reason to cite other references, for the following exposition does not pretend to achieve new results, but only to provide a scheme of analysis useful for the purposes of this work.

1. It should be emphatically stated that the present discussion is concerned only with a brief summary of the *sociological* aspects of these phenomena, so far as they are relevant to its context. The *economic* aspect is included only insofar as it is expressed in what are formally sociological categories. The presentation would be economic in the *sub-stantive* sense only if the price and market conditions, which so far have been dealt with only on the theoretical level, were brought in. But these substantive aspects of the general problem could be worked into such a summary introduction only in the form of terse theses, which would involve some very dubious distortions. The explanatory methods of *pure* economics are as tempting as they are misleading. To take an example: It might be argued that for the development of medieval, corporately regulated, but "free" labor the decisive period should be seen in the "dark" ages from the tenth to the twelfth century, and in particular in the situation during that period of the skilled (peasant, mining, and artisan) labor force whose production activity was oriented to the reve-nue chances of the feudal lords with rights over the land, the persons, and the courts—powers which were fighting for their separate interests and competing for these revenue sources. The decisive period for the development of capitalism could be claimed to be the great chronic price revolution of the sixteenth century. The argument would be that this led both to an absolute and a relative increase in the prices of almost all products of the soil in the West, and hence—on the basis of well-known principles of agricultural economics—provided both incentives and pos-sibilities for market production and thus for production on a large scale; in part, as in England, this took the form of capitalistic enterprise, and in part, as in the lands between the Elbe river and Russia, that of *corvée*-labor estates. For non-agricultural products, this inflation signified in most cases a rise in absolute prices, but, it would be argued, rarely one in relative prices; typically, relative prices for industrial goods would fall, thus stimulating, so far as the necessary organizational and other external and subjective preconditions were given, attempts to create market enterprises able to stand up under competitive conditions. The claim that these preconditions were not given in Germany would be adduced to account for the economic decline which started there about that time. The later consequence of all this, the argument would run, was the development of capitalist industrial entrepreneurship. A neces-sary prerequisite for this would be the development of mass markets. An indication that this was actually happening could be seen in certain changes of English commercial policy, to say nothing of other phenom-ena.

In order to verify *theoretical* reasoning about the *substantive* economic conditions of the development of economic structure, theses such as these and similar ones would have to be utilized. But this is simply not admissible. These and numerous other equally controversial theories, even so far as they could be proved not to be wholly erroneous, cannot be incorporated into the present scheme which is intentionally limited to sociological *concepts*. In renouncing any attempt of this sort, however, the following exposition in this chapter explicitly repudiates any claim to concrete "explanation" and restricts itself to working out a sociological typology. The same is true of the previous discussion in that it consciously omitted to develop a theory of money and price determination. This must be strongly emphasized. For only the facts of the economic situation provide the flesh and blood for a genuine explanation of also that process of development relevant for sociological theory. What can be done here is only to supply a scaffolding adequate to provide the analysis with relatively unambiguous and definite concepts.

It is obvious not only that no attempt is made here to do justice to the historical aspect of economic development, but also that the typology of the genetic sequence of possible forms is neglected. The present aim is only to develop a schematic system of classification.

2. A common and justified objection to the usual terminology of economics is that it frequently fails to make a distinction between the business "establishment" (*Betrieb*) and the "firm" (*Unternehmung*).[27] In the area of economically oriented action, "establishment" is a *technical* category which designates the continuity of the combination of certain types of services with each other and with material means of production. The antithesis of this category is either intermittent action, or action which is constitutionally discontinuous (such as is found in every household). By contrast, the antithesis to "firm," which is a category of *economic* orientation (to profit), is the "budgetary unit" (*Haushalt*), which is economically oriented to provision for needs. But the classification in terms of "firm" and "budgetary unit" is not exhaustive, for there exist actions oriented to acquisition which cannot be subsumed under the category "firm." All activity in which earnings are due purely to "work," such as the activity of the writer, the artist, the civil servant, is neither the one nor the other. The drawing and consumption of rents and annuities, however, obviously belong into the category of "budgetary administration."

In spite of this distinction [between the "establishment" and the "firm"], we have in the earlier discussion used the term "profit-making establishment" (*Erwerbsbetrieb*) wherever continuously coordinated, uninterrupted entrepreneurial activity was meant;[28] such activity is in fact unthinkable without the constitution of an "establishment," if only one consisting of nothing but the entrepreneur's own activity without the aid of a staff. Our concern so far was mainly to stress the separation of the household (budgetary unit) and the continuously organized business establishment. It should now be noted that use of the term "profit-making establishment" as a substitute for "continuously organized business firm" is fitting and unambiguous only in the simplest case where the technical unit, the "establishment," coincides with the economic unit, the "firm."

In the market economy this need not be the case, for several technically separate "establishments" can be combined into a single "firm." The latter is not, of course, constituted through the mere relationship of the various technical units to the same entrepreneur, but through the fact that in their exploitation for profit these units are oriented to a coordinated plan; hence transitional forms are possible. When the term "establishment" or "enterprise" (*Betrieb*) is used by itself, it will always refer to such *technical* units consisting of buildings, equipment, labor, and a *technical* management, the latter possibly heterocephalous and heteronomous—units such as exist even in the communist economy (as the terminology presently in use also recognizes). The term "profit-making establishment or enterprise" will henceforth be used only in cases where the technical and the economic unit (the "firm") are identical.

The relation between "establishment" and "firm" raises particularly difficult terminological questions in the analysis of such categories as "factory" and "putting-out enterprise." The latter is quite clearly a type of "firm." In terms of "establishments," it consists of two types of units: a commercial establishment, and establishments which are component parts of the workers' households (in the absence of larger workshops such as might be organized by master craftsmen as intermediaries under a "hiring-boss" system); the household establishments perform certain specified functions for the commercial establishment, and vice versa. Viewed only from the point of view of "establishments," the process as a whole cannot be understood at all; for this it is necessary to employ additional categories, such as: market, firm, household (of the individual workers), commercial exploitation of purchased services.

The concept of "factory" could, as has been proposed, be defined in entirely non-economic terms as a mode of technical organization, leaving aside consideration of the status of the workers, whether free or unfree, the mode of division of labor, involving the extent of internal technical specialization, and the type of means of production, whether machines or tools. That is, it would be defined simply as an organized workshop. However, it would seem necessary in addition to include in the definition the mode of appropriation of premises and means of production—namely: to *one* owner—, for otherwise the concept would become as vague as that of the *ergasterion*.[29] But once this is done, it would as a matter of principle seem more expedient to classify "factory" and "putting-out enterprise" as two strictly *economic* categories of the "firm" conducted on the basis of capital accounting. In a fully socialist order the category "factory" could then occur as little as that of "putting-out enterprise," but only such categories as: workshops, buildings, tools, shop labor services and domestic labor services of all kinds.

3. The question of stages of economic development will be considered only insofar as it is absolutely necessary, and then only incidentally. The following points will suffice for the present.

It has fortunately become more common lately to distinguish types of economic system from types of economic policy.[30] The stages which Schönberg first suggested and which, in a somewhat altered form, have become identified with Schmoller's name, "domestic economy," "village economy," with the further stages of "seigneurial and princely patrimonial household economy," "town economy," "territorial economy," and "national economy,"[31] were in his terminology defined by the type of organization regulating economic activity. But it is not claimed that even the *types* of regulation, to which economic activity has been subjected by the different organizations thus classified in terms of the extent of their jurisdiction, were at all different. Thus the so-called territorial economic policies in Germany consisted to a large extent simply of an adoption of the measures developed in the town economy. Furthermore, such innovations as did occur were not greatly different from the "mercantilist" policies of those of the patrimonial states which had already achieved a relatively high level of rationality; they were thus to that extent "national economic policies," to use the common term, which, however, is not very appropriate. This classification, further, clearly does not claim that the inner structure of the economic system, the modes in which work roles were assigned, differentiated, and combined, the ways in which these different functions were divided between independent economic units, and the modes of appropriation of control over labor, means of production, and opportunities for profit, in any way were correlated with the dimensions of the organizations which were (potential) agents of an economic policy; above all this classification does not claim that they always changed in the same direction with changes in these dimensions. A comparison of the Western World with Asia, and of the modern West with that of Antiquity, would show the untenability of such an assumption. At the same time, in considering economic structure, it is by no means legitimate to ignore the existence or absence of organizations with substantive powers of regulation of economic activity, nor to ignore essential purposes of their regulation. The modes of profit-making activity are strongly influenced by such regulation, but it is by no means only political organizations which are important in this respect.

4. In this connection, as well as others, the purpose of the discussion has been to determine the optimum conditions for the *formal* rationality of economic activity and its relation to the various types of *substantive* demands which may be made on the economic system.

16. Types of the Technical Division of Labor

From a *technical* point of view the division of labor may be classified as follows: (1) In the first place, it may vary according to modes of differentiation and combination of work services as such: (a) They may vary according to the type of functions (*Leistungen*) undertaken by the same person. He may combine managerial functions with those of carrying out specifications; or his work may be specialized in terms of one or the other.

The distinction is naturally relative. It is common for an individual who normally supervises to take a hand in the work from time to time, as in the case of the peasants with larger holdings. The type cases of combination of the two functions are: The small peasant, the independent artisan, or the small boatman.

Further, a given individual may (b) perform functions which are *technically* different and contribute to different results, or he may perform only technically specialized functions. In the first case, the lack of specialization may be due to the technical level of work which does not permit further dividing up, to seasonal variation, or to the exploitation of labor services as a side line at times when they are not taken up by their primary occupation. In the second case, the function may be specialized in terms of the product in such a way that the same worker carries out all the processes necessary for this product, though they differ technically from each other. In a sense, this involves a combination of different functions and will be called the "specification of function." On the other hand, the functions may be differentiated according to the type of work, so that the product is brought to completion only by combining, simultaneously or successively, the work of a number of persons. This is the "specialization of function." The distinction is to a large extent relative, but it exists in principle and is historically important.

The case where there is little division of labor because of the low technical level is typical of primitive household economies. There, with the exception of the differentiation of sex roles (of which more in Part Two, ch. III) every individual performs every function as the occasion arises. Seasonal variation has been common in the alternation of agricultural work in the summer with the crafts in the winter. An example of side lines is the tendency for urban workers to take up agricultural work at certain times, such as the harvest, and also the various cases of secondary functions undertaken in otherwise free time, which is common even in modern offices.

The case of specification of function is typical of the occupational structure of the Middle Ages: a large number of crafts, each of which specialized in the production of a single article, completely unperturbed by the technical heterogeneity of the functions involved. There was thus a combination of functions. The specialization of functions, on the other hand, is crucial to the modern development of the organization of labor. There are, however, important physiological and psychological reasons why it has virtually never been pushed to the absolute extreme of isolation, even on the highest levels of specialization. There is almost always an element of specification of function involved. It is not, however, as in the Middle Ages, oriented to the final product.

(2) The differentiation and combination of different functions may further vary according to the modes in which the services of a plurality of persons are combined to achieve a co-ordinated result. There are two

main possibilities: (a) the "accumulation" of functions; that is the employment of a number of persons all performing the same function to achieve a result. This may take the form either of identical, but technically independent efforts co-ordinated in parallel, or of identical efforts organized technically into a single collective effort.

Examples of the first case are the functions performed by mowers or road pavers, several of whom work in parallel. The second type was exemplified on a grand scale in ancient Egypt in such cases as the transportation of huge stones by thousands of workers, large numbers of them performing the same acts, such as pulling on ropes, on the same object.

The second type, (b) is the "combination" of functions—that is, of efforts which are qualitatively different, and thus specialized—in order to achieve a result. These efforts may be technically independent and either simultaneous or successive; or they may involve technically organized co-operation in the simultaneous performance of technically complementary efforts.

1. A particularly simple example of simultaneous, technically independent functions is furnished by the parallel spinning of the warp and the woof for a given cloth. In the same class are to be placed a very large number of processes which are, from a technical point of view, undertaken independently, but are all designed as part of the production of the same final product.

2. An example of the successive type of technically independent processes is furnished by the relation of spinning, weaving, fulling, dyeing, and finishing. Similar examples are to be found in every industry.

3. The combination of specialized functions is found all the way from the case of an assistant holding a piece of iron while a blacksmith forges it, a case which is repeated in every modern foundry, to the complicated situations, which, though not specific to modern factories, are an important characteristic of them. One of the most highly developed types outside the factory is the organization of a symphony orchestra or of the cast of a theatrical production.

17. *Types of the Technical Division of Labor— (Continued)*

The division of labor efforts varies also, from a technical point of view, in terms of the extent and nature of combinations with complementary material means of production.

1. Forms may vary according to whether they consist purely in personal services, as in the case of wash-women, barbers, the performance of

actors, or whether they produce or transform goods by "working up" or transporting raw materials. The latter may consist in construction work, as that of plasterers, decorators, and stucco workers, in production of commodities and in transport of commodities. There are many transitional forms between them.

2. They may be further distinguished according to the stage at which they stand in the progression from original raw material to consumption: thus, from the original products of agriculture and mining to goods which are not only ready to be consumed, but available at the desired place for consumption.

3. The forms may further vary according to the ways in which they use: (a) Fixed plant and facilities (*Anlagen*). These may consist in sources of power; that is, means of harnessing energy, either that of natural forces, such as the power of water, wind, or heat from fire, or that which is produced mechanically, especially steam and electrical power, or in special premises for work, or they may use (b) implements of work (*Arbeitsmittel*), which include tools, apparatus, and machines. In some cases only one or another of these means of production may be used, or none. "Tools" are those aids to labor, the design of which is adapted to the physiological and psychological conditions of manual labor. "Apparatus" is something which is "tended" by the worker. "Machines" are mechanized apparatus. These rather vague distinctions have a certain significance for characterizing epochs in the development of industrial technology.

The use of mechanized sources of power and of machinery, characteristic of modern industry, is from a *technical* point of view due to their specific productivity and the resulting saving of human labor, and also to the uniformity and calculability of performance, both in quality and quantity. It is thus rational only where there exists a sufficiently wide demand for the particular types of products. In the case of a market economy, this means adequate purchasing power for the relevant goods; and this in turn depends on a certain type of income distribution.

It is quite out of the question here to undertake to develop even the most modest outline of a theory of the evolution of the technology and economics of tools and machinery. The concept of "apparatus" refers to such things as the type of loom which was operated by a foot-pedal and to numerous other similar devices. These already involve a certain relative independence on the part of the mechanical process, as distinguished from the functioning of the human or, in some cases, the animal organism. Without such apparatus—which included in particular various devices for moving materials in mines—machines, with their importance in modern technology, would never have come into existence. Leonardo's famous inventions were types of apparatus.

18. *Social Aspects of the Division of Labor*

From the social point of view, types of the division of labor may be classified in the following way: In the first place, according to the ways in which qualitatively different, especially complementary functions, are distributed among more or less autocephalous and autonomous economic units, which may further be distinguished economically according to whether these are budgetary units or profit-making enterprises. There are two polar possibilities:

(1) A "unitary" economy (*Einheitswirtschaft*) where the specialization (or specification) of functions is wholly internal, completely heterocephalous and heteronomous and determined on a purely technical basis. The same would be true of the co-ordination of functions. A unitary economy may, from an economic point of view, be either a budgetary unit or a profit-making enterprise.

On the largest possible scale, a communist national economy would be a unitary budgetary economy; on the smallest scale it was the primitive family unit, which included all or the great majority of production functions in a "closed household economy." The type case of a "unitary" profit-making enterprise with purely internal specialization and co-ordination of functions is naturally the great vertical combination[32] which treats with outsiders only as an integrated unit. These two distinctions will suffice for the moment as a treatment of the development of autonomous unitary economy.

(2) The distribution of functions may, on the other hand, take place between autocephalous economic units. (a) It may consist in the specialization or specification of functions between heteronomous, but autocephalous units which are oriented to an order established by agreement or imposed. The order, in turn, may be substantively oriented in a variety of ways. Its main concern may be to provide for the needs of a superior economic unit, which may be the budgetary unit (household) of a lord, an *oikos,* or it may be oriented to profit-making for an economic unit controlled by a political body or lord. The order may, on the other hand, be concerned with providing for the needs of the members of some closed group (*genossenschaftlicher Verband*). From an economic point of view, this may be accomplished either in the "budgetary" (household) or in the "profit-making" mode. The organization in all these cases may either be confined to the mere regulation of economic activity or it may, at the same time, be engaged in economic action on its own account. (b) The other main type is the specialization of autocephalous and autonomous units in a market economy, which are oriented on the one hand substantively only to their own self-interest, formally only to the

order of an organization such as the laissez-faire state, which enforces only formal, rather than substantive rules (See above, chap. II, sec. 5:d).

1. A typical example of the organization which, limiting its function to the regulation of economic activity, takes the form of a budgetary unit administered by an association of the members under case 2(a), is the organization of village handicrafts in India ("establishment"). An organization with autocephalous but heteronomous units oriented in their economic activity to the household of a lord, as under 2(a), may be illustrated by structures which provide for the household wants of princes or landlords (in the case of princes, also for the political wants) by means of contributions from the individual holdings of subjects, dependents, serfs, slaves, cottars, or sometimes "demiurgic" (see below) village artisans, such are found everywhere in the world. The exactions of services or products for a landlord or a town corporation should usually be classified as "mere regulation of economic activity," insofar as they usually served only fiscal, not substantive ends. A case of market order with units oriented to profit-making for the lord exists where putting-out type production tasks contracted for are reallocated to the individual households.

The types where there is specialization and specification of function between heteronomous units under the aegis of a co-operative organization can be illustrated by the specialization common in many very old small-scale industries. The Solingen metal trades were originally organized in terms of a voluntary association determining the division of labor by agreement. It was only later that they became organized in terms of domination, namely as a "putting-out industry." The type where the autocephalous economic units are subject only to regulation by an organization is illustrated by innumerable cases of the rules established by village communities and town corporations for the regulation of trade, so far at least as these have a substantive influence on the processes of production.

The case of specialization as between autonomous and autocephalous units in a market economy is best illustrated by the modern economic order.

2. A few further details may be added. The order of the organizations which attempt to provide for the wants of their members on a budgetary basis is "budgetary" in a particular way—that is, it is oriented to the prospective needs of the individual members, not of the organized group, such as a village itself. Specified service obligations of this kind will be called "demiurgic liturgies,"[33] and this type of provision for needs, correspondingly, "demiurgic provision." It always is a question of corporate regulation governing the division of labor and, in some cases, the mode of combination of labor services.

This term will not, on the other hand, be applied to an organization, whether it is based on domination or on voluntary co-operation, if it carries on economic activity on its own account, contributions to which are sub-allocated on a specialized basis. The type cases of this category are the specialized and specified contributions in kind of *corvée* estates (*Fronhöfe*), seigneurial estates, and other types of large household units. But sub-allocated obligations are also common in various types of organizations which are not primarily oriented to economic ends, such as the households of princes, political groups and the budgetary administration of local communities. These contributions are generally for the benefit of the budgetary needs of the governing authority or for corporate purposes. These in-kind obligations of services and products imposed on peasants, artisans, and tradesmen will be called "*oikos* liturgies in kind" when they are owed to the household establishment of an individual, and "corporate liturgies in kind" when they are payable to the budgetary unit of an organization as such. The principle governing this mode of provision for the budgetary needs of an organization engaged in economic action, is called "liturgical provision." This mode of organization has played an exceedingly important historical role and will have to be discussed frequently. In political organizations, it held the place of modern "public finances," and in economic groups it made possible a decentralization of the main household by providing for its needs through actors who were no longer maintained and utilized in it. Each sub-unit managed its own affairs, but assumed the obligation to fulfill certain functions for the central unit and to that extent was dependent on it. Examples are peasants and serfs subject to various kinds of labor services and payments in kind; craftsmen attached to an estate; and a large number of other types. Rodbertus[34] was the first to apply the term "*oikos*" to the large-scale household economies of Antiquity. He accepted as the principal criterion the essential autarky of want satisfaction through utilization of the services of household members or of dependent labor, material means of production being made available on a non-exchange basis. It is a fact that the landed estates, and still more the royal households, of Antiquity, especially of the New Kingdom in Egypt, were cases where the greater part of the needs of the unit were provided by services and payments in kind, which were obligations of dependent household units, although the degree of approach to the pure type varies widely. The same phenomena are to be found at times in China and India, and to a less extent in our own Middle Ages, beginning with the *capitulare de villis*.[35] It is true that exchange with the outside was generally not entirely lacking, but it tended to have the character of budgetary exchange. Obligations to money payment have also not been uncommon, but have generally played a subsidiary part in the main provision for needs and have tended to be traditionally fixed. For the economic units subject to liturgical obligations it also has not been uncommon to be involved in exchange relations. But the decisive point is that the bulk of the subsistence of these units was covered by the in-kind benefits—either in the form of certain quotas of products, or in that of the use of pieces of land—which they received in compensation for the liturgical deliveries imposed on them. There are, of course, many transitional forms. But in each case there is some kind of regulation of functions by an organization which is concerned with the mode of division of labor and of its co-ordination.

3. The cases where an organization regulating economic activity is oriented to considerations of economic profit are well illustrated by those economic regulations of the communes of medieval Europe, and by the guilds and castes of China and India, which restricted the number of master craftsmen and their functions and also the techniques of the crafts, that is, the way in which labor was oriented in the handicrafts. They belonged to this type so far as the rules were intended not primarily to secure provision of the consumer with the products of the craftsmen, but, as was often though not always the case, to secure the market position of the artisans by maintaining the quality of performance and by dividing up the market. Like every other type of economic regulation, this type also involved limitations on market freedom and hence on the fully autonomous business orientation of the craftsmen. It was unquestionably intended to maintain the "livings" for the existing craft shops, and to that extent, in spite of its apparent "business" character, it was more closely related to the budgetary mode of orientation.

4. The case of an organization itself engaged in economic activity with an orientation to profit-making can be illustrated, apart from the pure type of putting-out industry already discussed, by the agricultural estates of the German East with a labor force holding small plots of estate land on a service tenure and entirely oriented to the order of the estate (*Instleute*), or by those of the German North-West with similar types of tenant labor (*Heuerlinge*) who, however, hold their plots on a rental basis. The agricultural estates, just like the putting-out industries, are profit-making organizations of the landlord and the entrepreneur, respectively. The economic units of the tenants and home-industry workers are oriented, both in the imposed division of functions and in the mode of combining work efforts, as in the whole of their economic conduct, primarily to the obligations which the order of the estate or the putting-out relationship dictates to them. Apart from that, they are households. Their acquisitive efforts are not autonomous, but heteronomous efforts oriented to the enterprise of the landlord or the entrepreneur. Depending upon the degree to which this orientation is substantively standardized, the division of functions may approach the purely technical type of division within one and the same enterprise which is typical of the factory.

19. *Social Aspects of the Division of Labor—* (*Continued*)

From a social point of view, the modes of the division of labor may be further classified according to the mode in which the economic advantages, which are regarded as returns for the different functions, are appropriated. Objects of appropriation may be: the opportunities of disposing of, and obtaining a return from, human labor services (*Leistungsverwertungschancen*); the material means of production;[36] and the opportunities for profit from managerial functions.[37] (On the sociological concept of appropriation, see above, chap. I, sec. 10).

When the utilization rights for labor services are appropriated, the services themselves may either, (1) go to an individual recipient (a lord) or to an organization, or (2) they may be sold on the market. In either case one of the following four, radically different, possibilities may apply:

(a) Monopolistic appropriation of the opportunities for disposal of labor services by the individual worker himself: the case of "craft-organized free labor." The appropriated rights may either be hereditary and alienable, in which case type (1) above is illustrated by the Indian village artisan and type (2) by certain medieval non-personal craft rights; or they may be strictly personal and inalienable, as under type (1) all "rights to an office"; or, finally, they may be hereditary, but inalienable, as under types (1) and (2) certain medieval, but above all Indian, craft rights, and medieval "offices" of the most diverse kind. In all these cases appropriation may be unconditional or subject to certain substantive conditions.

(b) The second possibility is that the right of utilization of labor services is appropriated to an "owner" of the worker: the case of "unfree labor." The property rights in the worker may be both hereditary and alienable—the case of slavery proper. Or, though it is hereditary, it may not be freely alienable, but, e.g., only together with the material means of production, particularly the land. This includes serfdom and hereditary dependency.

> The appropriation of the use of labor by a lord may be limited by substantive conditions, as in serfdom. The worker cannot leave his status of his own free will, but neither can it arbitrarily be taken from him.

The appropriated rights of disposal of labor services may be used by the owner for purposes of budgetary administration, as a source of income in kind or in money, or a source of labor services in his household, as in the case of domestic slaves or serfs. Or it may be used as a means of profit. In that case the dependent may be obligated to deliver goods or to work on raw materials provided by the owner. The owner will then sell the product. This is unfree domestic industry. He may, finally, use his laborer in an organized shop—a slave or serf workshop.

> The person herein designated as the "owner" may be involved in the work process himself in a managerial capacity or even in part as a work-

er, but this need not be true. It may be that his position as owner, *ipso facto,* makes him the managing agent. But this is by no means necessary and is very generally not the case.

The use of slaves and serfs, the latter including various types of dependents, as part of a process of budgetary administration and as source of rent revenue, but not as workers in a profit-making enterprise, was typical of Antiquity and of the early Middle Ages. There are, for instance, cuneiform inscriptions which mention slaves of a Persian prince who were bound out as apprentices, possibly to be used later for labor services in the household, but perhaps to be set to work in substantive freedom for their own customers, making a regular payment to the owner (an early equivalent of the Greek ἀποφορά, the Russian *obrok,* and the German *Hals-* or *Leibzins*). Though by no means without exception, this tended to be the rule for Greek slaves; and in Rome this type of independent economic activity with a *peculium* or *merx peculiaris* and, naturally, payments to the owner, found reflection in various legal institutions. In the Middle Ages, body serfdom (*Leib-herrschaft*) frequently involved merely a right to claim payments from otherwise almost independent persons. This was usual in western and southern Germany. In Russia, also, *de facto* limitation to the receipt of these payments (*obrok*) from an otherwise independent serf was, if not universal, at least very common, although the legal status of these persons remained precarious.

The use of unfree labor for "business" purposes has taken the following principal forms, particularly in the domestic industries on seigneurial estates, including various royal estates, among them probably those of the Pharaohs: (1) Unfree obligation to payments in kind—the delivery of goods in kind, the raw material for which was produced by the workers themselves as well as worked on by them. Flax is an example; (2) unfree domestic industry—work on material provided by the lord. The product could be sold at least in part for money by the lord. But in many cases, as in Antiquity, the tendency was to confine market sale to occasional instances. In early modern times, however, particularly in the German-Slavic border regions this was not the case; it was there, though not only there, that domestic industries developed on the estates of landlords. The utilization in a continuous organization could take the form of unfree home-industry labor or of unfree workshop labor. Both forms are common. The latter was one of the various forms of the *ergasterion* of Antiquity. It was found on the estates of the Pharaohs, in temple workshops, and according to the testimony of tomb frescoes, also on the estates of private owners or lords, in the Orient, in Greece (Demosthenes' shops in Athens), in the Roman estate workshops (see the description by Gummerus), in the Carolingian *genitium* (that is, a *gynaik-eion*), and in more recent times for example in the Russian serf factories (see Tugan-Baranovskii's book on the Russian factory).[38]

(c) The third possibility is the absence of any sort of appropriation: formally "free" labor, in this sense that the services of labor are the subject of a contractual relationship which is formally free on both sides. The contract may, however, be substantively regulated in various ways through a conventional or legal order governing the conditions of labor.

Freely contracted labor may be used in various ways. In the first place, in a budgetary unit, as occasional labor (what Bücher calls *Lohnwerk*), either in the household of the employer (*Stör*) or in that of the worker himself (*Heimwerk* in Bücher's terminology). Or it may be permanent, again performed in the household of the employer, as in the case of domestic service, or in that of the worker, as typical of the colonate. It may, on the other hand, be used for profit, again on an occasional or a permanent basis; and in both cases either in the worker's own home or on premises provided by the employer. The latter is true of workers on an estate or in a workshop, but especially of the factory.

> Where the worker is employed in a budgetary unit, he is directly in the service of a consumer who supervises his labor. Otherwise, he is in the service of a profit-making entrepreneur. Though the form is often legally identical, economically the difference is fundamental. *Coloni* may be in either status; but it is more typical for them to be workers in an *oikos*.

(d) The fourth possibility is that opportunities for disposal of labor services may be appropriated by an organization of workers, either without any appropriation by the individual worker or with important limitations on such appropriation. This may involve absolute or relative closure against outsiders and also prohibition of the dismissal of workers from employment by management without consent of the workers, or at least some kind of limitations on power of dismissal.

> Examples of the type of appropriation involving closure of the group are castes of workers or the type of miners' association found in the Medieval mining industry, the organized groups or retainers sometimes found at courts, or the "thresher tenure" (*Dreschgärtner*) on landed estates in Germany. This type of appropriation is found throughout the social history of all parts of the world in an endless variety of forms. The second type involving limitations on powers of dismissal, which is also very widespread, plays an important part in the modern situation in the "closed shop" of trade unions and especially in the "works councils."

Every form of appropriation of jobs in profit-making enterprises by workers, like the converse case of appropriation of the services of workers by owners, involves limitations on the free recruitment of the labor force. This means that workers cannot be selected solely on grounds of their technical efficiency, and to this extent there is a limitation on the *formal* rationalization of economic activity. Appropriation of jobs also imposes substantive limitations on *technical* rationality, namely: (1) if the exploitation for profit of the products of labor is appropriated by an owner, through the tendency to restrict the work effort, either by tradition, or by convention, or by contract; also through the reduction or complete disappearance (if the worker is fully owned, a slave) of the worker's own interest in optimal effort; (2) if the exploitation for profit of the products is also appropriated by the workers, there may be a conflict of the worker's self-interest, which lies in the maintenance of his traditional mode of life, with the attempts of his employer to get him to produce at the optimum technical level or to use other means of production in place of labor. For employers, there is always the possibility of transforming their exploitation of labor into a mere source of income. Any appropriation of the exploitation of products by the workers thus generally leads under otherwise favorable circumstances to a more or less complete expropriation of the owner from management. But it also regularly tends to place workers in a state of dependence on people with whom they deal who enjoy a more favorable market position. These, such as putting-out entrepreneurs, then tend to assume a managerial position.

     1. The very opposite forms of appropriation—that of jobs by workers and that of workers by owners—nevertheless have in practice very similar results. This should not be surprising. In the first place, the two tendencies are very generally formally related. This is true when appropriation of the workers by an owner coincides with appropriation of opportunities for jobs by a closed organization of workers, as has happened in the manor associations. In such cases it is natural that exploitation of labor services should, to a large extent, be stereotyped; hence, that work effort should be restricted and that the workers have little self-interest in the output. The result is generally a successful resistance of workers against any sort of technical innovation. But even where this does not occur, the fact that workers are appropriated by an owner means in practice that he is obliged to make use of this particular labor force. He is not in a position, like the modern factory manager, to select according to technical needs, but must utilize those he has without selection. This is particularly true of slave labor. Any attempt to exact performance from appropriated workers beyond that which has become traditionally established encounters traditional obstacles. These could only be overcome by the most ruthless methods, which are not without their danger from the point of view of the owner's self-interest, since they might undermine the traditionalistic bases of his authority. Hence almost universally the work effort of appropriated workers has shown a tendency to restriction. Even where, as was particularly true of eastern Europe at the beginning of the modern age, this was broken by the power of the lords, the development of higher technical levels of production was impeded by the absence of the selective process and by the absence of any element of self-interest or own risk-taking on the part of the appropriated workers.

When jobs have been formally appropriated by workers, the same result has come about even more rapidly.

2. Appropriation by workers was typical for the development in the early Middle Ages (10th to 13th century). The Carolingian *Beunden*[39] and all other beginnings of large-scale agricultural enterprise declined and disappeared. The rents and dues paid to landlords and lords holding rights over persons became stereotyped at a low level; and an increasing proportion of the products in kind, in agriculture and mining, and of the money proceeds from the handicrafts, went to the workers. In just this form this development was peculiar to the Western world. The principal circumstances which favored it were as follows: (a) The fact that the propertied classes were heavily involved in political and military activity; (b) the absence of a suitable administrative staff. These two circumstances made it impossible for them to utilize these workers in any other way than as a source of rent payments; (c) the fact that the freedom of movement of workers between the potential employers competing for their services could not easily be restricted; (d) the numerous opportunities of opening up new land, new mines, and new local markets; (e) the primitive level of the technical tradition. The more the appropriation of profit opportunities *by* the workers replaced the appropriation *of* workers *by* owners, the more the owners were dispossessed of their rights of control and became mere recipients of rents and dues. Classical examples are the mining industry and the English guilds. Even at this early period the process tended to go further, to the point of redemption or repudiation of the obligation to make payments to a lord altogether, on the principle that "A townsman is a freeman." Almost immediately all this led to a differentiation of the opportunities of making profit by market transactions, arising either from within the group of workers themselves or from without through the development of trade.

20. *Social Aspects of the Division of Labor: The Appropriation of the Material Means of Production*

The material means of production may be appropriated by workers as individuals or as organizations, by owners, or by regulating groups consisting of third parties.

When appropriated by workers, it may be by the individual worker who then becomes the "owner" of the material means of production; or the appropriation may be carried out by a completely or relatively closed group of workers so that, though the individual worker is not the owner, the organization is. Such an organization may carry out its functions as a unitary economy on a "communist" basis, or with appropriation of shares (*genossenschaftlich*). In all these cases, appropriation may be used for the purposes of budgetary administration or for profit making.

Appropriation of the means of production by individual workers may exist in a system of complete market freedom of the small peasants, artisans, boatmen, or carters, or under the aegis of a regulating group. Where it is not the individual but an organization which owns the means of production, there is a wide variety of possibilities, varying particularly with the extent to which the system is of a budgetary or a profit-making character. The household economy, which is in principle not necessarily by origin or in fact communistic (see Part Two, ch. III), may be oriented wholly to provision for its own needs. Or it may, perhaps only occasionally, dispose of surpluses of certain types of raw material accumulated by virtue of a favorable location, or of products derived from some particular technical skill, as a means to better provision. This occasional sale may then develop into a regular system of profit-making exchange. In such cases it is common for "tribal" crafts to develop, with interethnic functional specialization and trade between the tribes, since the chances of finding a market often depend on maintaining a monopoly, which in turn is usually secured by inherited trade secrets. From this may develop ambulatory crafts or possibly pariah[40] crafts or, where these groups are united in a political structure and where there are ritual barriers between the ethnic elements, castes, as in India.

The case where members of the group possess appropriated shares is that of "producers' co-operation."[41] Household economies may, with the development of money accounting, approach this type. Otherwise, it is occasionally found as an organization of workmen. It was of great significance in one important case, that of the mining industry of the early Middle Ages.

Since appropriation by organized groups of workers has already been dealt with, appropriation by "owners" or organized groups of them can only mean the expropriation of the workers from the means of production, not merely as individuals, but as a whole. An owner may in this connection appropriate one or more of the following items: land, including water; subterranean wealth; sources of power; work premises; labor equipment, such as tools, apparatus and machinery; and raw materials. In any given case all these may be concentrated in a single ownership or they may be appropriated by different owners. The owners may employ the means of production they appropriate in a context of budgetary administration, either as means to provide for their own needs or as sources of income by lending them out. In the latter case, the loans may in turn be used by the borrower for budgetary purposes or as means for earning a profit, either in a profit-making establishment without capital accounting or as capital goods (in their own enterprise). Finally, the owner may use them as capital goods in his own enterprise.

The appropriating agency may be an organization engaged in economic activity. In this case, all the alternatives just outlined are open to it.

It is, finally, also possible that the means of production should be appropriated by an organization which only *regulates* economic activity, which does not itself use them as capital goods or as a source of income, but places them at the disposal of its members.

I. When *land* is appropriated by individual economic units, it is usually for the period of actual cultivation until the harvest or, so far as, by virtue of clearing or irrigation, land is itself an artifact, for the period of continuous cultivation. It is only when scarcity of land has become noticeable that it is common for rights of cultivation, pasturage and use of timber to be reserved to the members of a settlement group, and for the extent of their use to be limited.

(1) When that happens, appropriation may be carried out by an organization. This may be of differing sizes, according to the mode of use, to which the land is put—for gardens, meadows, arable land, pastures, or woodland. These have been appropriated by progressively larger groups, from the individual household to the whole tribe. Typical cases are the appropriation of arable land, meadows, and pastures by a kinship group or a neighborhood group, usually a village. Woodland has usually been appropriated by broader territorial groups, differing greatly in character and extent. The individual household has typically appropriated garden land and the area around the house and has had shares in the arable fields and meadows. The system of shares may find expression (i) in the *de facto* egalitarianism of the assignment of newly tilled fields where cultivation is "ambulatory" (as in the so-called field-grass husbandry), or (ii) in rationally systematic redistribution under sedentary cultivation. The latter is usually the consequence of either fiscal claims for which the village members are collectively held responsible, or of political claims of the members for equality. The unit of the production organization has usually been the household (on which see Part Two, ch. III and IV).

(2) Appropriation of the land may also be to a lord or seigneur (*Grundherr*). This seigneurial position, as will be discussed later, may be based primarily on the individual's position of authority in a kinship group or as tribal chieftain with claims to exact labor services (see Part Two, ch. IV), or on fiscal or military authority, or on some form of organization for the systematic exploitation of new land or an irrigation project. Seigneurial domination over land (*Grundherrschaft*) may be made a source of utilities by the employment of the unfree labor of slaves or serfs. This, in turn, may be administered as part of a budgetary unit, through deliveries in kind or labor services, or as a means of profit, as a "plantation." On the other hand, it may be exploited with free labor. Here again it may be treated in budgetary terms, drawing income from the land in the form of payments in kind or from share-cropping by tenants or of money rents from tenants. In both cases the equipment used may be provided by the tenant himself, or by the seigneur (colo-

nate). A lord may also exploit his holdings as a source of profit in the form of a large-scale rational economic enterprise.

Where the land is used as part of a budgetary economy with unfree labor, the lord is apt to be bound traditionally in his exploitation of it, both with respect to his labor personnel, which is not subject to selection, and to their functions. The use of unfree labor in a profit-making establishment, the "plantation," occurred only in a few cases, notably in Antiquity in Carthage and in Rome, and in modern times in the plantations of colonial areas and in the Southern States of North America. The use of land in large-scale profit-making enterprises with free labor has occurred only in the modern Western World. It is the mode of development of the medieval landlordship or seigneurie (*Grundherrschaft*), in particular the way in which it was broken up, which has been most decisive in determining the modern forms of land appropriation. The modern pure type knows only the following categories: the owner of the land, the capitalistic tenant, and the propertyless agricultural laborer. But this pure type is exceptional, found principally in England.

II. Sources of wealth adapted to exploitation by *mining* may be appropriated in the following ways: (a) By the owner of the land, who in the past has usually been a seigneur; (b) by a political overlord (owner of the regal prerogatives or "royalties"); (c) by any person discovering deposits worthy of mining (*Bergbaufreiheit*); (d) by an organization of workers; and (e) by a profit-making enterprise. Seigneurs and owners of "royalties" may administer their holdings themselves, as they did occasionally in the early Middle Ages; or they may use them as a source of income, by leasing them to an organized group of workers or to any discoverer whatever or to anyone who was a member of a given group. This was the case with the "freed mountains" (*gefreite Berge*) of the Middle Ages and was the origin of the institution of "mining freedom" (*Bergbaufreiheit*).[42]

In the Middle Ages, the groups of organized mine workers were typically closed membership groups with shares held by the members, where each member was under obligation, either to the seigneurial owner, or to the other members collectively responsible to him, to work in the mine. This obligation was balanced by a right to a share in the products. There was also a type of a pure "owners" association, each sharing in the proceeds or the contributions required due to losses. The tendency was for the seigneurial owners to be progressively expropriated in favor of the workers; but these, in turn, as their need for investment in installations increased, became more and more dependent on groups with command over capital goods. Thus in the end, the appropriation took the form of a capitalistic *Gewerkschaft*, a limited liability company.

III. Means of production which are *fixed installations*, such as sources of power, particularly water power, "mills" for various different purposes, and workshops, sometimes including the fixed apparatus in them, have in the past, particularly in the Middle Ages, generally been appropriated in one of the following ways: (a) by princes or seigneurs; (b) by towns (either as economically active or merely regulating organizations); (c) by associations of workers, such as guilds (as "regulating" groups), without the development, in any of them, of a unified production organization (*Betrieb*).

In the first two cases, they were usually exploited as a source of income, a charge being made for their use. This has often been combined with interdiction of rival facilities and the compulsory use of those belonging to the lord. Each production unit would make use of the facilities in turn, according to need or, under certain circumstances, it was made the monopoly of a closed, regulative group. Baking ovens, various kinds of grinding mills for grain or oil, fulling mills, polishing installations, slaughter-houses, dye-works, bleaching installations, forges—which were usually, to be sure, leased—, breweries, distilleries, other installations including particularly shipyards in the possession of the Hanseatic towns, and all kinds of market stalls have been appropriated in this pre-capitalistic way, to be exploited by allowing workers to use them in return for a payment; they were thus used as part of the budgetary wealth (*Vermögen*), rather than as capital of the owners (individuals or organizations, including town corporations). This type of production and budgetary exploitation of fixed installations as a source of investment income for the owning individual or group, or possibly production by a producers' co-operative group, has preceded the creation of "fixed capital" of individual business units. Those *using* such installations have tended to treat them in part as means of meeting their own household needs, especially in the case of baking ovens and of brewing and distilling installations, and in part for profit-making operations.

IV. For maritime transport the typical arrangement in the past has been the appropriation of the *ship* by a plurality of owners, who tended to become more and more sharply differentiated from the actual seafarers. The fact that the organization of maritime enterprise then tended to develop into a system of risk-sharing with shippers, in which ship owners, officers, and even the crew, were associated as shippers of freight, did not, however, produce any fundamentally new forms of *appropriation*. It affected only the forms of settling accounts and hence the distribution of profit-making possibilities.

V. Today, it is usual for the installations of all kinds and the tools to be appropriated under *one* controlling agency, as is essential to the modern factory; but in earlier times, this has been exceptional. In particular, the economic character of the Greek and Byzantine *ergasterion* and the corresponding Roman *ergastulum* has been highly ambiguous, a fact which historians have persistently ignored. It was a "workshop" which might, (i) be a part of a budgetary unit in which slaves would carry out production for the owner's own needs, as for the needs of a landed estate, or subsidiary production of goods for sale. But (ii) the workshop might also be used as a source of rent revenue, part of the holdings of a private individual or of an organization, which latter might be a town, as was true of the *ergasteria* of the Piraeus. Such *ergasteria* would then be leased to individuals or to organized closed groups of workers. Thus, when it is stated that an *ergasterion* was exploited, especially a municipal one, it is always necessary to inquire further to whom it belonged and who was the owner of the other means of production necessary for the work process. Did free labor work there? Did they work for their own profit? Or did slaves work there, in which case it is necessary to know who their owners were, and whether they were working on their own account, making ἀποφορά payments to their master, or directly for their master. According to the ways in which these questions are answered, the structure would be radically different from an economic point of view. In the great majority of cases, as late as the Byzantine and Mohammedan types, the *ergasterion* seems to have been primarily a source of rent revenue, and was hence fundamentally different from the modern factory or even its early predecessors. From an economic point of view, this category is, in its economic ambiguity, most closely comparable to the various types of mills found in the Middle Ages.

VI. Even in cases where the workshop and the means of production are appropriated by an individual owner who hires labor, the situation is not, from an economic point of view, necessarily what would usually be called a "factory" today. For this it would be necessary in addition to have the use of mechanical power, of machinery, and of an elaborate internal differentiation and combination of functions. The factory today is a category of the capitalistic economy. Hence in the present discussion the concept "factory" will be confined to a type of establishment which is at least potentially under the control of a profit-making firm with fixed capital, which thus takes the form of an organized workshop with internal differentiation of function, with the appropriation of *all* non-human means of production and with a high degree of mechanization of the work process by the use of mechanical power and machinery. The great workshop of "Jack of Newbury"[43] of the early sixteenth century, which was sung about by balladeers of a later day, did not have any of these features. It is alleged to have contained hundreds of hand looms, which were his property and for the workers of which he bought the raw materials, and also all manner of "welfare" arrangements. But each worker worked independently as if he were at home. Internal differentiation and combination of functions could, to be sure, exist in an Egyptian, Greek, Byzantine or Mohammedan *ergasterion* which a master worked with his unfree laborers. But the Greek texts show clearly that even in such cases is was common for the master to be content with the payment of an ἀποφορά from each worker and perhaps a higher one from the foreman. This alone is sufficient to warn us not to consider such a structure economically equivalent to a factory or even to a workshop like that of "Jack of Newbury." The closest approximation to the factory in the usual sense is found in royal manufactories, like the imperial Chinese porcelain manufactory and the European manufactories of court luxuries, which were modelled on it, and especially those for the production of military equipment. No one can be blamed for calling these "factories." And the Russian workshops operating with serf labor seem at first sight to stand even closer to the modern factory. Here the appropriation of the workers themselves is added to that of the means of production. Nevertheless, for present purposes the concept "factory" will, for the reasons stated, be limited to organized workshops where the material means of production are fully appropriated by an owner, but the workers are not; where there is internal specialization of functions, and where mechanical power and machines which must be "tended" are used. All other types of organized workshops will be designated by that word, with the appropriate adjectives.

21. *Social Aspects of the Division of Labor: The Appropriation of Managerial Functions*

(1) In all cases of the management of traditional budgetary (household) units, it is typical for the appropriation of managerial functions to take place either by the titular head himself, such as the head of the family or the kinship group, or by members of an administrative staff appointed for the management of the unit, as in the case of service fiefs of household officials.

(2) In the case of profit-making enterprises, it occurs in the following situations: (a) When management and ordinary labor are entirely or very nearly identical. In this case there is usually also appropriation of the material means of production by the worker. This type of appropriation may be unlimited, that is, hereditary and alienable on the part of the individual, with or without a guaranteed market. It may, on the other hand, be appropriation to an organized group, with appropriation of the function by the individual restricted to personal tenure[44] or subject to substantive regulation, thus limited and dependent on various conditions. Again, a market may or may not be guaranteed. (b) Where management and ordinary work are separated, there may be a monopolistic appropriation of entrepreneurial functions in various possible forms, notably to closed membership groups, such as guilds, or to monopolies granted by the political authority.

(3) In cases where managerial functions are, from a formal point of view, wholly unappropriated, the appropriation of the means of production or of the credit necessary for securing control over them is in practice, in a capitalistic form of organization, identical with appropriation of control of management by the owners of the means of production. Owners can, in such cases, exercise their control by personally managing the business or by appointment of the actual managers. Where there is a plurality of owners, they will co-operate in the selection. These points are so obvious that there is no need of comment.

Wherever there is appropriation of technically complementary means of production, it generally means, in practice, at least some degree of effective voice in the selection of management and, to a relative extent at least, the expropriation of the workers from management. The expropriation of the individual workers, however, does not necessarily imply the expropriation of workers in general. Though they are formally expropriated, it is possible for an association of workers to be in fact in a position to exact for itself an effective share in management or in the selection of managing personnel.

22. *The Expropriation of Workers from the Means of Production*

The expropriation of the individual worker from ownership of the means of production is determined by purely *technical* factors in the following cases: (a) if the means of production require the services of many workers, at the same time or successively; (b) if sources of power can be rationally exploited only by using them simultaneously for many similar types of work under a unified control; (c) if a technically rational organization of the work process is possible only by combining many complementary processes under continuous common supervision; (d) if special technical training is needed for the management of co-ordinated processes of labor which, in turn, can only be exploited rationally on a large scale; (e) if unified control over the means of production and raw materials creates the possibility of subjecting labor to a stringent discipline and hence of controlling the speed of work and of attaining standardization of effort and of product quality.

These factors, however, do not exclude the possibility of appropriation by an organized group of workers, a producers' co-operative. They necessitate only the separation of the *individual* worker from the means of production.

The expropriation of workers *in general,* including clerical personnel and technically trained persons, from possession of the means of production has its *economic* reasons above all in the following factors: (a) The fact that, other things being equal, it is generally possible to achieve a higher level of economic rationality if the management has extensive control over the selection and the modes of use of workers, as compared with the situation created by the appropriation of jobs or the existence of rights to participate in management. These latter conditions produce technically irrational obstacles as well as economic irrationalities. In particular, considerations appropriate to small-scale budgetary administration and the interests of workers in the maintenance of jobs ("livings") are often in conflict with the rationality of the organization. (b) In a market economy a management which is not hampered by any established rights of the workers, and which enjoys unrestricted control over the goods and equipment which underlie its borrowings, is of superior credit-worthiness. This is particularly true if the management consists of individuals experienced in business affairs and with a good reputation for "safety" derived from their continuous conduct of business. (c) From a historical point of view, the expropriation of labor has arisen since the sixteenth century in an economy characterized by the progressive extensive and intensive expansion of the market system on the one hand, because of the sheer superiority and actual indispensability of a type of management oriented to the particular market situations, and on the other because of the structure of power relationships in the society.

In addition to these general conditions, the effect of the fact that enterprise has been oriented to the exploitation of market advantages has in the following ways favored such expropriation: (a) because it put a premium on capital accounting—which can be effected in the technically most rational manner only with full appropriation of capital goods to the owner—as against any type of economic behavior with less rational accounting procedures; (b) because it put a premium on the purely commercial qualities of the management, as opposed to the technical ones, and on the maintenance of technical and commercial secrets; (c) because it favored a speculative business policy, which again requires expropriation. Further, and in the last analysis quite regardless of the degree of technical rationality, this expropriation is made possible, (d) by the sheer bargaining superiority which in the labor market any kind of property ownership grants vis-à-vis the workers, and which in the commodity markets accrues to any business organization working with capital accounting, owned capital equipment and borrowed funds vis-à-vis any type of competitor operating on a lower level of rationality in methods of calculation or less well situated with respect to capital and credit resources. The fact that the maximum of *formal* rationality in capital accounting is possible only where the workers are subjected to domination by entrepreneurs, is a further specific element of *substantive* irrationality in the modern economic order. Finally, (e), a further economic reason for this expropriation is that free labor and the complete appropriation of the means of production create the most favorable conditions for discipline.

23. *The Expropriation of Workers from the Means of Production—(Continued)*

The expropriation of *all* the workers from the means of production may in practice take the following forms: (1) Management is in the hands of the administrative staff of an organization. This would be true very particularly also of any rationally organized socialist economy, which would retain the expropriation of all workers and merely bring it to completion by the expropriation of the private owners. (2) Managerial functions are, by virtue of their appropriation of the means of production, exercised by the owners or by persons they appoint. The appropriation of control over the persons exercising managerial authority by the interests of ownership may have the following forms: (a) Management by one or more entrepreneurs who are at the same time owners —the immediate appropriation of entrepreneurial functions. This situation, however, does not exclude the possibility that a wide degree of control over the policies of management may rest in hands outside the enterprise, by virtue of their powers over credit or financing—for instance, the bankers or financiers who finance the enterprise; (b) separation of managerial functions from appropriated ownership, especially through limitations of the functions of owners to the appointment of management and through shared free (that is, alienable) appropriation of the enterprise as expressed by shares of the nominal capital (stocks, mining shares). This state, which is related to the purely personal form of appropriation through various types of intermediate forms, is rational in the *formal* sense in that it permits, in contrast to the case of permanent and hereditary appropriation of the management itself of accidentally inherited properties, the selection for managerial posts of the persons best qualified from the point of view of profitability. But in practice it may mean a number of things, such as: That control over the managerial position may come, through appropriation, into the hands of "outside interests" representing the resources of a budgetary unit, or mere wealth (*Vermögen;* see above, ch. II, sec. 10), and seeking above all a high rate of income; or that control over the managerial position comes, through temporary stock acquisitions, into the hands of speculative "outside interests" seeking gains only through the resale of their shares; or that disposition over the managerial position comes into the hands of outside business interests, by virtue of power over markets or over credit, such as banks or "financiers," which may pursue their own business interests, often foreign to those of the organization as such.

We call "outside interests" those which are not primarily oriented to the long-run profitability of the enterprise. This may be true of any kind of budgetary "wealth" interests. It is particularly true, however, of interests which consider their control over the plant and capital goods of the enterprise or of a share in it not as a permanent investment, but as a means of making a purely short-run speculative profit. The types of outside interest which are most readily reconciled with those of the enterprise—that is, its interests in present *and* long-run profitability—are those seeking only income (*rentiers*).

The fact that such "outside" interests can affect the mode of control over managerial positions, even and especially when the highest degree of *formal* rationality in their selection is attained, constitutes a further element of *substantive* irrationality specific to the modern economic order. These might be entirely private "wealth" interests, or business interests which are oriented to ends having no connection whatsoever with the organization, or finally, pure gambling interest. By gaining control of shares, all of these can control the appointment of the managing personnel and, more important, the business policies imposed on this management. The influence exercised by speculative interests outside the producing organizations themselves on the market situation, especially that for capital goods, and thus on the orientation of the production of goods, is *one* of the sources of the phenomena known as the "crises" of the modern market economy. This cannot, however, be further discussed here.

24. *The Concept of Occupation and Types of Occupational Structure*

The term "occupation" (*Beruf*) will be applied to the mode of specialization, specification, and combination of the functions of an individual so far as it constitutes for him the basis of a continuous opportunity for income or earnings. The distribution of occupations may be achieved in the following ways: (1) by means of a heteronomous assignment of functions and of provisions for maintenance within an organization regulating economic activity—unfree differentiation of occupations—or through autonomous orientation to the state of the market for occupational services—free differentiation of occupations; (2) it may rest on the specification or the specialization of functions; (3) it may involve economic exploitation of the services by their bearers on either an autocephalous or a heterocephalous basis.

The structure of occupational differentiation and that of opportunities for business income are closely related. This will be discussed in relation to the problems of "class" and "status" stratification.

On occupation as a basis of status, and on classes in general, see chap. IV, below.[45]

1. Unfree organization of occupations exists in cases where there is compulsory assignment of functions within the organization of a royal estate, a state, a feudal manor, or a commune on the basis of liturgies or of the *oikos* type of structure. The free type of distribution arises from the successful offer of occupational services on the labor market or successful application for free "positions."

2. As was pointed out above in sec. 16, specification of functions was typical of the handicrafts in the Middle Ages; specialization is characteristic of the modern rational business organization. The distribution of occupations in a market economy consists to a large extent of technically irrational specification of functions, rather than of rational specialization of functions, because such an economy is oriented to the market situation and hence to the interests of purchasers and consumers. This orientation determines [the uses to which] the entire bundle of labor services offered by a given productive unit will be put in a manner often different from the specialization of functions [of the given labor force], thus making necessary modes of combination of functions which are technically irrational.

3. Cases of autocephalous occupational specialization are the independent "business" of an artisan, a physician, a lawyer, or an artist. The factory worker and the government official, on the other hand, occupy heterocephalous occupational positions.

The occupational structure of a given social group may vary in the following ways: (a) According to the degree in which well-marked and stable occupations have developed at all. The following circumstances are particularly important in this connection: the development of consumption standards, the development of techniques of production, and the development of large-scale budgetary units in the case of unfree occupational organization, or of market systems in that of free organization; (b) according to the mode and degree of occupational specification or specialization of individual economic units. This will be decisively influenced by the market situation for the services or products of specialized units, which is in turn dependent on adequate purchasing power. It will also be influenced by the mode of distribution of control over capital goods; (c) according to the extent and kind of continuity or change in occupational status. This in turn depends above all on two factors: on the one hand, on the amount of training required for the specialized functions, and on the other hand the degree of stability or instability of opportunities for earnings from them. The latter is in turn dependent on the type and stability of distribution of income and on the state of technology.

Finally, it is always important in studying occupational structure to know the status stratification, with the attendant status-tied types of education and other advantages and opportunities which it creates for certain kinds of skilled occupations.

It is only functions which require a certain minimum of training and for which opportunity of continuous remuneration is available which become the objects of independent and stable occupations. The choice of occupation may rest on tradition, in which case it is usually hereditary; on goal-oriented rational considerations, especially the possibility of returns; on charismatic or on affectual grounds; and finally, in particular, on grounds of prestige with particular reference to status. Originally, the more directly individual "callings" have been dependent primarily on charismatic (magical) elements, while all the rest of the occupational structure, so far as in a differentiated form it existed at all, was traditionally fixed. The requisite charismatic qualities, so far as they were not specifically personal, tended to become the object of a traditional "training" in closed groups, or of hereditary transmission. Individual occupations which were not of a strictly charismatic character first appeared on a liturgical basis in the large-scale households of princes and landed lords, and then in the market economy of the towns. Alongside of this, however, a large role in their development was always played by the literary forms of education with a high status esteem, which arose in close connection with magical, ritual, or priestly ("clerical") professional training.

From what has been said it will be seen that occupational specialization does not necessarily imply continuous rendering of services, either on a liturgical basis for an organization—in a royal household or a workshop—or for a completely free market. Other forms are not only possible but common: (1) Propertyless occupationally specialized workers may be employed on an occasional basis as needed in the service of a relatively stable group of either consumers in household units or employers in profit-making enterprises. In the case of work for *households,* we have the possibility of the expropriation from the worker of at least the raw materials (and hence of the control over the final product); services may be rendered on this basis either on the consumer's premises (*Stör*), whether it be by itinerant workers or by sedentary workers moving around the households of a local clientele, or on the workers' premises: shop or household ("wage work" [in Bücher's terminology][46]). In either case the consumer household provides the raw materials, but it is customary for the worker to own his tools—the mower his scythe, the seamstress her sewing equipment, etc. The cases of *Stör* involve temporary membership in the consumer's household.

The case, contrasting with the above, in which the worker owns *all* means of production, Bücher terms "price work."

Occupationally specialized workers may be employed on an occasional basis by *profit-making enterprises* when at least the raw material, and thus also control over the product, belongs to the employer. In this case there may be migratory labor for a variety of different employers in different units, or occasional or seasonal work for an employer, the work being done in the worker's own household. Migratory harvest labor is an example of the first type. The second type may be illustrated by any type of occasional work at home which supplements the work in the workshop.

Occupational specialization without continuous engagement of the types noted above can also exist if: (2) Economic activity is conducted with appropriated means of production and (i) there is capital accounting and *partial* appropriation—especially, appropriation restricted to the fixed installations—by owners. Examples are workshops and factories transforming raw materials owned by others (*Lohnfabriken*) and, above all, factories producing under contract for an outside entrepreneur who takes charge of sales and other entrepreneurial functions (*verlegte Fabriken*); the former have existed for a long time, while the latter have recently become common. Or, if (ii) there is complete appropriation of the means of production by the workers, with the following possibilities: (a) in small-scale units without capital accounting, either producing for households ("price work" for customers), or producing for commercial enterprises. The latter is a case of domestic industry without expropriation of the means of production. The worker is formally a free craftsman, but is actually bound to a monopolistic group of merchants who are buyers for his product; (b) on a large scale with capital accounting and production for a fixed group of purchasers. This is usually, though not always, the result of market regulation by cartels.

Finally, it must be pointed out that not every case of acquisitive action is necessarily part of an occupational profit-making activity; nor is it necessary that involvement in acquisitive action, however frequent, should imply a continuous specialization with a constant meaningful orientation. With respect to the first observation, we note that "occasional acquisition" is found as a result of the disposal of surpluses produced in a budgetary unit. Corresponding to these is occasional trading of goods by large-scale budgetary units, especially seigneurial estates. From this starting point, it is possible to develop a continuous series of possible "occasional acquisitive acts," such as the occasional speculation of a *rentier*, occasional publication of an article or a poem by a person who is not a professional author, and similar modern phenomena, to the case where such things constitute a "subsidiary occupaiton" (*Nebenberuf*).

As to the second observation, it should be remembered that there are ways of making a living which are continually shifting and fundamentally unstable. A person may shift continually from one type of "occasional" profitable activity to another; or even between normal legitimate earning and begging, stealing, or highway robbery.

The following must be treated in special terms: (a) Support from purely charitable sources; (b) maintenance in an institution on other than a charitable basis, notably a penal institution; (c) regulated acquisition by force; and (d) criminal acquisition; that is, acquisition by force or fraud in violation of the rules of an order. The cases of (b) and (d) are of relatively little interest; (a) has often been of tremendous importance for hierocratic groups, such as mendicant orders; while (c) has been crucial for many political groups in the form of the booty gained from war, and in both cases the economy was profoundly affected. It is characteristic of both these cases that they lie outside the realm of economic activity as such. Hence this is not the place to enter into a more detailed classification. The forms will be treated elsewhere. For reasons which are in part the same, the earnings of civil servants, including military officers, have been mentioned below (sec. 38) only in order to give them a place as a sub-type of the earnings of labor, but without going into the details. To do this, it would be necessary to discuss the structure of relations of domination in the context of which these types of earnings are to be placed.

24a. *The Principal Forms of Appropriation and of Market Relationship*

According to the theoretical schemes which have been developed starting with sec. 15, the classification of the modes of appropriation in their technical, organizational aspects, and of the market relationships, is exceedingly complex. But actually, only a few of the many theoretical possibilities play a really dominant role.

(1) With respect to agricultural land: (a) There is the "ambulatory" cultivation by household units, which changes its location whenever the land has been exhausted. The land is usually appropriated by the tribe while its use is temporarily or permanently appropriated by neighborhood groups, with only temporary appropriation of the use of land to individual households.

The extent of the household group may vary from the individual conjugal family, through various types of extended family groups, to organized kin groups or a widely extended household community. (Agriculture is "ambulatory" as a rule only in relation to arable land, much less commonly and at longer intervals for farmyard sites.)

(b) Sedentary agriculture. The use of arable fields, meadows, pastures, woodland, and water is usually regulated by territorial or village associations for the smaller family household. Gardens and the land immediately surrounding the buildings are normally appropriated by the immediate family; arable fields, usually meadows, and pastures, by the village organization; woodland, by more extensive territorial groups. Redistribution of land is usually possible according to the law, but has generally not been systematically carried through and is hence usually obsolete. Economic activities have generally been regulated by a system of rules applying to the whole village. This is a "primary village economy."

It is only in exceptional cases, such as China, that the extended kinship group has constituted an economic unit. Where this is the case, it has generally taken the form of a rationalized organization, such as a clan association.

(c) Seigneurial rights over land (*Grundherrschaft*) and persons (*Leibherrschaft*) with a central manor of the lord (*Fronhof*) and dependent peasant farms obligated to deliveries in kind and labor services. The land itself and the workers are appropriated by the lord, the *use* of the land and rights to work by the peasants. This is a simple case of *manorial organization based on income in kind*.

(d) Seigneurial or fiscal monopoly of control over the land, with collective responsibility of the peasant community for meeting fiscal obligations. This leads to communal control over and regular systematic redistribution of the land. The land is, as a correlate of the fiscal burden, by decree permanently appropriated to the organized peasant community, not to the individual household; the latter enjoys only rights of use and these are subject to redistribution. Economic activity is regulated by the rules imposed by the manorial or the political lord. This is *manorial* or *fiscal field community (Feldgemeinschaft)*.

(e) *Unrestricted seigneurial land proprietorship* with exploitation of the dependent peasants as a source of rent income. The land is appropriated by the lord; but *coloni*,[47] sharecroppers, or tenants paying money rent carry out the actual economic activities.

(f) The *plantation*. The land is freely appropriated and worked by purchased slaves. The owner uses both as means of profit-making in a capitalistic enterprise with unfree labor.

(g) The "*estate economy*" (*Gutswirtschaft*). The land is appropriated to owners who either draw rent from it by leasing it to large-scale tenant farmers or farm it themselves for profit. In either case free labor is used, living in their own homesteads or those supplied by the landlord, and—in both cases again—conducting some agricultural production or, in the marginal case, none at all on own account.

(h) Absence of seigneurial ownership (*Grundherrschaft*): a peasant economy with appropriation of the land by the farmer (peasant). In practice this form of appropriation may mean that the land farmed is predominantly inherited land, or, on the other hand, that land lots are freely bought and sold. The former is typical of settlements with scattered farms and large-scale peasant proprietors; the latter, where settlement is in villages and the scale is small.[48]

Where tenants pay a money rent and where peasant proprietors buy and sell land, it is necessary to presuppose an adequate local market for the products of peasant agriculture.

(2) In the field of industry and transport, including mining, and of trade:

(a) *Household industry* carried on primarily as a means of occasional exchange of surpluses, only secondarily as a means of profit. This may involve an *inter-ethnic division of labor*, out of which in turn *caste occupations* have occasionally developed. In both cases appropriation of the sources of raw materials, and hence of the raw material production, is normal; purchase of raw materials and transformation of non-owned raw material ("wage work") are secondary phenomena. In the case of inter-ethnic specialization, *formal* appropriation is often absent. There is, however, generally, and in the case of caste, always, hereditary appropriation of the opportunities for earnings from specified functions by kinship or household groups.

(b) *"Tied" craft production* directly for customers: specification of functions in the service of an organized group of consumers. This may be a dominating group (*oikos* or seigneurial specification), or it may be a closed membership group (demiurgic specification).

There is no market sale. In the first case, we find organization of functions on a budgetary basis, or of labor in a workshop, as in the *ergasterion* of the lord. In the second case, there is hereditary appropriation of the status of the workers which may, however, become alienable, and work is carried out for an appropriated group of customers (consumers). There are the following very limited possibilities of development: (i) Appropriated (*formally* unfree) workers who are carriers of specified functions—of a trade—may be used either as a source of income payments to their owner, in which case they are usually and in spite of their formal servility *substantively* free, working in most cases directly for their own customers (rent slaves); or again, they might be used as unfree domestic craft producers, producing for the owner's profit; or, finally, as workers in the owner's workshop or *ergasterion*, also producing for profit. (ii) This may also develop into a liturgical specification of functions for fiscal purposes, similar to the type of caste occupations.

In the field of mining, there are similar forms, notably the use of unfree labor, slaves or serfs, in productive units controlled by princes or seigneurial owners.

In inland transportation, it is common for transportation installations [roads] to be appropriated by a seigneurial owner as a source of rent revenue. Maintenance services are then compulsorily imposed on specified small peasant holdings. Another possibility is small-scale caravan trade regulated by closed membership groups. The traders would then appropriate the goods themselves.

In the field of maritime transportation: (i) The ownership of ships by an *oikos,* a seigneur or a patrician trading on own account; (ii) co-operative construction and ownership of ships, captain and crew participating in trade on their own account, small travelling merchants constituting the shippers, all parties sharing the risks, and voyages made in strictly regulated "caravans." In all these cases "trade" was still identical with inter-local trade, that is, with transport.

(c) *Free non-agricultural trades.* Free production for consumers in return for a wage, either on the customer's premises or on that of the worker. Usually the raw materials were appropriated by the customer, the tools by the worker, premises and installations, if any were involved, by a lord as a source of income or by organized groups with rights of use in rotation. Another possibility is that both raw materials and tools should be appropriated by the worker who thus managed his own work, whereas premises and stationary equipment belonged to an organized group of workers, such as a guild. In all these cases, it is usual for the regulation of profit-making activity to be carried on by guilds.

In mining, deposits have usually been appropriated by political authorities or by seigneurial owners as sources of rent, while the rights of exploitation have been appropriated by organized groups of workers. Mining operations have been regulated on a guild basis with participation in the work an obligation of the members to the lord, who was interested in the rent, and to the working group (*Berggemeinde*), which was collectively responsible to him and had an interest in the proceeds.

In the field of inland transport, we find boatmen and teamster guilds with fixed rotation of travel assignments among the members and regulation of their opportunities for profit.

In the field of maritime transport, shared ownership of ships, travelling in convoys, and travelling merchants acting as *commenda* partners for businessmen staying at home are typical everywhere.

There are the following stages in the development toward capitalism:

(a) Effective monopolization of money capital by entrepreneurs, used as a means to make advances to labor. Connected with this is the assumption of powers of management over the process of production by virtue of the extension of credit, and of control over the product in spite of the fact that appropriation of the means of production has continued formally in the hands of the workers, as in the handicrafts and in mining; (b) appropriation of the right of marketing products on the basis of previous monopolization both of knowledge of the market and hence of market opportunities and of money capital. This was made possible by the imposition of a monopolistic system of guild regulation or by privileges granted by the political authority in return for periodical payments or for loans; (c) the subjective disciplining of workers who stood in a dependent relationship in the putting-out system, via the supply of raw materials and apparatus by the entrepreneur. A special case is that of the rational monopolistic organization of domestic industries on the basis of privileges granted in the interests of public finances or of the employment of the population. The conditions of work were thereby regulated by imposition from above as part of the concession which made profit-making activity possible; (d) the development of workshops *without* a rational specialization of labor in the process of production, by means of the appropriation by the entrepreneur of all the material means of production. In mining this included the appropriation by individual owners of mineral deposits, galleries, and equipment. In transportation, shipping enterprises fell into the hands of large owners. The universal result was the expropriation of the workers from the means of production; (e) the final step in the transition to capitalistic organization of production was the mechanization of the productive process and of transportation, and its orientation to capital accounting. All material means of production become fixed or working capital; all workers become "hands." As a result of the transformation of enterprises into associations of stock holders, the manager himself becomes expropriated and assumes the formal status of an "official." Even the owner becomes effectively a trustee of the suppliers of credit, the banks.

Of all these various types, the following instances may be noted:

1. In agriculture, type (a), migratory agriculture, is universal. But the sub-type where the effective unit has been the large-scale household or kinship group, is found only occasionally in Europe, quite frequently in East Asia, particularly China. Type (b), sedentary agriculture with land-use-regulating village associations, has been common in Europe and India. Type (c), seigneurial rights over the land with restrictions due to mutual obligations, has been found everywhere and is still common in some parts of the Orient. Type (d), seigneurial or fiscal rights over the land with systematic redistribution of the fields by the peasants, has existed in the more seigneurial type in Russia and in a variant involving the redistribution of land rents in India,[49] and in the more fiscal form in East Asia, the Near East, and Egypt. Type (e), unrestricted seigneurial land ownership drawing rent from small tenants, is typical of Ireland,

but also occurs in Italy, southern France, China, and the eastern parts of the Hellenistic world in Antiquity. Type (f), the plantation with unfree labor, was characteristic of Carthage and Rome in Antiquity, of modern colonial areas, and of the Southern States of the United States. Type (g), the "estate economy" in the form which involves separation of ownership and exploitation, has been typical of England; in the form of owner management, of eastern Germany, parts of Austria, Poland, and western Russia. Finally, type (h), peasant proprietorship, has been found in France, southern and western Germany, parts of Italy, Scandinavia, with certain limitations in south-western Russia, and with modifications particularly in modern China and India.

These wide variations in the forms which the organization of agriculture has finally assumed are only partially explicable in economic terms, that is, from such factors as the difference between the cultivation of forest clearings and of areas requiring irrigation. Special historical circumstances played a large role, and especially the forms taken by political and fiscal obligations and military organization.

2. In the field of industry, the following outline of the distribution of types may be given. Our knowledge of the situation in transportation and mining is not sufficiently complete to give such an outline for those fields.

(a) The first type, tribal crafts, has been found universally; (b) organization on the basis of occupational castes became general only in India. Elsewhere it has existed only for occupations considered discreditable and sometimes ritually impure; (c) the organization of industry on the basis of the *oikos* is found in all royal households in early times, but has been most highly developed in Egypt. It has also existed on seigneurial manors all over the world. Production by demiurgic crafts was occasionally found everywhere, including the Western World, but has developed into a pure type only in India. The special case of the use of control over unfree persons simply as a source of rent was common in Mediterranean Antiquity. The liturgical specification of functions was characteristic of Egypt, of the Hellenistic period, of the later Roman Empire, and has been found at times in China and India; (d) the free handicraft organization with guild regulations is classically illustrated in the European Middle Ages and became the predominant form only there. It has, however, been found all over the world; and guilds, in particular, have developed very widely, especially in China and the Near East. It is notable, however, that this type was entirely absent from the economic organization of the period of Mediterranean "classical" Antiquity. In India, the caste took the place of the guild. Of the stages in the development toward capitalism, only the second was reached on a large scale outside the Western World. This difference cannot be explained entirely in purely economic terms.

25. Conditions Underlying the Calculability of the Productivity of Labor

1. In the three typical communist forms of organization, noneconomic motives play a predominant part (see below, sec. 26). But apart from these cases, there are three primary conditions affecting the optimization of calculable performance by labor engaged in carrying out specifications: (a) The optimum of aptitude for the function; (b) the optimum of skill acquired through practice; (c) the optimum of inclination for the work.

Aptitude, regardless of whether it is the product of hereditary or environmental and educational influences, can only be determined by testing. In business enterprises in a market economy this usually takes the form of a trial period. The Taylor system involves an attempt to work out rational methods of accomplishing this.

Practice, and the resulting skill, can only be perfected by rational and continuous specialization. Today, it is worked out on a basis which is largely empirical, guided by considerations of minimizing costs in the interest of profitability, and limited by these interests. Rational specialization with reference to physiological conditions is only in its beginnings (witness again the Taylor system).

Inclination to work may be oriented to any one of the ways which are open to any other mode of action (see above, ch. I, sec. 2). But in the specific sense of incentive to execute one's own plans or those of persons supervising one's work, it must be determined either by a strong self-interest in the outcome, or by direct or indirect compulsion. The latter is particularly important in relation to work which executes the dispositions of others. This compulsion may consist in the immediate threat of physical force or of other undesirable consequences, or in the probability that unsatisfactory performance will have an adverse effect on earnings.

The second type, which is essential to a market economy, appeals immensely more strongly to the worker's self-interest. It also necessitates freedom of selection according to performance, both qualitatively and quantitatively, though naturally from the point of view of its bearing on profit. In this sense it has a higher degree of formal rationality, from the point of view of technical considerations, than any kind of direct compulsion to work. It presupposes the expropriation of the workers from the means of production by owners is protected by force. As compared with direct compulsion to work, this system involves the transferral, in addition to the responsibility for reproduction (in the family), of part of the worries about selection according to aptitude to the workers themselves. Further, both the need for capital and the capital risks are, as compared with the use of unfree labor, lessened and made more calculable. Finally, through the payment of money wages on a large scale, the market for goods which are objects of mass consumption is broadened.

Other things being equal, positive motives for work are, in the absence of direct compulsion, not obstructed to the same extent as they are for unfree labor. It is true, however, that whenever technical specialization has reached very high levels, the extreme monotony of operations tends to limit incentives to purely material wage considerations. Only when wages are paid in proportion to performance on a piece-rate basis is there an incentive to increasing productivity. In the capitalistic system, the most immediate bases of willingness to work are opportunities for high piece-rate earnings and the danger of dismissal.

The following observations may be made about the situation of free labor separated from the means of production: (a) Other things being equal, the likelihood that people will be willing to work on *affectual* grounds is greater in the case of specification of functions than in that of specialization of functions. This is true because the product of the individual's own work is more clearly evident. In the nature of the case, this is almost equally true wherever the quality of the product is important; (b) *traditional* motivations to work are particularly common in agriculture and in home industries—both cases where also the *general* attitude toward life is traditional. It is characteristic of this that the level of performance is oriented either to products which are stereotyped in quantity and quality or to a traditional level of earnings, or both. Where such an attitude exists, it is difficult to manage labor on a rational basis, and production cannot be increased by such incentives as piece rates. Experience shows, on the other hand, that a traditional patriarchal relationship to a lord or owner is capable of maintaining a high level of affectual incentive to work; (c) motivations based on *absolute values* are usually the result of religious orientations or of the high social esteem in which the particular form of work as such is held. Observation seems to show that all other sources of motivations directed to ultimate values are only transitional.

It goes without saying that the "altruistic" concern of the worker for his own family is a typical element of duty contributing to willingness to work generally.

2. The appropriation of the means of production and personal con-

trol, however formal, over the process of work constitute one of the strongest incentives to unlimited willingness to work. This is the fundamental basis of the extraordinary importance of small units in agriculture, whether in the form of small-scale proprietorship or small tenants who hope to rise to the status of owner. The classical locus of this type of organization is China. The corresponding phenomenon in the functionally specified skilled trades is most marked in India, but it is very important in all parts of Asia and also in Europe in the Middle Ages. In the latter case, the most crucial conflicts have been fought out over the issue of formal autonomy of the individual worker. The existence of the small peasant in a sense depends directly on the absence of capital accounting and on retaining the unity of household and enterprise. His is a specified and not a specialized function, and he tends both to devote more intensive labor to it and to restrict his standard of living in the interest of maintaining his formal independence. In addition, this system of agriculture makes possible the use of all manner of by-products and even "waste" in the household in a way which would not be possible in a larger farm unit. All the information we have available goes to show that capitalistic organization in agriculture is, where management is in the hands of the owner, far more sensitive to cyclical movements than small-scale peasant farming (see the author's figures in the *Verhandlungen des deutschen Juristentags,* vol. xxiv). [49a]

In industry, the corresponding small-scale type has retained its importance right up to the period of mechanization and of the most minute specialization and combination of functions. Even as late as the sixteenth century, as actually happened in England [1555], it was possible simply to forbid the operation of workshops like that of "Jack of Newbury" without catastrophic results for the economic situation of the workers. This was true because the combination in a single shop of looms, appropriated by one owner and operated by workers, could not, under the market conditions of the time, without any far-reaching increase in the specialization and co-ordination of labor functions, lead to an improvement in the prospect of profit for the entrepreneur large enough to compensate with certainty for the increase in risk and the cost of operating the shop. Above all, in industry an enterprise with large investments in fixed capital is not only, as in agriculture, sensitive to cyclical fluctuations, but also in the highest degree to every form of irrationality—that is, lack of calculability—in public administration and the administration of justice, as it existed everywhere outside the modern Western World. It has hence been possible, as in the competition with the Russian "factory" and everywhere else, for decentralized domestic industry to dominate the field. This was true up to the point, which was reached *before* the introduction of mechanical power and machine tools, where, with the broadening of market opportunities, the need for exact cost accounting and standardization of product became marked. In combination with technically rational apparatus, using water power and horse-gins, this led to the development of economic enterprises with internal specialization. Mechanical motors and machines could then be fitted in. Until this point had been reached, it was possible for all the large-scale industrial establishments, which occasionally had appeared all over the world, to be eliminated again without any serious prejudice to the economic situation of all those involved in them and without any serious danger to the interest of consumers. This situation changed only with the appearance of the factory. But willingness to work on the part of factory labor has been primarily determined by a combination of the transfer of responsibility for maintenance to the workers personally and the corresponding powerful indirect compulsion to work, as symbolized in the English workhouse system, and it has permanently remained oriented to the compulsory guarantee of the property system. This is demonstrated by the marked decline in willingness to work at the present time which resulted from the collapse of this coercive power in the [1918] revolution.

26. *Forms of Communism*

Communist arrangements for the communal or associational organization of work which are indifferent to calculation are not based on a consideration of means for obtaining an optimum of provisions, but, rather, on direct feelings of mutual solidarity. They have thus tended historically, up to the present, to develop on the basis of common value attitudes of a primarily non-economic character. There are three main types: (1) The household communism of the family, resting on a traditional and affectual basis; (2) the military communism of comrades in an army; (3) the communism based on love and charity in a religious community.

Cases (2) and (3) rest primarily on a specific emotional or charismatic basis. Always, however, they either (a) stand in direct conflict with the rational or traditional, economically specialized organization of their environment; such communist groups either work themselves or, in direct contrast, are supported purely by contributions from patrons, or both. Or (b) they may constitute a budgetary organization of privileged persons, ruling over other household units which are excluded from their organization, and are supported by voluntary contributions or liturgies of the latter. Or (c) finally, they are consumer household units, distinct from any profit-making enterprises but drawing income from them, and thus in an associative relationship with them.

The first of these modes of support (a) is typical of communities based on religious belief or some *Weltanschauung*—such as monastic communities which renounce the world altogether or carry on communal labor, sectarian groups and utopian socialists.

The second mode (b) is typical of military groups which rest on a wholly or partially communistic basis. Examples are the "men's house" in many primitive societies, the Spartan *syssitia,* the Ligurian pirate groups, the entourage of Calif Omar, the communism, in consumption and partly in requisitioning, of armies in the field in every age. A similar state of affairs is found in authoritarian religious groups—as in the Jesuit state in Paraguay and communities of mendicant monks in India and elsewhere.

The third mode (c) is typical of family households in a market economy.

Willingness to work and consumption without calculation within these communities are a result of the non-economic attitudes characteristic of them. In the military and religious cases, they are to an appreciable extent based on a feeling of separateness from the ordinary everyday world and of conflict with it. Modern communist movements are, so far as they aim for a communist organization of the masses, dependent on "value-rational" appeals to their disciples, and on arguments from expediency (*zweckrational*) in their [external] propaganda. In both cases, thus, they rest their position on specifically *rational* considerations and, in contrast to the military and religious communities, on considerations concerned with the everyday profane world.[50] Their prospects of success under ordinary conditions rest on entirely different subjective conditions than those of groups which are oriented to exceptional activities, to otherworldly values, or to other primarily non-economic considerations.

27. *Capital Goods and Capital Accounting*

The embryonic forms of capital goods are typically found in commodities traded in inter-local [as against local] or inter-tribal exchange, provided that "trade" (see sec. 29) appears as an activity clearly distinct from the mere procurement of goods on a household (budgetary) basis. For the swapping (*Eigenhandel*) of household economies—trading-off of surpluses—cannot be oriented to capital accounting. The inter-tribally sold products of household, clan or tribal crafts are *commodities,* while the means of procurement, as long as they remain one's own output, are only tools or raw materials, but not capital goods. The same goes for the market products and means of procurement of the peasant and the feudal lord as long as economic activity is not oriented to capital accounting, if only in its most primitive forms such as were incipient already in [the manual on estate management of the elder] Cato.

It is obvious that the internal movement of goods within the domain of a feudal lord or of an *oikos,* including occasional exchange and the common forms of internal exchange of products, is the antithesis of trade based on capital accounting. The trade engaged in by an *oikos,* like that of the Pharaohs, even when it is not concerned solely with provision for need and thus does not act as a budgetary unit but as one oriented to profit, is not for present purposes necessarily capitalistic. This would only be the case if it were oriented to capital accounting, particularly to an ex-ante estimate in money of the chances of profit from a transaction. Such estimates were made by the professional travelling merchants, whether they were engaged in selling on *commenda* basis for others, or in disposing of goods co-operatively marketed by an organized group. It is here, in the form of "occasional" enterprise, that the source of capital accounting and of the use of goods as capital is to be found.

Human beings (slaves and serfs) and fixed installations of all types which are used by seigneurial owners as sources of rent are, in the nature of the case, only rent-producing household property and not capital goods, similar to the securities which today yield interest or dividends for a private investor oriented to obtain an income from his wealth and perhaps some speculative gains. Investment of this household type should be clearly distinguished from the temporary investment of business capital by an enterprise. Goods which a lord over land or persons receives from his dependents in payment of the obligations due him by virtue of his seigneurial powers, and then puts up for sale, are not capital goods for the present terminological purposes, but only commodities. In such cases capital accounting—and above all, estimates of cost—are lacking in principle, not merely in practice. On the other hand, where slaves are used in an enterprise as a means of profit, particularly where there is an organized slave market and widespread purchase and sale of slaves, they do constitute capital goods. Where corvée-based production units (*Fronbetriebe*) work with a labor force of (hereditary) dependents who are not freely alienable and transferable, we shall not talk of capitalistic economic establishments, but of profit-making economic establishments with bound labor, regardless of whether we are dealing with agricultural production or unfree household industry. The decisive aspect is whether the tie is mutual—whether the lord is also bound to the worker.

In industry, production for sale by free workers with their own raw materials and tools ("price work") is a case of small-scale capitalistic enterprise. The putting-out industry is capitalistic, but decentralized; whereas every case of an organized workshop under capitalistic control is centralized capitalistic organization. All types of "wage work" of occasional workers, whether in the employer's or in the worker's home, are mere forms of dependent work which are sometimes exploited in the interest of the budgetary economy, sometimes in the interest of the employer's profit.

The decisive point is thus not so much the empirical fact, but rather the theoretical possibility of the use of capital accounting.

28. *The Concept of Trade and Its Principal Forms*

In addition to the various types of specialized and specified functions, which have already been discussed, every market economy (even, normally, one subject to substantive regulation) knows another function: namely mediation in the process of disposing of a producer's own control over goods or acquiring such control from others. This function can be carried out in any one of the following forms: (1) By the members of the administrative staff of an organized economic group, in return for payments in kind or in money which are fixed or vary with the services performed; (2) by an organized group created especially to provide for the selling and purchasing needs of its members; (3) by the members of a specialized occupational group working for their own profit and remunerated by fees or commissions without themselves acquiring control of the goods they handle; they act, that is, as agents, but in terms of a wide variety of legal forms; (4) by a specialized occupational group engaged in trade as a capitalistic profit-making enterprise (trade on own account). Such persons purchase goods with the expectation of being able to resell them at a profit, or sell for future delivery with the expectation of being able to cover their obligations before that date at a profitable figure. This may be done by buying and selling entirely freely in the market or subject to substantive regulation; (5) by a continuous regulated process, under the aegis of an organized political group, of expropriation of goods against compensation and of voluntary or enforced disposal of these goods to customers, again against compensation: compulsory trade; (6) by the professional lending of money or procurement of credit for the purpose of effectuating business payments or for the acquisition of means of production on credit; such transactions may be with business enterprises or with other organized groups, particularly political bodies. The economic function of the credit may be to finance current payments or the acquisition of capital goods.

Cases (4) and (5), and only these, will be called "trade." Case (4) is "free" trade, case (5) "compulsory monopolistic" trade.

Type (1) is illustrated for budgetary units by the *negotiatores* and *actores* who have acted on behalf of princes, landlords, monasteries, etc., and for profit-making enterprises by various types of travelling salesmen; type (2) is illustrated by various kinds of co-operative buying and selling agencies, including consumers' co-operative societies; type (3) includes brokers, commission merchants, forwarding agents, insurance agents, and various other kinds of agents; type (4) is illustrated for the case of free market transactions by modern trade, and for the regulated case by various types of heteronomously imposed or autonomously agreed divisions of the market with an allocation of the transactions with certain customers or of the transactions in certain commodities, or by the substantive regulation of the terms of exchange by the order of a political body or some other type of co-operative group; type (5) is illustrated by the state monopoly of the grain trade.

29. The Concept of Trade and Its Principal Forms— (Continued)

Free trade on own account (type 4), which alone will be dealt with for the present, is always a matter of profit-making enterprise, never of budgetary administration. It is hence under all normal conditions, if not always, a matter of earning money profits by contracts of purchase and sale. It may, however, be carried on (a) by an organization subsidiary to a budgetary economy, or (b) it may be an inseparable part of a total function through which goods are brought to a state of local consumability.

Case (a) is illustrated by members of a budgetary unit designated specifically to dispose of surpluses of that unit's production on their own account. If, however, it is a matter simply of "occasional" sale by *different* members at *different* times, it is not even a subsidiary enterprise, but where the members in question devote themselves entirely and on their own financial responsibility to sale or purchase, it is an example of the type (4), though somewhat modified. If, on the other hand, they act for the account of the unit as a whole, it is a case of the type (1).

Case (b) is illustrated by peddlers and other small traders who travel *with* their goods, and who thus primarily perform the function of transporting goods to the place of sale. They have hence been mentioned above in connection with the function of transportation. Travelling *commenda* traders may be a transitional form between types (3) and

(4). Whether the transportation service is primary and the trading profit secondary, or *vice versa,* is generally quite indefinite. In any case, all persons included in these categories are "traders."

Trade on the individual's own account (type 4) is always carried on on the basis of appropriation of the means of procurement, even though his control may be made possible only by borrowing. It is always the trader who bears the capital risk on his own account; and, correspondingly, it is he who, by virtue of his appropriation of the means of procurement, enjoys the opportunity for profit.

Specialization and specification of functions in the field of free trade on own account may take place in a variety of different ways. From an economic point of view, it is for the present most important to distinguish them according to the types of economic unit between which the merchant mediates: (i) Trade between households (budgetary units) with a surplus and other households which consume the surplus; (ii) trade between profit-making enterprises, themselves producers or merchants, and households (budgetary units) which consume the product. The latter include, of course, all types of organizations, in particular, political bodies; (iii) trade between one profit-making enterprise and another.

The first two cases come close to what is usually called "retail trade," which involves sale to consumers without reference to the sources from which the goods were obtained. The third case corresponds to "wholesale trade."

Trade may be oriented to the market or to customers. In the former case it may be a consumers' market, normally with the goods actually present. It may, on the other hand, be a market for business enterprises, in which case the goods may actually be present, as at fairs and expositions (usually though not necessarily, seasonal), or the goods may not be present, as in trade on commodity exchanges (usually, though not necessarily, permanent). If trade is oriented directly to customers, providing for the needs of a relatively fixed group of purchasers, it may be to households (budgetary units), as in retail trade, or to profit-making enterprises. The latter may in turn be producing units or retail enterprises or, finally, other wholesale enterprises. There may be various levels of middlemen in this sense, varying from the one nearest the producers to the one who sells to the retailer.

According to the geographical source of the goods disposed of, trade may be "interlocal" or "local."

The merchant may be in a position in fact to secure purchases on his own terms from the economic units which sell to him—putting-out trade. He may, on the other hand, be in a position to dictate the terms of his sales to the economic units which buy from him—traders' monopoly.

The first type is closely related to the putting-out organization of industry and is generally found combined with it. The second is "substantively regulated" trade, a variety of type (4).

It goes without saying that every market-oriented business enterprise must dispose of its own goods, even if it is primarily a producing enterprise. This type of marketing is not, however, "mediation" in the sense of the above definition so long as no members of the administrative staff are specialized for this and only this purpose (such as travelling salesman). Only then is a specialized "trading" function being performed. There are, of course, all manner of transitional forms.

The calculations underlying trading activity will be called "speculative" to the extent to which they are oriented to possibilities, the realization of which is regarded as fortuitous and is in this sense uncalculable. In this sense the merchant assumes the burden of "uncertainty."[51] The transition from rational calculation to what is in this sense speculative calculation is entirely continuous, since no calculation which attempts to forecast future situations can be completely secured against unexpected "accidental" factors. The distinction thus has reference only to a difference in the *degree* of rationality.

The forms of technical and economic specialization and specification of function in trade do not differ substantially from those in other fields. The department store corresponds to the factory in that it permits the most extensive development of internal specialization of function.

29a. *The Concept of Trade and Its Principal Forms—* (*Concluded*)

The term "banks" will be used to designate those types of profit-making "trading" enterprise which make a specialized function of administering or procuring money.

Money may be administered for private households by taking private deposit accounts and caring for the property of private individuals. It may also be administered for political bodies, as when a bank carries the account of a government, and for profit-making enterprise, by carrying business deposits and their current accounts.

Money may be procured for the needs of budgetary units, as in extending private consumption credit to private individuals, or in extending credit to political bodies. It may be procured for profit-making enterprises for the purpose of making payments to third persons, as in the creation of bills of exchange or the provision of checks or drafts for remittances. It may also be used to make advances on future payments due from customers, especially in the form of the discounting of bills of exchange. It may, finally, be used to give credit for the purchase of capital goods.

Formally, it is indifferent whether the bank (1) advances this money from its own funds or promises to make it available on demand, as in the provision for over-drafts of a current account, and whether the loan is or is not accompanied by a pledge or any other form of security provided by the borrower; or, (2) whether the bank, by some type of guarantee or in some other manner, influences others to grant the funds.

In practice, the business policy of banks is normally aimed to make a profit by relending funds which have been lent to them or placed at their disposal.

The funds which a bank lends may be obtained from stocks of bullion or of coin from the existing mints which it holds on credit, or by its own creation of certificates (*banco*-money) or of means of circulation (bank notes), or, finally, from the deposits of private individuals who have placed their money at its disposal.

Whether a bank borrows on its own to obtain the funds it lends out or creates means of circulation, it must, if it is acting rationally, attempt to provide for coverage to maintain its liquidity—that is, it must keep a sufficient stock of cash reserves or arrange the terms of credit granted in such a manner that it can always meet its normal payment obligations.

As a rule, the observance of liquidity ratios by money-creating (i.e., note-issuing) banks is provided for in imposed regulations by organizations (merchant guilds or political bodies). These regulations are at the same time usually designed to protect the chosen monetary system of an area as far as possible against changes in the substantive validity of the money, and thus to protect the (formal) rationality of the economic calculations of budgetary units, above all those of the political body, and of profit-making enterprises against disturbances from (substantive) irrationalities. In particular, the most stable rate of exchange possible for one's own money against the monies of other monetary areas, with which trade or credit relations exist or are desired, is usually striven for. This type of monetary policy, which attempts to control the factors of irrationality in the monetary field, will, following G. F. Knapp, be called "lytric" policy. In the strictly laissez-faire state, this is the most important function in the realm of economic policy which the state would undertake. In its rational form this type of policy is entirely restricted to the modern state.

The policy measures of the Chinese with respect to copper and paper money and the Roman coinage policy will be discussed at the proper point, but they did not constitute a modern lytric monetary policy. Only the *banco*-money policy of the Chinese guilds, which formed the model

for the Hamburg *banco* mark, came up to modern standards of rationality.[52]

The term "financing" (*Finanzierungsgeschäfte*) will be applied to all
business transactions which are oriented to obtaining control, in one of
the following ways, of favorable opportunities for profit-making by business enterprise, regardless of whether they are carried on by banks or by
other agencies, including individuals, as an occasional source of profit
or as a subsidiary enterprise, or as part of the speculative operations of a
"financier": (a) through the transformation of rights to appropriated
profit opportunities into securities or other negotiable instruments, and
by the acquisition of these securities, either directly or through such
subsidiary enterprises as are described below under (c); (b) by the systematic tender (or, occasionally, refusal) of business credit; (c) through
compulsory joining, if necessary or desired, of hitherto competing enterprises, either (i) in the form of monopolistic regulation of enterprises
at the same stage of production (cartellization), or (ii) in the form of
monopolistic fusion under one management of hitherto competing enterprises for the purpose of weeding out the least profitable ones (merger),
or (iii) in the not necessarily monopolistic form of the fusion of specialized enterprises at successive stages of a production process (vertical combination), or finally (iv) in the form of an attempted domination of
many enterprises through operations with their shares (trusts, holding
companies) or the creation of new enterprises for the purpose of increasing profits or merely to extend personal power (financing as such).

> Of course, financing operations are often carried out by banks and,
> as a general rule, unavoidably involve their participation. But the main
> control often lies in the hands of stock brokers, like Harriman, or of
> individual large-scale entrepreneurs in production, like Carnegie. The
> formation of cartels is also often the work of large-scale entrepreneurs,
> like Kirdorf; while that of trusts is more likely to be the work of "finan-
> ciers," like Gould, Rockefeller, Stinnes, and Rathenau. This will be
> further discussed below.

30. *The Conditions of Maximum Formal Rationality of Capital Accounting*

The following are the principal conditions necessary for obtaining a
maximum of formal rationality of capital accounting in production enterprises: (1) complete appropriation of all material means of production
by owners and the complete absence of all formal appropriation of opportunities for profit in the market; that is, market freedom; (2) complete

autonomy in the selection of management by the owners, thus complete absence of formal appropriation of rights to managerial functions; (3) complete absence of appropriation of jobs and of opportunities for earning by workers and, conversely, the absence of appropriation of workers by owners. This implies free labor, freedom of the labor market, and freedom in the selection of workers; (4) complete absence of substantive regulation of consumption, production, and prices, or of other forms of regulation which limit freedom of contract or specify conditions of exchange. This may be called substantive freedom of contract; (5) complete calculability of the technical conditions of the production process; that is, a mechanically rational technology; (6) complete calculability of the functioning of public administration and the legal order and a reliable purely formal guarantee of all contracts by the political authority. This is a formally rational administration and law; (7) the most complete separation possible of the enterprise and its conditions of success and failure from the household or private budgetary unit and its property interests. It is particularly important that the capital at the disposal of the enterprise should be clearly distinguished from the private wealth of the owners, and should not be subject to division or dispersion through inheritance. For large-scale enterprises, this condition tends to approach an optimum from a formal point of view: in the fields of transport, manufacture, and mining, if they are organized in corporate form with freely transferrable shares and limited liability, and in the field of agriculture, if there are relatively long-term leases for large-scale production units; (8) a monetary system with the highest possible degree of formal rationality.

Only a few points are in need of comment, though even these have already been touched on.

(1) With respect to the freedom of labor and of jobs from appropriation, it is true that certain types of unfree labor, particularly full-fledged slavery, have guaranteed what is formally a more complete power of disposal over the worker than is the case with employment for wages. But there are various reasons why this is less favorable to rationality and efficiency than the employment of free labor: (a) The amount of capital which it was necessary to invest in human resources through the purchase and maintenance of slaves has been much greater than that required by the employment of free labor; (b) the capital risk attendant on slave ownership has not only been greater but specifically irrational in that slave labor has been exposed to all manner of non-economic influences, particularly to political influence in a very high degree; (c) the slave market and correspondingly the prices of slaves have been particularly subject to fluctuation, which has made a balancing of profit and loss on a rational basis exceedingly difficult; (d) for similar reasons,

particularly involving the political situation, there has been a difficult problem of recruitment of slave labor forces; (e) when slaves have been permitted to enjoy family relationships, this has made the use of slave labor more expensive in that the owner has had to bear the cost of maintaining the women and of rearing children. Very often, he has had no way in which he could make rational economic use of these elements as part of his labor force; (f) hence the most complete exploitation of slave labor has been possible only when they were separated from family relationships and subjected to a ruthless discipline. Where this has happened it has greatly accentuated the difficulties of the problem of recruitment; (g) it has in general been impossible to use slave labor in the operation of tools and apparatus, the efficiency of which required a high level of responsibility and of involvement of the operator's self-interest; (h) perhaps most important of all has been the impossibility of selection, of employment only after trying out in the job, and of dismissal in accordance with fluctuations of the business situation or when personal efficiency declined.

Hence the employment of slave labor has only been possible in general under the following conditions: (a) Where it has been possible to maintain slaves very cheaply; (b) where there has been an opportunity for regular recruitment through a well-supplied slave market; (c) in agricultural production on a large scale of the plantation type, or in very simple industrial processes. The most important examples of this type of relatively successful use of slaves are the Carthaginian and Roman plantations, those of colonial areas and of the Southern United States, and the Russian "factories." The drying up of the slave market, which resulted from the pacification of the Empire, led to the decay of the plantations of Antiquity.[53] In North America, the same situation led to a continual search for cheap new land, since it was impossible to meet the costs of slaves and pay a land rent at the same time. In Russia, the serf "factories" were barely able to meet the competition of the *kustar* type of household industry and were totally unable to compete with free factory labor. Even before the emancipation of the serfs, petitions for permission to dismiss workers were common, and the factories decayed with the introduction of shops using free labor.

When workers are employed for wages, the following advantages to industrial profitability and efficiency are conspicuous: (a) Capital risk and the necessary capital investment are smaller; (b) the costs of reproduction and of bringing up children fall entirely on the worker. His wife and children must seek employment on their own account; (c) largely for this reason, the risk of dismissal is an important incentive to the maximization of production; (d) it is possible to select the labor force according to ability and willingness to work.

(2) The following comment may be made on the separation of enterprise and household. The separation in England of the producing farm *enterprise,* leasing the land and operating with capital accounting, from the entailed *ownership* of the land is by no means fortuitous, but

is the outcome of an undisturbed development over centuries which was characterized by the absence of an effective protection of the status of peasants. This in turn was a consequence of the country's insular position. Every joining of the *ownership* of land with the *cultivation* of the land turns the land into a capital good for the economic unit, thus increasing the capital requirements and the capital risks of this unit. It impedes the separation of the household from the economic establishment; the settlements paid out at inheritance, for instance, burden the resources of the enterprise. It reduces the liquidity of the entrepreneur's capital and introduces a number of irrational factors into his capital accounting. Hence the separation of landownership from the organization of agricultural production is, from a formal point of view, a step which promotes the rationality of capital accounting. It goes without saying, however, that any substantive evaluation of this phenomenon is quite another matter, and its conclusions may be quite different depending on the values underlying the judgment.

3 1 . *The Principal Modes of Capitalistic Orientation of Profit-Making*

The "capitalistic" orientation of profit-making activity (in the case of rationality, this means: the orientation to capital accounting) can take a number of qualitatively different forms, each of which represents a definite type:

1. It may be orientation to the profit possibilities in continuous buying and selling on the market ("trade") with free exchange—that is, absence of formal and at least relative absence of substantive compulsion to effect any given exchange; or it may be orientation to the profit possibilities in continuous production of goods in enterprises with capital accounting.

2. It may be orientation to the profit possibilities in trade and speculation in different currencies, in the taking over of payment functions of all sorts and in the creation of means of payment; the same with respect to the professional extension of credit, either for consumption or for profit-making purposes.

3. It may be orientation to opportunities for predatory profit from political organizations or persons connected with politics. This includes the financing of wars or revolutions and the financing of party leaders by loans and supplies.

4. It may be orientation to the profit opportunities in continuous business activity which arise by virtue of domination by force or of a position of power guaranteed by the political authority. There are two

main sub-types: colonial profits, either through the operation of plantations with compulsory deliveries or compulsory labor or through monopolistic and compulsory trade, and fiscal profits, through the farming of taxes and of offices, whether at home or in colonies.

5. It may be orientation to profit opportunities in unusual transactions with political bodies.

6. It may be orientation to profit opportunities of the following types: (a) in purely speculative transactions in standardized commodities or in the securities of enterprises; (b) in the execution of the continuous financial operations of political bodies; (c) in the promotional financing of new enterprises in the form of sale of securities to investors; (d) in the speculative financing of capitalistic enterprises and of various other types of economic organization with the purpose of a profitable regulation of market situations or of attaining power.

Types (1) and (6) are to a large extent peculiar to the modern Western World. The other types have been common all over the world for thousands of years wherever the possibilities of exchange and money economy (for type 2) and money financing (for types 3–5) have been present. In the Western World they have not had such a dominant importance as modes of profit-making as they had in Antiquity, except in restricted areas and for relatively brief periods, particularly in times of war. Where large areas have been pacified for a long period, as in the Chinese and later Roman Empire, these types have tended to decline, leaving only trade, money changing, and lending as forms of capitalistic acquisition. For the capitalistic financing of political activities was everywhere the product of the competition of states with one another for power, and of the corresponding competition for capital which moved freely between them. All this ended only with the establishment of the unified empires.

The point of view here stated has, if the author's memory is accurate, been previously put forward in the clearest form by J. Plenge in his *Von der Diskontpolitik zur Herrschaft über den Geldmarkt* (Berlin 1913). Before that a similar position seems to have been taken only in the author's article, *"Agrarverhältnisse im Altertum,"* 1909 [reprinted in *GAzSW,* 1924; cf. 275ff.]

It is only in the modern Western World that rational capitalistic enterprises with fixed capital, free labor, the rational specialization and combination of functions, and the allocation of productive functions on the basis of capitalistic enterprises, bound together in a market economy, are to be found. In other words, we find the capitalistic type of organization of labor, which in formal terms is purely voluntary, as the typical and dominant mode of providing for the wants of the masses of the population,

with expropriation of the workers from the means of production and appropriation of the enterprises by security owners. It is also only here
that we find public credit in the form of issues of government securities,
the "going public" of business enterprises, the floating of security issues and
financing carried on as the specialized function of rational business
enterprises, trade in commodities and securities on organized exchanges,
money and capital markets, monopolistic organizations as a form of rational business organization of the entrepreneurial *production* of goods,
and not only of the trade in them.

This difference calls for an explanation and the explanation cannot
be given on economic grounds alone. Types (3) to (5) inclusive will be
treated here together as "politically oriented capitalism." The whole of
the later discussion will be devoted particularly to the problem of explaining the difference. In general terms, it is possible only to make the following statements:

1. It is clear from the very beginning that the politically oriented
events and processes which open up these profit opportunities exploited
by political capitalism are irrational from an economic point of view—
that is, from the point of view of orientation to market advantages and
thus to the consumption needs of budgetary units.

2. It is further clear that purely speculative profit opportunities and
pure consumption credit are irrational from the point of view both
of want satisfaction and of the production of goods, because they are determined by the fortuitous distribution of ownership and of market advantages. The same may also be true of opportunities for promotion and
financing, under certain circumstances; but this is not necessarily always
the case.

Apart from the rational capitalistic enterprise, the modern economic
order is unique in its monetary system and in the commercialization of
ownership shares in enterprises through the various forms of securities.
Both these peculiarities must be discussed—first the monetary system.

32. *The Monetary System of the Modern State and the Different Kinds of Money: Currency Money*

1. (a) The modern state has universally assumed the monopoly of
regulating the monetary system by statute; and (b) almost without exception, the monopoly of creating money, at least for coined money.

Originally, purely fiscal considerations were decisive in the creation
of this monopoly—seigniorage (minting fees) and other profits from

coinage. This was the motive for the prohibition of the use of foreign money. But the monopolization of issue of money has not been universal even up into the modern age. Thus, up until the currency reform [of 1871–1873] foreign coins were current in Bremen.

(c) With the increasing importance of its taxation and its own economic enterprises, the state has become both the largest receiver and the largest maker of payments in the society, either through its own pay offices or through those maintained on its behalf. Quite apart from the monopoly of monetary regulation and issue, because of the tremendous importance of the financial transactions of the state the behavior of the state treasurers in their monetary transactions is of crucial significance for the monetary system—above all, what kind of money they *actually* have at hand and hence can pay out, and what kind of money they force on the public as legal tender, and further, what kind of money they *actually* accept and what kind they partially or fully repudiate.

> Thus, paper money is partially repudiated if customs duties have to be paid in gold, and was fully repudiated (at least ultimately) in the case of the *assignats* of the French Revolution, the money of the Confederate States of America, and that issued by the Chinese Government during the Tai Ping Rebellion.

In terms of its legal properties, money can be defined as a "legal means of payment" which everyone, including also and especially the public pay offices, is obligated to accept and to pay, either up to a given amount or without limit. In terms of the behavior of the state (*regiminal*) it may be defined as that money which public pay offices accept in payment and for which they in turn enforce acceptance in their payments; legal compulsory money is that money, in particular, which they impose in their payments. The "imposition" may occur by virtue of existing legal authority for reasons of monetary policy, as in the case of the [German silver] Taler and the [French silver] five-franc piece after the discontinuance—as we know, never really put into effect—of the coining of silver [1871 and 1876]; or it may occur because the state is incapable of paying in any other means of payment. In the latter case, an existing legal authority to enforce acceptance may now be employed for the first time, or an *ad hoc* legal authority may be created, as is almost always true in cases of resort to paper money. In this last case, what usually happens is that a means of exchange, which was previously by law or *de facto* redeemable in definitive money, whether its acceptance could be legally imposed or not, will now be *de facto* imposed and by the same token become *de facto* unredeemable.

By passing a suitable law, a state can turn any object into a "legal means of payment" and any chartal object into "money" in the sense of a means of payment. It can establish for them any desired set of "value scales" or, in the case of "market money," "currency relations" [see above, ch. II, sec. 6]. There are, however, certain formal disturbances of the monetary system in these cases which the state can either not suppress at all or only with great difficulties:

(a) In the case of administrative money, the forgery of notes, which is almost always very profitable; and (b) with all forms of metallic money, the non-monetary use of the metal as a raw material, where its products have a high value. This is particularly true when the metal in question is in an undervalued currency relation to others. It is also, in the case of market money, exceedingly difficult to prevent the export of the coins to other countries where that currency metal has a higher value. Finally, it is difficult to compel the offer of a legal monetary metal for coinage where it is undervalued with respect to the currency money (coins or paper).

With paper money the rate of exchange of one currency unit of the metal with its nominal equivalent of paper always becomes too unfavorable for the metal when redeemability of the notes is suspended, and this is what happens when it is no longer possible to make payments in metal money.

The exchange ratios between several kinds of market money may be determined (a) by fixing the relation for each particular case; (b) by establishing rates periodically; and (c) by legal establishment of permanent rates, as in bimetallism.

In cases (a) and (b) it is usual that only one metal is the effective currency (in the Middle Ages it was silver), while the others are used as trading coins with varying rates. The complete separation of the specific modes of use of different types of market money is rare in modern monetary systems, but has at times been common, as in China and in the Middle Ages.

2. The definition of money as a legal means of payment and as the creature of the "lytric" administration of political bodies is, from a sociological point of view, not exhaustive. This definition, to put it in G. F. Knapp's words, starts from "the fact of the existence of debts,"[54] especially of tax debts to the state and of interest debts of the state. What is relevant for the legal discharge of such debts is the continuity of the *nominal* unit of money, even though the monetary material may have changed, or, if the nominal unit should change, the "historical definition" of the new nominal unit. Beyond that, the individual today values the nominal unit of money as a certain proportional part of his nominal money income, and not as a chartal piece of metal or note.

The state can through its legislation—or its administrative staff through the actual behavior of its pay offices—indeed dictate the *formal* validity of the "currency" of the monetary area which it rules.

Provided, that is, that it employs modern methods of administration. It was not, however, possible at all times, for instance, in China. There in earlier times it has generally not been possible because payments by and to the government were too small in relation to the total field of transactions. Even recently it appears that the Chinese Government has not been able to make silver into a "limited money" currency with a gold reserve because it was not sufficiently powerful to suppress the counterfeiting which would undoubtedly have ensued.

However, it is not merely a matter of dealing with existing debts, but also with exchange in the present and the contraction of new debts to be paid in the future. But in this connection the orientation of the parties is primarily to the status of money as a means of exchange [see above, ch. II, sec. 6], and thus to the probability that it will be at some future time acceptable in exchange for specified or unspecified goods in price relationships which are capable of approximate estimate.

1. Under certain circumstance, it is true, the probability that urgent debts can be paid off to the state or private individuals from the proceeds may also be importantly involved. This case may, however, be left out of account here because it only arises in emergency situations.

2. In spite of the fact that it is otherwise absolutely correct and brilliantly executed, hence of permanently fundamental importance, it is at this point that the incompleteness of G. F. Knapp's *Staatliche Theorie des Geldes* becomes evident.

Furthermore, the state on its part needs the money which it receives through taxation or from other sources also as a means of exchange, though not only for that purpose, but often in fact to a very large extent for the payment of interest on its debt. But its creditors, in the latter case, will then wish to employ it as a means of exchange; indeed this is the main reason why they desire money. And it is almost always true that the state itself needs money to a large degree, sometimes even entirely, as a means of exchange to cover future purchases of goods and supplies in the market. Hence, however necessary it is to distinguish it analytically, it is not, after all, the fact that money is a means of payment which is decisive.

The exchange possibility of money against other specific goods, which rests on its valuation in relation to marketable goods, will be called its "substantive" validity, as opposed to its formal, legal validity as a means of payment and the frequently existing legal compulsion for its formal use as a means of exchange.

In principle, as an observable fact, a monetary unit has a substantive valuation only in relation to definite types of goods and only for each separate individual as his own valuation on the basis of the marginal utility of money for him, which will vary with his income. This marginal utility is changed for the individual with any increase in the quantity of money at his disposal. Thus the marginal utility of money to the issuing authority falls, not only, but above all, when it creates administrative money and uses it for obtaining goods by exchange or forces it on the public as a means of payment. There is a secondary change in the same direction for those persons who deal with the state and who, because of the higher prices resulting from the lowered marginal utility of money to public bodies, become the possessors of larger money stocks. The "purchasing power" now at their disposal—that is, the lowering of the marginal utility of money for these possessors—can in turn result in an increase in prices paid to those from whom *they* purchase, etc. If, on the other hand, the state were to withdraw from circulation part of the notes it receives—that is, if it should not pay them out again, but destroy them—the result would be that the marginal utility of money of its lessened money stocks would rise, and it would have to curtail its expenditures correspondingly, that is, it would reduce its demand prices appropriately. The results would be the exact opposite of those just outlined. It is hence possible for administrative money, though by no means only this, to have an important effect on the price structure in any given monetary area. (The speed at which this will occur and the different ways in which it affects different goods cannot be discussed here).

3. A cheapening and increase in the supply, or vice versa, a rise in cost and curtailment of the supply in the production of monetary metals could have a similar effect in *all* countries using it for monetary purposes. Monetary and non-monetary uses of metals are closely interdependent, but the only case in which the non-monetary use of the metal has been decisive for its valuation as money has been that of copper in China. Gold will enjoy an equivalent valuation in the nominal unit of gold money less costs of coining as long as it is used as a means of payment between monetary areas and is also the market money in the monetary areas of the leading commercial powers. In the past this was true also of silver and would be today if silver were still in the same position as gold. A metal which is not used as a means of payment between monetary areas, but constitutes market money in some of them, will naturally have a definite value in terms of the nominal monetary unit of those areas. But these in turn will, according to the costs of adding to the supply and according to the quantities in circulation, and, finally, according

to the so-called "balance of payments," have a fluctuating exchange relationship to other currencies. Finally, a precious metal which is universally used for restricted coinage into administrative money, but not as market money, is primarily valued on the basis of its non-monetary use. The question is always whether the metal in question can be profitably produced and at what rate. When it is completely demonetized, this valuation depends entirely on its money cost of production reckoned in international means of payment in relation to the non-monetary demand for it. If, on the other hand, it is used universally as market money and as an international means of payment, its valuation will depend on costs in relation primarily to the monetary demand for it. When, finally, it has a limited use as market or administrative money, its valuation will be determined in the long run by whichever of the two demands for it, as expressed in terms of international means of payment, is able to afford better to pay the costs of production. If its use as market money is limited to a particular monetary area, it is unlikely in the long run that its monetary use will be decisive for the valuation, for the exchange rate of such special-standard areas to other monetary areas will tend to fall, and it is only when international trade is completely cut off—as in China and Japan in the past, and in the areas still actually cut off from each other after the war today—that this will not affect domestic prices. The same is true for the case of a metal used as regulated [i.e., limited coinage] administrative money; the strictly limited possibility of the use of the metal as money could be decisive for its valuation only if it would be minted in great quantities. The long-run outcome would in this case, however, be similar to that of a metal used as market money only in a restricted area.

Though it was temporarily realized in practice in China, the monopolization of the total production and use of a monetary metal is essentially a theoretical, limiting case. If several competing monetary areas are involved and wage labor is used, it does not alter the situation as much as possibly might be expected. For if all payments by government agencies were made in terms of this metal, every attempt to limit its coinage or to tax it very heavily, which might well yield large profit, would have the same result as it did in the case of the very high Chinese seigniorage. First, in relation to the metal the money would become very highly valued, and if wage labor were used, mining operations would to a large extent become unprofitable. As the amount in circulation declined, there would result a "contra-inflation"; and it is possible, as actually happened in China where this led at times to complete freedom of coinage, that this would go so far as to induce the use of money substitutes and a large extension of the area of natural economy. This also happened in China. If a market economy were to be maintained, it would be hardly possible for monetary policy in the long run to act otherwise than as if free coinage were legally in force. The only difference is that minting would no longer be left to the initiative of interested parties. With complete socialism, on the other hand, the problem of money would cease to be significant and the precious metals would hardly be produced at all.

4. The fact that the precious metals have normally become the monetary standard and the material from which money is made is historically an outcome of their function as ornaments and hence, specifically, as gifts. But apart from purely technical factors, this use was also determined by the fact that they were goods which were typically dealt with by weight. Their maintenance in this function is not at first sight obvious since today, for all except the smallest payments, everyone normally uses notes, especially bank-notes, and expects to receive them in payment. There are, however, important motives underlying retention of metal standards.

5. In all modern states, not only is the issue of money in the form of notes legally regulated, but it is monopolized by the state. It is either carried out directly by the state itself, or by one or a few issuing agencies enjoying special privileges but subject to the control of the state—the banks of issue.

6. The term "public currency money" (*regiminales Kurantgeld*)[55] will be applied only to money which is actually paid out by public agencies and acceptance of which is enforced. On the other hand, any other money which, though not paid out under compulsory acceptance, is used in transactions between private individuals by virtue of formal legal provisions, will be called "accessory standard money." Money which must legally be accepted in private transactions only up to a given maximum amount, will be called "change" (*Scheidegeld*). (This terminology is based on that of Knapp. This is even more definitely true in what follows.)

"Definitive" currency money means public currency money; whereas any type of money is to be called "provisional" currency money so far as it is in fact effectively exchangeable for or redeemable in terms of definitive currency.

7. In the long run, public currency money must naturally coincide with the effective currency. It cannot be a possibly separate, merely "official" legal tender currency. Effective currency, however, is necessarily one of three things: (a) free market money; (b) unregulated; or (c) regulated administrative money. The public treasury does not make its payments simply by deciding to apply the rules of a monetary system which somehow seems to it ideal, but its acts are determined by its own financial interests and those of important economic groups.

With regard to its chartal form, an effective standard money may be metallic money or note money.[56] Only metallic money can be a free market money, but this is not necessarily the case for all metallic money.

It is free market money when the lytric administration will coin any quantity of the standard metal or will exchange it for chartal coins— "hylodromy."[57] According, then, to the precious metal which is chosen as the standard, there will be an effective gold, silver, or copper standard. Whether the lytric administration is in fact in a position to maintain an actual hylodromic system does not depend simply on its own desires, but on whether individuals are interested in presenting metal for coinage.

It is thus possible for hylodromy to exist "officially" without existing "effectively." Whatever the official position may be, it is not effective (a) when, given hylodromy with several metals, one or more of these is at the official rate *under*valued with respect to the market price of the raw material. In that case, naturally, only the *over*valued metal will be offered to the mint for coinage and to creditors in payments. If the public pay offices do not participate in this trend, the *over*valued coins will pile up in their hands until they, too, have nothing else to offer in their payments. If the price relation is rigidly enough maintained, the *under*valued coins will then be melted down, or they will be exchanged by weight, as commodities, against the coins of the *over*valued metal.

(b) Hylodromy is also not effective if persons making payments, including especially public agencies under stress of necessity, continually and on a large scale make use of their formal right or usurped power to compel acceptance of another means of payment, whether metal or notes, which is not presently provisional [i.e. redeemable] money, but either has been accessory money or, if previously provisional, has ceased to be redeemable because of the insolvency of the issuing agency.

In case (a) hylodromy always ceases, and the same thing happens in case (b) when accessory forms of money or forms which are no longer effectively provisional are forced on the public persistently on a large scale.

The outcome in case (a) is to confine the maintenance of the fixed rate to the overvalued metal, which then becomes the only free market money; the result is thus a new· metallic standard. In case (b) the accessory metal or notes which are no longer effectively provisional become the standard money. In the first case we get a "restricted money" standard; in the second, a paper standard.

It is also possible for hylodromy to be effective without being official in the sense of being legally established.

An example is the competition of the various coining authorities in the Middle Ages, determined by their fiscal interest in seigniorage, to mint as much as possible of the monetary metals. There was no formal establishment of hylodromy at that time, but the actual situation was much as if there had been.

In view of what has just been said, a "monometallic legal standard," which may be gold, silver, or copper, will be said to exist when one metal is by law hylodromic. A "multimetallic legal standard," on the other hand, exists when more than one metal is used (it may be two or three) and they are freely coined in a fixed ratio to each other. A "parallel legal standard" exists when several metals are freely coinable *without* a fixed ratio. A standard metal and a metallic standard will only be spoken of for that metal which is effectively hylodromic, and thus, in practice, constitutes actual market money.

Legally, all countries of the Latin Union were under bimetallism until the suspension of the free coinage of silver, which followed the German currency reform [1871]. But effectively, as a rule, only the metal which was for the time being overvalued was actually a standard metal. The legal stabilization of the exchange ratio, however, worked so well that the change was often scarcely noted and there seemed to be effective bimetallism. But insofar as the ratio shifted, the coins of the undervalued money became accessory money. (This account of the matter coincides closely with that of Knapp). At least where there is competition between several autocephalous and autonomous minting agencies, bimetallism is an effective monetary state only as a transitory phenomenon and is usually only a legal, as opposed to an effective, state of affairs.

The fact that the undervalued metal is not brought to the mint is naturally the result not of administrative action, but of the changed market situation in relation to the persistence of the legal coinage ratio of the metals. It would, of course, be possible for the mint to continue to coin that metal at a loss as administrative money, but since the non-monetary uses of the money are more profitable, it could not be kept in circulation.

33. *Restricted Money*

Any type of metallic money which is not hylodromic will be called "restricted money" (*Sperrgeld*) if it is currency money. Restricted money may circulate as accessory money; that is, having a fixed relationship to some other currency money in the same monetary area. This latter may be another form of restricted money, paper money, or a market money.

Or restricted money may be oriented to an international standard. This is the case when it is the sole currency money in its own area, and provision is made for having international means of payment available for making payments abroad, either in coin or in bullion. This is a "convertible restricted money" standard with a reserve fund of foreign exchange.

(a) Restricted money will be called "particular" when it is the only currency money, but is not oriented to an international standard.

> Restricted money may then be valued internationally *ad hoc* each time international means of payment or foreign exchange is bought; or, when this is possible, it may be given a fixed relation to the international standard. Talers and silver five-franc pieces were restricted money with a fixed relation to the currency money of the same country; both were accessory money. The Dutch silver gulden has been oriented to the international gold standard after having been "particular" for a short time after the restriction of coinage, and now the rupee is in the same position. This is also true of the Chinese dollar which, since the coinage regulation of 24 May 1910, is "particular" as long as hylodromy, which is not mentioned in the statute, does also *de facto* not exist. The orientation to the international gold standard, as recommended by the American Commission, was rejected.

In the case of a "restricted" money, free coinage at fixed rates (hylodromy) would be very profitable to the private owners of the precious metals. Nevertheless, and precisely for this reason, restriction is maintained because it is feared that the introduction of hylodromy of the metal of the formerly restricted money would lead to abandonment as unprofitable of the hylodromy of the other metal which was fixed in too low a ratio to it. The monetary stock of this metal, which would now become "obstructed" (see next paragraph), would be put to more profitable non-monetary uses. The reason why a rational lytric administration wishes to avoid this is that the other metal, which would be forced out, is an international means of payment.

(b) Restricted currency money will be called "obstructed" market money when, contrary to the case just cited, free coinage exists legally, but is unprofitable to private business and hence does not take place. This lack of profitability may rest on an unfavorable relation between the market price of the metal and its monetary ratio to the market money, if a metal, or to paper money. Such money must at some time in the past have been market money; but, with multimetallism, changes in the relative market prices of the metals or, with multi- or monometallism, financial catastrophes, must have made the payment of metallic money by the government impossible and must have forced it to adopt paper money and to make it irredeemable. In consequence the private business preconditions of effective hylodromy have ceased to exist. This money will then no longer be used in transactions—at least, insofar as action is rational.

(c) Apart from restricted currency money, which alone has been called "restricted money" here, there may be restricted "change" money —that is, money which must be accepted as means of payment only up to a given amount. Usually, though not necessarily, it is then intentionally coined at a rate which overvalues it in relation to standard coin to protect it from being melted down. Usually, then, it has the status of provisional money in that it is redeemable at certain places. (This case is a phenomenon of everyday experience and has no special importance for present purposes.)

All "change" money and many types of restricted metallic money occupy a place in monetary systems similar to that of note (today: paper) money. They differ from it only in that the monetary metal has a non-monetary use which is of some importance. Restricted metallic money is very nearly a means of circulation when it is provisional money; that is, when there is adequate provision for redemption in market money.

34. *Note Money*

Note money naturally is always administrative money. For the purposes of a sociological theory of money, it is always the specific chartal form of the document including the specific formal meaning printed on it which constitutes "money," and not the claim to something else which it may, though it need not, represent. Indeed, in the case of unredeemable paper money, such a claim is altogether absent.

From a formal legal point of view, note money may consist in (at least officially) redeemable certificates of indebtedness, acknowledged by a private individual, as in the case of the English goldsmiths in the seventeenth century, by a privileged bank, as in the case of bank-notes, or by a political body, as in the case of government notes. If it is effectively redeemable and thus functions only as a circulating medium or provisional money, it may be fully covered—thus constituting a certificate—or it may be covered only sufficiently to meet normal demands for redemption, which makes it a circulating medium. Coverage may be in terms of specified weights of bullion (as in the case of a *banco-currency*) or of metal coin.

It is almost always the case that note money has first been issued as a reedemable form of provisional money. In modern times, it has been typically a medium of circulation, almost always in the form of bank-notes. They have therefore been denominated in terms of units of an existing metallic standard.

1. The first part of the last paragraph, naturally, is not true of cases where one form of note money has been replaced by another; for example, where government notes have been replaced by bank-notes, or vice versa. But this is not a case of a primary issue of money.

2. It is of course true that means of exchange and of payment may exist which do not take a chartal form, i.e., are not coins or notes or other material objects. There is no doubt of this. It is not, however, expedient to speak of these as "money," but to use the term "unit of account" or some other term which, according to the particular case, is appropriate. It is characteristic of money that it is associated with particular quantities of chartal artifacts. This is a property which is very far from being merely external or of secondary importance.

If what has previously been provisional money has its redeemability suspended, it is important to distinguish whether the interested parties regard this as a temporary measure or as definitive for as long as they can predict. In the first case it would be usual, since metallic money or bullion is sought after for all international payments, for the note money to fall to a discount in relation to its nominal metal equivalent. This is not, however, by any means inevitable; and the discount is often moderate. The discount may, however, become large if the need for foreign exchange is very acute. In the second case, after a time a definitive "paper money standard" will develop. Then it is no longer appropriate to speak of a "discount" on the monetary unit, but rather, at least in the usage of the past, of "debasement."

It is not beyond the range of possibilities that the market price of the metal of the former market money, which is now obstructed, and in terms of which the issue is denominated, may for some reason fall radically relative to international means of payment, while the fall in the value of the paper currency is less marked. This must have the result (as it actually did in Austria and Russia) that what was earlier the nominal unit in terms of weight of the metal (of silver in those two cases) could now be purchased with a smaller nominal amount in the notes, which had now become independent of it. That is readily understandable. Thus, even though in the initial stages of a pure paper standard the unit of paper money is probably without exception valued in international exchange at a lower figure than the same nominal amount of metal, because this step always results from inability to pay, the subsequent development depends, as in the cases of Austria and Russia, on the development of the balance of payments which determines the foreign demand for domestic means of payment, on the amount of paper money issued, and on the degree of success with which the issuing authority is able to obtain an adequate supply of international means of payment. These three factors can (and in fact at times did) shape up in such a way that the exchange rate against the international means of payment —in this case: gold—of the paper money is increasingly stabilized or even rises, while at the same time the earlier standard metal falls in price relative to the international standard. In the case of silver, this happened (vis-à-vis gold) because of the increased and cheapened pro- duction of the metal and because of its progressive demonetization. A true independent paper standard exists in the case where there is no longer any prospect of effective resumption of redemption in terms of metal at the former rate.

35. *The Formal and Substantive Validity of Money*

It is true that by law and administrative action a state can today insure the *formal* validity of a type of money as the standard in its own area of power, provided it remains itself in a position to make payments in this money.

It will not remain in a position to do this if it has allowed what was previously an accessory or provisional type of money to become free market money (in the case of a metallic money) or autonomous paper money (in the case of note money). This is because these types of money will then accumulate in the hands of the government until it commands no other kind and is hence forced to impose them in its own payments. (Knapp has rightly maintained that this is the normal process in the case of "obstructional" changes in the standard.)

But naturally this formal power implies nothing as to the *substantive* validity of money; that is, the rate at which it will be accepted in ex- change for commodities. Nor does it yield any knowledge of whether and to what extent the monetary authorities can influence its substantive validity. Experience shows that it is possible for the political authority to attain, by such measures as the rationing of consumption, the control of production, and the enforcement of maximum or minimum prices, a high degree of control of this substantive validity, at least with respect to goods or services which are present or produced within its own terri- tory. It is equally demonstrable from experience, however, that there are exceedingly important limits to the effectiveness of this kind of control, which will be discussed elsewhere. But in any case, such measures obviously do not belong in the category of monetary administration. The rational type of modern monetary policy has, on the contrary, had quite a different aim. The tendency has been to attempt to influence the sub- stantive valuation of domestic currency in terms of foreign currency, that is, the market price of the home currency expressed in units of foreign currencies, usually to maintain stability or in some cases to attain the highest possible ratio. Among the interests determining such policy are those of prestige and political power. But on the economic side, the decisive ones are financial interest, with particular reference to future foreign loans, and other very powerful business interests, notably of importers and of industries which have to use raw materials from abroad. Finally, the interests as consumers of those elements in the population which purchase imported goods are involved. Today there can be no doubt that "lytric" policy is in fact primarily concerned with regulation of the foreign exchanges.

Both this and what follows are closely in agreement with Knapp. Both in its form and content, his book is one of the greatest masterpieces of German literary style and scientific acumen. It is unfortunate that most of the specialist critics have concentrated on the problems which he deliberately ignored—a small number indeed (although in some cases not altogether unimportant).

While England probably still came into the gold standard somewhat reluctantly, because silver, which was desired as the official standard, was undervalued by the official ratio, all the other states in the modern world with a modern form of organization have chosen their monetary standard with a view to the most stable possible exchange relation with the English gold standard. They chose either a pure gold standard, a gold standard with restricted accessory silver money, or a restricted silver or regulated note standard with a lytric policy concerned primarily with the maintenance of gold reserves for international payments. The adoption of pure paper standards has always been a result of political catastrophe, wherever this has been the only way to meet the problem of inability to pay in what was previously the standard money. This is happening on a large scale today.[58]

It seems to be true that for the purpose of stabilizing foreign exchange in relation to gold, the free coinage of fixed rates of gold in one's own monetary system is not the only possible means. The parity of exchange between different types of hylodromic chartal gold coinage can in fact become seriously disturbed, although it is true that the possibility of obtaining international means of payment in case of need by means of exporting and recoining gold is always greatly improved by internal hylodromy and can be temporarily negated only through natural obstacles to trade or embargoes on the export of gold as long as this hylodromy exists. But on the other hand it is also true, as experience shows, that under normal peace-time conditions it is quite possible for an area with a well-ordered legal system, favorable conditions of production and a lytric policy which is deliberately oriented to procuring adequate foreign exchange for international payments, to maintain a relatively stable exchange rate. Yet, if other things are equal, this involves markedly higher burdens to state finances and to persons in need of gold. Exactly the same would be true, of course, if silver were the principal means of payment in international transactions and were recognized as such in the principal trading nations of the world.

36. Methods and Aims of Monetary Policy

Among the more elementary of the typical methods (specific measures will not in general be dealt with here) of lytric policy in relation to foreign exchange are the following:

(a) In countries with gold hylodromy: (1) The backing of the circulating medium, so far as it is not covered by gold, with commercial paper; that is, claims to payments for goods which have been sold, which are guaranteed by safe persons or, in other words, proved entrepreneurs. The transactions of the note issuing banks on their own account are as far as possible limited to dealing with such bills, to making loans on the security of stocks of goods, to the receipt of deposits, the clearing of check payments, and, finally, acting as financial agent for the state; (2) the "discount policy" of the banks of issue. This consists in raising the rate of interest charged on bills discounted when there is a probability that payments abroad will create a demand for gold sufficient to threaten the internal stock of gold, especially that in the hands of the issuing bank. The purpose is to encourage owners of foreign balances to take advantage of the higher rate of interest and to discourage domestic borrowing.

(b) In areas with a restricted metal standard other than gold or with a paper standard, the following are the principal measures: (1) Discount policy similar to that described under (a:2) in order to check undue expansion of credit; (2) a gold-premium policy. This is a measure which is also common in gold-standard areas with an accessory restricted silver currency; (3) a deliberate policy of gold purchases and deliberate control of the foreign exchange rate by purchase and sale of foreign bills.

This policy is in the first instance oriented purely to lytric considerations, but under certain circumstances it may come to involve substantive regulation of economic activity. The note-issuing banks occupy a position of great power in the system of commercial banks, since the latter are often dependent on the credit extended by the bank of issue.

The bank of issue may influence the other banks to regulate the money market, that is, the conditions on which short-term credit is given, in a uniform way, and from there proceed to a deliberate regulation of business credit, thereby influencing the direction of the production of goods. This is, within the framework of a capitalistic economic order, the closest approach to a planned economy. It is formally merely a matter of voluntary adjustments, but actually involves substantive regulation of economic activity within the territory controlled by the political authority in question.

These measures were all typical before the war. They were used in the interest of a monetary policy which was primarily oriented to the stabilization of a currency or, in case changes were desired, as in countries with restricted or paper money, at most to attempts to bring about a gradual rise in the foreign exchange value of the currency. It was, thus, in the last analysis, oriented to the hylodromic monetary systems of the most important trading nations.

But strong interests exist which desire just the reverse policy. They favor a lytric policy of the following type: (1) Measures which would lead to a fall in the foreign exchange price of their own money in order to improve the position of exporting interests; (2) by increasing the issue of money through free coinage of silver in addition to gold (which would have meant *instead of* it), and even in some cases deliberate issue of paper money, to decrease the value of money in relation to domestic goods and thereby, what is the same thing, to raise the money prices of domestic goods. The object has been to improve prospects for profit in the production of such goods, an increase in the price of which as reckoned in terms of domestic currency was thought to be the first consequence of the increase of the amount of domestic money in circulation and of the attendant fall in its foreign exchange value. The intended process is termed "inflation."

The following points may be noted: (1) though its quantitative importance is still controversial, it is very probable that with any type of hylodromy a very great cheapening in the production of the precious metal or other source of increase in its supply, as through very cheap forced seizures, will lead to a noticeable tendency toward a rise in the prices at least of many products in areas where that metal is the monetary standard, and in differing degrees of all products. (2) It is at the same time an undoubted fact that, in areas with an independent paper standard, situations of severe financial pressure, especially war, lead the monetary authorities to orient their policy overwhelmingly to the financial requirements of the war. It is equally clear that countries with hylodromy or with restricted metallic money have, in similar circumstances, not only suspended redemption of their notes in circulation, but have gone further to establish a definitive and pure paper standard. But in the latter case, the metal money, now become accessory money, could, because its premium in relation to notes is ignored, only be used for non-monetary purposes. It thus disappeared from circulation. Finally, it is a fact that in cases of such shifts to a pure paper standard, occurring along with unlimited issue of paper money, inflation has in fact ensued with all its consequences on a colossal scale.

When all these processes are compared, it will be seen that so long as freely coined market money exists, the possibility of inflation will be narrowly limited. This will be true in the first place for mechanical reasons: though it is somewhat elastic, the quantity of the precious metal in question available for monetary use is ultimately firmly limited. Secondly, there are economic reasons in that here the creation of money takes place on the initiative of private interests, so that the demand for coinage is oriented to the needs of the market system for means of payment. Inflation, then, is only possible if restricted metal money (such as today silver in gold-standard countries) is thrown open to free coinage. However, if the restricted metal can be produced very cheaply and in large quantities, the effect may be very great.

Inflation through an increase in the quantity of "means of circulation" is conceivable only as the result of a very gradual increase in the circulation through a lengthening of credit terms. The limits are elastic, but in the last resort this process is strictly limited by the necessity for maintaining the solvency of the note-issuing bank. There is acute danger of inflation only if there is danger that the bank will become insolvent. Normally this is likely to occur only where there is a paper standard resulting from war needs. (Cases like the gold inflation of Sweden during the war, resulting from the export of war materials, are the result of such special circumstances that they need not be considered here.)

Where an independent paper standard has once been established, there may not be any greater danger of inflation itself (since in time of war almost all countries soon go over to a paper standard), but in general there is a noticeably greater possibility of the development of the consequences of inflation. The pressure of financial difficulties and of the increased wage and salary demands and other costs which are caused by the higher prices will noticeably strengthen the tendency of financial administrations to continue the inflation even if there is no absolute necessity to do so and in spite of the possibility to suppress it if strong sacrifices are incurred. The differences in this respect between paper currency and other currencies is, even if only quantitative, certainly noticeable, as the financial conduct [during and after the War] of the

Allies as a group, of Germany, and of both Austria and Russia finally, can show.

Lytric policy may thus, especially in the case of accessory restricted metal or of paper money, be an inflationary policy. In a country which, like the United States, has had relatively so little interest in the foreign exchange value of her money, this has been true for a time under quite normal conditions without being based on any motives derived from financial needs of the state. In a number of countries which fell into inflationary measures during the War, the pressure of necessity has been such as to lead to the continuance of an inflationary policy afterwards.

This is not the place to develop a theory of inflation. Inflation always means, in the first place, a particular way of increasing the purchasing power of certain interests. We will only note that any lytric policy oriented to the *substantive* rationality of a planned economy, which it would seem to be far easier to develop with administrative and especially paper money, is at the same time far more likely to come to serve interests which, from the point of view of exchange rate stabilization, are irrational. For *formal* rationality (of the market-economy type) of lytric policy, and hence of the monetary system, can, in conformity with the definition of "rationality" consistently held to here, only mean: the exclusion of all such interests which are either not market-oriented, like the financial interests of the state, or are not interested in the maintenance of stable exchange relations with other currencies as an optimum basis for rational calculation, but which, on the contrary, are primarily oriented to the creation of purchasing power for certain interest groups by means of inflation and to its maintenance even if there is no longer any need for the issue of new money from the point of view of public finances. Whether especially this latter process is to be praised or censured is, naturally, not a question capable of solution on empirical grounds. Of its empirical existence there can be no doubt.

It is furthermore true that proponents of a point of view which is oriented to *substantive* social ideals can find a very important opening for criticism in the very fact that the creation of money and currency is, in a pure market economy, made an object of the play of interests oriented only to profitability, and is not considered in terms of the "right" volume or the "right" type of money. They might with reason argue that it is only administrative money which can be "managed," but not market money. Thus the use of administrative money, especially paper money, which can be cheaply produced in any desired form and quantity is, from the point of view of a *substantive* rationality, whatever its goals, the only correct way to handle the monetary question. This argument is conclusive in formal logical terms. Its value, however, is naturally limited in view of the fact that in the future as in the past it will be the "interests" of individuals rather than the "ideas" of an economic administration which will rule the world.[59] Thus, the possibility of conflict between *formal* rationality in the present sense and the *substantive* rationality which could theoretically be constructed for a lytric authority entirely free of any obligation to maintain hylodromy of a metal, has been demonstrated also for this point. That was the sole purpose of this discussion.

> It is evident that this whole treatment of money consists only in a kind of discussion with Knapp's magnificent book, *Die Staatliche Theorie des Geldes,* a discussion which is, however, confined to points relevant to the present problems and carried out on a highly schematic basis, entirely neglecting the finer points. Quite at variance with its author's intentions, though perhaps not entirely without fault on his part, the work immediately was utilized in support of value judgments. It was naturally greeted with especial warmth by the Austrian lytric administration, with its partiality to paper money. Events have by no means disproved Knapp's theory in any point, though they have shown, what was known beforehand, that it is incomplete in its treatment of the *substantive* validity of money. It will now be necessary to justify this statement in more detail.

36a. Excursus: *A Critical Note on the "State Theory of Money"*

Knapp victoriously demonstrates that in every case the recent monetary policy both of states themselves and of agencies under the direction of the state have, in their efforts to adopt a gold standard or some other standard approximating this as closely as possible, been primarily concerned with the exchange value of their currency in terms of others, particularly the English. The object has been to maintain a certain exchange parity with the English gold standard, the money of the world's largest trading area which was universally used as a means of payment in international trade. To accomplish this, Germany first demonetized silver; then France, Switzerland, and the other countries of the Latin Union, Holland, and finally India ceased to treat silver as market money and made it into restricted money. Apart from this they undertook indirectly gold-hylodromic measures to provide for foreign payments in gold. Austria and Russia did the same, in that the lytric administration of these countries using unredeemable, independent paper money took indirectly gold-hylodromic measures so as to be in a position to make at least foreign payments in gold at any time. They were thus concerned entirely with obtaining the greatest possible stability of their foreign exchange rates. Knapp concludes from this that stabilization of the foreign exchange rate is the only factor which makes the particular monetary material and hylodromy at all significant. He concludes that this end of foreign exchange rate stability is served just as well by the indirectly hylodromic measures of the paper currency administrations (as in Austria and Russia) as by directly hylodromic measures. His claim is not, to be sure, strictly and literally true under *ceteris paribus* conditions for areas of full hylodromy in the same metal. For, as long as two areas which maintain a hylodromic coinage in the same metal refrain from embargoes on the exportation of the monetary metal, whether they are both gold-standard or silver-standard countries, the fact of the existence of the same hylodromy on both sides undoubtedly facilitates the maintenance of exchange parity considerably. Yet, under normal conditions Knapp's conclusion is to a large extent correct. But this does not prove that in the choice of a monetary material—above all today in the choice between a metal, whether gold or silver, and note money—this would be the only set of considerations which could be important. (The special circumstances which are involved in bimetallism and restricted money have already been discussed and can reasonably be left aside here.)

Such a claim would imply that a paper standard and a metallic standard behave in all other respects in the same way. But even from a formal point of view the difference is significant. Paper money is necessarily a form of administrative money, which may be true of metallic money, but is not necessarily so. It is impossible for paper money to be "freely coined." The difference between depreciated paper money, such as the *assignats*, and the type of depreciation of silver which might at some future time result from its universal demonetization, making it exclusively an industrial raw material, is not negligible; it is true, however, that Knapp occasionally grants this. Paper has been and is today (1920) by no means a freely available good, just as the precious metals are not. But the difference, both in the objective possibility of increased production and in the costs of production in relation to probable demand, is enormous, since the production of metals is to a relative degree so definitely dependent on the existence of mineral deposits. This difference justifies the proposition that a lytric administration was, before the war, in a position to produce paper money, if it so desired, in unlimited quantities. This is a significant difference even from copper, as used in China, certainly from silver, and very decidedly from gold. The costs would be, relatively speaking, negligible. Furthermore, the nominal value of the notes could be determined arbitrarily and need bear no particular relation to the amount of paper used. In the case of metallic money, this last has been true only of its use as "change" money; thus not in any comparable degree or sense. It was certainly not true of currency metal. In the latter case, the available quantity was indeed somewhat elastic, but nevertheless immensely more rigidly limited than the produceability of paper. This fact has imposed limits on the arbitrariness of monetary policy. It is of course true that, so far as the lytric administration has been oriented exclusively to the maintenance of the greatest possible stability of foreign exchange rates, it would be subject to very definite normative limitations on its creation of note money, even though not to technical limitations. This is the answer Knapp might well give, and in giving it he would be right, although only from a formal point of view. And how about fully "independent" paper money? The situation is the same, Knapp would say, pointing to Austria and Russia: "only" the purely technical limitations imposed by the scarcity of monetary metals are absent. The question is, whether this absence is an altogether unimportant difference—a question which Knapp ignores. "Against death," he might say, meaning that of a currency, "no potion has yet been found." If the present (1920) absolute and abnormal obstruction of paper production be ignored, there unquestionably have been and still are certain factors tending to unlimited issue of paper money. In the first place, there are the interests of those in political authority who, as Knapp also assumes, bear ultimate responsibility for monetary policy, and there are also certain private interests. Both are not of necessity primarily concerned with the maintenance of stable foreign exchange rates. It is even true, at least temporarily, that their interests might lie in the directly opposite direction. These interests can, either from within the political and monetary administration or by exercising a strong pressure on it, have an important influence on policy which would lead to "inflation" or what Knapp, who strictly avoids the term, could only describe as a case of the issue of paper money which is not "admissible" because it is not oriented to the international rate of exchange.

There are, in the first place, financial temptations to resort to inflation. An average depreciation of the German mark by inflation to 1/20th of its former value in relation to the most important domestic commodities and property objects would—once profits and wages had become adapted to this level of prices—mean, it may here be assumed, that all internal commodities and labor services would nominally be valued 20 times as high as before. This would further mean, for those in this fortunate situation, a reduction of the war debt to 1/20th of its original level. The state, which would receive a proportionate increase in its income from taxation as nominal money incomes rose, would at least enjoy important relief from this source. This is indeed an attractive prospect. It is clear that someone would have to bear the costs, but it would be neither the state nor one of these two categories of private individuals, entrepreneurs and wage earners. The prospect is even more attractive of being able to pay old foreign debts in a monetary unit which can be manufactured at will and at negligible cost. Apart from the possibility of political intervention, there is of course the objection that the use of this policy toward foreign loans would endanger future credit. But the state is often more concerned with the present than with the more or less remote future. Furthermore, there are entrepreneurs who would be only too glad to see the prices of their products increased twenty-fold through inflation if, as is altogether possible, the nominal wages of workers, because of lack of bargaining power or through lack of understanding of the situation or for any other reason, were to increase "only" five- or possibly ten-fold.

It is usual for acute inflation from public finance motives of this kind to be sharply disapproved by experts in economic policy. It is certainly not compatible with Knapp's form of exchange-rate oriented monetary policy. On the other hand, a deliberate but very gradual increase of the volume of means of circulation, of the type which is sometimes undertaken by central banks by facilitating the extension of credit, is often looked upon favorably as a means of stimulating speculative attitudes. By holding out prospect of greater profits, it is held to stimulate the spirit of enterprise and with that an increase in capitalistic production by encouraging the investment of free money in profit-making enterprise, rather than its investment in fixed-interest securities. We have to ask, however, what is the effect of this more conservative policy on the stability of the exchange rate? Its direct effect—that is, the consequences of the stimulation of the spirit of enterprise—may be to create a more favorable balance of payment, or at least to check the fall in the foreign exchange position of the domestic currency. How often this works out and how strong the influence is, is, of course, another question. Also, no attempt will here be made to discuss whether the effects of a moderate increase in the volume of currency caused by state requirements for money would be similar. The costs of such an expansion of the stock of currency money, which would be relatively harmless to the foreign exchange position, would be gradually paid by the same groups which would be subject to "confiscation" in a case of acute inflation. This includes all those whose nominal income remains the same or who have securities with a constant nominal value, above all, the receivers of fixed-interest bond income, and those who earn salaries which are "fixed" in that they can be raised only through a severe struggle. It is thus not possible to interpret Knapp as meaning that it is only the stability of foreign exchange which is significant as a criterion for the management of paper money; indeed, he does not claim this. Nor is it legitimate to believe, as he does, that there is a very high probability that this will empirically be the only criterion. It cannot, however, be denied that it would indeed be the decisive criterion of a lytric policy which is completely rational in Knapp's sense, that is, one which seeks as far as possible to prevent disturbances of the price relations resulting from monetary policies (a definition which Knapp does not himself spell out). But it cannot be admitted, and Knapp does not claim this either, that the practical significance of the kind of monetary policy formulated is limited to the question of the stability of foreign exchange rates.

Inflation has here been spoken of as a source of price revolutions or at least slow price level increases, and it has been pointed out that it may be caused by the desire to bring about such price level changes. Naturally, an inflation so extensive as to create a price revolution will inevitably upset the stability of foreign exchange; though this is by no means necessarily true of gradual increases in the circulating medium. Knapp would admit that. He obviously assumes, and rightly, that there is no place in his theory for a currency policy concerned with commodity prices, whether it be revolutionary, evolutionary, or conservative. Why does he do this? Presumably for the following formal reasons:

The exchange relationship between the standards of two or more countries is expressed daily in a small number of formally unambiguous and uniform market prices of currencies, which can be used as a guide to a rational lytric policy. It is further possible for a lytric authority, especially one concerned with the means of circulation, to make certain estimates (but only *estimates,* based on anterior demand conditions periodically observed in the market) of the probable fluctuations of a given stock of means of payment which will be required, for payment purposes alone, by a given population linked in market relationships over a certain future period, provided conditions in general remain approximately unchanged. But it is not possible to estimate in the same sense, quantitatively, the effect on prices—revolutionary or gradual increase, or perhaps a decrease—of a currency expansion or contraction over a certain future period. To do this, it would, in the case of inflation, to which attention will be confined, be necessary to know the following additional facts: (1) The existing distribution of income; (2) connected with this, the present policy conclusions derived therefrom of the different individuals engaged in economic activity; (3) the channels the inflationary process would follow, that is, who would be the primary and subsequent recipients of newly-issued money. This would involve knowing the sequence in which nominal incomes are raised by the inflation and the extent to which this would take place; (4) the way in which the newly-created demand for goods would be exercised, for consumption, for building up property investments, or for new capital. This would be important quantitatively, but even more so qualitatively; (5) the direction of the consequent changes in prices and of the further income changes resulting in turn, and all the innumerable further attendant phenomena of purchasing power redistribution, and also the volume of the (possible) stimulated increase in goods production. All these are data which would depend entirely on the decisions made by individuals when faced with the new economic situation. And these decisions would in turn react on the expectations as to prices of other individuals; only the consequent struggle of interests can determine the actual future prices. In such a situation there can clearly be no question of forecasting in the form of such predictions as that the issue of an additional billion of currency units would result in increases in the pig-iron price of "X" or in the grain price of "Y." The prospect is made even more difficult by the fact that it is possible temporarily to establish effective price regulation of domestic commodities, even though these can only be maximum and not minimum prices and their effectiveness is definitely limited. But even if this impossible task of calculating specific prices were accomplished, it would be of relatively little use. This would only determine the amount of money required as a means of payment, but in addition to this, and on a much larger scale, money would be required in the form of credit as a means of obtaining capital goods. Here, possible consequences of a proposed inflationary measure are involved which are inaccessible to any kind of accurate forecasting. It is thus understandable that, all things considered, Knapp should have entirely neglected the possibility of inflationary price policies being used in the modern market economy as a deliberate rational policy comparable to that of maintenance of foreign exchange stability.

But historically the existence of such policies is a fact. To be sure, in a crude form and under much more primitive conditions of money economy, inflation and deflation have been repeatedly attempted with the Chinese copper currency, though they have led to serious failures. In America, inflation has been proposed. Knapp, however, since his book operates on the basis only of what he calls demonstrable assumptions, contents himself with giving the advice that the state ought to be careful in the issue of independent paper money. Since he is entirely oriented to the criterion of exchange rate stability, this advice *appears* to be relatively unequivocal; inflationary debasement and depreciation in foreign exchange are usually very closely associated. But they are not identical, and it is far from true that every inflation is primarily caused by the foreign exchange situation. Knapp does not explicitly admit, but neither does he deny, that an inflationary money regime has been urged for reasons of price policy among others by the American silver producers during the free silver campaign and by the farmers who demanded "greenbacks," but not only in these cases. It is probably comforting to him that it has never been successful over a long period.

But the situation is by no means so simple as this. Whether or not they have been *intended* simply to raise the price level, inflations of this sort have in fact often taken place; and even in the Far East, to say nothing of Europe, such catastrophes as met the *assignats* are by no means unknown. This is a fact which a *substantive* theory of money must deal with. Knapp, of all people, certainly would not maintain that there is no difference whatever between the depreciation of silver and the depreciation of the *assignats*. Even formally this is not the case. What has been depreciated is not silver coin, but, on the contrary, the raw silver for industrial purposes. Coined chartal silver, on the contrary, being restricted, has often had the opposite fate. On the other hand, it was not the paper available for industrial purposes which was "depreciated," but only the chartal *assignats*. It is true, as Knapp would rightly point out, that they would fall to zero or to their values to collectors or as museum pieces only when they had finally been repudiated by the state. Thus even this results from a "state" action. This may be granted, but their material value may have fallen to a minute proportion of what it formerly was, before their formal repudiation, in spite of the fact that they were still nominally valid for making payments of public obligations.

But quite apart from such catastrophes, history provides a considerable number of examples of inflation, and, on the other hand, in China, of deflationary movements as a result of non-monetary use of monetary metals. It is necessary to do more than merely to note that under some circumstances certain kinds of money which were not accessory before, have become so, have tended to accumulate in the hands of the state, and have rendered obstructional changes in the standard necessary. A substantive theory of money should at least formulate the question as to how prices and income, and hence the whole economic system, are influenced in such cases, even though it is, for the reasons which have been given, perhaps questionable how far it will be able to achieve a theoretical solution. Similarly, a problem is suggested by the fact that, as a result of relative decline in the prices of either silver or gold in terms of the other, France, which has been formally a country of bimetallism, in fact has operated at times on a gold standard alone, and at others on a silver standard, while the other metal became accessory. In such a case it is not sufficient merely to call attention to the fact that the resulting price changes originate from a *monetary* source. The same is true in other cases where the monetary material has been changed. We also want to know what are the sources of an increase in the supply of a precious metal, whether it has stemmed from booty (as in the case of Cortez and Pizarro), from enrichment through trade (as in China early in the Christian era and since the sixteenth century), or from an increase of production. So far as the latter is the source, has production merely increased, or has it also become cheaper, and why? What is the part which may have been played by changes in the non-monetary uses of the metal? It may be that for a particular economic area, as, for instance, the Mediterranean area in Antiquity, a definitive export has taken place to an entirely distinct area like China or India, as happened in the early centuries of the Christian era. Or the reasons may lie wholly or partly in a change in the monetary demand arising from changes in customs touching the use of money, such as use in small transactions. How all these and various other possibilities tend to affect the situation is a subject which ought to be discussed in a monetary theory.

Finally, it is necessary to discuss the regulation of the "demand" for money in a market economy, and to inquire into the meaning of this concept. One thing is clear, that it is the actual demand for means of payment on the part of the parties to market relationships which determines the creation of free market money under free coinage. Furthermore, it is the effective demand for means of payment and, above all, for credit, on the part of market participants, in combination with care for the solvency of the banks of issue and the norms which have been established with this in view, which determines the policies for means of circulation of modern banks of issue. All this is oriented to the requirements of interested parties, as is in conformity with the general character of the modern economic order.

It is only this which, under the formal legal conditions of our economic system, can correctly be called "demand for money." This concept is thus quite indifferent with respect to substantive criteria, as is the related one of effective demand for goods. In a market economy there is an inherent limit to the creation of money only in the case of metallic money. But it is precisely the existence of this limit, as has already been pointed out, which constitutes the significance of the precious metals for monetary systems. The restriction of standard money to a material which is not capable of unlimited production at will, particularly to one of the precious metals, in combination with the "coverage" of means of circulation by this standard, sets a limit to any sort of creation of money. Even though it does not exclude a certain elasticity and does not make an evolutionary type of credit inflation altogether impossible, it still has a significant degree of rigidity. Where money is made out of a material which is, for practical purposes, capable of unlimited production, like paper, there is no such mechanical limit. In this case, there is no doubt that it is the free decision of the political authorities which is the regulator of the quantity of money, unimpeded by any such mechanical restraints. That, however, means, as has been indicated, determination by their conception of the financial interests of the political authority or even, under certain circumstances, the purely personal interests of the members of the administrative staff, as was true of the use of the printing presses by the Red armies. The significance of metallic standards today lies precisely in the elimination of these interests from influence on the monetary situation, or more precisely, since they may always try to influence the state, urging it to abandon metal in favor of a pure paper standard, in a certain restraint on such interests. In spite of the mechanical character of its operation, a metallic standard nevertheless makes possible a higher degree of formal rationality in a market economy because it permits action to be oriented wholly to market advantages. It is, of course, true, as demonstrated by the experience of Austria and Russia, that the monetary policy of lytric authorities under a pure paper standard is not necessarily oriented either to the purely personal interests of the authority or the administrative staff, or to the financial interests of the state (which would mean the least expensive creation of the greatest possible volume of means of payment, without concern for what happens to the currency as a means of exchange). But the danger that such an orientation should become dominant is, nonetheless, continually present under a paper standard, while in a hylodromic system (free market money) it does not exist in a comparable sense. From the point of view of the formal order of a market economy, the existence of this danger is an "irrational" factor present in any form of monetary system other than a hylodromic standard. This is true in spite of the fact that it may be readily admitted that, on account of its mechanical character, such a monetary system itself possesses only a relative degree of formal rationality. So much Knapp could and should admit.

However incredibly primitive the older forms of the quantity theory of money were, there is no denying that any inflation with the issue of paper money determined by financial needs of the state is in danger of causing "debasement" of the currency. Nobody, not even Knapp, would deny this. But his reasons for dismissing it as unimportant are thoroughly unconvincing. The "amphitropic" position of each individual, meaning

that every man is both a debtor and creditor, which Knapp in all seri-
ousness puts forward as proof of the absolute indifference of any currency "debasement,"[60] is, as we now all know from personal experience,
a mere phantom. What becomes of this position, not only for the *rentier,*
but also for every one on a fixed salary, whose income remains constant
in nominal units or, at best, is doubled if state finances and the mood
of the bureaucracies permit, while his expenditures may, in nominal
units, have increased twenty-fold, as it happens to us nowadays? What
becomes of it for any long-term creditor? Such radical alterations in the
(substantive) validity of money today produce a chronic tendency
toward social revolution, even if many entrepreneurs are in a position
to profit from the international exchange situation, and if some (very
few) workers are powerful enough to secure increases in their nominal
wages. It is, of course, open to anyone to welcome this revolutionary
effect and the accompanying tremendous unsettlement of the market
economy. Such an opinion cannot be scientifically refuted. Rightly or
wrongly, some can hope that this tendency will lead to the transformation of a market economy into socialism. Or some may expect proof for
the thesis that only a regulated economy with small-scale production
units is capable of substantive rationality, regardless of the sacrifices its
establishment would entail. It is impossible for science to decide such
questions, but at the same time it is its duty to state the facts about these
effects as clearly and objectively as possible. Knapp's assumption that
people are both debtors and creditors in the same degree, which in the
generalized form he gives the proposition is quite untenable, serves only
to obscure the situation. There are particular errors in his work, but the
above seems to be the most important element of *incompleteness* in his
theory. It is this which has led also some scholars who otherwise would
have no reason to be hostile to his work, to attack his theory on grounds
of "principle."

37. *The Non-Monetary Significance of Political Bodies for the Economic Order*

The significance for the economic system apart from the monetary
order of the fact that autonomous political organizations exist lies above
all in the following aspects:

(1) In the fact that, other things being nearly equal, they tend to
prefer their own subjects as sources of supply for the utilities they need.
The impact of this fact is the greater, the more the economy of these

political bodies has a monopolistic character or that of a system of budgetary satisfaction of needs; hence it is presently on the increase.

(2) In the possibility deliberately to encourage, restrain, or regulate
trade transactions across its boundaries on the basis of some substantive
criteria—that is, to conduct a foreign trade policy.

(3) In the possibility of various types of formal and substantive
regulation of economic activity by political bodies, differing in stringency
and in type.

(4) In the important consequences of the very great differences in
the structure of authority and of political power and in the closely related structure of administration and of social classes, especially of those
which enjoy the highest prestige, and of the attitudes toward earning
and profit-making which derive from these.

(5) In the competition among the directing authorities of these
political bodies to increase their own power and to provide the members
under their authority with means of consumption and acquisition and
with the corresponding opportunities for earnings and profits.

(6) In the differences in ways in which these bodies provide for
their own needs. On this see the following section.

38. *The Financing of Political Bodies*

The most direct connection between the economic system and primarily non-economic organizations lies in the way in which they secure
the means of carrying on their corporate activity as such; that is, the
activity of the administrative staff itself and that which is directed by it
(see chap. I, sec. 12). This mode of provision may be called "financing"
in the broadest sense, which includes the provision of goods in kind.

Financing—that is, the provision of corporate activity with economically scarce means—may, considering only the simplest types, be
organized in the following ways:

(1) Intermittently, based either on purely voluntary or on compulsory contributions or services. Voluntary "intermittent" financing may
take one of three forms:

(a) That of large gifts or endowments.[61] This is typical in relation
to charitable, scientific, and other ends which are primarily neither
economic nor political.

(b) That of begging. This is typical of certain kinds of ascetic communities.

In India, however, we also find secular castes of beggars, and elsewhere, particularly in China, organized groups of beggars are found.

Begging may in these cases be extensively monopolized and systematized with territorial assignments. Also, because response is regarded as a duty or as meritorious, begging may lose its intermittent character and in fact tend to become a tax-like source of income.

(c) That of gifts, which are formally voluntary, to persons recognized as politically or socially superior. This includes gifts to chiefs, princes, patrons, feudal lords over land or persons. Because of the fact that they have become conventional, these may in fact be closely approximated to compulsory payments. But usually, they are not worked out on a basis of rational expediency, but are generally made on certain traditional occasions, such as particular anniversaries or on the occasion of events of family or political significance.

Intermittent financing may, on the other hand, be based on compulsory contributions.

The type case for compulsory "intermittent" financing is furnished by such organizations as the *Camorra* in southern Italy and the *Mafia* in Sicily, and similar organized groups elsewhere. In India there have existed ritually separated castes of "thieves" and "robbers," and in China sects and secret societies with a similar method of economic provision. The payments are "intermittent" only on the surface, because they are formally illegal. In practice they often assume the character of periodic "subscriptions," paid in exchange for the rendering of certain services—notably, of a guarantee of security. About twenty years ago, a Neapolitan manufacturer replied to my doubts concerning the effectiveness of the *Camorra* with respect to business enterprises: "Signore, la Camorra mi prende X lire nel mese, ma garantisce la sicurezza,—lo Stato me ne prende 10 · X, e garantisce: niente." [Sir, the *Camorra* takes X lire a month from me, but guarantees me security; the state takes ten times that amount, and guarantees me nothing.] The secret societies typical of Africa—perhaps rudiments of the former "men's house"—operate in a similar way (as secret courts), thus insuring security. Political groups may, like the Ligurian "pirate state," rest primarily on the profits of booty, but this has never been the exclusive source of support over a long period.

(2) Financing may, on the other hand, be organized on a permanent basis.

A.—This may take place without any independent economic production on the part of the organization. It may then consist in contributions of goods, which may be based on a money economy. If so, money contributions are collected and provisions are obtained by the money purchase of the necessary utilities. In this case, all compensation of members of the administrative staff takes the form of money salaries. Contributions of goods may, on the other hand, be organized on the basis of a natural economy. Then, members are assessed with specific contributions in kind. Within this category, there are the following sub-types: the administrative staff may be provided for by benefices in kind and the needs of the group met in the same way. On the other hand, the contributions which were collected in kind may be sold wholly or in part for money and provision made in monetary terms.

Whether in money or in kind, the principal elementary types of contribution are the following:

(a) Taxes; that is, contributions which may be a proportion of all possessions (in the money economy: of wealth), or of all receipts (in the money economy: of incomes), or, finally, only of the means of production or from certain kinds of profit-making enterprises (so-called "yield taxes").

(b) Fees; that is, payments for using or taking advantage of facilities provided by the organization, of its property or of its services.

(c) "Imposts" on such things as specific types of use or consumption of commodities, specific kinds of transactions, above all, the transportation of goods (customs) and the turn-over of goods (excise duties and sales tax).

Contributions may be collected by the organization itself or leased out ("farmed") or lent out or pledged. The leasing of collection for a fixed sum of money ("tax farming") may have a rational effect on the fiscal system since it may be the only possible way to budget accounts. Lending and pledging are usually irrational from the fiscal point of view, normally resulting from financial necessity or usurpation on the part of the administrative staff, a result of the absence of a dependable administrative organization.

A permanent appropriation of the receipts from contributions by creditors of the state, by private guarantors of the army or of tax payments, by unpaid mercenary captains (*condottieri*) and soldiers, and, finally, by holders of rights to official positions, will be called the granting of benefices (*Verpfründung*). This may in turn take the form of individual appropriation or collective appropriation with freedom of replacement from the group which has collectively carried out the appropriation.

Financing without any economic production on the part of the organization itself may also take place by the imposition of obligations to personal services; that is, direct personal services with specification of the work to be done.

B.—Permanent financing may further, contrary to the above cases, be based on the existence of a productive establishment under the direct control of the organization. Such an establishment may be a budgetary unit, as an *oikos* or a feudal domain, or it may be a profit-making enterprise, which, in turn, may compete freely with other profit-making enterprises or be a monopoly.

Once more, exploitation may be directly under the administration of the organization or it may be farmed out, leased, or pledged.

C.—Finally, it is possible for financing to be organized "liturgically" by means of burdens which are associated with privileges. These may involve "positive privileges," as when a group is freed from the burden of making particular contributions, or (possibly identical with the former case) "negative privileges," as when certain burdens are placed on particular groups. The latter are usually either status groups (*Stände*) or property or income classes. Finally, the liturgic type may be organized "correlatively" by associating specific monopolies with the burden of performing certain services or supplying certain goods. This may take the form of organization of "estates," that is, of compulsorily forming the members of the organization into hereditarily closed liturgical classes on the basis of property and occupation, each enjoying status privileges. Or it may be carried out capitalistically, by creating closed guilds or cartels, with monopolistic rights and a corresponding obligation to make money contributions.

This very rough classification applies to all kinds of organizations. Examples, however, will be given only in terms of political bodies.

The system of provision through money contributions without economic production is typical of the modern state. It is, however, quite out of the question to attempt here even a summary analysis of modern systems of taxation. What will first have to be discussed at length is the "sociological location" of taxation—that is, the type of structure of domination that has typically led to the development of certain kinds of contributions (as, e.g., fees, excises, or taxes).

Contributions in kind, even in the case of fees, customs, excises, and sales taxes, were common throughout the Middle Ages. Their commutation into money payments is a relatively modern phenomenon.

Deliveries of goods in kind are typical in the form of tribute or of assessments of products laid upon dependent economic units. The transportation of in-kind contributions is possible only for small political units or under exceptionally favorable transportation conditions, as were provided by the Nile and the Chinese Grand Canal. Otherwise it is necessary for the contributions to be converted into money if the final recipient is to benefit from them. This was common in Antiquity. It is also possible for them to be exchanged, according to the distance they have to be transported, into objects with higher price-to-weight ratios. This is said to have been done in ancient China.

Examples of obligations to personal service are obligations to military service, to serve in courts and on juries, to maintain roads and bridges, to work on a dyke or in a mine, and all sorts of compulsory service for corporate purposes which are found in various types of organizations. The type case is furnished by the "*corvée* state," of which the best example is the New Kingdom of ancient Egypt. Similar conditions were found at some periods in China, to a lesser extent in India and to a still less extent in the late Roman Empire and in many organizations of the early Middle Ages. Support by the granting of benefices is illustrated by the following cases: (1) In China, collectively to the body of successful examinees for official positions; (2) in India, to the private guarantors of military services and tax payments; (3) to unpaid *condottieri* and mercenary soldiers, as in the late Caliphate and under the regime of the Mamelukes; (4) to creditors of the state, as in the sale of offices common everywhere.

Provision from the organization's own productive establishment administered on a budgetary basis is illustrated by the exploitation of domains under direct control for the household of the king, and in the obligation of subjects to compulsory services if used, as in Egypt, to produce goods needed by the court or for political purposes in directly controlled production establishments. Modern examples are factories maintained by the state for the manufacture of munitions or of military clothing.

The use of productive establishments for profit in free competition with private enterprise is rare, but has occurred occasionally, as, for instance, in the case of the [Prussian] *Seehandlung*.[62] On the other hand, the monopolistic type is very common in all periods of history, but reached its highest development in the Western World from the sixteenth to the eighteenth centuries.

Positive privileges on a liturgical basis are illustrated by the exemption of the *literati* in China from feudal obligations. There are similar exemptions of privileged groups from the more menial tasks all over the world. In many countries educated people have been exempt from military service.

Negative privilege is to be found in the extra liturgical burdens placed upon wealth in the democracies of Antiquity. It is also illustrated by the burden placed on the classes who did not enjoy the exemptions in the cases just mentioned.

To take the "correlative" case under (C.) above: the subjection of privileged classes to specified liturgical obligations is the most important form of systematic provision for public needs on a basis other than that of regular taxation. In China, India, and Egypt, the countries with the earliest development of "hydraulic" bureaucracy, liturgical organization was based on obligations to deliveries and services in kind. It was in part taken over from these sources by the Hellenistic states and by the late Roman Empire, though there, to be sure, to an important extent it took the form of liturgical obligations to pay money taxes rather than contributions in kind. This type of provision always involves the organization of the population in terms of occupationally differentiated classes. It is by no means out of the question that it might reappear again in the modern world in this form if public provision by taxation should fall

down and the satisfaction of private wants by capitalistic enterprise becomes subject to extensive regulation by the state. Up until now, the
financial difficulties of the modern state could be adequately met by the
compulsory creation of producer cartels with monopoly rights in exchange against money contributions; an example could be the compulsory control of the gunpowder factories in Spain with monopoly protection against new foundations and a continuous high contribution to the
state treasury. The idea is suggestive: one might proceed in the same
way in the "socialization" of the capitalistic enterprises of individual
branches, by imposing compulsory cartels or combinations with obligations to pay large sums in taxes. Thus they could be made useful for
fiscal purposes, while production would continue to be oriented rationally to the price situation.

39. *Repercussions of Public Financing on Private Economic Activity*

The way in which political and hierocratic bodies provide for their
corporate needs has very important repercussions on the structure of
private economic activity. A state based exclusively on money contributions, conducting the collection of the taxes (but no other economic
activity) through its own staff, and calling on personal service contributions only for political and judicial purposes, provides an optimal
environment for a rational market-oriented capitalism. A state which
collects money taxes by tax farming is a favorable environment for the
development of politically oriented capitalism, but it does not encourage
the orientation of profit-making activity to the market. The granting of
rights to contributions and their distribution as benefices normally tends
to check the development of capitalism by creating vested interests in the
maintenance of existing sources of fees and contributions. It thus tends
to stereotyping and traditionalizing of the economic system.

A political body based purely on deliveries in kind does not promote
the development of capitalism. On the contrary, it hinders it to the
extent to which it involves rigid binding of the structure of production
in a form which, from a point of view of profit-making enterprise, is
irrational.

A system of provision by compulsory services in kind hinders the
development of market capitalism above all through the confiscation of
the labor force and the consequent impediments to the development of a
free labor market. It is unfavorable to politically oriented capitalism because it removes the typical prospective advantages which enable it to
develop.

Financing by means of monopolistic profit-making enterprises has in common with the use of contributions in kind which are sold for money and with liturgical obligations on property, the fact that they are all unfavorable to the development of a type of capitalism which is autonomously oriented to the market. On the contrary, they tend to repress it by fiscal measures which, from the point of view of the market, are irrational, such as the establishment of privileges and of opportunities for money making through other channels. They are, on the other hand, under certain conditions favorable to politically oriented capitalism.

What is important for profit-making enterprises with fixed capital and careful capital accounting is, in formal terms, above all, the calculability of the tax load. Substantively, it is important that there shall not be unduly heavy burdens placed on the capitalistic employment of resources, which means, above all, on market turnover. On the other hand, speculative trade capitalism is compatible with any form of organization of public finances which does not, through tying it to liturgical obligations, directly inhibit the trader's exploitation of goods as commodities.

Though important, the form of organization of the obligations imposed by public finance is not sufficient to determine completely the orientation of economic activity. In spite of the apparent absence of all the more important obstacles of this type, no important development of rational capitalism has occurred in large areas and for long periods. On the other hand, there are cases where, in spite of what appear to be very serious obstacles placed in its way by the system of public finances, such a development has taken place. Various factors seem to have played a part. Substantively, state economic policy may be very largely oriented to non-economic ends. The development of the intellectual disciplines, notably science and technology, is important. In addition, obstructions due to certain value-attitudes derived from ethical and religious sources have tended to limit the development of an autonomous capitalistic system of the modern type to certain areas. It must, furthermore, not be forgotten that forms of establishment and of the firm must, like technical products, be "invented." In an historical analysis, we can only point out certain circumstances which exert negative influences on the relevant thought processes—that is, influences which impede or even obstruct them—or such which exert a positive, favoring influence. It is not, however, possible to prove a strictly inevitable causal relationship in such cases, any more than it is possible in any other case of strictly individual events.[63]

Apropos of the last statement, it may be noted that the concrete individual events also in the field of the natural sciences can be rigorously reduced to their particular causal components only under very special circumstances. There is thus no difference in principle between the field of action and other fields.[64]

At this point it is possible to give only a few provisional indications of the fundamentally important interrelationships between the form of organization and administration of political bodies and the economic system.

1. Historically, the most important case of obstruction of the development of market capitalism by turning public contributions into privately held benefices is China. The conferring of contributions as fiefs, which often cannot be differentiated from this, had the same effect in the Near East since the time of the Caliphs. Both will be discussed in the proper place. Tax farming is found in India, in the Near East, and in the Western World in Antiquity and the Middle Ages. Particularly, however, in Antiquity, as in the development of the Roman class of tax-farming financiers, the *equites,* it became decisive in determining the mode of orientation of capitalistic acquisition. In India and the Near East, on the other hand, it was more important in determining the development and distribution of wealth, notably of land ownership.

2. The most important case in history of the obstruction of capitalistic development by a liturgical organization of public finance is that of later Antiquity. It was perhaps also important in India after the Buddhist era and at certain periods in China. This also will be discussed later.

3. The most important historical case of the monopolistic diversion of capitalism is, after the Hellenistic, especially the Ptolemaic precursors, the period of royal monopolies and monopolistic concessions in early modern times, which again will be discussed in the proper place. A prelude to this development might be seen in certain measures introduced by Emperor Frederick II in Sicily, perhaps following a Byzantine model, and its final struggle in the conflict of the Stuarts with the Long Parliament.[65]

This whole discussion in such an abstract form has been introduced only in order to make an approximately correct formulation of problems possible. But before returning to the stages of development of economic activity and the conditions underlying that development, it is necessary to undertake a strictly sociological analysis of the non-economic components.

40. *The Influence of Economic Factors on the Formation of Organizations*

Economic considerations have one very general kind of sociological importance for the formation of organizations if, as is almost always true, the directing authority and the administrative staff are remunerated.

If this is the case, an overwhelmingly strong set of economic interests become bound up with the continuation of the organization, even though its primary ideological basis may in the meantime have ceased to exist.

It is an everyday occurrence that organizations of all kinds which, even in the eyes of the participants, have become "meaningless," continue to exist because an executive secretary or some other official makes his "living" in this manner and otherwise would have no means of support.

Every advantage which is appropriated, or even under certain circumstances one which has not been formally appropriated, *may* have the effect of stereotyping existing forms of social action. Among the opportunities for economic profit or earnings in the field of the peaceful provision for everyday wants, it is in general *only* the opportunities open to profit-making enterprise which constitute autonomous forces that are in a rational sense *revolutionary;* but even of them this is not always true.

For example, the interests of bankers in maintaining their commissions long obstructed the recognition of endorsements on bills of exchange. Similar cases of the obstruction of formally rational institutions by vested interests, which may well be interests in capitalistic profits, will frequently be met with below. They are, however, appreciably rarer than obstructions resulting from such factors as appropriation of benefices, status advantages, and various economically irrational forces.

4 1 . *The Mainspring of Economic Activity*

All economic activity in a market economy is undertaken and carried through by individuals acting to provide for their own ideal or material interests. This is naturally just as true when economic activity is oriented to the patterns of order of organizations, whether they themselves are partly engaged in economic activity, are primarily economic in character, or merely regulate economic activity. Strangely enough, this fact is often not taken account of.

In an economic system organized on a socialist basis, there would be no fundamental difference in this respect. The decision-making, of course, would lie in the hands of the central authority, and the functions of the individual engaged in the production of goods would be limited to the performance of "technical" services; that is, to "labor" in the sense of the term employed here. This would be true so long as the individuals were being administered "dictatorially," that is, by autocratic determination from above in which they had no voice. But once any right of "co-determination" were granted to the population, this would immediately make possible, also in a formal sense, the fighting out of interest conflicts centering on the manner of decision-making and, above all, on the question of how much should be saved (i.e., put aside from current production). But this is not the decisive point. What is decisive is that in socialism, too, the individual will under these conditions ask first whether to him, personally, the rations allotted and the work assigned, as compared with other possibilities, appear to conform with his own interests. This is the criterion by which he would orient his behavior, and violent power struggles would be the normal result: struggles over the alteration or maintenance of rations once allotted—as, for instance, over ration supplements for heavy labor; appropriations or expropriations of particular jobs, sought after because of extra remuneration or pleasant working conditions; work cessations, such as in strikes or lock-outs; restrictions of production to enforce changes in the conditions of work in particular branches; boycotts and the forcible dismissal of unpopular supervisors— in short, appropriation processes of all kinds and interest struggles would also then be the normal phenomena of life. The fact that they would for the most part be fought out through organized groups, and that advantages would be enjoyed on the one hand by the workers engaged in the most essential services, on the other hand by those who were physically strongest, would simply reflect the existing situation. But however that might be, it would be the interests of the individual, possibly organized in terms of the similar interests of many individuals as opposed to those of others, which would underlie all action. The *structure* of interests and the relevant situation would be different, and there would be other *means* of pursuing interests, but this fundamental factor would remain just as relevant as before. It is of course true that economic action which is oriented on purely ideological grounds to the interests of others does exist. But it is even more certain that the mass of men do not act in this way, and it is an induction from experience that they cannot do so and never will.

In a completely socialized planned economy there would be scope only for the following: (a) the distribution of real goods on the basis of planned rationed needs; (b) the production of these goods according to a plan of production. "Income" as a category of the money economy would necessarily disappear, but rationed "receipts" would be possible.

In a market economy the striving for *income* is necessarily the ultimate driving force of all economic activity. For every disposition, insofar as it makes a claim on goods or utilities which are not available to the actor in a form fully ready for whatever use he intends, presupposes the acquisition of and disposition over future income, and practically every existing power of control over goods and services presupposes previous income. All business profits of enterprises will at some stage and in some form be turned into the income of economically acting individuals. In a "regulated economy" the principal aim of the regulations is generally to affect in some manner the distribution of income. (In a "natural economy" we find no "income" in the usage of the present terminology; instead there are "receipts" in the form of goods and services which cannot be valued in terms of a unitary means of exchange.)

Income and receipts may, from a sociological point of view, take the following principal forms and be derived from the following principal sources:

A.—Incomes and receipts from personal services derived from specialized or specified functions:

(1) Wages: (a) Freely determined wage incomes or receipts contracted at fixed rates per time period; (b) the same, determined on some established scale (salaries or in-kind remuneration of public officials and civil servants); (c) the labor return of hired workers on contracted piece rates; (d) entirely open labor returns.

(2) Gains: (a) Free exchange profits deriving from the procurement of goods and services on an entrepreneurial basis; (b) the same, but regulated. In cases (a) and (b), "incomes" are calculated as net returns after the deduction of costs. (c) Predatory gains; (d) Gains derived from positions of political authority, fee incomes of an office, bribes, tax farming, etc., obtained by the appropriation of power. In cases (c) and (d), costs will be deducted to calculate "income" only if the activity is conducted as a continuous organized mode of acquisition; otherwise the gross revenue is usually considered "income."

B.—Income and receipts from property, derived from the exploitation of control over important means of production:

(1) Those in which "income" is normally calculated as "net rent" after the deduction of costs. (a) Rent obtained from the ownership of human beings, as in the case of slaves, serfs or freedmen. These may be receipts in money or in kind; they may be fixed in amount or consist in shares of the source's earnings after the deduction of costs of maintenance. (b) Appropriated revenues derived from positions of political authority (after the deduction of the costs of administration). (c) Rental revenues derived from the ownership of land (*métayage* payments or fixed rents per unit of time, either in kind or in money, seigneurial rent revenues—after deduction of land taxes and costs of maintenance). (d) House rents after deduction of expenses. (e) Rent receipts from appropriated monopolies (feudal *banalités*, patent royalties after the deduction of fees).

(2) Property income and receipts normally not requiring deduction

of costs from gross revenues: (a) Investment income (interest paid to households or profit-making enterprises in return for the right to utilize their resources or capital—see above, ch. II, sec. 11). (b) "Interest" from cattle loans (*Viehrenten*).[66] (c) "Interest" from other loans of concrete objects, and contracted "annuities in kind" (*Deputatrenten*). (d) Interest on money loans. (e) Money interest on mortgages. (f) Money returns from securities, which may consist in fixed interest or in dividends varying with profitability. (g) Other shares in profits, such as shares in the proceeds of "occasional" profit-making ventures and in profits from rational speculative operations, and shares in the rational long-run profit-making activities of all sorts of enterprises.

All "gains" and the dividend incomes from shares are either not contracted (as to rate or amount) in advance, or only indirectly contracted incomes (namely, through the agreement on prices or piece rates). Fixed interest and wages, leases of land, and house rents are contracted incomes. Income from the exercise of power, from ownership of human beings, from seigneurial authority over land, and predatory incomes all involve appropriation by force. Income from property may be divorced from any occupation in case the recipient lets others utilize the property. Wages, salaries, labor profits, and entrepreneurial profits are, on the other hand, occupational incomes. Other types of property incomes and gains may be either one or the other. An exhaustive classification is not intended here.

Of all types of incomes, it is particularly those from business profits and the contracted piece rate or free labor incomes which have a dynamic, revolutionary significance for economic life. Next to these stand incomes derived from free exchange and, in quite different ways, under certain circumstances, the "predatory" incomes.

Those having a static, conservative influence on economic activity are above all incomes drawn in accordance with a predetermined scale, namely salaries, wages reckoned per unit of working time, gains from the exploitation of office powers, and normally all kinds of fixed interest and rents.[67]

The *economic* source of "incomes" (in an exchange economy) lies in a great majority of cases in the exchange situation on the market for goods and labor services. Thus, in the last analysis, it is determined by consumers' demand, in connection with the more or less strong natural or statutory monopolistic position of the parties to market relationships.

The economic source of "receipts" (in a natural economy) generally lies in the monopolistic appropriation of opportunities to exploit property or services for a return.

The underpinning of all these incomes is nothing but the *possibility* of violence in the defence of appropriated advantages (see above, ch. II, sec. 1, pt. 4). Predatory incomes and related modes of acquisition are the return on *actual* violence. An exhaustive classification had to be foregone in this very rough first sketch.

In spite of many disagreements on particular points, I consider the sections on "income" in R. Liefmann's works to be among the most valuable of his contributions.[68] The problems of economic theory involved cannot be explored any further here; the interrelations between the economic dynamics and the social order will have to be discussed time and again.

NOTES

Unless otherwise indicated, notes are by Parsons.

1. In the economic sense.

2. Robert Liefmann, *Grundsätze der Volkswirtschaftslehre*, vol. I, 3rd ed. (Stuttgart 1923), p. 74ff. and *passim*. (Wi)

3. See Franz Oppenheimer, *System der Soziologie*, Part III, *Theorie der reinen und politischen Ökonomie*, 5th ed. (Jena 1923), pp. 146–152. (Wi)

4. The German word *Technik* which Weber uses here covers both the meanings of the English word "technique" and of "technology." Since the distinction is not explicitly made in Weber's terminology, it will have to be introduced according to the context in the translation.

5. The term *Verfügungsgewalt*, of which Weber makes a great deal of use, is of legal origin, implying legally sanctioned powers of control and disposal. This, of course, has no place in a purely economic conceptual scheme but is essential to a sociological treatment of economic systems. It is another way of saying that concretely economic action depends on a system of property relations.

6. This is one of the many differences between China and the Western World which Weber related to the difference of orientation to economic activities, growing out of the religious differences of the two civilizations. See his *The Religion of China: Confucianism and Taoism*, transl. H. H. Gerth (Glencoe, Ill. 1951).

7. *Beschaffung*. Weber uses this term, which could be translated variously as "making available," "bringing forth," "providing," etc., throughout this chapter in combinations where today the term "production" has become usual, and we normally translate it in this way. However, the term does cover, beyond production in the narrow sense, also all manner of activities which make available goods, services, money, or anything else useful—that is, transport (as noted here), trade, banking, etc. Wherever it was necessary to indicate this wider meaning clearly, we have translated the term as "procurement." (Wi)

8. It is a striking fact that, particularly in primitive society, a very large proportion of economically significant exchange is formally treated as an exchange of gifts. A return gift of suitable value is definitely obligatory but the specific characteristic of purely economically rational exchange, namely bargaining, is not only absent but is specifically prohibited.

9. The type case Weber has in mind is the relation of the state to the modern system of property and contract. Whether or not private citizens will engage in any given activity is not determined by the law. The latter is restricted

to the enforcement of certain formal rules governing whoever does engage in such activities.

10. This is a term which is not in general use in German economics, but which Weber took over, as he notes below, from G. F. Knapp. There seems to be no suitable English term and its use has hence been retained.

11. *Theorie des Geldes und der Umlaufsmittel* (Munich 1912). English edition: *The Theory of Money and Credit*, trsl. H. E. Batson (London 1934; 2d rev. ed., New Haven 1953). (Wi)

12. English edition: *The State Theory of Money*, abridged ed., trsl. by H. M. Lucas and J. Bonar, publ. for the Royal Economic Society (London 1924). (Wi)

13. Weber, as will become clear further on in this chapter, in common with many of his contemporaries (including the leaders of the Bolshevik revolution in Russia) strongly identified "socialism" and "communism" with the absence of money and monetary categories (money prices, money wages, etc.). In the event, these categories were, of course, used in the Communist countries even in the substantial absence of free markets, although their use was attended by many difficulties, as yet unresolved, in the determination of rational prices. This is true for the internal economy of these countries, but particularly true for the exchange relations *between* the Communist countries (coexisting "communist organizations") which are mentioned here. For the state of the debate in Weber's day, see F. A. Hayek (ed.), *Collectivist Economic Planning* (London 1935); an appreciation of Weber's contribution, p. 32ff. (Wi)

14. The concept *Haushalt*, as distinguished from *Erwerb*, is central to Weber's analysis in this context. He means by it essentially what Aristotle meant by the "management of a household" (Jowett's translation). It is a question of rational allocation of resources in providing for a given set of needs. The concept of budget and budgetary management seems to be the closest English equivalent in common use.

15. Corresponding to the distinction of *Haushalt* and *Erwerb*, Weber distinguishes *Vermögen* and *Kapital*. They are, of course, classes of property distinguished in terms of their function in the management of an economic unit. There is no English equivalent of *Vermögen* in this sense, and it has seemed necessary to employ the more general term "wealth." Where there is danger of confusion, it will be amplified as "budgetary wealth."

16. In common usage the term *Erwerben* would perhaps best be translated as "acquisition." This has not, however, been used, as Weber is here using the term in a technical sense as the antithesis of *Haushalten*. "Profit-Making" brings out this specific meaning much more clearly.

17. Since Weber wrote, there has been an extensive discussion of the problem of whether rational allocation of resources was possible in a completely socialistic economy in which there were no independent, competitively determined prices. The principal weight of technical opinion seems at present to take the opposite position from that which Weber defends here. A discussion of the problem will be found in Oskar Lange and F. M. Taylor, *On the Economic Theory of Socialism*, edited by B. E. Lippincott (Minneapolis 1938). This book includes a bibliography on the subject.

18. For the relevant articles by K. Rodbertus, see *Jahrbücher für National-ökonomie und Statistik*, vols. IV, V, and VIII (1865–1869); K. Bücher, *Industrial Evolution*, trsl. S. M. Wickett (New York 1901). (Wi)

19. On *banco*-currencies, see *Economic History*, 189f; on the Egyptian "grain deposit banks," *ibid.*, 59. (Wi)

20. Otto Neurath, *Bayerische Sozialisierungserfahrungen*, Vienna 1920; *id.*,

Vollsozialisierung. Von der nächsten u. übernächsten Zukunft (*Deutsche Gemeinwirtschaft,* vol. 15; Jena 1920), and bibliography given there. Neurath, incidentally, had not only written about and agitated for economic socialization, but also briefly worked as director of the Bavarian *Zentralwirtschaftsamt,* the agency in charge of socialization plans, during the *Räterepublik* or "soviet" phase of the Bavarian revolutionary regime in the spring of 1919; when he was brought to trial after the suppression of the revolution, Weber testified in his defense. See A. Mitchell, *Revolution in Bavaria 1918–1919* (Princeton 1965), pp. 293–305; Marianne Weber, *Max Weber* (Tübingen 1926), pp. 673 & 677; Ernst Niekisch, *Gewagtes Leben* (Köln 1958), pp. 53–57. (Wi)

21. J. C. L. Simonde de Sismondi, Essay X ("De la condition des cultivateurs dans la Campagne de Rome") in his *Études sur l'Économie Politique,* vol. II (Paris 1838); W. Sombart, *Die römische Campagna. Eine sozialökonomische Studie* (Leipzig 1888). (Wi)

22. Oppenheimer, who was for part of his life associated with the Henry George movement, saw the ultimate basis of capitalism in the appropriation of land; he was himself the founder of a "free land" movement. (Wi)

23. English translation in F. A. Hayek (ed.), *Collectivist Economic Planning* (London 1935). (Wi)

24. Weber seems to have said in this passage in a somewhat involved way what has come to be generally accepted among the more critical economic theorists and the welfare economists. A simpler way of stating the same point is provided by the doctrine of maximum satisfaction. This states the conditions under which, to use Weber's phrase, formal and substantive rationality would coincide. It is generally conceded that among these conditions is the absence of certain types of inequality of wealth. One of the best statements of the problem is that of Frank H. Knight in his essay "The Ethics of Competition," which is reprinted in the book of that title. The problem of the relations of formal and substantive rationality has for Weber, however, wider ramifications.

25. Proposals for the introduction of a planned economy made in the early summer of 1919 by the first *Reichswirtschaftsminister* of the Weimar Republic, the Social Democrat Rudolf Wissell and his Undersecretary Wichard von Moellendorff. After the rejection of his plans, Wissell resigned in July of that year and was replaced by an opponent of planning. Cf. Arthur Rosenberg, *A History of the German Republic,* trsl. I. F. D. Morrow and M. Sieveking (London 1936), 108ff. The text of the proposals is included in Wissell's justification of his conduct of office: *Praktische Wirtschaftspolitik. Unterlagen zur Beurteilung einer fünfmonatlichen Wirtschaftsführung* (Berlin 1919), and in part also in *Deutsche Gemeinwirtschaft,* vols. 9 and 10 (Jena 1919). (Wi)

26. English ed.: *Industrial Evolution,* transl. (from the 3rd German edition, 1900) by S. Morley Wickoff (New York 1901). (Wi)

27. In a good deal of his discussion, Weber uses the term *Betrieb* in a context where this distinction is not important. To avoid a confusion of terms, it has in general been found most convenient to translate *Betrieb* as "enterprise" (cf. the definition of "enterprise" as continuous rational activity, above, ch. I:15). But wherever the distinction made here is important in the context, the term "establishment" is used. *Unternehmen* has for the same reason been translated as "firm." (Wi)

28. See above note. In most cases it has so far seemed best to translate *Erwerbsbetrieb* with "enterprise."

29. See below, ch. II, sec. 20, point V. (Wi)

30. Weber here sides with Karl Bücher against a theory of developmental

stages propounded mainly by Gustav Schmoller, who defines stages in terms of ruling groups. Cf. Schmoller, "Städtische, territoriale und staatliche Wirtschaftspolitik," *Jahrb. f. Gesetzgebung, Verwaltung u. Volkswirtschaft*, VIII (1884), 4ff. and II (1904), 668ff.; Bücher, "The Rise of the National Economy," in his *Industrial Evolution, op. cit.*, 83–149. For the polemic between Schmoller and Bücher, see *Jb. f. G., V. & V.*, XVII and XVIII (1893–1894). See also below, Part Two, ch. XVI:i:4. (Wi)

31. The corresponding German terms are: *Hauswirtschaft, Dorfwirtschaft, grundherrliche* and *patrimonialfürstliche Haushaltswirtschaft, Stadtwirtschaft, Territorialwirtschaft,* and *Volkswirtschaft.*

32. What Weber apparently has in mind is the type of "trust" which controls all stages of the process of production from raw material to the finished product. Thus many of our steel enterprises have not only blast furnaces and rolling mills, but coal mines, coke ovens, railways and ships, and iron ore mines. The most notable example in Germany in Weber's time was the Stinnes combine.

33. The *demiurgoi* were the public craftsmen ("those who work for the people") of ancient Greece. Whether they were really on an annual retainer, rather than being paid for the individual job, is still controversial (cf. M. I. Finley, *The World of Oddyseus* [New York 1959], 51f.); Weber himself usually cites the public artisans of Indian villages as an example (e.g., *Economic History*, 34f., 103f.) (Wi)

34. K. Rodbertus, "Zur Geschichte der römischen Tributsteuern seit Augustus," *Jahrbücher f. Nationalök. u. Statistik*, IV (1865); cf. also *Economic History*, 108. (Wi)

35. Carolingian Imperial regulation prescribing detailed management procedures for the royal estates (*villae*). (Wi)

36. Discussed in sec 20, below. (Wi)

37. Discussed in sec. 21, below. (Wi)

38. On Demosthenes' shops and the Carolingian women's house (*genitium*), see *Economic History*, 104ff.; on Roman estate shops, H. Gummerus, *Der römische Gutsbetrieb als wirtschaftl. Organismus nach den Werken des Cato, Varro und Columella* (Leipzig 1906); on the Russian serf factory, see M. I. Tugan-Baranovskii, *Geschichte der russischen Fabrik*, transl. B. Minzes (Berlin 1900). (Wi)

39. *Beunden* were plots of land exempt from the cultivation regulations (crop rotation, grazing rights, etc.) of the village (*Mark-*) association; in contrast to ordinary arable, they could be fenced. *Herrenbeunden*, or unrestricted seigneurial farms operated by a special official (*Beundehofmann*), are found in early documents. J. & W. Grimm, *Deutsches Wörterbuch*, I (Leipzig 1854). (Wi)

40. The term *Paria* is used by Weber in a technical sense to designate a group occupying the same territorial area as others, but separated from them by ritual barriers which severely limit social intercourse between the groups. It has been common for such groups to have specialized occupations, particularly occupations which are despised in the larger society.

41. What is ordinarily called a "producers' co-operative association" would be included in this type, but Weber conceives the type more broadly. In certain respects, for instance, the medieval village community could be considered an example.

42. On the "freed mountains" and "mining freedom," see *Economic History*, 142f. (Wi)

43. His real name was John Winchcombe. See W. J. Ashley, *An Introduc-*

tion to English Economic History and Theory, II (London 1893), 229f. and 255f., who reprints part of the poem; also *Economic History*, 132. (Wi)

44. That is without rights of inheritance or alienation. See above chap. I, sec. 10.

45. This chapter is, however, a mere fragment which Weber intended to develop on a scale comparable with the others. Hence most of the material to which this note refers was probably never written down.

46. For a discussion of *Stör*, "wage work," and "price work," see Karl Bücher, *Industrial Evolution, op. cit.*, chap. 4. (Wi)

47. On *coloni*, see *Economic History*, 56, 73. (Wi)

48. It seems curious that in this classification Weber failed to mention the type of agricultural organization which has become predominant in the staple agricultural production of much of the United States and Canada. Of the European types this comes closest to large-scale peasant proprietorship, but is much more definitely oriented to the market for a single staple, such as wheat. Indeed, in many respects this type of farm is closely comparable to some kinds of small-scale industrial enterprise.

49. On this peculiar phenomenon, see *Economic History*, 35. (Wi)

49a. Memorandum on the question of a legal provision to protect the home-steads of smallholders against legal execution ("Empfiehlt sich die Einführung eines Heimstättenrechtes, insbesondere zum Schutz des kleinen Grundbesitzes gegen Zwangsvollstreckung?") in *Deutscher Juristentag* XXIV (1897), *Verhandlungen*, II, 15–32. (W)

50. Weber uses the term *Alltag* in a technical sense, which is contrasted with *Charisma*. The antithesis will play a leading role in chap. III. In his use of the terms, however, an ambiguity appears of which he was probably not aware. In some contexts, *Alltag* means routine, as contrasted with things which are exceptional or extraordinary and hence temporary. Thus, the charismatic movement led by a prophet is, in the nature of the case, temporary, and if it is to survive at all must find a routine basis of organization. In other contexts, *Alltag* means the profane, as contrasted with the sacred. The theoretical significance of this ambiguity has been analysed in [Parsons,] *Structure of Social Action*, chap. xvii.

51. There are several different factors involved in the inability to predict future events with complete certainty. Perhaps the best known analysis of these factors is that of F. H. Knight in his *Risk, Uncertainty and Profit*.

52. On the Chinese and Hamburg *banco*-money (deposit certificates), see *Economic History*, 189f. (Wi)

53. In a well-known essay, "The Social Causes of the Decay of Ancient Civilization," (*J. of General Education*, V, 1950, 75–88), Weber attributed to this factor an important role in the economic decline and through this the cultural changes of the Roman Empire.

54. G. F. Knapp, *The State Theory of Money, op. cit.*, 11. (Wi)

55. For the exact definition of "currency money," see Knapp, *The State Theory of Money*, 100ff. (Wi)

56. Note money is discussed in sec. 34, below; metal money in this and the following section. (Wi)

57. Most of the special terminology employed here was coined by Knapp, but never came to be really widely used. "Lytric," from the Greek *lytron* = means of payment, designates specifically the agencies or institutions connected with payments or regulating payment instruments. "Hylodromy," literally the rate of exchange (*Kurs* = *dromos*) of currency metals (matter = *hyle*), Knapp defines

as a state characterized by "the deliberate fixing of the price of a hylic metal" (Knapp, *The State Theory of Money*, 79). (Wi)

58. It should be borne in mind that this was written in 1919 or 1920. The situation has clearly been radically changed by the developments since that time.

59. This is an application of Weber's general theory of the relations of interests and ideas, which is much further developed in his writings on the Sociology of Religion. The most important point is that he refused to accept the common dilemma that a given act is motivated either by interests or by ideas. The influence of ideas is rather to be found in their function of defining the situations in which interests are pursued. Beside in Weber's own works, this point is developed in [Parsons'] article "The Role of Ideas in Social Action," *American Sociological Review*, October 1938.

60. Knapp, *The State Theory of Money*, 48. (Wi)

61. *Mäzenatisch*. This term is commonly used in German but not in the precise sense which Weber gives it here. There seems to be no equivalent single term in English, so the idea has been conveyed by a phrase.

62. For the complex history of this institution, the later *Preussische Staatsbank*, see W. O. Henderson, *The State and the Industrial Revolution in Prussia, 1740–1870* (Liverpool 1958), 119–147. Founded in 1772 by Frederick II as a primarily government-owned overseas trade agency, the *Seehandlung* eventually turned into a fully government-owned commercial bank used to float state loans and, to some extent, to finance desired industrial development. (Wi)

63. The methodological problems touched here have been further discussed in various of the essays collected in the volume *GAzW*. The most essential point is that Weber held that no scientific analysis in the natural or the social field ever exhausts the concrete individuality of the empirical world. Scientific conceptual schemes and the causal explanations attained through their use are always in important respects abstract.

64. Cf. Weber's essay on "Roscher und Knies und die logischen Probleme der historischen Nationalökonomie," *GAzW*, 2nd ed., 1951, 56, 64ff. (Wi)

65. See *Economic History*, 213 and 256f. (Wi)

66. On cattle loans, see *Economic History*, 56 and 201. (Wi)

67. The distinction here made between those types of economic interest having a dynamic and a static influence on economic activity respectively, is strikingly similar to that made by Pareto between "speculators" and "rentiers;" see *The Mind and Society*, especially secs. 22, 34ff.

68. See Robert Liefmann, *Ertrag und Einkommen auf Grundlage einer rein subjektiven Wertlehre* (Jena 1907); Liefmann, *Grundsätze der Volkswirtschaftslehre* (Stuttgart 1919), vol. II, parts VIII–IX, esp. 636–710. (Wi)

CHAPTER III

THE TYPES OF LEGITIMATE DOMINATION

i

The Basis of Legitimacy

1. Domination and Legitimacy

Domination was defined above (ch. I:16) as the probability that certain specific commands (or all commands) will be obeyed by a given group of persons. It thus does not include every mode of exercising "power" or "influence" over other persons. Domination ("authority")[1] in this sense may be based on the most diverse motives of compliance: all the way from simple habituation to the most purely rational calculation of advantage. Hence every genuine form of domination implies a minimum of voluntary compliance, that is, an *interest* (based on ulterior motives or genuine acceptance) in obedience.

Not every case of domination makes use of economic means; still less does it always have economic objectives. However, normally the rule over a considerable number of persons requires a staff (cf. ch. I:12), that is, a *special* group which can normally be trusted to execute the general policy as well as the specific commands. The members of the administrative staff may be bound to obedience to their superior (or superiors) by custom, by affectual ties, by a purely material complex of interests, or by ideal (*wertrationale*) motives. The quality of these motives largely determines the type of domination. *Purely* material interests and calculations of advantages as the basis of solidarity between the chief and his administrative staff result, in this as in other connexions, in a relatively unstable situation. Normally other elements, affectual and ideal, supplement such interests. In certain exceptional cases the former alone may be decisive. In everyday life these relationships, like others, are governed by custom and material calculation of advantage. But custom, personal advantage, purely affectual or ideal motives of solidarity, do not form a sufficiently reliable basis for a given domination. In addition there is normally a further element, the belief in *legitimacy*.

Experience shows that in no instance does domination voluntarily limit itself to the appeal to material or affectual or ideal motives as a basis for its continuance. In addition every such system attempts to establish and to cultivate the belief in its legitimacy. But according to the kind of legitimacy which is claimed, the type of obedience, the kind of administrative staff developed to guarantee it, and the mode of exercising authority, will all differ fundamentally. Equally fundamental is the variation in effect. Hence, it is useful to classify the types of domination according to the kind of claim to legitimacy typically made by each. In doing this, it is best to start from modern and therefore more familiar examples.

1. The choice of this rather than some other basis of classification can only be justified by its results. The fact that certain other typical criteria of variation are thereby neglected for the time being and can only be introduced at a later stage is not a decisive difficulty. The legitimacy of a system of control has far more than a merely "ideal" significance, if only because it has very definite relations to the legitimacy of property.

2. Not every claim which is protected by custom or law should be spoken of as involving a relation of authority. Otherwise the worker, in his claim for fulfilment of the wage contract, would be exercising authority over his employer because his claim can, on occasion, be enforced by order of a court. Actually his formal status is that of party to a contractual relationship with his employer, in which he has certain "rights" to receive payments. At the same time the concept of an authority relationship (*Herrschaftsverhältnis*) naturally does not exclude the possibility that it has originated in a formally free contract. This is true of the *authority* of the employer over the worker as manifested in the former's rules and instructions regarding the work process; and also of the *authority* of a feudal lord over a vassal who has freely entered into the relation of fealty. That subjection to military discipline is formally "involuntary" while that to the discipline of the factory is voluntary does not alter the fact that the latter is also a case of subjection to *authority*. The position of a bureaucratic official is also entered into by contract and can be

freely resigned, and even the status of "subject" can often be freely entered into and (in certain circumstances) freely repudiated. Only in the limiting case of the slave is formal subjection to authority absolutely involuntary.

On the other hand, we shall not speak of formal domination if a monopolistic position permits a person to exert economic power, that is, to dictate the terms of exchange to contractual partners. Taken by itself, this does not constitute authority any more than any other kind of influence which is derived from some kind of superiority, as by virtue of erotic attractiveness, skill in sport or in discussion. Even if a big bank is in a position to force other banks into a cartel arrangement, this will not alone be sufficient to justify calling it an authority. But if there is an immediate relation of command and obedience such that the management of the first bank can give orders to the others with the claim that they shall, and the probability that they will, be obeyed regardless of particular content, and if their carrying out is supervised, it is another matter. Naturally, here as everywhere the transitions are gradual; there are all sorts of intermediate steps between mere indebtedness and debt slavery. Even the position of a "salon" can come very close to the border-line of authoritarian domination and yet not necessarily constitute "authority." Sharp differentiation in concrete fact is often impossible, but this makes clarity in the analytical distinctions all the more important.

3. Naturally, the legitimacy of a system of domination may be treated sociologically only as the probability that to a relevant degree the appropriate attitudes will exist, and the corresponding practical conduct ensue. It is by no means true that every case of submissiveness to persons in positions of power is primarily (or even at all) oriented to this belief. Loyalty may be hypocritically simulated by individuals or by whole groups on purely opportunistic grounds, or carried out in practice for reasons of material self-interest. Or people may submit from individual weakness and helplessness because there is no acceptable alternative. But these considerations are not decisive for the classification of types of domination. What is important is the fact that in a given case the particular claim to legitimacy is to a significant degree and according to its type treated as "valid"; that this fact confirms the position of the persons claiming authority and that it helps to determine the choice of means of its exercise.

Furthermore, a system of domination may—as often occurs in practice —be so completely protected, on the one hand by the obvious community of interests between the chief and his administrative staff (bodyguards, Pretorians, "red" or "white" guards) as opposed to the subjects, on the other hand by the helplessness of the latter, that it can afford to drop even the pretense of a claim to legitimacy. But even then the mode of legitimation of the relation between chief and his staff may vary widely according to the type of basis of the relation of the authority between them, and, as will be shown, this variation is highly significant for the structure of domination.

4. "Obedience" will be taken to mean that the action of the person obeying follows in essentials such a course that the content of the command may be taken to have become the basis of action for its own sake. Furthermore, the fact that it is so taken is referable only to the formal obligation, without regard to the actor's own attitude to the value or lack of value of the content of the command as such.

5. Subjectively, the causal sequence may vary, especially as between "intuition" and "sympathetic agreement." This distinction is not, however, significant for the present classification of types of authority.

6. The scope of determination of social relationships and cultural phenomena by virtue of domination is considerably broader than appears at first sight. For instance, the authority exercised in the schools has much to do with the determination of the forms of speech and of written language which are regarded as orthodox. Dialects used as the "chancellery language" of autocephalous political units, hence of their rulers, have often become orthodox forms of speech and writing and have even led to the formation of separate "nations" (for instance, the separation of Holland from Germany). The rule by parents and the school, however, extends far beyond the determination of such cultural patterns, which are perhaps only apparently formal, to the formation of the young, and hence of human beings generally.

7. The fact that the chief and his administrative staff often appear formally as servants or agents of those they rule, naturally does nothing whatever to disprove the quality of dominance. There will be occasion later to speak of the substantive features of so-called "democracy." But a certain minimum of assured power to issue commands, thus of domination, must be provided for in nearly every conceivable case.

2. *The Three Pure Types of Authority*

There are three pure types of legitimate domination. The validity of the claims to legitimacy may be based on:

1. Rational grounds—resting on a belief in the legality of enacted rules and the right of those elevated to authority under such rules to issue commands (legal authority).

2. Traditional grounds—resting on an established belief in the sanctity of immemorial traditions and the legitimacy of those exercising authority under them (traditional authority); or finally,

3. Charismatic grounds—resting on devotion to the exceptional sanctity, heroism or exemplary character of an individual person, and of the normative patterns or order revealed or ordained by him (charismatic authority).

In the case of legal authority, obedience is owed to the legally established impersonal order. It extends to the persons exercising the authority of office under it by virtue of the formal legality of their commands and only within the scope of authority of the office. In the case of traditional authority, obedience is owed to the *person* of the chief who occupies the traditionally sanctioned position of authority and who is (within its sphere) bound by tradition. But here the obligation of obedience is a matter of personal loyalty within the area of accustomed obligations. In the case of charismatic authority, it is the charismatically qualified leader as such who is obeyed by virtue of personal trust in his revelation, his heroism or his exemplary qualities so far as they fall within the scope of the individual's belief in his charisma.

1. The usefulness of the above classification can only be judged by its results in promoting systematic analysis. The concept of "charisma" ("the gift of grace") is taken from the vocabulary of early Christianity. For the Christian hierocracy Rudolf Sohm, in his *Kirchenrecht,* was the first to clarify the substance of the concept, even though he did not use the same terminology. Others (for instance, Holl in *Enthusiasmus und Bussgewalt*) have clarified certain important consequences of it. It is thus nothing new.

2. The fact that none of these three ideal types, the elucidation of which will occupy the following pages, is usually to be found in historical cases in "pure" form, is naturally not a valid objection to attempting their conceptual formulation in the sharpest possible form. In this respect the present case is no different from many others. Later on (sec. 11 ff.) the transformation of pure charisma by the process of routinization will be discussed and thereby the relevance of the concept to the understanding of empirical systems of authority considerably increased. But even so it may be said of every historical phenomenon of authority that it is not likely to be "as an open book." Analysis in terms of sociological types has, after all, as compared with purely empirical historical investigation, certain advantages which should not be minimized. That is, it can in the particular case of a concrete form of authority determine what conforms to or approximates such types as "charisma," "hereditary charisma," "the charisma of office," "patriarchy," "bureaucracy," the authority of status groups, and in doing so it can work with relatively unambiguous concepts. But the idea that the whole of concrete historical reality can be exhausted in the conceptual scheme about to be developed is as far from the author's thoughts as anything could be.

ii

Legal Authority With a Bureaucratic Administrative Staff

Note: The specifically modern type of administration has intentionally been taken as a point of departure in order to make it possible later to contrast the others with it.

3. *Legal Authority: The Pure Type*

Legal authority rests on the acceptance of the validity of the following mutually inter-dependent ideas.

1. That any given legal norm may be established by agreement or by imposition, on grounds of expediency or value-rationality or both, with a claim to obedience at least on the part of the members of the organization. This is, however, usually extended to include all persons within the sphere of power in question—which in the case of territorial bodies is the territorial area—who stand in certain social relationships or carry out forms of social action which in the order governing the organization have been declared to be relevant.

2. That every body of law consists essentially in a consistent system of abstract rules which have normally been intentionally established. Furthermore, administration of law is held to consist in the application of these rules to particular cases; the administrative process in the rational pursuit of the interests which are specified in the order governing the organization within the limits laid down by legal precepts and following principles which are capable of generalized formulation and are approved in the order governing the group, or at least not disapproved in it.

3. That thus the typical person in authority, the "superior," is himself subject to an impersonal order by orienting his actions to it in his own dispositions and commands. (This is true not only for persons exercising legal authority who are in the usual sense "officials," but, for instance, for the elected president of a state.)

4. That the person who obeys authority does so, as it is usually stated, only in his capacity as a "member" of the organization and what he obeys is only "the law." (He may in this connection be the member

of an association, of a community, of a church, or a citizen of a state.)

5. In conformity with point 3, it is held that the members of the organization, insofar as they obey a person in authority, do not owe this obedience to him as an individual, but to the impersonal order. Hence, it follows that there is an obligation to obedience only within the sphere of the rationally delimited jurisdiction which, in terms of the order, has been given to him.

The following may thus be said to be the fundamental categories of rational legal authority:

(1) A continuous rule-bound conduct of official business.

(2) A specified sphere of competence (jurisdiction). This involves: (a) A sphere of obligations to perform functions which has been marked off as part of a systematic division of labor. (b) The provision of the incumbent with the necessary powers. (c) That the necessary means of compulsion are clearly defined and their use is subject to definite conditions. A unit exercising authority which is organized in this way will be called an "administrative organ" or "agency" (*Behörde*).

> There are administrative organs in this sense in large-scale private enterprises, in parties and armies, as well as in the state and the church. An elected president, a cabinet of ministers, or a body of elected "People's Representatives" also in this sense constitute administrative organs. This is not, however, the place to discuss these concepts. Not every administrative organ is provided with compulsory powers. But this distinction is not important for present purposes.

(3) The organization of offices follows the principle of hierarchy; that is, each lower office is under the control and supervision of a higher one. There is a right of appeal and of statement of grievances from the lower to the higher. Hierarchies differ in respect to whether and in what cases complaints can lead to a "correct" ruling from a higher authority itself, or whether the responsibility for such changes is left to the lower office, the conduct of which was the subject of the complaint.

(4) The rules which regulate the conduct of an office may be technical rules or norms.[2] In both cases, if their application is to be fully rational, specialized training is necessary. It is thus normally true that only a person who has demonstrated an adequate technical training is qualified to be a member of the administrative staff of such an organized group, and hence only such persons are eligible for appointment to official positions. The administrative staff of a rational organization thus typically consists of "officials," whether the organization be devoted to political, hierocratic, economic—in particular, capitalistic—or other ends.

(5) In the rational type it is a matter of principle that the members of the administrative staff should be completely separated from owner-

ship of the means of production or administration. Officials, employees, and workers attached to the administrative staff do not themselves own the non-human means of production and administration. These are rather provided for their use, in kind or in money, and the official is obligated to render an accounting of their use. There exists, furthermore, in principle complete separation of the organization's property (respectively, capital), and the personal property (household) of the official. There is a corresponding separation of the place in which official functions are carried out—the "office" in the sense of premises—from the living quarters.

(6) In the rational type case, there is also a complete absence of appropriation of his official position by the incumbent. Where "rights" to an office exist, as in the case of judges, and recently of an increasing proportion of officials and even of workers, they do not normally serve the purpose of appropriation by the official, but of securing the purely objective and independent character of the conduct of the office so that it is oriented only to the relevant norms.

(7) Administrative acts, decisions, and rules are formulated and recorded in writing, even in cases where oral discussion is the rule or is even mandatory. This applies at least to preliminary discussions and proposals, to final decisions, and to all sorts of orders and rules. The combination of written documents and a continuous operation by officials constitutes the "office" (*Bureau*)[3] which is the central focus of all types of modern organized action.

(8) Legal authority can be exercised in a wide variety of different forms which will be distinguished and discussed later. The following ideal-typical analysis will be deliberately confined for the time being to the administrative staff that is most unambiguously a structure of domination: "officialdom" or "bureaucracy."

In the above outline no mention has been made of the kind of head appropriate to a system of legal authority. This is a consequence of certain considerations which can only be made entirely understandable at a later stage in the analysis. There are very important types of rational domination which, with respect to the ultimate source of authority, belong to other categories. This is true of the hereditary charismatic type, as illustrated by hereditary monarchy, and of the pure charismatic type of a president chosen by a plebiscite. Other cases involve rational elements at important points, but are made up of a combination of bureaucratic and charismatic components, as is true of the cabinet form of government. Still others are subject to the authority of the chiefs of other organizations, whether their character be charismatic or bureaucratic; thus the formal head of a government department under a parliamentary regime may be a minister who occupies his position because of his authority in a party. The type of rational, legal administrative staff is capable of application in all kinds of situations and contexts. It is the most important mechanism for the administration of everyday affairs. For in that sphere, the exercise of authority consists precisely in administration.

4. *Legal Authority: The Pure Type (Continued)*

The purest type of exercise of legal authority is that which employs a bureaucratic administrative staff. Only the supreme chief of the organization occupies his position of dominance (*Herrenstellung*) by virtue of appropriation, of election, or of having been designated for the succession. But even *his* authority consists in a sphere of legal "competence." The whole administrative staff under the supreme authority then consists, in the purest type, of individual officials (constituting a "monocracy" as opposed to the "collegial" type, which will be discussed below) who are appointed and function according to the following criteria:

(1) They are personally free and subject to authority only with respect to their impersonal official obligations.

(2) They are organized in a clearly defined hierarchy of offices.

(3) Each office has a clearly defined sphere of competence in the legal sense.

(4) The office is filled by a free contractual relationship. Thus, in principle, there is free selection.

(5) Candidates are selected on the basis of technical qualifications. In the most rational case, this is tested by examination or guaranteed by diplomas certifying technical training, or both. They are *appointed*, not elected.

(6) They are remunerated by fixed salaries in money, for the most part with a right to pensions. Only under certain circumstances does the employing authority, especially in private organizations, have a right to terminate the appointment, but the official is always free to resign. The salary scale is graded according to rank in the hierarchy; but in addition to this criterion, the responsibility of the position and the requirements of the incumbent's social status may be taken into account (cf. ch. IV).

(7) The office is treated as the sole, or at least the primary, occupation of the incumbent.

(8) It constitutes a career. There is a system of "promotion" according to seniority or to achievement, or both. Promotion is dependent on the judgment of superiors.

(9) The official works entirely separated from ownership of the means of administration and without appropriation of his position.

(10) He is subject to strict and systematic discipline and control in the conduct of the office.

This type of organization is in principle applicable with equal facility to a wide variety of different fields. It may be applied in profit-making business or in charitable organizations, or in any number of other types of private enterprises serving ideal or material ends. It is equally applicable to political and to hierocratic organizations. With the varying degrees of approximation to a pure type, its historical existence can be demonstrated in all these fields.

1. For example, bureaucracy is found in private clinics, as well as in endowed hospitals or the hospitals maintained by religious orders. Bureaucratic organization is well illustrated by the administrative role of the priesthood (*Kaplanokratie*) in the modern [Catholic] church, which has expropriated almost all of the old church benefices, which were in former days to a large extent subject to private appropriation. It is also illustrated by the notion of a [Papal] universal episcopate, which is thought of as formally constituting a universal legal competence in religious matters. Similarly, the doctrine of Papal infallibility is thought of as in fact involving a universal competence, but only one which functions "ex cathedra" in the sphere of the office, thus implying the typical distinction between the sphere of office and that of the private affairs of the incumbent. The same phenomena are found in the large-scale capitalistic enterprise; and the larger it is, the greater their role. And this is not less true of political parties, which will be discussed separately. Finally, the modern army is essentially a bureaucratic organization administered by that peculiar type of military functionary, the "officer."

2. Bureaucratic authority is carried out in its purest form where it is most clearly dominated by the principle of appointment. There is no such thing as a hierarchical organization of elected officials. In the first place, it is impossible to attain a stringency of discipline even approaching that in the appointed type, since the subordinate official can stand on his own election and since his prospects are not dependent on the superior's judgment. (On elected officials, see below, sec. 14.)

3. Appointment by free contract, which makes free selection possible, is essential to modern bureaucracy. Where there is a hierarchical organization with impersonal spheres of competence, but occupied by unfree officials—like slaves or *ministeriales,* who, however, function in a formally bureaucratic manner—the term "patrimonial bureaucracy" will be used.

4. The role of technical qualifications in bureaucratic organizations is continually increasing. Even an official in a party or a trade-union organization is in need of specialized knowledge, though it is usually developed by experience rather than by formal training. In the modern

state, the only "offices" for which no technical qualifications are required are those of ministers and presidents. This only goes to prove that they are "officials" only in a formal sense, and not substantively, just like the managing director or president of a large business corporation. There is no question but that the "position" of the capitalistic entrepreneur is as definitely appropriated as is that of a monarch. Thus at the top of a bureaucratic organization, there is necessarily an element which is at least not purely bureaucratic. The category of bureaucracy is one applying only to the exercise of control by means of a particular kind of administrative staff.

5. The bureaucratic official normally receives a fixed salary. (By contrast, sources of income which are privately appropriated will be called "benefices" (*Pfründen*)—on this concept, see below, sec. 8.) Bureaucratic salaries are also normally paid in money. Though this is not essential to the concept of bureaucracy, it is the arrangement which best fits the pure type. (Payments in kind are apt to have the character of benefices, and the receipt of a benefice normally implies the appropriation of opportunities for earnings and of positions.) There are, however, gradual transitions in this field with many intermediate types. Appropriation by virtue of leasing or sale of offices or the pledge of income from office are phenomena foreign to the pure type of bureaucracy (cf. *infra*, sec. 7a: III:3).

6. "Offices" which do not constitute the incumbent's principal occupation, in particular "honorary" offices, belong in other categories, which will be discussed later (sec. 19f.). The typical "bureaucratic" official occupies the office as his principal occupation.

7. With respect to the separation of the official from ownership of the means of administration, the situation is exactly the same in the field of public administration and in private bureaucratic organizations, such as the large-scale capitalistic enterprise.

8. Collegial bodies will be discussed separately below (section 15). At the present time they are rapidly decreasing in importance in favor of types of organization which are in fact, and for the most part formally as well, subject to the authority of a single head. For instance, the collegial "governments" in Prussia have long since given way to the monocratic "district president" (*Regierungspräsident*). The decisive factor in this development has been the need for rapid, clear decisions, free of the necessity of compromise between different opinions and also free of shifting majorities.

9. The modern army officer is a type of appointed official who is clearly marked off by certain status distinctions. This will be discussed elsewhere (ch. IV). In this respect such officers differ radically from elected military leaders, from charismatic *condottieri* (sec. 10), from the type of officers who recruit and lead mercenary armies as a capitalistic enterprise, and, finally, from the incumbents of commissions which have been purchased (sec. 7a). There may be gradual transitions between these types. The patrimonial "retainer," who is separated from the means

of carrying out his function, and the proprietor of a mercenary army for capitalistic purposes have, along with the private capitalistic entrepreneur, been pioneers in the organization of the modern type of bureaucracy. This will be discussed in detail below.

5. *Monocratic Bureaucracy*

Experience tends universally to show that the purely bureaucratic type of administrative organization—that is, the monocratic variety of bureaucracy—is, from a purely technical point of view, capable of attaining the highest degree of efficiency and is in this sense formally the most rational known means of exercising authority over human beings. It is superior to any other form in precision, in stability, in the stringency of its discipline, and in its reliability. It thus makes possible a particularly high degree of calculability of results for the heads of the organization and for those acting in relation to it. It is finally superior both in intensive efficiency and in the scope of its operations, and is formally capable of application to all kinds of administrative tasks.

The development of modern forms of organization in all fields is nothing less than identical with the development and continual spread of bureaucratic administration. This is true of church and state, of armies, political parties, economic enterprises, interest groups, endowments, clubs, and many others. Its development is, to take the most striking case, at the root of the modern Western state. However many forms there may be which do not appear to fit this pattern, such as collegial representative bodies, parliamentary committees, soviets, honorary officers, lay judges, and what not, and however many people may complain about the "red tape," it would be sheer illusion to think for a moment that continuous administrative work can be carried out in any field except by means of officials working in offices. The whole pattern of everyday life is cut to fit this framework. If bureaucratic administration is, other things being equal, always the most rational type from a technical point of view, the needs of mass administration make it today completely indispensable. The choice is only that between bureaucracy and dilettantism in the field of administration.

The primary source of the superiority of bureaucratic administration lies in the role of technical knowledge which, through the development of modern technology and business methods in the production of goods, has become completely indispensable. In this respect, it makes no difference whether the economic system is organized on a capitalistic or a socialistic basis. Indeed, if in the latter case a comparable level of technical efficiency were to be achieved, it would mean a tremendous increase in the importance of professional bureaucrats.

When those subject to bureaucratic control seek to escape the influence of the existing bureaucratic apparatus, this is normally possible only by creating an organization of their own which is equally subject to bureaucratization. Similarly the existing bureaucratic apparatus is driven to continue functioning by the most powerful interests which are material and objective, but also ideal in character. Without it, a society like our own—with its separation of officials, employees, and workers from ownership of the means of administration, and its dependence on discipline and on technical training—could no longer function. The only exception would be those groups, such as the peasantry, who are still in possession of their own means of subsistence. Even in the case of revolution by force or of occupation by an enemy, the bureaucratic machinery will normally continue to function just as it has for the previous legal government.

The question is always who controls the existing bureaucratic machinery. And such control is possible only in a very limited degree to persons who are not technical specialists. Generally speaking, the highest-ranking career official is more likely to get his way in the long run than his nominal superior, the cabinet minister, who is not a specialist.

Though by no means alone, the capitalistic system has undeniably played a major role in the development of bureaucracy. Indeed, without it capitalistic production could not continue and any rational type of socialism would have simply to take it over and increase its importance. Its development, largely under capitalistic auspices, has created an urgent need for stable, strict, intensive, and calculable administration. It is this need which is so fateful to any kind of large-scale administration. Only by reversion in every field—political, religious, economic, etc.—to small-scale organization would it be possible to any considerable extent to escape its influence. On the one hand, capitalism in its modern stages of development requires the bureaucracy, though both have arisen from different historical sources. Conversely, capitalism is the most rational economic basis for bureaucratic administration and enables it to develop in the most rational form, especially because, from a fiscal point of view, it supplies the necessary money resources.

Along with these fiscal conditions of efficient bureaucratic administration, there are certain extremely important conditions in the fields of communication and transportation. The precision of its functioning requires the services of the railway, the telegraph, and the telephone, and becomes increasingly dependent on them. A socialistic form of organization would not alter this fact. It would be a question (cf. ch. II, sec. 12) whether in a socialistic system it would be possible to provide conditions for carrying out as stringent a bureaucratic organization as has been possible in a capitalistic order. For socialism would, in fact, require a still higher degree of formal bureaucratization than capitalism. If this should prove not to be possible, it would demonstrate the existence of another of those fundamental elements of irrationality—a conflict between formal and substantive rationality of the sort which sociology so often encounters.

Bureaucratic administration means fundamentally domination through knowledge. This is the feature of it which makes it specifically rational. This consists on the one hand in technical knowledge which, by itself, is sufficient to ensure it a position of extraordinary power. But in addition to this, bureaucratic organizations, or the holders of power who make use of them, have the tendency to increase their power still further by the knowledge growing out of experience in the service. For they acquire through the conduct of office a special knowledge of facts and have available a store of documentary material peculiar to themselves. While not peculiar to bureaucratic organizations, the concept of "official secrets" is certainly typical of them. It stands in relation to technical knowledge in somewhat the same position as commercial secrets do to technological training. It is a product of the striving for power.

Superior to bureaucracy in the knowledge of techniques and facts is only the capitalist entrepreneur, within his own sphere of interest. He is the only type who has been able to maintain at least relative immunity from subjection to the control of rational bureaucratic knowledge. In large-scale organizations, all others are inevitably subject to bureaucratic control, just as they have fallen under the dominance of precision machinery in the mass production of goods.

In general, bureaucratic domination has the following social consequences:

(1) The tendency to "levelling" in the interest of the broadest possible basis of recruitment in terms of technical competence.

(2) The tendency to plutocracy growing out of the interest in the greatest possible length of technical training. Today this often lasts up to the age of thirty.

(3) The dominance of a spirit of formalistic impersonality: "*Sine ira et studio,*" without hatred or passion, and hence without affection or enthusiasm. The dominant norms are concepts of straightforward duty without regard to personal considerations. Everyone is subject to formal equality of treatment; that is, everyone in the same empirical situation. This is the spirit in which the ideal official conducts his office.

The development of bureaucracy greatly favors the levelling of status, and this can be shown historically to be the normal tendency. Conversely, every process of social levelling creates a favorable situation for the development of bureaucracy by eliminating the office-holder who rules by virtue of status privileges and the appropriation of the means and powers of administration; in the interests of "equality," it also eliminates those who can hold office on an honorary basis or as an avocation by virtue of their wealth. Everywhere bureaucratization foreshadows mass democracy, which will be discussed in another connection.

The "spirit" of rational bureaucracy has normally the following general characteristics:

(1) Formalism, which is promoted by all the interests which are concerned with the security of their own personal situation, whatever this may consist in. Otherwise the door would be open to arbitrariness and hence formalism is the line of least resistance.

(2) There is another tendency, which is apparently, and in part genuinely, in contradiction to the above. It is the tendency of officials to treat their official function from what is substantively a utilitarian point of view in the interest of the welfare of those under their authority. But this utilitarian tendency is generally expressed in the enactment of corresponding regulatory measures which themselves have a formal character and tend to be treated in a formalistic spirit. (This will be further discussed in the Sociology of Law). This tendency to substantive rationality is supported by all those subject to authority who are not included in the group mentioned above as interested in the protection of advantages already secured. The problems which open up at this point belong in the theory of "democracy."

iii

Traditional Authority

6. *The Pure Type*

Authority will be called traditional if legitimacy is claimed for it and believed in by virtue of the sanctity of age-old rules and powers. The masters are designated according to traditional rules and are obeyed because of their traditional status (*Eigenwürde*). This type of organized rule is, in the simplest case, primarily based on personal loyalty which results from common upbringing. The person exercising authority is not a "superior," but a personal master, his administrative staff does not consist mainly of officials but of personal retainers, and the ruled are not "members" of an association but are either his traditional "comrades" (sec. 7a) or his "subjects." Personal loyalty, not the official's impersonal duty, determines the relations of the administrative staff to the master.

Obedience is owed not to enacted rules but to the person who occupies a position of authority by tradition or who has been chosen for it by the traditional master. The commands of such a person are legitimized in one of two ways:

a) partly in terms of traditions which themselves directly determine the content of the command and are believed to be valid within certain limits that cannot be overstepped without endangering the master's traditional status;

b) partly in terms of the master's discretion in that sphere which tradition leaves open to him; this traditional prerogative rests primarily on the fact that the obligations of personal obedience tend to be essentially unlimited.

Thus there is a double sphere:

a) that of action which is bound to specific traditions;

b) that of action which is free of specific rules.

In the latter sphere, the master is free to do good turns on the basis of his personal pleasure and likes, particularly in return for gifts—the historical sources of dues (*Gebühren*). So far as his action follows principles at all, these are governed by considerations of ethical common sense, of equity or of utilitarian expediency. They are not formal principles, as in the case of legal authority. The exercise of power is oriented toward the consideration of how far master and staff can go in view of the subjects' traditional compliance without arousing their resistance. When resistance occurs, it is directed against the master or his servant personally, the accusation being that he failed to observe the traditional limits of his power. Opposition is not directed against the system as such—it is a case of "traditionalist revolution."

In the pure type of traditional authority it is impossible for law or administrative rule to be deliberately created by legislation. Rules which in fact are innovations can be legitimized only by the claim that they have been "valid of yore," but have only now been recognized by means of "Wisdom" [the *Weistum* of ancient Germanic law]. Legal decisions as "finding of the law" (*Rechtsfindung*) can refer only to documents of tradition, namely to precedents and earlier decisions.

7. *The Pure Type* (*Continued*)

The master rules with or without an administrative staff. On the latter case, see sec. 7a:I.

The typical administrative staff is recruited from one or more of the following sources:

(I) From persons who are already related to the chief by traditional ties of loyalty. This will be called patrimonial recruitment. Such persons may be

- a) kinsmen,
- b) slaves,
- c) dependents who are officers of the household, especially *ministeriales,*
- d) clients,
- e) *coloni,*
- f) freedmen;

(II) Recruitment may be extra-patrimonial, including

- a) persons in a relation of purely personal loyalty such as all sorts of "favorites,"
- b) persons standing in a relation of fealty to their lord (vassals), and, finally,
- c) free men who voluntarily enter into a relation of personal loyalty as officials.

On I.a) Under traditionalist domination it is very common for the most important posts to be filled with members of the ruling family or clan.

b) In patrimonial administrations it is common for slaves and freedmen to rise even to the highest positions. It has not been rare for Grand Viziers to have been at one time slaves.

c) The typical household officials have been the following: the senechal, the marshal, the chamberlain, the carver (*Truchsess*), the majordomo, who was the head of the service personnel and possibly of the vassals. These are to be found everywhere in Europe. In the Orient, in addition, the head eunuch, who was in charge of the harem, was particularly important, and in African kingdoms, the executioner. Furthermore, the ruler's personal physician, the astrologer and similar persons have been common.

d) In China and in Egypt, the principal source of recruitment for patrimonial officials lay in the clientele of the king.

e) Armies of *coloni* have been known throughout the Orient and were typical of the Roman nobility. (Even in modern times, in the Mohammedan world, armies of slaves have existed.)

On II.a) The regime of favorites is characteristic of every patrimonial rule and has often been the occasion for traditionalist revolutions.

b) The vassals will be treated separately.

c) Bureaucracy has first developed in patrimonial states with a body of officials recruited from extra-patrimonial sources; but, as will be shown soon, these officials were at first personal followers of their master.

In the pure type of traditional rule, the following features of a bureaucratic administrative staff are absent:

a) a clearly defined sphere of competence subject to impersonal rules,

b) a rationally established hierarchy,

c) a regular system of appointment on the basis of free contract, and orderly promotion,

d) technical training as a regular requirement,

e) (frequently) fixed salaries, in the type case paid in money.

On a): In place of a well-defined functional jurisdiction, there is a conflicting series of tasks and powers which at first are assigned at the master's discretion. However, they tend to become permanent and are often traditionally stereotyped. These competing functions originate particularly in the competition for sources of income which are at the disposal of the master himself and of his representatives. It is often in the first instance through these interests that definite functional spheres are first marked off and genuine administrative organs come into being.

At first, persons with permanent functions are household officials. Their (extra-patrimonial) functions outside the administration of the household are often in fields of activity which bear a relatively superficial analogy to their household function, or which originated in a discretionary act of the master and later became traditionally stereotyped. In addition to household officials, there have existed primarily only persons with *ad hoc* commissions.

> The absence of distinct spheres of competence is evident from a perusal of the list of the titles of officials in any of the ancient Oriental states. With rare exceptions, it is impossible to associate with these titles a set of rationally delimited functions which have remained stable over a considerable period.
>
> The process of delimiting permanent functions as a result of competition among and compromise between interests seeking favors, income, and other forms of advantage is clearly evident in the Middle Ages. This phenomenon has had very important consequences. The financial interests of the powerful royal courts and of the powerful legal profession in England were largely responsible for vitiating or curbing the influence of Roman and Canon law. In all periods the irrational division of official functions has been stereotyped by the existence of an established set of rights to fees and perquisites.

On b): The question of who shall decide a matter or deal with appeals—whether an agent shall be in charge of this, and which one, or whether the master reserves decision for himself—is treated either traditionally, at times by considering the provenience of certain legal norms and precedents taken over from the outside (*Oberhof-System*);[3a] or entirely on the basis of the master's discretion in such manner that all agents have to yield to his personal intervention.

> Next to the traditionalist system of the [precedent-setting outside] "superior" court (*Oberhof*) we find the principle of Germanic law, deriving from the ruler's political prerogative, that in his presence the jurisdiction of any court is suspended. The *ius evocandi* and its modern derivative, chamber justice (*Kabinettsjustiz*), stem from the same source and the ruler's discretion. Particularly in the Middle Ages the *Oberhof* was very often the agency whose writ declared and interpreted the law, and accordingly the source from which the law of a given locality was imported.

On c): The household officials and favorites are often recruited in a purely patrimonial fashion: they are slaves or dependents (*ministeriales*) of the master. If recruitment has been extra-patrimonial, they have tended to be benefice-holders whom he can freely remove. A fundamental change in this situation is first brought about by the rise of free vassals and the filling of offices by a contract of fealty. However, since fiefs are by no means determined by functional considerations, this does not alter the situation with respect to a) and b) [the lack of definite spheres of competence and clearly determined hierarchical relationships]. Except under certain circumstances when the administrative staff is organized on a prebendal basis, "promotion" is completely up to the master's discretion (see sec. 8).

On d): Rational technical training as a basic qualification for office is scarcely to be found among household officials and favorites. However, a fundamental change in administrative practice occurs wherever there is even a beginning of technical training for appointees, regardless of its content.

> For some offices a certain amount of empirical training has been necessary from very early times. This is particularly true of the art of reading and writing which was originally truly a rare "art." This has often, most strikingly in China, had a decisive influence on the whole development of culture through the mode of life of the literati. It eliminated the recruiting of officials from intra-patrimonial sources and thus limited the ruler's power by confronting him with a status group (cf. sec. 7a: III).

On e): Household officials and favorites are usually supported and equipped in the master's household. Generally, their dissociation from the lord's own table means the creation of benefices, at first usually benefices in kind. It is easy for these to become traditionally stereotyped in amount and kind. In addition, or instead of them, the officials who live outside the lord's household and the lord himself count on various fees, which are often collected without any regular rate or scale, being agreed upon from case to case with those seeking favors. (On the concept of benefices see sec. 8.)

7a. *Gerontocracy, Patriarchalism and Patrimonialism*

I. *Gerontocracy* and *primary patriarchalism* are the most elementary types of traditional domination where the master has no personal administrative staff.

The term gerontocracy is applied to a situation where so far as rule over the group is organized at all it is in the hands of elders—which originally was understood literally as the eldest in actual years, who are the most familiar with the sacred traditions. This is common in groups which are not primarily of an economic or kinship character. "Patriarchalism" is the situation where, within a group (household) which is usually organized on both an economic and a kinship basis, a particular individual governs who is designated by a definite rule of inheritance. Gerontocracy and patriarchalism are frequently found side by side. The decisive characteristic of both is the belief of the members that domination, even though it is an inherent traditional right of the master, must definitely be exercized as a joint right in the interest of all members and is thus not freely appropriated by the incumbent. In order that this shall be maintained, it is crucial that in both cases there is a complete absence of a personal (patrimonial) staff. Hence the master is still largely dependent upon the willingness of the members to comply with his orders since he has no machinery to enforce them. Therefore, the members (*Genossen*) are not yet really subjects (*Untertanen*).

Their membership exists by tradition and not by enactment. Obedience is owed to the master, not to any enacted regulation. However, it is owed to the master only by virtue of his traditional status. He is thus on his part strictly bound by tradition.

> The different types of gerontocracy will be discussed later. Elementary patriarchalism is related to it in that the patriarch's authority carries strict obligations to obedience only within his own household. Apart from this, as in the case of the Arabian Sheik, it has only an exemplary effect, in the manner of charismatic authority, or must resort to advice and similar means of exerting influence.

II. *Patrimonialism* and, in the extreme case, *sultanism* tend to arise whenever traditional domination develops an administration and a military force which are purely personal instruments of the master. Only then are the group members treated as subjects. Previously the master's authority appeared as a pre-eminent group right, now it turns into his personal right, which he appropriates in the same way as he would any ordinary object of possession. In principle, he can exploit his right like any economic asset—sell it, pledge it as security, or divide it by inheritance. The primary external support of patrimonial power is provided by slaves (who are often branded), *coloni* and conscripted subjects, but also by mercenary bodyguards and armies (patrimonial troops); the latter practice is designed to maximize the solidarity of interest between master and staff. By controlling these instruments the ruler can broaden the range of his arbitrary power and put himself in a position to grant grace and favors at the expense of the traditional limitations of patriarchal and gerontocratic structures. Where domination is primarily traditional, even though it is exercised by virtue of the ruler's personal autonomy, it will be called *patrimonial authority;* where it indeed operates primarily on the basis of discretion, it will be called *sultanism.* The transition is definitely continuous. Both forms of domination are distinguished from elementary patriarchalism by the presense of a personal staff.

> Sometimes it appears that sultanism is completely unrestrained by tradition, but this is never in fact the case. The non-traditional element is not, however, rationalized in impersonal terms, but consists only in an extreme development of the ruler's discretion. It is this which distinguishes it from every form of rational authority.

III. *Estate-type domination (ständische Herrschaft)*[4] is that form of patrimonial authority under which the administrative staff appropriates particular powers and the corresponding economic assets. As in all similar cases (cf. ch. II, sec. 19), appropriation may take the following forms:

a) Appropriation may be carried out by an organized group or by a category of persons distinguished by particular characteristics, or

b) it may be carried out by individuals, for life, on a hereditary basis, or as free property.

Domination of the estate-type thus involves:

a) always a limitation of the lord's discretion in selecting his administrative staff because positions or seigneurial powers have been appropriated by

α) an organized group,

β) a status group (see ch. IV), or

b) often—and this will be considered as typical—appropriation by the individual staff members of

α) the positions, including in general the economic advantages associated with them,

β) the material means of administration,

γ) the governing powers.

Those holding appropriated positions may have originated historically 1) from members of an administrative staff which was not previously an independent status group, or 2) before the appropriation, they may not have belonged to the staff.

Where governing powers are appropriated, the costs of administration are met indiscriminately from the incumbent's own and his appropriated means. Holders of military powers and seigneurial members of the "feudal" army (*ständisches Heer*) equip themselves and possibly their own patrimonial or feudal contingents. It is also possible that the provision of administrative means and of the administrative staff itself is appropriated as the object of a profit-making enterprise, on the basis of fixed contributions from the ruler's magazines or treasury. This was true in particular of the mercenary armies in the sixteenth and seventeenth century in Europe—examples of "capitalist armies."

Where appropriation is complete, all the powers of government are divided between the ruler and the administrative staff members, each on the basis of his personal rights (*Eigenrecht*); or autonomous powers are created and regulated by special decrees of the ruler or special compromises with the holders of appropriated rights.

On 1): An example are the holders of court offices which have become appropriated as fiefs. An example for 2) are seigneurs who appropriated powers by virtue of their privileged position or by usurpation, using the former as a legalization of the latter.

Appropriation by an *individual* may rest on

1. leasing,
2. pledging as security,
3. sale,
4. privileges, which may be personal, hereditary or freely appropriated, unconditional or subject to the performance of certain functions; such a privilege may be

    a) granted in return for services or for the sake of "buying" compliance, or

    b) it may constitute merely the formal recognition of actual usurpation of powers;

5. appropriation by an organized group or a status group, usually a consequence of a compromise between the ruler and his administrative staff or between him and an unorganized status group; this may

    α) leave the ruler completely or relatively free in his selection of individuals, or

    β) it may lay down rigid rules for the selection of incumbents;

6. fiefs, a case which we must deal with separately.

1. In the cases of gerontocracy and pure patriarchalism, so far as there are clear ideas on the subject at all, the means of administration are generally appropriated by the group as a whole or by the participating households. The administrative functions are performed on behalf of the group as a whole. Appropriation by the master personally is a phenomenon of patrimonialism. It may vary enormously in degree to the extreme cases of a claim to full proprietorship of the land (*Bodenregal*) and to the status of master over subjects treated as negotiable slaves. Estate-type appropriation generally means the appropriation of at least part of the means of administration by the members of the administrative staff. In the case of pure patrimonialism, there is complete separation of the functionary from the means of carrying out his function. But exactly the opposite is true of the estate-type of patrimonialism. The person exercising governing powers has personal control of the means of administration—if not all, at least of an important part of them. In full possession of these means were the feudal knight, who provided his own equipment, the count, who by virtue of holding his fief took the court fees and other perquisites for himself and met his feudal obligations from his own means (including the appropriated ones), and the Indian *jagirdar*, who provided and equipped a military unit from the proceeds of his tax benefice. On the other hand, a colonel who recruited a mercenary regiment on his own account, but received certain payments from the royal exchequer and covered his deficit either by curtailing the service or from booty or requisitions, was only partly in possession of the means of administration and was subject to certain regulations. By contrast, the Pharaoh, who organized armies of slaves or *coloni*, put his clients in command of them, and clothed, fed and equipped them from his own storehouses, was acting as a patrimonial lord in full personal control of the means of administration. It is not always the formal mode of organization which is decisive. The Mamelukes were formally purchased slaves. In fact, however, they monopolized the powers of government as completely as any group of *ministeriales* has ever monopolized the service fiefs.

There are examples of service land appropriated by a closed group without any individual appropriation. Where this occurs, land may be freely granted to individuals by the lord as long as they are members of the group (case III:a:α) or the grant may be subject to regulations specifying qualifications (case III:a:β). Thus, military or possibly ritual qualifications have been required of the candidates, but once they are given, close blood relations have had priority. The situation is similar in the case of manorial or guild artisans or of peasants whose services have been attached for military or administrative purposes.

2. Appropriation by lease, especially tax farming, by pledging as security, or by sale, have been found in the Occident, but also in the Orient and in India. In Antiquity, it was not uncommon for priesthoods to be sold at auction. In the case of leasing, the aim has been partly a practical financial one to meet stringencies caused especially by the costs of war. It has partly also been a matter of the technique of

financing, to insure a stable money income available for budgetary uses. Pledging as security and sale have generally arisen from the first aim. In the Papal States the purpose was also the creation of rents for nephews (*Nepotenrenten*). Appropriation by pledging played a significant role in France as late as the eighteenth century in filling judicial posts in the *parlements*. The appropriation of officers' commissions by regulated purchase continued in the British army well into the nineteenth century. Privileges, as a sanction of usurpation, as a reward, or as an incentive for political services, were common in the Middle Ages in Europe as well as elsewhere.

8. *Patrimonial Maintenance: Benefices and Fiefs*

The patrimonial retainer may receive his support in any of the following ways:

a) by living from the lord's table,
b) by allowances (usually in kind) from the lord's magazines or treasury,
c) by rights of land use in return for services ("service-land"),
d) by the appropriation of property income, fees or taxes,
e) by fiefs.

We shall speak of *benefices* insofar as the forms of maintenance b) through d) are always newly granted in a traditional fashion which determines amount or locality, and insofar as they can be appropriated by the individual, although not hereditarily. When an administrative staff is, in principle, supported in this form, we shall speak of *prebendalism*. In such a situation there may be a system of promotion on a basis of seniority or of particular objectively determined achievements, and it may also happen that a certain social status and hence a sense of status honor (*Standesehre*) are required as a criterion of eligibility. (On the concept of the status group: *Stand*, see ch. IV.)

Appropriated seigneurial powers will be called a *fief* if they are granted primarily to particular qualified individuals by a contract and if the reciprocal rights and duties involved are primarily oriented to conventional standards of status honor, particularly in a military sense. If an administrative staff is primarily supported by fiefs, we will speak of [Western] *feudalism* (*Lehensfeudalismus*).

The transition between fiefs and military benefices is so gradual that at times they are almost indistinguishable. (This will be further discussed below in ch. IV.)

In cases d) and e), sometimes also in c), the individual who has appropriated governing powers pays the cost of his administration, possibly of military equipment, in the manner indicated above, from the proceeds of his benefice or fief. His own authority may then become patrimonial (hence, hereditary, alienable, and capable of division by inheritance.)

1. The earliest form of support for royal retainers, household officials, priests and other types of patrimonial (for example, manorial) retainers has been their presence at the lord's table or their support by discretionary allowances from his stores. The "men's house," which is the oldest form of professional military organizations—to be dealt with later—, very often adheres to the consumptive household communism of a ruling stratum. Separation from the table of the lord (or of the temple or cathedral) and the substitution of allowances or service-land has by no means always been regarded with approval. It has, however, usually resulted from the establishment of independent families. Allowances in kind granted to such temple priests and officials constituted the original form of support of officials throughout the Near East and also existed in China, India, and often in the Occident. The use of land in return for military service is found throughout the Orient since early Antiquity, and also in medieval Germany, as a means of providing for *ministeriales,* manorial officials and other functionaries. The income sources of the Turkish *spahis,* the Japanese *samurai,* and various similar types of Oriental retainers and knights are, in the present terminology, "benefices" and not "fiefs," as will be pointed out later. In some cases they have been derived from the rents of certain lands; in others, from the tax income of certain districts. In the latter case, they have generally been combined with appropriation of governmental powers in the same district. The concept of the fief can be further developed only in relation to that of the state. Its object may be a manor—a form of patrimonial domination —or it may be any of various kinds of claims to property income and fees.

2. The appropriation of property income and rights to fees and the proceeds of taxes in the form of benefices and fiefs of all sorts is widespread. In India, particularly, it became an independent and highly developed practice. The usual arrangement was the granting of rights to these sources of income in return for the provision of military contingents and the payment of administrative costs.

9. *Estate-Type Domination and Its Division of Powers*

In the pure type, patrimonial domination, especially of the estate-type, regards all governing powers and the corresponding economic rights as privately appropriated economic advantages. This does not mean that these powers are qualitatively undifferentiated. Some important ones are appropriated in a form subject to special regulations. In particular, the appropriation of judicial and military powers tends to be treated as a legal basis for a privileged status position of those appropriating them, as compared to the appropriation of purely economic advantages having to do with the income from domains, from taxes, or perquisites. Within the latter category, again, there tends to be a differentiation of those which are primarily patrimonial from those which are primarily extra-patrimonial or fiscal in the mode of appropriation. For our terminology the decisive fact is that, regardless of content, governing powers and the related emoluments are treated as private rights.

> In his *Der deutsche Staat des Mittelalters,* von Below is quite right in emphasizing that the appropriation of judicial authority was singled out and became a source of privileged status, and that it is impossible to prove that the medieval political organization had either a purely patri-monial or a purely feudal character. Nevertheless, so far as judicial authority and other rights of a purely political origin are treated as private rights, it is for present purposes terminologically correct to speak of patrimonial domination. The concept itself, as is well known, has been most consistently developed by Haller in his *Restauration der Staatswissenschaften.* Historically there has never been a purely patri-monial state.[5]

IV. We shall speak of the *estate-type division of powers* (*ständische Gewaltenteilung*) when organized groups of persons privileged by ap-propriated seigneurial powers conclude *compromises* with their ruler. As the occasion warrants, the subject of such compromises may be political or administrative regulations, concrete administrative decisions or super-visory measures. At times the members of such groups may participate directly on their own authority and with their own staffs.

> 1. Under certain circumstances, groups, such as peasants, which do not enjoy a privileged social position, may be included. This does not, however, alter the concept. For the decisive point is the fact that the members of the privileged group have independent rights. If socially privileged groups were absent, the case would obviously belong under another type.
> 2. The type case has been fully developed only in the Occident. We must deal separately and in detail with its characteristics and with the reasons for its development.
> 3. As a rule, such a status group did not have an administrative staff of its own, especially not one with independent governing powers.

9a. Traditional Domination and the Economy

The primary effect of traditional domination on economic activities is usually in a very general way to strengthen traditional attitudes. This is most conspicuous under gerontocratic and purely patriarchal domina-tion, which cannot use an administrative machinery against the members of the group and hence is strongly dependent for its own legitimacy upon the safeguarding of tradition in every respect.

I. Beyond this, the typical mode of financing a traditional structure of domination affects the economy (cf. ch. II, sec. 38). In this respect, patrimonialism may use a wide variety of approaches. The following, however, are particularly important:

A. An *oikos* maintained by the ruler where needs are met on a liturgical basis wholly or primarily in kind (in the form of contributions and compulsory services). In this case, economic relationships tend to be strictly tradition-bound. The development of markets is obstructed, the use of money is primarily consumptive, and the development of capitalism is impossible.

B. Provisioning the services of socially privileged groups has very similar effects. Though not necessarily to the same extent, the development of markets is also limited in this case by the fact that the property and the productive capacity of the individual economic units are largely pre-empted for the ruler's needs.

C. Furthermore, patrimonialism can resort to monopolistic want satisfaction, which in part may rely on profit-making enterprises, fee-taking or taxation. In this case, the development of markets is, according to the type of monopolies involved, more or less seriously limited by irrational factors. The important openings for profit are in the hands of the ruler and of his administrative staff. Capitalism is thereby either directly obstructed, if the ruler maintains his own administration, or is diverted into political capitalism, if there is tax farming, leasing or sale of offices, and capitalist provision for armies and administration (see ch. II, sec. 31).

Even where it is carried out in money terms, the financing of patrimonialism and even more of sultanism tends to have irrational consequences for the following reasons:

1) The obligations placed on sources of direct taxation tend both in amount and in kind to remain bound to tradition. At the same time there is complete freedom—and hence arbitrariness—in the determination of a) fees and b) of newly imposed obligations, and c) in the organization of monopolies. This element of arbitrariness is at least claimed as a right. It is historically most effective in case a), because the lord and his staff must be asked for the "favor" of action, far less effective in case b), and of varying effectiveness in case c).

2) Two bases of the rationalization of economic activity are entirely lacking; namely, a basis for the calculability of obligations and of the extent of freedom which will be allowed to private enterprise.

D. In individual cases, however, patrimonial fiscal policy may have a rationalizing effect by systematically cultivating its sources of taxation and by organizing monopolies rationally. This, however, is "accidental" and dependent on specific historical circumstances, some of which existed in the Occident.

If there is estate-type division of powers, fiscal policy tends to be a result of compromise. This makes the burdens relatively predictable and eliminates or at least sharply limits the ruler's powers to impose new burdens and, above all, to create monopolies. Whether the resulting fiscal policy tends to promote or to limit rational economic activity depends largely on the type of ruling group; primarily, it depends on whether it is a *feudal* or a *patrician* stratum. The dominance of the feudal stratum tends, because the structure of feudalized powers of government is normally patrimonial, to set rigid limits to the freedom of acquisitive activity and the development of markets. It may even involve deliberate attempts to suppress them to protect the power of the feudal stratum. The predominance of a patrician [urban] stratum may have the opposite effect.

1. What has been said above must suffice for the present. It will be necessary to return to these questions repeatedly in different connections.

2. Examples for IA): the *oikos* of ancient Egypt and in India; IB): large parts of the Hellenistic world, the late Roman Empire, China, India, to some extent Russia and the Islamic states; IC): Ptolemaic Egypt, to some extent the Byzantine Empire, and in a different way the regime of the Stuarts in England; ID): the Occidental patrimonial states in the period of "enlightened despotism," especially Colbert's policies.

II. It is not only the financial policy of most patrimonial regimes which tends to restrict the development of rational economic activity, but above all the general character of their administrative practices. This is true in the following respects:

a) Traditionalism places serious obstacles in the way of formally rational regulations, which can be depended upon to remain stable and hence are calculable in their economic implications and exploitability.

b) A staff of officials with formal technical training is typically absent.

(The fact that it developed in the patrimonial states of the Occident is, as will be shown, accounted for by unique conditions. This stratum developed for the most part out of sources wholly different from the general structure of patrimonialism.)

c) There is a wide scope for actual arbitrariness and the expression of purely personal whims on the part of the ruler and the members of his administrative staff. The opening for bribery and corruption, which is simply a matter of the disorganization of an unregulated system of fees, would be the least serious effect of this if it remained a constant quantity, because then it would become calculable in practice. But it tends to be a matter which is settled from case to case with every individual official and thus highly variable. If offices are leased, the incumbent is put in a position where it is to his immediate interest to get back the capital he has invested by any available means of extortion, however irrational.

d) Patriarchalism and patrimonialism have an inherent tendency to regulate economic activity in terms of utilitarian, welfare or absolute values. This tendency stems from the character of the claim to legitimacy and the interest in the contentment of the subjects. It breaks down the type of *formal* rationality which is oriented to a technical legal order. This type of influence is decisive in the case of hierocratic patrimonialism. In the case of pure sultanism, on the other hand, it is fiscal arbitrariness which is likely to be most important.

For all these reasons, under the dominance of a patrimonial regime only certain types of capitalism are able to develop:

a) capitalist trading,

b) capitalist tax farming, lease and sale of offices,

c) capitalist provision of supplies for the state and the financing of wars,

d) under certain circumstances, capitalist plantations and other colonial enterprises.

All these forms are indigenous to patrimonial regimes and often reach a very high level of development. This is not, however, true of the type of profit-making enterprise with heavy investments in fixed capital and a rational organization of free labor which is oriented to the market purchases of private consumers. This type of capitalism is altogether too sensitive to all sorts of irrationalities in the administration of law, administration and taxation, for these upset the basis of *calculability*.

The situation is fundamentally different only in cases where a patrimonial ruler, in the interest of his own power and financial provision, develops a rational system of administration with technically specialized officials. For this to happen, it is necessary 1) that technical training should be available; 2) there must be a sufficiently powerful incentive to embark on such a policy—usually the sharp competition between a plurality of patrimonial powers within the same cultural area; 3) a very special factor is necessary, namely, the participation of urban communes as a financial support in the competition of the patrimonial units.

1. The major forerunners of the modern, specifically Western form of capitalism are to be found in the organized urban communes of Eu-

rope with their particular type of relatively rational administration. Its primary development took place from the sixteenth to the eighteenth centuries within the framework of the class structure and political organization (*ständischen politischen Verbände*) of Holland and England, which were distinguished by the unusual power of the bourgeois strata and the preponderance of their economic interests. The fiscal and utilitarian imitations, which were introduced into the purely patrimonial or largely feudal (*feudal-ständisch*) states of the Continent, have in common with the Stuart system of monopolistic industry the fact that they do not stand in the main line of continuity with the later autonomous capitalistic development. This is true in spite of the fact that particular measures of agricultural and industrial policy—so far and because they were oriented to English, Dutch, and later to French, models—played a very important part in creating some of the essential conditions for this later development. All this will be discussed further on.

2. In certain fields the patrimonial states of the Middle Ages developed a type of formally rational administrative staff which consisted especially of persons with legal training both in the civil and the canon law, and which differed fundamentally from the corresponding administrative staffs in political bodies of any other time or place. It will be necessary later to inquire more fully into the sources of this development and into its significance. For the present it is not possible to go beyond the very general observations introduced above.

iv

Charismatic Authority

1 0. *Charismatic Authority and Charismatic Community*

The term "charisma" will be applied to a certain quality of an individual personality by virtue of which he is considered extraordinary and treated as endowed with supernatural, superhuman, or at least specifically exceptional powers or qualities. These are such as are not accessible to the ordinary person, but are regarded as of divine origin or as exemplary, and on the basis of them the individual concerned is treated as a "leader." In primitive circumstances this peculiar kind of quality is thought of as resting on magical powers, whether of prophets, persons with a reputation for therapeutic or legal wisdom, leaders in the hunt, or heroes in war. How the quality in question would be ultimately judged from any ethical, aesthetic, or other such point of view is naturally entirely indifferent for purposes of definition. What is alone important is how the individual is actually regarded by those subject to charismatic authority, by his "followers" or "disciples."

> For present purposes it will be necessary to treat a variety of different types as being endowed with charisma in this sense. It includes the state of a "berserk" whose spells of maniac passion have, apparently wrongly, sometimes been attributed to the use of drugs. In medieval Byzantium a group of these men endowed with the charisma of fighting frenzy was maintained as a kind of weapon. It includes the "shaman," the magician who in the pure type has to be subject to epileptoid seizures as a means of falling into trances. Another type is represented by Joseph Smith, the founder of Mormonism, who may have been a very sophisticated swindler (although this cannot be definitely established). Finally it includes the type of *littérateur,* such as Kurt Eisner,[6] who is overwhelmed by his own demagogic success. Value-free sociological analysis will treat all these on the same level as it does the charisma of men who are the "greatest" heroes, prophets, and saviors according to conventional judgements.

I. It is recognition on the part of those subject to authority which is decisive for the validity of charisma. This recognition is freely given and guaranteed by what is held to be a proof, originally always a miracle, and consists in devotion to the corresponding revelation, hero worship, or absolute trust in the leader. But where charisma is genuine, it is not this which is the basis of the claim to legitimacy. This basis lies rather in the conception that it is the duty of those subject to charismatic authority to recognize its genuineness and to act accordingly. Psychologically this recognition is a matter of complete personal devotion to the possessor of the quality, arising out of enthusiasm, or of despair and hope.

> No prophet has ever regarded his quality as dependent on the attitudes of the masses toward him. No elective king or military leader has ever treated those who have resisted him or tried to ignore him otherwise than as delinquent in duty. Failure to take part in a military expedition under such leader, even though the recruitment is formally voluntary, has universally met with disdain.

II. If proof and success elude the leader for long, if he appears deserted by his god or his magical or heroic powers, above all, if his leadership fails to benefit his followers, it is likely that his charismatic authority will disappear. This is the genuine meaning of the divine right of kings (*Gottesgnadentum*).

> Even the old Germanic kings were sometimes rejected with scorn. Similar phenomena are very common among so-called primitive peoples.

In China the charismatic quality of the monarch, which was transmitted unchanged by heredity, was upheld so rigidly that any misfortune whatever, not only defeats in war, but drought, floods, or astronomical phenomena which were considered unlucky, forced him to do public penance and might even force his abdication. If such things occurred, it was a sign that he did not possess the requisite charismatic virtue and was thus not a legitimate "Son of Heaven."

III. An organized group subject to charismatic authority will be called a charismatic community (*Gemeinde*). It is based on an emotional form of communal relationship (*Vergemeinschaftung*). The administrative staff of a charismatic leader does not consist of "officials"; least of all are its members technically trained. It is not chosen on the basis of social privilege nor from the point of view of domestic or personal dependency. It is rather chosen in terms of the charismatic qualities of its members. The prophet has his disciples; the warlord his bodyguard; the leader, generally, his agents (*Vertrauensmänner*). There is no such thing as appointment or dismissal, no career, no promotion. There is only a call at the instance of the leader on the basis of the charismatic qualification of those he summons. There is no hierarchy; the leader merely intervenes in general or in individual cases when he considers the members of his staff lacking in charismatic qualification for a given task. There is no such thing as a bailiwick or definite sphere of competence, and no appropriation of official powers on the basis of social privileges. There may, however, be territorial or functional limits to charismatic powers and to the individual's mission. There is no such thing as a salary or a benefice.

Disciples or followers tend to live primarily in a communistic relationship with their leader on means which have been provided by voluntary gift. There are no established administrative organs. In their place are agents who have been provided with charismatic authority by their chief or who possess charisma of their own. There is no system of formal rules, of abstract legal principles, and hence no process of rational judicial decision oriented to them. But equally there is no legal wisdom oriented to judicial precedent. Formally concrete judgments are newly created from case to case and are originally regarded as divine judgments and revelations. From a substantive point of view, every charismatic authority would have to subscribe to the proposition, "It is written . . . but I say unto you . . ." The genuine prophet, like the genuine military leader and every true leader in this sense, preaches, creates, or demands *new* obligations—most typically, by virtue of revelation, oracle, inspiration, or of his own will, which are recognized by the members of the religious, military, or party group because they come from such a source. Recognition is a duty. When such an authority comes into conflict with the competing authority of another who also claims charismatic sanction, the only recourse is to some kind of a contest, by magical means or an actual physical battle of the leaders. In principle, only one side can be right in such a conflict; the other must be guilty of a wrong which has to be expiated.

Since it is "extra-ordinary," charismatic authority is sharply opposed to rational, and particularly bureaucratic, authority, and to traditional authority, whether in its patriarchal, patrimonial, or estate variants, all of which are everyday forms of domination; while the charismatic type is the direct antithesis of this. Bureaucratic authority is specifically rational in the sense of being bound to intellectually analysable rules; while charismatic authority is specifically irrational in the sense of being foreign to all rules. Traditional authority is bound to the precedents handed down from the past and to this extent is also oriented to rules. Within the sphere of its claims, charismatic authority repudiates the past, and is in this sense a specifically revolutionary force. It recognizes no appropriation of positions of power by virtue of the possession of property, either on the part of a chief or of socially privileged groups. The only basis of legitimacy for it is personal charisma so long as it is proved; that is, as long as it receives recognition and as long as the followers and disciples prove their usefulness charismatically.

> The above is scarcely in need of further discussion. What has been said applies to purely plebiscitary rulers (Napoleon's "rule of genius" elevated people of humble origin to thrones and high military commands) just as much as it applies to religious prophets or war heroes.

IV. Pure charisma is specifically foreign to economic considerations. Wherever it appears, it constitutes a "call" in the most emphatic sense of the word, a "mission" or a "spiritual duty." In the pure type, it disdains and repudiates economic exploitation of the gifts of grace as a source of income, though, to be sure, this often remains more an ideal than a fact. It is not that charisma always demands a renunciation of property or even of acquisition, as under certain circumstances prophets and their disciples do. The heroic warrior and his followers actively seek booty; the elective ruler or the charismatic party leader requires the material means of power. The former in addition requires a brilliant display of his authority to bolster his prestige. What is despised, so long as the genuinely charismatic type is adhered to, is traditional or rational everyday economizing, the attainment of a regular income by continuous economic activity devoted to this end. Support by gifts, either on a grand scale involving donation, endowment, bribery and honoraria, or by begging, constitute the voluntary type of support. On the other hand, "booty" and extortion, whether by force or by other means, is the typical form of charismatic provision for needs. From the point of view of rational economic activity, charismatic want satisfaction is a typical anti-economic force. It repudiates any sort of involvement in the everyday routine world. It can only tolerate, with an attitude of complete emotional indifference, irregular, unsystematic acquisitive acts. In that it relieves the recipient of economic concerns, dependence on property income can be the economic basis of a charismatic mode of life for some groups; but that is unusual for the normal charismatic "revolutionary."

> The fact that incumbency of church office has been forbidden to the Jesuits is a rationalized application of this principle of discipleship. The fact that all the "virtuosi" of asceticism, the mendicant orders, and fighters for a faith belong in this category, is quite clear. Almost all prophets have been supported by voluntary gifts. The well-known saying of St. Paul, "If a man does not work, neither shall he eat," was directed against the parasitic swarm of charismatic missionaries. It obviously has nothing to do with a positive valuation of economic activity for its own sake, but only lays it down as a duty of each individual somehow to provide for his own support. This because he realized that the purely charismatic parable of the lilies of the field was not capable of literal application, but at best "taking no thought for the morrow" could be hoped for. On the other hand, in a case of a primarily artistic type of charismatic discipleship it is conceivable that insulation from economic struggle should mean limitation of those really eligible to the "economically independent"; that is, to persons living on income from property. This has been true of the circle of Stefan George, at least in its primary intentions.

V. In traditionalist periods, charisma is *the* great revolutionary force. The likewise revolutionary force of "reason" works from *without*: by altering the situations of life and hence its problems, finally in this way changing men's attitudes toward them; or it intellectualizes the individual. Charisma, on the other hand, *may* effect a subjective or *internal* reorientation born out of suffering, conflicts, or enthusiasm. It may then result in a radical alteration of the central attitudes and directions of action with a completely new orientation of all attitudes toward the different problems of the "world."[7] In prerationalistic periods, tradition and charisma between them have almost exhausted the whole of the orientation of action.

V

The Routinization of Charisma

11. *The Rise of the Charismatic Community and the Problem of Succession*

In its pure form charismatic authority has a character specifically foreign to everyday routine structures. The social relationships directly involved are strictly personal, based on the validity and practice of charismatic personal qualities. If this is not to remain a purely transitory phenomenon, but to take on the character of a permanent relationship, a "community" of disciples or followers or a party organization or any sort of political or hierocratic organization, it is necessary for the character of charismatic authority to become radically changed. Indeed, in its pure form charismatic authority may be said to exist only *in statu nascendi*. It cannot remain stable, but becomes either traditionalized or rationalized, or a combination of both.

The following are the principal motives underlying this transformation: (a) The ideal and also the material interests of the followers in the continuation and the continual reactivation of the community, (b) the still stronger ideal and also stronger material interests of the members of the administrative staff, the disciples, the party workers, or others in continuing their relationship. Not only this, but they have an interest in continuing it in such a way that both from an ideal and a material point of view, their own position is put on a stable everyday basis. This means, above all, making it possible to participate in normal family relationships or at least to enjoy a secure social position in place of the kind of discipleship which is cut off from ordinary worldly connections, notably in the family and in economic relationships.

These interests generally become conspicuously evident with the disappearance of the personal charismatic leader and with the problem of *succession*. The way in which this problem is met—if it is met at all and the charismatic community continues to exist or now begins to emerge —is of crucial importance for the character of the subsequent social relationships. The following are the principal possible types of solution:—

(a) The *search* for a new charismatic leader on the basis of criteria of the qualities which will fit him for the position of authority.

This is to be found in a relatively pure type in the process of choice of a new Dalai Lama. It consists in the search for a child with characteristics which are interpreted to mean that he is a reincarnation of the Buddha. This is very similar to the choice of the new Bull of Apis.

In this case the legitimacy of the new charismatic leader is bound to certain distinguishing characteristics; thus, to rules with respect to which a tradition arises. The result is a process of traditionalization in favor of which the purely personal character of leadership is reduced.

(b) *Revelation* manifested in oracles, lots, divine judgments, or other techniques of selection. In this case the legitimacy of the new leader is dependent on the legitimacy of the *technique* of his selection. This involves a form of legalization.

It is said that at times the *Shofetim* [Judges] of Israel had this character. Saul is said to have been chosen by the old war oracle.

(c) Designation on the part of the original charismatic leader of his own successor and his recognition on the part of the followers.

This is a very common form. Originally, the Roman magistracies were filled entirely in this way. The system survived most clearly into later times in the appointment of the *dictator* and in the institution of the *interrex*.[8]

In this case legitimacy is *acquired* through the act of designation.

(d) Designation of a successor by the charismatically qualified administrative staff and his recognition by the community. In its typical form this process should quite definitely not be interpreted as "election" or "nomination" or anything of the sort. It is not a matter of free selection, but of one which is strictly bound to objective duty. It is not to be determined merely by majority vote, but is a question of arriving at the correct designation, the designation of the right person who is truly endowed with charisma. It is quite possible that the minority and not the majority should be right in such a case. Unanimity is often required. It is obligatory to acknowledge a mistake and persistence in error is a serious offense. Making a wrong choice is a genuine wrong requiring expiation. Originally it was a magical offence.

Nevertheless, in such a case it is easy for legitimacy to take on the character of an acquired right which is justified by standards of the correctness of the process by which the position was acquired, for the most part, by its having been acquired in accordance with certain formalities such as coronation.

This was the original meaning of the coronation of bishops and kings in the Western world by the clergy or the high nobility with the "consent" of the community. There are numerous analogous phenomena all over the world. The fact that this is the origin of the modern conception of "election" raises problems which will have to be gone into later.[9]

(e) The conception that charisma is a quality transmitted by heredity; thus that it is participated in by the kinsmen of its bearer, particularly by his closest relatives. This is the case of *hereditary charisma*. The order of hereditary succession in such a case need not be the same as that which is in force for appropriated rights, but may differ from it. It is also sometimes necessary to select the proper heir within the kinship group by some of the methods just spoken of.

> Thus in certain African states brothers have had to fight for the succession. In China, succession had to take place in such a way that the relation of the living group to the ancestral spirits was not disturbed. The rule either of seniority or of designation by the followers has been very common in the Orient. Hence, in the House of Osman, it used to be obligatory to kill off all other possible aspirants.

Only in Medieval Europe and in Japan, elsewhere sporadically, has the principle of primogeniture, as governing the inheritance of authority, become clearly established. This has greatly facilitated the consolidation of political groups in that it has eliminated struggle between a plurality of candidates from the same charismatic family.

In the case of hereditary charisma, recognition is no longer paid to the charismatic qualities of the individual, but to the legitimacy of the position he has acquired by hereditary succession. This may lead in the direction either of traditionalization or of legalization. The concept of divine right is fundamentally altered and now comes to mean authority by virtue of a personal right which is not dependent on the recognition of those subject to authority. Personal charisma may be totally absent.

> Hereditary monarchy is a conspicuous illustration. In Asia there have been very numerous hereditary priesthoods; also, frequently, the hereditary charisma of kinship groups has been treated as a criterion of social rank and of eligibility for fiefs and benefices.

(f) The concept that charisma may be transmitted by ritual means from one bearer to another or may be created in a new person. The concept was originally magical. It involves a dissociation of charisma from a particular individual, making it an objective, transferrable entity. In particular, it may become the *charisma of office*. In this case the belief in legitimacy is no longer directed to the individual, but to the acquired qualities and to the effectiveness of the ritual acts.

> The most important example is the transmission of priestly charisma by anointing, consecration, or the laying on of hands; and of royal au-

thority, by anointing and by coronation. The *character indelebilis* thus acquired means that the charismatic qualities and powers of the office are emancipated from the personal qualities of the priest. For precisely this reason, this has, from the Donatist and the Montanist heresies down to the Puritan revolution, been the subject of continual conflicts. The "hireling" of the Quakers is the preacher endowed with the charisma of office.

12. *Types of Appropriation by the Charismatic Staff*

Concomitant with the routinization of charisma with a view to insuring adequate succession, go the interests in its routinization on the part of the administrative staff. It is only in the initial stages and so long as the charismatic leader acts in a way which is completely outside everyday social organization, that it is possible for his followers to live communistically in a community of faith and enthusiasm, on gifts, booty, or sporadic acquisition. Only the members of the small group of enthusiastic disciples and followers are prepared to devote their lives purely idealistically to their call. The great majority of disciples and followers will in the long run "make their living" out of their "calling" in a material sense as well. Indeed, this must be the case if the movement is not to disintegrate.

Hence, the routinization of charisma also takes the form of the appropriation of powers and of economic advantages by the followers or disciples, and of regulating recruitment. This process of traditionalization or of legalization, according to whether rational legislation is involved or not, may take any one of a number of typical forms.

1. The original basis of recruitment is personal charisma. However, with routinization, the followers or disciples may set up norms for recruitment, in particular involving training or tests of eligibility. Charisma can only be "awakened" and "tested"; it cannot be "learned" or "taught." All types of magical asceticism, as practiced by magicians and heroes, and all novitiates, belong in this category. These are means of closing the administrative staff. (On the charismatic type of education, see ch. IV below [unfinished].)

Only the proved novice is allowed to exercise authority. A genuine charismatic leader is in a position to oppose this type of prerequisite for membership; his successor is not free to do so, at least if he is chosen by the administrative staff.

This type is illustrated by the magical and warrior asceticism of the "men's house" with initiation ceremonies and age groups. An individual who has not successfully gone through the initiation, remains a "woman"; that is, he is excluded from the charismatic group.

2. It is easy for charismatic norms to be transformed into those defining a traditional social status (on a hereditary charismatic basis). If the leader is chosen on a hereditary basis, the same is likely to happen in the selection and deployment of the staff and even the followers. The term "clan state" (Geschlechterstaat) will be applied when a political body is organized strictly and completely in terms of this principle of hereditary charisma. In such a case, all appropriation of governing powers, of fiefs, benefices, and all sorts of economic advantages follow the same pattern. The result is that all powers and advantages of all sorts become traditionalized. The heads of families, who are traditional gerontocrats or patriarchs without personal charismatic legitimacy, regulate the exercise of these powers which cannot be taken away from their family. It is not the type of position he occupies which determines the rank of a man or of his family, but rather the hereditary charismatic rank of his family determines the position he will occupy.

Japan, before the development of bureaucracy, was organized in this way. The same was undoubtedly true of China as well where, before the rationalization which took place in the territorial states, authority was in the hands of the "old families." Other types of examples are furnished by the caste system in India, and by Russia before the mestnichestvo was introduced. Indeed, all hereditary social classes with established privileges belong in the same category.

3. The administrative staff may seek and achieve the creation and appropriation of individual positions and the corresponding economic advantages for its members. In that case, according to whether the tendency is to traditionalization or legalization, there will develop (a) benefices, (b) offices, or (c) fiefs. In the first case a prebendal organization will result; in the second, patrimonialism or bureaucracy; in the third, feudalism. These revenue sources become appropriated and replace provision from gifts or booty without settled relation to the everyday economic structure.

Case (a), benefices, may consist in rights to the proceeds of begging, to payments in kind, or to the proceeds of money taxes, or finally, to the proceeds of fees. The latter may result from the former through the regulation of the original provision by free gifts or by "booty" in terms of a rational organization or finance.

Regularized begging is found in Buddhism; benefices in kind, in the Chinese and Japanese "rice rents"; support by money taxation has been the rule in all the rationalized conquest states. The last case is common everywhere, especially on the part of priests and judges and, in India, even the military authorities.

Case (b), the transformation of the charismatic mission into an office, may have more of a patrimonial or more of a bureaucratic character. The former is much the more common; the latter is found principally in Antiquity and in the modern Western world. Elsewhere it is exceptional.

In case (c), only land may be appropriated as a fief, whereas the position as such retains its originally charismatic character, or powers and authority may be fully appropriated as fiefs. It is difficult to distinguish the two cases. However, orientation to the charismatic character of the position was slow to disappear, also in the Middle Ages.

1 2a. *Status Honor and the Legitimation of Authority*

For charisma to be transformed into an everyday phenomenon, it is necessary that its anti-economic character should be altered. It must be adapted to some form of fiscal organization to provide for the needs of the group and hence to the economic conditions necessary for raising taxes and contributions. When a charismatic movement develops in the direction of prebendal provision, the "laity" becomes differentiated from the "clergy"—derived from κλῆρος, meaning a "share"—, that is, the participating members of the charismatic administrative staff which has now become routinized. These are the priests of the developing "church." Correspondingly, in a developing political body—the "state" in the rational case—vassals, benefice-holders, officials or appointed party officials (instead of voluntary party workers and functionaries) are differentiated from the "tax payers."

> This process is very conspicuous in Buddhism and in the Hindu sects—see the Sociology of Religion below. The same is true in all conquest states which have become rationalized to form permanent structures; also of parties and other originally charismatic structures.

It follows that, in the course of routinization, the charismatically ruled organization is largely transformed into one of the everyday authorities, the patrimonial form, especially in its estate-type or bureaucratic variant. Its original peculiarities are apt to be retained in the charismatic status honor acquired by heredity or office-holding. This applies to all who participate in the appropriation, the chief himself and the members of his staff. It is thus a matter of the type of prestige enjoyed by ruling groups. A hereditary monarch by "divine right" is not a simple patrimonial chief, patriarch, or sheik; a vassal is not a mere household retainer or official. Further details must be deferred to the analysis of status groups.

As a rule, routinization is not free of conflict. In the early stages personal claims on the charisma of the chief are not easily forgotten and the conflict between the charisma of the office or of hereditary status with personal charisma is a typical process in many historical situations.

1. The power of absolution—that is, the power to absolve from mortal sins—was held originally only by personal charismatic martyrs or ascetics, but became transformed into a power of the office of bishop or priest. This process was much slower in the Orient than in the Occident because in the latter is was influenced by the Roman conception of office. Revolutions under a charismatic leader, directed against hereditary charismatic powers or the powers of office, are to be found in all types of organizations, from states to trade unions. (This last is particularly conspicuous at the present time [1918/20].) The more highly developed the interdependence of different economic units in a monetary economy, the greater the pressure of the everyday needs of the followers of the charismatic movement becomes. The effect of this is to strengthen the tendency to routinization, which is everywhere operative, and as a rule has rapidly won out. Charisma is a phenomenon typical of prophetic movements or of expansive political movements in their early stages. But as soon as domination is well established, and above all as soon as control over large masses of people exists, it gives way to the forces of everyday routine.

2. One of the decisive motives underlying all cases of the routinization of charisma is naturally the striving for security. This means legitimization, on the one hand, of positions of authority and social prestige, on the other hand, of the economic advantages enjoyed by the followers and sympathizers of the leader. Another important motive, however, lies in the objective necessity of adapting the order and the staff organization to the normal, everyday needs and conditions of carrying on administration. In this connection, in particular, there are always points at which traditions of administrative practice and of judicial decision can take hold as these are needed by the normal administrative staff and those subject to its authority. It is further necessary that there should be some definite order introduced into the organization of the administrative staff itself. Finally, as will be discussed in detail below, it is necessary for the administrative staff and all its administrative practices to be adapted to everyday economic conditions. It is not possible for the costs of permanent, routine administration to be met by "booty," contributions, gifts, and hospitality, as is typical of the pure type of military and prophetic charisma.

3. The process of routinization is thus not by any means confined to the problem of succession and does not stop when this has been solved. On the contrary, the most fundamental problem is that of making a transition from a charismatic administrative staff, and the corresponding principles of administration, to one which is adapted to everyday conditions. The problem of succession, however, is crucial because through it occurs the routinization of the charismatic focus of the structure. In it, the character of the leader himself and of his claim to legitimacy is altered. This process involves peculiar and characteristic conceptions which are understandable only in this context and do not apply to the problem of transition to traditional or legal patterns of order and types or administrative organization. The most important of the modes of meeting the problem of succession are the charismatic designation of a successor and hereditary charisma.

4. As has already been noted, the most important historical example of designation by the charismatic leader of his own successor is Rome. For the *rex,* this arrangement is attested by tradition; while for the appointment of the *dictator* and of the co-emperor and successor in the Principate, it has existed in historical times. The way in which all the higher magistrates were invested with the *imperium* shows clearly that they also were designated as successors by the military commander, subject to recognition by the citizen army. The fact that candidates were examined by the magistrate in office and that originally they could be excluded on what were obviously arbitrary grounds shows clearly what was the nature of the development.

5. The most important examples of designation of a successor by the charismatic followers of the leader are to be found in the election of bishops, and particularly of the Pope, by the original system of designation by the clergy and recognition by the lay community. The investigations of U. Stutz have made it probable that the election of the German king was modelled on that of the bishops.[10] He was designated by a group of qualified princes and recognized by the "people," that is, those bearing arms. Similar arrangements are very common.

6. The classical case of the development of hereditary charisma is that of caste in India. All occupational qualifications, and in particular all the qualifications for positions of authority and power, have there come to be regarded as strictly bound to the inheritance of charisma. Eligibility for fiefs, involving governing powers, was limited to members of the royal kinship group, the fiefs being granted by the eldest of the group. All types of religious office, including the extraordinarily important and influential position of *guru,* the *directeur de l'âme,* were treated as bound to hereditary charismatic qualities. The same is true of all sorts of relations to traditional customers and of all positions in the village organization, such as priest, barber, laundryman, watchman, etc. The foundation of a sect always meant the development of a hereditary hierarchy, as was true also of Taoism in China. Also in the Japanese

"feudal" state, before the introduction of a patrimonial officialdom on the Chinese model, which then led to prebends and a new feudalization, social organization was based purely on hereditary charisma.

This kind of hereditary charismatic right to positions of authority has been developed in similar ways all over the world. Qualification by virtue of individual achievement has been replaced by qualification by birth. This is everywhere the basis of the development of hereditary aristocracies, in the Roman nobility, in the concept of the *stirps regia*, which Tacitus describes among the Germans, in the rules of eligibility to tournaments and monasteries in the late Middle Ages, and even in the genealogical research conducted on behalf of the *parvenu* aristocracy of the United States. Indeed, this is to be found everywhere where hereditary status groups have become established.

Relationship to the economy: The process of routinization of charisma is in very important respects identical with adaptation to the conditions of the economy, since this is the principal continually operating force in everyday life. Economic conditions in this connection play a leading role and do not constitute merely a dependent variable. To a very large extent the transition to hereditary charisma or the charisma of office serves as a means of legitimizing existing or recently acquired powers of control over economic goods. Along with the ideology of loyalty, which is certainly by no means unimportant, allegiance to hereditary monarchy in particular is very strongly influenced by the consideration that all inherited and legitimately acquired property would be endangered if people stopped believing in the sanctity of hereditary succession to the throne. It is hence by no means fortuitous that hereditary monarchy is more adequate to the propertied strata than to the proletariat.

Beyond this, it is not possible to say anything in general terms, which would at the same time be substantial and valuable, on the relations of the various possible modes of adaptation to the economic order. This must be reserved to the more detailed treatment. The development of a prebendal structure, of feudalism, and the appropriation of all sorts of advantages on a hereditary charismatic basis may in all cases have the same stereotyping effect on the economic order if they develop from charismatic starting points as if they developed from early patrimonial or bureaucratic stages. In economic respects, too, the revolutionary impact of charisma is usually tremendous; at first, it is often destructive, because it means new modes of orientation. But routinization leads to the exact reverse.

The economics of charismatic revolutions will have to be discussed separately; it is a different matter altogether.

vi
Feudalism

12*b*. *Occidental Feudalism and Its Conflict with Patrimonialism*

The case noted above, under sec. 12:3c [the fief], requires separate discussion. This is because a structure of domination may develop out of it which is different both from patrimonialism and from genuine or hereditary charisma and which has had a very great historical significance, namely, feudalism. We will distinguish two types: the one based on fiefs (*Lehensfeudalismus*) and the other based on benefices (prebendal feudalism). All other forms in which the use of land is granted in exchange for military service really have a patrimonial character and hence will not be treated here separately. For the different kinds of benefices will be discussed later in detail.

A. A fief involves the following elements:

(1) The appropriation of powers and rights of exercising authority. Appropriation as a fief may apply only to powers relevant within a master's household or it may be extended to include those of a political association. The latter type may be restricted to economic rights—that is, fiscal rights—or it may also include political powers proper. Fiefs are granted in return for specific services. Normally they are primarily of a military character, but they may also include administrative functions. The grant of the fief takes a very specific form. It is carried out

(2) on a purely personal basis for the lifetime of the lord and of the recipient of the fief, his vassal.

(3) The relationship is established by a contract, thus it is supposed that the vassal is a free man.

(4) If feudalism is based on fiefs, the recipient adheres to the style of life of a knightly status group.

(5) The contract of fealty is not an ordinary business contract, but establishes a solidary, fraternal relationship which involves reciprocal obligations of loyalty, to be sure, on a legally unequal basis. These obligations are upheld by

(a) knightly status honor, and (b) are clearly delimited.

The transition pointed out above at the end of section 12 [i.e., from

mere appropriation of land to full appropriation of powers] takes place
a) when fiefs are appropriated hereditarily, subject only to the condition
that each new vassal have the necessary qualifications and will pledge
fealty to his lord, and the existing vassals will do so to a new lord; *β*)
when the feudal administrative staff compels the lord to fill every
vacancy (*Leihezwang*), since all fiefs are considered part of the maintenance fund for the members of the knightly status group.

The first step took place relatively early in the Middle Ages; the
second, later on. The struggle of kings and princes with their vassals
were above all directed, though not usually explicitly, toward the
elimination of this principle, since it prevented the rise of a patrimonial
regime.

B. If an administration is based completely on the granting of fiefs
—and *Lehensfeudalismus* has never been historically realized in the pure
type any more than has pure patrimonialism—, this involves the following features:

(1) The authority of the lord is reduced to the likelihood that the
vassals will remain faithful to their oaths of fealty.

(2) The political association is completely replaced by a system of
relations of purely personal loyalty between the lord and his vassals and
between these in turn and their own sub-vassals (sub-infeudation) and
so on. Only a lord's own vassals are bound to fealty to him; whereas they
in turn can claim the fealty of their own vassals, and so on.

(3) Only in the case of a "felony" does the lord have a right to
deprive his vassal of his fief, and the same in turn applies to the vassal
in his relation to his own vassal. When such a case, however, arises, in
enforcing his rights against a vassal who has broken the oath of fealty,
the lord is dependent on the help of his other vassals or on the passivity
of the sub-vassals of the guilty party. Either source of support can only
be counted on when the relevant group recognizes that a felony has
actually been committed. However, even then the overlord cannot count
on the non-interference of sub-vassals unless he has at least been able to
secure recognition on their part of the principle that a struggle against
an overlord is an exceptional state. Overlords have always attempted to
establish this principle but not always with success.

(4) There is a hierarchy of social rank corresponding to the hierarchy of fiefs through the process of sub-infeudation—the order of the
Heerschilde in the Mirror of Saxon Law (*Sachsenspiegel*). This is not,
however, a judicious and administrative hierarchy. For whether an order
or a decision can be challenged and to what authority appeal can be made
is in principle a matter for the respective court of appeals (*Oberhof*)

and does not depend on the hierarchy of feudal relationships. (It is theoretically possible for the *Oberhof* authority to be granted to a status-equal of the local judicial lord, but in practice this was not the case.)

(5) The elements in the population who do not hold fiefs involving patrimonial or political authority are "subjects" (*Hintersassen*); that is, they are patrimonial dependents. They are dependent on the holders of fiefs to the extent that their traditional status determines or permits it, or so far as the coercive power in the hands of the possessors of military fiefs compels it, since they are to a large extent defenseless. Just as the supreme lord is under obligation to grant land in fief, those who do not hold fiefs are always under the authority of a lord; in both cases the rule is: *nulle terre sans seigneur*. The sole survival of the old immediate political powers of the ruler is the principle, which is almost always recognized, that political authority, particularly judicial authority, is turned over to the ruler whenever he is personally present.

(6) Powers over the household (inluding domains, slaves and serfs), the fiscal rights of the political group to the receipt of taxes and contributions, and specifically political powers of jurisdiction and compulsion to military service—thus powers over free men—all become objects of feudal grants in the same way. However, as a rule the strictly political powers are subject to special regulation.

> In ancient China the granting of economic income in fiefs and of territorial authority were distinguished in name as well as in fact. The distinctions in name are not found in the European Middle Ages, but there were clear distinctions in the holder's status and in numerous other particular points.

It is not usual for political powers to be fully appropriated in the same way as property rights in fiefs. Numerous transitional forms and irregularities remain. One conspicuous difference is the existence of a status distinction between those enjoying only economic or fiscal rights and those with strictly political powers, notably judicial and military authority. Only the latter are *political* vassals.

It goes without saying that whenever *Lehensfeudalismus* is highly developed, the overlord's authority is precarious. This is because it is very dependent on the voluntary obedience and hence the purely personal loyalty of the members of the administrative staff, who, by virtue of the feudal structure, are themselves in possession of the means of administration. Hence, the latent struggle for authority becomes chronic between the lord and his vassal, and the ideal extent of feudal authority has never been effectively carried out in practice or remained effective on a permanent basis.

Rather, the feudal lord may attempt to improve his position in one of the following ways:

(a) He may not rely on the purely personal loyalty of his vassals, but may attempt to secure his position by limiting or forbidding sub-infeudation.

> This was common in Western feudalism, but often was initiated by the administrative staff in the interest of their own power. The same was true of the alliance of princes in China in 630 B.C.

He may attempt to establish the principle that the fealty of a sub-vassal to his immediate lord is void in case of war against the higher lord.

Or, if possible, the attempt is made to obligate the sub-vassal to direct fealty to him, the liege lord.

(b) The feudal chief may seek to implement his control of the administration of political powers in a variety of ways. He may grant all the subjects a right of appeal to him or his courts. He may station supervising agents at the courts of his political vassals. He may attempt to enforce a right to collect taxes from the subjects of all his vassals. He may appoint certain officials of the political vassals. Finally, he may attempt to enforce the principle that all political authority is forfeited to him in his personal presence or beyond that to any agent he designates and that he, as the supreme lord, is entitled to try any case in his own court at will.

(c) It is possible for a supreme lord to attain and maintain his power against vassals, as well as against other types of holders of appropriated authority, only if he creates or re-creates an administrative staff under his personal control and organizes it in an appropriate manner. There are three main possibilities.

(1) It may be a patrimonial staff. (This was to a large extent what happened in the European Middle Ages and in Japan in the *Bakufu* of the *Shogun,* who exercised a very effective control over the feudal *Daimyos.*)

(2) It may be an extra-patrimonial staff recruited from a status group with literary education.

> The principal examples are clerical officials, whether Christian or Brahman; *kayasths* (Buddhist, Lamaist, or Mohammedan);[10a] or humanists, such as the Confucian scholars in China. On the peculiarities of such groups and their immense importance for cultural development, see ch. IV [unfinished].

(3) Or it may be a group of technically trained officials, particularly legal and military specialists.

This was proposed in China in the eleventh century by Wang An Shi, but by that time it was directed against the classical scholars and not the feudal magnates. In the Occident, such a bureaucracy was recruited for civil administration from university-trained men. In the Church the primary training was in the Canon Law, in the State, the Roman Law. In England, it was the Common Law, which had, however, been rationalized under the influence of Roman modes of thought. In this development lie some origins of the modern Western state. The development of Western military organization took a somewhat different course. The feudal organization was first replaced by capitalistic military entrepreneurs, the *condottieri*. These structures were in turn appropriated by the territorial princes with the development of a rational administration of royal finance from the seventeenth century on. In England and France, it happened somewhat earlier.

This struggle of the feudal chief with his feudal administrative staff in the Western World, though not in Japan, largely coincided with his struggle against the power of corporately organized privileged groups (*Stände-Korporationen*). In modern times it everywhere issued in the ruler's victory, and that meant in bureaucratic administration. This happened first in the Western World, then in Japan; in India, and perhaps also in China, it happened in the wake of foreign rule. Along with purely historical power constellations, economic conditions have played a very important part in this process in the Western World. Above all, it was influenced by the rise of the bourgeoisie in the towns, which had an organization peculiar to Europe. It was in addition aided by the competition for power by means of rational—that is, bureaucratic—administration among the different states. This led, from fiscal motives, to a crucially important alliance with capitalistic interests, as will be shown later.

12c. *Prebendal Feudalism and Other Variants*

Not every kind of "feudalism" involves the fief in the Occidental sense. In addition, there is above all:

A. prebendal feudalism, which has a fiscal basis.

This was typical of the Islamic Near East and of India under the Moguls. On the other hand, *ancient* Chinese feudalism before the time of Shi Huang Ti had at least in part a structure of fiefs, though benefices were also involved. Japanese feudalism also involved fiefs, but they were subject in the case of the *Daimyos* to a rather stringent control on the part of the supreme lord (*Bakufu*), and the fiefs of the Samurai and the Buke were really benefices of *ministeriales* (although they often came to be appropriated) which were registered according to their yield in terms of rice rent (*kokudaka*).

Prebendal feudalism exists when (1) benefices which are valued and granted according to the income they yield are appropriated and where (2) appropriation is, in principle, though not always effectively, carried out only on a personal basis in accordance with services, thus involving the possibility of promotion. (This was, at least from the legal point of view, true of the benefices held by the Turkish *sipahi*.)

Finally and above all, (3) it does not involve primarily a free relation of personal fealty arising from a contract of personal loyalty with the lord as the basis of a particular fief. It is rather a matter primarily of fiscal considerations in the context of a system of financing which is otherwise patrimonial, often sultanistic. This is for the most part made evident by the fact that the prebends are assessed according to their tax value.

It is very common for the *Lehensfeudalismus* to originate in a system of want satisfaction of the political group on the basis of a purely natural economy and in terms of personal obligations (personal services and military services). The principal motive is to replace the insufficiently trained popular levy, whose members can no longer equip themselves and are needed in the economy, with a well-trained and equipped army of knights who are bound to their chief by personal honor. Prebendal feudalism, on the other hand, usually originates in the reversion from monetary financing to financing in kind. The following are the principal reasons leading to such a policy:—

(a) The transfer of the risk involved in fluctuating income to an entrepreneur; that is, a sort of tax farming.

α) Rights to such income may be transferred in return for undertaking to supply certain particular army contingents, such as cavalry, sometimes war chariots, armored troops, supply trains, or artillery, for a patrimonial army. (This was common in the Chinese Middle Ages. Quotas for the army in each of the different categories were established for a particular territorial area.)

Either in addition to this or alone, prebendal feudalism may be established as a means of β) meeting the costs of civil administration and of γ) securing tax payments for the royal treasury. (This was common in India.)

δ) In return for these various services, in the first instance to enable those who undertook them to meet their obligations, an appropriation of governmental power in varying degrees and respects was permitted. Such appropriation has usually been for a limited period and subject to repurchase. But when means to do this have been lacking, it has often in fact been definitive. Those who hold such definitively appropriated powers then become, at the very least, landlords, as opposed to mere land-owners, and often come into the possession of extensive political powers.

> This process has been typical above all of India. It is the source of the powers over land of the *Zamindars,* the *Jagirdars,* and the *Tuluk-dars.* It is also found in a large part of the Near East, as C. H. Becker has clearly shown—he was the first to understand the difference from the European fief.[11] The primary basis lies in the leasing of taxes. As a secondary consequence, it developed into a "manorial" system. The Rumanian Boyars—the descendants of the most heterogeneous society the world has ever seen, of Jews, Germans, Greeks, and various others —were also tax farmers who on this basis appropriated governing authority.

(b) Inability to pay the contingents of a patrimonial army may lead to an usurpation of the sources of taxation on their part, which is subsequently legalized. The result is that appropriation of the land and of the subjects is carried out by the officers and members of the army. (This was true of the famous Khans of the empire of the Caliphs. It was the source or the model for all forms of Oriental appropriation, including the Mameluke army, which was formally composed of slaves.)

It is by no means inevitable that this should lead to systematic registration as a basis for the granting of benefices. But this is a readily available course and has often actually been followed out. (We shall not yet discuss how far the "fiefs" of the Turkish *sipahi* were genuine fiefs or whether they were closer to benefices. From a legal point of view, promotion according to achievement was possible.)

It is clear that the two types of feudalism are connected by gradual imperceptible transitions and that it is seldom possible to classify cases with complete definiteness under one category or the other. Furthermore, prebendal feudalism is closely related to a purely prebendal organization, and there are also gradual transitions in this direction.

According to an imprecise terminology, in addition to the fief resting on a free contract with the lord and the feudal benefice, there is:

B. so-called "polis" feudalism, resting on a real or fictitious "synoikism" of landlords. These enjoy equal rights in the conduct of a purely military mode of life with high status honor. The economic aspect of the *kleros* is the plot of land which is appropriated by qualified persons on a personal basis and passed on by individual hereditary succession. It is cultivated by the services of unfree persons—assigned as the property of the status group—and forms the basis of provision of military equipment.

This type is found only in Greece, in fully developed form, only in Sparta, and originated out of the "men's house." It has been called "feudalism" because of the set of conventions regulating status honor and of the element of chivalry in the mode of life of a group of land-lords. This is hardly legitimate usage. In Rome the term *fundus* corresponds to the Greek *kleros*. There is, however, no information available about the organization of the *curia* (*co-viria* equals the Greek *andreion*, the "men's house). We do not know how far it was similar to the Greek.)

The term "feudal" is often used in a very broad sense to designate all military strata, institutions and conventions which involve any sort of status privileges. This usage will be avoided here as entirely too vague.

C. The second doubtful type is called feudalism for the opposite reason. The fief is present but, on the other hand, is not acquired by a free contract (fraternization either with a lord or with equals), but is bestowed by the order of a patrimonial chief. On the other hand, it may not be administered in the spirit of a knightly mode of life. Finally, both criteria may be absent. Thus there may be service fiefs held by dependent knights; or, conversely, fiefs may be freely acquired but their holders are not subject to a code of chivalry. Finally, fiefs may be granted to clients, coloni, or slaves who are employed as fighting forces. All these cases will be treated here as *benefices*.

The case of dependent knights is illustrated by Occidental and Oriental *ministeriales*, in Japan by the Samurai. Freely recruited soldiers without a chivalrous code are known to the Orient; this was probably the origin of the Ptolemaic military organization. When the hereditary appropriation of service land has led further to the appropriation of the military function as such, the end result is a typical liturgical organization of the state. The third type, the use of unfree military forces, is typical of the so-called warrior caste of ancient Egypt, of the Mame-lukes of medieval Egypt, and of various other unfree Oriental and Chinese warriors. These have not always been granted rights in land, but such an arrangement is common.

In such cases, it is imprecise to speak of "feudalism," since it involves military status groups, which, at least from a formal point of view, occupy a negatively privileged position. They will be discussed in Chapter IV.

13. Combinations of the Different Types of Authority

The above discussion makes it quite evident that "ruling organizations" which belong only to one or another of these pure types are very exceptional. Furthermore, in relation to legal and traditional authority especially, certain important types, such as the collegial form and some aspects of the feudal, have either not been discussed at all or have been barely suggested. In general, it should be kept clearly in mind that the basis of every authority, and correspondingly of every kind of willingness to obey, is a *belief,* a belief by virtue of which persons exercising authority are lent prestige. The composition of this belief is seldom altogether simple. In the case of "legal authority," it is never purely legal. The belief in legality comes to be established and habitual, and this means it is partly traditional. Violation of the tradition may be fatal to it. Furthermore, it has a charismatic element, at least in the negative sense that persistent and striking lack of success may be sufficient to ruin any government, to undermine its prestige, and to prepare the way for charismatic revolution. For monarchies, hence, it is dangerous to lose wars since that makes it appear that their charisma is no longer genuine. For republics, on the other hand, striking victories may be dangerous in that they put the victorious general in a favorable position for making charismatic claims.

Groups approximating the purely traditional type have certainly existed. But they have never been stable indefinitely and, as is also true of bureaucratic authority, have seldom been without a head who had a personally charismatic status by heredity or office. Under certain circumstances, the charismatic chief can be different from the traditional one. Everyday economic needs have been met under the leadership of traditional authorities; whereas certain exceptional ones, like hunting and the quest of "booty" in war, have had charismatic leadership. The idea of the possibility of "legislation" is also relatively ancient, though for the most part it has been legitimized by oracles. Above all, however, whenever the recruitment of an administrative staff is drawn from extrapatrimonial sources, the result is a type of official which can be differentiated from those of legal bureaucracies only in terms of the ultimate basis of their authority and not in terms of formal status.

Similarly, entirely pure charismatic authority, including the hereditary charismatic type, etc., is rare. It is not impossible, as in the case of Napoleon, for the strictest type of bureaucracy to issue directly from a charismatic movement; or, if not that, all sorts of prebendal and feudal types of organization. Hence, the kind of terminology and classification set forth above has in no sense the aim—indeed, it could not have it—to be exhaustive or to confine the whole of historical reality in a rigid scheme. Its usefulness is derived from the fact that in a given case it is possible to distinguish what aspects of a given organized group can legitimately be identified as falling under or approximating one or another of these categories. For certain purposes this is unquestionably an important advantage.

For all types of authority the fact of the existence and continual functioning of an administrative staff is vital. For the habit of obedience cannot be maintained without organized activity directed to the application and enforcement of the order. It is, indeed, the existence of such activity which is usually meant by the term "organization."[12] For this to exist in turn, it is essential that there should be an adequate degree of the solidarity of interests, both on the ideal and material levels, of the members of the administrative staff with their chief. It is fundamental in understanding the relation of the chief to these members that, so far as this solidarity exists, the chief is stronger than any individual member but is weaker than the members taken together. It is, however, by all means necessary for the members of an administrative staff to enter into a deliberate agreement in order to obstruct or even consciously oppose their chief so successfully that the leadership of the chief becomes impotent. Similarly, any individual who sets out to destroy a rulership must, if he is going to take over the position of power, build up an administrative staff of his own, unless he is in a position to count on the connivance and co-operation of the existing staff against their previous leader.

Solidarity of interest with a chief is maximized at the point where both the legitimacy of the status of the members and the provision for their economic needs is dependent on the chief retaining his position. For any given individual, the possibility of escaping this solidarity varies greatly according to the structure. It is most difficult where there is complete separation from the means of administration, thus in purely traditional patriarchal structures, under pure partimonialism and in bureaucratic organizations resting on formal rules. It is easiest where fiefs or benefices have been appropriated by socially privileged groups.

It is most important, finally, to realize that historical reality involves a continuous, though for the most part latent, conflict beween chiefs and their administrative staffs for appropriation and expropriation in relation to one another. For almost all of cultural development, it has been crucial in what way this struggle has worked out and what has been the character of the stratum of officials dependent upon the chief which has helped him win out in his struggle against the feudal classes or other groups enjoying appropriated powers. In different cases it has been ritually trained literati, the clergy, purely secular clients, household officials, legally trained persons, technically specialized financial officials, or private *honoratiores*, (about whom more will be said later).

One of the reasons why the character of these struggles and of their outcome has been so important, not only to the history of administration as such, but to that of culture generally, is that the type of education has been determined by them and with it the modes of status group formation.

1. Both the extent and the way in which the members of an administrative staff are bound to their chief will vary greatly according to whether they receive salaries, opportunities for profit, allowances, or fiefs. It is, however, a factor common to all of these that anything which endangers the legitimacy of the chief who has granted and who guarantees them, tends at the same time to endanger the legitimacy of these forms of income and the positions of power and prestige which go with membership in the administrative staff. This is one of the reasons why legitimacy, which is often so much neglected in analysing such phenomena, plays a crucially important role.

2. The history of the dissolution of the old system of domination legitimate in Germany up until 1918 is instructive in this connection. The War, on the one hand, went far to break down the authority of tradition; and the German defeat involved a tremendous loss of prestige for the government. These factors combined with systematic habituation to illegal behavior, undermined the amenability to discipline both in the army and in industry and thus prepared the way for the overthrow of the older authority. At the same time, the way in which the old administrative staff continued to function and the way in which its order was simply taken over by the new supreme authorities, is a striking example of the extent to which, under rationalized bureaucratic conditions, the individual member of such a staff is inescapably bound to his technical function. As it has been noted above, this fact is by no means adequately explained by the private economic interests of the members —their concern for their jobs, salaries, and pensions—although it goes without saying that these considerations were not unimportant to the great majority of officials. In addition to this, however, the disinterested ideological factor has been crucial. For the breakdown of administrative organization would, under such conditions, have meant a breakdown of the provision of the whole population, including, of course, the officials themselves, with even the most elementary necessities of life. Hence an appeal was made to the sense of duty of officials, and this was successful. Indeed the objective necessity of this attitude has been recognized even by the previous holders of power and their sympathizers.

3. In the course of the past revolution in Germany, a new administrative staff came into being in the Soviets of workers and soldiers. In the first place it was necessary to develop a technique of organizing these new staffs. Furthermore, their development was closely dependent on the War, notably the possession of weapons by the revolutionary element. Without this factor the revolution would not have been possible at all. (This and its historical analogies will be discussed below.) It was only by the rise of charismatic leaders against the legal authorities and

by the development around them of groups of charismatic followers, that it was possible to take power away from the old authorities. It was furthermore only through the maintenance of the old bureaucratic organization that power once achieved could be retained. Previous to this situation every revolution which has been attempted under modern conditions has failed completely because of the indispensability of trained officials and of the lack of its own organized staff. The conditions under which previous revolutions have succeeded have been altogether different. (See below, the chapter on the theory of revolutions. [Unwritten].)

4. The overthrow of authority on the initiative of the administrative staff has occurred in the past under a wide variety of conditions. Some form of association of the members of the staff has always been a necessary prerequisite. According to the circumstances, it might have more the character of a limited conspiracy or more that of a general solidarity. This is peculiarly difficult under the conditions to which the modern official is subject; but as the Russian case has shown, it is not altogether impossible. As a general rule, however, such association does not go further than the kind which is open to workers through the ordinary procedure of the strike.

5. The patrimonial character of a body of officials is above all manifested in the fact that admission involves a relation of personal dependency. In the Carolingian system, one became a *puer regis,* under the Angevins, a *familiaris.* Survivals of this have persisted for a very long time.

vii

The Transformation of Charisma in a Democratic Direction

14. Democratic Legitimacy, Plebiscitary Leadership and Elected Officialdom[13]

The basically authoritarian principle of charismatic legitimation may be subject to an anti-authoritarian interpretation, for the validity of charismatic authority rests entirely on recognition by the ruled, on "proof" before their eyes. To be sure, this recognition of a charismatically qualified, and hence legitimate, person is treated as a duty. But when the charismatic organization undergoes progressive rationalization, it is readily possible that, instead of recognition being treated as a consequence of legitimacy, it is treated as the basis of legitimacy: *democratic legitimacy*. Then designation of a successor by an administrative staff becomes "preselection," by the predecessor himself "nomination," whereas recognition by the group becomes an "election." The personally legitimated charismatic leader becomes leader by the grace of those who follow him since the latter are formally free to elect and even to depose him— just as the loss of charisma and its efficacy had involved the loss of genuine legitimacy. Now he is the freely elected leader.

Correspondingly, the recognition of charismatic decrees and judicial decisions on the part of the community shifts to the belief that the group has a right to enact, recognize, or appeal laws, according to its own free will, both in general and for an individual case. Under genuinely charismatic authority, on the other hand, conflicts over the correct law may actually be decided by a group vote, but this takes place under the pressure of feeling that there can be only *one* correct decision, and it is a matter of duty to arrive at this. However, in the new interpretation the treatment of law approaches the case of legal authority. The most important transitional type is the legitimation of authority by plebiscite: *plebiscitary leadership*. The most common examples are the modern party leaders. But it is always present in cases where the chief feels himself to be acting on behalf of the masses and is indeed recognized by them. Both the Napoleons are classical examples, in spite of the fact that legitimation by plebiscite took place only after they seized power by force. The second Napoleon also resorted to the plebiscite after a severe loss of prestige. Regardless of how its real value as an expression of the popular will may be regarded, the plebiscite has been the specific means of deriving the legitimacy of authority from the confidence of the ruled, even though the voluntary nature of such confidence is only formal or fictitious.

Once the elective principle has been applied to the chief by a reinterpretation of charisma, it may be extended to the administrative staff. Elective officials whose legitimacy is derived from the confidence of the ruled and who are therefore subject to recall, are typical of certain democracies, for instance, the United States. They are not "bureaucratic" types. Because they have an independent source of legitimacy, they are not strongly integrated into a hierarchical order. To a large extent their "promotion" and assignment is not influenced by their superiors. (There are analogies in other cases where several charismatic structures, which are qualitatively heterogeneous, exist side by side, as in the relations of the Dalai Lama and the Tashi Lama.) Such an administrative structure is greatly inferior as a precision instrument compared to the bureaucratic type with its appointed officials.

1. Plebiscitary democracy—the most important type of *Führer-Demokratie*—is a variant of charismatic authority, which hides behind a legitimacy that is *formally* derived from the will of the governed. The leader (demagogue) rules by virtue of the devotion and trust which his political followers have in him personally. In the first instance his power extends only over those recruited to his following, but if they can hand over the government to him he controls the whole polity. The type is best illustrated by the dictators who emerged in the revolutions of the ancient world and of modern times: the Hellenic *aisymnetai,* tyrants and demagogues; in Rome Gracchus and his successors; in the Italian city states the *capitani del popolo* and mayors; and certain types of political leaders in the German cities such as emerged in the democratic dictatorship of Zürich. In modern states the best examples are the dictatorship of Cromwell, and the leaders of the French Revolution and of the First and Second Empire. Wherever attempts have been made to legitimize this kind of exercise of power, legitimacy has been sought in recognition by the sovereign people through a plebiscite. The leader's personal administrative staff is recruited in a charismatic form usually from able people of humble origin. In Cromwell's case, religious qualifications were taken into account. In that of Robespierre along with personal dependability also certain "ethical" qualities. Napoleon was concerned only with personal ability and adaptability to the needs of his imperial "rule of genius."

At the height of revolutionary dictatorship the position of a member of the administrative staff tends to be that of a person entrusted *ad hoc* with a specific task, subject to recall. This was true of the role of the agents of the "Committee of Public Safety." When a certain kind of municipal "dictators" have been swept into power by the reform movements in American cities the tendency has been to grant them freedom to appoint their own staff. Thus both traditional legitimacy and formal legality tend to be equally ignored by the revolutionary dictator. The tendency of patriarchal authorities, in the administration of justice and in their other functions, has been to act in accordance with substantive ideas of justice, with utilitarian considerations and in terms of reasons of state. These tendencies are paralleled by the revolutionary tribunals and by the substantive postulates of justice of the radical democracy of Antiquity and of modern socialism (of which more will be said in the Soc. of Law, ch. VIII: *vii*). The process of routinization of revolutionary charisma then brings with it changes similar to those brought about by the corresponding process in other respects. Thus the development of a professional army in England goes back to the voluntary army of the faithful in the days of Cromwell. Similarly, the French system of administration by prefects is derived from the charismatic administration of the revolutionary democratic dictatorship.

2. The introduction of elected officials always involves a radical alteration in the position of the charismatic leader. He becomes the "servant" of those under his authority. There is no place for such a type in a technically rational bureaucratic organization. Since he is not ap-

pointed and promoted by his superiors and his position is derived from the votes of the ruled, he is likely to be little interested in the prompt and strict observance of discipline which would be likely to win the favor of superiors. The tendency is rather for electoral positions to become autocephalous spheres of authority. It is in general not possible to attain a high level of technical administrative efficiency with an elected staff of officials. (This is illustrated by a comparison of the elected officials in the individual states in the United States with the appointed officials of the Federal Government. It is similarly shown by comparing the elected municipal officials with the administration of the reform mayors with their own appointed staffs.) It is necessary to distinguish the type of plebiscitary democracy from that which attempts to dispense with leadership altogether. The latter type is characterized by the attempt to minimize the domination of man over man.

It is characteristic of the *Führerdemokratie* that there should in general be a highly emotional type of devotion to and trust in the leader. This accounts for a tendency to favor the type of individual who is most spectacular, who promises the most, or who employs the most effective propaganda measures in the competition for leadership. This is a natural basis for the utopian component which is found in all revolutions. It also dictates the limitations on the level of rationality which, in the modern world, this type of administration can attain. Even in America it has not *always* come up to expectations.

Relationship to the economy: 1. The anti-authoritarian direction of the transformation of charisma normally leads into the path of rationality. If a ruler is dependent on recognition by plebiscite he will usually attempt to support his regime by an organization of officials which functions promptly and efficiently. He will attempt to consolidate the loyalty of those he governs either by winning glory and honor in war or by promoting their material welfare, or under certain circumstances, by attempting to combine both. Success in these will be regarded as proof of the charisma. His first aim will be the destruction of traditional, feudal, patrimonial, and other types of authoritarian powers and privileges. His second aim will have to be to create economic interests which are bound up with his regime as the source of their legitimacy. So far as, in pursuing these policies, he makes use of the formalization and legalization of law he may contribute greatly to the formal rationalization of economic activity.

2. On the other hand, plebiscitary regimes can easily act so as to weaken the formal rationality of economic activity so far as their interests in legitimacy, being dependent on the faith and devotion of the masses, forces them to impose substantive ideas of justice in the economic sphere. This will result in an administration of justice emancipated from formal procedures, as it happens under revolutionary tribunals, war-time ration-

ing and in other cases of limited and controlled production and consumption. This tendency, which is by no means confined to the modern socialist type, will be dominant insofar as the leader is a "social dictator." The causes and consequences of this type cannot yet be discussed.

3. The presence of elective officials is a source of disturbance to formally rational economic life. This is true in the first place because such officials are primarily elected according to party affiliations and not technical competence. Secondly, the risks of recall or failure of re-election make it impossible to pursue a strictly objective course of decision and administration, without regard to such consequences. There is, however, one case where the unfavorable effects for the rationality of economic activity are not evident. This is true where there is a possibility of applying the economic and technical achievements of an old culture to new areas. In this case, the means of production are not yet appropriated and there is a sufficiently wide margin so that the almost inevitable corruption of officials can be taken account of as one of the cost factors, and large-scale profits still be attained [as in the United States].

On 1. The classical example of a favorable effect on economic rationality is to be found in the two Napoleonic regimes. Napoleon I introduced the *Code Napoléon,* compulsory division of estates by inheritance and everywhere destroyed the traditional authorities. It is true that his regime created what almost amounted to fiefs for his deserving followers, and that the soldiers got almost everything, the citizen nothing. But this was compensated for by *la gloire* and, on the whole, the small bourgeois were tolerably well off. Under Napoleon III there was continued adherence to the motto of the era of Louis Philippe: "enrichissez-vous"; grand-scale building; the *Crédit Mobilier,* with its well-known scandal.

On 2. The tendencies of "social dictatorship" are classically illustrated by the Greek democracy of the Periclean age and its aftermath. In Rome the jurors who tried a case were bound by the instructions of the *praetor,* and decisions followed the formal law. But in the Greek *heliaia*-court decisions were made in terms of "substantive" justice—in effect, on the basis of sentimentality, flattery, demagogic invectives and jokes. This can be clearly seen in the court orations of the Athenian rhetors. Analogous phenomena are found in Rome only in the case of political trials, such as Cicero participated in. The consequence was that the development of formal law and formal jurisprudence in the Roman sense became impossible. For the *heliaia* was a "people's court" directly comparable to the revolutionary tribunals of the French Revolution and of the Soviet phase of the revolution in Germany. The jurisdiction of these lay tribunals was by no means confined to politically relevant cases. On the other hand, no revolutionary movement in England has ever interfered with the administration of justice except in cases of major political significance. However, it is true that there was a considerable arbitrary element in the decisions of the justices of the peace, but only insofar as they concerned pure "police" cases *not* involving interests of the propertied.

On 3. The United States of America is the classical example. As late as the early 1900's the author inquired of American workers of English origin why they allowed themselves to be governed by party henchmen who were so often open to corruption. The answer was, in the first place, that in such a big country even though millions of dollars were stolen or embezzled there was still plenty left for everybody, and secondly that these professional politicians were a group which even workers could treat with contempt whereas technical officials of the German type would as a group "lord it over" the workers.

A specialized discussion of relations of economic activity will have to be left for the more detailed treatment below [Part Two].

viii

Collegiality and the Division of Powers

15. Types of Collegiality and of the Division of Powers

On either a traditional or a rational basis authority may be limited and controlled by certain specific means.

> The present concern is not with the limitations of authority as such, whether it is determined by tradition or by law. This has already been discussed (secs. 3ff.). Just now it is rather a question of specific social relationships and groups which have the function of limiting authority.

1. Patrimonial and feudal regimes generally have their authority limited by the privileges of status groups. This type of limitation is most highly developed when there is an estate-type division of powers. This situation has already been discussed (sec. 9:IV).

2. A bureaucratic organization may be limited and indeed must be by agencies which act on their own authority alongside the bureaucratic hierarchy. This limitation is inherent in the fully developed legality type so that administrative action can be restricted to what is in conformity with rules. Such limiting agencies have the following principal functions:

(a) supervision of adherence to the rules, if need be, through an inquiry;

(b) a monopoly of creation of the rules which govern the action of officials completely, or at least of those which define the limits of their independent authority;

(c) above all a monopoly of the granting of the means which are necessary for the administrative function. These modes of limitation will be discussed separately below (sec. 16).

3. It is possible for any type of authority to be deprived of its monocratic character by the *principle of collegiality*. This may, however, occur in a variety of ways with widely varying significance. The following are the principal types:

(a) It may be that alongside the monocratic holders of governing powers there are other monocratic authorities which, by tradition or legislation, are in a position to delay or to veto acts of the first authority. This is the case of "veto collegiality" (*Kassationskollegialität*).

> The most important examples in Antiquity are the [Roman] tribune and, in its origins, the [Spartan] ephor, in the Middle Ages the *capitano del popolo*, and, in the period after November 9, 1918 until the regular administration was again emancipated from this control, the [German revolutionary] "Councils of Workers and Soldiers" whose delegates (*Vertrauensmänner*) were entitled to "countersign" official acts.

(b) The second type is precisely the opposite of this, namely the arrangement that the acts of an authority which is not monocratic must be carried out only after previous consultation and a vote. That is, their acts are subject to the rule that a plurality of individuals must co-operate for the act to be valid: the case of "functional collegiality." This cooperation may follow (α) the principle of unanimity or (β) of decision by majority.

(c) In effect closely related to case (a) is that in which, in order to weaken monocratic power, a plurality of monocratic officials exists, each of whom has equal authority, without specification of function. If a conflict arises over the same function, there must be a resort either to mechanical means such as lots, rotation, or oracles, or some controlling agency (2a) must intervene. In effect the tendency is for each member of the collegial body to have a power of veto over the others. (The most important example is the collegiality of the Roman magistrates, such as the consuls and the praetors.)

(d) A type which is closely related to case (b) is that in which, although there is an actually monocratic *primus inter pares*, his acts are normally subject to consultation with formally equal members, and disagreement in important matters may lead to breaking up of the collegial body by resignation, thus endangering the position of the monocratic chief. This may be called "functional collegiality with a preeminent head."

The most important example is that of the position of the British Prime Minister in relation to his cabinet. This organization has, as is well known, changed greatly in the course of its history. The above formulation, however, is substantially correct for most cases in the period of cabinet government.

Advisory collegial bodies do not necessarily involve a weakening of the power of an autocratic chief but may well lead to a tempering of the exercises of authority in the direction of rationalization. It is, however, also possible that in effect they should gain the upper hand over the chief. This is particularly true if they are representative of well-established status groups. The following are the more important types:

(e) The case noted above under (d) is closely related to that in which a body whose functions are formally only advisory is attached to a monocratic chief. Even though he is not formally bound to follow their advice but only to listen to it, the failure of his policies if this occurs may be attributed to neglect of this advice.

The most important case is that of the Roman Senate as a body advisory to the magistrates. From this there developed an actual dominance over the magistrates, chiefly through the Senate's control of finance. The Senate was probably actually only an advisory body in the early days, but through the actual control of finance and still more through the fact that senators and the formally elected magistrates belonged to the same status group, a situation developed in which the magistrates were in fact bound by the resolutions of the Senate. The formula "*Si eis placeret,*" in which the traditional lack of formal obligation was expressed, came to mean something analogous to "if you please" accompanied by something like a command.

(f) A somewhat different type is found in the case where a collegial body is made up of individuals with specified functions. In such a case the preparation and presentation of a subject is assigned to the individual technical expert who is competent in that field or possibly to several experts, each in a different aspect of the field. Decisions, however, are taken by a vote of the body as a whole.

Most councils of state and similar bodies in the past have more or less closely approximated to this type. This was true of the English Privy Council in the period before the development of cabinet government. Though at times their power has been very great, they have never succeeded in expropriating monarchs. On the contrary, under certain circumstances the monarch has attempted to secure support in his council of state in order to free himself from the control of cabinets which were made up of party leaders. This attempt was made in England, but without success. This type is also an approximately correct description of the ministries or cabinets made up of specialized officials which hereditary monarchs or elective presidents of the American type have appointed for their own support.

(g) A collegial body, the members of which have specified functions, may be a purely advisory body. In this case—as in (e)—it is open to the chief to accept or reject their recommendations, according to his own free decision.

The only difference is the extreme specialization of functions. This case was approached by the Prussian organization under Frederick William I [1713-40] and is always favorable to consolidating the power of the chief.

(h) The direct antithesis of rationally specialized collegiality is a traditional collegial body consisting of "elders." Their collegial function is primarily to guarantee that the law which is applied is really authentically traditional. Sometimes such bodies have a veto power as a means of upholding the genuine tradition against untraditional legislation. (Examples: *gerousia* [council of elders] in many cases in Antiquity; for veto power, the Areopagus in Athens and the *patres* in Rome, the latter, however, belong primarily in type (l) below.)

(i) One way of weakening domination is by applying the collegial principle to the highest authority whether its supremacy be formal or substantive. Several variations of this type are found, resembling the types d) through g). The powers of individual members of such bodies may be assumed in rotation or may be distributed on a permanent basis. Such bodies are collegial so long as there is a formal requirement that legitimate acts require the participation of all the members.

One of the most important examples is the Swiss Federal Council, the members of which do not have clearly defined specialized functions, while to some extent the principle of rotation is involved. Another example is found in the revolutionary councils of "People's Commissars" in Russia, Hungary, and for a short time in Germany. In the past such bodies as the "Council of Eleven" in Venice and the colleges of "Ancients" [in other Italian city states] belong in this category.

A great many cases of collegiality in patrimonial or feudal organizations belong in one or another of the following categories:

1) The estate-type division of powers ("estate collegiality").

2) The collegial organization of patrimonial officials which the chief has organized in order to counterbalance the power of organized privileged groups. This is often the position of the councils of state discussed above under (f).

3) Advisory bodies or sometimes bodies with executive authority over which the chief presides or the meetings of which he attends or from

which at least he receives reports. Such bodies are generally made up either of technical experts or of persons of high social prestige or both. In view of the increasingly specialized considerations involved in the functions of government he may hope, through the advice of such bodies, to attain a level of information sufficiently above pure dilettantism so that an intelligent personal decision is possible (case g) above).

In cases of the third type the chief is naturally interested in having heterogeneous and even opposed elements represented, whether this heterogeneity is one of technical opinions or of interest. This is because, on the one hand, he is concerned with the widest possible range of information, and on the other with being in a position to play the opposing interests off against each other.

In the second type, on the contrary, the chief is often, though not always, concerned with uniformity of opinions and attitudes. This is a main source of the "solidary" ministries and cabinets in so-called Constitutional states or others with an effective separation of powers. In the first case the collegial body which represents the appropriated interests will naturally lay stress on uniformity of opinion and solidarity. It is not, however, always possible to attain this, since every kind of appropriation through social privilege creates conflicting interests.

> The first of these types is illustrated by the assemblies of estates and the assemblies of vassals which preceded them frequently not only in Europe but elsewhere—for instance in China. The second type is well illustrated by the administrative, mostly collegial organs which were formed in the early stages of the modern monarchies and which were primarily composed of legal and financial experts. The third type is illustrated by the councils of state of the same monarchies and is also found in other parts of the world. As late as the eighteenth century it was not unknown for an archbishop to have a seat in the English cabinet. Typically, these bodies have been composed of dignitaries such as *Räte von Haus aus*,[14] and typically have had a mixture of *honoratiores* and specialized officials.

(k) Where there is a conflict of interests of status groups it may work out to the advantage of a chief through negotiation and struggle with the various groups. For organizations which are composed of delegated representatives of conflicting interests, whether their basis be in ideal causes, in power, or in economic advantage, may at least in external form be collegial bodies. What goes on within the body is then supposedly a process of adjustment of these conflicts of interest by compromise. (This is the case of "compromise-oriented collegiality," in contrast to office and parliamentary collegiality.)

This type is present in a crude form wherever there is an estate-type division of powers in such a way that decisions can only be arrived at by a compromise between the privileged groups. A more highly rationalized form is built up when the delegated members of the collegial bodies are selected in terms of their permanent status or class position, or in terms of the specific interests they represent. In such a body, unless its character is radically changed, action cannot result from a "vote" in the ordinary sense but is the outcome of a compromise which is either negotiated among the interests themselves or is imposed by the chief after the case for each of the groups involved has been considered.

> The peculiar structure of the *Ständestaat* will be discussed more in detail below (ch. XIII). The above formulation applies to such situations as arose through the separation of the bodies representing different social groups. Thus in England the House of Lords was separated from the House of Commons, while the Church did not participate in Parliament at all but had its separate "Convocations." In France, the division came to be that of the nobility, the clergy, and the *tiers état*, while in Germany there were various more complex divisions. These divisions made it necessary to arrive at decisions by a process of compromise, first within one estate and then between estates. The decisions were then generally submitted to the king as recommendations which he was not necessarily bound to follow. Today the theory of representation by occupational groups is very much in vogue. The advocates of this proposal for the most part fail to see that even under these conditions compromises rather than majority decisions would be the only feasible means (see sec. 22 below). Insofar as free workers' councils were the bodies concerned, the tendency would be for questions to be settled in terms of the relative economic power of different groups, and not by majority vote.

(l) A related case is "voting collegiality," where collegial bodies which decide things by vote have been formed out of previously autocephalous and autonomous groups and a (variously gradated) right to a voice in decision-making has been appropriated by the leaders or the delegates of the component groups ("merger collegiality").

> Examples are found in the representation of the phylae, the phratries, and the clans in the governing bodies of ancient city-states, in the medieval clans in the time of the *consules,* in the *mercadanza* of the guilds, in the delegates of the crafts (*Fachräte*) to the executive council of a federation of trade unions, in the federal council or senate in federal states, and finally in the distribution of appointments to cabinet posts in coalition ministries. This last case is particularly clear in the case of Switzerland, where posts are distributed in proportion to the number of votes for each party.

(m) A rather special case is the "voting collegiality" of elected parliamentary bodies which is hence in need of separate treatment. Its composition rests on one of two bases. It is either based on leadership, in which case the particular members constitute the following of leaders, or it is composed of collegial party groups without subordination to a specific leader (*führerloser Parlamentarismus*). To understand this it is necessary to discuss the structure of parties (see sec. 18 below).

Except in the case of the monocratic type of "veto collegiality," collegiality almost inevitably involves obstacles to precise, clear, and above all, rapid decision. In certain irrational forms it also places obstacles in the way of technical experts, but in introducing specialized officials monarchs have often found this consequence not altogether unwelcome. With the progressive increase in the necessity for rapid decision and action, however, the importance of this type of collegiality has declined.

Generally speaking, where collegial bodies have had executive authority the tendency has been for the position of the leading member to become substantively and even formally pre-eminent. This is true of the positions of the Bishop and the Pope in the church and of the Prime Minister in cabinets. Any interest in reviving the principle of collegiality in actual executive functions is usually derived from the interest in weakening the power of persons in authority. This, in turn, is derived from mistrust and jealousy of monocratic leadership, not so much on the part of those subject to authority, who are more likely to demand a "leader," as on the part of the members of the administrative staff. This is not only or even primarily true of negatively privileged groups but is, on the contrary, typical of those enjoying positive privileges. Collegiality is in no sense specifically "democratic." Where privileged groups have had to protect their privileges against those who were excluded from them they have always attempted to prevent the rise of monocratic power. Indeed, they have had to do so because such a power could base itself on the support of the underprivileged. Thus, while on the one hand they have tended to enforce strict equality within the privileged group they have tended to set up and maintain collegial bodies to supervise or even to take over power.

> Examples are Sparta, Venice, the Roman Senate before the time of the Gracchi and in Sulla's days, England repeatedly in the eighteenth century, Berne and other Swiss cantons, the medieval patrician towns with their collegial consuls, and the *mercadanza* which comprised the merchant guilds, but not those of the craft workers. The latter very easily became the prey of *nobili* and *signori*.

Collegiality favors greater thoroughness in the weighing of administrative decisions. Apart from the considerations already discussed, where this is more important than precision and rapidity, collegiality tends to be resorted to even to-day. Furthermore, it divides personal responsibility, indeed in the larger bodies this disappears almost entirely, whereas in monocratic organizations it is perfectly clear without question where responsibility lies. Large-scale tasks which require quick and consistent solutions tend in general, for good technical reasons, to fall into the hands of monocratic "dictators," in whom all responsibility is concentrated.

It is impossible for either the internal or the foreign policy of great states to be strongly and consistently carried out on a collegial basis. The dictatorship of the proletariat for the purpose of carrying out the nationalization of industry requires an individual "dictator" with the confidence of the masses. The "masses" as such are not necessarily adverse to this but the people holding power in Parliaments, parties, or, what makes very little difference, in "Soviets," cannot put up with such a dictator. This type has emerged only in Russia through the help of military force and supported by the interests of the peasants in the solidary maintenance of their newly acquired control of the land.

Finally, a few remarks may be made which partly summarize and partly supplement what has already been said. From a historical point of view, collegiality has had two principal kinds of significance:

a) It has involved a plurality of incumbents of the same office, or a number of persons in offices whose spheres of authority were directly competing, each with a mutual power of veto. This is primarily a matter of a technical separation of powers in order to minimize authority. The most conspicuous instance of this type of collegiality is that of the Roman magistrates. Their most important significance lay in the fact that every official act was subject to intercession by a magistrate with equal authority, thus greatly limiting the power of any one magistrate. But the magistracy remained an individual office merely multiplied in several copies.

b) The second main type has been that involving collegial decision. In such cases an administrative act is only legitimate when it has been produced by the cooperation of a plurality of people according to the principle of unanimity or of majority. This is the type of collegiality which is dominant in modern times, though it was also known in Antiquity. It may involve collegiality 1) of governmental leadership, 2) of administrative agencies, 3) of advisory bodies.

1) Collegiality in the supreme authority may be derived from the following considerations:—

(a) Its basis may lie in the fact that the governing authority (*Herrschaftsverband*) has arisen from the *Vergemeinschaftung* or *Vergesellschaftung* of previously autocephalous groups and that each of these demands its share of power. This was true of the "synoikism" of the ancient city states with their councils organized on the basis of clans, phratries, and phylae. It was true of the medieval towns with a council representing the important noble families, and of the medieval guild federations, in the *Mercadanza* with the council of the "*Ancients*" or guild deputies. It is also found in the bodies representing the component states in modern federal states and in the collegial structure of the ministries which have been built up by party coalitions (see again the increasing importance of proportional division in Switzerland). Collegiality in this case is a particular case of the representation of status or territorial groups.

(b) It may, secondly, be based on the absence of a leader. This may in turn result from mutual jealousy among those competing for leadership or from the attempt of the subjects to minimize the authority of any individual. It has appeared in most revolutions from a combination of these factors, in such forms as a council of officers or even soldiers of revolutionary troops or the Committee of Public Safety or the Councils of People's Commissars. In times of peace it has been mostly this last motive, antipathy to the individual "strong man," which has underlain the establishment of collegial bodies. Examples are Switzerland and the new constitution of Baden in 1919. (In the last case it was the socialists who most strongly manifested this antipathy; for fear of an "elected monarch" they sacrificed the strict administrative unification which was an absolutely essential condition of successful nationalization. The most decisive influence in this was the attitude of party officials in trade unions, local communities, and party headquarters, all of whom were suspicious of the powers of leadership.)

(c) The third basis may lie in the independent social position of the status groups primarily available for positions of power and monopolizing these positions. In this case collegiality is the product of an aristocratic regime. Every socially privileged class fears the type of leader who seeks support in the emotional devotion of the masses just as much as the type of democracy without leaders fears the rise of "demagogues." The senatorial regime in Rome, various attempts to rule through closed councils, and the Venetian and similar constitutions all belong in this category.

(d) The fourth basis may lie in the attempt of monarchs to counteract increasing expropriation at the hands of a technically trained bureaucracy. In the modern Western state, modern administrative organization was first introduced at the top with the establishment of collegial bodies. This was similar to what happened to the patrimonial states of the Orient, in China, Persia, the empire of the Caliphs, and in the Ottoman Empire, all of which served as models for Europe. A monarch is not only afraid of the power of particular individuals but hopes above all to be in a position, in the votes and counter-votes of a collegial body, to hold the balance himself. Furthermore, since he tends to become more and more of a dilettante he can also hope in this way to have a better comprehension of the details of administration than if he abdicated in favor of individual officials. (Generally speaking the functions of the highest bodies have been a mixture of advisory and executive elements. It is only in the field of finance, where arbitrariness has particularly irrational consequences, that, as in the case of the [1495–97] reform of Emperor Maximilian, the power of the monarch was immediately clipped by the professional officialdom. In this case there were powerful factors forcing the monarch to give way.)

(e) Another basis lies in the need to reconcile the points of view of different technical specialists and divergent interests, whether material or personal, by collegial discussion, that is, to make compromise possible. This has been particularly true in the organization of municipal affairs, which have on the one hand involved highly technical problems which could be appraised in local terms, and on the other hand have tended to rest heavily on the compromise of material interests. This has been true at least so long as the masses have put up with control by the strata privileged through property and education. The collegiality of ministries rests, from a technical point of view, on a similar basis. In Russia and to a less extent in Imperial Germany, however, it has not been possible to attain effective solidarity between the different parts of the government. The result has been bitter conflict between the different agencies.

The basis in cases (a), (c), and (d) is purely historical. Bureaucratic authority in the modern world has, wherever it has developed in large-scale associations such as states or metropolitan cities, led to a weakening of the role of collegiality in effective control. Collegiality unavoidably obstructs the promptness of decision, the consistency of policy, the clear responsibility of the individual, and ruthlessness to outsiders in combination with the maintenance of discipline within the group. Hence for these and certain other economic and technical reasons in all large states which are involved in world politics, where collegiality has been retained at all, it has been weakened in favor of the prominent position of the political leader, such as the Prime Minister. Incidentally a similar process has taken place in almost all of the large patrimonial organizations, particularly those which have been strictly Sultanistic. There has again and again been the need for a leading personality such as the Grand Vizier in addition to the monarch, unless a regime of favorites has provided a substitute. One person must carry the responsibility, but from a legal point of view the monarch himself could not do this.

2) Collegiality as employed in agencies acting under the direction of higher authorities has been primarily intended to promote objectivity and integrity and to this end to limit the power of individuals. As in respect to the highest authority it has almost everywhere, for the same reasons, given way to the technical superiority of monocratic organizations. This process is illustrated by the fate of the *Regierungen* [provincial "governments"] in Prussia.

3) In purely advisory bodies, collegiality has existed at all times and will probably always continue to exist. It has played a very important part historically. This has been particularly true in cases where the power structure was such that "advice" submitted to a magistrate or a monarch was for practical purposes binding. In the present discussion it is not necessary to carry the analysis further.

The type of collegiality under discussion here is always collegiality in the exercise of authority. It is thus a matter of bodies which either are administrative or which directly influence administrative agencies (through advice). The behavior of assemblies representing status groups and of parliamentary bodies will be taken up later. [See below, sec. *x* of this chapter.]

From a historical point of view it is in terms of collegiality that the concept of an "administrative agency" first came to be fully developed. This is because collegiality has always been linked with a separation of the sphere of office of the members from their private affairs, of public and private staff, and finally of the means of administration from personal property. It is thus by no means fortuitous that the history of modern administration in the Western World begins with the development of collegial bodies composed of technical specialists. Collegial administration has also been the beginning of every permanent organization of patrimonial, feudal, or other types of traditional political structures though in a different way. Only collegial bodies of officials, which were capable of standing together, could gradually expropriate the Occidental monarch, who had become a "dilettante." If officials had been merely individual appointees, the obligation of personal obedience would have made it far more difficult to maintain consistent opposition to irrational decisions of the monarch. When it became evident that a transition to the rule of technical bureaucracy was inevitable, the monarch regularly attempted to extend the system of advisory collegial bodies in the form of councils of state, in order to remain the master in spite of his lack of technical competence by playing off the internal dissensions of these bodies against each other. It was only after rational technical bureaucracy had come to be finally and irrevocably supreme that a need has been felt, particularly in relation to parliaments, for solidarity of the highest collegial bodies under monocratic direction through a prime minister. These bodies were intended to cover the ruler, who in turn protected them. With the latest development the general tendency of monocracy, and hence bureaucracy, in the organization of administration has become definitely victorious.

1. The significance of collegiality in the early stages of the development of modern administration is particularly evident in the struggle which the financial bodies created by Emperor Maximilian to meet the emergencies of the Turkish invasions carried on against his tendency to go over the heads of his officials and to issue orders and pledge securities for loans in accordance with every momentary whim. It was in the sphere of finance that the expropriation of the monarch began, for it was here in the first place that he lacked technical competence. This development occurred first in the Italian city states with their commercially organized system of accounting, then in the Burgundian and French Kingdoms, in the German territorial states, and independently of these in the Norman state of Sicily and in England. In the Near East

the Divans played a similar role, as did the Yamen in China and the Bakufu in Japan. In these cases, however, no rationally trained group of technically competent officials was available, and it was necessary to resort to the empirical knowledge of "experienced" officials. This accounts for the fact that a rationally bureaucratic system did not result. In Rome a somewhat similar role was played by the Senate.

2. The role of collegiality in promoting the separation of the private household from the sphere of office is somewhat similar to that played by the large-scale voluntary trading companies in the separation of the household and the profit-making enterprise on the one hand, of personal property and capital on the other.

16. The Functionally Specific Division of Powers

4.[15] It is further possible for authoritative powers to be limited by a functionally specific separation of powers. This means entrusting different individuals with specifically differentiated "functions" and the corresponding powers. In the strictly legal type—as in the constitutional separation of powers—these functions are rationally determined. It follows that in questions which involve two or more authorities it is only by means of a compromise between them that legitimate measures can be taken.

1. Functionally specific separation of powers differs from that based on status groups in that powers are divided in terms of their functionally objective character. This involves some kind of "constitution," which need not, however be formally enacted or written. The setup is such either that different types of measures have to be undertaken by different authorities or that the same type involves the cooperation by informal compromise of a plurality of agencies. It is not merely spheres of competence which are separated in this case but also the ultimate powers.

2. The functionally specific separation of powers is not wholly a modern phenomenon. The division of an independent political authority and an equally independent hierocratic authority instead of either caesaropapism or theocracy belongs in this category. Similarly, there is a certain sense in which the specified spheres of competence of the different Roman magistracies may be thought of as a kind of "separation of powers." The same is true of the specialized charismata of Lamaist Buddhism. In China the Confucian Hanlin Academy and the "censors" had a position which, in relation to the Emperor, was largely independent. In most patrimonial states, but also in the Roman Principate it has been usual for the administration of justice and the civil aspect of finance to be separated from the military establishment, at least in the lower

reaches. But in these cases the concept of separation of powers loses all precision. It is best to restrict its application to the supreme authority itself. If this restriction is accepted then the rational, formally enacted constitutional form of the separation of powers is entirely a modern phenomenon. In a constitutional but non-parliamentary state a budget can be put through only by a process of compromise between the legal authorities, such as the crown, and one or more legislative chambers.

Historically, the separation of powers in Europe developed out of the old system of estates. Its theoretical basis for England was first worked out by Montesquieu and then by Burke. Further back the division of powers began in the process of appropriation of governing powers and of the means of administration by privileged groups. Another important factor lay in the increasing financial needs of the monarchs, both the recurring needs arising from the social and economic development and the exceptional ones of war time. They could not be met without the consent of privileged groups, even though the latter were often the first to insist that they be met. In this situation it was necessary for the estates to reach a compromise, which was the historical origin of compromises over the budget and over legislation. The latter phenomena do not, however, belong in the context of the separation of powers as between estates but to the constitutional type.

3. The constitutional separation of powers is a specifically unstable structure. What determines the actual power structure is the answer to the question what would happen if a constitutionally necessary compromise, such as that over the budget, were not arrived at. An English king who attempted to rule without a budget today would risk his crown, whereas in pre-revolutionary Germany a Prussian king would not, for under the German system the position of the dynasty was dominant.

17. The Relations of the Political Separation of Powers to the Economy

1. Collegiality of legal bodies with rationally defined functions may be favorable to objectivity and the absence of personal influences in their administrative actions. Even if such collegiality has a negative influence because it functions imprecisely, the general effect may favor the rationality of economic activity. On the other hand, the big capitalistic interests of the present day, like those of the past, are apt, in political life —in parties and in all other connections that are important to them—to prefer monocracy. For monocracy is, from their point of view, more "discreet." The monocratic chief is more open to personal influence and is more easily swayed, thus making it more readily possible to influence the

administration of justice and other governmental activity in favor of such powerful interests. This is also in accord with German experience.

Conversely, the type of collegiality involving mutual veto powers or that in which collegial bodies have arisen out of the irrational appropriation of power of a traditional administrative staff may have irrational consequences. The type of collegiality of financial bodies, which originated specialized officialdom, has on the whole certainly been favorable to the formal rationalization of economic activity.

> In the United States the monocratic "party boss," rather than the official party organs which are often collegial, was preferred by the big contributors. This accounts for his indispensability. For the same reason, in Germany large sections of so-called "heavy industry" have favored bureaucratic domination rather than parliamentary government with its collegial system.

2. Like every form of appropriation, the separation of powers creates established spheres of authority which, though they may not yet be rational, still introduce an element of calculability into the functioning of the administrative apparatus. Hence, the separation of powers is generally favorable to the formal rationalization of economic activity. Movements which, like the Soviet type, the French Convention, and the Committee of Public Safety, aim to abolish the separation of powers, are definitely concerned with a more or less "just" economic distribution. Accordingly, they work against formal rationalization.

(All details must wait for the extended analyses.)

ix

Parties

18. *Definition and Characteristics*[16]

The term "party" will be employed to designate associations, membership in which rests on formally free recruitment. The end to which its activity is devoted is to secure power within an organization for its leaders in order to attain ideal or material advantages for its active members. These advantages may consist in the realization of certain objective policies or the attainment of personal advantages or both. Parties may have an ephemeral character or may be organized with a view to permanent activity. They may appear in all types of organizations and may themselves be organized in any one of a large variety of forms. They may consist of the following of a charismatic leader, of traditional retainers, or of purpose- or value-rational adherents. They may be oriented primarily to personal interests or to objective policies. Officially or merely in fact, they may be solely concerned with the attainment of power for their leaders and with securing positions in the administrative staff for their own members. (Then they are "patronage parties".) They may, on the other hand, predominantly and consciously act in the interests of a status group or a class or of certain objective policies or of abstract principles. (In the latter case they are called "ideological parties.") The attainment of positions in the administrative staff for their members is, however, at the least a secondary aim and objective programs are often merely a means of persuading outsiders to participate.

By definition a party can exist only *within* an organization, in order to influence its policy or gain control of it. Federations of party groups which cut across several corporate bodies are, however, not uncommon.

A party may employ any one of the conceivable means of gaining power. In cases where the government is determined by a formally free ballot and legislation is enacted by vote they are primarily organizations for the attraction of votes. Where voting takes a course in accord with legitimate expectations they are legal parties. The existence of legal parties, because of the fact that their basis is fundamentally one of voluntary adherence, always means that the business of politics is the pursuit of *interests*. (It should, however, be noted that in this context, "interests" is by no means necessarily an economic category. In the first instance, it is a matter of political interests which rest either on an ideological basis or on an interest in power as such.)

In this case the political enterprise is in the hands of:

a) party leaders and their staffs, whereas

b) active party members have for the most part merely the function of acclaiming their leaders. Under certain circumstances, however, they may exercise some forms of control, participate in discussion, voice complaints, or even initiate resolutions within the party;

c) the inactive masses of electors or voters (*Mitläufer*) are merely objects whose votes are sought at election time. Their attitudes are important only for the agitation of the competing parties;

d) contributors to party funds usually remain behind the scenes.

Apart from formally organized legal parties in a polity, there are the following principal types:

a) Charismatic parties arising from disagreement over the charismatic quality of the leader or over the question of who, in charismatic terms, is to be recognized as the correct leader. They create a schism.

b) Traditionalistic parties arising from controversy over the way in which the chief exercises his traditional authority in the sphere of his arbitrary will and grace. They arise in the form of movements to obstruct innovations or in open revolt against them.

c) Parties organized about questions of faith (*Glaubensparteien*). These are usually, though not necessarily, identical with a). They arise out of a disagreement over the content of doctrines or declarations of faith. They take the form of heresies, which are to be found even in rational parties such as the socialist.

d) Appropriation parties [or spoils-oriented parties] arising from conflict with the chief and his administrative staff over the filling of positions in the administrative staff. This type is very often, though by no means necessarily, identical with b).

Structurally, parties may conform to the same types as any other organizations. They may thus be charismatically oriented by devotion to the leader, with the plebiscite as an expression of confidence. They may be traditional with adherence based on the social prestige of the chief or of an eminent neighbor, or they may be rational with adherence to a leader and staff set up by a "constitutional process" of election. These differences may apply both to the basis of obedience of the members, and of the administrative staff. Further elaboration must be reserved to the Sociology of the State. [The *Staatssoziologie* was never written.]

It is of crucial importance for the economic aspect of the distribution of power and for the determination of party policy by what method the party activities are financed. Among the possibilities are small contributions from the masses of members and sympathizers; large contributions from disinterested sympathizers with its cause; direct or indirect sell-out to interested parties; or taxation either of elements under obligation to the party, including its members, or of its defeated opponents. These details, too, belong in the *Staatssoziologie*.

1. As has been pointed out, parties can exist by definition only within an organization, whether political or other, and only when there is a struggle for its control. Within a party there may be and very often are sub-parties; for example, as ephemeral structures they are typical in the nomination campaigns of presidential candidates of the American parties. On a permanent basis an example is the "Young Liberals" in Germany. Parties which extend to a number of different polities are illustrated by the Guelphs and Ghibellines in Italy in the thirteenth century and by the modern socialists.

2. The criterion of formally voluntary solicitation and adherence in terms of the rules of the group within which the party exists is treated here as the crucial point. It involves a distinction of major sociological significance from all associations which are prescribed and controlled by the polity. Even where the order of the polity takes notice of the existence of parties, as in the United States and in the German system of proportional representation, the voluntarist component remains. It remains even if an attempt is made to regulate their constitution. But when a party becomes a closed group which is incorporated by law into the administrative staff, as was true of the Guelphs in the Florentine statutes of the thirteenth century, it ceases to be a party and becomes a part of the polity.

3. Under genuinely charismatic domination, parties are necessarily schismatic sects. Their conflict is essentially over questions of faith and, as such, is basically irreconcilable. The situation in a strictly patriarchal body may be somewhat similar. Both these types of parties, at least in the pure form, are radically different from parties in the modern sense. In the usual kind of hereditary monarchy and estate-type organization, it is common for groups of retainers, composed of pretenders to fiefs and offices, to rally around a pretender to the throne. Personal followings are also common in organizations of *honoratiores* such as the aristocratic city states. They are, however, also prominent in some democracies. The modern type of party does not arise except in the legal state with a representative constitution. It will be further analyzed in the Sociology of the State.

4. The classic example of parties in the modern state organized primarily around patronage are the two great American parties of the last generation. Parties primarily oriented to issues and ideology have been the older type of Conservatism and Liberalism, bourgeois Democracy, later the Social Democrats and the [Catholic] Center Party. In all, except the last, there has been a very prominent element of class interest. After the Center attained the principal points of its original program, it became very largely a pure patronage party. In all these types, even those which are most purely an expression of class interests, the (ideal and material) interests of the party leaders and the staff in power, office, and remuneration always play an important part. There is a tendency for the interests of the electorate to be taken into account only so far as their neglect would endanger electoral prospects. This fact is one of the sources of public opposition to political parties as such.

5. The different forms which the internal organization of parties take will be dealt with separately in the proper place. One fact, however, is common to all these forms, namely, that there is a central group of individuals who assume the active direction of party affairs, including the formulation of programs and the selection of candidates. There is, secondly, a group of "members" whose role is notably more passive, and finally, the great mass of citizens whose role is only that of objects of solicitation by the various parties. They merely choose between the

various candidates and programs offered by the different parties. Given the voluntary character of party affiliation this structure is unavoidable. It is this which is meant by the statement that party activity is a matter of "play of interests." (As has already been stated, it is political interests and not economic interests which are involved.) The role of interests in this sense is the second principal point of attack for the opposition to parties as such. In this respect, there is a *formal* similarity between the party system and the system of capitalistic enterprise which rests on the recruitment of formally free labor.

6. The role in party finance of large-scale contributors is by no means confined to the "bourgeois" parties. Thus Paul Singer was a contributor to the Social Democratic party (and, by the way, humanitarian causes) of grand style (and purest motives so far as is known). His whole position as chairman of the party rested on this fact. Furthermore, the parties of the Russian revolution in the Kerensky stage were partly financed by very large Moscow business interests. Other German parties on the "right" have been financed by heavy industry, while the Center party occasionally had large contributions from Catholic millionaires.

For reasons which are readily understandable, the subject of party finances, though one of the most important aspects of the party system, is the most difficult to secure information about. It seems probable that in certain special cases a "machine" has actually been "bought." Apart from the role of individual large contributors, there are two basic alternatives: On the one hand, as in the English system, the electoral candidate may carry the burden of campaign expenses, with the result that the candidates are selected on a plutocratic basis. On the other hand, the costs may be borne by the "machine," in which case the candidates become dependent on the party organization. Parties as permanent organizations have always varied between these two fundamental types, in the thirteenth century in Italy just as much as today. These facts should not be covered up by fine phrases. Of course, there are limits to the power of party finance. It can only exercise an influence insofar as a "market" exists, but as in the case of capitalistic enterprise, the power of the seller as compared with the consumer has been tremendously increased by the suggestive appeal of advertising. This is particularly true of "radical" parties regardless of whether they are on the right or the left.

X

Direct Democracy and Representative Administration [17]

19. The Conditions of Direct Democracy and of Administration by Notables

Though a certain minimum of imperative powers in the execution of measures is unavoidable, certain organizations may attempt to reduce it as far as possible. This means that persons in authority are held obligated to act solely in accordance with the will of the members and in their service by virtue of the authority given by them. In small groups where all the members can be assembled at a single place, where they know each other and can be treated socially as equals this can be attained in a high degree. It has, however, been attempted in large groups, notably the corporate cities and city states of the past and certain regional groups.

The following are the principal technical means of attaining this end: (a) Short terms of office, if possible only running between two general meetings of the members; (b) Liability to recall at any time; (c) The principle of rotation or of selection by lot in filling offices so that every member takes a turn at some time. This makes it possible to avoid the position of power of technically trained persons or of those with long experience and command of official secrets; (d) A strictly defined mandate for the conduct of office laid down by the assembly of members. The sphere of competence is thus concretely defined and not of a general character; (e) A strict obligation to render an accounting to the general assembly; (f) The obligation to submit every unusual question which has not been foreseen to the assembly of members or to a committee representing them; (g) The distribution of powers between a large number of offices each with its own particular function; (h) The treatment of office as an avocation and not a full time occupation.

If the administrative staff is chosen by ballot, the process of election takes place in the assembly of members. Administration is primarily oral, with written records only so far as it is necessary to have a clear record of certain rights. All important measures are submitted to the assembly.

This and similar types of administration, as long as the assembly of members is effective, will be called "direct" or "immediate democracy."

1. The North American "township" and the smaller Swiss Cantons such as Glarus, Schwyz, and Appenzell are all, on account of their size alone, on the borderline of applicability of immediate democracy. The Athenian democracy actually overstepped this boundary to an important extent, and the *parlamentum* of the early medieval Italian cities still more radically. Voluntary associations, guilds, scientific, academic, and athletic associations of all sorts often have this form. It is, however, also applicable to the internal organization of aristocratic groups of masters who are unwilling to allow any individual to hold authority over them.

2. In addition to the small scale of the group in numbers or territorial extent, or still better in both, as essential conditions of immediate democracy, is the absence of qualitative functions which can only be adequately handled by professional specialists. Where such a group of professional specialists is present, no matter how strongly the attempt is made to keep them in a dependent position, the seeds of bureaucratization are present. Above all, such persons can neither be appointed nor dismissed according to the procedures appropriate to immediate democracy.

3. Closely related to the rational forms of immediate democracy is the primitive gerontocratic or patriarchal group. This is because those holding authority are expected to administer it in the "service" of the members. However, there are two principal differences: governing powers are normally appropriated and action is strictly bound to tradition. Immediate democracy is either a form of organization of rational groups or may become a rational form. The transitional types will be discussed presently.

20. *Administration by Notables*

Notables (*honoratiores*) are persons (1) whose economic position permits them to hold continuous policy-making and administrative positions in an organization · without (more than nominal) remuneration; (2) who enjoy social prestige of whatever derivation in such a manner that they are likely to hold office by virtue of the member's confidence, which at first is freely given and then traditionally accorded.

Most of all, the notable's position presupposes that the individual is able to live *for* politics without living *from* politics. He must hence be able to count on a certain level of provision from private sources. This condition is most likely to be met by receivers of property income of all sorts, such as landowners, slaveowners, and owners of cattle, real estate, or securities. Along with these, people with a regular occupation are in a favorable position if their occupation is such as to leave them free for political activity as an avocation. This is particularly true of persons whose occupational activity is seasonal, notably agriculture, of lawyers, who have an office staff to depend on, and certain others of the free professions. It is also to a large extent true of patrician merchants whose business is not continuously exacting. The most unfavorably situated are independent industrial entrepreneurs and industrial workers. Every type of immediate democracy has a tendency to shift to a form of government by notables. From an ideal point of view this is because they are held to be especially well-qualified by experience and objectivity. From a material point of view this form of government is especially cheap, indeed, sometimes completely costless. Such a person is partly himself in possession of the means of administration or provides them out of his own private resources, while in part they are put at his disposal by the organization.

1. The classification of notables as a status group will be undertaken later [ch. IV]. The primary basis in all primitive societies is wealth, which is often sufficient to make a man a "chief." In addition to this, according to different circumstances, hereditary charisma or economic availability may be more prominent.

2. In the American township the tendency has been to favor actual rotation on grounds of natural rights. As opposed to this the immediate democracy of the Swiss Cantons has been characterized by recurrence of the same names and, still more, families among the office holders. The fact that some persons were economically more available than others became also important in the Germanic communes (*Dinggemeinden*), and in the initially, at least in some cases, strictly democratic North-German towns this was one of the sources for the rise of the *meliores,* and hence of the patriciate, who monopolized the city councils.

3. Administration by notables is found in all kinds of organizations. It is, for instance, typical of political parties which are not highly bureaucratized. It always means an extensive rather than intensive type of administration. When there are very urgent economic or administrative needs for precise action, though it is free to the group as such, it is hence often very expensive for individual members.

Both immediate democracy and government by notables are technically inadequate, on the one hand in organizations beyond a certain limit of size, constituting more than a few thousand full-fledged members, or on the other hand, where functions are involved which require technical training or continuity of policy. If, in such a case, permanent technical officials are appointed alongside of shifting heads, actual power will normally tend to fall into the hands of the former, who do the real work, while the latter remain essentially dilettantes.

A typical example is to be found in the situation of the annually elected head (*Rektor*) of the German university, who administers academic affairs only as a sideline, *vis-á-vis* the syndics, or under certain circumstances even the permanent officials in the university administration (*Kanzlei*). Only an autonomous university president with a long term of office like the American type would, apart from very exceptional cases, be in a position to create a genuinely independent self-government of a university which went beyond phrase-making and expressions of self-importance. In Germany, however, both the vanity of academic faculties and the interests of the state bureaucracy in their own power stand in the way of any such development. Varying according to particular circumstances, similar situations are to be found everywhere.

Immediate democracy and government by notables exist in their genuine forms, free from *Herrschaft*, only so long as parties which contend with each other and attempt to appropriate office do not develop on a permanent basis. If they do, the leader of the contending and victorious party and his staff constitute a structure of domination, regardless of how they attain power and whether they formally retain the previous mode of administration.

(Indeed, this is a relatively common form of destroying the old ways.)

xi

Representation

21. *The Principal Forms and Characteristics*

The primary fact underlying representation is that the action of certain members of an organization, the "representatives," is considered binding on the others or accepted by them as legitimate and obligatory (cf. ch. I, sec. 11). Within the structures of domination, representation takes a variety of typical forms.

1. *Appropriated representation.* In this case the chief or a member of the administrative staff holds appropriated rights of representation. In this form it is very ancient and is found in all kinds of patriarchal and charismatic groups. The power of representation has a traditionally limited scope.

> This category covers the sheiks of clans and chiefs of tribes, the headmen of castes in India, hereditary priests of sects, the *patel* of the Indian village, the *Obermärker*, hereditary monarchs, and all sorts of similar patriarchal or patrimonial heads of organizations. Authority to conclude contractual agreements and to agree on binding rules govern-

ing their relations with the elders of neighboring tribes exists in what are otherwise exceedingly primitive conditions, as in Australia.

2. Closely related to appropriated representation is *estate-type representation*. This does not constitute representation so far as it is a matter primarily of representing and enforcing appropriated rights or privileges. It may, however, have a representative character and be recognized as such, so far as the effect of the decisions of such bodies as estates extends beyond the personal holders of privileges to the unprivileged groups. This may not be confined to the immediate retainers but may include others who are not in the socially privileged group. These others are regularly bound by the action involved, whether this is merely taken for granted or a representative authority is explicitly claimed.

> This is true of all feudal courts and assemblies of privileged estates, and included the Estates of the late Middle Ages in Germany and of more recent times. In Antiquity and in non-European areas this institution occurs only sporadically and has not been a universal stage of development.

3. The radical antithesis of this is *"instructed" representation*. In this case elected representatives or representatives chosen by rotation or lot or in any other manner exercise powers of representation which are strictly limited by an imperative mandate and a right of recall. This type of "representative" is, in effect, an agent of those he represents.

> The imperative mandate has had for a very long time a place in the most various organizations. For instance, the elected representatives of the communes in France were almost always bound by the *cahiers de doléances*. At the present time this type of representation is particularly prominent in the Soviet type of republican organization where it serves as a substitute for immediate democracy, since the latter is impossible in a mass organization. Instructed mandates are certainly to be found in all sorts of organizations outside the Western World, both in the Middle Ages and in modern times, but nowhere else have they been of great historical significance.

4. *Free representation*. The representative, who is generally elected (and possibly subject to rotation), is not bound by instruction but is in a position to make his own decisions. He is obligated only to express his own genuine conviction, and not to promote the interests of those who have elected him.

Free representation in this sense is not uncommonly an unavoidable consequence of the incompleteness or absence of instructions, but in other cases it is the deliberate object of choice. In so far as this is true, the representative, by virtue of his election, exercises authority over the electors and is not merely their agent. The most prominent example of this type is modern parliamentary representation. It shares with legal authority the general tendency to impersonality, the obligation to conform to abstract norms, political or ethical.

This feature is most pronounced in the case of the parliaments, the representative bodies of the modern political organizations. Their function is not understandable apart from the voluntaristic intervention of the parties. It is the parties which present candidates and programs to the politically passive citizens. They also, by the process of compromise and balloting within the parliament, create the norms which govern the administrative process. They subject the administration to control, support it by their confidence, or overthrow it by withdrawal of confidence whenever, by virtue of commanding a majority of votes, they are in a position to do this.

The party leader and the administrative staff which is appointed by him, consisting of ministers, secretaries of state, and sometimes undersecretaries, constitute the political administration of the state, that is, their position is dependent upon the electoral success of their party, and an electoral defeat forces their resignation. Where party government is fully developed they are imposed on the formal head of the state, the monarch, by the party composition of the parliament. The monarch is expropriated from the actual governing power and his role is limited to two things.

1.) By negotiation with the parties, he selects the effective head and formally legitimizes his position by appointment.

2.) He acts as an agency for legalizing the measures of the party chief who at the time is in power.

The "cabinet" of ministers, a committee of the majority party, may be organized in a monocratic or a more collegial form. The latter is unavoidable in coalition cabinets, whereas the former is more precise in its functioning. The cabinet protects itself from the attacks of its followers who seek office and its opponents by the usual means, by monopolizing official secrets and maintaining solidarity against all outsiders. Unless there is an effective separation of powers, this system involves the complete appropriation of all powers by the party organization in control at the time; not only the top positions but often many of the lower offices become benefices of the party followers. This may be called *parliamentary cabinet government.*

The facts are in many respects best presented in the brilliantly polemical attack on the system by W. Hasbach [*Die parlamentarische Kabinettsregierung,* 1919] which has erroneously been called a "political description." The author in his own essay, *Parlament und Regierung im neugeordneten Deutschland,* has been careful to emphasize that it is a polemical work which has arisen out of the particular situation of the time.

Where the appropriation of power by the party government is not complete but the monarch or a corresponding elected president enjoys independent power especially in appointments to office, including military officers, there is a *constitutional government.* This is likely to be found where there is a formal separation of powers. A special case is an *elective presidency combined with a representative parliament.*

The executive authorities or the chief executive of a parliamentary organization may also be chosen by parliament itself: this is *purely representative government.*

The governing powers of representative bodies may be both limited and legitimized where direct canvassing of the masses of members of the groups is permitted through the *referendum.*

1. It is not representation as such but free representation in conjunction with the presence of parliamentary bodies which is peculiar to the modern Western World. Only relatively small beginnings are to be found in Antiquity and elsewhere in such forms as assemblies of delegates in the confederations of city states. But in principle the members of these bodies were usually bound by instructions.

2. The abolition of imperative mandates has been very strongly influenced by the positions of the monarchs. The French kings regularly demanded that the delegates to the Estates General should be elected on a basis which left them free to vote for the recommendations of the king. If they had been bound by imperative mandates, the king's policy would have been seriously obstructed. In the English Parliament, as will be pointed out below, both the composition and the procedure of the body led to the same result. It is connected with this fact that right up to the Reform Bill of 1867, the members of Parliament regarded themselves as a specially privileged group. This is shown clearly by the rigorous exclusion of publicity. (As late as the middle of the eighteenth century, heavy penalties were laid upon newspapers which reported the transactions of Parliament.) The theory came to be that the parliamentary deputy was a "representative" of the people as a whole and that hence he was not bound by any specific mandates, was not an "agent" but a person in authority (*Herr*). This theory was already well developed in the literature before it received its classical rhetorical form in the French Revolution.

3. It is not yet possible at this point to analyse in detail the process by which the English king and certain others following his example came to be gradually expropriated by the unofficial cabinet system which represented only party groups. This seems at first sight to be a very peculiar development in spite of the universal importance of its consequences. But in view of the fact that bureaucracy was relatively undeveloped in

England, it is by no means so "fortuitous" as has often been claimed. It is also not yet possible to analyse the partly plebiscitarian and partly representative American system of functional separation of powers and the place in it of the referendum (which is essentially an expression of mistrust of corrupt legislative bodies). Also Swiss democracy, and the related forms of purely representative democracy which have recently appeared in some of the German states, will have to be left aside for the present. The purpose of the above discussion was only to outline a few of the most important types.

4. So-called constitutional monarchy, which is above all characterized by appropriation of the power of patronage including the appointment of ministers and of military commanders by the monarch, may come to be very similar to a purely parliamentary regime of the English type. Conversely, the latter by no means necessarily excludes a politically gifted monarch like Edward VII from effective participation in political affairs. He need not be a mere figurehead. Details will be given below.

5. Groups governed by representative bodies are by no means necessarily democratic in the sense that all their members have equal rights. Quite the contrary, it can be shown that the classic soil for the growth of parliamentary government has tended to be an aristocratic or plutocratic society. This was true of England.

Relations to the economic order: These are highly complex and will have to be analyzed separately. For the present primary purposes only the following general remarks will be made:

1. One factor in the development of free representation was the undermining of the economic basis of the older status groups. This made it possible for persons with demagogic gifts to pursue their career regardless of their social position. The source of this undermining process was modern capitalism.

2. Calculability and reliability in the functioning of the legal order and the administrative system is vital to rational capitalism. This need led the bourgeoisie to attempt to impose checks on patrimonial monarchs and the feudal nobility by means of a collegial body in which the bourgeois had a decisive voice, which controlled administration and finance and could exercise an important influence on changes in the legal order.

3. When this transition was taking place, the proletariat had not yet become a political power and did not yet appear dangerous to the bourgeoisie. Furthermore, there was no hesitation in eliminating any threat to the power of the propertied class by means of property qualifications for the franchise.

4. The formal rationalization of the economic order and the state, which was favorable to capitalistic development, could be strongly pro-

moted by parliaments. Furthermore, it seemed relatively easy to secure influence on party organizations.

5. The development of demagogy in the activities of the existing parties was a function of the extension of the franchise. Two main factors have tended to make monarchs and ministers everywhere favorable to universal suffrage, namely, the necessity for the support of the proletariat in foreign conflict and the hope, which has proved to be unjustified, that, as compared to the bourgeoisie, they would be a conservative influence.

6. Parliaments have tended to function smoothly as long as their composition was drawn predominantly from the classes of wealth and culture, that is, as they were composed of *honoratiores*. Established social status rather than class interests as such underlay the party structure. The conflicts tended to be only those between different forms of wealth, but with the rise of class parties to power, especially the proletarian parties, the situation of parliaments has changed radically. Another important factor in the change has been the bureaucratization of party organizations, with its specifically plebiscitary character. The member of parliament thereby ceases to be "master" of the electors and becomes merely a "servant" of the leaders of the party machine. This will have to be discussed more in detail elsewhere.

22. *Representation by the Agents of Interest Groups*

A fifth type of representation is that by the agents of interest groups. This term will be applied to the type of representative body where the selection of members is not a matter of free choice, but where the body consists of persons who are chosen on the basis of their occupations or their social or class membership, each group being represented by persons of its own sort. At the present time the tendency of this type is to representation on an occupational basis.

This kind of representation may, however, have a very different significance, according to certain possible variations within it. In the first place, it will differ widely according to the specific occupations, status groups and classes which are involved, and, secondly, according to whether direct balloting or compromise is the means of settling differences. In the first connection its significance will vary greatly according to the numerical proportions of the different categories. It is possible for such a system to be radically revolutionary or extremely conservative in its character. In every case it is a product of the development of powerful parties representing class interests.

As a rule, this kind of representation is propagated with a view toward disenfranchising certain strata:

(a) either by distributing mandates among the occupations and thus *in fact* disenfranchising the numerically superior masses; or

(b) by *openly and formally* limiting suffrage to the non-propertied and thus by disenfranchising those strata whose power rests on their economic position (the case of a state of Soviets).

It is, at least, the theory that this type of representation weakens the exclusive sway of party interests, though, if experience so far is conclusive, it does not eliminate it. It is also theoretically possible that the role of campaign funds can be lessened, but it is doubtful to what degree this is true. Representative bodies of this type tend toward the absence of effective individual leadership (*Führerlosigkeit*), for the professional representative of an interest group is likely to be the only person who can devote his whole time to his function; among the non-propertied strata this task hence devolves upon the paid secretaries of the organized interest groups.

1. Representation where compromise has provided the means of settling differences is characteristic of all the older historical bodies of "estates." Today it is dominant in the labor-management committees and wherever negotiations between the various separate authorities is the order of the day. It is impossible to assign a numerical value to the "importance" of an occupational group. Above all the interests of the masses of workers on the one hand and of the increasingly smaller number of entrepreneurs, who are likely both to be particularly well informed and to have strong personal interests, somehow have to be taken account of regardless of numbers. These interests are often highly antagonistic, hence majority voting among elements which in status and class affiliation are highly heterogeneous, is exceedingly artificial. The ballot as a basis of final decision is characteristic of settling and expressing the compromise of *parties*. It is not, however, characteristic of the occupational interest groups.

2. The ballot is adequate in social groups where the representation consists of elements of roughly equal social status. Thus the so-called Soviets are made up only of workers. The prototype is the *mercadanza* of the time of the guilds' struggle [for power]. It was composed of delegates of the individual guilds who decided matters by majority vote. It was, however, in fact in danger of secession if certain particularly powerful guilds were out-voted. Even the participation of white-collar workers in Soviets raises problems. It has been usual to put mechanical limits to their share of votes. If representatives of peasants and craftsmen are admitted, the situation becomes still more complicated, and if the so-called "higher" professions and business interests are brought in, it is impossible for questions to be decided by ballot. If a labor-management body is organized in terms of equal representation, the tendency is for

"yellow" unions to support the employers and certain types of employers to support the workers. The result is that the elements which are most lacking in class loyalty (*Klassenwürde*) have the most decisive influence.

But even purely proletarian "Soviets" would in settled times be subject to the development of sharp antagonism between different groups of workers, which would probably paralyze the Soviets in effect. In any case, however, it would open the door for adroit politics in playing the different interests off against each other. This is the reason why the bureaucratic elements have been so friendly to the idea. The same thing would be likely to happen as between representatives of peasants and of industrial workers. Indeed any attempt to organize such representative bodies otherwise than on a strictly revolutionary basis comes down in the last analysis only to another opportunity for electoral manipulation in different forms.

3. The probability of the development of representation on an occupational basis is by no means low. In times of the stabilization of technical and economical development it is particularly high, but in such situations the importance of parties will be reduced at any rate. Unless this situation arises, it is obvious that occupational representative bodies will fail to eliminate parties. On the contrary, as can be clearly seen at the present time, all the way from the "Works Councils" to the Federal Economic Council in Germany, a great mass of new benefices for loyal party henchmen are being created and made use of. Politics is penetrating into the economic order at the same time that economic interests are entering into politics. There are a number of different possible value attitudes toward this situation, but this does not alter the facts.

Genuine parliamentary representation with the voluntaristic play of interests in the political sphere, the resulting plebiscitary party organization with its consequences, and the modern idea of *rational* representation by interest groups, are all peculiar to the Western World. None of these is understandable apart from the peculiar Western development of status groups and classes. Even in the Middle Ages the seeds of these phenomena were present in the Western World, and *only* there. It is only in the Western World that "cities" and "estates" (*rex et regnum*), "bourgeois" and "proletarians" have existed.

NOTES

Unless otherwise indicated, all notes are by Parsons.

1. Weber put *Autorität* in quotation marks and parentheses behind *Herrschaft*, referring to an alternative colloquial term, but the sentence makes it clear that this does not yet specify the basis of compliance. However, the chapter is devoted to a typology of legitimate domination, which will alternatively be translated as authority. The chapter begins with a reformulation of ch. X in Part Two,

and then presents a concise classification of the more descriptive exposition in chs. XI–XVI. (R)

2. Weber does not explain this distinction. By a "technical rule" he probably means a prescribed course of action which is dictated primarily on grounds touching efficiency of the performance of the immediate functions, while by "norms" he probably means rules which limit conduct on grounds other than those of efficiency. Of course, in one sense all rules are norms in that they are prescriptions for conduct, conformity with which is problematical.

3. It has seemed necessary to use the English word "office" in three different meanings, which are distinguished in Weber's discussion by at least two terms. The first is *Amt,* which means "office" in the sense of the institutionally defined status of a person. The second is the "work premises," as in the expression "he spent the afternoon in his office." For this Weber uses *Bureau* as also for the third meaning which he has just defined, the "organized work process of a group." In this last sense an office is a particular type of "enterprise," or *Betrieb* in Weber's sense. This use is established in English in such expressions as "the District Attorney's Office has such and such functions." Which of the three meanings is involved in a given case will generally be clear from the context.

3a. Under the *Oberhof* system, appeal against the local court's decision lay not to the court of the territorial prince but to that of one of the major independent cities with whose legal system the locality had originally been endowed by its ruler. Important "superior courts" (*Oberhöfe*) of this type for large parts of Germany and some areas in the Slavic East were the courts of Freiburg, Lübeck, Magdeburg, and other towns. Cf. H. Mitteis, *Deutsche Rechtsgeschichte* (5th ed., München 1958), 159, 190. (Wi)

4. As Parsons noted, "the term *Stand* with its derivatives is perhaps the most troublesome single term in Weber's text. It refers to a social group the members of which occupy a relatively well-defined common status, particularly with reference to social stratification, though this reference is not always important. In addition to common status, there is the further criterion that the members of a *Stand* have a common mode of life and usually more or less well-defined code of behavior" (Parsons, ed., *Theory,* 347). Parsons chose "decentralized authority" for "estate-type domination" because the members of the administrative staff are independent of their master. However, since the term *ständisch* derives from a specific historical context, even though Weber uses it often in a generic sense, it appeared appropriate to use the English equivalent "estate," which can denote both the medieval Estates and high social rank. *Stand* alone, however, will usually be translated as "status group" or "socially privileged group." (R)

5. Cf. Georg v. Below, *Der deutsche Staat des Mittelalters,* 1914 (sec. ed., 1925); *id., Territorium und Stadt* (sec. ed., 1923), 161ff; *id., Vom Mittelalter bis zur Neuzeit,* 1924; for a critique, see Ernst Kern, *Moderner Staat und Staatsbegriff,* 1949. Karl Ludwig v. Haller, *Restauration der Staatswissenschaft* (sec. ed., vols. 1–4, 1820–22, vol. 5, 1834, vol. 6, 1825). (W)

6. Kurt Eisner, a brilliant Social Democratic (not Communist) intellectual proclaimed the Bavarian Republic in Nov. 1918. He was murdered on Feb. 21, 1919. When the death sentence of the murderer, Count Arco, was commuted to a life sentence in Jan. 1920, Weber announced at the beginning of one of his lectures that he favored Arco's execution on substantive and pragmatic grounds. In the next lecture this resulted in a packed audience and noisy right-wing demonstration, which prevented Weber from lecturing. See now the account of two eyewitnesses in René König and Johannes Winckelmann, eds., *Max Weber*

zum Gedächtnis. Special issue 7 of the *Kölner Zeitschrift für Soziologie,* 1963, 24–29. On this period, cf. also the references in ch. II, n. 20. (R)

7. Weber here uses *Welt* in quotation marks, indicating that it refers to its meaning in what is primarily a religious context. It is the sphere of "worldly" things and interests as distinguished from transcendental religious interests.

8. Cf. Theodor Mommsen, *Abriss des römischen Staatsrechts.* First ed. 1893, sec. ed., 1907, 102ff, 162f. (W)

9. Cf. Fritz Rörig, *Geblütsrecht und freie Wahl in ihrer Auswirkung auf die deutsche Geschichte* (Abhandlungen der Berliner Akademie, 1945/6, Philosophische-Historische Klasse Nr. 6). (W)

10. The works of Ulrich Stutz are listed in Brunner-v. Schwerin, *Grundzüge der deutschen Rechtsgeschichte.* 8th ed. (1930), paragraph 33, 137. (W)

10a. On the *kayasth,* a caste of scribes in Bengal and elsewhere in India, cf. Weber, *Religion of India,* 75f., 298. (Wi)

11. See. C. H. Becker, *Islamstudien* (Leipzig: Quelle und Meyer, 1924), I, ch. 9. (R)

12. For the older definition of "organization," see Part Two, ch. X:3. Weber's definition of *Organisation* refers to the activities of a staff or apparatus, including the sharing of executive powers with the "master" (chief, head). This definition comes close to that of "organized action" (*Verbandshandeln*) in sec. 12, ch. I. The term *Verband,* which I prefer to render as "organization," is more broadly defined, since rules may be enforced by a head alone. Usually, however, a *Verband* has a staff, and Weber almost always uses the term in this sense. Hence, the terminological difference between *Verband* and *Organisation* can be disregarded most of the time. This is an additional reason for rendering *Verband,* which Weber uses much more frequently than *Organisation,* as "organization" in English. (R)

13. Weber titled both headings "The Anti-Authoritarian (*herrschaftsfremde*) Reinterpretation of Charisma," because recognition by the followers may become the *formal* basis of legitimacy, in contrast to the earlier stage in which charisma claims legitimacy and recognition on its own grounds. Since Weber's meaning of "anti-authoritarian" is not obvious without explanation, more descriptive titles were chosen. (R)

14. German territorial princes, since the thirteenth and fourteenth centuries, occasionally called on feudal and ecclesiastic notables for advice. As these counselors were only visiting at court, they were called *Räte von Haus aus,* or *familiares domestici, consiliarii,* etc.; cf. Georg Ludwig von Maurer, *Geschichte der Fronhöfe, der Bauernhöfe und der Hofverfassung in Deutschland* (Erlangen, 1862), II, 237, 240ff, 312f. (GM)

15. This continues the enumeration at the beginning of sec. 15. (R)

16. For the early formulation, see Part Two, ch. IX:6e. (R)

17. For the early formulation, see Part Two, ch. X:2. (R)

CHAPTER IV

STATUS GROUPS
AND CLASSES[1]

1. Class Situation and Class Types

"Class situation" means the typical probability of
1. procuring goods
2. gaining a position in life and
3. finding inner satisfactions,

a probability which derives from the relative control over goods and skills and from their income-producing uses within a given economic order.

"Class" means all persons in the same class situation.

a) A *"property* class" is primarily determined by property differences,

b) A *"commercial* class" by the marketability of goods and services,

c) A *"social* class" makes up the totality of those class situations within which individual and generational mobility is easy and typical.

Associations of class members—class organizations—may arise on the basis of all three types of classes. However, this does not necessarily happen: "Class situation" and "class" refer only to the same (or similar) interests which an individual shares with others. In principle, the various controls over consumer goods, means of production, assets, resources and skills each constitute a *particular* class situation. A *uniform* class situation prevails only when completely unskilled and propertyless persons are dependent on irregular employment. Mobility among, and stability of, class positions differs greatly; hence, the unity of a social class is highly variable.

2. *Property Classes*

The primary significance of a positively privileged property class lies in

α) its exclusive acquisition of high-priced consumers goods,

β) its sales monopoly and its ability to pursue systematic policies in this regard,

γ) its monopolization of wealth accumulation out of unconsumed surpluses,

δ) its monopolization of capital formation out of savings, i.e., of the utilization of wealth in the form of loan capital, and its resulting control over executive positions in business,

ε) its monopolization of costly (educational) status privileges.

I. Positively privileged property classes are typically *rentiers*, receiving income from:

a) men (the case of slave-owners),

b) land,

c) mines,

d) installations (factories and equipment),

e) ships,

f) creditors (of livestock, grain or money),

g) securities.

II. Negatively privileged property classes are typically

a) the unfree (see under "Status Group"),

b) the declassed (the *proletarii* of Antiquity), c) debtors,

d) the "paupers".

In between are the various "middle classes" (*Mittelstandsklassen*), which make a living from their property or their acquired skills. Some of them may be "commercial classes" (entrepreneurs with mainly positive privileges, proletarians with negative ones). However, not all of them fall into the latter category (witness peasants, craftsmen, officials).

The mere differentiation of property classes is not "dynamic," that is, it need not result in class struggles and revolutions. The strongly privileged class of slave owners may coexist with the much less privileged peasants or even the declassed, frequently without any class antagonism and sometimes in solidarity (against the unfree). However, the juxtaposition of property classes *may* lead to revolutionary conflict between

1. land owners and the declassed or

2. creditor and debtors (often urban patricians versus rural peasants or small urban craftsmen).

These struggles need not focus on a change of the economic system, but may aim primarily at a redistribution of wealth. In this case we can speak of "property revolutions" (*Besitzklassenrevolutionen*).

A classic example of the lack of class conflict was the relationship of the "poor white trash" to the plantation owners in the Southern States. The "poor white trash" were far more anti-Negro than the plantation owners, who were often imbued with patriarchal sentiments. The major examples for the struggle of the declassed against the propertied date back to Antiquity, as does the antagonism between creditors and debtors and land owners and the declassed.

3. *Commercial Classes*

The primary significance of a positively privileged commercial class lies in

a) the monopolization of entrepreneurial management for the sake of its members and their business interests,

β) the safeguarding of those interests through influence on the economic policy of the political and other organizations.

I. Positively privileged commercial classes are typically *entrepreneurs*:

a) merchants,

b) shipowners,

c) industrial and

d) agricultural entrepreneurs,

e) bankers and financiers, *sometimes* also

f) professionals with sought-after expertise or privileged education (such as lawyers, physicians, artists), or

g) workers with monopolistic qualifications and skills (natural, or acquired through drill or training).

II. Negatively privileged commercial classes are typically *laborers* with varying qualifications:

a) skilled

b) semi-skilled

c) unskilled.

In between again are "middle classes": the self-employed farmers and craftsmen and frequently:

a) public and private officials.

b) the last two groups mentioned in the first category [i.e., the "liberal professions" and the labor groups with exceptional qualifications].

4. Social Classes

Social classes are
a) the working class as a whole—the more so, the more automated the work process becomes,
  b) the petty bourgeoisie,
  c) the propertyless intelligentsia and specialists (technicians, various kinds of white-collar employees, civil servants—possibly with considerable social differences depending on the cost of their training),
  d) the classes privileged through property and education.

The unfinished last part of Karl Marx's *Capital* apparently was intended to deal with the issue of class unity in the face of skill differentials. Crucial for this differentiation is the increasing importance of semi-skilled workers, who can be trained on the job in a relatively short time, over the apprenticed and sometimes also the unskilled workers. Semi-skilled qualification too can often become monopolistic (weavers, for example, sometimes achieve their greatest efficiency after five years). It used to be that every worker aspired to be a self-employed small businessman. However, this is less and less feasible. In the generational sequence, the rise of groups a) and b) into c) (technicians, white-collar workers) is relatively the easiest. Within class d) money increasingly buys *everything*, at least in the sequence of generations. In banks and corporations, as well as in the higher ranks of the civil service, class c) members have a chance to move up into class d).

Class-conscious organization succeeds most easily
a) against the immediate economic opponents (workers against entrepreneurs, but *not* against stockholders, who truly draw "unearned" incomes, and also *not* in the case of peasants confronting manorial lords);
  b) if large numbers of persons are in the same class situation,
  c) if it is technically easy to organize them, especially if they are concentrated at their place of work (as in a "workshop community"),
  d) if they are led toward readily understood goals, which are imposed and interpreted by men outside their class (intelligentsia).

5. Status and Status Group (Stand)

"Status" (*ständische Lage*) shall mean an effective claim to social esteem in terms of positive or negative privileges; it is typically founded on
a) style of life, hence
  b) formal education, which may be

a) empirical training or

β) rational instruction, and the corresponding forms of behavior,

c) hereditary or occupational prestige.

In practice, status expresses itself through

a) connubium,

β) commensality, possibly

γ) monopolistic appropriation of privileged modes of acquisition or the abhorrence of certain kinds of acquisition,

δ) status conventions (traditions) of other kinds.

Status *may* rest on class position of a distinct or an ambiguous kind. However, it is not solely determined by it: Money and an entrepreneurial position are not in themselves status qualifications, although they may lead to them; and the lack of property is not in itself a status disqualification, although this may be a reason for it. Conversely, status may influence, if not completely determine, a class position without being identical with it. The class position of an officer, a civil servant or a student may vary greatly according to their wealth and yet not lead to a different status since upbringing and education create a common style of life.

A "status group" means a plurality of persons who, within a larger group, successfully claim

a) a special social esteem, and possibly also

b) status monopolies.

Status groups may come into being:

a) in the first instance, by virtue of their own style of life, particularly the type of vocation: "self-styled" or occupational status groups,

b) in the second instance, through hereditary charisma, by virtue of successful claims to higher-ranking descent: hereditary status groups, or

c) through monopolistic appropriation of political or hierocratic powers: political or hierocratic status groups.

The development of hereditary status groups is generally a form of the (hereditary) appropriation of privileges by an organization or qualified individuals. Every definite appropriation of political powers and the corresponding economic opportunities tends to result in the rise of status groups, and vice-versa.

Commercial classes arise in a market-oriented economy, but status groups arise within the framework of organizations which satisfy their wants through monopolistic liturgies, or in feudal or in *ständisch-patrimonial* fashion. Depending on the prevailing mode of stratification, we shall speak of a "status society" or a "class society." The status group comes closest to the social class and is most unlike the commercial class. Status groups are often created by property classes.

Every status society lives by conventions, which regulate the style of life, and hence creates economically irrational consumption patterns and fetters the free market through monopolistic appropriations and by curbing the individual's earning power. More on that separately.

NOTES

1. For the early formulation of class and status, see Part Two, ch. IX:6. (R)

PART TWO

The Economy and the Arena of

Normative and De Facto Powers

CHAPTER I

THE ECONOMY AND SOCIAL NORMS

1. Legal Order and Economic Order

A. THE SOCIOLOGICAL CONCEPT OF LAW. When we speak of "law," "legal order," or "legal proposition" (*Rechtssatz*), close attention must be paid to the distinction between the legal and the sociological points of view. Taking the former, we ask: What is intrinsically valid as law? That is to say: What significance or, in other words, what *normative* meaning ought to be attributed in correct logic to a verbal pattern having the form of a legal proposition. But if we take the latter point of view, we ask: What *actually* happens in a group owing to the *probability* that persons engaged in social action (*Gemeinschaftshandeln*), especially those exerting a socially relevant amount of power, subjectively consider certain norms as valid and practically act according to them, in other words, orient their own conduct towards these norms? This distinction also determines, in principle, the relationship between *law* and *economy*.

The juridical point of view, or, more precisely, that of legal dogmatics[1] aims at the correct meaning of propositions the content of which constitutes an order supposedly determinative for the conduct of a defined group of persons: in other words, it tries to define the facts to which this order applies and the way in which it bears upon them. Toward this end, the jurist, taking for granted the empirical validity of the legal propositions, examines each of them and tries to determine its logically correct meaning in such a way that all of them can be combined in a system which is logically coherent, i.e., free from internal contradictions. This system is the "legal order" in the juridical sense of the word.

Sociological economics (*Sozialökonomie*), on the other hand, considers actual human activities as they are conditioned by the necessity to take into acount the facts of economic life. We shall apply the term *economic order* to the distribution of the actual control over goods and services, the distribution arising in each case from the particular mode of balancing interests consensually; moreover, the term shall apply to the manner in which goods and services are indeed used by virtue of these powers of disposition, which are based on *de facto* recognition (*Einverständnis*).

It is obvious that these two approaches deal with entirely different problems and that their subjects cannot come directly into contact with one another. The ideal "legal order" of legal theory has nothing directly to do with the world of real economic conduct, since both exist on different levels. One exists in the realm of the "ought," while the other deals with the world of the "is." If it is nevertheless said that the economic and the legal order are intimately related to one another, the latter is understood, not in the legal, but in the sociological sense, i.e., as being *empirically* valid. In this context "legal order" thus assumes a totally different meaning. It refers not to a set of norms of logically demonstrable correctness, but rather to a complex of actual determinants (*Bestimmungsgründe*) of human conduct. This point requires further elaboration.

The fact that some persons act in a certain way because they regard it as prescribed by legal propositions (*Rechtssätze*) is, of course, an essential element in the actual emergence and continued operation of a "legal order." But, as we have seen already in discussing the significance of the "existence" of rational norms,[2] it is by no means necessary that all, or even a majority, of those who engage in such conduct, do so from this motivation. As a matter of fact, such a situation has never occurred. The broad mass of the participants act in a way corresponding to legal norms, not out of obedience regarded as a legal obligation, but either because the environment approves of the conduct and disapproves of its opposite, or merely as a result of unreflective habituation to a regularity of life that has engraved itself as a custom. If the latter attitude were universal, the law would no longer "subjectively" be regarded as such, but would be observed as custom. As long as there is a chance that a coercive apparatus will enforce, in a given situation, compliance with those norms, we nevertheless must consider them as "law." Neither is it necessary— according to what was said above—that all those who share a belief in certain norms of behavior, actually live in accordance with that belief at all times. Such a situation, likewise, has never obtained, nor need it obtain, since, according to our general definition, it is the "orientation" of an action toward a norm, rather than the "success" of that norm that is decisive for its validity. "Law," as understood by us, is simply an "order" endowed with certain specific guarantees of the probability of its empirical validity.

The term "guaranteed law" shall be understood to mean that there exists a "coercive apparatus" (in the sense defined earlier),[3] that is, that there are one or more persons whose special task it is to hold themselves ready to apply specially provided means of coercion (legal coercion) for the purpose of norm enforcement. The means of coercion may be physical or psychological, they may be direct or indirect in their operation, and they may be directed, as the case may require, against the participants in the consensual group (*Einverständnisgemeinschaft*) or the association (*Vergesellschaftung*), the organization (*Verband*) or the institution (*Anstalt*), within which the order is (empirically) valid; or they may be aimed at those outside. These means are the "legal regulations" of the group in question.

By no means all norms which are consensually valid in a group—as we shall see later—are "legal norms." Nor are all official functions of the persons constituting the coercive apparatus of a community concerned with legal coercion; we shall rather consider as legal coercion only those actions whose intention is the enforcement of conformity to a norm as such, i.e., because of its being formally accepted as binding. The term will not be applied, however, where conformity of conduct to a norm is sought because of considerations of expediency or other material circumstances. It is obvious that the effectuation of the validity of a norm may in fact be pursued for the most diverse motives. However, we shall designate it as "guaranteed law" only in those cases where there exists the probability that coercion will be applied for the norm's sake. As we shall have opportunity to see, not all law is guaranteed law. We shall speak of law—albeit in the sense of "indirectly guaranteed" or "unguaranteed" law—also in all those cases where the validity of a norm consists in the fact that the mode of orientation of an action toward it has some "legal consequences"; i.e., that there are other norms which associate with the "observance" or "infringement" of the primary norm certain probabilities of consensual action guaranteed, in their turn, by legal coercion. We shall have occasion to illustrate this case which occurs in a large area of legal life. However, in order to avoid further complication, whenever we shall use the term "law" without qualification, we shall mean norms which are directly guaranteed by legal coercion.

Such "guaranteed law" is by no means in all cases guaranteed by "violence" (*Gewalt*) in the sense of the prospect of physical coercion. In our terminology, law, including "guaranteed law" is not characterized by violence or, even less, by that modern technique of effectuating claims of private law through bringing "suit" in a "court," followed by coercive execution of the judgment obtained. The sphere of "public" law, i.e., the norms governing the conduct of the organs of the state and other state-oriented activities, recognizes numerous rights and legal norms, upon the infringement of which a coercive apparatus can be set in motion only through "complaint" or through "remonstance" by members of a limited group of persons, and often without any means of physical coercion. Sociologically, the question of whether or not guaranteed law exists in such a situation depends on the availability of an organized coercive apparatus for the nonviolent exercise of legal coercion. This apparatus must also possess such power that there is in fact a significant probability that the norm will be respected because of the possibility of recourse to such legal coercion.

Today legal coercion by violence is the monopoly of the state. All other groups applying legal coercion by violence are today considered as heteronomous and mostly also as heterocephalous. This is the outcome, however, of certain stages of development. We shall speak of "state" law, i.e., of law guaranteed by the state, only when legal coercion is exercised through the specific, i.e., normally directly *physical,* means of coercion of the political community. Thus, the existence of a "legal norm" in the sense of "state law" means that the following situation obtains: In the case of certain events occurring there is general agreement that certain organs of the community can be expected to go into official action, and the very expectation of such action is apt to induce conformity with the commands derived from the generally accepted interpretation of that legal norm; or, where such conformity has become unattainable, at least to effect reparation or indemnification. The event inducing this conse-quence, the legal coercion by the state, may consist in certain human acts, for instance, the conclusion or the breach of a contract, or the com-mission of a tort. But this type of occurence constitutes only a special instance, since, upon the basis of some empirically valid legal proposi-tion, the coercive instruments of the political powers against persons and things may also be applied where, for example, a river has risen above a certain level. It is in no way inherent, however, in the validity of a legal norm as normally conceived, that those who obey do so, predomi-nantly or in any way, because of the availability of such a coercive appara-tus as defined above. The motives for obedience may rather be of many different kinds. In the majority of cases, they are predominantly utilitarian or ethical or subjectively conventional, i.e., consisting of the fear of dis-approval by the environment. The nature of these motives is highly relevant in determining the kind and the degree of validity of the law itself. But in so far as the formal sociological concept of guaranteed law, as we intend to use it, is concerned, these psychological facts are irrelevant. In this connection nothing matters except that there be a sufficiently high probability of intervention on the part of a specially designated group of persons, even in those cases where nothing has occurred but the sheer fact of a norm infringement, i.e., on purely formal grounds.

The empirical validity of a norm as a legal norm affects the interests of an individual in many respects. In particular, it may convey to an individual certain calculable chances of having eonomic goods available or of acquiring them under certain conditions in the future. Obviously, the creation or protection of such chances is normally one of the aims of law enactment by those who agree upon a norm or impose it upon others. There are two ways in which such a "chance" may be attributed. The attribution may be a mere by-product of the empirical validity of the norm; in that case the norm is not *meant* to guarantee to an individual the chance which happens to fall to him. It may also be, however, that the norm is specifically meant to provide to the individual such a guaranty, in other words, to grant him a "right." Sociologically, the statement that someone has a right by virtue of the legal order of the state thus normally means the following: He has a chance, factually guaranteed to him by the consensually accepted interpretation of a legal norm, of invoking in favor of his ideal or material interests the aid of a "coercive apparatus" which is in special readiness for this purpose. This aid consists, at least normally, in the readiness of certain persons to come to his support in the event that they are approached in the proper way, and that it is shown that the recourse to such aid is actually guaranteed to him by a "legal norm." Such guaranty is based simply upon the "validity" of the legal proposition, and does not depend upon questions of expediency, discretion, grace, or arbitrary pleasure.

A law, thus, is valid wherever legal help in this sense can be obtained in a relevant measure, even though without recourse to physical or other drastic coercive means. A law can also be said to be valid, viz., in the case of unguaranteed law, if its violation, as, for instance, that of an electoral law, induces, on the ground of some empirically valid norm, legal consequences, for instance, the invalidation of the election, for the execution of which an agency with coercive powers has been established.

For purposes of simplification we shall pass by those "chances" which are produced as mere "by-products." A "right," in the context of the "state," is guaranteed by the coercive power of the political authorities. Wherever the means of coercion which constitute the guaranty of a "right" belong to some authority other than the political, for instance, a hierocracy, we shall speak of "extra-state law."

B. STATE LAW AND EXTRA-STATE LAW. A discussion of the various categories of such extra-state law would be out of place in the present context. All we need to recall is that there exist nonviolent means of coercion which may have the same or, under certain conditions, even greater effectiveness than the violent ones. Frequently, and in fairly large areas even regularly, the threat of such measures as the exclusion from an organization, or a boycott, or the prospect of magically conditioned advantages or disadvantages in this world, or of reward and punishment in the next, are under certain cultural conditions more effective in producing a certain behavior than a political apparatus whose coercive functioning is not always predictable with certainty. Legal forcible coercion exercised by the coercive apparatus of the political community has often come off badly as compared with the coercive power of other, e.g., religious, authorities. In general, the actual scope of its efficiency depends on the circumstances of each concrete case. Within the realm of sociological reality, legal coercion continues to exist, however, as long as some socially *relevant* effects are produced by its power machinery.

The assumption that a state "exists" only if the coercive means of the political community are superior to *all* other communities, is not sociological. "Ecclesiastical law" is still law even where it comes into conflict with "state" law, as it has happened many times and as it is bound to happen again in the case of the relations between the modern state and certain churches, for instance, the Roman-Catholic. In imperial Austria, the Slavic *Zadruga* not only lacked any kind of legal guaranty by the state, but some of its norms were outright contradictory to the official law. Since the consensual action constituting a *Zadruga* has at its disposal its own coercive apparatus for the enforcement of its norms, these norms are to be considered as "law." Only the state, if invoked, would refuse recognition and proceed, through its coercive power, to break it up.

Outside the sphere of the European-Continental legal system, it is no rare occurrence at all that modern state law explicitly treats as "valid" the norms of other organizations and reviews their concrete decisions. American law thus protects labor union labels or regulates the conditions under which a candidate is to be regarded as validly nominated by a party. English judges intervene, on appeal, in the judicial proceedings of a club. Even on the Continent German judges investigate, in defamation cases, the propriety of the rejection of a challenge to a duel, even though duelling is forbidden by law. We shall not enter into a casuistic inquiry of the extent to which such norms thus become "state law." For all the reasons given above and, in particular, for the sake of terminological consistency, we categorically deny that "law" exists only where legal coercion is guaranteed by the political authority. For us, there is no practical reason for such a terminology. A "legal order" shall rather be said to exist wherever coercive means, of a physical or psychological kind, are available; i.e., wherever they are at the disposal of one or more persons who hold themselves ready to use them for this purpose in the case of certain events; in other words, wherever we find a consociation specifically dedicated to the purpose of "legal coercion." The possession of such an apparatus for the exercise of physical coercion has not always been the monopoly of the political community. As far as psychological coercion is concerned, there is no such monopoly even today, as demonstrated by the importance of law guaranteed only by the church.

We have also indicated already that direct guaranty of law and of rights by a coercive apparatus constitutes only one instance of the existence of "law" and of "rights." Even within this limited sphere the coercive apparatus can take on a great variety of forms. In marginal cases, it may consist in the consensually valid chance of coercive intervention by *all* the members of the community in the event of an infringement of a valid norm. However, in that case one cannot properly speak of a "coercive apparatus" unless the conditions under which participation in such coercive intervention is to be obligatory, are firmly fixed. In those cases where the protection of rights is guaranteed by the organs of the political authority, the coercive apparatus may be reinforced by pressure groups: the strict regulations of associations of creditors and landlords, especially their blacklists of unreliable debtors or tenants, often operate more effectively than the prospect of a lawsuit. It goes without saying that this kind of coercion may be extended to claims which the state does not guarantee at all; such claims are nevertheless based on *rights* even though they are guaranteed by authorities other than the state. The law of the state often tries to obstruct the coercive means of other associations; the English Libel Act thus tries to preclude blacklisting by excluding the defense of truth. But the state is not always successful. There are groups stronger than the state in this respect, for instance, those status groups which rely on the "honor code" of the duel as the means of resolving conflicts. With courts of honor and boycott as the coercive means at their disposal, they usually succeed in compelling the fulfillment of obligations as "debts of honor," for instance, gambling debts or the duty to engage in a duel; such debts are intrinsically connected with the specific purposes of the group in question, but, as far as the state is concerned, they are not recognized, or are even proscribed. But the state has been forced, as least partially, to trim its sails.

It would indeed be distorted legal reasoning to demand that such a specific delict as duelling be punished as "attempted murder" or assault and battery. Those crimes are of a quite different character. But it remains a fact that in Germany the readiness to participate in a duel is still a *legal* obligation imposed by the state upon its army officers even though the duel is expressly forbidden by the Criminal Code. The state itself has connected legal consequences with an officer's failure to comply with the honor code. Outside of the status group of army officers the situation is different, however. The typical means of statutory coercion applied by "private" organizations against refractory members is exclusion from the corporate body and its tangible or intangible advantages. In the professional organizations of physicians and lawyers as well as in social or political clubs, it is the *ultima ratio*. The modern political organization has to a large extent usurped the application of these measures of coercion. Thus, recourse to them has been denied to the physicians and lawyers in Germany; in England the state courts have been given jurisdiction to review, on appeal, exclusions from clubs; and in America the courts have power over political parties as well as the right of reviewing, on appeal, the legality of the use of a union label.

This conflict between the means of coercion of various organizations is as old as the law itself. In the past it has not always ended with the triumph of the coercive means of the political body, and even today this has not always been the outcome. A businessman, for instance, who has violated a cartel agreement, has no remedy against a systematic attempt to drive him out of business by underselling. Similarly, there is no protection against being blacklisted for having availed oneself of the plea of illegality of a contract in futures. In the Middle Ages the prohibitions of resorting to the ecclesiastical court contained in the statutes of certain merchants' guilds were clearly invalid from the point of view of canon law, but they persisted nonetheless.[4]

To a considerable extent the state must tolerate the coercive power of organizations even in cases where it is directed not only against members, but also against outsiders on whom the organization tries to impose its own norms. Illustrations are afforded by the efforts of cartels to force outsiders into membership, or by the measures taken by creditors' associations against debtors and tenants.

An important marginal case of coercively guaranteed law, in the sociological sense, is presented by that situation which may be regarded as the very opposite of that which is presented by the modern political communities as well as by those religious communities which apply their own "laws." In the modern communities the law is guaranteed by a "judge" or some other "organ" who is an impartial and disinterested umpire rather than a person who would be characterized by a special relationship with one or the other of the parties. In the situation which we have in mind the means of coercion are provided by those very persons who are linked to the party by close personal relationship, for example, as members of his kinship group. Just as war under modern international law, so under these conditions "vengeance" and "feud" are the only, or at least, the normal, forms of law enforcement. In this case, the "right" of the individual consists, sociologically seen, in the mere probability that the members of his kinship group will respond to their obligation of supporting his feud and blood vengeance (an obligation originally guaranteed by fear of the wrath of supernatural authorities) and that they will possess strength sufficient to support the right claimed by him even though not necessarily to achieve its final triumph.

The term "legal relationship" will be applied to designate that situation in which the content of a right is constituted by a relationship, i.e., the actual or potential actions of concrete persons or of persons to be identified by concrete criteria. The rights contained in a legal relationship may vary in accordance with the actually occurring actions. In this sense a state can be designated as a legal relationship, even in the hypothetical marginal case in which the ruler alone is regarded as endowed with rights (the right to give orders) and where, accordingly, the opportunities of all the other individuals are reduced to reflexes of his regulations.

2. *Law, Convention, and Custom*[5]

A. SIGNIFICANCE OF CUSTOM IN THE FORMATION OF LAW. Law, convention, and custom belong to the same continuum with imperceptible transitions leading from one to the other. We shall define *custom* (*Sitte*) to mean a typically uniform activity which is kept on the beaten track simply because men are "accustomed" to it and persist in it by unreflective imitation. It is a collective way of acting (*Massenhandeln*), the perpetuation of which by the individual is not "required" in any sense by anyone.

Convention, on the other hand, shall be said to exist wherever a certain conduct is sought to be induced without, however, any coercion, physical or psychological, and, at least under normal circumstances, without any direct reaction other than the expression of approval or disapproval on the part of those persons who constitute the environment of the actor.

"Convention" must be strictly distinguished from *customary law*. We shall abstain here from criticizing this not very useful concept.[6] According to the usual terminology, the validity of a norm as customary law consists in the very likelihood that a coercive apparatus will go into action for its enforcement although it derives from mere consensus rather than from enactment. Convention, on the contrary, is characterized by the very absence of any coercive apparatus, i.e., of any, at least relatively clearly delimited, group of persons who would continuously hold themselves ready for the special task of legal coercion through physical or psychological means.

The existence of a mere custom, even unaccompanied by convention, can be of far-reaching economic signifiance. The level of economic need, which constitutes the basis of all "economic activity," is comprehensively conditioned by mere custom. The individual might free himself of it without arousing the slightest disapproval. In fact, however, he cannot escape from it except with the greatest difficulty, and it does not change except where it comes gradually to give way to the imitation of the different custom of some other social group.

We shall see[7] that the uniformity of mere usages can be of importance in the formation of social groups and in facilitating intermarriage. It may also give a certain, though rather intangible, impetus toward the formation of feelings of "ethnic" identification and, in that way, contribute to the creation of community. At any rate, adherence to what has as such become customary is such a strong component of all conduct and, consequently, of all social action, that legal coercion, where it transforms a custom into a legal obligation (by invocation of the "usual") often adds practically nothing to its effectiveness, and, where it opposes custom, frequently fails in the attempt to influence actual conduct. Convention is equally effective, if not even more. In countless situations the individual depends on his environment for a spontaneous response not guaranteed by any earthly or transcendental authority. The existence of a "convention" may thus be far more determinative of his conduct than the existence of legal enforcement machinery.

Obviously, the borderline between custom and convention is fluid. The further we go back in history, the more we find that conduct, and particularly social action, is determined in an ever more comprehensive sphere exclusively by orientation to what is customary. The more this is so, the more disquieting are the effects of any deviation from the customary. In this situation, any such deviation seems to act on the psyche of the average individual like the disturbance of an organic function. This, in turn, seems to reinforce custom.

Present ethnological literature does not allow us to determine very clearly the point of transition from the stage of mere custom to the, at first vaguely and dimly experienced, "consensual" character of social action, or, in other words, to the conception of the binding nature of certain accustomed modes of conduct. Even less can we trace the changes of the scope of activities with respect to which this transition took place. We shall thus by-pass this problem. It is entirely a question of terminology and convenience at which point of this continuum one shall assume the existence of the subjective conception of a "legal obligation." Objectively the chance of the factual occurrence of a violent reaction against certain types of conduct has always been present among human beings as well as among animals. It would be far-fetched, however, to assume in every such case the existence of a consensually valid norm, or that the action in question would be directed by a clearly conceived conscious purpose. Perhaps, a rudimentary conception of "duty" may be determinative in the behavior of some domestic animals to a greater extent than may be found in aboriginal man, if we may use this highly ambiguous concept in what is in this context a clearly intelligible sense. We have no access, however, to the "subjective" experiences of the first *homo sapiens* and such concepts as the allegedly primordial, or even *a priori,* character of law or convention are of no use whatsoever to empirical sociology. It is not due to the assumed binding force of some rule or norm that the conduct of primitive man manifests certain external factual regularities, especially in his relation to his fellows. On the contrary, those organically conditioned regularities which we have to accept as psychophysical reality, are primary. It is from them that the concept of "natural norms" arises. The inner orientation towards such regularities contains in itself very tangible inhibitions against "innovations," a fact which can be observed even today by everyone in his daily experiences, and it constitutes a strong support for the belief in such binding norms.

    B. CHANGE THROUGH INSPIRATION AND EMPATHY. In view of such observation we must ask how anything new can ever arise in this world, oriented as it is toward the regular as the empirically valid. No doubt innovations have been induced from the outside, i.e., by changes in the external conditions of life. But the response evoked by external change may be the extinction of life as well as its reorientation; there is no way of foretelling. Furthermore, external change is by no means a necessary precondition for innovation: in some of the most significant cases, it has not even been a contributing factor in the establishment of a new order. The evidence of ethnology seems rather to show that the most important source of innovation has been the influence of individuals who have experienced certain "abnormal" states (which are frequently, but not always, regarded by present-day psychiatry as pathological) and hence have been capable of exercising a special influence on others. We are not discussing here the origin of these experiences which appear to be "new" as a consequence of their "abnormality," but rather their effects. These influences which overcome the inertia of the customary may originate from a variety of psychological occurrences. To Hellpach[8] we owe the distinction between two categories which, despite the possibility of intermediate forms, nonetheless appear as polar types. The first, inspiration, consists in the sudden awakening, through drastic means, of the awareness that a certain action "ought" to be done by him who has this experience. In the other form, that of empathy or identification, the influencing person's attitude is emphatically experienced by one or more others. The types of action which are produced in these ways may vary greatly. Very often, however, a collective action (*massenhaftes Gemein-schaftshandeln*) is induced which is oriented toward the influencing person and his experience and from which, in turn, certain kinds of consensus with corresponding contents may be developed. If they are "adapted" to the external environment, they will survive. The effects of "empathy" and, even more so, of "inspiration" (usually lumped together under the ambiguous term "suggestion") constitute the major sources for the realization of actual innovations whose establishment as regularities will, in turn, reinforce the sense of "oughtness," by which they may possibly be accompanied. The feeling of oughtness—as soon as it has developed any conceptual meaning—may undoubtedly appear as something primary and original even in the case of innovation. Particularly in the case of "inspiration" it may constitute a psychological component. It is confusing, however, when imitation of new conduct is regarded as the basic and primary element in its diffusion. Undoubtedly, imitation is of extraordinary importance, but as a general rule it is secondary and constitutes only a special case. If the conduct of a dog, man's oldest companion, is "inspired" by man, such conduct, obviously, cannot be described as "imitation of man by dog." In a very large number of cases, the relation between the persons influencing and those influenced is exactly of this kind. In some cases, it may approximate "empathy," in others, "imitation," conditioned either by rational purpose or in the ways of "mass psychology."

In any case, however, the emerging innovation is most likely to produce consensus and ultimately law, when it derives from a strong inspiration or an intensive identification. In such cases a convention will result or, under certain circumstances, even consensual coercive action against deviants. As long as religious faith is strong, convention, the approval or disapproval by the environment, engenders, as historical experience shows, the hope and faith that the supernatural powers too will reward or punish those actions which are approved or disapproved in this world. Convention, under appropriate conditions, may also produce the further belief that not only the actor himself but also those around him may have to suffer from the wrath of those supernatural powers, and that, therefore, reaction is incumbent upon all, acting either individually or through the coercive apparatus of some organization. In consequence of the constant recurrence of a certain pattern of conduct, the idea may arise in the minds of the guarantors of a particular norm, that they are confronted no longer with mere custom or convention, but with a legal obligation requiring enforcement. A norm which has attained such practical validity is called customary law. Eventually, the interests involved may engender a rationally considered desire to secure the convention, or the obligation of customary law, against subversion, and to place it explicitly under the guarantee of an enforcement machinery, i.e., to transform it into enacted law. Particularly in the field of the internal distribution of power among the organs of an institutional order experience reveals a continuous scale of transitions from norms of conduct guaranteed by mere convention to those which are regarded as binding and guaranteed by law. A striking example is presented by the development of the British "constitution."

C. BORDERLINE ZONES BETWEEN CONVENTION, CUSTOM AND LAW. Finally, any rebellion against convention may lead the environment to make use of its coercively guaranteed rights in a manner detrimental to the rebel; for instance, the host uses his right as master of the house against the guest who has merely infringed upon the conventional rules of social amenity; or a war lord uses his legal power of dismissal against the officer who has infringed upon the code of honor. In such cases the conventional rule is, in fact, indirectly supported by coercive means. The situation differs from that of "unguaranteed" law insofar as the initiation of the coercive measures is a factual, but not a legal, consequence of the infringement of the convention, although the legal right to exclude anyone from his house belongs to the master as such. But a directly unguaranteed legal proposition draws its validity from the fact that its violation engenders consequences somehow *via* a guaranteed legal norm. Where, on the other hand, a legal norm refers to "good morals" (*die guten Sitten*),[9] i.e., conventions worthy of approval, the fulfillment of the conventional obligations has also become a legal obligation and we have a case of indirectly guaranteed law.

There are also numerous instances of intermediate types, as, for example, the courts of love of the Troubadours of Provence which had "jurisdiction" in matters of love;[10] or the "judge" in his original role as arbitrator seeking to procure a settlement between feuding antagonists, perhaps also rendering a verdict, but lacking coercive powers of his own; or, finally, modern international courts of arbitration. In such cases, the amorphous approval or disapproval of the environment has crystallized into a set of commands, prohibitions, and permissions authoritatively promulgated, i.e., a concretely organized pattern of psychic coercion. Excepting situations of mere play, as, for instance, the courts of love, such cases may be classified as "law" provided the judgment is normally backed not only by the personal, and therefore irrelevant, opinion of the judge, but by, at least, some boycott as self-help of the kinship group, the state, or some other group of persons whose right has been violated, as in the last two of the illustrations above.

According to our definition, the fact that some type of conduct is "approved" or "disapproved" by ever so many persons is insufficient to constitute it as a "convention"; it is essential that such attitudes are likely to find expression in a specific environment. This latter term is, of course, not meant in any geographical sense. But there must be some test for defining that group of persons which constitutes the environment of the person in question. It does not matter in this context whether the test is constituted by profession, kinship, neighborhood, status group, ethnic group, religion, political allegiance, or anything else. Nor does it matter that the membership is changeable or unstable. For the existence of a convention in our sense it is not required that the environment be constituted by an organization (as we understand that term). The very opposite is frequently the case. But the validity of law, presupposing, as we have seen, the existence of an enforcement machinery, is necessarily a corollary of organizational action. (Of course, this does not mean that only organizational action—or even mere social action—is legally regulated by organization.) In this sense the organization may be said to be the "sustainer" of the law.

On the other hand, we are far from asserting that legal rules, in the sense here used, would offer the only standard of subjective orientation for social, consensual, rationally controlled, organizational or institutional action, which, we must remember, is nothing but a segment of sociologically relevant conduct in general. If the order of an organization is understood to be characteristic of, or indispensable to, the actual course of social action, then this order is only to a small extent the result of an orientation toward legal rules. To the extent that the regularities are consciously oriented towards rules at all and do not merely spring from unreflective habituation, they are of the nature of "custom" and "convention"; often they are predominantly rational maxims of purposeful self-interested action, on the effective operation of which each participant is counting for his own conduct as well as that of all others. This expectation is, indeed, justified objectively, especially since the maxim, though lacking legal guaranties, often constitutes the subject matter of some association or consensus. The chance of legal coercion which, as already mentioned, motivates even "legal" conduct only to a slight extent, is also objectively an ultimate guaranty for no more than a fraction of the actual course of consensually oriented conduct.

It should thus be clear that, from the point of view of sociology, the transitions from mere usage to convention and from it to law are fluid.

3. Excursus *in Response to Rudolf Stammler*

Even from a non-sociological point of view it is wrong to distinguish between law and ethics by asserting that legal norms regulate mere external conduct, while moral norms regulate only matters of conscience. The law, it is true, does not always regard the intention of an action as relevant, and there have been legal propositions and legal systems in which legal consequences, including even punishment, are merely determined by external events. But this situation is not the normal one. Legal consequences attach to *bona* or *mala fides,* or intention, or moral turpitude, and a good many other purely subjective factors. Moral commandments, on the other hand, are aiming at overcoming in external conduct those anti-normative impulses which form part of the "mental attitude."

From the normative point of view we should thus distinguish between the two phenomena not as external and subjective, but as representing different degrees of normativeness.

From the sociological point of view, however, ethical validity is normally identical with validity "on religious grounds" or "by virtue of convention." Only an abstract standard of conduct subjectively conceived as derived from ultimate axioms could be regarded as an exclusively ethical norm, and this only in so far as this conception would acquire practical significance in conduct. Such conceptions have in fact often had real significance. But wherever this has been the case, they have been a relatively late product of philosophical reflection. In the past, as well as in the present, "moral commandments" in contrast to legal commands are, from a sociological point of view, normally either religiously or conventionally conditioned maxims of conduct. They are not distinguished from law by hard and fast criteria. There is no socially important moral commandment which has not been a legal command at one time or another.

Stammler's distinction between convention and legal norm according to whether or not the fulfillment of the norm is dependent upon the free will of the individual[11] is of no use whatsoever. It is incorrect to say that the fulfillment of conventional "obligations," for instance of a rule of social etiquette, is not "imposed" on the individual, and that its non-fulfillment would simply result in, or coincide with, the free and voluntary separation from a voluntary consociation. It may be admitted that there are norms of this kind, but they exist not only in the sphere of convention, but equally in that of law. The *clausula rebus sic stantibus* in fact often lends itself to such use. At any rate, the distinction between conventional rule and legal norm in Stammler's own sociology is not centered on this test. Not only the theoretically constructed anarchical society, the "theory" and "critique" of which Stammler has elaborated with the aid of his scholastic concepts, but also a good number of consociations existing in the real world have dispensed with the legal character of their conventional norms. They have done so on the assumption that the mere fact of the social disapproval of norm infringement with its, often very real, indirect consequences will suffice as a sanction. From the sociological point of view, legal order and conventional order do thus not constitute any basic contrast, since, quite apart from obvious cases of transition, convention, too, is sustained by psychological as well as (at least indirectly) physical coercion. It is only with regard to the sociological *structure* of coercion that they differ: The conventional order lacks specialized personnel for the implementation of coercive power (enforcement machinery: priests, judges, police, the military, etc.).

Above all, Stammler confuses the ideal validity of a norm with the assumed validity of a norm in its actual influence on empirical action. The former can be deduced systematically by legal theorists and moral philosophers; the latter, instead, ought to be the subject of empirical observation. Furthermore, Stammler confuses the normative regulation of conduct by rules whose "oughtness" is factually accepted by a sizable number of persons, with the factual regularities of human conduct. These two concepts are to be strictly separated, however.

It is by way of conventional rules that merely factual regularities of action, i.e., usages, are frequently transformed into binding norms, guaranteed primarily by psychological coercion. Convention thus makes tradition. The mere fact of the regular recurrence of certain events somehow confers on them the dignity of oughtness. This is true with regard to natural events as well as to action conditioned organically or by unreflective imitation of, or adaptation to, external conditions of life. It applies to the accustomed course of the stars as ordained by the divine powers, as well as to the seasonal floods of the Nile or the accustomed way of remunerating slave laborers, who by the law are unconditionally surrendered to the power of their masters.

Whenever the regularities of action have become conventionalized, i.e., whenever a statistically frequent action (*Massenhandeln*) has become a consensually oriented action (*Einverständnishandeln*)—this is, in our terminology, the real meaning of this development—we shall speak of "tradition."

It cannot be overstressed that the mere habituation to a mode of action, the inclination to preserve this habituation, and, much more so, tradition, have a formidable influence in favor of a habituated legal order, even where such an order originally derives from legal enactment. This influence is more powerful than any reflection on impending means of coercion or other consequences, considering also the fact that at least some of those who act according to the "norms" are totally unaware of them.

The transition from the merely unreflective formation of a habit to the conscious acceptance of the maxim that action should be in accordance with a norm is always fluid. The mere statistical regularity of an action leads to the emergence of moral and legal convictions with corresponding contents. The threat of physical and psychologial coercion, on the other hand, imposes a certain mode of action and thus produces habituation and thereby regularity of action.

Law and convention are intertwined as cause and effect in the actions of men, with, against, and beside, one another. It is grossly misleading to consider law and convention as the "forms" of conduct in contrast with its "substance" as Stammler does. The belief in the legal or conventional oughtness of a certain action is, from a sociological point of view, merely a superadditum increasing the degree of probability with which an acting person can calculate certain *consequences* of his action. Economic theory therefore properly disregards the character of the norms to some extent. For the economist the fact that someone "possesses" something simply means that he can count on other persons not to interfere with his disposition over the object. This mutual respect of the right of disposition may be based on a variety of considerations. It may derive from deference to conventional or legal norms, or from considerations of self-interest on the part of each participant. Whatever the reason, it is of no primary concern to economic theory. The fact that a person "owes" something to another can be translated, sociologically, into the following terms: a certain commitment (through promise, tort, or other cause) of one person to another; the expectation, based thereon, that in due course the former will yield to the latter his right of disposition over the goods concerned; the existence of a chance that this expectation will be fulfilled. The psychological motives involved are of no primary interest to the economist.

An exchange of goods means: the transfer of an object, according to an agreement, from the factual control of one person to that of another, this transfer being based on the assumption that another object is to be transferred from the factual control of the second to that of the first. Of those who take part in a debtor-creditor relationship or in a barter, each one expects that the other will conform to his own intentions. It is not necessary, however, to assume conceptually any "order" outside or above the two parties to guarantee, command, or enforce compliance by means of coercive machinery or social disapproval. Nor is it necessary to assume the subjetive belief of either or both parties in any "binding" norm. For the partner to an exchange can depend on the other partner's *egoistic interest* in the future continuation of exchange relationships or other similar motives to offset his inclination to break his promise—a fact which appears tangibly in the so-called "silent trade" among primitive peoples as well as in modern business, especially on the stock exchange.

Assuming purely expediential rationality, each participant can and does, in fact, depend on the probability that under normal circumstances the other party will act "as if" he accepted as "binding" the norm that one has to fulfill his promises. Conceptually this is quite sufficient. But it goes without saying that it makes a difference whether the partner's expectation in this respect is supported by one or both of the following guaranties: 1. the factually wide currency, in the environment, of the subjective belief in the objective validity of such a norm (consensus); 2. even more so, the creation of a conventional guaranty through regard for social approval or disapproval, or of a legal guaranty through the existence of enforcement machinery.

Can it be said that a stable private economic system of the modern type would be "unthinkable" without legal guaranties? As a matter of fact we see that in most business transactions it never occurs to anyone even to think of taking legal action. Agreements on the stock exchange, for example, take place between professional traders in such forms as in the vast majority of cases exclude "proof" in cases of bad faith: the contracts are oral, or are recorded by marks and notations in the trader's own notebook. Nevertheless, a dispute practically never occurs. Likewise, there are organizations pursuing purely economic ends the rules of which nonetheless dispense entirely, or almost entirely, with legal protection from the state. Certain types of "cartels" were illustrative of this class of organization. It often happened also that agreements which had been concluded and were valid according to private law were rendered inoperative through the dissolution of the organization, as there was no longer a formally legitimated plaintiff. In these instances, the organization with its own coercive apparatus had a system of "law" which was totally lacking in the power of forcible legal coercion. Such coercion, at any rate, was available only so long as the organization was in existence. As a result of the peculiar subjective attitude of the participants, cartel contracts often had not even any effective conventional guarantee. However, they often functioned nonetheless for a long time and quite efficiently in consequence of the convergent interests of all the participants.

Despite all such facts, it is obvious that forcible legal guarantee, especially where exercised by the state, is not a matter of indifference to such organizations. Today economic exchange is quite overwhelmingly guaranteed by the threat of legal coercion. The normal intention in an act of exchange is to acquire certain subjective "rights," i.e., in sociological terms, the probability of support of one's power of disposition by the coercive apparatus of the state. Economic goods today are normally at the same time *legitimately acquired rights*; they are the very building material for the universe of the economic order. Nonetheless, even today they do not constitute the total range of objects of exchange.

Economic opportunities which are not guaranteed by the legal order, or the guaranty of which is even refused on grounds of policy by the legal order, can and do constitute objects of exchange transactions which are not only not illegitimate but perfectly legitimate. They include, for instance, the transfer, against compensation, of the goodwill of a business. The sale of a goodwill today normally engenders certain private law claims of the purchaser against the seller, namely, that he will refrain from certain actions and will perform certain others, for instance, "introduce" the purchaser to the customers. But the legal order does not enforce the claims against third parties. Yet, there have been and still are cases in which the coercive apparatus of the political authority is available for the exercise of direct coercion in favor of the owner or purchaser of a "market," as for instance in the case of a guild monopoly or some other legally protected monopoly. It is well known that Fichte[12] considered it as the essential characteristic of modern legal development that, in contrast to such cases, the modern state guarantees only claims on concrete usable goods or labor services. Besides, so-called "free competition" finds its legal expression in this very fact. Yet, although such "opportunities" have remained objects of economic exchange even without legal protection against third parties, the absence of legal guaranties has nevertheless far-reaching economic consequences. But from the point of view of economics and sociology it remains a fact that, on general principle, at least, the interference of legal guaranties merely increases the degree of certainty with which an economically relevant action can be calculated in advance.

The legal regulation of a subject matter has never been carried out in all its implications anywhere. This would require the availability of some human agency which in every case of the kind in question would be regarded as being capable of determining, in accordance with some conceived norm, what ought to be done "by law." We shall by-pass here the interaction between consociation and legal order: as we have seen elsewhere, any rational consociation, and therefore, any order of social and consensual action is posterior in this respect. Nor shall we discuss here the proposition that the development of social and consensual action continually creates entirely new situations and raises problems which can be solved by the accepted norms or by the usual logic of jurisprudence only in appearance or by spurious reasoning (cf. in this respect the thesis of the "free-law" movement).

We are concerned here with a more basic problem: It is a fact that the most "fundamental" questions often are left unregulated by law even in legal orders which are otherwise thoroughly rationalized. Let us illustrate two specific types of this phenomenon:

(1) A "constitutional" monarch dismisses his responsible minister and fails to replace him by any new appointee so that there is no one to countersign his acts. What is to be done "by law" in such a situation? This question is not regulated in any constitution anywhere in the world. What is clear is no more than that certain acts of the government cannot be "validly" taken.

(2) Most constitutions equally omit consideration of the following question: What is to be done when those parties whose agreement is necessary for the adoption of the budget are unable to reach an agreement?

The first problem is described by Jellinek as "moot" for all practical purposes.[13] He is right. What is of interest to us is just to know why it is "moot." The second type of "constitutional gap," on the other hand, has become very practical, as is well known.[14] If we understand "constitution," in the sociological sense, as the modus of distribution of power which determines the possibility of regulating social action, we may, indeed, venture the proposition that any community's constitution *in the sociological sense* is determined by the fact of where and how its constitution *in the juridical sense* contains such "gaps," especially with regard to basic questions. At times such gaps of the second type have been left intentionally where a constitution was rationally enacted by consensus or imposition. This was done simply because the interested party or parties who exercised the decisive influence on the drafting of the constitution in question expected that he or they would ultimately have sufficient power to control, in accordance with their own desires, that portion of social action which, while lacking a basis in any enacted norm, yet had to be carried on somehow. Returning to our illustration: they expected to govern without a budget.

Gaps of the first type mentioned above, on the other hand, usually remain open for another reason: Experience seems to teach convincingly that the self-interest of the party or parties concerned (in our example, of the monarch) will at all times suffice so to condition his way of acting that the "absurd" though legally possible situation (in our example, the lack of a responsible minister) will never occur. Despite the "gap," general consensus considers it as the unquestionable "duty" of the monarch to appoint a minister. As there are legal consequences attached to this duty, it is to be considered as an "indirectly guaranteed legal obligation." Such ensuing legal consequences are: the impossibility of executing certain acts in a valid manner, i.e., of attaining the possibility of having them guaranteed through the coercive apparatus. But for the rest, it is not established, either by law or convention, what is to be done to carry on the administration of the state in case the ruler should not fulfill this duty; and since this case has never occurred thus far, there is no custom either which could become the source for a decision. This situation constitutes a striking illustration of the fact that law, convention, and custom are by no means the only forces to be counted on as guarantee for such conduct of another person as is expected of, promised by, or otherwise regarded as due from, him. Beside and above these, there is another force to be reckoned with: the other person's self-interest in the continuation of a certain consensual action as such. The certainty with which the monarch's compliance with an assumedly binding duty can be anticipated is no doubt greater, but only by a matter of degree, than the certainty— if we may return now to our previous example—with which a partner to an exchange counts, and in the case of continued intercourse, may continue to count, upon the other party's conduct to conform with his own expectations. This certainty exists even though the transaction in question may lack any normative regulation or coercive guaranty.

What is relevant here is merely the observation that the legal as well as the conventional regulation of consensual or rationally regulated action may be, as a matter of principle, incomplete and, under certain circumstances, will be so quite consciously. While the orientation of social action to a norm is constitutive of consociation in any and every case, the coercive apparatus does not have this function with regard to the totality of all stable and institutionally organizational action. If the absurd case of illustration (1) were to occur, it would certainly set legal speculation to work immediately and then perhaps,.a conventional, or even legal, regulation would come into existence. But in the meantime the problem would already have been actually solved by some social or consensual or rationally regulated action the details of which would depend upon the nature of the concrete situation. Normative regulation is one important causal component of consensual action, but it is not, as claimed by Stammler, its universal "form."

For a discipline such as sociology, which searches for empirical regularities and types, the legal guarantees and their underlying normative conceptions are of interest both as consequences and as causes or concomitant causes of certain regularities of human action which are as such directly relevant to sociology, or of regularities of natural occurrences engendered by human action which as such are indirectly relevant to sociology.

Factual regularities *of* conduct ("customs") can, as we have seen, become the source of rules *for* conduct ("conventions," "law"). The reverse, however, may be equally true. Regularities may be produced by legal norms, acting by themselves or in combination with other factors. This applies not only to those regularities which directly realize the content of the legal norm in question, but equally to regularities of a different kind. The fact that an official, for example, goes to his office regularly every day is a direct consequence of the order contained in a legal norm which is accepted as "valid" in practice. On the other hand, the fact that a traveling salesman of a factory visits the retailers regularly each year for the solicitation of orders is only an indirect effect of legal norms, viz., of those which permit free competition for customers and thus necessitate that they be wooed. The fact that fewer children die when nursing mothers abstain from work as a result of a legal or conventional "norm" is certainly a consequence of the validity of that norm. Where it is an enacted legal norm, this result has certainly been one of the rationally conceived ends of the creators of that norm; but it is obvious that they can decree only the abstention from work and not the lower death rate. Even with regard to directly commanded or prohibited conduct, the practical effectiveness of the validity of a coercive norm is obviously problematic. Observance follows to an "adequate" degree, but never without exceptions. Powerful interests may indeed induce a situation in which a legal norm is violated, without ensuing punishment, not only in isolated instances, but prevalently and permanently, in spite of the coercive apparatus on which the "validity" of the norm is founded. When such a situation has become stabilized and when, accordingly, prevailing practice rather than the pretense of the written law has become normative of conduct in the conviction of the participants, the guaranteeing coercive power will ultimately cease to compel conduct to conform to the latter. In such case, the legal theorist speaks of "derogation through customary law."

"Valid" legal norms, which are guaranteed by the coercive apparatus of the political authority, and conventional rules may also coexist, however, in a state of chronic conflict. We have observed such a situation in the case of the duel, where private revenge has been transformed by convention. And while it is not at all unusual that legal norms are rationally enacted with the purpose of changing existing "customs" and conventions, the normal development is more usually as follows: a legal order is empirically "valid" owing not so much to the availability of coercive guaranties as to its habituation as "usage" and its "routinization." To this should be added the pressure of convention which, in most cases, disapproves any flagrant deviation from conduct corresponding to that order.

For the legal theorist the (ideological) validity of a legal norm is conceptually the *prius*. Conduct which is not directly regulated by law is regarded by him as legally "permitted" and thus equally affected by the legal order, at least ideologically. For the sociologist, on the other hand, the legal, and particularly the rationally enacted, regulation of conduct is empirically only one of the factors motivating social action; moreover, it is a factor which usually appears late in history and whose effectiveness varies greatly. The beginnings of actual regularity and "usage," shrouded in darkness everywhere, are attributed by the sociologist, as we have seen, to the instinctive habituation of a pattern of conduct which was "adapted" to given necessities. At least initially, this pattern of conduct was neither conditioned nor changed by an enacted norm. The increasing intervention of enacted norms is, from our point of view, only one of the components, however characteristic, of that process of rationalization and association whose growing penetration into all spheres of social action we shall have to trace as a most essential dynamic factor in development.

4. *Summary of the Most General Relations Between Law and Economy*

In sum, we can say about the most general relationships between law and economy, which alone concern us here, the following:

(1) Law (in the sociological sense) guarantees by no means only economic interests but rather the most diverse interests ranging from the most elementary one of protection of personal security to such purely ideal goods as personal honor or the honor of the divine powers. Above all, it guarantees political, ecclesiastical, familial, and other positions of authority as well as positions of social preëminence of any kind which may indeed be economically conditioned or economically relevant in the most diverse ways, but which are neither economic in themselves nor sought for preponderantly economic ends.

(2) Under certain conditions a "legal order" can remain unchanged

while economic relations are undergoing a radical transformation. In theory, a socialist system of production could be brought about without the change of even a single paragraph of our laws, simply by the gradual, free contractual acquisition of all the means of production by the political authority. This example is extreme; but, for the purpose of theoretical speculation, extreme examples are most useful. Should such a situation ever come about—which is most unlikely, though theoretically not unthinkable—the legal order would still be bound to apply its coercive machinery in case its aid were invoked for the enforcement of those obligations which are characteristic of a productive system based on private property. Only, this case would never occur in fact.[15]

(3) The legal status of a matter may be basically different according to the point of view of the legal system from which it is considered. But such differences [of legal classification] need not have any relevant economic consequences provided only that on those points which generally are relevant economically, the *practical* effects are the same for the interested parties. This not only is possible, but it actually happens widely, although it must be conceded that any variation of legal classification may engender some economic consequences somewhere. Thus totally different forms of action would have been applicable in Rome depending on whether the "lease" of a mine were to be regarded legally as a lease in the strict sense of the term, or as a purchase. But the practical effects of the difference for economic life would certainly have been very slight.[16]

(4) Obviously, legal guaranties are directly at the service of economic interests to a very large extent. Even where this does not seem to be, or actually is not, the case, economic interests are among the strongest factors influencing the creation of law. For, any authority guaranteeing a legal order depends, in some way, upon the consensual action of the constitutive social groups, and the formation of social groups depends, to a large extent, upon constellations of material interests.

(5) Only a limited measure of success can be attained through the threat of coercion supporting the legal order. This applies especially to the economic sphere, owing to a number of external circumstances as well as to its own peculiar nature. It would be quibbling, however, to assert that law cannot "enforce" any particular economic conduct, on the ground that we would have to say, with regard to all its means of coercion, that *coactus tamen voluit* ("Although coerced, it was still his will.") For this is true, without exception, of all coercion which does not treat the person to be coerced simply as an inanimate object. Even the most drastic means of coercion and punishment are bound to fail where the subjects remain recalcitrant. In many spheres such a situation would always mean that the participants have not been educated to

acquiescence. Such education to acquiescence in the law of the time and place has, as a general rule, increased with growing pacification. Thus it should seem that the chances of enforcing economic conduct would have increased, too. Yet, the power of law over economic conduct has in many respects grown weaker rather than stronger as compared with earlier conditions. The effectiveness of maximum price regulations, for example, has always been precarious, but under present-day conditions they have an even smaller chance of success than ever before.

Thus the measure of possible influence on economic activity is not simply a function of the general level of acquiescence towards legal co-ercion. The limits of the actual success of legal coercion in the economic sphere rather arise from two main sources. One is constituted by the limitations of the economic capacity of the persons affected. There are limits not only to the stock itself of available goods, but also to the way in which that stock can possibly be used. For the patterns of use and of relationship among the various economic units are determined by habit and can be adjusted to heteronomous norms, if at all, only by difficult reorientations of all economic dispositions, and hardly without losses, which means, never without frictions. These difficulties increase with the degree of development and universality of a particular form of consensual action, namely, the interdependence of the individual economic units in the market, and, consequently, the dependence of every one upon the conduct of others. The second source of the limitation of successful legal coercion in the economic sphere lies in the relative proportion of strength of private economic interests on the one hand and interests promoting conformance to the rules of law on the other. The inclination to forego economic opportunity simply in order to act legally is obviously slight, unless circumvention of the formal law is strongly disapproved by a powerful convention, and such a situation is not likely to arise where the interests affected by a legal innovation are widespread. Besides, it is often not difficult to disguise the circumvention of a law in the economic sphere. Quite particularly insensitive to legal influence are, as experience has shown, those effects which derive directly from the ultimate sources of economic action, such as the estimates of economic value and the formation of prices. This applies particularly to those situations where the determinants in production and consumption do not lie within a com-pletely transparent and directly manageable complex of consensual con-duct. It is obvious, besides, that those who continuously operate in the market have a far greater rational knowledge of the market and interest situation than the legislators and enforcement officers whose interest is only formal. In an economy based on all-embracing interdependence on the market the possible and unintended repercussions of a legal measure must to a large extent escape the foresight of the legislator simply because they depend upon private interested parties. It is those private interested parties who are in a position to distort the intended meaning of a legal norm to the point of turning it into its very opposite, as has often happened in the past. In view of these difficulties, the extent of factual impact of the law on economic conduct cannot be determined generally, but must be calculated for each particular case. It belongs thus to the field of case studies in social economics. In general, no more can be asserted than that, from a purely theoretical point of view, the complete monopolization of a market, which entails a far greater perspicuity of the situation, technically facilitates the control by law of that particular sector of the economy. If it, nevertheless, does not always in fact increase the opportunities for such control, this result is usually due either to legal particularism arising from the existence of competing political associations, or to the power of the private interests amenable to the monopolistic control and thus resisting the enforcement of the law.

(6) From the purely theoretical point of view, legal guaranty *by the state* is not indispensable to any basic economic phenomenon. The protection of property, for example, can be provided by the mutual aid system of kinship groups. Creditors' rights have sometimes been protected more efficiently by a religious community's threat of excommunication than by political bodies. "Money," too, has existed in almost all of its forms, without the state's guaranty of its acceptability as a means of payment. Even "chartal" money, i.e., money which derives its character as means of payment from the marking of pieces rather than from their substantive content, is conceivable without the guaranty by the state. Occasionally chartal money of non-state origin appeared even in spite of the existence of an apparatus of legal coercion by the state: the ancient Babylonians, for instance, did not have "coins" in the sense of a means of payment constituting legal tender by proclamation of the political authority, but contracts were apparently in use under which payment was to be made in pieces of a fifth of a shekel designated as such by the stamp of a certain "firm" (as we would say).[17] There was thus lacking any guaranty "proclaimed" by the state; the chosen unit of value was derived, not from the state, but from private contract. Yet the means of payment was "chartal" in character, and the state guaranteed coercively the concrete deal.

Conceptually the "state" thus is not indispensable to any economic activity. But an economic system, especially of the modern type, could certainly not exist without a legal order with very special features which could not develop except in the frame of a public legal order. Present-day economic life rests on opportunities acquired through contracts. It is true, the private interests in the obligations of contract, and the common interest of all property holders in the mutual protection of property are still considerable, and individuals are still markedly influenced by convention and custom even today. Yet, the influence of these factors has declined due to the disintegration of tradition, i.e., of the tradition-determined relationships as well as of the belief in their sacredness. Furthermore, class interests have come to diverge more sharply from one another than ever before. The tempo of modern business communication requires a promptly and predictably functioning legal system, i.e., one which is guaranteed by the strongest coercive power. Finally, modern economic life by its very nature has destroyed those other associations which used to be the bearers of law and thus of legal guaranties. This has been the result of the development of the market. The universal predominance of the market consociation requires on the one hand a legal system the functioning of which is *calculable* in accordance with rational rules. On the other hand, the constant expansion of the market, which we shall get to know as an inherent tendency of the market consociation, has favored the monopolization and regulation of all "legitimate" coercive power by *one* universalist coercive institution through the disintegration of all particularist status-determined and other coercive structures which have been resting mainly on economic monopolies.

NOTES

Unless otherwise indicated, notes are by Rheinstein. For full references of works mentioned, see Sociology of Law, ch. VIII:*i*, n. 1.

1. Legal dogmatics (*dogmatische Rechtswissenschaft*)—the term frequently used in German to mean the legal science of the law itself as distinguished from such ways of looking upon law from the outside as philosophy, history, or sociology of law.

2. See now Part One, ch. I:5, but the reference is presumably to "Some Categories of Interpretive Sociology," *GAzW* 443. (R)

3. See *op. cit.*, 445, 447f., 466. (R)

4. Cf. below, ch. VIII:*v*:8.

5. This is an early formulation of the relationship between usage, custom, interest constellation, law and convention, repeated in Part I, sec. 4–6. (R)

6. Cf. below, ch. VIII:*iii*:1.

7. Cf. Part Two, ch. IV:2. (W)

8. Willy Hellpach (1877–1955), professor of medicine, known by his highly original investigations on the influence of meteorological and geographic phenomena upon the mind. See his "Die geistigen Epidemien," *Die Gesellschaft*, XI, 1906.

9. Cf. German Civil Code, Sec. 138: "A transaction which is contrary to good morals is void"; Sec. 826: "One who causes harm to another intentionally and in a manner which is against good morals, has to compensate the other for such harm."

10. The "courts of love" (*cours d'amour*) belonged to the amusements of polite society at the high period of chivalry and the troubadours (twelfth to thir-

teenth century). They are reported to have consisted of circles of ladies who were organized in the way of courts and rendered judgments and opinions in matters of courtly love and manners. They flourished in southern France, especially Provence, where they came to an end with the collapse of Provençal society in the "crusade" against the Albigensian heretics. In the late Middle Ages, a brilliant court of love is reported to have flourished for some years at the Burgundian court; cf. HUIZINGA, WANING OF THE MIDDLE AGES (1924), c. 8, p. 103. On the courts of love in general, see CAPEFIGUE, LES COURS D'AMOUR (1863); RAJNA, LE CORTI D'AMORE (1890); and the article by F. Bonnardot in 2 LA GRANDE ENCYCLOPÉDIE 805, with further literature.

11. Rudolf Stammler, *Wirtschaft und Recht nach der materialistischen Geschichtsauffassung* (1896), 12.

12. Joh. Gottlieb Fichte, *Der geschlossene Handelsstaat* (1800), Bk. I, c. 7.

13. GESETZ UND VERORDNUNG (1887) 295; VERFASSUNGSÄNDERUNG UND VERFASSUNGSWANDEL (1906) 43.

14. The situation arose in Prussia when the predominantly liberal Diet early in 1860 refused to pass Bismarck's budget because of its disapproval of his policy of armaments (so-called Era of Conflict or *Konfliktsperiode*). In Austria, too, Parliament (*Reichsrat*) repeatedly was unable to reach agreement on a budget during that period of conflict between the several ethnic groups of the Monarchy which preceded the outbreak of World War I.

15. The norms of the legal order existing before the total socialization took place could also be applied after its occurrence, if legal title to the various means of production were to be ascribed not to one single, central public authority but to formally autonomous public institutions or corporations which are to regulate their relationships to each other by contractual transactions, subject to the directions of, and control by, the central planning authority. Such a situation does indeed exist in the Soviet Union. Cf. H. J. BERMAN, JUSTICE IN RUSSIA (1950), and review by Rheinstein (1951) 64 HARV. L. REV. 1387.

16. Cf. in American law the controversy as to the correct legal classification of a mining or oil and gas lease: does the transaction create a profit a prendre, or does it give to the "lessee" the title to the minerals, or does it result in the creation of a leasehold interest in the strict sense of the term? As in Rome, the "proper" classification may be relevant in some practical respect as, for instance, with regard to the question of whether, in the case of the death of the lessee—if he should ever be an individual!—his interest descends as real, or is to be distributed as personal, property. In the former case it would, ordinarily, not be touched for the payment of debts of the deceased until all the personal property has been exhausted; in the latter, the "lease" would be immediately available for the creditors along with the other "personal" assets of the decedent. But, by and large, the economic situation is one and the same whichever of the various legal classifications is applied.

17. No reference to a practice of the kind mentioned could be located except the following passage in B. MAISSNER, BABYLONIEN UND ASSYRIEN (1920) 356: "As one could not generally rely upon the weight and fineness of the silver and thus had to check (*xâtu*), one preferred to receive silver bearing a stamp (*kanku*) by which the weight and fineness would be guaranteed. In contracts from the period of the first Babylonian dynasty we find shekels mentioned 'with a stamp'(?) of Babylon (Vorderasiatische Bibliothek VI, No. 217, 15) or shekels 'from the city of Zahan' or 'from Grossippar' (Brit. Mus. Cuneiform Tablets IV, 47, 19a)."

CHAPTER 11

THE ECONOMIC
RELATIONSHIPS OF
ORGANIZED GROUPS

1. Economic Action and Economically Active Groups

Most social groups engage in economic activities. Contrary to an unsuitable usage, we shall not consider every instrumental (*zweckrationale*) action as economic. Thus, praying for a spiritual good is not an economic act, even though it may have a definite purpose according to some religious doctrine. We also shall not include every economizing activity, neither intellectual economizing in concept formation nor an esthetic "economy of means"; artistic creations are often the highly unprofitable outcome of ever-renewed attempts at simplification. Just as little is the mere adherence to the technical maxim of the "optimum"—the relatively greatest result with the least expenditure of means—an economic act; rather, it is a matter of purpose-rational technique. We shall speak of economic action only if the satisfaction of a need depends, in the actor's judgment, upon relatively *scarce* resources and a *limited* number of possible actions, and if this state of affairs evokes specific reactions. Decisive for such rational action is, of course, the fact that this scarcity is *subjectively* presumed and that action is oriented to it.

We will not deal here with any detailed "casuistry" and terminology. However, we will distinguish two types of economic action: (1) The first is the satisfaction of one's own wants, which may be of any conceivable kind, ranging from food to religious edification, if there is a scarcity of goods and services in relation to demand. It is conventional to think particularly of everyday needs—the so-called material needs—when the term "economy" is used. However, prayers and masses too *may* become economic objects if the persons qualified to say them are in short supply and can only be secured for a price, just like the daily bread. Bushmen drawings, to which a high artistic value is often attributed, are not economic objects, not even products of labor in the economic sense, yet artistic products that are rated much lower become economic objects if they are relatively scarce. (2) The second type of economic action concerns profit-making by controlling and disposing of scarce goods.

Social action (*soziales Handeln*) may be related to the economy in diverse ways.[1]

Rationally controlled action (*Gesellschaftshandeln*) may be oriented, in the actor's eyes, to purely economic results—want satisfaction or profit-making. In this case an *"economic group"* comes into being. However, rationally controlled action may use economic operations as a means for achieving different goals. In this case we have a *"group with secondary economic interests"* (*wirtschaftende Gemeinschaft*). Social action may also combine economic and non-economic goals, or none of these cases may occur. The dividing line between groups with primary and secondary economic interests is fluid. Strictly speaking, the first state of affairs prevails only in those groups that strive for profit by taking advantage of scarcity conditions, that is, profit-making enterprises, for all groups oriented merely toward want satisfaction resort to economic action only so far as the relation of supply and demand makes it necessary. In this regard, there is no difference between the economic activities of a family, a charitable endowment, a military administration, or an association for joint forest clearing or hunting. To be sure, there seems to be a difference between social action that comes into being essentially for the sake of satisfying economic demands, as in the case of forest clearing, and action with goals (such as military training) that necessitates economic activities merely because of scarcity conditions. But in reality this distinction is very tenuous and can be clearly drawn only to the extent that social action would remain the same in the absence of any scarcity.

Social action that constitutes a group neither with primary nor secondary economic interests may in various respects be influenced by scarcity factors and to that extent be economically determined. Conversely, such action may also determine the nature and course of economic activities. Most of the time both influences are at work. Social action unrelated to either of the two groups is not unusual. Every joint walk may be an example. Groups that are economically unimportant are quite frequent. However, a special case of economically relevant groups consists of those whose norms regulate the economic behavior of the participants but whose organs do not continuously direct economic activities through immediate participation, concrete instructions or injunctions: These are *"regulatory groups."* They include all kinds of political and many religious groups, and numerous others, among them those associated specifically for the sake of economic regulation (such as cooperatives of fishermen or peasants).

As we have said, groups that are not somehow economically determined are extremely rare. However, the degree of this influence varies widely and, above all, the economic determination of social action is ambiguous—contrary to the assumption of so-called historical materialism. Phenomena that must be treated as constants in economic analysis are very often compatible with significant structural variations—from a sociological viewpoint—among the groups that comprise them or coexist with them, including groups with primary and secondary economic interests. Even the assertion that social structures and the economy are "functionally" related is a biased view, which cannot be justified as an historical generalization, if an unambiguous interdependence is assumed. For the forms of social action follow "laws of their own," as we shall see time and again, and even apart from this fact, they may in a given case always be co-determined by other than economic causes. However, at some point economic conditions tend to become causally important, and often decisive, for almost all social groups, at least those which have major cultural significance; conversely, the economy is usually also influenced by the autonomous structure of social action within which it exists. No significant generalization can be made as to when and how this will occur. However, we can generalize about the degree of elective affinity between concrete structures of social action and concrete forms of economic organization; that means, we can state in general terms whether they further or impede or exclude one another—whether they are "adequate" or "inadequate" in relation to one another. We will have to deal frequently with such relations of adequacy. Moreover, at least some generalization can be advanced about the manner in which economic interests tend to result in social action of a certain type.

2. *Open and Closed Economic Relationships*

One frequent economic determinant is the competition for a livelihood—offices, clients and other remunerative opportunities. When the number of competitors increases in relation to the profit span, the participants become interested in curbing competition. Usually one group of competitors takes some externally identifiable characteristic of another group of (actual or potential) competitors—race, language, religion, local or social origin, descent, residence, etc.—as a pretext for attempting their exlusion. It does not matter which characteristic is chosen in the individual case: whatever suggests itself most easily is seized upon. Such group action may provoke a corresponding reaction on the part of those against whom it is directed.

In spite of their continued competition against one another, the jointly acting competitors now form an "interest group" toward outsiders; there is a growing tendency to set up some kind of association with rational regulations; if the monopolistic interests persist, the time comes when the competitors, or another group whom they can influence (for example, a political community), establish a legal order that limits competition through formal monopolies; from then on, certain persons are available as "organs" to protect the monopolistic practices, if need be, with force. In such a case, the interest group has developed into a *"legally privileged group"* (*Rechtsgemeinschaft*) and the participants have become *"privileged members"* (*Rechtsgenossen*). Such closure, as we want to call it, is an ever-recurring process; it is the source of property in land as well as of all guild and other group monopolies.

The tendency toward the monopolization of specific, usually economic opportunities is always the driving force in such cases as: "co-operative organization," which always means closed monopolistic groups, for example, of fishermen taking their name from a certain fishing area; the establishment of an association of engineering graduates, which seeks to secure a legal, or at least factual, monopoly over certain positions;[2] the exclusion of outsiders from sharing in the fields and commons of a village; "patriotic" associations of shop clerks;[3] the *ministeriales,* knights, university graduates and craftsmen of a given region or locality; ex-soldiers entitled to civil service positions—all these groups first engage in some joint action (*Gemeinschaftshandeln*) and later perhaps an explicit association. This monopolization is directed against competitors who share some positive or negative characteristics; its purpose is always the closure of social and economic opportunities to *outsiders*. Its extent may vary widely, especially so far as the group member shares in the apportionment of monopolistic advantages. These may remain open to all monopoly holders, who can therefore freely compete with one another; witness the holders of occupational patents (graduates entitled to certain positions or master-craftsmen privileged with regard to customers and the employment of apprentices). However, such opportunities may also be "closed" to *insiders*. This can be done in various ways: (a) Positions may be rotated: the short-run appointment of some holders of office benefices had this purpose; (b) Grants may be revocable, such as the individual disposition over fields in a strictly organized rural commune, for example, the Russian *mir;*[4] (c) Grants may be for life, as is the rule for all prebends, offices, monopolies of master-craftsmen, rights in using the commons, and originally also for the apportionment of fields in most village communes; (d) The member and his heirs may get definite grants with the stipulation that they cannot be given to others or only to group members: witness the κλῆρος (the warrior prebend of Antiquity), the service fiefs of the *ministeriales,* and monopolies on hereditary offices and crafts; (e) Finally, only the number of shares may be limited, but the holder may freely dispose of his own without the knowledge or permission of the other group members, as in a stockholding company. These different stages of internal closure will be called stages in the *appropriation* of the social and economic opportunities that have been monopolized by the group.

If the appropriated monopolistic opportunities are released for exchange outside the group, thus becoming completely "free" property, the old monopolistic association is doomed. Its remnants are the appropriated powers of disposition which appear on the market as "acquired rights" of individuals. For all property in natural resources developed historically out of the gradual appropriation of the monopolistic shares of group members. In contrast to the present, not only concrete goods but also social and economic opportunities of all kinds were the object of appropriation. Of course, manner, degree, and ease of the appropriation vary widely with the technical nature of the object and of the opportunities, which may lend themselves to appropriation in very different degrees. For example, a person subsisting by, or gaining an income from, the cultivation of a given field is bound to a concrete and clearly delimited material object, but this is not the case with customers. Appropriation is not motivated by the fact that the object produces a yield only through amelioration, hence that to some extent it is the product of the user's labor, for this is even more true of an acquired clientele, although in a different manner; rather, customers cannot be "registered" as easily as real estate. It is quite natural that the extent of an appropriation depends upon such differences among objects. Here, however, we want to emphasize that the process is in principle the same in both cases, even though the pace of appropriation may vary: monopolized social and economic opportunities are "closed" even to insiders. Hence, groups differ in varying degrees with regard to external or internal "openness" or "closure."

3. Group Structures and Economic Interests: Monopolist versus Expansionist Tendencies

This monopolistic tendency takes on specific forms when groups are formed by persons with shared qualities *acquired* through upbringing, apprenticeship and training. These characteristics may be economic qualifications of some kind, the holding of the same or of similar offices, a knightly or ascetic way of life, etc. If in such a case an association results from social action, it tends toward the *guild*. Full members make a vocation out of monopolizing the disposition of spiritual, intellectual, social and economic goods, duties and positions. Only those are admitted to the unrestricted practice of the vocation who (1) have completed a novitiate in order to aquire the proper training, (2) have proven their qualification, and (3) sometimes have passed through further waiting periods and met additional requirements. This development follows a typical pattern in groups ranging from the juvenile student fraternities, through knightly associations and craft-guilds, to the qualifications required of the modern officials and employees. It is true that the interest in guaranteeing an efficient performance may everywhere have some importance; the participants may desire it for idealistic or materialistic reasons in spite of their possibly continuing competition with one another: local craftsmen may desire it for the sake of their business reputation, *ministeriales* and knights of a given association for the sake of their professional reputation and also their own military security, and ascetic groups for fear that the gods and demons may turn their wrath against all members because of faulty manipulations. (For example, in almost all primitive tribes, persons who sang falsely during a ritual dance were originally slain in expiation of such an offense.)[5] But normally this concern for efficient performance recedes behind the interest in limiting the supply of candidates for the benefices and honors of a given occupation. The novitiates, waiting periods, masterpieces and other demands, particularly the expensive entertainment of group members, are more often economic than professional tests of qualification.

Such monopolistic tendencies and similar economic considerations have often played a significant role in *impeding* the expansion of a group. For example, Attic democracy increasingly sought to limit the number of those who could share in the advantages of citizenship, and thus limited its own political expansion. The Quaker propaganda was brought to a standstill by an ultimately similar constellation of economic interests. The Islamic missionary ardor, originally a religious obligation, found its limits in the conquering warriors' desire to have a non-Islamic, and hence underprivileged, population that could provide for the maintenance of the privileged believers—the type case for many similar phenomena.

On the other hand, it is a typical occurrence that individuals live by representing group interests or, in some other manner, ideologically or economically from the existence of a group. Hence social action may be propagated, perpetuated and transformed into an association in cases in which this might not have happened otherwise. This kind of interest may have the most diverse intellectual roots: In the 19th century the Romantic ideologists and their epigoni awakened numerous declining language groups of "interesting" peoples to the purposive cultivation of their language. German secondary and university teachers helped save small Slavic language groups, about whom they felt the intellectual need to write books.

However, such purely ideological group existence is a less effective lever than economic interest. If a group pays somebody to act as a continuous and deliberate "organ" of their common interests, or if such interest representation pays in other respects, an association comes into being that provides a strong guarantee for the continuance of concerted action under all circumstances. Henceforth, some persons are professionally interested in the retention of the existing, and the recruitment of new, members. It does not matter here whether they are paid to represent (hidden or naked) sexual interests[6] or other "non-material" or, finally, economic interests (trade unions, management associations and similar organizations), whether they are public speakers paid by the piece or salaried secretaries. The pattern of intermittent and irrational action is replaced by a systematic rational "enterprise," which continues to function long after the original enthusiasm of the participants for their ideals has vanished.

In various ways capitalist interests proper may have a stake in the propagation of certain group activities. For example, [in Imperial Germany] the owners of German "Gothic" type fonts want to preserve this "patriotic" kind of lettering [instead of using Latin *Antiqua*]; similarly, innkeepers who permit Social Democratic meetings even though their premises are kept off limits for military personnel have a stake in the size of the party's membership. Everybody can think of many examples of this type for every kind of social action.

Whether we deal with employees or capitalist employers, all these instances of economic interest have one feature in common: The interest in the substance of the shared ideals necessarily recedes behind the interest in the persistence or propaganda of the group, irrespective of the content of its activities. A most impressive example is the complete disappearance of ideological substance in the American parties, but the greatest example, of course, is the age-old connection between capitalist interests and the expansion of political communities. On the one hand, these communities can exert an extraordinary influence on the economy, on the other they can extract tremendous revenues, so that the capitalist interests can profit most from them: directly by rendering paid services or making advances on expected revenues, and indirectly through the exploitation of objects within the realm of the political community. In Antiquity and at the beginning of modern history the focus of capitalist acquisition centered on such politically determined "imperialist" profits, and today again capitalism moves increasingly in this direction. Every expansion of a country's power sphere increases the profit potential of the respective capitalist interests.

These economic interests, which favor the expansion of a group, may not only be counteracted by the monopolistic tendencies discussed above, but also by other economic interests that originate in a group's closure and exclusiveness. We have already stated in general terms that voluntary organizations tend to transcend their rational primary purpose and to create relationships among the participants that may have quite different goals: As a rule, an overarching communal relationship (*über-greifende Vergemeinschaftung*) attaches itself to the association (*Vergesellschaftung*). Of course, this is not always true; it occurs only in cases in which social action presupposes some personal, not merely business, contacts. For example, a person can acquire stocks irrespective of his personal qualities, merely by virtue of an economic transaction, and generally without the knowledge and consent of the other stockholders. A similar orientation prevails in all those associations that make membership dependent upon a purely formal condition or achievement and do not examine the individual himself. This occurs very often in certain purely economic groups and also in some voluntary political organizations; in general, this orientation is everywhere the more likely, the more rational and specialized the group purpose is. However, there are many associations in which admission presupposes, expressly or silently, qualifications and in which those overarching communal relationships arise. This, of course, happens particularly when the members make admission dependent upon an investigation and approval of the candidate's personal qualities. At least as a rule, the candidate is scrutinized not only with regard to his usefulness for the organization but also "existentially," with regard to personal characteristics esteemed by the members.

We cannot classify here the various modes of association according to the degree of their exclusiveness. It suffices to say that such selectness exists in associations of the most diverse kinds. Not only a religious sect, but also a social club, for instance, a veterans' association or even a bowling club, as a rule admit nobody who is personally objectionable to the members. This very fact "legitimizes" the new member toward the outside, far beyond the qualities that are important to the group's purpose. Membership provides him with advantageous connections, again far beyond the specific goals of the organization. Hence, it is very common that persons belong to an organization although they are not really interested in its purpose, merely for the sake of those economically valuable legitimations and connections that accrue from membership. Taken by themselves, these motives may contain a strong incentive for joining and hence enlarging the group, but the opposite effect is created by the members' interest in monopolizing those advantages and in increasing their economic value through restriction to the smallest possible circle. The smaller and the more exclusive such a circle is, the higher will be both the economic value and the social prestige of membership.

Finally, we must briefly deal with another frequent relationship between the economy and group activities: the deliberate offer of economic advantages in the interest of preserving and expanding a primarily non-economic group. This happens particularly when several similar groups compete for membership: witness political parties and religious communities. American sects, for instance, arrange artistic, athletic and other entertainment and lower the conditions for divorced persons remarrying; the unlimited underbidding of marriage regulations was only recently curbed by regular cartelization. In addition to arranging excursions and similar activities, religious and political parties establish youth groups and women chapters and participate eagerly in purely municipal or other basically non-political activities, which enable them to grant economic favors to local private interests. To a very large extent, the invasion of municipal, co-operative or other agencies by such groups has a direct economic motivation: it helps them to maintain their functionaries through office benefices and social status and to shift the operating costs to these other agencies. Suitable for this purpose are jobs in municipalities, producers' and consumers' co-operatives, health insurance funds, trade unions and similar organizations; and on a vast scale, of course, political offices and benefices or other prestigious or remunerative positions that can be secured from the political authorities—professorships included. If a group is sufficiently large in a system of parliamentary government, it can procure such support for its leaders and members, just like the political parties, for which this is essential.

In the present context we want to emphasize only the general fact that non-economic groups also establish economic organizations, especially for propaganda purposes. Many charitable activities of religious groups have such a purpose, and this is even more true of the Christian,

Liberal, Socialist and Patriotic trade unions and mutual benefit funds, of savings and insurance institutes and, on a massive scale, of the consumers' and producers' co-operatives. Some Italian co-operatives, for instance, demanded the certification of confession before hiring a worker. In Germany [before 1918] the Poles organized credit lending, mortgage payments and farm acquisition in an unusually impressive fashion; during the Revolution of 1905/6 the various Russian parties immediately pursued similarly modern policies. Sometimes commercial enterprises are established: banks, hotels (like the socialist *Hôtellerie du Peuple* in Ostende) and even factories (also in Belgium). If this happens, the dominant groups in a political community, particularly the civil service, resort to similar methods in order to stay in power, and organize everything from economically advantageous "patriotic" associations and activities to state-controlled loan associations (such as the *Preussenkasse*). The technical details of such propagandistic methods do not concern us here.

In this section we merely wanted to state in general terms, and to illustrate with some typical examples, the coexistence and opposition of expansionist and monopolist economic interests within diverse groups. We must forego any further details since this would require a special study of the various kinds of associations. Instead, we must deal briefly with the most frequent relationship between group activities and the economy: the fact that an extraordinarily large number of groups have secondary economic interests. Normally, these groups must have developed some kind of rational association; exceptions are those that develop out of the household (see ch. IV:2 below).

4. *Five Types of Want Satisfaction by Economically Active Groups*

Social action that has become rational association will have an established order for want satisfaction if it requires goods and services for its operations. In principle, there are five typical ways of securing these goods and services—as far as possible, the examples will be taken from political groups, since they have the most highly developed arrangements:

(1) The *oikos* type with its collective natural economy. The group members must render fixed personal services, which may be equal for all or specialized (for instance, universal conscription of all able-bodied men or specialized military duties as craftsmen—(*Ökonomiehand-werker*); moreover, they must meet the material needs by fixed payments

in kind (for the royal table or the military administration). Thus, these goods and services are not produced for the market but for the group's collective economy (for instance, a self-sufficient manorial or royal household—the pure type of the *oikos*—or a military administration that is completely dependent upon services and payments in kind, as—approximately—in ancient Egypt).

(2) *Market-oriented assessments* that make it possible for a group to meet its demands by buying equipment and employing workers, officials and mercenaries; these assessments may be compulsory taxes, regular dues, or fees at certain occasions; they may also be tributes from persons who are not otherwise group members, but who (a) benefit from certain advantages and opportunities (such as a Registry Office for real estate or some other agency) or physical facilities (such as roads)—the principle involved is that of a compensation for services rendered: fees in the technical sense; tributes may also be levied on persons who (b) simply happen to be within the group's power sphere (contributions from persons who are merely residents, duties from persons and goods passing through the group's territory).

(3) *Production for the market*: an enterprise sells its products and services and surrenders its profits to the group of which it is a part. The enterprise may not have a formal monopoly (witness the Prussian *See-handlung* and the *Grande Chartreuse*), or it may be of the monopolist type that has been frequent in the past and the present (such as the post office). Obviously, every kind of combination is possible between these three, logically most consistent types. Money may be substituted for payments in kind, natural products may be sold on the market, capital goods may be secured directly by payments in kind or bought with the help of assessments. As a rule, the components of these types are combined with one another.

(4) The *maecenatic type*: Voluntary contributions are made by persons who can afford them and who have material or ideal interests in the group, whether or not they are members in other respects. (In the case of religious and political groups, the typical forms here are religious endowments, political subsidies by big contributors, but also the mendicant orders and the [not-so-] voluntary "gifts" to princes in early historical times.) There are no fixed rules and obligations and no necessary connections between contributions and other forms of participation: the sponsor may remain completely outside the group.

(5) *Contributions and services linked to positive and negative privileges.* (a) The positive variant occurs primarily when a certain economic or social monopoly is guaranteed or, conversely, when certain

privileged status groups or monopolized groups are completely or partly exempt. Hence contributions and services are not required according to general rules from the various property and income strata or the—at least in principle—freely accessible kinds of property and occupation; rather, they are required according to the specific economic and political powers and monopolies that have been granted to an individual or a group by the larger community. (Examples are manorial estates, tax privileges or special levies for guilds or certain status groups.) The point is that these demands are raised as a correlate of, or compensation for, the guarantee or appropriation of privileges. Thus, the method of want satisfaction creates or stabilizes a monopolistic differentiation of the group by virtue of the closure of the social and economic opportunities granted to its various strata. An important special case are the many diverse forms of feudal or patrimonial administration, with their linkage to appropriated power positions that permit the necessary amount of concerted action. (In the *Ständestaat* the prince must meet the costs of government from his patrimonial possessions, just like the feudal participants in political or patrimonial power and status, the vassals, *ministeriales* etc., must use their own means.) Most of the time, this mode of want satisfaction involves contributions in kind. However, under capitalism analogous phenomena may occur: for example, in one way or another, the political authorities may guarantee a monopoly to a group of entrepreneurs and in return impose contributions directly or through taxation. This method, which was widespread during the mercantilist era, is presently quite important again—witness the liquor tax in Germany.[7]

(b) Want satisfaction through negative privileges is called *liturgy*: We speak of *class liturgy*, if economically costly obligations are tied to a certain size or amount of property that is not privileged by any monopoly; at best, those affected can take turns. Examples are the *trierarchoi* and *choregoi* in Athens and the compulsory tax-farmers in the Hellenistic states. We speak of *status liturgy*, if the obligations are linked to monopolistic groups in such a manner that the members cannot withdraw unilaterally and hence remain collectively liable for satisfying the needs of the larger political unit. Examples are the compulsory guilds of ancient Egypt and late Antiquity; the hereditary attachment of the Russian peasants to the village, which is collectively liable for taxes; the more or less strict immobility of *coloni* and peasants throughout history, with their collective liability for paying taxes and, possibly, for providing recruits; and the Roman *decuriones*, who were collectively responsible for the taxes which they had to levy.

As a rule, the last type (5) of want satisfaction is inherently limited to compulsory associations, especially the political ones.

5. *Effects of Want Satisfaction and Taxation on Capitalism and Mercantilism*

The various modes of want satisfaction, always the result of struggles between different interests, often exert a far-reaching influence beyond their direct purpose. This may lead to a considerable degree of economic regulation: witness in particular the liturgical modes of want satisfaction. Even when this is not directly the case, these modes may strongly affect the development and the direction of the economy. For example, status-liturgy greatly contributed to the "closure" of social and economic opportunities, to the stabilization of status groups, and thus to the elimination of private capital formation. Moreover, if a political community satisfies its wants by public enterprises or by production for the market, private capitalism also tends to be eliminated. Monopolistic want satisfaction, too, affects private capitalism, but it may stimulate as well as impede private capital formation. This depends upon the particular nature of the state-sponsored monopolies. Ancient capitalism was suffocated because the Roman empire resorted increasingly to status-liturgy and partly also to public want satisfaction. Today, capitalist enterprises run by municipalities or the state in part redirect and in part displace private capitalism: the fact that the German exchanges have not quoted rail stocks since the railroads were nationalized is not only important for their position but also for the nature of property formation.[8] Private capitalism is retarded (for example, the growth of private distilleries), if monopolies are protected by the state and stabilized with state subsidies (as in the case of the German liquor tax). Conversely, during the Middle Ages and in early modern times, the trade and colonial monopolies at first facilitated the rise of capitalism, since under the given conditions only monopolies provided a sufficient profit span for capitalist enterprises. But later—in England during the 17th century—these monopolies impeded capitalist profit interests and provoked so much bitter opposition that they collapsed. Thus, the effect of tax-based monopolies is equivocal. However, clearly favorable to capitalist development has been want satisfaction through taxation and the market; in the extreme case, the open market is used as much as possible for administrative needs, including the recruitment and training of troops by private entrepreneurs, and all means are secured through tax monies. This presupposes, of course, a fully developed money economy and also a strictly rational and efficient administration: a bureaucracy.

This precondition is particularly important with regard to the taxation of personal ("mobile") property, a difficult undertaking everywhere, especially in a democracy. We must deal briefly with these difficulties, since they have greatly affected the rise of modern capitalism. Even where the propertyless strata are dominant, the taxation of personal property meets certain limits as long as the propertied can freely leave the community. The degree of mobility depends not only on the relative importance of membership in this particular community for the propertied, but also on the nature of the property. Within compulsory associations, particularly political communities, all property utilization that is largely dependent on real estate is stationary, in contrast to personal property which is either monetary or easily exchangeable. If propertied families leave a community, those staying behind must pay more taxes; in a community dependent on a market economy, and particularly a labor market, the have-nots may find their economic opportunities so much reduced that they will abandon any reckless attempt at taxing the haves or will even deliberately favor them. Whether this will indeed happen, depends upon the economic structure of the community. In democratic Athens such considerations were outweighed by the incentives for taxing the propertied, since the Athenian state lived largely from the tributes of subjects and had an economy in which the labor market (in the modern sense of the term) did not yet determine the class situation of the masses.

Under modern conditions the reverse is usually true. Today communities in which the propertyless have seized power are often very cautious toward the propertied. Municipalities under socialist control, such as the city of Catania, have attracted factories with substantial tax-benefits, because the socialist rank and file were more interested in better job opportunities and in directly ameliorating their class situation, than in "just" property distribution and "equitable" taxation. Likewise, in spite of conflicting interests in a given case, landlords, speculators in building land, retailers and craftsmen tend to think first of their immediate class-determined interests; therefore, all kinds of mercantilism have been a frequent, though highly varied, phenomenon in all types of communities. This is all the more so since those concerned with the relative power position of a community also have an interest in preserving the tax base and great fortunes capable of granting them loans; hence, they are forced to treat personal property cautiously. Thus, even where the have-nots are in control, personal property may either expect mercantilist privileges or at least exemption from liturgies and taxes, *provided* a plurality of communities competes with one another among which the property owners can choose their domicile. One example is the United States, in which the separatism of the individual states led to the failure of all serious attempts at unifying consumer interests; more limited, but still pertinent is the case of the municipalities of a country, and finally there are the independent countries themselves.

For the rest, the method of taxation depends, of course, very much on the relative power position of the various groups in a community, and on the nature of the economic system. Every increase of want satisfaction in kind favors the liturgical method. Thus, in Egypt the liturgical system originated in the Pharaonic period, and the course of the late Roman liturgical state, which was modelled after the Egyptian example, was determined by the largely natural economy of the conquered inland areas and the relative decline of the capitalist strata; in turn, these strata lost their former importance because the political and administrative transformation of the Empire eliminated the tax-farmer and the exploitation of the subjects through usury.

If personal ("mobile") property is dominant, the propertied everywhere unburden themselves of liturgical want satisfaction and shift the tax burden to the masses. In Rome military service used to be liturgically classified according to property and to involve the self-equipment of the propertied citizens; then, however, the knightly strata were freed from military service and replaced by the state-equipped proletarian army, elsewhere the mercenary army, the costs of which were met by mass taxation. Instead of satisfying extraordinary public wants through the property tax or compulsory loans without interest, that is, through the liturgical liability of the propertied, the Middle Ages everywhere resorted to interest-bearing loans, land mortgages, customs and other assessments; thus, the propertied used pressing public needs as a source for profit and rent. Sometimes these practices would almost reduce a city's administration and tax system to an instrument of state creditors, as it happened for a time in Genoa.

Finally, at the beginning of modern history, the various countries engaged in the struggle for power needed ever more capital for political reasons and because of the expanding money economy. This resulted in that memorable alliance between the rising states and the sought-after and privileged capitalist powers that was a major factor in creating modern capitalism and fully justifies the designation "mercantilist" for the policies of that epoch. This usage is justified even though, in Antiquity and modern times, "mercantilism," as the protection of personal ("mobile") property, existed wherever several political communities competed with one another by enlarging their tax base and by promoting capital formation for the sake of obtaining private loans. The fact that "mercantilism" at the beginning of modern history had a specific character and specific effects had two reasons: (1) the political structure of the competing states and of their economy—this will be treated later—, and (2) the novel structure of emergent modern capitalism, especially industrial capitalism, which was unknown to Antiquity and in the long run profited greatly from state protection. At any rate, from that time dates that European competitive struggle between large, approximately equal and purely political structures which has had such a global impact. It is well known that this political competition has remained one of the most important motives of the capitalist protectionism that emerged then and today continues in different forms. Neither the trade nor the monetary policies of the modern states—those policies most closely linked to the central interests of the present economic system—can be understood without this peculiar political competition and "equilibrium" among the European states during the last five hundred years—a phenomenon which Ranke recognized in his first work as the world-historical distinctiveness of this era.[9]

NOTES

1. This sentence appears to be a later insertion. The term *soziales Handeln* does not recur in the chapter; rather, Weber uses the older equivalent *Gemein-schaftshandeln*.

2. As is his wont, Weber uses the name of a given association in a generic sense, but also with an undertone of irony. In this case he refers to the *Verband der Diplomingenieure*, the association of engineering graduates from the Technical Colleges (*Hochschulen*), which ranked lower in prestige than the older universities. Such graduates often took pains to differentiate themselves from the products of engineering schools without university status and protected diplomas.

3. The Patriotic Association of Business Clerks was a union of white-collar employees who emphasized their social distance from the working class by pronounced nationalism. The association remained a prominent right-wing organization in the Weimar Republic.

4. Cf. Weber, *Economic History*, 30f.

5. Weber speaks later (ch. VI:8) of this as a practice among American Indians; Fischoff translates instead "India," but Ralph Linton locates the practice in Polynesia; see *The Tree of Culture* (New York: Knopf, 1955), 192.

6. Weber may refer here to contemporary events: female lecturers advocating free love and the right to illegitimate children, and a Freudian psychiatrist who proclaimed "sexual communism," appeared in Heidelberg and aroused his ire. However, Weber was by no means anti-feminist. When his wife organized a convention of the *Bund deutscher Frauenvereine* in Heidelberg in 1910, a faculty member attacked this meeting in a newspaper article as an assembly of spinsters, widows, Jewesses and sterile women—the last category obviously meant to include Marianne Weber. Weber wrote his wife's public defense, but this led to allegations that he was hiding behind her and refusing to duel in her behalf. The upshot was one of Weber's several involved lawsuits. Weber also helped Else von Richthofen, his first female doctorate candidate, to become the first female factory inspector in the state of Baden in 1900. (Her sister was the wife of D. H. Lawrence.) See Marianne Weber, *Max Weber*, 263f, 411ff and 472ff.

7. The Liquor Tax of 1909 was a major factor in ending the coalition between Liberals and Conservatives in the Reichstag and in precipitating Chancellor Bülow's resignation. At issue was a tax reform which would pay for the mounting military expenditures and at the same time distribute more equitably the tax burden among the various social strata.

8. In 1875, about half of the rapidly growing German railroads were still in private hands. Railshares were a major object of speculation before the great crash of 1873. The Prussian state, which had built railroads since 1847, embarked on large-scale nationalization after 1878. However, the interest in preventing further stock speculations was less important than were military considerations. Cf. Gustav Stolper, *German Economy: 1870–1940.* (New York: Reynal & Hitchcock, 1940), 72f.

9. Leopold von Ranke, *Histories of the Latin and Teuton Nations: 1495–1514* (London, 1909), G. R. Dennis, trans. First published in the summer of 1824. Cf. Theodore von Laue, *Leopold Ranke: The Formative Years* (Princeton: University Press, 1950), 24–32.

CHAPTER III

HOUSEHOLD, NEIGHBORHOOD AND KIN GROUP[1]

1. *The Household: Familial, Capitalistic and Communistic Solidarity*

An examination of the specific, often highly complex effects of the ways in which social groups satisfy their economic wants does not belong into this general review, and concrete individual instances will be considered merely as examples.

While abandoning any attempt to systematically classify the various kinds of groups according to the structure, content and means of social action—a task which belongs to general sociology—, we turn to a brief elucidation of those types of groups which are of the greatest importance for our exposition. Only the relationship of the economy to "society"—in our case, the general structures of human groups—will be discussed here and not the relationship between the economic sphere and specific areas of culture—literature, art, science, etc. Contents and directions of social action are discussed only insofar as they give rise to specific forms that are also economically relevant. The resulting boundary is no doubt quite fluid. At any rate, we shall be concerned only with certain universal types of groups. What follows is only a general characterization. Concrete historical forms of these groups will be discussed in greater detail in connection with "authority" [ch. X–XV].

The relationships between father, mother and children, established by a stable sexual union, appear to us today as particularly "natural" relationships. However, separated from the household as a unit of economic maintenance, the sexually based relationship between husband and wife, and the physiologically determined relationship between father and children are wholly unstable and tenuous. The father relationship cannot exist without a stable economic household unit of father and mother; even where there is such a unit the father relationship may not always be of great import. Of all the relationships arising from sexual intercourse, only the mother-child relationship is "natural," because it is a biologically based household unit that lasts until the child is able to search for means of subsistence on his own.

Next comes the sibling group, which the Greeks called *homogalaktes* [literally: persons suckled with the same milk]. Here, too, the decisive point is not the fact of the common mother but that of common maintenance. Manifold group relationships emerge, in addition to sexual and physiological relationships, as soon as the family emerges as a specific social institution. Historically, the concept of the family had several meanings, and it is useful only if its particular meaning is always clearly defined. More will be said later on about this.

Although the grouping of mother and children must be regarded as (in the present sense) the most primitive sort of family, it does not mean —indeed, it is unimaginable—that there ever were societies with maternal groupings only. As far as it is known, wherever the maternal grouping prevails as a family type, group relationships, economic and military, exist among men as well, and so do those of men with women (both sexual and economic). The pure maternal grouping as a normal, but obviously secondary, form is often found precisely where men's everyday life is confined to the stable community of a "men's house," at first for military purposes, later on for other reasons. Men's houses [*Männerhäuser*] can be found in various countries as a specific concomitant and a resultant of militaristic development.

One cannot think of marriage as a mere combination of sexual union and socialization agency involving father, mother, and children. The concept of marriage can be defined only with reference to other groups and relationships besides these. Marriage as a social institution comes into existence everywhere only as an antithesis to sexual relationships which are *not* regarded as marriage. The existence of a marriage means that (1) a relationship formed against the will of the wife's or the husband's kin will not be tolerated and may even be avenged by an organization, such as in olden times the kinsmen of the husband or of the wife or both. (2) It means especially that only children born of stable sexual relationships within a more inclusive economic, political, religious, or other community to which one or both parents belong will be treated, by virtue of their descent, as equal members of an organization—house, village, kin, political group, status group, religious group; while descendants who are a product of other sexual relationships will not be treated in such a manner. This and nothing else is the meaning of the distinction between birth in wedlock and out of wedlock. The prerequisites of a legitimate marriage, the classes of persons not allowed to enter into stable relationships with each other, the kinds of permission and kinds of kinship or other connections required for their validity, the usages which must be observed—all these matters are regulated by the "sacred" traditions and the laws of those groups. Thus, it is the regulations of groups other than mere sexual groupings and sibling communities of experience which endow the marriage with its specific quality. We do not intend to expound here the anthropologically very significant development of these regulations, since it is only their most important economic aspects which concern us.

Sexual relationships and the relationships between children based on the fact of their common parent or parents can engender social action only by becoming the normal, though not the only, bases of a specific economic organization: the household.

The household cannot be regarded as simply a primitive institution. Its prerequisite is not a "household" in the present-day sense of the word, but rather a certain degree of organized cultivation of soil.

The household does not seem to have existed in a primitive economy of hunters and nomads. However, even under the conditions of a technically well-advanced agriculture, the household is often secondary with respect to a preceding state which accorded more power to the inclusive kinship and neighborhood group on the one hand, and more freedom to the individual vis-a-vis the parents, children, grandchildren, and siblings on the other hand. The almost complete separation of the husband's and wife's means and belongings, which was very frequent especially where social differentiation was low, seems to point in this direction, as does the occasional custom according to which man and wife were seated back to back during their meals or even took their meals separately, and the fact that within the political group there existed independent organizations of women with female chieftains alongside the men's organizations. However, one should not infer from such facts the existence of an individualistic primitive condition. Rather, conditions that are due to a certain type of military organization, such as the man's absence from the house for his military service, lead to a "manless" household management by the wives and mothers. Such conditions were residually preserved in the family structure of the Spartans, which was based on the man's absence from the home and separation of belongings.

The size and inclusiveness of the household varies. But it is the most widespread economic group and involves continuous and intensive social action. It is the fundamental basis of loyalty and authority, which in turn is the basis of many other groups. This "authority" is of two kinds: (1) the authority derived from superior strength; and (2) the authority derived from practical knowledge and experience. It is, thus, the authority of men as against women and children; of the able-bodied as against those of lesser capability; of the adult as against the child; of the old as against the young. The "loyalty" is one of subjects toward the holders of authority and toward one another. As reverence for ancestors, it finds its way into religion; as a loyalty of the patrimonial official, retainer, or vassal, it becomes a part of the relationships originally having a domestic character.

In terms of economic and personal relationships, the household in its "pure," though not necessarily primitive, form implies solidarity in dealing with the outside and communism of property and consumption of everyday goods within (household communism). The principle of solidarity in facing the outside world was still found in its pure form in the periodically contractually regulated households as entrepreneurial units in the medieval cities of northern and central Italy, especially those most advanced in capitalist economy. All members of the household, including at times even the clerks and apprentices who were members by contract, were jointly responsible to the creditors. This is the historic source of the joint liability of the owners of a private company for the debts incurred by the firm. This concept of joint liability was of great importance in the subsequent development of the legal forms of modern capitalism.[2]

There was nothing corresponding to our law of inheritance in the old household communism. In its place there was, rather, the simple idea that the household is "immortal." If one of its members dies, or is expelled (after committing an inexpiable ill deed), or is permitted to join another household (by adoption), or is dismissed (*emancipatio*), or leaves out of his own accord (where this is permitted), he cannot possibly lay claim to his "share." By leaving the household he has relinquished his share. If a member of the household dies, the joint economy of the survivors simply goes on. The Swiss *Gemeinderschaften* operate in such a way to the present day.[3]

The principle of household communism, according to which everybody contributes what he can and takes what he needs (as far as the supply of goods suffices), constitutes even today the essential feature of our family household, but is limited in the main to household consumption.

Common residence is an essential attribute of the pure type of household. Increase in size brings about a division and creation of separate households. In order to keep the property and the labor force intact, a compromise based on local decentralization without partition can be adopted. Granting some special privileges to the individual household is an inevitable consequence of such a solution. Such a partition can be carried to a complete legal separation and independence in the control of the business, yet at the same time a surprisingly large measure of household communism can still be preserved. It happens in Europe, particularly in the Alpine countries (cf. Swiss hotel-keepers' families), and also in the large family firms of international trade that, while the household and household authority have outwardly completely disappeared, a communism of risk and profit, i.e., sharing of profit and loss of otherwise altogether independent business managements, continues to exist.

I have been told about conditions in international houses with earnings amounting to millions, whose capital belongs for the most part, but not exclusively, to relatives of varying degree and whose management is predominantly, but not solely, in the hands of the members of the family. The individual establishments operate in very diverse lines of business; they possess highly variable amounts of capital and labor force; and they achieve widely variable profits. In spite of this, after the deduction of the usual interest on capital, the annual returns of all the branches are simply thrown into one hopper, divided into equal portions, and allotted according to an amazingly simple formula (often by the number of heads). The household communism on this level is being preserved for the sake of mutual economic support, which guarantees a balancing of capital requirements and capital surplus between the business establishments and spares them from having to solicit credit from outsiders. The "calculative spirit" thus does not extend to the distribution of balance-sheet results, but it dominates all the more within the individual enterprise: even a close relative without capital and working as an employee will not be paid more than any other employee, because calculated costs of operation cannot be arbitrarily altered in favor of one individual without creating dissatisfaction in others. Beyond the balance sheet, those lucky enough to participate enter the "realm of equality and brotherhood."

2. *The Neighborhood: An Unsentimental Economic Brotherhood*

The household meets the everyday demands for goods and labor. In a self-sufficient agrarian economy a good deal of the extraordinary demands at special occasions, during natural calamities and social emergencies are met by social action that transcends the individual household: the assistance of the neighborhood. For us, the neighborhood is not only the "natural" one of the rural settlement but every permanent or ephemeral community of interest that derives from physical proximity; of course, if not specified further, we refer most of the time to the neighborhood of households settled close to one another.

The group of neighbors may take on different forms depending on the type of settlement: scattered farms, a village, a city street or a slum; neighborly social action may have different degrees of intensity and, especially in the modern city, it may be almost non-existent. To be sure, the extent of mutual help and of sacrifices that even today occurs frequently in the apartment houses of the poor may be astonishing to one who discovers it for the first time. However, not only the fleeting "togetherness" in streetcar, railroad or hotel, but also the enduring one in an apartment house is by and large oriented toward maintaining the greatest possible *distance* in spite (or because) of the physical proximity, and some social action is likely only in cases of common danger. We cannot discuss here why this attitude has become so conspicuous under modern conditions as a result of the specific sense of individual dignity created by them. Suffice it to note that the same ambivalence has always occurred in the stable rural neighborhood: the individual peasant does not like any interference with his affairs, no matter how well-meant it may be. Neighborly co-operation is an exception, although it recurs regularly. It is always less intensive and more discontinuous than the social action of the household, and the circle of participants is far more unstable. For in general, the neighborhood group is merely based on the simple fact that people happen to reside close to one another. In the self-sufficient rural economy of early history the typical neighborhood is the village, a group of households bordering upon each other. However, the neighborhood may also be effective beyond the fixed boundaries of other, in particular political, structures. In practice, neighborhood means mutual dependence in case of distress, especially when the transportation technology is undeveloped. The neighbor is the typical helper in need, and hence neighborhood is brotherhood, albeit in an unpathetic, primarily economic sense. If the household is short of means, mutual help may be requested: the loans of implements and goods free of charge, and "free labor for the asking" (*Bittarbeit*) in case of urgent need. This mutual help is guided by the primeval popular ethics which is as unsentimental as it is universal: "Do unto others as you would have them do unto you." (This is also nicely indicated by the Roman term *mutuum* for an interest-free loan.) For everybody may get into a situation in which he needs the help of others. If a compensation is provided, it consists in feasting the helpers, as in the typical case of neighborly help for house construction (still practiced in the German East). If an exchange takes place, the maxim applies: "Brothers do not bargain with one another." This eliminates the rational market principle of price determination.

Neighborliness is not restricted to social equals. Voluntary labor (*Bittarbeit*), which has great practical importance, is not only given to the needy but also to the economic powers-that-be, especially at harvest time, when the big landowner needs it most. In return, the helpers expect that he protect their common interests against other powers, and also that he grant surplus land free of charge or for the usual labor assistance —the *precarium* was land for the asking. The helpers trust that he will give them food during a famine and show charity in other ways, which he indeed does since he too is time and again dependent on them. In time this purely customary labor may become the basis of manorial services and thus give rise to patrimonial domination if the lord's power and the indispensability of his protection increase, and if he succeeds in turning custom into a right.

Even though the neighborhood is the typical locus of brotherhood, neighbors do not necessarily maintain "brotherly" relations. On the contrary: Wherever popularly prescribed behavior is vitiated by personal enmity and conflicting interests, hostility tends to be extreme and lasting, exactly because the opponents are aware of their breach of common ethics and seek to justify themselves, and also because the personal relations had been particularly close and frequent.

The neighborhood may amount to an amorphous social action, with fluctuating participation, hence be "open" and intermittent. Firm boundaries tend to arise only when a closed association emerges, and this occurs as a rule when the neighborhood becomes an economic group proper or an economically regulatory group. This may happen for economic reasons, in the typical fashion familiar to us; for example, when pastures and forests become scarce, their use may be regulated in a "co-operative" (*genossenschaftlich*) manner, that means, monopolistically. However, the neighborhood is not necessarily an economic, or a regulatory, group, and where it is, it is so in greatly varying degrees. The neighborhood may regulate the behavior of its members either through an association of its own: witness the *Flurzwang* [the compulsory regulation of tilling and crop rotation under the open-field system]; or a regulation may be imposed by outsiders (individuals or communities), with whom the neighbors are associated economically or politically (for example, the landlords of tenement houses). But all of this is not essential for neighborly social action. Even in the self-sufficient household economy of early times, there is no necessary identity among neighborhood, the forest regulations of political communities, especially the village, the territorial economic association (for example, the *Markgemeinschaft*) and the polity; they may be related in very diverse ways. The size of the territorial economic associations may vary according to the objects they comprise. Fields, pastures, forests and hunting grounds are often controlled by different groups, which overlap with one another and with the polity. Wherever peaceful activities are the primary means of making a living, the agent of joint work, the household, is likely to have control, and wherever maintenance depends upon land seized by force, the polity, and more so for extensively used land, such as hunting grounds and forests, than for pastures and fields.

Furthermore, the individual types of possessions tend to become scarce at different historical stages and hence subject to regulatory association; forests may still be free objects when pastures and fields are already economic ones and their use has been regulated and appropriated. Hence, diverse territorial associations may appropriate different kinds of land.

The neighborhood is the natural basis of the local community (*Gemeinde*)—a structure which arises only, as we shall see later [cf. ch. XVI, "The City"], by virtue of political action comprising a *multitude* of neighborhoods. Moreover, the neighborhood may itself become the basis of political action, if it controls a territory such as a village; and in the course of organizational rationalization, it may engage in activities of all kinds (from public schools and religious functions to the systematic settling of necessary crafts), or the polity may impose them as an obligation. But the essence of neighborly social action is merely that sombre economic brotherhood practiced in case of need.

3. *The Regulation of Sexual Relations in the Household*

We shall now return to the household, the most "natural" of the externally closed types of social action. Typically, the development from the primeval household communism runs counter to the kind of communism described in the previous example [in sec. 1], when profits and losses were shared in spite of the separation of the households; rather, typical is the internal weakening of household communism, that means, the progress of internal closure in the face of the continued external unity of the household.

The earliest substantial inroads into unmitigated communist house authority proceed not directly from economic motives but apparently from the development of exclusive sexual claims of the male over women subjected to their authority. This may result in a highly casuistic but strictly enforced regulation of sex relations, especially if social action is not much rationalized in other respects. It is true that sexual rights sometimes occur in "communist" form (polyandry), but in all known instances such polyandric rights constitute only a relative communism: a limited number of men (brothers or the members of a men's house) are exclusive co-owners by virtue of the common acquisition of a woman.

Nowhere do we find unregulated, amorphous sexual promiscuity within the house, even if sexual relations between siblings are a recognized institution; at least nowhere on a normative basis. On the contrary, any kind of communist sexual freedom is most thoroughly banished from a house in which there is communist property ownership. The [younger] members of such a household could adjust to this because their sexual attraction to one another was minimized by having grown up together. Subsequent normative elaboration was obviously in the interest of safeguarding solidarity and domestic peace in the face of jealousies. Where the members of the house belong to different sibs because of sib exogamy and hence would be free to engage in sexual relations, they are nevertheless forced to avoid one another because house exogamy is older than sib exogamy and persists next to it. The beginnings of regulated exogamy can perhaps be found in exchange arrangements of households and of sibs, which resulted from their division. At any rate, sexual relations are even disapproved of among close relatives among whom this would be permissible according to the sib code (for example, among very close paternal relatives under rules of matrilineal exogamy). As an institution, the marriage between siblings and relatives is commonly limited to socially prominent families, especially royal houses; its purpose is the preservation of economic resources, probably also the avoidance of struggles among pretenders, and finally the purity of the blood—hence it is a secondary phenomenon.

As a rule, then, a man acquires exclusive sexual rights over a woman when he takes her into his house or enters her house if his means are insufficient. Of course, this exclusiveness, too, has often enough been precarious vis-à-vis the autocratic head of the house. Notorious are the liberties, for example, which the father-in-law of an extended Russian family could take up until modern times. Normally, however, the household differentiates itself into permanent sexual unions with their offspring. In our times, the household consists of the parents and their children, together with the personal servants and at most a spinster relative. However, the household of earlier periods was not always very large; often it was small if finding sustenance required dispersion. However, history has known many households ("extended families") based on parent and child relations but comprising grandchildren, brothers, cousins and outsiders, to a degree which has become very rare in advanced countries. The extended family prevails where a large number of hands are required, hence where agriculture is intensive, and also where property is intended to remain concentrated in the interest of social and economic dominance, hence in aristocratic and plutocratic strata.

Apart from the very early closure of sexual relations within the household, the sexual sphere was further narrowed, especially at otherwise low levels of cultural differentiation, by structures that overlapped with domestic authority. In fact, one can say that these imposed the first decisive limitations on domestic authority. As blood relationships gain importance, incest transcends the house to include other relatives and becomes subject to casuistic regulation by the *kin group* (*Sippe*).

4. *The Kin Group and Its Economic Effects on the Household*

The kin group is not as "natural" a group as the household or the neighborhood. As a rule, its social action is discontinuous and lacks association; in fact, the kin group proves that social action is possible even if the participants do not know one another and action is merely passive (refraining from sexual relations, for example). The kin group presupposes the existence of others within a larger community. It is the natural vehicle of all fealty (*Treue*). Friendship is originally an artificial blood brotherhood. The vassal as well as the modern officer are not only subordinates but also the lord's brothers, "comrades" (that means, "roommates," originally household members). Substantively, the kin group competes with the household in the sphere of sexual relations and in-group solidarity; it is a protective group, which substitutes for our detective force and vice squad; and it is also a group of expectant heirs made up of those former household members who left when it was divided or when they married, and of their descendants. Hence with the kin group begins inheritance outside the household. Since members are committed to blood revenge, the in-group solidarity of the kin group may become more important than loyalty toward partiarchal authority.

We should keep in mind that the kin group is not an extended or decentralized household or a superordinate structure uniting several households: that may be the case, but as a rule it is not. Whether a particular kin group cuts across the households or comprises all members depends upon its structure, which may assign father and children to different groups, as we shall see later. Kin membership may not mean more than that marriage within the group is prohibited (exogamy); in this case the members may have common marks of identification and may believe in common descent from a natural object, most of the time an animal, which the members are usually not allowed to eat (totemism).

Furthermore, the kin members are forbidden to engage in combat with one another; they must practice blood revenge and be collectively liable to it, at least in the case of close relatives. Blood revenge in turn requires the joint declaration of a feud in case of a homicide and establishes the right and the duty of the kin members to receive and to pay a compensation (*Wergild*). The kin group is also open to Divine revenge in case of perjury, since it provides oath-bound witnesses at a trial. In this manner the kin group guarantees the security and legal personality of the individual.

Finally, the neighborhood established by a settlement (a village, a rural commune of villages—*Markgenossenschaft*) may coincide with the kin group; then the household is indeed a unit of the kin group. Even if this is not the case, the kin members often retain very palpable rights in relation to domestic authority: a veto against the sale of property, the right of participating in the selling of daughters into marriage and of receiving part of the bridal price, the rights of providing a legal guardian, etc.

Collective selfhelp is for the kin group the most typical means of reacting to infringements upon its interests. The oldest procedures approximating a trial are compulsory arbitration of conflict *within* the household or the kin group, either by the household head or the kin elder who best knows the customs, and mutually agreed arbitration *between* several households and kin groups. The kin group competes with political groups as an independent, overlapping group deriving from common descent, which may be actual, fictitious or artificially created through blood brotherhood; it is a complex of obligations and loyalties between persons who may belong not only to different households but also to different political and even language groups. The kin group may be completely unorganized, a kind of passive counter-image of the authoritarian household. For its normal functioning it does not require a leader with powers of control; indeed, as a rule, the kin group is merely an amorphous circle of persons who may be identified positively by forming a religious community and negatively by their refraining from the violation or consumption of a joint sacred object (taboo); we shall deal later [ch. VI] with the religious rationale for such behavior. It seems scarcely possible to assume, as Gierke has done, that kin groups with some kind of continuous government are the older form; rather, the reverse is the rule:

kin groups become associations only when it seems desirable to erect economic or social monopolies against outsiders. If the kin group has a head and functions as a political group, it may serve originally extraneous purposes of a political, military or economic nature; in this case it becomes part of a heterogeneous social structure—witness the *gens* as a subdivision of the *curia* or the [Germanic] "sibs" as military units.

Especially in periods in which social action is otherwise scarcely developed, household, kin group, neighborhood and political community typically overlap in such a manner that the members of a household and a village may belong to different kin groups, and the kin members to different political and even language communities. Hence it is possible that neighbors or members of the same political group and even of the same household are expected to practice blood revenge against one another. These drastically conflicting obligations were removed only when the political community gradually monopolized the use of physical force. However, if political action occurs only intermittently, when there is an external threat or booty seekers associate, the kin group's importance and the rationalization of its structure and obligations may approximate scholastic casuistry (as for example in Australia).

The manner in which the kin groups are organized and regulate sexual relations is important because of the repercussions on the composition and the economic structure of the households. Domestic authority over a child derives from matrilineal or patrilineal descent, and this in turn defines the other households in which the child has a property share, in particular access to economic opportunities which these households appropriated within economic, status, or political groups. Hence those other groups are interested in the manner in which household membership is established; in any given case the prevailing order is a resultant of the economic and also the political interests of all groups involved. It should be clearly understood from the beginning that as soon as a household becomes part of other groups that control economic and other opportunities, it cannot freely attribute membership, the less so the more limited these opportunities become. Patrilineal or matrilineal descent and their consequences are determined by the most diverse interests, which cannot be analyzed here in detail. In the case of matrilineal descent the child is protected and disciplined by the mother's brothers, apart from his father, and also receives his inheritance from them (*avunculate*); the mother exercises domestic authority only in rare cases subject to special conditions. In a patrilineal system, the child is subject to the power of his paternal relatives, apart from his father's, and he inherits from them. Today kinship and succession are as a rule cognate, that means, there is no difference between the father's and the mother's side, whereas domestic authority is exercised by the father or, if he is not there, often by a close relative who is appointed as a guardian and supervised by the public authorities; however, in the past patrilineal and matrilineal principles were often mutually exclusive. This did not necessarily mean that only one applied in a given group to all households; one principle might apply in one household, the other in another one. In the simplest case this competition of the two principles originated in property differentiation. Like all children, daughters are considered economic assets of the household into which they are born. The household decides their disposition. The head might offer them to his guests, just like his own wife, or he might permit sexual relations temporarily or permanently in exchange for goods and services. This "prostitution" of female household members accounts for many cases that are subsumed under the imprecise collective name of *matriarchy* (*Mutterrecht*): Husband and wife each remain members of their own household, the children belong to the mother's household, and the father is for them an alien who merely pays "alimony" (in modern terminology) to the household head. Hence husband, wife and children do not form a household of their own.

However, if there is such a household it may have a patrilineal or matrilineal basis. The man who can afford to pay cash for a woman takes her out of her household and kin group into his own. In this case the woman and her children are fully owned by the man's household. However, a man who cannot pay for a woman whom he desires must join her household, if its head permits the union, either temporarily in order to work off her price ("service marriage") or permanently, and then the woman's household retains control over her and the children. Thus the head of a well-to-do household buys women from less prosperous households for himself and his sons (so-called *diga*-marriage) or forces impecunious suitors to join his own household (*bina*-marriage). Hence patrilineal and matrilineal descent and the domestic authority of the father's or the mother's household may exist side by side for different persons within the *same* household. In this simple case patrilineal descent is always linked to control by the father's household, and vice versa. This relationship grows more complex when the husband takes the wife into his household and thus places her under its authority, but when matrilineal attribution remains, that means, when the children belong to the mother's kin group as her exogamous sex group and are subject to the rules of blood revenge and inheritance of her group. As a technical term, *matriarchy* ("mother right") should be restricted to this phenomenon. To be sure, as far as we know, matriarchy does not occur in this form in which the father's relation to the children is extremely restricted because they are legally aliens in spite of his authority. However, there are various intermediate stages: The mother's house may yield her to the father's household and yet retain certain rights in her and her children. Frequently matrilineal rules of kin exogamy apply because superstitious fear of incest persists; moreover, matrilineal rules of succession are often retained in varying degrees. This is likely to give rise to many conflicts between the two kin groups, the outcome of which depends very much on the land holdings, the influence of the village neighborhood and the role of military associations.

NOTES

1. The chapter titles of chs. III and IV and the subheadings were chosen by the English editor in an attempt to make clearer the content of the various sections and to come closer to Weber's original outline, which envisaged a chapter on "Household, Oikos and Enterprise," to be followed by "Neighborhood, Kin Group and Community." However, the text reverses some of the chapter sequence, unless the changes were made by the original editors.

For another discussion of marriage and kinship in relation to economic factors, see Weber's *Economic History,* 37–53, and Marianne Weber's *Ehefrau und Mutter in der Rechtsentwicklung* (1907); for other background literature, see below, Soc. of Law, ch. VIII: *ii*, nn. 18, 70–74.

2. On this point, see Weber's dissertation: *Zur Geschichte der Handelsgesellschaften im Mittelalter* (Stuttgart 1889), reprinted in *GAzSW*, 312–443, esp. ch. III ("Die Familien- und Arbeitsgemeinschaften").

3. Cf. Eugen Huber, *System and Geschichte des Schweizer Privatrechts* (1893), vol. IV, and Max Huber, *Gemeinderschaften der Schweiz* (Breslau 1897).

CHAPTER IV

HOUSEHOLD, ENTERPRISE AND OIKOS

1. *The Impact of Economic, Military and Political Groups on Joint Property Law and Succession in the Household*

Unfortunately, the relationships between kin group, village, the "commune" of villages (*Markgenossenschaft*) and political association belong to the most obscure and least investigated areas of ethnography and economic history. Not one case has been completely elucidated, neither the primitive stages of civilized peoples nor the so-called primitive tribes (*Naturvölker*), not even the American Indians, in spite of Morgan's research. The neighborhood organization of a village may originate in a given case in the division of the inheritance of a household. When nomadic cultivation is replaced by permanent agriculture, land may be assigned on a kinship basis, since the latter is usually taken into account in military organization; thus the territory of a village (*Dorfgemarkung*) may be considered kin property. This seems to have happened in ancient Germanic times, since the sources speak of *genealogiae* as the owners of village territory even when it appears that the land was not occupied by a noble family with its retainers. However, this was probably not the rule. As far as we know, the military bodies of a hundred or a thousand men, which developed from cadres into territorial units, were not unambiguously linked to the kin groups, and neither were the latter to the "rural communes" (*Markgemeinschaften*).

We can make only three generalizations: (1) Land may be primarily a place to work on. In this case all land and all yield belong to the women's kin groups, as long as cultivation is primarily women's work.

The father does not leave any land to his children, since it is handed down through the mother's house and kin group; the paternal inheritance comprises only military equipment, weapons, horses and tools of male crafts. In pure form this case is rare. (2) Conversely, land may be considered male property won and defended by force; unarmed persons, especially women, cannot have a share in it. Hence, the father's local political association may be interested in retaining his sons as military manpower; since the sons join the father's military group, they inherit the land from him, and only movable property from the mother. (3) The neighborhood composed of a village or a "rural commune" (*Markgenossenschaft*) always controls the land gained through joint deforestation, that means, through men's work, and does not permit its inheritance by children who do not continuously fulfill their obligations toward the association. The clash of these practices, and possibly of even more complex ones, may have very diverse results. However, we cannot make a fourth generalization that might suggest itself in view of these practices: that the primarily military character of a group points unambiguously to the predominance of the father's house and of male ("agnatic") family and property attribution. Rather this depends on the type of military organization. The able-bodied age-groups may permanently live in barracks; typical examples are the "men's house" described by Schurtz or the Spartan *syssitiae*.[1] In this case the men's absence frequently establishes the household as a "maternal grouping" in which children and property are attributed to the maternal household, or the woman achieves at least a relative domestic independence, as it is reported for Sparta. The numerous means that were specifically invented to intimidate and rob women—for example, the periodic predatory exploits of the *duk-duk*—[2] are an attempt by the men who have left the household to strengthen their threatened authority.

However, when the members of a military caste were landowners living dispersed in the countryside, the patriarchal and agnatic structure of household and kin group became usually predominant. As far as our historical knowledge goes, the empire-building peoples of the Far East and India, the Near East, the Mediterranean and the European North developed patrilineal descent and exclusively agnatic attribution of kinship and property; contrary to a frequent assumption, the Egyptians also had patrilineal descent even though they did not have agnatic attribution. The major reason for this phenomenon is that great empires cannot be maintained in the long run by small monopolistic, staff-like groups of warriors who live closely together in the manner of "men's houses"; in a natural economy empire-building requires as a rule the patrimonial and seigneurial control of the land, even if this subjection proceeds from

groups of closely settled warriors, as in Antiquity. The manorial administration develops quite naturally out of the patriarchal household that is
turned into an apparatus of domination; everywhere the manor originates
in patriarchal authority. Hence, there is no serious evidence for the
assertion that the predominance of patrilineal descent among those
peoples was ever preceded by another order, ever since kinship relations
among them had been regulated by any law at all. Particularly worthless
is the hypothesis of a once universal prevalence of matriarchal marriage.
This construct confuses very heterogeneous phenomena: it blurs the difference between primitive conditions under which parent-child relations
are not legally regulated at all, hence the mother is indeed closer to the
children whom she feeds and rears, and a *legal* arrangement deserving
the name "matriarchy" (*Mutterrecht*). Equally erroneous is the idea
that marriage by abduction was a universal intermediate stage between
"matriarchy" and "patriarchy." A woman can be legitimately acquired
from another household only through exchange or purchase. Abduction
results in feud and restitution. It is true that for the hero the abducted
woman is a trophy, just like the scalp of the enemy, but we cannot say
that actual abduction was a stage in legal history.

Because of the very predominance of patriarchy, property law develops in the great empires in the direction of steadily *weakening* unlimited patriarchal power. Since legal restraints were originally missing,
no distinction was made between "legitimate" and "illegitimate" children; in the Germanic law of the Middle Ages the master's right to
identify "his" child was a residue of the once unlimited power of the
patriarch. This state of affairs was definitely changed only with the intervention of political and economic groups, which made membership dependent upon "legitimate" descent, that means, on permanent relations
with women from their own circle. The most important stage in the
development of this principle, the very distinction between "legitimate"
and "illegitimate" children and the protection of the right of succession
for the former, is usually reached when the propertied or status-privileged
strata no longer regard women merely as chattel and begin to protect
by contract daughters, and their children, against the original discretion
of the buyer. From then on his property is supposed to be inherited only
by the children from this marriage. Hence the motivating force of this
development is not the man's but the woman's interest in "legitimate"
children. As status aspirations and the corresponding costs of living rise,
the woman, who is now regarded as a luxury possession, receives a
dowry; at the same time this represents the compensation for her share in
the household—a purpose clearly stipulated in ancient Oriental and
Hellenic law—and provides her with the material means of destroying the

husband's unlimited discretion, since he must return the dowry if he divorces her. In time, this purpose was achieved, in different degrees and not always through formal law, but often so successfully that only an endowed marriage was considered a marriage proper (ἔγγραφος γάμος in Egypt).

We cannot deal here further with the development of joint property rights. Decisive changes occur wherever the military importance of land declines as a possession taken by force or as the basis of maintaining able-bodied men (capable of equipping themselves); then real estate can be used primarily for economic purposes, especially in the cities, and daughters too can succeed to land. The compromise between the interests of husband and wife and of their kin varies greatly depending on whether the family lives primarily from joint *labor earnings* or from rent-producing *property*.

In the Occidental Middle Ages the institution of joint property prevailed in the former case and that of joint administration (actually the administration and utilization of the wife's property by the husband) in the latter; in addition, since the feudal families did not want to release any land, widows were maintained through a rent attached to family holdings, as it occurred typically in England (dower marriage). For the rest the most diverse determinants may come into play. The social conditions of the Roman and English nobility were similar in some respects, but very different in others. Whereas in ancient Rome the wife became economically and personally emancipated by virtue of the freely dissolvable marriage, yet was completely unprotected as a widow and had no legal control whatsoever over her children, in England the wife remained under coverture which prevented any economic and legal independence and made it almost impossible for her to dissolve the feudal "dower marriage." The difference seems to have been owing to the more developed urban character of the Roman nobility, on the one hand, and the impact of Christian patriarchalism in the English family on the other. Whereas feudal marriage law persisted in England and French marriage law was shaped by petty-bourgeois and militaristic considerations—in the *Code Napoléon* through the personal influence of its creator—, bureaucratic states (such as Austria and Russia) have minimized sex differences in the joint property law; this levelling tends to go furthest where militarism has receded most in the ruling classes. With the advance of the market economy the marital property structure is also strongly influenced by the need to protect creditors. The manifold arrangements deriving from these factors do not belong in the present context.

The "legitimate" marriage that developed out of the wife's interests does not necessarily lead to a speedy adoption of monogamy. The wife whose children are privileged in relation to succession may be distinguished as the "chief wife" in a circle of other wives, as it was the case in the Orient, in Egypt and in most civilized Asian areas. This type of semi-polygamy was of course everywhere a privilege of the propertied strata. The ownership of several wives is lucrative only when women still do most of the agricultural work, at most when their textile production is especially profitable (as is still assumed in the Talmud); for example, the possession of a large number of women is considered a profitable capital investment by the chieftains in Caffraria; this presupposes, of course, that the man has the necessary means to buy women. But polygamy is too costly for all middle-income groups in an economy in which male work predominates, and especially in social strata in which women work only as dilettantes or for luxury needs in jobs considered beneath the dignity of freemen. Monogamy was institutionalized first among the Hellenes (even though the royal families did not consistently adhere to it as late as the period of the Diadochs) and among the Romans; it fitted into the household structure of the emergent urban patriciate. Subsequently Christianity raised monogamy to an absolute norm for ascetic reasons, in contrast to at least the early stages of all other religions. In the main, polygamy persisted in those cases in which the strictly patriarchal structure of political authority helped to preserve the discretion of the household head.

The institution of the dowry affects the development of the household in two ways: (1) As against the children of concubines, the "legitimate" children achieve special legal status as the sole inheritors of the paternal property; (2) the husband's economic position tends to be differentiated according to the wife's dowry, which in turn depends on her family's wealth. It is true that the dowry becomes formally subject to the husband's discretion (especially in Roman law), but in fact it tends to be set aside as a "special account." Thus the calculating spirit enters into the relations between the family members.

However, at this stage other economic motives have usually begun this dissolution of the household. Undifferentiated communism was economically deflected at such an early stage that it existed historically perhaps only in marginal cases. In principle, artifacts such as tools, arms, jewelry and clothes may be used by their producer alone or preferentially, and they are inherited not necessarily by the group but by other qualified individuals. (Examples are riding horse and sword, in the Middle Ages the *Heergewäte*, the *Gerade*, etc.) These incipient forms of the individual right to succession developed very early even under authoritarian house communism; however, their beginnings probably antecede the household itself and are found wherever tools are produced by individuals. In the case of arms, the same development was probably owing to the intervention of military powers interested in equipping the most able-bodied men.

2. *The Disintegration of the Household: The Rise of the Calculative Spirit and of the Modern Capitalist Enterprise*

In the course of cultural development, the internal and external determinants of the weakening of household authority gain ascendancy. Operating from within, and correlated with the quantitative growth of economic means and resources, is the development and differentiation of abilities and wants. With the multiplication of life chances and opportunities, the individual becomes less and less content with being bound to rigid and undifferentiated forms of life prescribed by the group. Increasingly he desires to shape his life as an individual and to enjoy the fruits of his own abilities and labor as he himself wishes.

The disintegration of the household authority is furthered by a number of other groups. One factor is the fiscal interest in a more intensive exploitation of the individual taxpayer. These groups may work contrary to the household's interests in keeping property intact for the sake of military self-equipment. The usual consequence of these disintegrative tendencies is, in the first place, the increasing likelihood of division in case of inheritance or marriage of children. In the early times of relatively primitive agriculture, employment of mass labor was the only means of increasing land yields. As a result, the household grew in size. However, the development of individualized production brought about a decrease in the size of households, which continued until the family of parents and children constitutes the norm today.

The function of the household has changed so radically that it is becoming increasingly inopportune for an individual to join a large communistic household. An individual no longer gets protection from the household and kinship groups but rather from political authority, which exercises compulsory jurisdiction. Furthermore, household and occupation become ecologically separated, and the household is no longer a unit of common production but of common consumption. Moreover, the individual receives his entire education increasingly from outside his home and by means which are supplied by various enterprises: schools, bookstores, theaters, concert halls, clubs, meetings, etc. He can no longer regard the household as the bearer of those cultural values in whose service he places himself.

This decrease in the size of households is not due to a growing "sub-jectivism," understood as a stage of social psychological development, but to the *objective* determinants of its growth. It should not be overlooked that there exist also hindrances to this development, particularly on the highest levels of the economic scale. In agriculture, the possibility of unrestricted splitting up of landed estates is tied in with certain tech-nological conditions. An integrated estate, even a large one, with valuable buildings on it, can be partitioned only at a loss. The division is tech-nically facilitated by mixed holdings and village settlement. Isolated loca-tion makes such a partition difficult. Separate farms and large estates, operated with an intensive expenditure of capital, therefore tend to be inherited by one individual. A small farm, operated with intensive ex-penditure of labor on scattered holdings, has a tendency to continuous splintering. In addition, the separate farm and large estate are much more suitable objects from which to extract payments in favor of movable property [i.e., money lenders] in the form of permanent or long-term mortgages, and they are thus kept intact for the benefit of the creditors.

Large property-holding, being a determinant of position and prestige, is conducive to the desire to keep it intact in the family. A small farm, on the other hand, is merely a place where work is done. There is an ap-positeness between the seigneurial standard of life, with its fixed con-ventions, and the large household. Given the spaciousness of, say, a castle and the almost inevitable "inner distance" even between the closest relatives, these large households do not restrain the freedom that the individual demands to such an extent as does the middle-class house-hold, which may consist of an equally large number of persons but occupies a smaller space and lacks the aristocratic sense of distance, and whose members, moreover, typically have far more differentiated life interests than do those of an estate-seated gentry family. Today, the large household provides an appropriate way of life, aside from the seigneurial one, only for the highly intense ideological community of a sect, whether religious, social-ethical or artistic—corresponding to the monasteries and the cloister-like communities of the past.

Even where the household unit remains outwardly intact, the internal dissolution of household communism by virtue of the growing sense of calculation (*Rechenhaftigkeit*) goes on irresistibly in the course of cul-tural development. Let us look at the consequences of this factor in somewhat greater detail.

As early as in the large capitalistic households of medieval cities— for example, in Florence—every person had his own account. He has pocket money (*danari borsinghi*) at his disposal. Specific limits are set for certain expenditures—for example, if he invites a visitor for a stay. The member must settle his account in the same way as do partners in any modern trading company. He has capital shares "in" the house and [separate "outside"] wealth (*fuori della compagnia*) which the house controls and for which it pays him interest, but which is not regarded as working capital proper and therefore does not share in the profit.[3] Thus, a rational association takes the place of the "natural" participation in the household's social action with its advantages and obligations. The individual is born into the household, but even as a child he is already a potential business partner of the rationally managed enterprise. It is evident that such conduct became possible only within the framework of a money economy, which therefore plays a crucial role in the internal dissolution of the household. The money eonomy makes possible an objective calculation both of the productive performances and of the consumption of the individuals, and for the first time makes it possible for them to satisfy their wants freely, through the indirect exchange medium of money.

The parallelism of money economy and attenuation of household authority is, of course, far from complete. Domestic authority and household are relatively independent of economic conditions, in spite of the latters' great importance, and appear "irrational" from an economic point of view; in fact, they often shape economic relationships because of their own historic structure. For example, the *patria potestas,* which the head of a Roman family retained until the end of his life, had economic and social as well as political and religious roots (the preservation of a patrician household, military affiliation according to kinship and, probably, house, and the father's position as house priest). The *patria potestas* persisted during the most diverse economic stages before it was finally attenuated under the Empire, even toward the children. In China, the same situation was perpetuated by the principle of filial piety, which was carried to an extreme by the code of duties and furthered by the state and the bureaucratic status ethic of Confucianism, in part for reasons of political domestication. This principle led not only to economically untenable consequences (as in the mourning regulations) but also to politically questionable results (for example, large-scale office vacancies, because piety toward the late father—originally, fear of the dead man's envy—forbade the use of his property and the occupation of his office).

Economic factors originally determined to a large extent whether a property was inherited by one person or principal heir or whether it was divided. This practice varies with economic influences, but it cannot be explained solely by economic factors, and especially not by modern economic conditions. This was demonstrated particularly in the recent studies of Sering and others.[4] Under identical conditions and in contiguous areas, there exist often quite disparate systems, affected especially by different ethnic composition, e.g., Poles and Germans. The far-reaching economic consequences of these differing structures were caused by factors that could be regarded as economically "irrational" from the very beginning, or that became irrational as a consequence of changes in economic conditions.

In spite of all, the economic realities intervene in a compelling manner. First, there are characteristic differences depending on whether economic gain is attributed to common work or to common property. If the former situation obtains, the household authority is usually basically unstable, no matter how autocratic it may be. Mere separation from the parental household and the establishment of an independent household is sufficient for a person to be set free from the household authority. This is mostly the case in the large households of primitive agricultural peoples. The *emancipatio legis Saxonicae* of the German law clearly has its economic foundation in the importance of personal labor, which prevailed at the time.

On the other hand, the household authority is typically stable wherever ownership of livestock, and property in general, forms the prime economic basis. This is particularly true when land ceases to be abundant and becomes a scarce commodity. For reasons already alluded to, family and lineage cohesion is generally an attribute of the landed aristocracy. The man without any landed property or with only little of it is also without lineage group.

The same difference is to be found in the capitalistic stage of development. The large households of Florence and other parts of northern Italy practiced the principle of joint responsibility and of maintaining the property intact. In the trading places of the Mediterranean, especially in Sicily and southern Italy, the exact opposite was the case: each adult member of the household could at any time request his share while the legator was still alive. Nor did joint personal liability to the outsiders exist. In the family enterprises of northern Italy, the inherited capital represented the basis of economic power to a greater degree than did the personal business activities of the partners. The opposite was true in southern Italy, where common property was treated as a product of common work. With the increasing importance of capital, the former practice gained ascendancy. In this case, the capitalist economy, a "later" stage in terms of a theory of development starting with undifferentiated social action, determines a theoretically "earlier" structure in which the household members are more tightly bound to the household and subjected to household authority.

However, at the same time a far more significant, and *uniquely Occidental,* transformation of domestic authority and household was under way in these Florentine and other business-oriented medieval houses.

The entire economic arrangements of such large households were periodically regulated by *contract*. Whereas, originally, the personal funds and the business organization were regulated by the same set of rules, the situation gradually changed. Continuous capitalist acquisition became a special vocation performed in an increasingly separate enterprise. An autonomous rational association emerged out of the social action of the household, in such a way that the old identity of household, workshop and office fell apart, which had been taken for granted in the undifferentiated household as well as the ancient *oikos,* to be discussed in the next section. First, the household ceased to exist as a necessary basis of rational business association. Henceforth, the partner was not necessarily—or typically—a house member. Consequently, business assets had to be separated from the private property of the partners. Similarly, a distinction began to be made between the business employees and the domestic servants. Above all, the commercial debts had to be distinguished from the private debts of the partners, and joint responsibility had to be limited to the former, which were identified as such by being contracted under the "firm," the business name.

This whole development is obviously a precise parallel to the separation of the bureaucratic office as a "vocation" from private life, the "bureau" from the private household, the official assets and liabilities from private property, and the official dealings from private dealings; this will be discussed in the analysis of authority [chapter XI]. The capitalist enterprise, created by the household which eventually retreats from it, thus is related from the very beginning to the "bureau" and the now obvious bureaucratization of the private economy.

But the factor of decisive importance in this development is not the spatial differentiation or separation of the household from the work-shop and the store. This is rather typical of the bazaar system of the Islamic cities in the Orient, which rests throughout on the separation of the castle (*kasbah*), bazaar (*suk*), and residences. What is crucial is the separation of household and business for accounting and legal purposes, and the development of a suitable body of laws, such as the commercial register, elimination of dependence of the association and the firm upon the family, separate property of the private firm or limited partnership, and appropriate laws on bankruptcy. This fundamentally important development is the characteristic feature of the Occident, and it is worthy of note that the legal forms of our present commercial law were almost all developed as early as the Middle Ages—whereas they were almost entirely foreign to the law of Antiquity with its capitalism that was quantitatively sometimes much more developed. This is one of the many phenomena characterizing most clearly the qualitative uniqueness of the development of modern capitalism, since both the concentration of the family property for the purpose of mutual economic support and the development of a "firm" from a family name existed, for example, in China as well. There, too, the joint liability of the family stands behind the debts of the individual. The name used by a company in commercial transactions does not provide information about the actual proprietor: there, too, the "firm" is related to the business organization and not to the household. But the laws on private property and bankruptcy as they were developed in Europe seem to be absent in China, where two things are of special relevance: Association and credit, until the modern era, were to a large degree dependent on the kinship group. Likewise, the keeping of the property intact in the well-to-do kinship groups and the mutual granting of credit within the kinship groups served different purposes. They were concerned not with capitalistic profit but with raising money to cover the costs of family members' preparation for the examinations and afterwards for the purchase of an office. The incumbency of the office then offered the relatives an opportunity to recover their expenses with a profit from the legal and illegal revenues that the office afforded. Furthermore, these relatives could benefit from the protection of the office-holder. It was the chances of the politically rather than economically determined gain that were conducive to the "capitalistic" cohesion of the family, especially one that was well-off economically.

The capitalistic type of association which corresponds to our joint-stock company and is completely detached, at least formally, from kinship and personal ties has its antecedents in Antiquity only in the area of politically oriented capitalism, i.e., in companies of tax-farmers. In the Middle Ages, such associations were also organized in part for colonizing ventures—such as the big partnerships of the *maone* in Genoa —and in part for state credit—such as the Genoese group of creditors which for all practical purposes held the municipal finances under sequester. In the realm of private enterprise, a purely commercial and capitalistic type of association initially developed only in the form of *ad hoc* groupings in long-distance trade, such as the *commenda* association which can be found already in Old Babylonian law and later quite universally: A financier entrusts his capital to a travelling merchant for a concrete voyage, with profit or loss distribution on this basis. This is the form typical for the period of "intermittent trade" (*Gelegenheitshandel*). Enterprises in the form of joint-stock corporations which were monopolistically privileged by the political powers, especially colonial undertakings, constituted the transition to the application of such organizational types also in purely private business.

3. *The Alternative Development: The* Oikos

These kinds of undertakings which, as the basis of a capitalist enterprise, constitute its most radical separation from the original identity with the household do not particularly concern us at this point. Rather, we shall turn to a radically different way in which a household may evolve. The disintegration of the household and of domestic authority because of exchange with the outside, and the resulting rise of the capitalist enterprise proceed in juxtaposition to the household's internal evolution into an *oikos,* as Rodbertus called it.[5] This is not simply any large household or one which produces on its own various products, agricultural or industrial; rather, it is the authoritarian household of a prince, manorial lord or patrician. Its dominant motive is not capitalistic acquisition but the lord's organized want satisfaction in kind. For this purpose, he may resort to any means, including large-scale trade. Decisive for him is the utilization of property, not capital investment. The essence of the oikos is organized want satisfaction, even if market-oriented enterprises are attached to it. Of course, there is a scale of imperceptible transitions between the two modes of economic orientation, and often also a more or less rapid transformation from one into the other. In reality, if there is a relatively developed technology, the oikos is rarely a purely collective natural economy; for it can exist purely only if it permanently eliminates all exchange, and practices, or at least aims at, autarky, hence if it is a self-sufficient economy so far as possible. In this case an apparatus of house-dependent labor, which often is highly specialized, produces all the goods and personal services, economic, military and sacral, which the ruler requires. His own land provides the raw materials, his workshops with their personally unfree labor supply all other materials. The remaining services are provided by servants, officials, house priests and warriors. Exchange takes place only if surplus is to be dumped or if goods simply cannot be procured in any other way. This state of affairs was approximated to a considerable extent by the royal economies of the Orient, especially of Egypt, and to a lesser degree by the households of the Homeric aristocrats and princes; those of the Persian and Frankish kings also appear quite similar. In the Roman empire the landed estates moved increasingly in this direction as they grew in size, the slave supply fell off and capitalist acquisition was curbed by bureaucracy and liturgy. But the medieval manor took the opposite course with the increasing importance of trade, the cities and the money economy. However, in all these cases the oikos was never really self-sufficient. The Pharaoh engaged in foreign trade just as did the majority of the early princes and aristocrats of the Mediterranean; their treasuries depended heavily upon trade proceeds. As early as the Frankish kingdom the seigneurs received substantial amounts of money or various tributes which had cash-value. The *capitularia* took for granted that the royal *fisci* were free to sell whatever was not needed by the court and the army. In all better known cases only a part of the unfree work-force of the big owners of land and people was completely tied to their household. Those most strictly attached to the household were the personal servants and the workers who labored in the master's self-sufficient household and were wholly maintained by him: the case of *autarkic utilization of labor*. However, another group of strictly attached workers consists of those who produced for the market; the Carthaginian, Sicilian and Roman plantation owners employed their barrack slaves in this fashion, as did the father of Demosthenes with the slaves in his two *ergasteria* or, in modern times, the Russian landlords with the peasants in their factories: these are cases of the *capitalist utilization of unfree labor*. However, many slaves on the plantations and in the *ergasteria* were bought on the market, hence they were not "produced" in the household. Unfree workers born in the master's household presuppose some kind of unfree "family," and this implies an attenuation of attachment and normally also of the full exploitation of labor power. Therefore, the majority of these hereditarily unfree workers is not employed in centralized enterprises, but surrenders only part of their work capacity to the master, and pays him more or less arbitrary and traditionally fixed taxes in kind or in coin. Whether the master prefers to use his unfree workers as a work-force or as a source of revenue depends above all on what yields most to him in a given situation. Barrack slaves without families can be replaced only if they are very cheap and plentiful; this presupposes continuous slavery wars and low food costs (a Southern climate). Hereditarily attached peasants, moreover, can pay money taxes only if there is a (local) market, and this in turn requires a degree of urban development. Where this was low, and the harvest yield could be fully used only through export, as in the German and European East at the beginning of modern times (in contrast to the West) and in the "Black Earth" regions of Russia in the nineteenth century, the forced labor of the peasants was the only way of making money. In this way large-scale market-oriented enterprise developed within the oikos. The owner of an oikos may become almost indistinguishable, or wholly identical, with a capitalist entrepreneur, if he establishes large industrial undertaking with his own unfree labor, or rented unfree or even free workers; he may use the latter two groups either partly or exclusively, and he may run his own or rented *ergasteria*. A major example for this transformation are the creators of the Silesian *starost* [i.e., village steward] industries.[6]

Ultimately, the oikos is defined only by the rent-producing utilization of property, but in terms of the owner's primary interest this meaning may become practically indistinguishable from, or outright identical with, entrepreneurial capital proper. The manorial origin of the *starost*-industry is visible only because of the particular combination of enterprises: large-scale lumbering with brick-yards, distilleries, sugar refineries, coal mines, that means, of enterprises that are not integrated, along technically or economically suggested, horizontal or vertical lines, like the modern combines and mixed firms. However, a manorial lord who adds a foundry or a steelmill to his coal mines, or a lumbermill and papermill to his lumbering operations may in practice bring about the same result. Only the starting point, not the end product are different. In the ancient *ergasteria,* too, we find incipient combinations based on the possession of raw materials. The father of Demosthenes, who descended from a family of Attic merchants, was an importer of ivory which he sold τῷ βουλομένῳ [i.e., to anyone desiring it, to any comer] and which was used as inlay for knife handles and furniture. He eventually trained slaves to manufacture knives in his own workshop and, in addition, had to take over the *ergasterion,* that means, mostly the slaves, of a bankrupt cabinet-maker. He combined these holdings into both a cutlery and a furniture *ergasterion.* The *ergasterion* developed further during the Hellenistic period, especially in Alexandria, up until early Islamic times. The use of unfree craftsmen as a source of rent was widely known throughout Antiquity, both in the Orient and the Occident, during the early Middle Ages, and in Russia until the emancipation of the serfs. The master may rent his slaves, as Nikias did with masses of unskilled slaves for the mine-owners. He may turn them into skilled craftsmen, a practice found in all Antiquity, from a contract in which [the Persian] crown prince Kambyses [6th century B.C.] is mentioned as the owner of the trainer, up to the [late Roman] pandects, but it is also found in Russia as late as the 18th and 19th century. The master may also leave it to the slaves, after he arranged for their training, to work for their own account in exchange for a rent (Greek: *apophora,* Babylonian: *mandaku,* German: *Halssteuer,* Russian: *obrok*). The master may also provide them with a workshop and capital equipment (*peculium*) as well as working capital (*merx peculiaris*). Historically, we find all imaginable transitions from almost total mobility to complete regimentation in barracks. A more detailed description of the "enterprises" emerging within the oikos and run by either the master or the unfree belongs into a different set of topics. However, the transformation of the oikos into a patrimonial rulership will be discussed in the analysis of the forms of domination.

NOTES

1. Heinrich Schurtz, *Altersklassen und Männerbünde* (1902). (W)—For further literature, see Soc. of Law, ch. VIII:*ii*, n. 13.

2. *Duk-Duk:* secret society of the New Britain Archipelago N.E. of New Guinea. Cf. Graf von Pfeil, "Duk-Duk," 27 *Journal of Anthropol. Institut.*, 181; E. A. Weber, *The Duk-Duk* (1929). (Rh) For a more detailed description of the Duk-Duk, see below, ch. IX:2.

3. Cf. Weber, *Handelsgesellschaften*, ch. V, in GAzSW, 411ff.

4. See, e.g., Max Sering et al., *Die Vererbung des ländlichen Grundbesitzes im Königreich Preussen* (Berlin: Parey, 1908). Cf. also *GAzSW*, 463f.

5. Karl Johann Rodbertus (1805–75), who championed a conservative form of socialism, advanced the theory that all of Antiquity should be classified as falling into the stage of the "*oikos* economy," a concept created by him; cf. Weber, *Agrarverhältnisse*, in GAzSW, 7, and *supra*, Part One, ch. II, n. 34.

6. The term could not be traced, but elsewhere Weber refers to "the typical *starost*-industry of Silesia and Bohemia—thus styled, as is well known, by Engel— which is a form of 'wealth-utilization,' as contrasted to the 'capital-utilization' of bourgeois industry . . ." (*AfS*, Vol. 38 [1914], 544). The reference might be to the famous Prussian statistician Ernst Engel (1821–1896). On this phenomenon and the origin of Silesian and Bohemian linen industry, see also *Economic History*, 104; Arthur Salz, *Geschichte der böhmischen Industrie in der Neuzeit* (Munich: Duncker & Humblot, 1913), 365–383.

CHAPTER V

ETHNIC GROUPS

1. "Race" Membership[1]

A much more problematic source of social action than the sources analyzed above is "race identity": common inherited and inheritable traits that actually derive from common descent. Of course, race creates a "group" only when it is subjectively perceived as a common trait: this happens only when a neighborhood or the mere proximity of racially different persons is the basis of joint (mostly political) action, or conversely, when some common experiences of members of the same race are linked to some antagonism against members of an *obviously* different group. The resulting social action is usually merely negative: those who are obviously different are avoided and despised or, conversely, viewed with superstitious awe. Persons who are externally different are simply despised irrespective of what they accomplish or what they are, or they are venerated superstitiously if they are too powerful in the long run. In this case antipathy is the primary and normal reaction. However, this antipathy is shared not just by persons with anthropological similarities, and its extent is by no means determined by the degree of anthropological relatedness; furthermore, this antipathy is linked not only to inherited traits but just as much to other visible differences.

If the degree of objective racial difference can be determined, among other things, purely physiologically by establishing whether hybrids reproduce themselves at approximately normal rates, the subjective aspects, the reciprocal racial attraction and repulsion, might be measured by finding out whether sexual relations are preferred or rare between two groups, and whether they are carried on permanently or temporarily and irregularly. In all groups with a developed "ethnic" consciousness the existence or absence of intermarriage (*connubium*) would then be a normal consequence of racial attraction or segregation. Serious research on the sexual attraction and repulsion between different ethnic groups is only incipient, but there is not the slightest doubt that racial factors,

[385]

that means, common descent, influence the incidence of sexual relations and of marriage, sometimes decisively. However, the existence of several million mulattoes in the United States speaks clearly against the assumption of a "natural" racial antipathy, even among quite different races. Apart from the laws against biracial marriages in the Southern states, sexual relations between the two races are now abhorred by both sides, but this development began only with the Emancipation and resulted from the Negroes' demand for equal civil rights. Hence this abhorrence on the part of the Whites is socially determined by the previously sketched tendency toward the monopolization of social power and honor, a tendency which in this case happens to be linked to race.

The *connubium* itself, that means, the fact that the offspring from a permanent sexual relationship can share in the activities and advantages of the father's political, economic or status group, depends on many circumstances. Under undiminished patriarchal powers, which we treat elsewhere, the father was free to grant equal rights to his children from slaves. Moreover, the glorification of abduction by the hero made racial mixing a normal event within the ruling strata. However, patriarchal discretion was progressively curtailed with the monopolistic closure, by now familiar to us, of political, status or other groups and with the monopolization of marriage opportunities; these tendencies restricted the *connubium* to the offspring from a permanent sexual union within the given political, religious, economic and status group. This also produced a high incidence of inbreeding. The "endogamy" of a group is probably everywhere a secondary product of such tendencies, if we define it not merely as the fact that a permanent sexual union occurs primarily on the basis of joint membership in some association, but as a process of social action in which only endogamous children are accepted as full members. (The term "sib endogamy" should not be used; there is no such thing unless we want to refer to the levirate marriage and arrangements in which daughters have the right to succession, but these have secondary, religious and political origins.) "Pure" anthropological types are often a secondary consequence of such closure; examples are sects (as in India) as well as pariah peoples, that means, groups that are socially despised yet wanted as neighbors because they have monopolized indispensable skills.

Reasons other than actual racial kinship influence the degree to which blood relationship is taken into account. In the United States the smallest admixture of Negro blood disqualifies a person unconditionally, whereas very considerable admixtures of Indian blood do not. Doubtlessly, it is important that Negroes appear esthetically even more alien than Indians, but it remains very significant that Negroes were slaves and hence disqualified in the status hierarchy. The conventional *connubium* is far less impeded by anthropological differences than by status differences, that means, differences due to socialization and upbringing (*Bildung* in the widest sense of the word). Mere anthropological differences account for little, except in cases of extreme esthetic antipathy.

2. *The Belief in Common Ethnicity: Its Multiple Social Origins and Theoretical Ambiguities*

The question of whether conspicuous "racial" differences are based on biological heredity or on tradition is usually of no importance as far as their effect on mutual attraction or repulsion is concerned. This is true of the development of endogamous conjugal groups, and even more so of attraction and repulsion in other kinds of social intercourse, i.e., whether all sorts of friendly, companionable, or economic relationships between such groups are established easily and on the footing of mutual trust and respect, or whether such relationships are established with difficulty and with precautions that betray mistrust.

The more or less easy emergence of social circles in the broadest sense of the word (*soziale Verkehrsgemeinschaft*) may be linked to the most superficial features of historically accidental habits just as much as to inherited racial characteristics. That the different custom is not understood in its subjective meaning since the cultural key to it is lacking, is almost as decisive as the peculiarity of the custom as such. But, as we shall soon see, not all repulsion is attributable to the absence of a "consensual group." Differences in the styles of beard and hairdo, clothes, food and eating habits, division of labor between the sexes, and all kinds of other visible differences can, in a given case, give rise to repulsion and contempt, but the actual extent of these differences is irrelevant for the emotional impact, as is illustrated by primitive travel descriptions, the Histories of Herodotus or the older prescientific ethnography. Seen from their positive aspect, however, these differences may give rise to consciousness of kind, which may become as easily the bearer of group relationships as groups ranging from the household and neighborhood to political and religious communities are usually the bearers of shared customs. All differences of customs can sustain a specific sense of honor or dignity in their practitioners. The original motives or reasons for the inception of different habits of life are forgotten and the contrasts are then perpetuated as conventions. In this manner, any group can create customs, and it can also effect, in certain circumstances very decisively, the selection of anthropological types. This it can do by providing favorable chances of survival and reproduction for certain hereditary qualities and traits. This holds both for internal assimilation and for external differentiation.

Any cultural trait, no matter how superficial, can serve as a starting point for the familiar tendency to monopolistic closure. However, the universal force of imitation has the general effect of only gradually changing the traditional customs and usages, just as anthropological types are changed only gradually by racial mixing. But if there are sharp boundaries between areas of observable styles of life, they are due to conscious monopolistic closure, which started from small differences that were then cultivated and intensified; or they are due to the peaceful or warlike migrations of groups that previously lived far from each other and had accommodated themselves to their heterogeneous conditions of existence. Similarly, strikingly different racial types, bred in isolation, may live in sharply segregated proximity to one another either because of monopolistic closure or because of migration. We can conclude then that similarity and contrast of physical type and custom, regardless of whether they are biologically inherited or culturally transmitted, are subject to the same conditions of group life, in origin as well as in effectiveness, and identical in their potential for group formation. The difference lies partly in the differential instability of type and custom, partly in the fixed (though often unknown) limit to engendering new hereditary qualities. Compared to this, the scope for assimilation of new customs is incomparably greater, although there are considerable variations in the transmissibility of traditions.

Almost any kind of similarity or contrast of physical type and of habits can induce the belief that affinity or disaffinity exists between groups that attract or repel each other. Not every belief in tribal affinity, however, is founded on the resemblance of customs or of physical type. But in spite of great variations in this area, such a belief can exist and can develop group-forming powers when it is buttressed by a memory of an actual migration, be it colonization or individual migration. The persistent effect of the old ways and of childhood reminiscences continues as a source of native-country sentiment (*Heimatsgefühl*) among emigrants even when they have become so thoroughly adjusted to the new country that return to their homeland would be intolerable (this being the case of most German-Americans, for example).

In colonies, the attachment to the colonists' homeland survives despite considerable mixing with the inhabitants of the colonial land and despite profound changes in tradition and hereditary type as well. In case of political colonization, the decisive factor is the need for political support. In general, the continuation of relationships created by marriage is important, and so are the market relationships, provided that the "customs" remained unchanged. These market relationships between the homeland and the colony may be very close, as long as the consumer standards remain similar, and especially when colonies are in an almost absolutely alien environment and within an alien political territory.

The belief in group affinity, regardless of whether it has any objective foundation, can have important consequences especially for the formation of a political community. We shall call "ethnic groups" those human groups that entertain a subjective belief in their common descent because of similarities of physical type or of customs or both, or because of memories of colonization and migration; this belief must be important for the propagation of group formation; conversely, it does not matter whether or not an objective blood relationship exists. Ethnic membership (*Gemeinsamkeit*) differs from the kinship group precisely by being a presumed identity, not a group with concrete social action, like the latter. In our sense, ethnic membership does not constitute a group; it only facilitates group formation of any kind, particularly in the political sphere. On the other hand, it is primarily the political community, no matter how artificially organized, that inspires the belief in common ethnicity. This belief tends to persist even after the disintegration of the political community, unless drastic differences in the custom, physical type, or, above all, language exist among its members.

This artificial origin of the belief in common ethnicity follows the previously described pattern [cf. chapter II:3] of rational association turning into personal relationships. If rationally regulated action is not widespread, almost any association, even the most rational one, creates an overarching communal consciousness; this takes the form of a brotherhood on the basis of the belief in common ethnicity. As late as the Greek city state, even the most arbitrary division of the polis became for the member an association with at least a common cult and often a common fictitious ancestor. The twelve tribes of Israel were subdivisions of a political community, and they alternated in performing certain functions on a monthly basis. The same holds for the Greek tribes (*phylai*) and their subdivisions; the latter, too, were regarded as units of common ethnic descent. It is true that the original division may have been induced by political or actual ethnic differences, but the effect was the same when such a division was made quite rationally and schematically, after the break-up of old groups and relinquishment of local cohesion, as it was done by Cleisthenes. It does not follow, therefore, that the Greek polis was actually or originally a tribal or lineage state, but that ethnic fictions were a sign of the rather low degree of rationalization of Greek political life. Conversely, it is a symptom of the greater rationalization of Rome that its old schematic subdivisions (*curiae*) took on religious importance, with a pretense to ethnic origin, to only a small degree.

The belief in common ethnicity often delimits "social circles," which in turn are not always identical with endogamous connubial groups, for greatly varying numbers of persons may be encompassed by both. Their similarity rests on the belief in a specific "honor" of their members, not shared by the outsiders, that is, the sense of "ethnic honor" (a phenomenon closely related to status honor, which will be discussed later). These few remarks must suffice at this point. A specialized sociological study of ethnicity would have to make a finer distinction between these concepts than we have done for our limited purposes.

Groups, in turn, can engender sentiments of likeness which will persist even after their demise and will have an "ethnic" connotation. The political community in particular can produce such an effect. But most directly, such an effect is created by the *language group,* which is the bearer of a specific "cultural possession of the masses" (*Massenkultur-gut*) and makes mutual understanding (*Verstehen*) possible or easier.

Wherever the memory of the origin of a community by peaceful secession or emigration ("colony," *ver sacrum,* and the like) from a mother community remains for some reason alive, there undoubtedly exists a very specific and often extremely powerful sense of ethnic identity, which is determined by several factors: shared political memories or, even more importantly in early times, persistent ties with the old cult, or the strengthening of kinship and other groups, both in the old and the new community, or other persistent relationships. Where these ties are lacking, or once they cease to exist, the sense of ethnic group membership is absent, regardless of how close the kinship may be.

Apart from the community of language, which may or may not coincide with objective, or subjectively believed, consanguinity, and apart from common religious belief, which is also independent of consanguinity, the ethnic differences that remain are, on the one hand, esthetically conspicuous differences of the physical appearance (as mentioned before) and, on the other hand and of equal weight, the perceptible differences in the *conduct of everyday life.* Of special importance are precisely those items which may otherwise seem to be of small social relevance, since when ethnic differentiation is concerned it is always the conspicuous differences that come into play.

Common language and the ritual regulation of life, as determined by shared religious beliefs, everywhere are conducive to feelings of ethnic affinity, especially since the intelligibility of the behavior of others is the most fundamental presupposition of group formation. But since we shall not consider these two elements in the present context, we ask: what is it that remains? It must be admitted that palpable differences in dialect and differences of religion in themselves do not exclude sentiments of common ethnicity. Next to pronounced differences in the economic way of life, the belief in ethnic affinity has at all times been affected by outward differences in clothes, in the style of housing, food and eating habits, the division of labor between the sexes and between the free and the unfree. That is to say, these things concern one's conception of what is correct and proper and, above all, of what affects the individual's sense of honor and dignity. All those things we shall find later on as objects of specific differences between status groups. The conviction of the excellence of one's own customs and the inferiority of alien ones, a conviction which sustains the sense of ethnic honor, is actually quite analogous to the sense of honor of distinctive status groups.

The sense of ethnic honor is a specific honor of the masses (*Massenehre*), for it is accessible to anybody who belongs to the subjectively believed community of descent. The "poor white trash," i.e., the propertyless and, in the absence of job opportunities, very often destitute white inhabitants of the southern states of the United States of America in the period of slavery, were the actual bearers of racial antipathy, which was quite foreign to the planters. This was so because the social honor of the "poor whites" was dependent upon the social *déclassement* of the Negroes.

And behind all ethnic diversities there is somehow naturally the notion of the "chosen people," which is merely a counterpart of status differentiation translated into the plane of horizontal co-existence. The idea of a chosen people derives its popularity from the fact that it can be claimed to an equal degree by any and every member of the mutually despising groups, in contrast to status differentiation which always rests on subordination. Consequently, ethnic repulsion may take hold of all conceivable differences among the notions of propriety and transform them into "ethnic conventions."

Besides the previously mentioned elements, which were still more or less closely related to the economic order, conventionalization (a term expounded elsewhere) may take hold of such things as a hairdo or style of beard and the like. The differences thereof have an "ethnically" repulsive effect, because they are thought of as symbols of ethnic membership. Of course, the repulsion is not always based merely on the "symbolic" character of the distinguishing traits. The fact that the Scythian women oiled their hair with butter, which then gave off a rancid odor, while Greek women used perfumed oil to achieve the same purpose, thwarted—according to an ancient report—all attempts at social intercourse between the aristocratic ladies of these two groups. The smell of

butter certainly had a more compelling effect than even the most prominent racial differences, or—as far as I could see—the "Negro odor," of
which so many fables are told. In general, racial qualities are effective only
as limiting factors with regard to the belief in common ethnicity, such as
in case of an excessively heterogeneous and esthetically unaccepted
physical type; they are not positively group-forming.

Pronounced differences of custom, which play a role equal to that
of inherited physical type in the creation of feelings of common ethnicity and notions of kinship, are usually caused, in addition to linguistic
and religious differences, by the diverse economic and political conditions
of various social groups. If we ignore cases of clear-cut linguistic boundaries and sharply demarcated political or religious communities as a
basis of differences of custom—and these in fact are lacking in wide areas
of the African and South American continents—then there are only
gradual transitions of custom and no immutable ethnic frontiers, except
those due to gross geographical differences. The sharp demarcations of
areas wherein ethnically relevant customs predominate, which were not
conditioned either by political or economic or religious factors, usually
came into existence by way of migration or expansion, when groups of
people that had previously lived in complete or partial isolation from
each other and became accommodated to heterogeneous conditions of
existence came to live side by side. As a result, the obvious contrast
usually evokes, on both sides, the idea of blood disaffinity (*Blutsfremd-
heit*), regardless of the objective state of affairs.

It is understandably difficult to determine in general—and even in a
concrete individual case—what influence specific ethnic factors (i.e.,
the belief in a blood relationship, or its opposite, which rests on similarities, or differences, of a person's physical appearance and style of life)
have on the formation of a group.

There is no difference between the ethnically relevant customs and
customs in general, as far as their effect is concerned. The belief in
common descent, in combination with a similarity of customs, is likely
to promote the spread of the activities of one part of an ethnic group
among the rest, since the awareness of ethnic identity furthers imitation.
This is especially true of the propaganda of religious groups.

It is not feasible to go beyond these vague generalizations. The content of joint activities that are possible on an ethnic basis remains indefinite. There is a corresponding ambiguity of concepts denoting
ethnically determined action, that means, determined by the belief in
blood relationship. Such concepts are *Völkerschaft*, *Stamm* (tribe),
Volk (people), each of which is ordinarily used in the sense of an ethnic
subdivision of the following one (although the first two may be used in

reversed order). Using such terms, one usually implies either the existence of a contemporary political community, no matter how loosely organized, or memories of an extinct political community, such as they are preserved in epic tales and legends; or the existence of a linguistic or dialect group; or, finally, of a religious group. In the past, cults in particular were the typical concomitant of a tribal or *Volk* consciousness. But in the absence of the political community, contemporary or past, the external delimitation of the group was usually indistinct. The cult communities of Germanic tribes, as late as the Burgundian period [6th century A.D.], were probably rudiments of political communities and therefore pretty well defined. By contrast, the Delphian oracle, the undoubted cultic symbol of Hellenism, also revealed information to the barbarians and accepted their veneration, and it was an organized cult only among some Greek segments, excluding the most powerful cities. The cult as an exponent of ethnic identity is thus generally either a remnant of a largely political community which once existed but was destroyed by disunion and colonization, or it is—as in the case of the Delphian Apollo—a product of a *Kulturgemeinschaft* brought about by other than purely ethnic conditions, but which in turn gives rise to the belief in blood relationship. All history shows how easily political action can give rise to the belief in blood relationship, unless gross differences of anthropological type impede it.

3. Tribe and Political Community: The Disutility of the Notion of "Ethnic Group"

The tribe is clearly delimited when it is a subdivision of a polity, which, in fact, often establishes it. In this case, the artificial origin is revealed by the round numbers in which tribes usually appear, for example, the previously mentioned division of the people of Israel into twelve tribes, the three Doric *phylai* and the various *phylai* of the other Hellenes. When a political community was newly established or reorganized, the population was newly divided. Hence the tribe is here a political artifact, even though it soon adopts the whole symbolism of blood-relationship and particularly a tribal cult. Even today it is not rare that political artifacts develop a sense of affinity akin to that of blood relationship. Very schematic constructs such as those states of the United States that were made into squares according to their latitude have a strong sense of identity; it is also not rare that families travel from New York to Richmond to make an expected child a "Virginian."

Such artificiality does not preclude the possibility that the Hellenic *phylai,* for example, were at one time independent and that the polis used them schematically when they were merged into a political association. However, tribes that existed before the *polis* were either identical with the corresponding political groups which were subsequently associated into a *polis,* and in this case they were called *ethnos,* not *phyle;* or, as it probably happened many times, the politically unorganized tribe, as a presumed "blood community," lived from the memory that it once engaged in joint political action, typically a single conquest or defense, and then such political memories constituted the tribe. Thus, the fact that tribal consciousness was primarily formed by common political experiences and not by common descent appears to have been a frequent source of the belief in common ethnicity.

Of course, this was not the only source: Common customs may have diverse origins. Ultimately, they derive largely from adaptation to natural conditions and the imitation of neighbors. In practice, however, tribal consciousness usually has a political meaning: in case of military danger or opportunity, it easily provides the basis for joint political action on the part of tribal members or *Volksgenossen* who consider one another as blood relatives. The eruption of a drive to political action is thus one of the major potentialities inherent in the rather ambiguous notions of tribe and people. Such intermittent political action may easily develop into the moral duty of all members of tribe or people (*Volk*) to support one another in case of a military attack, even if there is no corresponding political association; violators of this solidarity may suffer the fate of the [Germanic, pro-Roman] sibs of Segestes and Inguiomer—expulsion from the tribal territory—, even if the tribe has no organized government. If the tribe has reached this stage, it has indeed become a continuous political community, no matter how inactive in peacetime, and hence unstable, it may be. However, even under favorable conditions the transition from the habitual to the customary and therefore obligatory is very fluid. All in all, the notion of "ethnically" determined social action subsumes phenomena that a rigorous sociological analysis—as we do not attempt it here—would have to distinguish carefully: the actual subjective effect of those customs conditioned by heredity and those determined by tradition; the differential impact of the varying content of custom; the influence of common language, religion and political action, past and present, upon the formation of customs; the extent to which such factors create attraction and repulsion, and especially the belief in affinity or disaffinity of blood; the consequences of this belief for social action in general, and specifically for action on the basis of shared custom or blood relationship, for diverse sexual relations, etc.—all of this would have to be studied in detail. It is certain that in this process the collective term "ethnic" would be abandoned, for it is unsuitable for a really rigorous analysis. However, we do not pursue sociology for its own sake and therefore limit ourselves to showing briefly the diverse factors that are hidden behind this seemingly uniform phenomenon.

The concept of the "ethnic" group, which dissolves if we define our terms exactly, corresponds in this regard to one of the most vexing, since emotionally charged concepts: the *nation,* as soon as we attempt a sociological definition.

4. *Nationality and Cultural Prestige*[2]

The concept of "nationality" shares with that of the "people" (*Volk*) —in the "ethnic" sense—the vague connotation that whatever is felt to be distinctively common must derive from common descent. In reality, of course, persons who consider themselves members of the same nationality are often much less related by common descent than are persons belonging to different and hostile nationalities. Differences of nationality may exist even among groups closely related by common descent, merely because they have different religious persuasions, as in the case of Serbs and Croats. The concrete reasons for the belief in joint nationality and for the resulting social action vary greatly.

Today, in the age of language conflicts, a shared common language is pre-eminently considered the normal basis of nationality. Whatever the "nation" means beyond a mere "language group" can be found in the specific objective of its social action, and this can only be the *autonomous polity.* Indeed, "nation state" has become conceptually identical with "state" based on common language. In reality, however, such modern nation states exist next to many others that comprise several language groups, even though these others usually have one official language. A common language is also insufficient in sustaining a sense of national identity (*Nationalgefühl*)—a concept which we will leave undefined for the present. Aside from the examples of the Serbs and Croats, this is demonstrated by the Irish, the Swiss and the German-speaking Alsatians; these groups do not consider themselves as members, at least not as full members, of the "nation" associated with their language. Conversely, language differences do not necessarily preclude a sense of joint nationality: The German-speaking Alsatians considered themselves—and most of them still do—as part of the French "nation," even though not in the same sense as French-speaking nationals. Hence there are qualitative degrees of the belief in common nationality.

Many German-speaking Alsatians feel a sense of community with the French because they share certain customs and some of their "sensual culture" (*Sinnenkultur*)—as Wittich in particular has pointed out—and also because of common political experiences. This can be understood by any visitor who walks through the museum in Colmar, which is rich in relics such as tricolors, *pompier* and military helmets, edicts by Louis Philippe and especially memorabilia from the French Revolution; these may appear trivial to the outsider, but they have sentimental value for the Alsatians.[3] This sense of community came into being by virtue of common political and, indirectly, social experiences which are highly valued by the masses as symbols of the destruction of feudalism, and the story of these events takes the place of the heroic legends of primitive peoples. *La grande nation* was the liberator from feudal servitude, she was the bearer of civilization (*Kultur*), her language was *the* civilized language; German appeared as a dialect suitable for everyday communication. Hence the attachment to those who speak the language of civilization is an obvious parallel to the sense of community based on common language, but the two phenomena are not identical; rather, we deal here with an attitude that derives from a partial sharing of the same culture and from shared political experiences.

Until a short time ago most Poles in Upper Silesia had no strongly developed sense of Polish nationality that was antagonistic to the Prussian state, which is based essentially on the German language. The Poles were loyal if passive "Prussians," but they were not "Germans" interested in the existence of the *Reich;* the majority did not feel a conscious or a strong need to segregate themselves from German-speaking fellow-citizens. Hence, in this case there was no sense of nationality based on common language, and there was no *Kulturgemeinschaft* in view of the lack of cultural development.

Among the Baltic Germans we find neither much of a sense of nationality amounting to a high valuation of the language bonds with the Germans, nor a desire for political union with the *Reich;* in fact, most of them would abhor such a unification. However, they segregate themselves rigorously from the Slavic environment, and especially from the Russians, primarily because of status considerations and partly because both sides have different customs and cultural values which are mutually unintelligible and disdained. This segregation exists in spite of, and partly because of, the fact that the Baltic Germans are intensely loyal vassals of the Tsar and have been as interested as any "national" Russian (*Nationalrusse*) in the predominance of the Imperial Russian system, which they provide with officials and which in turn maintains their descendants. Hence, here too we do not find any sense of nationality in the modern meaning of the term (oriented toward a common language and culture). The case is similar to that of the purely proletarian Poles: loyalty toward the state is combined with a sense of group identity that is limited to a common language group within this larger community and strongly modified by status factors. Of course, the Baltic Germans are no longer a cohesive status group, even though the differences are not as extreme as within the white population of the American South.

Finally, there are cases for which the term nationality does not seem to be quite fitting; witness the sense of identity shared by the Swiss and the Belgians or the inhabitants of Luxemburg and Liechtenstein. We hesitate to call them "nations," not because of their relative smallness— the Dutch appear to us as a nation—, but because these neutralized states have purposively forsaken power. The Swiss are not a nation if we take as criteria common language or common literature and art. Yet they have a strong sense of community despite some recent disintegrative tendencies. This sense of identity is not only sustained by loyalty toward the body politic but also by what are perceived to be common customs (irrespective of actual differences). These customs are largely shaped by the differences in social structure between Switzerland and Germany, but also all other big and hence militaristic powers. Because of the impact of bigness on the internal power structure, it appears to the Swiss that their customs can be preserved only by a separate political existence.

The loyalty of the French Canadians toward the English polity is today determined above all by the deep antipathy against the economic and social structure, and the way of life, of the neighboring United States; hence membership in the Dominion of Canada appears as a guarantee of their own traditions.

This classification could easily be enlarged, as every rigorous sociological investigation would have to do. It turns out that feelings of identity subsumed under the term "national" are not uniform but may derive from diverse sources: Differences in the economic and social structure and in the internal power structure, with its impact on the customs, may play a role, but within the German *Reich* customs are very diverse; shared political memories, religion, language and, finally, racial features may be source of the sense of nationality. Racial factors often have a peculiar impact. From the viewpoint of the Whites in the United States, Negroes and Whites are not united by a common sense of nationality, but the Negroes have a sense of American nationality at least by claiming a right to it. On the other hand, the pride of the Swiss in their own distinctiveness, and their willingness to defend it vigorously, is neither qualitatively different nor less widespread than the same attitudes in any "great" and powerful "nation." Time and again we find that the concept "nation" directs us to political power. Hence, the concept seems to refer—if it refers at all to a uniform phenomenon—to a specific kind of pathos which is linked to the idea of a powerful political community of people who share a common language, or religion, or common customs, or political memories; such a state may already exist or it may be desired. The more power is emphasized, the closer appears to be the link between nation and state. This pathetic pride in the power of one's own community, or this longing for it, may be much more widespread in relatively small language groups such as the Hungarians, Czechs or Greeks than in a similar but much larger community such as the Germans 150 years ago, when they were essentially a language group without pretensions to national power.

NOTES

1. On race and civilization, see also Weber's polemical speech against A. Ploetz at the first meeting of the German Sociological Association, Frankfurt, 1910, in GAzSS, 456–62. Two years later, at the second meeting of the Association in Berlin, Weber took the floor again after a presentation by Franz Oppenheimer. Among other things, Weber said (*op. cit.,* 489):
"With race theories you can prove and disprove anything you want. It is a scientific crime to attempt the circumvention, by the uncritical use of completely unclarified racial hypotheses, of the sociological study of Antiquity, which of course is much more difficult, but by no means without hope of success; after all, we can no longer find out to what extent the qualities of the Hellenes and Romans rested on inherited dispositions. The problem of such relationships has not yet been solved by the most careful and toilsome investigations of living subjects, even if undertaken in the laboratory and with the means of exact experimentation."
2. Cf. the related section on "The Nation" in ch. IX:5.
3. See Werner Wittich, *Deutsche und französische Kultur im Elsass* (Strassburg: Schlesier und Schweikhardt, 1900), 38ff; for a French transl., see "Le génie national des races française et allemande en Alsace." *Revue internationale de Sociologie,* vol. X, 1902, 777–824 and 857–907, esp. 814ff. Cf. also Weber, *GAzRS,* I, 25, n. 1; *GAzSS,* 484. "Outsiders," in contrast to the pre-1914 custodian who showed Weber his greatest treasures, cherish the Colmar museum for one of the most powerful works of art of the late Middle Ages, Grünewald's "Isenheim Altar."

CHAPTER VI

RELIGIOUS GROUPS
(THE SOCIOLOGY
OF RELIGION)[1]

i

The Origins of Religion

1. *The Original This-Worldly Orientation of Religious and Magical Action*

To define "religion," to say what it *is*, is not possible at the start of a presentation such as this. Definition can be attempted, if at all, only at the conclusion of the study. The essence of religion is not even our concern, as we make it our task to study the conditions and effects of a particular type of social action.

The external courses of religious behavior are so diverse that an understanding of this behavior can only be achieved from the viewpoint of the subjective experiences, ideas, and purposes of the individuals concerned—in short, from the viewpoint of the religious behavior's "meaning" (*Sinn*).

The most elementary forms of behavior motivated by religious or magical factors are oriented to *this* world. "That it may go well with thee . . . and that thou mayest prolong thy days upon the earth" [Deut.

4:40] expresses the reason for the performance of actions enjoined by religion or magic. Even human sacrifices, although uncommon among urban peoples, were performed in the Phoenician maritime cities without any otherworldly expectations whatsoever. Furthermore, religiously or magically motivated behavior is relatively rational behavior, especially in its earliest manifestations. It follows rules of experience, though it is not necessarily action in accordance with a means-end schema. Rubbing will elicit sparks from pieces of wood, and in like fashion the mimetical actions of a magician will evoke rain from the heavens. The sparks resulting from twirling the wooden sticks are as much a "magical" effect as the rain evoked by the manipulations of the rainmaker. Thus, religious or magical behavior or thinking must not be set apart from the range of everyday purposive conduct, particularly since even the ends of the religious and magical actions are predominantly economic.

Only we, judging from the standpoint of our modern views of nature, can distinguish objectively in such behavior those attributions of causality which are "correct" from those which are "fallacious," and then designate the fallacious attributions of causality as irrational, and the corresponding acts as "magic." Quite a different distinction will be made by the person performing the magical act, who will instead distinguish between the greater or lesser ordinariness of the phenomena in question. For example, not every stone can serve as a fetish, a source of magical power. Nor does every person have the capacity to achieve the ecstatic states which are viewed, in accordance with primitive experience, as the pre-conditions for producing certain effects in meteorology, healing, divination, and telepathy. It is primarily, though not exclusively, these extraordinary powers that have been designated by such special terms as "mana," "orenda," and the Iranian "maga" (the term from which our word "magic" is derived). We shall henceforth employ the term "charisma" for such extraordinary powers.

Charisma may be either of two types. Where this appellation is fully merited, charisma is a gift that inheres in an object or person simply by virtue of natural endowment. Such primary charisma cannot be acquired by any means. But charisma of the other type may be produced artificially in an object or person through some extraordinary means. Even then, it is assumed that charismatic powers can be developed only in people or objects in which the germ already existed but would have remained dormant unless evoked by some ascetic or other regimen. Thus, even at the earliest stage of religious evolution there are already present *in nuce* all forms of the doctrine of religious grace, from that of *gratia infusa* to the most rigorous tenet of salvation by good works. The strongly naturalistic orientation (lately termed "pre-animistic") of the earliest religious phenomena is still a feature of folk religion. To this day, no decision of church councils, differentiating the "worship" of God from the "adoration" of the icons of saints, and defining the icons as merely a devotional means, has succeeded in deterring a south European peasant from spitting in front of the statue of a saint when he holds it responsible for withholding a favor even though the customary procedures were performed.

2. *The Belief in Spirits, Demons, and the Soul*

A process of abstraction, which only appears to be simple, has usually already been carried out in the most primitive instances of religious behavior which we examine. Already crystallized is the notion that certain beings are concealed "behind" and responsible for the activity of the charismatically endowed natural objects, artifacts, animals, or persons. This is the belief in spirits. At the outset, "spirit" is neither soul, demon, nor god, but something indeterminate, material yet invisible, nonpersonal and yet somehow endowed with volition. By entering into a concrete object, spirit endows the latter with its distinctive power. The spirit may depart from its host or vessel, leaving the latter inoperative and causing the magician's charisma to fail. In other cases, the spirit may diminish into nothingness, or it may enter into another person or thing.

That any particular economic conditions are prerequisites for the emergence of a belief in spirits does not appear to be demonstrable. But belief in spirits, like all abstraction, is most advanced in those societies within which certain persons possess charismatic magical powers that inhere only in those with special qualifications. Indeed it is this circumstance that lays the foundation for the oldest of all "vocations," that of the professional necromancer. In contrast to the ordinary person, the "layman" in the magical sense, the magician is permanently endowed with charisma. Furthermore, he has turned into an "enterprise" the distinctive subjective condition that notably represents or mediates charisma, namely ecstasy. For the layman, this psychological state is accessible only in occasional actions. Unlike the merely rational practice of wizardry, ecstasy occurs in a social form, the *orgy*, which is the primordial form of religious association. But the orgy is an occasional activity, whereas the enterprise of the magician is continuous and he is indispensable for its operation.

Because of the routine demands of living, the layman can experience ecstasy only occasionally, as intoxication. To induce ecstasy, he may employ any type of alcoholic beverage, tobacco, or similar narcotics—and especially music—all of which originally served orgiastic purposes. In addition to the rational manipulation of spirits in accordance with economic interests, the manner in which ecstasy was employed constituted another important, but historically secondary, concern of the magician's art, which, naturally enough, developed almost everywhere into a secret lore. On the basis of the experience with the conditions of orgies, and in all likelihood under the influence of his professional practice, there evolved the concept of "soul" as a separate entity present in, behind or near natural objects, even as the human body contains something that leaves it in dream, syncope, ecstasy, or death.

This is not the place to treat extensively the diversity of possible relationships between spiritual beings and the objects behind which they lurk and with which they are somehow connected. These spirits or souls may "dwell" more or less continuously and exclusively near or within a concrete object or process. But on the other hand, they may somehow "possess" types of events, things, or categories thereof, the behavior and efficacy of which they will decisively determine. These and similar views are properly called animistic. The spirits may temporarily "incorporate" themselves into things, plants, animals, or people; this is a further stage of abstraction, achieved only gradually. At the highest stage of abstraction, which is scarcely ever maintained consistently, spirits may be regarded as invisible essences that follow their own laws, and are merely "symbolized by" concrete objects. In between these extremes of naturalism and abstraction there are many transitions and combinations. Yet even at the first stage of the simpler forms of abstraction, there is present in principle the notion of "supersensual" forces that may intervene in the destiny of people in the same way that a man may influence the course of the world about him.

At these earlier stages, not even the gods or demons are yet personal or enduring, and sometimes they do not even have names of their own. A god may be thought of as a power controlling the course of one particular event (Usener's *Augenblicksgötter*),[2] to whom no one gives a second thought until the event in question is repeated. On the other hand, a god may be the power which somehow emanates from a great hero after his death. Either personification or depersonalization may be a later development. Then, too, we find gods without any personal name, who are designated only by the name of the process they control. At a later time, when the semantics of this designation is no longer understood, the designation of this process may take on the character of a proper name for the god. Conversely, the proper names of powerful chieftains or prophets have become the designations of divine powers, a procedure employed in reverse by myth to derive the right to transform purely divine appellations into personal names of deified heroes. Whether a given conception of a deity becomes enduring and therefore is always approached by magical or symbolic means, depends upon many different circumstances. The most important of these is whether and in what manner the magician or the secular chieftain accepts the god in question on the basis of their own personal experiences.

Here we may simply note that the result of this process is the rise on one hand of the idea of the "soul," and on the other of ideas of "gods," "demons," hence of "supernatural" powers, the ordering of whose relations to men constitutes the realm of religious behavior. At the outset, the soul is neither a personal nor yet an impersonal entity. It is frequently identified—in a naturalistic fashion—with something that disappears after death, e.g., with the breath or with the beat of the heart in which it resides and by the ingestion of which one may acquire the courage of his dead adversary. Far more important is the fact that the soul is frequently viewed as a heterogeneous entity. Thus, the soul that leaves man during dreams is distinguished from the soul that leaves him in ecstasy —when his heart beats in his throat and his breath fails, and from the soul that inhabits his shadow. Different yet is the soul that, after death, clings to the corpse or stays near it as long as something is left of it, and the soul that continues to exert influence at the site of the person's former residence, observing with envy and anger how the heirs are relishing what had belonged to it in its life. Still another soul is that which appears to the descendants in dreams or visions, threatening or counseling, or that which enters into some animal or into another person— especially a newborn baby—bringing blessing or curse, as the case may be. The conception of the "soul" as an independent entity set over against the "body" is by no means universally accepted, even in the religions of salvation. Indeed, some of these religions, such as Buddhism, specifically reject this notion.

3. Naturalism and Symbolism

What is primarily distinctive in this whole development is not the personality, impersonality or superpersonality of these supernatural powers, but the fact that new experiences now play a role in life. Before, only the things or events that actually exist or take place played a role in life; now certain experiences, of a different order in that they only signify something, also play a role. Thus magic is transformed from a direct manipulation of forces into a *symbolic activity*.

A notion that the soul of the dead must be rendered innocuous developed, beyond the direct fear of the corpse (a fear manifested even by animals), which direct fear often determined burial postures and procedures, e.g., the squatting posture, cremation, etc. After the development of ideas of the soul, the body had to be removed or restrained in the grave, provided with a tolerable existence, and prevented from becoming envious of the possessions enjoyed by the living; or its good will had to be secured in other ways, if the survivors were to live in peace. Of the various magical practices relating to the disposal of the dead, the notion with the most enduring economic consequences is that the corpse must be accompanied to the grave by all its personal belongings. This notion was gradually attenuated to the requirement that the goods of the deceased must not be touched for at least a brief period after his death, and frequently the requirement that the survivors must not even enjoy their own possessions lest they arouse the envy of the dead. The funerary prescriptions of the Chinese still fully retain this view, with consequences that are equally irrational in both the economic and the political spheres. (One of the interdictions during the mourning period related to the occupancy of a benefice; since the usufruct thereof constituted a possession, it had to be avoided.)

The development of a realm of souls, demons, and gods in turn affected the meaning of the magical arts. For these beings cannot be grasped or perceived in any concrete sense but possess a kind of transcendental existence which is normally accessible only through the mediation of symbols and meanings and which consequently appears to be shadowy and sometimes outright unreal. Since it is assumed that behind real things and events there is something else, distinctive and spiritual, of which real events are only the symptoms or indeed the symbols, an effort must be made to influence the spiritual power that expresses itself in concrete things. This is done through actions that address themselves to a spirit or soul, hence by instrumentalities that "mean" something, i.e., symbols. Thereafter, naturalism may be swept away by a flood of symbolic actions. The occurrence of this displacement of naturalism depends upon the pressure which the professional masters of such symbolism can put behind their belief and its intellectual elaboration, hence, on the power which they manage to gain within the community. The displacement of naturalism will depend upon the importance of magic for the economy and upon the power of the organization the necromancers succeed in creating.

The proliferation of symbolic acts and their supplanting of the original naturalism will have far-reaching consequences. Thus, if the dead person is accessible only through symbolic actions, and indeed if the god expresses himself only through symbols, then the corpse may be satisfied with symbols instead of real things. As a result, actual sacrifices may be replaced by shewbreads and puppet-like representations of the surviving wives and servants of the deceased. It is of interest that the oldest paper money was used to pay, not the living, but the dead. A similar substitution occurred in the relationships of men to gods and demons. More and more, things and events assumed meanings beyond the potencies that actually or presumably inhered in them, and efforts were made to achieve real effects by means of symbolically significant action.

Every purely magical act that had proved successful in a naturalistic sense was, of course, repeated in the form once established as effective. Subsequently, this principle extended to the entire domain of symbolic significances, since the slightest deviation from the ostensibly successful method might render the procedure inefficacious. Thus, all areas of human activity were drawn into this circle of magical symbolism. For this reason the greatest contrasts of purely dogmatic views, even within religions that have undergone rationalization, may be tolerated more easily than innovations in symbolism, which threaten the magical efficacy of action or even—and this is the new concept supervening upon symbolism—arouse the anger of a god or an ancestral spirit. Thus, the question whether the sign of the cross should be made with two or three fingers was a basic reason for the schism of the Russian church as late as the seventeenth century. Again, the fear of giving serious affront to two dozen saints by omitting the days sacred to them from the calendar year has hindered the reception of the Gregorian calendar in Russia until today. Among the magicians of the American Indians, faulty singing during ritual dances was immediately punished by the death of the guilty singer, to remove the evil magic or to avert the anger of the god.

The religious stereotyping of the products of pictorial art, the oldest form of stylization, was directly determined by magical conceptions and indirectly determined by the fact that these artifacts came to be produced professionally for their magical significance; professional production tended automatically to favor the creation of art objects based upon design rather than upon representational reproduction of the natural object. The full extent of the influence exerted by the religious factor in art is exemplified in Egypt, where the devaluation of the traditional religion by the monotheistic campaign of Amenhotep IV (Ikhnaton) immediately stimulated naturalism. Other examples of the religious stylization of art may be found in the magical uses of alphabetical symbols; the development of mimicry and dance as homeopathic, apotropaic, exorcistic, or magically coercive symbolism; and the stereotyping of admissible musical scales, or at least admissible musical keynotes (*râga* in India), in contrast to the chromatic scale. Another manifestation of such religious influence is found in the widespread substitutions of therapy based upon exorcism or upon symbolic homeopathy for the earlier empirical methods of medical treatment, which frequently were considerably developed but seemed only a cure of the symptoms, from the point of view of symbolism and the animistic doctrine of possession by spirits. From the standpoint of animistic symbolism's own basic assumptions its therapeutic methods might be regarded as rational, but they bear the same relation to empirical therapy as astrology, which grew from the same roots, bears to empirical computation of the calendar.

All these related phenomena had incalculable importance for the substantive evolution of culture, but we cannot pursue this here. The first and fundamental effect of religious views upon the conduct of life and therefore upon economic activity was generally stereotyping. The alteration of any practice which is somehow executed under the protection of supernatural forces may affect the interests of spirits and gods. To the natural uncertainties and resistances facing every innovator, religion thus adds powerful impediments of its own. The sacred is the uniquely unalterable.

The details of the transitions from pre-animistic naturalism to symbolism are altogether variable. When the primitive tears out the heart of a slain foe, or wrenches the sexual organs from the body of his victim, or extracts the brain from the skull and then mounts the skull in his home or esteems it as the most precious of bridal presents, or eats parts of the bodies of slain foes or the bodies of especially fast and powerful animals—he really believes that he is coming into possession, in a naturalistic fashion, of the various powers attributed to these physical organs. The war dance is in the first instance the product of a mixture of fury and fear before the battle, and it directly produces the heroic frenzy; to this extent it too is naturalistic rather than symbolic. The transition to symbolism is at hand insofar as the war dance (somewhat in the manner of our manipulations by "sympathetic" magic) mimetically anticipates victory and thereby endeavors to insure it by magical means, insofar as animals and men are slaughtered in fixed rites, insofar as the spirits and gods of the tribe are summoned to participate in the ceremonial repast, and insofar as the consumers of a sacrificial animal regard themselves as having a distinctively close kin relationship to one another because the "soul" of this animal has entered into them.

The term "mythological thinking" has been applied to the pattern of thought that is the basis of the fully developed realm of symbolic concepts, and considerable attention has been given to the detailed elucidation of its character. We cannot occupy ourselves with these problems here. Only one generally important aspect of this way of thinking is of concern to us: the significance of analogy, especially in its most effective form, the parable. Analogy has exerted a lasting influence upon, indeed has dominated not only forms of religious expression but also juristic thinking, even the treatment of precedents in purely empirical forms of law. The syllogistic constructions of concepts through rational subsumption only gradually replaced analogical thinking, which originated in symbolistically rationalized magic, whose structure is wholly analogical.

Gods, too, were not originally represented in human forms. To be sure they came to possess the form of enduring beings, which is essential for them, only after the suppression of the purely naturalistic view still evident in the Vedas (e.g., that a fire is the god, or is at least the body of a concrete god of fire) in favor of the view that a god, forever identical with himself, possesses all fires, produces or controls them, or somehow is incorporated in each of them. This abstract conception becomes really secure only through the continuing activity of a "cult" dedicated to one and the same god—through the god's connection with an enduring association of men, for which he has special significance as the enduring god. We shall presently consider this process further. Once this perseveration of the forms of the gods has been secured, the intellectual activity of those concerned in a professional way with such problems may be devoted to the systematization of these ideas.

4. Pantheon and Functional Gods

The gods frequently constituted an unordered miscellany of accidental entities, held together fortuitously by the cult, and this condition was by no means confined to periods of low social differentiation. Thus, even the gods of the Vedas did not form an orderly commonwealth. But as a rule there is a tendency for a pantheon to evolve once systematic thinking concerning religious practice and the rationalization of life generally, with its increasing demands upon the gods, have reached a certain level, the details of which may differ greatly from case to case. The emergence of a pantheon entails the specialization and characterization of the various gods as well as the allocation of constant attributes and the differentiation of their jurisdictions. Yet the increasing anthropomorphic personification of the gods is in no way identical with or parallel to the increasing delimitation of jurisdictions. Frequently the opposite is true. Thus, the scope of the Roman *numina* is incomparably more fixed and unequivocal than that of the Hellenic gods. On the other hand, the anthropomorphization and plastic representation of the latter as real personalities went very much further than in the authentic Roman religion.

Sociologically, the most important basis for this development is to be found in the fact that the genuine Roman view concerning the general nature of the supernatural tended to retain the pattern of a national religion appropriate to a peasantry and a landed gentry. On the other hand, Greek religion inclined to reflect the general structure of an interlocal regional knightly culture, such as that of the Homeric age with its heroic gods. The partial reception of these conceptions and their indirect influence on Roman soil changed nothing of the national religion, many of these conceptions attaining only an esthetic existence there. The primary characteristics of the Roman tradition were conserved virtually unchanged in ritual practices. In contrast to the Greek way, the Roman attitude also remained permanently adverse to religions of the orgiastic or mystery type (for reasons to be discussed later). Quite naturally, the capacity of magical powers to develop differentiated forms is much less elastic than the "jurisdiction" of a god conceived as a person. Roman religion remained *religio* (whether the word be derived etymologically from *religare* [to tie] or from *relegere* [to reconsider]); it denoted a tie with tested cultic formulae and a "consideration" for spirits (*numina*) of all types which are active everywhere.

The authentic Roman religion contained, besides the trend toward formalism which resulted from the factors just mentioned, another important characteristic trait that stands in contrast with Greek culture, namely a conception of the impersonal as having an inner relationship to the objectively rational. The *religio* of the Roman surrounded his entire daily life and his every act with the casuistry of a sacred law, a casuistry which temporally and quantitatively occupied his attention quite as much as the attention of the Jews and Hindus was occupied by their ritual laws, quite as much as the attention of the Chinese was occupied by the sacred laws of Taoism. The Roman priestly lists (*indigitamenta*)[3] contained an almost infinite number of gods, particularized and specialized. Every act and indeed every specific element of an act stood under the influence of special *numina*. It was therefore a precaution for one engaged in an important activity to invoke and honor, besides the *dii certi* to whom tradition had already assigned a fixed responsibility and influence, various ambiguous gods (*incerti*) whose jurisdiction was uncertain and indeed whose sex, effectiveness, and possibly even existence were dubious. As many as a dozen of the *dii certi*[4] might be involved in certain farming activities. While the Romans tended to regard the *ekstasis* (Latin: *superstitio*) of the Greeks as a mental alienation (*abalienatio mentis*) that was socially reprehensible, the casuistry of Roman *religio* (and of the Etruscan, which went even further) appeared to the Greek as slavish fear (*deisidaimonia*). The Roman interest in keeping the *numina* satisfied had the effect of producing a conceptual analysis of all individual actions into their components, each being assigned to the jurisdiction of a particular *numen* whose special protection it enjoyed.

Although analogous phenomena occurred in India and elsewhere, the listed number of spirits (*numina*) to be derived and formally listed (*indigitieren*) on the basis of purely conceptual analysis, and hence intellectual abstraction, was nowhere as large as among the Romans, for whom ritual practice was thoroughly concentrated upon this procedure. The characteristic distinction of the Roman way of life which resulted from this abstraction (and this provides an obvious contrast to the influence of Jewish and Asiatic rituals upon their respective cultures) was its ceaseless cultivation of a practical, rational casuistry of sacred law, the development of a sort of cautelary sacred jurisprudence[5] and the tendency to treat these matters to a certain extent as lawyers' problems. In this way, sacred law became the mother of rational juristic thinking. This essentially religious characteristic of Roman culture is still evident in the histories of Livy. In contrast to the practical orientation of the Jewish tradition, the Roman emphasis was always on the demonstration of the "correctness" of any given institutional innovation, from the point of view of sacred and national law. In Roman thought questions of juristic etiquette were central, not sin, punishment, penitence and salvation.

For the ideas of deity, however, to which we must here first devote our attention, it was relevant that both of those processes, anthropomorphization and the delimitation of jurisdictions, which ran partly parallel and partly in opposition to each other, contained the tendency to propel ever further the rationalization of the worship of the gods as well as of the very idea of god, even though the starting point was the given variety of deities. For our purposes here, the examination of the various kinds of gods and demons would be of only slight interest, although or rather because it is naturally true that they, like the vocabulary of a language, have been shaped directly by the economic situation and the historical destinies of different peoples. Since these developments are concealed from us by the mists of time, it is frequently no longer possible to determine the reasons for the predominance of one over another kind of deity. These may lie in objects of nature that are important to the economy, such as stellar bodies, or in organic processes that the gods and demons possess or influence, evoke or impede: disease, death, birth, fire, drought, rainstorm, and harvest failure. The outstanding economic importance of certain events may enable a particular god to achieve primacy within the pantheon, as for example the primacy of the god of heaven. He may be conceived of primarily as the master of light and warmth, but among groups that raise cattle he is most frequently conceived of as the lord of reproduction.

That the worship of chthonic deities such as Mother Earth generally presupposes a relative importance of agriculture is fairly obvious, but such parallelism is not always direct. Nor can it be maintained that the heavenly gods, as representatives of a heroes' paradise beyond the earth, have everywhere been noble gods rather than chthonic deities of the peasantry. Even less can it be maintained that the development of Mother Earth as a goddess parallels the development of matriarchal organization. Nevertheless, the chthonic deities who controlled the harvest have customarily borne a more local and popular character than the other gods. In any case, the inferiority of earth divinities to celestial personal gods who reside in the clouds or on the mountains is frequently determined by the development of a knightly culture, and there is a tendency to permit originally tellurian deities to take their place among the gods who are resident in the skies. Conversely, the chthonic deities frequently combine two functions in primarily agrarian cultures: they control the harvest, thus granting wealth, and they are also the masters of the dead who have been laid to rest in the earth. This explains why frequently, as in the Eleusinian mysteries, these two most important practical interests, namely earthly riches and fate in the hereafter, depend upon them. On the other hand, the heavenly gods are the lords of the stars in their courses. The fixed laws by which the celestial bodies are obviously regulated favor a development whereby the rulers of the celestial bodies become masters of everything that has or ought to have fixed laws, particularly of judicial decisions and morality.

Both the increasing objective significance of typical components and types of conduct, and subjective reflection about them, lead to functional specialization among the gods. This may be of a rather abstract type, as in the case of the gods of "incitation" (*Antreibens*) and many similar gods in India.[6] Or it may lead to qualitative specialization according to particular lines of activity, e.g., praying, fishing, or plowing. The classic paradigm of this fairly abstract form of deity-formation is the highest conception of the ancient Hindu pantheon, Brahma, as the lord of prayer. Just as the Brahmin priests monopolized the power of effective prayer, i.e., of the effective magical coercion of the gods, so did a god in turn now monopolize the disposition of this capacity, thereby controlling what is of primary importance in all religious behavior; as a result, he finally came to be the supreme god, if not the only one. In Rome, Janus, as the god of the correct "beginning" [of an action] who thus decides everything, achieved more unpretentiously a position of relatively universal importance.

Yet there is no concerted action, as there is no individual action, without its special god. Indeed, if an association is to be permanently guaranteed, it must have such a god. Whenever an organization is not the personal power base of an individual ruler, but genuinely an association of men, it has need of a god of its own.

5. Ancestor Cult and the Priesthood of the Family Head

To begin with, household and kin group need a god of their own, and they naturally turn to the spirits of the ancestors, actual or imaginary. To these are later added the *numina* and the gods of the hearth and the hearth fire. The importance attributed by the group to its cult, which is performed by the head of the house or *gens,* is quite variable and depends on the structure and practical importance of the family. A high degree of development in the domestic cult of ancestors generally runs parallel to a patriarchal structure of the household, since only in a patriarchal structure is the home of central importance for the men. But as the example of Israel demonstrates, the connection between these factors is not a simple one, for the gods of other social groups, especially those of a religious or political type, may by reason of their priests' power effectively suppress or entirely destroy the domestic cult and the priestly functioning of the family head.

But where the power and significance of the domestic cult and priesthood remain unimpaired, they naturally form an extremely strong personal bond, which exercises a profound influence on the family and the *gens,* unifying the members firmly into a strongly cohesive group. This cohesive force also exerts a strong influence on the internal economic relationships of the households. It effectively determines and stamps all the legal relationships of the family, the legitimacy of the wife and heirs, and the relation of sons to their father and of brothers to one another. From the viewpoint of the family and kin group, the religious reprehensibility of marital infidelity is that it may bring about a situation where a stranger, i.e., one not related by blood, might offer sacrifice to the ancestors of the kin group, which would tend to arouse their indignation against the blood relatives. For the gods and *numina* of a strictly personal association will spurn sacrifices brought by one lacking authorization. Strict observance of the principle of agnate relationship, wherever it is found, certainly is closely connected with this, as are all questions relating to the legitimation of the head of the household for his functioning as priest.

Similar sacral motivations have influenced the testamentary rights of succession of the eldest son, either as sole or preferred heir, though military and economic factors have also been involved in this matter. Furthermore, it is largely to this religious motivation that the Asiatic (Chinese and Japanese) family and clan, and that of Rome in the Occident, owe the maintenance of the patriarchal structure throughout all changes in economic conditions. Wherever such a religious bond of household and kin group exists, only two possible types of more inclusive associations, especially of the political variety, may emerge. One of these is the religiously dedicated confederation of actual or imaginary kin groups. The other is the patrimonial rule of a royal household over comparable households of the subjects, in the manner of an attenuated patriarchalism. Wherever the patrimonial rule of the royal household developed, the ancestors, the *numina, genii* or personal gods of that most powerful household took place beside the domestic gods belonging to subject households and thus lent a religious sanction to the position of the ruler. This was the case in the Far East, as in China, where the emperor as high priest monopolized the cult of the supreme spirits of nature. The sacred role of the *genius* of the Roman ruler (*princeps*), which resulted in the universal reception of the person of the emperor into the lay cult, was calculated to produce similar results.

6. *Political and Local Gods*

Where the development was in the direction of a religiously buttressed confederation, there developed a special god of the political organzation as such, as was the case with Yahweh. That he was a God of the federation—which according to tradition was an alliance between the Jews and the Midianites—led to a fateful consequence. His relation to the people of Israel, who had accepted him under oath, together with the political confederation and the sacred order of their social relationships, took the form of a covenant (*berith*), a contractual relationship imposed by Yahweh and accepted submissively by Israel. From this, various ritual, canonical, and ethical obligations which were binding upon the human partner were presumed to flow. But this contractual relationship also involved very definite promises by the Divine partner; it was deemed appropriate for the human partner to remind him of their inviolability, within the limits enjoined as proper vis-à-vis an omnipotent god. This is the primary root of the promissory character of Israelite religion, a character that despite numerous analogues is found nowhere else in such intensity.

On the other hand, it is a universal phenomenon that the formation of a political association entails subordination to its corresponding god. The Mediterranean *synoikism* as was always a reorganization, if not necessarily a new creation, of a cultic community under a *polis* deity. The classical bearer of the important phenomenon of a political local god was of course the *polis*, yet it was by no means the only one. On the contrary, every permanent political association had a special god who guaranteed the success of the political action of the group. When fully developed, this god was altogether exclusive with respect to outsiders, and in principle he accepted offerings and prayers only from the members of his group, or at least he was expected to act in this fashion. But since one could not be certain of this, disclosure of the method of effectively influencing the god was usually prohibited strictly. The stranger was thus not only a political, but also a religious alien. Even when the god of another group had the same name and attributes as that of one's own polity, he was still considered to be different. Thus the Juno of the Veientines is not that of the Romans, just as for the Neapolitan the Madonna of each chapel is different from the others; he may adore the one and berate or dishonor the other if she helps his competitors. An effort may be made to render the god disloyal to one's adversaries by promising him, for example, welcome and adoration in the new territory if only he will abandon the foes of the group in question (*evocare deos*). This invocation to the gods of a rival tribe to reject their group in behalf of another was practiced by Camillus before Veii.[7] The gods of one group might be stolen or otherwise acquired by another group, but this does not always accrue to the benefit of the latter, as in the case of the ark of the Israelites which brought plagues upon the Philistine conquerors.

In general, political and military conquest also entailed the victory of the stronger god over the weaker god of the vanquished group. Of course not every god of a political group was a local god, spatially anchored to the group's administrative center. The *lares* of the Roman family changed their venue as the family moved; the God of Israel was represented, in the narrative of the wandering in the wilderness, as journeying with and at the head of his people. Yet, in contradiction to this account, Yahweh was also represented—and this is his decisive hallmark—as a God from afar, a God of the nations who resided on Sinai, and who approached in the storm with his heavenly hosts (*zebaoth*) only when the military need of his people required his presence and participation. It probably has been assumed correctly that this particular quality of "effective influence from afar," which resulted from the reception of a foreign god by Israel, was a factor in the evolution of the concept of Yahweh as the universal and omnipotent God. For, as a rule, the fact that a god was regarded as a local deity, or that he sometimes demanded of his followers exclusive "monolatry" did not lead to monotheism, but rather tended to strengthen religious particularism. Conversely, the development of local gods resulted in an uncommon strengthening of political particularism.

This was true even of the *polis*, which was as exclusive of other communities as one church is toward another, and which was absolutely opposed to the formation of a unified priesthood overarching the various groupings. In marked contrast to our state, which is conceived as a compulsory territorial institution, the *polis*, as a result of this particularism, remained essentially a *personal* association of cultic adherents of the civic god. The *polis* was further organized internally into personal cultic associations of tribal, clan, and domestic gods, which were exclusive with respect to their individual cults. Moreover, the *polis* was also exclusive internally, with regard to those who stood apart from the particular cults of kin groups and households. Thus in Athens, a man who had no household god (*Zeus herkeios*) could not hold office, as was the case in Rome with anyone who did not belong to the association of the *patres*. The special plebeian official (*tribunus plebis*) was covered only by a human oath (*sacro sanctus*); he had no auspices, and hence no legitimate *imperium*, but only a *potestas*.[8]

The local geographical connection of the association's god reached its maximum development where the very site of a particular association came to be regarded as specifically sacred to the god. This was increasingly the case of Palestine in relation to Yahweh, with the result that the tradition depicted him as a god who, living far off but desiring to participate in his cultic association and to honor it, required cartloads of Palestinian soil to be brought to him.

The rise of genuinely local gods is associated not only with permanent settlement, but also with certain other conditions that mark the local association as an agency of political significance. Normally, the god of a locality and his cultic association reach fullest development on the foundation of the city as a separate political association with corporate rights, independent of the court and the person of the ruler. Consequently, such a full development of the local god is not found in India, the Far East, or Iran, and occurred only in limited measure in northern Europe, in the form of the tribal god. On the other hand, outside the sphere of autonomous cities this development occurred in Egypt, as early as the stage of zoolatric religion, in the interest of apportioning districts. From the city-states, local deities spread to confederacies such as those of the Israelites, Aetolians, etc., which were oriented to this model. From the viewpoint of the history of ideas, this concept of the association as the local carrier of the cult is an intermediate link between the strict patrimonial view of political action and the notion of the purely instrumental association and compulsory organization, such as the [Gierke and Preuss] view of the modern "territorial corporate organization" (*Gebietskörperschaft*).

Not only political associations but also occupational and vocational associations have their special deities or saints. These were still entirely absent in the Vedic pantheon, which was a reflection of that particular level of economic development. On the other hand, the ancient Egyptian god of scribes indicates bureaucratization, just as the presence all over the globe of special gods and saints for merchants and all sorts of crafts reflects increasing occupational differentiation. As late as the 19th century, the Chinese army carried through the canonization of its war god, signifying that the military was regarded as a special vocation among others. This is in contrast to the conception of the war gods of the ancient Mediterranean littoral and of the Medes, who were always great national gods.

7. *Universalism and Monotheism in Relation to Everyday Religious Needs and Political Organization*

Just as the forms of the gods vary, depending on natural and social conditions, so too there are variations in the potential of a god to achieve primacy in the pantheon, or to monopolize divinity. Only Judaism and Islam are strictly monotheistic in their essence. The Hindu and Christian forms of the sole or supreme deity are theological concealments of the fact that an important and unique religious interest, namely in salvation through the incarnation of a divinity, stands in the way of strict monotheism. The path to monotheism has been traversed with varying degrees of consistency, but nowhere—not even during the Reformation—was the existence of spirits and demons permanently eliminated; rather, they were simply subordinated unconditionally to the one god, at least in theory.

The decisive consideration was and remains: who is deemed to exert the stronger influence on the interests of the individual in his everyday life, the theoretically supreme god or the lower spirits and demons? If the spirits, then the religion of everyday life is decisively determined by them, regardless of the official god-concept of the ostensibly rationalized religion. Where a political god of a locality developed, it was natural enough that he frequently achieved primacy. Whenever a plurality of settled communities with established local gods expanded the area of the political association through conquest, the usual result was that various local gods of the newly amalgamated communities were thereupon associated into a religious totality. Within this amalgam, the empirical and functional specializations of the gods, whether original or subsequently determined by new experiences concerning the special spheres of the gods' influences, would reappear in a division of labor, with varying degrees of clarity.

The local deities of the most important political and religious centers (and hence of the rulers and priests in these centers), e.g., Marduk of Babel or Amon of Thebes, thus advanced to the rank of the highest gods, only to disappear again with the eventual destruction or removal of the residence, as happened in the case of Assur after the fall of the Assyrian empire. Once a political association came under the tutelage of a particular deity, its protection appeared inadequate until the gods of the individual members were also incorporated, "associated," and adopted locally in a sort of "synoikism." This practice, so common in Antiquity, was re-enacted when the great sacred relics of the provincial cathedrals were transferred to the capital of the unified Russian empire.[9]

The possible combinations of the various principles involved in the construction of a pantheon or in the achievement of a position of primacy by one or another god are almost infinite in number. Indeed, the jurisdictions of the divine figures are as fluid as those of the officials of patrimonial regimes. Moreover, the differentiation among jurisdictions of the various gods is intersected by the practice of religious attachment to a particularly reliable god, or courtesy to a particular god who happens to be invoked. He is then treated as functionally universal; thus all kinds of functions are attributed to him, even functions which have been assigned previously to other deities. This is the "henotheism" which Max Müller erroneously assumed to constitute a special stage of evolution.[10] In the attainment of primacy by a particular god, purely rational factors have often played an important role. Wherever a considerable measure of constancy in regard to certain prescriptions became clearly evident—most often in the case of stereotyped and fixed religious rites—and where this was recognized by rationalized religious thought, then those deities that evinced the greatest regularity in their behavior, namely the gods of heaven and the stars, had a chance to achieve primacy.

Yet in the religion of everyday life, only a comparatively minor role was played by those gods who, because they exerted a major influence upon universal natural phenomena, were interpreted by metaphysical speculation as very important and occasionally even as world creators. The reason for this is that these natural phenomena vary but little in their course, and hence it is not necessary to resort in everyday religious practice to the devices of sorcerers and priests in order to influence them. A particular god might be of decisive importance for the entire religion of a people (e.g., Osiris in Egypt) if he met a pressing religious need, in this case a soteriological one, yet he might not achieve primacy in the pantheon. Reason favored the primacy of universal gods; and every consistent crystallization of a pantheon followed systematic rational principles to some degree, since it was always influenced by professional sacerdotal rationalism or by the rational striving for order on the part of secular individuals. Above all, it is the aforementioned similarity of the rational regularity of the stars in their heavenly courses, as regulated by divine order, to the inviolable sacred social order in terrestrial affairs, that makes the universal gods the responsible guardians of both these phenomena. Upon these gods depend both rational economic practice and the secure, regulated hegemony (*Herrschaft*) of sacred norms in the community. The priests are the primary protagonists and representatives of these sacred norms. Hence the competition of the stellar deities Varuna and Mitra, the guardians of the sacred order, with the storm god Indra,[11] a formidable warrior and the slayer of the dragon, was a reflection of the conflict between the priesthood, striving for a firm regulation and control of life, and the powerful warlike nobility. Among this warrior class, the appropriate reaction to supernatural powers was to believe in a heroic god avid for martial exploits as well as in the disorderly irrationality of fate and adventuresomeness. We shall find this same contrast significant in many other contexts.

The ascension of celestial or astral gods in the pantheon is advanced by a priesthood's propagation of systematized sacred ordinances, as in India, Iran, or Babylonia, and is assisted by a rationalized system of regulated subordination of subjects to their overlords, such as we find in the bureaucratic states of China and Babylonia. In Babylonia, religion plainly evolved toward a belief in the dominion of the stars, particularly the planets, over all things, from the days of the week to the fate of the individual in the afterworld. Development in this direction culminates in astrological fatalism. But this development is actually a product of later sacerdotal lore, and it is still unknown to the national religion of the politically independent state. A god may dominate a pantheon without being an international or "universal" deity. But his dominance of a pantheon usually suggests that he is on his way to becoming that.

As reflection concerning the gods deepened, it was increasingly felt that the existence and nature of the deity must be established unequivocally and that the god should be "universal" in this sense. Among the Greeks, philosophers interpreted whatever gods were found elsewhere as equivalent to and so identical with the deities of the moderately organized Greek pantheon. This tendency toward universalization grew with the increasing predominance of the primary god of the pantheon, that is, as he assumed more of a "monotheistic" character. The growth of empire in China, the extension of the power of the Brahmin caste throughout all the varied political formations in India, and the development of the Persian and Roman empires favored the rise of both universalism and monotheism, though not always in the same measure and with quite different degrees of success.

The growth of empire (or comparable adjustment processes that tend in the same direction) has by no means been the sole or indispensable lever for the accomplishment of this development. In the Yahweh cult, the most important instance in the history of religion, there evolved at least a first approach to universalistic monotheism, namely monolatry, as a result of a concrete historic event—the formation of a confederacy. In this case, universalism was a product of international politics, of which the pragmatic interpreters were the prophetic protagonists of the cult of Yahweh and the ethics enjoined by him. As a consequence of their preaching, the deeds of other nations that were profoundly affecting Israel's vital interests also came to be regarded as wrought by Yahweh. At this point one can see clearly the distinctively and eminently *historical* character of the theorizing of the Hebrew prophets, which stands in sharp contrast to the speculations concerning nature characteristic of the priesthoods of India and Babylonia. Equally striking is the ineluctable obligation resulting from Yahweh's promises: the necessity of interpreting the entire history of the Hebrew nation as consisting of the deeds of Yahweh, and hence as constituting a pattern of "world history" in view of the many dire threats to the people's survival, the historical contradictions to the divine promises, as well as the inextricable linkage with the destinies of other nations. Thus, the ancient warrior god of the confederacy, who had become the local god of the city of Jerusalem, took on the prophetic and universalistic traits of transcendently sacred omnipotence and inscrutability.

In Egypt, the monotheistic, and hence necessarily universalistic, transition of Amenhotep IV (Ikhnaton) to the solar cult resulted from an entirely different situation. One factor was again the extensive rationalism of the priesthood, and in all likelihood of the laity as well, which was of a purely naturalistic character, in marked contrast to Israelite prophecy. Another factor was the practical need of a monarch at the head of a bureaucratic unified state to break the power of the priests by eliminating the multiplicity of their gods, and to restore the ancient power of the deified Pharaoh by elevating the monarch to the position of supreme solar priest. On the other hand, the universalistic monotheism of Christianity and Islam must be regarded as derivative of Judaism, while the relative monotheism of Zoroastrianism was in all likelihood determined at least in part by Near Eastern rather than intra-Iranian influences. All of these monotheisms were critically influenced by the distinctive character of "ethical" prophecy, rather than by the "exemplary" type—a distinction to be expounded later [*iii:* 5]. All other relatively monotheistic and universalistic developments are the products of the philosophical speculations of priests and laymen. They achieved practical religious importance only when they became associated with the quest for salvation. (We shall return to this matter later.)

Almost everywhere a beginning was made toward some form of consistent monotheism, but practical impediments thwarted this development in the workaday mass religion (*Alltagsreligion*), with the exceptions of Judaism, Islam, and Protestant Christianity. There are different reasons for the failure of a consistent monotheism to develop in different cultures, but the main reason was generally the pressure of the powerful material and ideological interests vested in the priests, who resided in the cultic centers and regulated the cults of the particular gods. Still another impediment to the development of monotheism was the religious need of the laity for an accessible and tangible familiar religious object which could be brought into relationship with concrete life situations or with definite groups of people to the exclusion of outsiders, an object which would above all be accessible to magical influences. The security provided by a tested magical manipulation is far more reassuring than the experience of worshipping a god who—precisely because he is omnipotent—is not subject to magical influence. The crystallization of developed conceptions of supernatural forces as gods, even as a single transcendent god, by no means automatically eliminated the ancient magical notions, not even in Christianity. It did produce, however, the possibility of a dual relationship between men and the supernatural. This must now be discussed.

NOTES

1. Since the Fischoff translation did not contain a footnote apparatus, an attempt had to be made to identify at least Weber's major references. Unless otherwise indicated, all notes are by Roth.

In this unfinished "chapter" on religious groupings, Weber provides a setting for his earlier writings on the "Protestant Ethic and the Spirit of Capitalism" and the 1906 version of "The Protestant Sects and the Spirit of Capitalism" (see Gerth and Mills, eds., *op. cit.*, 302–22). The proper place of the present study within his other studies in the sociology of religion is indicated in the introduction to the three-volume *Collected Essays in the Sociology of Religion* (see *The Protestant Ethic*, transl. T. Parsons, 13–31, esp. 29ff.), where Weber writes: "Some justification is needed for the fact that ethnographic material has not been utilized to anything like the extent which the value of its contributions naturally demands in any really thorough investigation, especially in Asiatic religions. This limitation has not only been imposed because human powers of work are restricted. This omission has also seemed to be permissible because we are here necessarily dealing with the religious ethics of the classes which were the culture-bearers of their respective countries. We are concerned with the influence which *their* conduct has had. Now it is quite true that this can only be completely known in all its details when the facts of ethnography and folklore have been compared with it. Hence we must expressly admit and emphasize that this is a gap to which the ethnographer will legitimately object. I hope to contribute something to the closing of this gap in a systematic study of the Sociology of Religion."

The present book-length chapter is part of this systematic study. However, the ethnographic treatment in the first three subchapters remains sketchy since Weber wants to press on to the core of his analysis. After working on the present chapter, Weber's next writing in this field was his essay on Confucianism (begun in 1913).

2. See Hermann Usener, *Götternamen. Versuch einer Lehre von der religiösen Begriffsbildung* (Bonn: Cohen, 1896), 279ff. (W)

3. Indigamenta: See Chantepie-Bertholet-Lehmann (abbr. Chant.), *Lehrbuch der Religionsgeschichte* (Tübingen: Mohr, 1925), 4th ed., vol. I, 69. (W) Weber used the earlier editions as one of his sources.

4. Cf. Chant., *op. cit.*, vol. II, 455f. (W)

5. On cautelary jurisprudence, see below, ch. VIII:*iii*:1.—Ludwig Deubner (in Chant., *loc. cit.*) emphasizes the magical nature of the Roman insistence on ritual correctness and rejects the interpretation of this practice as a "specifically juristic approach." However, this does not necessarily conflict with Weber's presentation which derives Roman legal rationalism from these magical sources.

6. Cf. Helmuth von Glasenapp, *Der Hinduismus* (Munich: Wolff, 1922), 25. (W)

7. According to legend, M. Furius Camillus was appointed dictator at a critical juncture in the long war with Veii ca. 400 B.C. The legend has certain parallels with the siege and capture of Troy. Camillus is alleged to have used a

secret passage to the altar of Juno in Veii in order to offer a sacrifice to her. The goddess changed her allegiance and was taken in triumph to Rome where she resided forever after on the Aventine Hill.

8. For a fuller discussion, see *The City*, ch. XVI:*iv*:4.

9. See also *infra*, 1174. Weber may have had in mind the transfer of important cult objects—such as the icon of the Madonna of Kazan (from Moscow) and the remains of Alexander Nevskii (from Vladimir)—to his newly founded capital city on the Neva by Peter the Great; cf. Anatole Leroy-Beaulieu, *The Empire of the Tsars and the Russians* (transl. Z. A. Ragozin; London 1898), III, 100f., 197f. In earlier centuries, similar moves played a role in the gradual ascendance of Moscow over the other *udel* principalities or reenforced it. Thus in 1395 the Madonna of Vladimir, the former seat of the Metropolitan, was transferred to Moscow, and at various times subjugated competing cities had to hand over their main church bells (Tver in 1340; Great Novgorod in 1478, Pskov in 1510—in the latter two cases, however, this was probably of more directly political significance, since these were the bells for the citizen assembly, the *veche*). At a later date, in the 1640s, the remains of several Russian Patriarchs were transferred for reburial in Moscow. Cf. Karl Stählin, *Geschichte Russlands* (Stuttgart 1923), I, 142, 164, 213, 238; Albert M. Ammann S.J., *Ostslawische Kirchengeschichte* (Vienna 1950), 42, 282.

10. See Max Müller, *Anthropological Religion* (London: Longmans, Green, 1892), 76. Müller's three stages are Henotheism (each god supreme in his own domain), Polytheism (one god supreme among many), Monotheism (the supremacy of the one and only god); see also *id.*, *Contributions to the Science of Mythology* (London: Longmans, Green, 1897), 138ff.

11. On Varuna, Mitra and Indra, cf. Weber, "Hinduismus und Buddhismus," in *GAzRS*, II, 29, 175 (*Religion of India*, 27, 170).

ii

Magic and Religion

1. *Magical Coercion Versus Supplication, Prayer and Sacrifice*[1]

A power conceived by analogy to man endowed with a soul may be coerced into the service of man, just as the naturalistic power of a spirit could be coerced. Whoever possesses the requisite charisma for employing the proper means is stronger even than the god, whom he can compel to do his will. In these cases, religious behavior is not worship of the god but rather coercion of the god,[2] and invocation is not prayer but rather the exercise of magical formulae. Such is one ineradicable basis of popular religion, particularly in India. Indeed, such magical coercion is universally diffused, and even the Catholic priest continues to practice something of this magical power in executing the miracle of the mass and in exercising the power of the keys. By and large this is the original, though not exclusive, origin of the orgiastic and mimetic components of the religious cult—especially of song, dance, drama, and the typical fixed formulae of prayer.

The process of anthropomorphization may also take the form of attributing to the gods the human behavior patterns appropriate to a mighty terrestrial potentate, whose discretionary favor can be obtained by entreaty, gifts, service, tributes, cajolery, and bribes. On the other hand, his favor may be earned as a consequence of the devotee's own faithfulness and good conduct in conformity with his will. In these ways, the gods are conceived by analogy to earthly rulers: mighty beings whose power differs only in degree, at least at first. As gods of this type evolve, worship of divinity comes to be regarded as a necessity.

Of course, the two characteristic elements of divine worship, prayer and sacrifice, have their origin in magic. In prayer, the boundary between magical formula and supplication remains fluid. The technically rationalized enterprise of prayer (in the form of prayer wheels and similar devices, or of prayer strips hung in the wind or attached to icons of gods or saints, or of carefully measured rosary bead counting—virtually all of which are products of the methodical compulsion of the gods by the Hindus) everywhere stands far closer to magic than to entreaty. Individual prayer as real supplication is found in religions that are otherwise undifferentiated, but in most cases such prayer has a purely business-like, rationalized form that sets forth the achievements of the supplicant in behalf of the god and then claims adequate recompense therefor.

Sacrifice, at its first appearance, is a magical instrumentality that in part stands at the immediate service of the coercion of the gods. For the gods also need the soma juice[3] of the sorcerer-priests, the substance which engenders their ecstasy and enables them to perform their deeds. This is the ancient notion of the Aryans as to why it is possible to coerce the gods by sacrifice. It may even be held that a pact can be concluded with the gods which imposes obligations on both parties; this was the fateful conception of the Israelites in particular. Still another view of sacrifice holds that it is a means of deflecting, through magical media, the wrath of the god upon another object, a scapegoat or above all a human sacrifice.

But another motive for sacrifice is of greater importance, and it is probably older too: the sacrifice, especially of animals, is intended as a *communio,* a ceremony of eating together which serves to produce a fraternal community between the sacrificers and the god. This represents a transformation in the significance of the even older notion that to rend and consume a strong (and later a sacred) animal enables the eaters to absorb its potencies. Some such older magical meaning—and there are various other possibilities—may still provide the act of sacrifice with its essential form, even after genuine cultic views have come to exert considerable influence. Indeed, such a magical significance may even regain dominance over the cultic meaning. The sacrificial rituals of the Brahmanas, and even of the Atharva Veda, were almost purely sorcery, in contrast to the ancient Nordic ones. On the other hand, there are many departures from magic, as when sacrifices are interpreted as tribute. First fruits may be sacrificed in order that the god may not deprive man of the enjoyment of the remaining fruits; and sacrifice is often interpreted as a self-imposed punishment or atonement that averts the wrath of the gods before it falls upon the sacrificer. To be sure, this does not yet involve any awareness of sin, and it initially takes place in a mood of cool and calculated trading, as for example in India.

An increasing predominance of non-magical motives is later brought about by the growing recognition of the power of a god and of his character as a personal overlord. The god becomes a great lord who may fail on occasion, and whom one cannot approach with devices of magical compulsion, but only with entreaties and gifts. But if these motives add anything new to mere wizardry, it is initially something as sober and rational as the motivation of magic itself. The pervasive and central theme is: *do ut des*. This aspect clings to the routine and the mass religious behavior of all peoples at all times and in all religions. The normal situation is that the burden of all prayers, even in the most other-worldly religions, is the aversion of the external evils of this world and the inducement of the external advantages of this world.

Every aspect of religious phenomena that points beyond evils and advantages in this world is the work of a special evolutionary process, one characterized by distinctively dual aspects. On the one hand, there is an ever-broadening rational systematization of the god concept and of the thinking concerning the possible relationships of man to the divine. On the other hand, there ensues a characteristic recession of the original, practical and calculating rationalism. As such primitive rationalism recedes, the significance of distinctively religious behavior is sought less and less in the purely external advantages of everyday economic success. Thus, the goal of religious behavior is successively "irrationalized" until finally otherworldly non-economic goals come to represent what is distinctive in religious behavior. But for this very reason the extra-economic evolution just described requires as one of its prerequisites the existence of specific personal carriers.

The relationships of men to supernatural forces which take the forms of prayer, sacrifice and worship may be termed "*cult*" (*Kultus*) and "*religion*," as distinguished from "*sorcery*," which is magical coercion. Correspondingly, those beings that are worshipped and entreated religiously may be termed "*gods*," in contrast to "*demons*," which are magically coerced and charmed. There may be no instance in which it is possible to apply this differentiation absolutely, since the cults we have just called "religious" practically everywhere contain numerous magical components. The historical development of the aforementioned differentiation frequently came about in a very simple fashion when a secular or priestly power suppressed a cult in favor of a new religion, with the older gods continuing to live on as demons.

2. *The Differentiation of Priests from Magicians*

The sociological aspect of this differentiation [into gods and demons] is the rise of the "priesthood" as something distinct from "practitioners of magic." Applied to reality, this contrast is fluid, as are almost all socio-logical phenomena. Even the theoretical differentiae of these types are not unequivocally determinable. Following the distinction between "cult" and "sorcery," one may contrast those professional functionaries who in-fluence the gods by means of worship with those magicians who coerce demons by magical means; but in many great religions, including Chris-tianity, the concept of the priest includes such a magical qualification.

Or the term "priest" may be applied to the functionaries of a regularly organized and permanent enterprise concerned with influencing the gods, in contrast with the individual and occasional efforts of magicians. Even this contrast is bridged over by a sliding scale of transitions, but as a pure type the priesthood is unequivocal and can be said to be characterized by the presence of certain fixed cultic centers associated with some actual cultic apparatus.

Or it may be thought that what is decisive for the concept of priest-hood is that the functionaries, regardless of whether their office is heredi-tary or personal, be actively associated with some type of social organiza-tion, of which they are employees or organs operating in the interests of the organization's members, in contrast with magicians, who are self-employed. Yet even this distinction, which is clear enough conceptually, is fluid in actuality. The sorcerer is not infrequently a member of an or-ganized guild, and is occasionally the member of a hereditary caste which may hold a monopoly of magic within the particular community. Even the Catholic priest is not always the occupant of an official post. In Rome he is occasionally a poor mendicant who lives a hand-to-mouth existence from the proceeds of single masses which he performs.

Yet another distinguishing quality of the priest, it is asserted, is his professional equipment of special knowledge, fixed doctrine, and voca-tional qualifications, which brings him into contrast with either sorcerers or prophets, who exert their influence by virtue of personal gifts (char-isma) made manifest in miracle and revelation. But this again is no simple and absolute distinction, since the sorcerer may sometimes be very learned, while deep learning need not always characterize priests. Rather, the distinction between priest and magician must be established qualita-tively with reference to the different nature of the learning in the two cases. As a matter of fact we must later, in our exposition of the forms of domination [see ch. XIV:9, and also ch. XV:4], distinguish the rational training and discipline of priests from the different preparation of charis-matic magicians. The latter preparation proceeds in part as an "awaken-ing" using irrational means and aiming at rebirth, and proceeds in part as a training in purely empirical lore. But in this case also, the two contrasted types flow into one another.

"Doctrine" has already been advanced as one of the fundamental traits of the priesthood. We may assume that the outstanding marks of doctrine are the development of a rational system of religious concepts and (what is of the utmost importance for us here) the development of a systematic and distinctively religious ethic based upon a consistent and stable doctrine which purports to be a "revelation." An example is found in Islam, which contrasted scriptural religion with simple paganism. But this description of priesthood and this assumption about the nature of doctrine would exclude from the concept of priesthood the Japanese Shinto priests and such functionaries as the mighty hierocrats of the Phoenicians. The adoption of such an assumption would have the effect of making the decisive characteristic of the priesthood a function which, while admittedly important, is not universal.

It is more correct for our purpose, in order to do justice to the diverse and mixed manifestations of this phenomenon, to set up as the crucial feature of the priesthood the specialization of a particular group of persons in the continuous operation of a cultic enterprise, permanently associated with particular norms, places and times, and related to specific social groups. There can be no priesthood without a cult, although there may well be a cult without a specialized priesthood. The latter was the case in China, where state officials and the heads of households exclusively conducted the services of the official gods and the ancestral spirits. On the other hand, both novitiate and doctrine are to be found among typical, pure magicians, as in the brotherhood of the Hametze among the Indians, and elsewhere in the world. These magicians may wield considerable power, and their essentially magical celebrations may play a central role in the life of their people. Yet they lack a continuously operative cult, and so the term "priests" cannot be applied to them.

A rationalization of metaphysical views and a specifically religious ethic are usually missing in the case of a cult without priests, as in the case of a magician without a cult. The full development of both a metaphysical rationalization and a religious ethic requires an independent and professionally trained priesthood, permanently occupied with the cult and with the practical problems involved in the cure of souls. Consequently, ethics developed into something quite different from a metaphysically rationalized religion in classic Chinese thought, by reason of the absence of an independent priesthood; and this also happened with the ethics of ancient Buddhism, which lacked both cult and priesthood.

Moreover, as we shall later explicate, the rationalization of religious life was fragmentary or entirely missing wherever the priesthood failed to achieve independent status and power, as in classical Antiquity.

Wherever a status group of primitive magicians and sacred musicians did rationalize magic, but failed to develop a genuinely priestly office (as was the case with the Brahmins in India), the priesthood developed in a peculiar way. However, not every priesthood developed what is distinctively new as against magic: a rational metaphysic and a religious ethic. Such developments generally presupposed the operation of one or both of two forces outside the priesthood: *prophets,* the bearers of metaphysical or religious-ethical revelation, and the *laity,* the non-priestly devotees of the cult.

Before we examine the manner in which these factors outside the priesthood influenced religion sufficiently to enable it to transcend the stages of magic, which are rather similar the world over, we must discuss some typical trends of religious evolution which are set in motion by the existence of vested interests of a priesthood in a cult.

3. Reactions to Success and Failure of Gods and Demons

Whether one should at all try to influence a particular god or demon by coercion or by entreaty is the most basic question, and the answer to it depends only upon proven effect. As the magician must keep up his charisma, so too the god must continually demonstrate his prowess. Should the effort to influence a god prove to be permanently inefficacious, then it is concluded that either the god is impotent or the correct procedure of influencing him is unknown, and he is abandoned. In China, to this day, a few striking successes suffice to enable a god to acquire prestige and power (*shen, ling*), thereby winning a sizeable circle of devotees. The emperor, as the representative of his subjects vis-à-vis the heavens, provides the gods with titles and other distinctions whenever they have proven their capacity. Yet a few striking disappointments subsequently will suffice to empty a temple forever. Conversely, the historical accident that Isaiah's steadfast prophecy actually came to fulfillment—God would not permit Jerusalem to fall into the hands of the Assyrian hordes, if only the Judean king remained firm—provided the subsequently unshakeable foundation for the position of this god and his prophets.

Something of this kind occurred earlier in respect to the pre-animistic fetish and the charisma of those possessing magical endowment. In the event of failure, the magician possibly paid with his life. On the other hand, priests have enjoyed the contrasting advantage of being able to deflect the blame for failure away from themselves and onto their god.

Yet even the priests' prestige is in danger of falling with that of their gods. However, priests may find ways of interpreting failures in such a manner that the responsibility falls, not upon the god, but upon the behavior of the god's worshippers. There might even arise from such interpretation the idea of worshipping the god, as distinct from coercing him. The problem of why the god has not hearkened to his devotees might then be explained by stating that they had not honored their god sufficiently, that they had not satisfied his desires for sacrificial blood or soma juice, or finally that they neglected him in favor of other gods. Even renewed and increased worship of the god is of no avail in some situations, and since the gods of the adversaries remain more powerful, the end of his reputation is at hand. In such cases, there may be a defection to the stronger gods, although there still remain methods of explaining the wayward conduct of the old god in such a way that his prestige might not dwindle and might even be enhanced. Under certain circumstances priests succeeded even in excogitating such methods. The most striking example is that of the priests of Yahweh, whose attachment to his people became, for reasons to be expounded later, ever stronger as Israel became increasingly enmeshed in the toils of tragedy. But for this to happen, a new series of divine attributes must evolve.

The qualitative superiority of anthropomorphically conceived gods and demons over man himself is at first only relative. Their passions and their avidity for pleasure are believed to be unlimited, like those of strong men. But they are neither omniscient nor omnipotent (obviously only one could possess these attributes), nor necessarily eternal (the gods of Babylon and of the Germans were not). However, they often have the ability to secure their glamorous existence by means of magical food and drink which they have reserved for themselves, much as human lives may be prolonged by the magical potions of the medicine man. The only qualitative differentiation that is made between these anthropomorphic gods and demons is that between powers useful to man and those harmful to man. Naturally, the powers useful to him are usually considered the good and high gods, who are to be worshipped, while the powers harmful to him are usually the lower demons, frequently endowed with incredible guile or limitless spite, who are not to be worshipped but magically exorcised.

Yet the differentiation did not always take place along this particular line, and certainly not always in the direction of degrading the masters of the noxious forces into demons. The measure of cultic worship that gods receive does not depend upon their goodness, nor even upon their cosmic importance. Indeed, some very great and good gods of heaven frequently lack cults, not because they are too remote from man, but because their influence seems equable, and by its very regularity appears to be so secure that no special intervention is required. On the other hand, powers of clearly diabolical character, such as Rudra, the Hindu god of pestilence, are not always weaker than the good gods, but may actually be endowed with a tremendous power potential.

4. Ethical Deities and Increasing Demands upon Them

In addition to the important qualitative differentiation between the good and diabolical forces, which assumed considerable importance in certain cases, there might develop within the pantheon gods of a distinctively ethical character—and this is particularly important to us at this point. The possibility that a god may possess ethical qualities is by no means confined to monotheism. Indeed, this possibility exists at various stages in the formation of a pantheon; but it is at the level of monotheism that this development has particularly far-reaching consequences. A specialized functional god of legislation and a god who controls the oracle will naturally be found very frequently among the ethical divinities.

The art of "divining" at first grows out of the magic based on the belief in spirits, who function in accordance with certain principles of order, as do living creatures. Once knowing how the spirits operate, one can predict their behavior from symptoms or omens that make it possible to surmise their intentions, on the basis of previous experience. Where one builds houses, graves and roads, and when one undertakes economic and political activities is decided by reference to that which experience has established as the favorable place or time. Wherever a social group, as for example the so-called priests of Taoism in China, makes its living from the practice of the diviner's art, its craft (*feng shui*) may achieve ineradicable power. When this happens, all efforts at economic rationalization founder against the opposition of the spirits. Thus, no location for a railroad or factory could be suggested without creating some conflict with them. Capitalism was able to cope with this factor only after it had reached its fullest power. As late as the Russo-Japanese War, the Japanese army seems to have missed several favorable opportunities because the diviners had declared them to be of ill omen. On the other hand, [the Spartan regent] Pausanias had already adroitly manipulated the omens, favorable and otherwise, at Plataea

[479 B.C.] to make them fit the requirements of military strategy. Whenever the political power appropriated judicial or legislative functions (e.g., transforming into a mandatory verdict an arbitrator's suggestion in case of a clan feud, or transforming into an orderly procedure the primordial lynch justice practiced by a threatened group in cases of religious or political malfeasance), the particular solution was almost always mediated by a divine revelation (a judgement of the god). Wherever diviners succeeded in appropriating the preparation and interpretation of the oracles or the divine judgements, they frequently achieved a position of enduring dominance.

Quite in keeping with the realities of actual life, the guardian of the legal order was nowhere necessarily the strongest god: neither Varuna in India nor Maat in Egypt, much less Lykos in Attica, Dike, Themis or even Apollo. What alone characterized these deities was their ethical qualification, which corresponded to the notion that the oracle or divine judgment somehow always revealed the truth. It was not because he was a deity that the ethical god was the guardian of morality and the legal order, for the anthropomorphic gods originally had but little to do with ethics, in fact less than human beings. Rather, the reason for such a god's ethical pre-eminence was that he had taken this particular type of behavior under his aegis.

Increased ethical demands were made upon the gods by men, parallel with four developments. First, the increasing power of orderly judicial determination within large and pacified polities, and hence increasing claims upon its quality. Second, the increasing scope of a rational comprehension of an enduring and orderly cosmos. (The cause of this is to be sought in the meteorological orientation of economic activity.) Third, the increasing regulation of ever new types of human relationships by conventional rules, and the increasing dependence of men upon the observance of these rules in their interactions with each other. Fourth, the growth in social and economic importance of the reliability of the given word—whether of friends, vassals, officials, partners in an exchange transaction, debtors, or whomever else; what is basically involved in these four developments is the increased importance of an ethical attachment of individuals to a cosmos of obligations, making it possible to calculate what the conduct of a given person may be.

Even the gods to whom one turns for protection are henceforth regarded as either subject to some moral order or—like the great kings —as the creators of such an order, which they made the specific content of their divine will. In the first case, a superordinate and impersonal power makes its appearance behind the gods, controlling them from within and measuring the value of their deeds. Of course, this supradivine power may take many different forms. It appears first as "fate." Among the Greeks fate (*moira*) is an irrational and, above all, ethically neutral predestination of the fundamental aspects of every man's destiny. Such predetermination is elastic within certain limits, but flagrant interferences with predestined fate may be very dangerous (ὑπέρμορον) even to the greatest of the gods. This provides one explanation for the failure of so many prayers. This kind of predestinarian view is very congenial to the normal psychological attitude of a military caste, which is particularly unreceptive to the rationalistic belief in an ethically concerned, yet impartial, wise and kindly "providence." In this we glimpse once again the deep sociological distance separating a warrior class from every kind of religious or purely ethical rationalism. We have already made brief reference to this cleavage, and we shall have occasion to observe it in many contexts.

Quite different is the impersonal power contemplated by bureaucratic or theocratic strata, e.g., the Chinese bureaucracy or the Hindu Brahmins. Theirs is the providential power of the harmonious and rational order of the world, which may in any given case incline to either a cosmic or an ethical and social format, although as a rule both aspects are involved. In Confucianism as in Taoism, this order has both a cosmic and a characteristic ethical-rational character; it is an impersonal, providential force that guarantees the regularity and felicitous order of world history. This is the view of a rationalistic bureaucracy. Even more strongly ethical is the Hindu *rita*, the impersonal power of the fixed order of religious ceremonial and the fixed order of the cosmos, and hence of human activity in general. This is the conception held by the Vedic priesthood, which practiced an essentially empirical art of influencing the god, more by coercion than by worship. Also to be included here is the later Hindu notion of a supradivine and cosmic all-unity, superordinate to the gods and alone independent of the senseless change and transitoriness of the entire phenomenal world—a conception entertained by speculative intellectuals who were indifferent to worldly concerns.

Even when the order of nature and of the social conditions which are normally considered parallel to it, especially law, are not regarded as superordinate to the gods, but rather as their creations (later we shall inquire under what circumstances this occurs), it is naturally postulated that god will protect against injury the order he has created. The intellectual implementation of this postulate has far-reaching consequences for religious behavior and for the general attitude toward the god. It stimulated the development of a religious ethic, as well as the differentiation of demands made upon man by god from demands made upon man by nature, which latter so often proved to be inadequate. Hitherto, there had been two primordial methods of influencing supernatural powers. One was to subject them to human purposes by means of magic. The other was to win them over by making oneself agreeable to them, not by the exercise of any ethical virtue, but by gratifying their egotistic wishes. To these methods was now added obedience to the religious law as the distinctive way to win the god's favor.

5. *Magical Origins of Religious Ethics and the Rationalization of Taboo*

To be sure, religious ethics do not really begin with this view. On the contrary, there was already another and highly influential system of religious ethics deriving from purely magical norms of conduct, the infraction of which was regarded as a religious abomination. Wherever there exists a developed belief in spirits, it is held that extraordinary occurrences in life, and sometimes even routine life processes, are generated by the entrance into a person of a particular spirit, e.g., in sickness, at birth, at puberty, or at menstruation. This spirit may be regarded as either sacred or unclean; this is variable and often the product of accident, but the practical effect is the same. In either case one must avoid irritating the spirit, lest it enter into the officious intruder himself, or by some magical means harm him or any other persons whom it might possess. As a result, the individual in question will be shunned physically and socially and must avoid contact with others and sometimes even with his body. In some instances, e.g., Polynesian charismatic princes, such a person must be carefully fed lest he magically contaminate his own food.

Naturally, once this set of notions has developed, various objects or persons may be endowed with the quality of taboo by means of magical manipulations invoked by persons possessing magical charisma; thereupon, contact with the new possessor of taboo will work evil magic, for his taboo may be transmitted. This charismatic power to transfer taboo underwent considerable systematic development, especially in Indonesia and the South Sea area. Numerous economic and social interests stood under the sanctions of taboos. Among them were the following: the conservation of forests and wild life (after the pattern of the prohibited forests of early medieval kings); the protection of scarce commodities against uneconomic consumption during periods of economic difficulty; the provision of protection for private property, especially for the property of privileged priests or aristocrats; the safeguarding of common war booty against individual plundering (as by Joshua in the case of Achan); and the sexual and personal separation of status groups in the interest of maintaining purity of blood or prestige. This first and most general instance of the direct harnessing of religion to extra-religious purposes also reveals the idiosyncratic autonomy of the religious domain, in the somewhat incredible irrationality of its painfully onerous norms, which applied even to the beneficiaries of the taboos.

The rationalization of taboos leads ultimately to a system of norms according to which certain actions are permanently construed as religious abominations subject to sanctions, and occasionally even entailing the death of the malefactor in order to prevent evil sorcery from overtaking the entire group because of the transgression of the guilty individual. In this manner there arises an ethical system, the ultimate warrant of which is taboo. This system comprises dietary restrictions, the proscription of work on taboo or "unlucky" days (the Sabbath was originally a taboo day of this type), and certain prohibitions against marriage to specified individuals, especially within the circle of one's blood relations. The usual process here is that something which has become customary, whether on rational grounds or otherwise, e.g., experiences relative to illness and other effects of evil sorcery, comes to be regarded as sacred.

In some fashion not clearly understood, there developed for certain groups a characteristic association between specific norms having the quality of taboo and various important in-dwelling spirits inhabiting particular objects or animals. Egypt provides the most striking example of how the incarnation of spirits as sacred animals may give rise to cultic centers of local political associations. Such sacred animals, as well as other objects and artifacts, may also become the foci of other social groupings, which in any particular case may be more natural or artificial in their generation.

6. Taboo Norms: Totemism and Commensalism

The most widespread of the social institutions which developed in this fashion is that known as *totemism*, which is a specific relationship of an object, usually a natural object and in the purest manifestations of totemism an animal, with a particular social group. For the latter, the totemic animal is a symbol of brotherhood; and originally the animal symbolized the common possession by the group of the spirit of the animal, after it had been consumed by the entire group. There are, of course, variations in the scope of this fraternalism, just as there are variations in the nature of the relationship of the members to the totemic object. In the fully developed type of totemism, the brotherliness of the group comprises all the fraternal responsibilities of an exogamous kin group, while the totemic relation involves a prohibition of slaying and consuming the totemic animal, except at the cultic meals of the group. These developments culminate in a series of quasi-cultic obligations following from the common, though not universal, belief that the group is descended from the totem animal.

The controversy concerning the development of these widely diffused totemic brotherhoods is still unresolved. For us it will suffice to say that the totems functionally are the animistic counterparts of the gods found in cultic associations which, as previously mentioned, are associated with the most diverse social groups, since non-empirical thinking can not do without a functional organization (*Zweckverband*) based on personal and religiously guaranteed fraternization, even if the organization is purely artificial. For this reason the regulation of sexual behavior, which the kin groups undertook to effect, especially attracted religious sanctions having the nature of taboo, which are best provided by totemism. But this system was not limited to the purposes of sexual regulation, nor was it confined to the kin group, and it certainly did not necessarily arise first in this context. Rather, it is a widely diffused method of placing fraternal groupings under magical sanctions. The belief in the universality of totemism, and certainly the belief in the derivation of virtually all social groups and all religions from totemism, constitutes a tremendous exaggeration that has been rejected completely by now. Yet totemism has frequently been very influential in producing a division of labor between the sexes which is guaranteed and enforced by magical motivations. Then too, totemism has frequently played a very important role in the development and regulation of barter as a regular intra-group phenomenon (as contrasted with trade outside the limits of the group).

Taboos, especially the dietary restrictions based on magic, show us a new source of the institution of commensality which has such far-reaching importance. We have already noted one source of this institution, namely the household. Another aspect is the restriction of commensality to comrades having equal magical qualifications, which is a consequence of the doctrine of impurity by taboo. These two facets of commensality may enter into competition or even conflict. For example, when a woman is descended from another kin group than that of her husband, there are frequently restrictions upon her sitting at the same table with him, and in some cases she is even prohibited from seeing him eat. Nor is commensality permitted to the king who is hedged in by taboos, or to members of privileged status groups such as castes, or religious communities, both of which are also under taboo. Furthermore, highly privileged castes must be shielded from the glances of "unclean" strangers during cultic repasts or even everyday meals. Conversely, the provision of commensality is frequently a method of producing religious fellowship, which may on occasion lead to political and ethnic alliances. Thus, the first great turning point in the history of Christianity was the communal feast arranged at Antioch between Peter and the uncircumcised proselytes, to which Paul, in his polemic against Peter, attributed such decisive importance.

7. *Caste Taboo, Vocational Caste Ethics, and Capitalism*

On the other hand, norms of taboo may give rise to extraordinarily severe impediments to the development of trade and of the market, and other types of social intercourse. The absolute impurity of those outside one's own religion, as taught by the Shiite sect of Islam, has created in its adherents crucial impediments to intercourse with others, even in recent times, though recourse has been made to fictions of all sorts to ease the situation. The caste taboos of the Hindus restricted intercourse among people far more forcefully than the *feng shui* system of spirit beliefs interfered with trade in China.[4] Of course, even in these matters there are natural limits to the power of religion in respect to the elementary needs of life. Thus, according to the Hindu caste taboo, "The hand of the artisan is always clean." Also clean are mines, workshops, and whatever merchandise is available for sale in stores, as well as whatever articles of food have been touched by mendicant students (ascetic disciples of the Brahmins). The only Hindu caste taboo that was apt to be violated in any considerable measure was the taboo on sexual relationships between castes, under the pressure of the wealthy classses' interest in polygamy. To some extent, it was permissible to take girls of lower castes as concubines. The caste system of labor in India, like the *feng shui* system in China, is being slowly but surely rendered illusory wherever railroad transportation develops.

In theory, these taboo restrictions of caste need not have rendered capitalism impossible. Yet it is perfectly obvious that economic rationalization would never have arisen originally where taboo had achieved such massive power. Despite all efforts to reduce caste segregation, certain psychological resistances based on the caste system remained operative, preventing artisans of different crafts from working together in the same factory. The caste system tends to perpetuate a specialization of labor of the handicraft type, if not by positive prescription, then as a consequence of its general spirit and presuppositions. The net effect of the religious sanction of caste upon the spirit of economic activity is diametrically opposite to that of rationalism. In the caste system particular crafts, insofar as they are the indicia of different castes, are assigned a religious sanction and the character of a sacred vocation. Even the most despised of Hindu castes, not excluding that of thieves, regards its own enterprise as ordained by particular gods or by a specific volition of a god, assigned to its members as their special mission in life; and each caste nourishes its feeling of worth by its technically expert execution of its assigned vocation.

But this vocational ethic of a caste system is—at least as far as the crafts are concerned—notably traditionalistic, rather than rational. It finds its fulfillment and confirmation in the absolutely qualitative perfection of the product fashioned by the craft. Very alien to its mode of thinking is the possibility of rationalizing the method of production, which is basic to all modern rational technology, or the possibility of systematically organizing a commercial enterprise along the lines of a rational business economy, which is the foundation of modern capitalism. One must go to the ethics of ascetic Protestantism to find any ethical sanction for economic rationalism and for the entrepreneur. Caste ethics glorifies the spirit of craftsmanship and enjoins pride, not in economic earnings measured by money, nor in the wonders of rational technology as applied in the rational use of labor, but rather in the personal virtuosity of the producer as manifested in the beauty and worth of the product appropriate to his particular caste.

Finally, we should note—in anticipation of our general argument about these relationships—that what was decisive for the Hindu caste system in particular was its connection with a belief in transmigration, and especially its connection with the tenet that any possible improvement in one's chances in subsequent incarnations depended on the faithful execution in the present lifetime of the vocation assigned one by virtue of his caste status. Any effort to emerge from one's caste, and especially to intrude into the sphere of activities appropriate to other and higher castes, was expected to result in evil magic and entailed the likelihood of unfavorable incarnation hereafter. This explains why, according to numerous observations on affairs in India, it is precisely the lowest classes, who would naturally be most desirous of improving their status in subsequent incarnations, that cling most steadfastly to their caste obligations, never thinking of toppling the caste system through social revolutions or reforms. Among the Hindus, the Biblical

emphasis echoed in Luther's injunction, "Remain steadfast in your vocation," was elevated into a cardinal religious obligation and was fortified
by powerful religious sanctions.

8. *From Magical Ethics to Conscience, Sin and Salvation*

Whenever the belief in spirits became rationalized into belief in
gods, that is, whenever the coercion of spirits gave way to the worship
of the gods who are served by a cult, the magical ethic of the spirit belief
underwent a transformation too. This reorientation developed through
the notion that whoever flouted divinely appointed norms would be
overtaken by the ethical displeasure of the god who had these norms
under his special care. This made possible the assumption that when
enemies conquered or other calamities befell one's group, the cause was
not the weakness of the god but rather his anger against his followers,
caused by his displeasure at their transgression against the laws under
his guardianship. Hence, the sins of the group were to blame if some
unfavorable development overtook it; the god might well be using the
misfortune to express his desire to chastise and educate his favorite
people. Thus, the prophets of Israel were always able to point out to
their people misdeeds in their own generation or in their ancestors', to
which God had reacted with almost inexhaustible wrath, as evidenced
by the fact that he permitted his own people to become subject to another people that did not worship him at all.

This idea, diffused in all conceivable manifestations wherever the
god concept has taken on universalistic lines, forms a religious ethic out
of the magical prescriptions which operate only with the notion of evil
magic. Henceforth, transgression against the will of god is an ethical sin
which burdens the conscience, quite apart from its direct results. Evils
befalling the individual are divinely appointed inflictions and the consequences of sin, from which the individual hopes to be freed by "piety"
(behavior acceptable to god) which will bring the individual salvation.
In the Old Testament, the idea of "salvation," pregnant with consequences, still has the elementary rational meaning of liberation from
concrete ills.

In its early stages, the religious ethic consistently shares another
characteristic with magic worship in that it is frequently composed of a
complex of heterogeneous prescriptions and prohibitions derived from
the most diverse motives and occasions. Within this complex there is,
from our modern point of view, little differentiation between important

and unimportant requirements; any infraction of the ethic constitutes sin. Later, a systematization of these ethical concepts may ensue, which leads from the rational wish to insure personal external pleasures for oneself by performing acts pleasing to the god, to a view of sin as the unified power of the anti-divine (diabolical) into whose grasp man may fall. Goodness is then envisaged as an integral capacity for an attitude of holiness, and for consistent behavior derived from such an attitude. During this process of transformation, there also develops a hope for salvation as an irrational yearning to be able to be good for its own sake, in order to gain the beneficent awareness of such virtuousness.

An almost infinite series of the most diverse conceptions, crossed again and again by purely magical notions, leads to the sublimation of piety as the enduring basis of a specific conduct of life, by virtue of the continuous motivation it engenders. Of course such a sublimation is extremely rare and is attained in its full purity only intermittently by everyday religion. We are still in the realm of "magic" if *sin* and *piety* are viewed as integral powers, envisaged as rather like material substances; at this stage, the nature of the "good" or "evil" of the acting person is construed after the fashion of a poison, a healing antidote, or a bodily temperature. Thus in India *tapas,* the power of the sacred which a man achieved by asceticism and contained within his body, originally denoted the heat engendered in fowls during their mating season, in the creator of the world at the cosmogony, and in the magician during his sacred hysteria induced by mortifications and leading to supernatural powers.

It is a long way from here to the notion that the person who acts with goodness has received into himself a special soul of divine provenience, and to the various forms of inward possession of the divine to be described later. So too, it is a far cry from the conception of sin as a poison in the body of the malefactor, which must be treated by magical means, to the conception of an evil demon which enters into possession of him, and on to the culminating conception of the diabolical power of the radical evil, with which the evildoer must struggle lest he succumb to its dangerous power.

By no means every ethic traversed the entire length of the road culminating in these conceptions. Thus, the ethics of Confucianism lack the concept of radical evil, and in general lack the concept of any integral diabolical power of sin. Nor was this notion contained in the ethics of Greece or Rome. In both those cases, there was lacking not only an independently organized priesthood, but also prophecy, that historical phenomenon which normally produced a centralization of ethics under the aegis of religious salvation. In India, prophecy was not absent, but as will be expounded later, it had a very special character and a very highly sublimated ethic of salvation.

Prophets and priests are the twin bearers of the systematization and rationalization of religious ethics. But there is a third significant factor of importance in determining the evolution of religious ethics: the laity, whom prophets and priests seek to influence in an ethical direction. We must now devote a brief examination to the interaction of these three factors.

NOTES

1. The first part of this section belongs to Weber's first section, if indeed the German paragraph division is that of the original manuscript. The section is here combined with the German §2, which has only two pages, and with §3 (seven pages).

2. Weber contrasts the conventional German term for attending "services," "*Gottesdienst*," with the term "*Gotteszwang*."

3. Cf. Weber, *The Religion of India*, 137f.

4. On the *feng shui*, see Weber, *The Religion of China*, 199, 214, 217, 276, 297.

iii

The Prophet

1 . Prophet versus Priest and Magician

What is a prophet, from the perspective of sociology? We shall forego here any consideration of the general question regarding the "bringer of salvation" (*Heilbringer*) as raised by Breysig.[1] Not every anthropomorphic god is a deified bringer of salvation, whether external or internal salvation. And certainly not every provider of salvation became a god or even a savior, although such phenomena were widespread.

We shall understand "prophet" to mean a purely individual bearer of charisma, who by virtue of his mission proclaims a religious doctrine or divine commandment. No radical distinction will be drawn between a "renewer of religion" who preaches an older revelation, actual or supposititious, and a "founder of religion" who claims to bring completely new deliverances. The two types merge into one another. In any case, the formation of a new religious community need not be the result of doctrinal preaching by prophets, since it may be produced by the activities of non-prophetic reformers. Nor shall we be concerned in this context with the question whether the followers of a prophet are more attracted to his person, as in the cases of Zoroaster, Jesus, and Muhammad, or to his doctrine, as in the cases of Buddha and the prophets of Israel.

For our purposes here, the personal call is the decisive element distinguishing the prophet from the priest. The latter lays claim to authority by virtue of his service in a sacred tradition, while the prophet's claim is based on personal revelation and charisma. It is no accident that almost no prophets have emerged from the priestly class. As a rule, the Indian teachers of salvation were not Brahmins, nor were the Israelite prophets priests. Zoroaster's case is exceptional in that there exists a possibility that he may have descended from the hieratic nobility. The priest, in clear contrast, dispenses salvation by virtue of his office. Even in cases in which personal charisma may be involved, it is the hierarchical office that confers legitimate authority upon the priest as a member of an organized enterprise of salvation.

But the prophet, like the magician, exerts his power simply by virtue of his personal gifts. Unlike the magician, however, the prophet claims definite revelations, and the core of his mission is doctrine or commandment, not magic. Outwardly, at least, the distinction is fluid, for the magician is frequently a knowledgeable expert in divination, and sometimes in this alone. At this stage, revelation functions continuously as oracle or dream interpretation. Without prior consultation with the magician, no innovations in social relations could be adopted in primitive times. To this day, in certain parts of Australia, it is the dream revelations of magicians that are set before the councils of clan heads for adoption, and it is a mark of secularization that this practice is receding.

On the other hand, it was only under very unusual circumstances that a prophet succeeded in establishing his authority without charismatic authentication, which in practice meant magic. At least the bearers of new doctrine practically always needed such validation. It must not be forgotten for an instant that the entire basis of Jesus' own legitimation, as well as his claim that he and only he knew the Father and that the way to God led through faith in him alone, was the magical charisma he felt within himself. It was doubtless this consciousness of power, more than anything else, that enabled him to traverse the road of the prophets. During the apostolic period of early Christianity and thereafter the figure of the wandering prophet was a constant phenomenon. There was always required of such prophets a proof of their possession of particular gifts of the spirit, of special magical or ecstatic abilities.

Prophets very often practiced divination as well as magical healing and counseling. This was true, for example, of the prophets (*nabi, nebiim*)² so frequently mentioned in the Old Testament, especially in the prophetic books and Chronicles. But what distinguishes the prophet, in the sense that we are employing the term, from the types just described is an economic factor, i.e., that his *prophecy is unremunerated.* Thus, Amos indignantly rejected the appellation of *nabi.* This criterion of gratuitous service also distinguishes the prophet from the priest. The typical prophet propagates ideas for their own sake and not for fees, at least not in any obvious or regulated form. The provisions enjoining the non-remunerative character of prophetic propaganda have taken various forms. Thus developed the carefully cultivated postulate that the apostle, prophet, or teacher of ancient Christianity must not "trade on" his religious proclamations. Also, limitations were set upon the length of the time he could enjoy the hospitality of his friends. The Christian prophet was enjoined to live by the labor of his own hands or, as among the Buddhists, only from alms which he had not specifically solicited. These injunctions were repeatedly emphasized in the Pauline epistles, and in another form in the Buddhist monastic regulations. The dictum "whosoever will not work, shall not eat" applied to missionaries; however, the prophesying free of charge is, of course, one of the chief reasons for the success of prophetic propaganda itself.

The period of the older Israelitic prophecy at about the time of Elijah was an epoch of strong prophetic propaganda throughout the Near East and Greece. Perhaps prophecy in all its forms arose, especially in the Near East, in connection with the reconstitution of the great world empires in Asia, and the resumption and intensification of international commerce after a long interruption. At that time Greece was exposed to the invasion of the Thracian cult of Dionysos, as well as to the most diverse types of prophecies. In addition to the semiprophetic social reformers, certain purely religious movements now broke into the simple magical and cultic lore of the Homeric priests. Emotional cults, emotional prophecy based on "speaking with tongues," and highly valued intoxicating ecstasy interrupted the unfolding of theological rationalism (Hesiod), the beginnings of cosmogonic and philosophic speculation, of philosophical mystery doctrines and salvation religions. The growth of these emotional cults paralleled both overseas colonization and, above all, the formation of cities and the transformation of the *polis* which resulted from the development of a citizen army.

It is not necessary to detail here these developments of the eighth and seventh centuries, so brilliantly analyzed by Rohde,[3] some of which reached into the sixth and even the fifth century. They were contemporary with Jewish, Persian, and Hindu prophetic movements, and probably also with the achievements of Chinese ethics in the pre-Confucian period, although we have only scant knowledge of the latter. These Greek "prophets" differed widely among themselves in regard to the economic criterion of professionalism, and in regard to the possession of a "doctrine." The Greeks also made a distinction between professional teaching and unremunerated propagandizing of ideas, as we see from the example of Socrates. In Greece, furthermore, there existed a clear differentiation between the only real congregational type of religion, namely Orphism with its doctrine of salvation, and every other type of prophecy and technique of salvation, especially those of the mysteries. The basis of this distinction was the presence in Orphism of a genuine doctrine of salvation.

2. *Prophet and Lawgiver*

Our primary task is to differentiate the various types of prophets from the sundry purveyors of salvation, religious or otherwise. Even in historical times the transition from the prophet to the law-giver is fluid, if one understands the latter to mean a personage who in a concrete case has been assigned the responsibility of codifying a law systematically or of reconstituting it, as was the case notably with the Greek *aisymnetai* (e.g., Solon, Charondas, etc.). In no case did such a lawgiver or his labor fail to receive divine approval, if only subsequently.

A lawgiver is quite different from the Italian *podestà*, who is summoned from outside the group, not for the purpose of creating a new social order, but to provide a detached, impartial arbitrator, especially when families of the same social rank feud with one another. On the other hand, lawgivers were generally, though not always, called to their office when social tensions were in evidence. This was apt to occur with special frequency in the one situation which commonly provided the earliest stimulus to a reform policy: the economic differentiation of the warrior class as a result of growing monetary wealth of one part and the debt enslavement of another; an additional factor was the dissatisfaction arising from the unrealized political aspirations of a rising commercial class which, having acquired wealth through economic activity, was now challenging the old warrior nobility. It was the function of the *aisymnetes* to resolve the conflicts between status groups and to produce a new sacred law of eternal validity, for which he had to secure divine approbation.

It is very likely that Moses was a historical figure, in which case he would be classified functionally as an *aisymnetes*. For the prescriptions of the oldest sacred legislation of the Hebrews presuppose a money economy and hence sharp conflicts of interests, whether impending or already existing, within the confederacy. It was Moses' great achievement to find a compromise solution of, or prophylactic for, these conflicts (e.g., the *seisachtheia* of the Year of Release)[4] and to organize the Israelite confederacy with an integral national god. In essence, his work stands midway between the functioning of an ancient *aisymnetes* and that of Muhammad. The reception of the law formulated by Moses stimulated a period of expansion of the newly unified people in much the same way that the compromise among status groups stimulated expansion in so many other cases, particularly in Athens and Rome. The scriptural dictum that "after Moses there arose not in Israel any prophet like unto him" means that the Jews never had another *aisymnetes*.

Not only were none of the prophets *aisymnetai* in this sense, but in general what normally passes for prophecy does not belong to this category. To be sure, even the later prophets of Israel were concerned with social reform. They hurled their "woe be unto you" against those who oppressed and enslaved the poor, those who joined field to field, and those who deflected justice by bribes. These were the typical actions leading to class stratification everywhere in the ancient world, and were everywhere intensified by the development of the city-state (*polis*). Jerusalem too had been organized into a city-state by the time of these later prophets. A distinctive concern with social reform is characteristic of Israelite prophets. This concern is all the more notable because such a trait is lacking in Hindu prophecy of the same period, although the conditions in India at the time of the Buddha have been described as relatively similar to those in Greece during the sixth century.

An explanation for Hebrew prophecy's concern for social reform is to be sought in religious grounds, which we shall set forth subsequently. But it must not be forgotten that in the motivation of the Israelite prophets these social reforms were only means to an end. Their primary concern was with foreign politics, chiefly because it constituted the theater of their god's activity. The Israelite prophets were concerned with social and other types of injustice as a violation of the Mosaic code primarily in order to explain god's wrath, and not in order to institute a program of social reform. It is noteworthy that the sole theoretician of social reform, Ezekiel, was a priestly theorist who can scarcely be categorized as a prophet at all. Finally, Jesus was not at all interested in social reform as such.

Zoroaster shared with his cattle-raising people a hatred of the despoiling nomads, but the heart of his message was essentially religious. His central concern was his struggle against the magical cult of ecstasy and for his own divine mission, which of course had incidental economic consequences. A similar primary focus upon religion appeared very clearly in the case of Muhammad, whose program of social reform, which Umar carried through consistently, was oriented almost entirely to the unification of the faithful for the sake of fighting the infidels and of maintaining the largest possible number of warriors.

It is characteristic of the prophets that they do not receive their mission from any human agency, but seize it, as it were. To be sure, usurpation also characterized the assumption of power by tyrants in the Greek *polis*. These Greek tyrants remind one of the legal *aisymnetai* in their general functioning, and they frequently pursued their own characteristic religious policies, e.g., supporting the emotional cult of Dionysos, which was popular with the masses rather than with the nobility. But the aforementioned assumption of power by the prophets came about as a consequence of divine revelation, essentially for religious purposes. Furthermore, their characteristic religious message and their struggle against ecstatic cults tended to move in an opposite direction from that taken by the typical religious policy of the Greek tyrants. The religion of Muhammad, which is fundamentally political in its orientation, and his position in Medina, which was in between that of an Italian *podestà* and that of Calvin at Geneva, grew primarily out of his purely prophetic mission. A merchant, he was first a leader of pietistic bourgeois conventicles in Mecca, until he realized more and more clearly that the ideal external basis for his missionizing would be provided by the organization of the interests of the warrior clans in the acquisition of booty.

3. *Prophet and Teacher of Ethics*

On the other hand, there are various transitional phases linking the prophet to the teacher of ethics, especially the teacher of social ethics. Such a teacher, full of new or recovered ancient wisdom, gathers disciples about him, counsels private persons, and advises princes in public affairs and possibly tries to make them establish a new ethical order. The bond between the teacher of religious or philosophical wisdom and his disciple is uncommonly strong and regulated in an authoritarian fashion, particularly in the sacred laws of Asia. Everywhere this bond is one of the firmest relationships of loyalty. Generally, training in magic and heroism is so regulated that the novice is assigned to a particularly experienced master or is permitted to seek out a master, as the young "fox" can choose the senior member (*Leibbursche*) in German fraternities. All the Greek poetry of pederasty derives from such a relationship of respect, and similar phenomena are to be found among Buddhists and Confucianists, indeed in all monastic education.

The most complete expression of this disciple–master relationship is to be found in the position of the *guru* in Hindu sacred law. Every young man belonging to polite society was unconditionally required to devote himself for many years to the instruction and direction of life provided by such a Brahminic teacher. The obligation of obedience to the *guru,* who had absolute power over his charges, a relationship comparable to that of the occidental *famulus* to his *magister,* took precedence over loyalty to family, just as the position of the court Brahmin (*purohita*) was officially regulated so as to raise his position far above that of the most powerful father confessor in the Occident. Yet the *guru* is, after all, only a teacher who transmits acquired, not only revealed, knowledge, and this by virtue of a commission and not on his own authority.

The philosophical ethicist and the social reformer are not prophets in our sense of the word, no matter how closely they may seem to resemble prophets. Actually, the oldest Greek sages, who like Empedocles and Pythagoras are wreathed in legend, stand closest to the prophets. Some of them left behind groups with a distinctive doctrine of salvation and conduct of life, and they laid some claim to the status of savior. Such intellectual teachers of salvation have parallels in India, but the Greek teachers fell far short of the Hindu teachers in consistently focusing both life and doctrine on salvation.

Even less can the founders and heads of the actual "schools of philosophy" be regarded as prophets in our sense, no matter how closely they may approach this category in some respects. From Confucius, in whose temple even the emperor makes his obeisance, graded transitions lead to Plato. But both of them were simply academic teaching philosophers, who differed chiefly in that Confucius was centrally concerned with influencing princes in the direction of particular social reforms, and Plato only occasionally.

What primarily differentiates such figures from the prophets is their lack of that vital emotional *preaching* which is distinctive of prophecy, regardless of whether this is disseminated by the spoken word, the pamphlet, or any other type of literary composition (e.g., the *suras* of Muhammad). The enterprise of the prophet is closer to that of the popular leader (*demagogos*) or political publicist than to that of the teacher. On the other hand, the activity of a Socrates, who also felt himself opposed to the professional teaching enterprise of the Sophists, must be distinguished conceptually from the activities of a prophet by the absence of a directly revealed religious mission. Socrates' "genius" (*daimonion*) reacted only to concrete situations, and then only to dissuade and admonish. For Socrates, this was the outer limit of his ethical and strongly utilitarian rationalism, which occupied for him the position that magical divination assumed for Confucius. For this reason, Socrates' *daimonion* cannot be compared at all to the conscience of a genuine religious ethic; much less can it be regarded as the instrument of prophecy.

Such a divergence from the characteristic traits of the Hebrew prophets holds true of all philosophers and their schools as they were known in China, India, ancient Hellas, and in the medieval period among Jews, Arabs, and Christians alike. All such philosophical schools were rather similar from a sociological point of view. In their mode of life, they may be nearer to the mystagogic-ritual prophecy of salvation, as in the case of the Pythagoreans, or to the exemplary prophecy of salvation (in the sense soon to be explained), as in the case of the Cynics, who protested against the sacramental grace of the mysteries as well as against wordly civilization, and who in this regard show certain affinities to Hindu and Oriental ascetic sects. But the prophet, in our special sense, is never to be found where the proclamation of a religious truth of salvation through personal revelation is lacking. In our view, this qualification must be regarded as the decisive hallmark of prophecy.

Finally, the Hindu reformers of religion such as Shankara and Ramanuja and their Occidental counterparts like Luther, Zwingli, Calvin, and Wesley are to be distinguished from the category of prophets by virtue of the fact that they do not claim to be offering a substantively new revelation or to be speaking in the name of a special divine injunction. This is what characterized the founder of the Mormon church, who resembled, even in matters of detail, Muhammad; above all, it characterized the Jewish prophets. The prophetic type is also manifest in Montanus and Novatianus, and in such figures as Mani and Marcion whose message had a more rational doctrinal content than did that of George Fox, a prophet type with emotional tendencies.[5]

4. *Mystagogue and Teacher*

When we have separated out from the category of prophet all the aforementioned types, which sometimes abut very closely, various others still remain. The first is that of the *mystagogue*. He performs sacraments, i.e., magical actions that contain the boons of salvation. Throughout the entire world there have been saviors of this type whose difference from the average magician is only one of degree, the extent of which is determined by the formation of a special *congregation* around him. Very frequently dynasties of mystagogues developed on the basis of a sacramental charisma which was regarded as hereditary. These dynasties maintained their prestige for centuries, investing their disciples with great authority and thus developing a kind of hierarchical position. This was especially true in India, where the title of *guru* was also used to designate distributors of salvation and their plenipotentiaries. It was likewise the case in China, where the hierarch of the Taoists and the heads of certain secret sects played just such hereditary roles. Finally, one type of exemplary prophet to be discussed presently was also generally transformed into a mystagogue in the second generation.

The mystagogues were also very widely distributed throughout the Near East, and they entered Greece in the prophetic age to which reference was made earlier. Yet the far more ancient noble families who were the hereditary incumbents of the Eleusinian mysteries also represented at least another marginal manifestation of the simple hereditary priestly families. Ethical doctrine was lacking in the mystagogue, who distributed magical salvation, or at least doctrine played only a very subordinate role in his work. Instead, his primary gift was hereditarily transmitted magical art. Moreover, he normally made a living from his art, for which there was a great demand. Consequently we must exclude him too from the conception of prophet, even though he sometimes revealed new ways of salvation.

5. Ethical and Exemplary Prophecy

Thus, there remain only two kinds of prophets in our sense, one represented most clearly by the Buddha, the other with especial clarity by Zoroaster and Muhammad. The prophet may be primarily, as in the last cases, an instrument for the proclamation of a god and his will, be this a concrete command or an abstract norm. Preaching as one who has received a commission from god, he demands obedience as an ethical duty. This type we shall term the "*ethical prophet.*" On the other hand, the prophet may be an exemplary man who, by his personal example, demonstrates to others the way to religious salvation, as in the case of the Buddha. The preaching of this type of prophet says nothing about a divine mission or an ethical duty of obedience, but rather directs itself to the self-interest of those who crave salvation, recommending to them the same path as he himself traversed. Our designation for this second type is that of the *"exemplary prophet."*

The exemplary type is particularly characteristic of prophecy in India, although there have been a few manifestations of it in China (e.g., Lao Tzu) and the Near East. On the other hand, the ethical type is confined to the Near East, regardless of racial differences there. For neither the Vedas nor the classical books of the Chinese—the oldest portions of which in both cases consist of songs of praise and thanksgiving by sacred singers, and of magical rites and ceremonies—makes it appear at all probable that prophecy of the ethical type, such as developed in the Near East or Iran, could ever have arisen in India or China. The decisive reason for this is the absence of a personal, transcendental, and ethical god. In India this concept was found only in a sacramental and magical form, and then only in the later and popular faiths. But in the religions of those social strata within which the decisive prophetic conceptions of Mahavira and Buddha were developed, ethical prophecy appeared only intermittently and was constantly subjected to reinterpretations in the direction of pantheism. In China the notion of ethical prophecy was altogether lacking in the ethics of the stratum that exercised the greatest influence in the society. To what degree this may presumably be associated with the intellectual distinctiveness of such strata, which was of course determined by various social factors, will be discussed later.

As far as purely religious factors are concerned, it was decisive for both India and China that the conception of a rationally regulated world had its point of origin in the ceremonial order of sacrifices, on the unalterable sequence of which everything depended: especially the indispensable regularity of meteorological processes; in animistic terms, what was involved here was the normal activity or inactivity of the spirits and demons. According to both classical and heterodox Chinese views, these processes were held to be insured by the ethically proper conduct of government that followed the correct path of virtue, the Tao; without this everything would fail, even according to Vedic doctrine. Thus, in India and China, Rita and Tao respectively represented similar superdivine, impersonal forces.

On the other hand, the personal, transcendental and ethical god is a Near-Eastern concept. It corresponds so closely to that of an all-powerful mundane king with his rational bureaucratic regime that a causal connection can scarcely be denied. Throughout the world the magician is in the first instance a rainmaker, for the harvest depends on timely and sufficient rain, though not in excessive quantity. Until the present time the pontifical Chinese emperor has remained a rainmaker, for in northern China, at least, the uncertainty of the weather renders dubious the operation of irrigation procedures, no matter how extensive they are. Of greater significance was the construction of defense walls, and internal canals, which became the real source of the imperial bureaucracy. The emperor sought to avert meteorological disturbances through sacrifices, public atonement, and various virtuous practices, e.g., the termination of abuses in the administration, or the organization of a raid on unpunished malefactors. For it was always assumed that the reason for the excitation of the spirits and the disturbances of the cosmic order had to be sought either in the personal derelictions of the monarch or in some manifestation of social disorganization. Again, rain was one of the rewards promised by Yahweh to his devotees, who were at that time primarily agriculturalists, as is clearly apparent in the older portions of the tradition. God promised neither too scanty rain nor yet excessive precipitation or deluge.

But throughout Mesopotamia and Arabia it was not rain that was the creator of the harvest, but artificial irrigation alone. In Mesopotamia, irrigation was the sole source of the absolute power of the monarch, who derived his income by compelling his conquered subjects to build canals and cities adjoining them, just as the regulation of the Nile was the source of the Egyptian monarch's strength. In the desert and semiarid regions of the Near East this control of irrigation waters was probably one source of the conception of a god who had created the earth and man out of nothing and not procreated them, as was believed elsewhere. A riparian economy of this kind actually did produce a harvest out of nothing, from the desert sands. The monarch even created law by legislation and rational codification, a development the world experienced for the first time in Mesopotamia. It seems quite reasonable, therefore, that as a result of such experiences the ordering of the world should be conceived as the law of a freely acting, transcendental and personal god.

Another, and negative, factor accounting for the development in the Near East of a world order that reflected the operation of a personal god was the relative absence of those distinctive strata who were the bearers of the Hindu and Chinese ethics, and who created the "godless" religious ethics found in those countries. But even in Egypt, where originally Pharaoh himself was a god, the attempt of Ikhnaton to produce an astral monotheism foundered because of the power of the priesthood, which had by then systematized popular animism and become invincible. In Mesopotamia the development of monotheism and demagogic prophecy was opposed by the ancient pantheon, which was politically organized and had been systematized by the priests; such a development was, furthermore, limited by the firm order of the state.

The kingdom of the Pharaohs and of Mesopotamia made an even more powerful impression upon the Iraelites than the great Persian monarch, the *basileus kat exochen,* made upon the Greeks (the strong impact of Cyrus upon the Greeks is mirrored, for instance, in the fact that a pedagogical treatise [by Xenophon] was formulated as a *Cyropaedia,* despite the defeat of this monarch). The Israelites had gained their freedom from the "house of bondage" of the earthly Pharaoh only because a divine king had come to their assistance. Indeed, their subsequent establishment of a worldly monarchy was expressly declared to be a defection from Yahweh, the real ruler of the people. Hebrew prophecy was completely oriented to a relationship with the great political powers of the time, the Great Kings, who as the rods of God's wrath first destroy Israel and then, as a consequence of divine intervention, permit Israelites to return from the Exile to their own land. In the case of Zoroaster too it seems that the range of his vision was oriented to the views of the civilized lands of the West.

Thus, the distinctive character of the earliest prophecy, in both its dualistic and monotheistic forms, seems to have been determined decisively—aside from the operation of certain other concrete historical influences—by the pressure of relatively contiguous great centers of highly controlled social organization upon less developed neighboring peoples. The latter tended to see in their own continuous peril from the pitiless bellicosity of terrible nations the anger and grace of a heavenly king.

6. The Nature of Prophetic Revelation: The World As a Meaningful Totality

Regardless of whether a particular religious prophet is predominantly of the ethical or predominantly of the exemplary type, prophetic revelation involves for both the prophet himself and for his followers—and this is the element common to both varieties—a unified view of the world derived from a consciously integrated meaningful attitude toward life. To the prophet, both the life of man and the world, both social and cosmic events, have a certain systematic and coherent meaning, to which man's conduct must be oriented if it is to bring salvation, and after which it must be patterned in an integrally meaningful manner. Now the structure of this meaning may take varied forms, and it may weld together into a unity motives that are logically quite heterogeneous. The whole conception is dominated, not by logical consistency, but by practical valuations. Yet it always denotes, regardless of any variations in scope and in measure of success, an effort to systematize all the manifestations of life; that is, to organize practical behavior into a direction of life, regardless of the form it may assume in any individual case. Moreover, this meaning always contains the important religious conception of the world as a cosmos which is challenged to produce somehow a "meaningful," ordered totality, the particular manifestations of which are to be measured and evaluated according to this postulate.

The conflict between empirical reality and this conception of the world as a meaningful totality, which is based on the religious postulate, produces the strongest tensions in man's inner life as well as in his external relationship to the world. To be sure, this problem is by no means dealt with by prophecy alone. Both priestly wisdom and secular philosophy, the intellectualist as well as the popular varieties, are somehow concerned with it. The ultimate question of all metaphysics has always been something like this: if the world as a whole and life in particular were to have a meaning, what might it be, and how would the world have to look in order to correspond to it? The religious problem of prophets and priests is the womb from which non-sacerdotal philosophy emanated, where it developed at all. Subsequently, priests and prophets had to cope with secular philosophy as a very important component of religious evolution. Hence, we must now examine more closely the mutual relationships of priests, prophets, and non-priests.

NOTES

1. See Kurt Breysig, *Die Entstehung des Gottesgedankens und der Heilbringer* (Berlin: Bondi, 1905). Breysig, who early used the term "sociology of religion," dealt with the Jewish prophets and Jesus in *Alterthum und Mittelalter als Vorstufen der Neuzeit*, vol. II of *Kulturgeschichte der Neuzeit* (Berlin: Bondi, 1901), chs. I and II. Breysig's ambitious effort can serve as a contemporary comparison to Weber's work; by its very descriptiveness and diffuseness it demonstrates the analytical strength of Weber's approach.

2. On the *nebiim,* see Weber, *Ancient Judaism,* IV:2.

3. See Erwin Rohde, *Psyche. The Cult of Souls and Belief in Immortality Among the Greeks* (London: Paul, Trench, Trubner, 1925).

4. "*Seisachtheia* of the Year of Release": i.e., the debt release of the sabbatical year enjoined by Moses; cf. Deut. 15:1–3. The Greek term *seisachtheia,* "shaking off" (a burden), designated the debt cancellation of the Solonic reform in sixth century Athens.

5. Montanus and Novatianus were Christian sect founders of the early church (late 2nd, early 3d cent.), Mani (A.D. 215–273) the Babylonian founder of Manichaeism. The fourth figure is given as Manus in the German text, but the context suggests a misreading of Marcion, the 2nd-century Bible critic and sect founder whose movement later merged with Manichaeism.

iv

The Congregation Between Prophet and Priest

1. The Congregation: The Permanent Association of Laymen

If his prophecy is successful, the prophet succeeds in winning permanent helpers. These may be *Sodalen* (as Bartholomae translates the term of the Gathas),[1] disciples (Old Testament and Hindu), comrades (Hindu and Islamic) or followers (Isaiah and the New Testament). In all cases they are personal devotees of the prophet, in contrast to priests and soothsayers who are organized into guilds or office hierarchies. We shall devote additional consideration to this relationship in our analysis of the forms of domination [below, ch. XV]. Moreover, in addition to these permanent helpers, who are active co-workers with the prophet in his mission and who generally also possess some special charismatic qualifications, there is a circle of followers comprising those who support him with lodging, money, and services and who expect to obtain their salvation through his mission. These may engage in intermittent social action (*Gelegenheitshandeln*) or associate themselves continuously in a *congregation* (*Gemeinde*).

A congregation in the specifically religious sense (for this term is [in German] also employed to denote the neighborhood that has been associated for economic or for fiscal or other political purposes) does not arise *solely* in connection with prophecy in the particular sense used here. Nor does it arise in connection with *every* type of prophecy. Primarily, a religious community arises in connection with a prophetic movement as a result of routinization (*Veralltäglichung*), i.e., as a result of the process whereby either the prophet himself or his disciples secure the permanence of his preaching and the congregation's distribution of grace, hence insuring also the economic existence of the enterprise and those who man it, and thereby monopolizing as well the privileges reserved for those charged with religious functions.

It follows from this primacy of routinization in the formation of religious congregations that they may also be formed around mystagogues and priests of nonprophetic religions. For the mystagogue, indeed, the presence of a congregation is a normal phenomenon. The magician, in contrast, exercises his craft independently or, if a member of a guild, serves a particular neighborhood or political group, not a specific religious congregation. The congregations of the mystagogues, like those of the Eleusinian practitioners of mysteries, generally remained an open group with changing membership. Whoever was desirous of salvation would enter into a relationship, generally temporary, with the mystagogue and his assistants. However, the Eleusinian mysteries were something like a regional community, independent of particular localities.

The situation was quite different in the case of exemplary prophets who unconditionally demonstrated the way of salvation by their personal example, as did, for example, the mendicant monks of Mahavira and the Buddha, who belonged to a narrower exemplary community. Within this narrower community the disciples, who might still have been personally associated with the prophet, would exert particular authority. Outside of the exemplary community, however, there were pious devotees (e.g., the *Upasakas* of India) who did not go the whole way of salvation for themselves, but sought to achieve a relative optimum of salvation by demonstrating their devotion to the exemplary saint. These devotees either lacked altogether any fixed status in the religious community, as was originally the case with the Buddhist *Upasakas,* or they were organized into some special group with fixed rules and obligations. This regularly happened when priests, priest-like counselors, or mystagogues like the Buddhist *bonzes* were separated out from the exemplary community and entrusted with cultic responsibilities (which did not exist in the earliest stages of Buddhism). But the prevailing Buddhist practice was the voluntary temporary association, which the majority of mystagogues and exemplary prophets shared with the temple priesthoods of particular deities from the organized pantheon. The economic existence of these congregations was secured by endowments and maintained by sacrificial offerings and other gifts provided by persons with religious needs.

At this stage there was still no trace of a permanent congregation of laymen. Our present conceptions of membership in a religious denomination are not applicable to the situation of that period. As yet the individual was a devotee of a god, approximately in the sense that an Italian is a devotee of a particular saint. Yet there is an almost ineradicable vulgar error that the majority or even all of the Chinese are to be regarded as Buddhists in religion. The source of this misconception is the fact that many Chinese, brought up in the Confucian ethic (which alone enjoys official approbation), consult Taoist divining priests before building a house and mourn deceased relatives according to the Confucian rule while also arranging for Buddhist masses to be performed in their memory. Apart from those who continuously participate in the cult of a god and possibly a narrow circle having a permanent interest in it, all that we have at this stage are drifting laymen, or if one is permitted to use metaphorically a modern political designation, "floating voters."

Naturally, this condition does not satisfy the interests of those who man the cult, if only because of purely economic considerations. Consequently, in this kind of situation they endeavor to create a congregation whereby the personal following of the cult will assume the form of a permanent organization and become a community with fixed rights and duties. Such a transformation of a personal following into a permanent congregation is the normal process by which the doctrine of the prophets enters into everyday life, as the function of a permanent institution. The disciples or apostles of the prophets thereupon become mystagogues, teachers, priests or pastors (or a combination of them all), serving an association dedicated to exclusively religious purposes, namely the *congregation of laymen*.

But the same result can be reached from other starting points. We have seen that the priests, whose function evolved from that of magicians to that of generic priesthood, were either scions of landed priestly families, domestic and court priests of landed magnates and princes, or trained priests of a sacrificial cult who organized into a status group. Individuals or groups applied to these priests for assistance as the need arose, but for the rest the priests could be engaged in any occupation not deemed dishonorable to their status group. One other possibility is that priests might become attached to particular organizations, vocational or otherwise, and especially to a political association. But in all these cases there is no actual congregation which is separate from all other associations.

Such a congregation may arise when a clan of sacrificing priests succeeds in organizing the particular followers of their god into an exclusive association. Another and more usual way for a religious community to arise is as a consequence of the destruction of a political association, wherever the religious adherents of the association's god and his priests continue as a religious congregation. The first of these types is to be found in India and the Near East, where it is connected, in numerous intermediate gradations, with the transition of mystagogic and exemplary prophecy or of religious reform movements into a permanent organization of congregations. Many small Hindu denominations developed as a result of such processes.

By contrast, the transition from a priesthood serving a polity into a religious congregation was associated primarily with the rise of the great world empires of the Near East, especially Persia. Political associations were annihilated and the population disarmed; their priesthoods, however, were assigned certain political powers and were rendered secure in their positions. This was done because the religious congregation was regarded as a valuable instrument for pacifying the conquered, just as the neighborhood association turned into a compulsory community was found to be useful for the protection of financial interests. Thus, by virtue of decrees promulgated by the Persian kings from Cyrus to Artaxerxes, Judaism evolved into a religious community under royal protection, with a theocratic center in Jerusalem. A Persian victory would have brought similar chances and opportunities to the Delphic Apollo and to the priestly families servicing other gods, and possibly also to the Orphic prophets. In Egypt, after the decline of political independence, the national priesthood built a sort of "church" organization, apparently the first of its kind, with synods. On the other hand, religious congregations in India arose in the more limited sense as exemplary congregations. There, the status unity of the Brahmins, as well as the unity of ascetic regulations, survived the multiplicity of ephemeral political structures, and as a consequence, the various systems of ethical salvation transcended all political boundaries. In Iran, the Zoroastrian priests succeeded during the course of the centuries in propagandizing a closed religious organization which under the Sassanids became a political "denomination" (*Konfession*). (The Achaemenids, as their documents demonstrate, were not Zoroastrians, but rather, followers of Mazda.)

The relationships between political authority and religious community, from which the concept of religious denomination derived, belong in the analysis of domination [cf. below, ch. XV]. At this point it suffices to note that *congregational religion* is a phenomenon of diverse manifestations and great fluidity. We want to use the term only when the laity has been organized permanently in such a manner that they can actively participate. A mere administrative unit which delimits the jurisdiction of priests is a *parish,* but not yet a congregational community. But even the concept of a parish, as a grouping different from the secular, political, or economic community, is missing in the religions of China and ancient India. Again, the Greek and other ancient phratries and similar cultic communities were not parishes, but political or other types of associations whose collective actions stood under the guardianship of some god. As for the parish of ancient Buddhism, moreover, this was only a district in which temporarily resident mendicant monks were required to participate in the semimonthly convocations.

In medieval Christianity in the Occident, in post-Reformation Lutheranism and Anglicanism, and in both Christianity and Islam in the Near East, the parish was essentially a passive ecclesiastical tax unit and the jurisdictional district of a priest. In these religions the laymen generally lacked completely the character of a congregation. To be sure, small vestiges of congregational rights have been retained in certain Oriental churches and have also been found in Occidental Catholicism and Lutheranism. On the other hand, ancient Buddhist monasticism, like the warriors of ancient Islam, and like Judaism and ancient Christianity, had religious congregations with varying degrees of organizational elaboration (which will not yet be discussed in detail). Furthermore, a certain actual influence of the laity may be combined with the absence of a regular local congregational organization. An example of this would be Islam, where the laity wields considerable power, particularly in the Shiite sect, even though this is not legally secure; the Shah usually would not appoint priests without being certain of the consent of the local laity.

On the other hand, it is the distinctive characteristic of every sect, in the technical sense of the term (a subject we shall consider later [see below, ch. XV:14]), that it is based on a restricted association of individual local congregations. From this principle, which is represented in Protestantism by the Baptists and Independents, and later by the Congregationalists, a gradual transition leads to the typical organization of the Reformed Church. Even where the latter has become a universal organization, it nevertheless makes membership conditional upon a contractual entry into some particular congregation. We shall return later to some of the problems which arise from these diversities. At the moment, we are particularly interested in just one consequence of the generally so very important development of genuine *congregational* religions: That the relationship between priesthood and laity within the community becomes of crucial significance for the practical effect of the religion. As the organization assumes the specific character of a congregation, the very powerful position of the priest is increasingly confronted with the necessity of keeping in mind the needs of the laity, in the interest of maintaining and enlarging the membership of the community. Actually, every type of priesthood is to some extent in a similar position. In order to maintain its own power, the priesthood must frequently meet the needs of the laity in a very considerable measure. The three forces operative within the laity with which the priesthood must come to grips are: (a) prophecy, (b) the traditionalism of the laity, and (c) lay intellectualism. In contrast to these forces, another decisive factor at work here derives from the necessities and tendencies of the priestly enterprise as such. A few words need to be said about this last factor in its relation to the first one.

As a rule, the ethical and exemplary prophet is himself a layman, and his power position depends on his lay followers. Every prophecy by its very nature devalues the magical elements of the priestly enterprise, but in very different degrees. The Buddha and others like him, as well as the prophets of Israel, rejected and denounced adherence to knowledgeable magicians and soothsayers (who are also called "prophets" in the Israelite sources), and indeed they scorned all magic as inherently useless. Salvation could be achieved only by a distinctively religious and meaningful relationship to the eternal. Among the Buddhists it was regarded as a mortal sin to boast vainly of magical capacities; yet the existence of the latter among the unfaithful was never denied by the prophets of either India or Israel, nor denied by the Christian apostles or the ancient Christian tradition. All prophets, by virtue of their rejection of magic, were necessarily skeptical of the priestly enterprise, though in varying degrees and fashions. The god of the Israelite prophets desired not burnt offerings, but obedience to his commandments. The Buddhist will get nowhere in his quest for salvation merely with Vedic knowledge and ritual; and the ancient sacrifice of *soma* was represented in the oldest *Gathas* as an abomination to Ahura-mazda.

Thus, tensions between the prophets, their lay followers and the representatives of the priestly tradition existed everywhere. To what degree the prophet would succeed in fulfilling his mission, or would become a martyr, depended on the outcome of the struggle for power, which in some instances, e.g., in Israel, was determined by the international situation. Apart from his own family, Zoroaster depended on the clans of the nobles and princes for support in his struggle against the nameless counter-prophet; this was also the case in India and with Muhammad. On the other hand, the Israelite prophets depended on the support of the urban and rural middle class. All of them, however, made use of the prestige which their prophetic charisma, as opposed to the technicians of the routine cults, had gained for them among the laity. The sacredness of a new revelation opposed that of tradition; and depending on the success of the propaganda by each side, the priesthood might compromise with the new prophecy, outbid its doctrine, or eliminate it, unless it were subjugated itself.

2. *Canonical Writings, Dogmas and Scriptural Religion*

In any case, the priesthood had to assume the obligation of codifying either the victorious new doctrine or the old doctrine which had maintained itself despite an attack by the prophets. The priesthood had to delimit what must and must not be regarded as sacred and had to infuse its views into the religion of the laity, if it was to secure its own position. Such a development might have causes other than an effort by hostile prophets to imperil the position of the priesthood, as for example in India, where this took place very early. The simple interest of the priesthood in securing its own position against possible attack, and the necessity of insuring the traditional practice against the scepticism of the laity might produce similar results. Wherever this development took place it produced two phenomena, viz., canonical writings and dogmas, both of which might be of very different scope, particularly the latter. *Canonical scriptures* contain the revelations and traditions themselves, whereas *dogmas* are priestly interpretations of their meaning.

The collection of the prophetic religious revelations or, in the other case, of the traditionally transmitted sacred lore, may take place in the form of oral tradition. Throughout many centuries the sacred knowledge of the Brahmins was transmitted orally, and setting it down in writing was actually prohibited. This of course left a permanent mark on the literary form of this knowledge and also accounts for the not inconsiderable discrepancies in the texts of individual schools (*Shakhas*), the reason being that this knowledge was meant to be possessed only by qualified persons, namely the twice-born. To transmit such knowledge to anyone who had not experienced the second birth and was excluded by virtue of his caste position (*Shudra*)[2] was a heinous sin. Understandably, all magical lore originally has this character of secret knowledge, to protect the professional interest of the guild. But there are also aspects of this magical knowledge which everywhere become the material for the systematic instruction of other members of the group-at-large. At the root of the oldest and most universally diffused magical system of education is the animistic assumption that just as the magician himself requires rebirth and the possession of a new soul for his art, so heroism rests on a charisma which must be aroused, tested, and instilled into the hero by magical manipulations. In this way, therefore, the warrior is reborn into heroism. Charismatic education in this sense, with its novitiates, trials of courage, tortures, gradations of holiness and honor, initiation of youths, and preparation for battle, is an almost universal institution of all societies which have experienced warfare.

When the guild of magicians finally develops into the priesthood, this extremely important function of educating the laity does not cease, and the priesthood always concerns itself with maintaining this function. More and more, secret lore recedes and the priestly doctrine becomes a scripturally established tradition which the priesthood interprets by means of dogmas. Such a scriptural religion subsequently becomes the basis of a system of education, not only for the professional members of the priestly class, but also for the laity, indeed especially for the laity.

Most, though not all, canonical sacred collections became officially closed against secular or religiously undesirable additions as a consequence of a struggle between various competing groups and prophecies for the control of the community. Wherever such a struggle failed to occur or wherever it did not threaten the content of the tradition, the formal canonization of the scriptures took place very slowly. The canon of the Jewish scriptures was not fixed until the year 90 A.D., shortly after the destruction of the theocratic state, when it was fixed by the synod of Jamnia perhaps as a dam against apostolic prophecies, and even then the canon was established only in principle. In the case of the Vedas the scriptural canon was established in opposition to intellectual heterodoxy. The Christian canon was formalized because of the threat to the piety of the petty-bourgeois masses from the intellectual salvation doctrine of the Gnostics. On the other hand, the soteriology of the intellectual classes of ancient Buddhism was crystallized in the Pali canon as a result of the danger posed by the missionizing popular salvation religion of the *Mahayana*. The classical writings of Confucianism, like the priestly code of Ezra, were imposed by political force. For this reason, the former never became sacred, and only at a late stage did the latter take on the quality of authentic sacredness, which is always the result of priestly activity. Only the Koran underwent immediate editing, by command of the Caliph, and became sacred at once, because the semi-literate Muhammad held that the existence of a holy book automatically carries with it the mark of prestige for a religion. This view of prestige was related to widely diffused notions concerning the taboo quality and the magical significance of scriptural documents. Long before the establishment of the biblical canon, it was held that to touch the Pentateuch and the authentic prophetic writings "rendered the hands unclean."

The details of this process and the scope of the writings that were taken into the canonical sacred scriptures do not concern us here. It was due to the magical status of sacred bards that there were admitted into the Vedas not only the heroic epics but also sarcastic poems about the intoxicated Indra, as well as other poetry of every conceivable content. Similarly, a love poem and various personal details involved with the prophetic utterances were received into the Old Testament canon. Finally, the New Testament included a purely personal letter of Paul, and the Koran found room in a number of *suras* for records of all-too-human family vexations in the life of its prophet.

The closing of the canon was generally accounted for by the theory that only a certain epoch in the past history of the religion had been blessed with prophetic charisma. According to the theory of the rabbis this was the period from Moses to Alexander, while from the Roman Catholic point of view the period was the Apostolic Age. On the whole, these theories correctly express recognition of the contrast between prophetic and priestly systematization. Prophets systematized religion with a view to unifying the relationship of man to the world, by reference to an ultimate and integrated value position. On the other hand, priests systematized the content of prophecy or of the sacred traditions by supplying them with a casuistical, rationalistic framework of analysis, and by adapting them to the customs of life and thought of their own stratum and of the laity whom they controlled.

The development of priestly education from the most ancient charismatic stage to the period of literary education has considerable practical importance in the evolution of a faith into a scriptural religion, either in the complete sense of an attachment to a canon regarded as sacred or in the more moderate sense of the authoritativeness of a scripturally fixed sacred norm, as in the case of the Egyptian Book of the Dead. As literacy becomes more important for the conduct of purely secular affairs, which therefore assume the character of bureaucratic administration and proceed according to regulations and documents, the education of even secular officials and educated laymen passes into the hands of literate priests, who may also directly occupy offices the functions of which involve the use of writing, as in the chancelleries of the Middle Ages. To what degree one or the other of these processes takes place depends also, apart from the degree to which the administration has become bureaucratized, on the degree to which other strata, principally the warrior nobles, have developed their own system of education and have taken it into their own hands. Later on we must discuss the bifurcation of educational systems which may result from this process. We must also consider the total suppression or nondevelopment of a purely priestly system of education, which may result from the weakness of the priests or from the absence of either prophecy or scriptural religion.

The establishment of a religious congregation provides the strongest stimulus, though not the only one, for the development of the substantive content of the priestly doctrine, and it creates the specific importance of dogmas. Once a religious community has become established it feels a need to set itself apart from alien competing doctrines and to maintain its superiority in propaganda, all of which tends to place the emphasis upon differential doctrines. To be sure, this process of differentiation may be considerably strengthened by nonreligious motivations. For example, Charlemagne insisted, for the Frankish church, on the doctrine of *filioque*, which created one of the differences between the oriental and occidental Christian churches. This, and his rejection of the canon favorable to the icons, had political grounds, being directed against the supremacy of the Byzantine church.[3] Adherence to completely incomprehensible dogmas, like the espousal of the Monophysite doctrine by great masses of people in the Orient and in Egypt, was the expression of an anti-imperial and anti-Hellenic separatist nationalism. Similarly, the monophysitic Coptic church later preferred the Arabs to the [East] Romans as overlords. Such trends occurred frequently.

But the struggles of priests against indifference, which they profoundly hate, and against the danger that the zeal of the membership would stagnate generally played the greatest role in pushing distinctive criteria and differential doctrines to the foreground. Another factor was emphasis on the importance of membership in a particular denomination and the priests' desire to make difficult the transference of membership to another denomination. The historical precedent was provided by the tattoo markings of fellow members of a totemistic or warrior clan, which had a magical basis. Closest to totemic tattoo, at least externally, was the differential body painting of the Hindu sects. The Jewish retention of circumcision and of the Sabbath taboo was also intended, as is repeatedly indicated in the Old Testament, to effect separation from other nations, and it indeed produced such an effect to an extraordinary degree. A sharp differentiation of Christianity from Judaism was produced by the Christian choice of the day of the sun god as a day of rest, although this choice might possibly be accounted for by the Christian reception of the soteriolial mythos of mystagogic Near Eastern salvation doctrines of solar religion. Muhammad's choice of Friday for weekly religious services was probably motivated primarily by his desire to segregate his followers from the Jews, after his missionary effort among them had failed. But his absolute prohibition of wine had too many analogies with comparable ancient and contemporary phenomena, e.g., among the Rechabites and Nazirites, to have been determined necessarily by his desire to erect a dam against Christian priests, who are under the obligation to take wine (at Holy Communion).

In India differential dogmas corresponding to exemplary prophecy had generally a more practical ethical character, while those having an affinity to mystagogy were more ritualistic. The notorious ten points which produced the great schism of Buddhism at the Council of Vesali involved mere questions of monastic regulations, including many public details which were emphasized only for the purpose of establishing the separation of the *Mahayana* organization.

Asiatic religions, on the other hand, knew practically nothing of dogma as an instrumentality of differentiation. To be sure, the Buddha enunciated his fourfold truth concerning the great illusions as the basis for the practical salvation doctrine of the noble eightfold path. But the comprehension of those truths for the sake of their practical consequences, and not as dogma in the Occidental sense, is the goal of the work of salvation. This is also the case with the majority of ancient Hindu prophecies.

In the Christian congregation one of the very first binding dogmas, characteristically, was God's creation of the world out of nothing, and consequently the establishment of a transcendental god in contradistinction to the gnostic speculation of the intellectuals. In India, on the other hand, cosmological and other metaphysical speculations remained the concern of philosophical schools, which were always permitted a very wide range of latitude in regard to orthodoxy, though not without some limitations. In China the Confucian ethic completely rejected all ties to metaphysical dogma, if only for the reason that magic and belief in spirits had to remain untouched in the interest of maintaining the cult of ancestors, which was the foundation of patrimonial-bureaucratic obedience (as expressly stated in the tradition).

Even within ethical prophecy and the congregational religion it produced, there was a wide diversity in the scope of proliferation of genuine dogmas. Ancient Islam contented itself with confessions of loyalty to god and to the prophet, together with a few practical and ritual primary commandments, as the basis of membership. But dogmatic distinctions, both practical and theoretical, became more comprehensive as priests, congregational teachers, and even the community itself became bearers of the religion. This holds for the later Zoroastrians, Jews, and Christians. But genuinely dogmatic controversy could arise in ancient Israel or Islam only in exceptional cases, since both these religions were characterized by a simplicity of doctrinal theology. In both religions the main area of dispute centered about the doctrine of grace, though there were subsidiary disputes about ethical practice and about ritual and legal questions. This is even truer of Zoroastrianism.

Only among the Christians did there develop a comprehensive, binding and systematically rationalized dogmatics of a theoretical type concerning cosmological matters, the soteriological *mythos* (Christology), and priestly authority (the sacraments). This Christian dogmatics developed first in the Hellenistic portion of the Roman empire, but in the Middle Ages the major elaborations occurred in the Occident. In general, theological development was far stronger in the Western than in the Eastern churches, but in both regions the maximum development of theology occurred wherever a powerful organization of priests possessed the greatest measure of independence from political authorities.

This Christian preoccupation with the formulation of dogmas was in Antiquity particularly influenced by the distinctive character of the intelligentsia which was a product of Greek education; by the special metaphysical presuppositions and tensions produced by the cult of

Christ; by the necessity of taking issue with the educated stratum which at first remained outside the Christian community; and by the ancient Christian church's hostility to pure intellectualism (which stands in such contrast to the position taken by the Asiatic religions). Socially, Christianity was a *congregational* religion comprising primarily petty-bourgeois laymen, who looked with considerable suspicion upon pure intellectualism, a phenomenon which had to be given considerable attention by the bishops. In the Orient, non-Hellenic petty-bourgeois circles increasingly supplied Christianity with its monks; this destroyed Hellenic culture in the Orient and brought to an end the rational construction of dogma there.

In addition, the mode of organization of the religious congregations was an important determinant. In ancient Buddhism, the complete and purposeful absence of all hierarchical organization would have handicapped any consensus concerning rational dogmatics, such as was produced in Christianity, even assuming that the salvation doctrine would have needed any such dogmatic consensus. Christianity found it necessary to postulate some power able to make decisions concerning the orthodoxy of doctrines, in order to protect the unity of the community against the intellectual activity of priests and against the competing lay rationalism which had been aroused by ecclesiastical education. The result of a long process of evolution, the details of which cannot be expounded here, was that the Roman church produced the infallible doctrinal office of its bishop, in the hope that God would not permit the congregation of the world capital to fall into error. Only in this case do we find a consistent doctrinal solution, which assumes the inspiration of the incumbent of the doctrinal office whenever a decision has to be rendered concerning doctrine.

On the other hand, Islam and the Eastern church, for various reasons to be explained below, retained as their basis for determining the validity of dogmatic truths the practice of depending on the consensus of the official bearers of the ecclesiastical teaching organization, who were primarily theologians or priests, as the case might be. Islam arrived at this position by holding fast to the assurance of its prophet that God would never permit the congregation of the faithful to fall into error. The Eastern church followed in this regard the model of the earliest practice of the Christian church. The net effect of this was to slow down the proliferation of dogma in these religious traditions. By contrast, the Dalai Lama has political powers and control over the church, but he has no doctrinal powers proper in view of the magical-ritualist character of Lamaism. Among the Hindus the power of excommunication entrusted to the *gurus* was largely employed for political reasons and only rarely for the punishment of dogmatic deviations.

3. *Preaching and Pastoral Care as Results of Prophetic Religion*

The work of the priests in systematizing the sacred doctrines was constantly nourished by the new material that was turned up in their professional practice, so different from the practice of magicians. In the ethical type of congregational religion something altogether new evolved, namely preaching, and something very different in kind from magical assistance, namely rational pastoral care.

Preaching, which in the true sense of the word is collective instruction concerning religious and ethical matters, is normally specific to prophecy and prophetic religion. Indeed, wherever it arises apart from these, it is an imitation of them. But as a rule, preaching declines in importance whenever a revealed religion has been transformed into a priestly enterprise by routinization, and the importance of preaching stands in inverse proportion to the magical components of a religion. Buddhism originally consisted entirely of preaching, so far as the laity was concerned. In Christianity the importance of preaching has been proportional to the elimination of the more magical and sacramental components of the religion. Consequently, preaching achieves the greatest significance in Protestantism, in which the concept of the priest has been supplanted altogether by that of the preacher.

Pastoral care, the religious cultivation of the individual, is also in its rationalized and systematized form a product of prophetically revealed religion; and it has its source in the oracle and in consultations with the diviner or necromancer. The diviner is consulted when sickness or other blows of fate have led to the suspicion that some magical transgression is responsible, making it necessary to ascertain the means by which the aggrieved spirit, demon, or god may be pacified. This is also the source of the confessional, which originally had no connection with ethical influences on life. The connection between confession and ethical conduct was first effected by ethical religion, particularly by prophecy. Pastoral care may later assume diverse forms. To the extent that it is a charismatic distribution of grace it stands in a close inner relationship to magical manipulations. But the care of souls may also involve the instruction of individuals regarding concrete religious obligations whenever certain doubts have arisen. Finally, pastoral care may in some sense stand midway between charismatic distribution of grace and instruction, entailing the distribution of personal religious consolation in times of inner or external distress.

Preaching and pastoral care differ widely in the strength of their practical influence on the conduct of life. Preaching unfolds its power most strongly in periods of prophetic excitation. In the treadmill of daily living it declines sharply to an almost complete lack of influence upon the conduct of life, for the very reason that the charisma of speech is an individual matter.

Pastoral care in all its forms is the priests' real instrument of power, particularly over the workaday world, and it influences the conduct of life most powerfully when religion has achieved an ethical character. In fact, the power of ethical religion over the masses parallels the development of pastoral care. Wherever the power of an ethical religion is intact, the pastor will be consulted in all the situations of life by both private individuals and the functionaries of groups, just as the professional divining priest would be consulted in the magical religions, e.g., the religion of China. Among these religious functionaries whose pastoral care has influenced the everyday life of the laity and the attitude of the power-holders in an enduring and often decisive manner have been the counseling rabbis of Judaism, the father confessors of Catholicism, the pietistic pastors of souls in Protestantism, the directors of souls in Counter-Reformation Catholicism, the Brahminic *purohitas* at the court, the *gurus* and *gosains* in Hinduism, and the *muftis* and dervish sheiks in Islam.

As for the conduct of the individual's private life, the greatest influence of pastoral care was exerted when the priesthood combined ethical casuistry with a rationalized system of ecclesiastical penances. This was accomplished in a remarkably skillful way by the occidental church, which was schooled in the casuistry of Roman law. It is primarily these practical responsibilities of preaching and pastoral care which stimulated the labors of the priesthood in systematizing the casuistical treatment of ethical commandments and religious truths, and indeed first compelled them to take an attitude toward the numerous problems which had not been settled in the revelation itself. Consequently, it is these same practical responsibilities of preaching and pastoral care which brought in their wake the substantive routinization of prophetic demands into specific prescriptions of a casuistical, and hence more rational, character, in contrast to the prophetic ethics. But at the same time this development resulted in the loss of that unity which the prophet had introduced into the ethics—the derivation of a standard of life out of a distinctive "meaningful" relationship to one's god, such as he himself had possessed and by means of which he assayed not the external appearance of a single act, but rather its meaningful significance for the total relationship to the god. As for priestly practice, it required both positive injunctions and a casuistry for the laity. For this reason the preoccupation of religion with an ethics of ultimate ends had necessarily to undergo a recession.

It is evident that the positive, substantive injunctions of the prophetic ethic and the casuistical transformation thereof by the priests ultimately derived their material from problems which the folkways, conventions, and factual needs of the laity brought to the priests for disposition in their pastoral office. Hence, the more a priesthood aimed to regulate the behavior pattern of the laity in accordance with the will of the god, and especially to aggrandize its status and income by so doing, the more it had to compromise with the traditional views of the laity in formulating patterns of doctrine and behavior. This was particularly the case when no great prophetic preaching had developed which might have wrenched the faith of the masses from its bondage to traditions based upon magic.

As the masses increasingly became the object of the priests' influence and the foundation of their power, the priestly labors of systematization concerned themselves more and more with the most traditional, and hence magical, forms of religious notions and practices. Thus, as the Egyptian priesthood pressed towards greater power, the animistic cult of animals was increasingly pushed into the center of religious interest, even though it is most likely that the systematic intellectual training of the priests had grown by comparison with earlier times. And so too in India, there was an increased systematization of the cult after the displacement by the Brahmins of the *hotar,* the sacred charismatic singer, from first place in the sacrificial ceremonial. The Atharva Veda is much younger than the Rig Veda as a literary product, and the Brahmanas are much younger still. Yet the systematized religious material in the Atharva Veda is of much older provenience than the rituals of the noble Vedic cults and the other components of the older Vedas; indeed, the Atharva Veda is a purely magical ritual to a far greater degree than the older Vedas. The process of popularization and transformation into magic of religion which had been systematized by the priests continued even further in the Brahmanas. The older Vedic cults are indeed, as Oldenberg[4] has emphasized, cults of the propertied strata, whereas the magical ritual had been the possession of the masses since ancient times.

A similar process appears to have taken place in regard to prophecy. In comparison with the intellectual contemplativeness of ancient Buddhism, which had achieved the highest peaks of sublimity, the *Mahayana* religion was essentially a popularization that increasingly tended to approach pure wizardry or sacramental ritualism. A similar fate overtook the doctrines of Zoroaster, Lao Tzu, and the Hindu religious reformers, and to some extent the doctrines of Muhammad as well, when the respective faiths of these founders became religions of laymen. Thus, the

Zend Avesta sanctioned the cult of *Haoma,* although it had been expressly and strongly combated by Zoroaster, perhaps eliminating merely a few of the bacchantic elements which he had denounced with special fervor. Hinduism constantly betrayed a growing tendency to slide over into magic, or in any case into a semi-magical sacramental soteriology. The propaganda of Islam in Africa rested primarily on a massive foundation of magic, by means of which it has continued to outbid other competing faiths despite the rejection of magic by earliest Islam.

This process, which is usually interpreted as a decline or petrifaction of prophecy, is practically unavoidable. The prophet himself is normally a righteous lay preacher of sovereign independence whose aim is to supplant the traditional ritualistic religious grace of the ecclesiastical type by organizing life on the basis of ultimate ethical principles. The laity's acceptance of the prophet, however, is generally based on the fact that he possesses a certain charisma. This usually means that he is a magician, in fact much greater and more powerful than other magicians, and indeed that he possesses unsurpassed power over demons and even over death itself. It usually means that he has the power to raise the dead, and possibly that he himself may rise from the grave. In short, he is able to do things which other magicians are unable to accomplish. It does not matter that the prophet attempts to deny such imputed powers, for after his death this development proceeds without and beyond him. If he is to continue to live on in some manner among large numbers of the laity, he must himself become the object of a cult, which means he must become the incarnation of a god. If this does not happen, the needs of the laity will at least insure that the form of the prophet's teaching which is most appropriate for them will survive by a process of selection.

Thus, these two types of influences, viz., the power of prophetic charisma and the enduring habits of the masses, influence the work of the priests in their systematization, though they tend to oppose one another at many points. But even apart from the fact that prophets practically always come out of lay groups or find their support in them, the laity is not composed of exclusively traditionalistic forces. The *rationalism of lay circles* is another social force with which the priesthood must take issue. Different social strata may be the bearers of this lay rationalism.

NOTES

1. See Christian Bartholomae, trans. and ed., *Die Gatha's des Awesta. Zarathushtra's Verspredigten* (Strassburg: Trübner, 1905), 130; *Sodalen* were the members of the first rank in Zoroastrianism; the second rank was constituted by the knights, the third by the peasants.

2. On the Shudras, cf. Weber, *The Religion of India*, 55ff.

3. In the Western church, the Nicene Creed was modified in the 9th century by the phrase "qui ex Patre *Filioque* procedit." Thus, belief was professed in the Father, the Son and the Holy Ghost proceeding from *both* of them. This addition became the subject of a long controversy between the Orthodox and the Western church.

4. Hermann Oldenberg, *Die Religion der Veda*, 1894, 4th ed., 1923. (W)

V

The Religious Propensities of Peasantry, Nobility and Bourgeoisie[1]

1. Peasant Religion and Its Ideological Glorification

The lot of peasants is so strongly tied to nature, so dependent on organic processes and natural events, and economically so little oriented to rational systematization that in general the peasantry will become a carrier of religion only when it is threatened by enslavement or proletarianization, either by domestic forces (financial or seigneurial) or by some external political power.

Ancient Israelite religious history already manifested both major threats to the peasant class: first, pressures from foreign powers that threatened enslavement, and second, conflicts between peasants and landed magnates (who in Antiquity resided in the cities). The oldest documents, particularly the *Song of Deborah*, reveal the typical elements of the struggle of a peasant confederacy, comparable to that of the Aetolians, Samnites, and Swiss. Another point of similarity with the Swiss situation is that Palestine possessed the geographical character of a land bridge, being situated on a great trade route which spanned the terrain from Egypt to the Euphrates. This facilitated early a money economy and culture contacts. The Israelite confederacy directed its efforts against both the Philistines and the Canaanite land magnates who dwelt in the cities. These latter were knights who fought with iron chariots, "warriors trained from their very youth," as Goliath was described, who sought to enslave and render tributary the peasantry of the mountain slopes where milk and honey flowed.

It was a most significant constellation of historical factors that this struggle, as well as the social unification and the expansion of the

Mosaic period, was constantly renewed under the leadership of the Yahweh religion's saviors ("messiahs," from *mashiah*, "the anointed one," as Gideon and others, the so-called "Judges," were termed). Because of this distinctive leadership, a religious concern that far transcended the level of the usual agrarian cults entered very early into the ancient religion of the Palestinian peasantry. But not until the city of Jerusalem had been conquered did the cult of Yahweh, with its Mosaic social legislation, become a genuinely ethical religion. Indeed, as the social admonitions of the prophets demonstrate, even here this took place partly under the influence of agrarian social reform movements directed against the urban landed magnates and financial nabobs, and by reference to the social prescriptions of the Mosaic law regarding the equalization of status groups.

But prophetic religion has by no means been the product of specifically agrarian influences. A typical plebeian fate was one of the dynamic factors in the moralism of the first and only theologian of official Greek literature, Hesiod. But he was certainly not a typical "peasant." The more agrarian the essential social pattern of a culture, e.g., Rome, India, or Egypt, the more likely it is that the agrarian element of the population will fall into a pattern of traditionalism and that at least the religion of the masses will lack ethical rationalization. Thus, in the later development of Judaism and Christianity, the peasants never appeared as the carriers of rational ethical movements. This statement is completely true of Judaism, while in Christianity the participation of the peasantry in rational ethical movements took place only in exceptional cases and then in a communist, revolutionary form. The puritanical sect of the Donatists in Roman Africa, the Roman province of greatest land accumulation, appears to have been very popular among the peasantry, but this was the sole example of peasant concern for a rational ethical movement in Antiquity. The Taborites, insofar as they were derived from peasant groups, the peasant protagonists of "divine right" in the German peasant war [of 1524/5], the English radical communist smallholders, and above all the Russian peasant sectarians—all these have origins in agrarian communism by virtue of the pre-existing, more or less developed communal ownership of land.[2] All these groups felt themselves threatened by proletarization, and they turned against the official church in the first instance because it was the recipient of tithes and served as a bulwark of the financial and landed magnates. The association of the aforementioned peasant groups with religious demands was possible only on the basis of an already existing ethical religion which contained specific promises that might suggest and justify a revolutionary natural law. More will be said about this in another context.

Hence, manifestations of a close relationship between peasant religion and agrarian reform movements did not occur in Asia, where the combination of religious prophecy with revolutionary currents, e.g., as in China, took a different direction altogether, and did not assume the form of a real peasant movement. Only rarely does the peasantry serve as the carrier of any other sort of religion than their original magic.

Yet the prophecy of Zoroaster apparently appealed to the (relative) rationalism of peasants who, having learned to work in an orderly fashion and to raise cattle, were struggling against the orgiastic religion of the false prophets, which entailed the torture of animals. This, like the cult of intoxication which Moses combated, was presumably associated with the bacchantic rending of live animals. In the religion of the Parsees, only the cultivated soil was regarded as pure from the magical point of view, and therefore only agriculture was absolutely pleasing to god. Consequently, even after the pattern of the religion established by the original prophecy had undergone considerable transformation as a result of its adaptation to the needs of everyday life, it retained a distinctive agrarian pattern, and consequently a characteristically anti-urban tendency in its doctrines of social ethics. But to the degree that the Zoroastrian prophecy set in motion certain economic interests, these were probably in the beginning the interests of princes and lords in the peasants' ability to pay taxes, rather than peasant interests. As a general rule, the peasantry remained primarily involved with weather magic and animistic magic or ritualism; insofar as it developed any ethical religion, the focus was on a purely formalistic ethic of *do ut des* in relation to both god and priests.

That the peasant has become the distinctive prototype of the pious man who is pleasing to god is a thoroughly modern phenomenon, with the exception of Zoroastrianism and a few scattered examples of opposition to urban culture and its consequences on the part of literati representing patriarchal and feudalistic elements, or conversely, of intellectuals imbued with *Weltschmerz*. None of the more important religions of Eastern Asia had any such notion about the religious merit of the peasant. Indeed, in the religions of India, and most consistently in the salvation religion of Buddhism, the peasant is religiously suspect or actually proscribed because of *ahimsâ*, the absolute prohibition against taking the life of any living thing.

The Israelite religion of preprophetic times was still very much a religion of peasants. On the other hand, in exilic times the glorification of agriculture as pleasing to God was largely the expression of opposition to urban development felt by literary or patriarchal groups. The actual religion had rather a different appearance, even at that time; and later on in the period of the Pharisees it was completely different in this regard. To the congregational piety of the *chaberim* the "rustic" was virtually identical with the "godless," the rural dweller being politically and religiously a Jew of the second class. For it was virtually impossible for a peasant to live a pious life according to the Jewish ritual law, just as in Buddhism and Hinduism. The practical consequences of postexilic theology, and even more so of the Talmudic theology, made it extremely difficult for a Jew to practice agriculture. Even now, the Zionist colonization of Palestine has met with an absolute impediment in the form of the sabbatical year, a product of the theologians of later Judaism. To overcome this difficulty, the eastern European rabbis, in contrast to the more doctrinaire leaders of German Jewish orthodoxy, have had to construe a special dispensation based on the notion that such colonizing is especially pleasing to God.

In early Christianity, it will be recalled, the rustic was simply regarded as the heathen (*paganus*). Even the official doctrine of the medieval churches, as formulated by Thomas Aquinas, treated the peasant essentially as a Christian of lower rank, at any rate accorded him very little esteem. The religious glorification of the peasant and the belief in the special worth of his piety is the result of a very modern development. It was characteristic of Lutheranism in particular—in rather strongly marked contrast to Calvinism, and also to most of the Protestant sects—as well as of modern Russian religiosity manifesting Slavophile influences. These are ecclesiastical communities which, by virtue of their type of organization, are very closely tied to the authoritarian interests of princes and noblemen upon whom they are dependent. In modern Lutheranism (for this was not the position of Luther himself) the dominant interest is the struggle against intellectualist rationalism and against political liberalism. In the Slavophile religious peasant ideology, the primary concern was the struggle against capitalism and modern socialism. Finally, the glorification of the Russian sectarians by the *narodniki* [populists] tries to link the anti-rationalist protest of intellectuals with the revolt of a proletarized class of farmers against a bureaucratic church serving the interests of the ruling classes, thereby surrounding both intellectual and agrarian protest with a religious aura. Thus, what was involved in all cases was very largely a reaction against the development of modern rationalism, of which the cities were regarded as the carriers.

In striking contrast to all this is the fact that in the past it was the city which was regarded as the site of piety. As late as the seventeenth century, Baxter saw in the relationships of the weavers of Kidderminster to the metropolis of London (made possible by the development of domestic industry) a definite enhancement of the weavers' piety. Actually, early Christianity was an urban religion, and, as Harnack decisively demonstrated, its importance in any particular city was in direct proportion to the size of the urban community.[3] In the Middle Ages too, fidelity to the church, as well as sectarian movements in religion, characteristically developed in the cities. It is highly unlikely that an organized congregational religion, such as early Christianity became, could have developed as it did apart from the community life of a city (notably in the sense found in the Occident). For early Christianity presupposed as already extant certain conceptions, viz., the destruction of all taboo barriers between kin groups, the concept of office, and the concept of the community as a compulsory organization (*Anstalt*) with specific functions. To be sure, Christianity, on its part, strengthened these conceptions and greatly facilitated the renewed reception of them by the growing European cities during the Middle Ages. But actually these notions fully developed nowhere else in the world but within the Mediterranean culture, particularly in Hellenistic and definitely in Roman urban law. What is more, the specific qualities of Christianity as an ethical religion of salvation and as personal piety found their real nurture in the urban environment; and it is there that they created new movements time and again, in contrast to the ritualistic, magical or formalistic re-interpretation favored by the dominant feudal powers.

2. *Aristocratic Irreligion versus Warring for the Faith*

As a rule, the warrior nobles, and indeed feudal powers generally, have not readily become the carriers of a rational religious ethic. The life pattern of a warrior has very little affinity with the notion of a beneficent providence, or with the systematic ethical demands of a transcendental god. Concepts like sin, salvation, and religious humility have not only seemed remote from all ruling strata, particularly the warrior nobles, but have indeed appeared reprehensible to its sense of honor. To accept a religion that works with such conceptions and to genuflect before the prophet or priest would appear plebeian and dishonorable to any martial hero or noble person, e.g., the Roman nobility of the age of Tacitus, or the Confucian mandarins. It is an everyday psychological event for the warrior to face death and the irrationalities of human destiny. Indeed, the chances and adventures of mundane existence fill his life to such an extent that he does not require of his religion (and accepts only reluctantly) anything beyond protection against evil magic or ceremonial rites congruent with his sense of status, such as priestly prayers for victory or for a blissful death leading directly into the hero's heaven.

As has already been mentioned in another connection, the educated Greek always remained a warrior, at least in theory. The simple animistic belief in the soul which left vague the qualities of existence after death and the entire question of the hereafter (though remaining certain that the most miserable status here on earth was preferable to ruling over Hades), remained the normal faith of the Greeks until the time of the complete destruction of their political autonomy. The only developments beyond this were the mystery religions, which provided means for ritualistic improvement of the human condition in this world and in the next; the only radical departure was the Orphic congregational religion, with its doctrine of the transmigration of souls.

Periods of strong prophetic or reformist religious agitation have frequently pulled the nobility in particular into the path of prophetic ethical religion, because this type of religion breaks through all classes and status groups, and because the nobility has generally been the first carrier of lay education. But presently the routinization of prophetic religion had the effect of eliminating the nobility from the circle of groups characterized by religious enthusiasm. This is already evident at the time of the religious wars in France in the conflicts of the Huguenot synods with a leader like Condé over ethical questions. Ultimately, the Scottish nobility, like the British and the French, was completely extruded from the Calvinist religion in which it, or at least some of its groups, had originally played a considerable role.

As a rule, prophetic religion is naturally compatible with the status feeling of the nobility when it directs its promises to the warrior in the cause of religion. This conception assumes the exclusiveness of a universal god and the moral depravity of unbelievers who are his adversaries and whose untroubled existence arouses his righteous indignation. Hence, such a notion is absent in the Occident of ancient times, as well as in all Asiatic religion until Zoroaster. Indeed, even in Parsism a direct connection between religious promises and war against religious infidelity is still lacking. It was Islam that first produced this conjunction of ideas.

The precursor and probable model for this was the promise of the Hebrew god to his people, as understood and reinterpreted by Muhammad after he had changed from a pietistic leader of a conventicle in Mecca to the *podestà* of Yathrib-Medina, and after he had finally been rejected as a prophet by the Jews. The ancient wars of the Israelite confederacy, waged under the leadership of various saviors operating under the authority of Yahweh, were regarded by the tradition as holy wars. This concept of a holy war, i.e., a war in the name of a god, for

the special purpose of avenging a sacrilege, which entailed putting the
enemy under the ban and destroying him and all his belongings completely, is not unknown in Antiquity, particularly among the Greeks.
But what was distinctive of the Hebraic concept is that the people of
Yahweh, as his special community, demonstrated and exemplified their
god's prestige against their foes. Consequently, when Yahweh became a
universal god, Hebrew prophecy and the religion of the Psalmists
created a new religious interpretation. The possession of the Promised
Land, previously foretold, was supplanted by the farther reaching promise of the elevation of Israel, as the people of Yahweh, above other
nations. In the future all nations would be compelled to serve Yahweh
and to lie at the feet of Israel.

On this model Muhammad constructed the commandment of the
holy war involving the subjugation of the unbelievers to political authority and economic domination of the faithful. If the infidels were
members of "religions with a sacred book," their extermination was not
enjoined; indeed, their survival was considered desirable because of the
financial contribution they could make. It was a Christian war of religion that first was waged under the Augustinian formula *coge intrare*,[4]
by the terms of which unbelievers or heretics had only the choice between conversion and extirpation. It will be recalled that Pope Urban
lost no time in emphasizing to the crusaders the necessity for territorial
expansion in order to acquire new benefices for their descendants. To
an even greater degree than the Crusades, religious war for the Muslims
was essentially an enterprise directed towards the acquisition of large
holdings of real estate, because it was primarily oriented to securing
feudal revenue. As late as the period of Turkish feudal law [participation
in] the religious war remained an important qualification for preferential
status in the distribution of *sipahi* prebends. Apart from the anticipated
master status that results from victory in a religious war, even in Islam
the religious promises associated with the propaganda for war—particularly the promise of an Islamic paradise for those killed in such a war
—should not be construed as promises of salvation in the genuine sense
of this term, just as Valhalla, or the paradise promised to the Hindu
kshatriya, or to the warrior hero who has become sated with life once
he has seen his grandson, or indeed any other hero heaven are not
equivalent to salvation. Moreover, those religious elements of ancient
Islam which had the character of an ethical religion of salvation largely
receded into the background as long as Islam remained essentially a
martial religion.

So, too, the religion of the medieval Christian orders of celibate

knights, particular the Templars, which were first called into being during the Crusades against Islam and which corresponded to the Islamic
warrior orders, had in general only a formal relation to salvation religion.
This was also true of the faith of the Hindu Sikhs, which was at first
strongly pacifist. But a combination of Islamic ideas and persecution
drove the Sikhs to the ideal of uncompromising religious warfare. Another instance of the relative meagerness of the relationship of a martial
faith to salvation religion is that of the warlike Japanese monks of Buddhism, who for a temporary period maintained a position of political
importance. Indeed, even the formal orthodoxy of all these warrior religionists was often of dubious genuineness.

Although a knighthood practically always had a thoroughly negative
attitude toward salvation and congregational religion, the relationship is
somewhat different in "standing" professional armies, i.e., those having
an essentially bureaucratic organization and "officers." The Chinese
army plainly had a specialized god as did any other occupation, a hero
who had undergone canonization by the state. Then, too, the passionate
participation of the Byzantine army in behalf of the iconoclasts was not
a result of conscious puritanical principles, but that of the attitude
adopted by the recruiting districts, which were already under Islamic
influence. But in the Roman army of the period of the Principate, from
the time of the second century, the congregational religion of Mithra,
which was a competitor of Christianity and held forth certain promises
concerning the world to come, played a considerable role, together with
certain other preferred cults, which do not interest us at this point.

Mithraism was especially important (though not exclusively so)
among the centurions, that is the subaltern officers who had a claim
upon governmental pensions. The genuinely ethical requirements of the
Mithraistic mysteries were, however, very modest and of a general
nature only. Mithraism was essentially a ritualistic religion of purity; in
sharp contrast to Christianity, it was entirely masculine, excluding
women completely. In general, it was a religion of salvation, and, as
already noted, one of the most masculine, with a hierarchical gradation
of sacred ceremonies and religious ranks. Again in contrast to Christianity, it did not prohibit participation in other cults and mysteries, which
was not an infrequent occurrence. Mithraism, therefore, came under
the protection of the emperors from the time of Commodus, who first
went through the initiation ceremonies (just as the kings of Prussia
were members of fraternal orders), until its last enthusiastic protagonist,
Julian. Apart from promises of a mundane nature which, to be sure,
were in this case as in all other religions linked with predictions regard-

ing the world beyond, the chief attraction of this cult for army officers was undoubtedly the essentially magical and sacramental character of its distribution of grace and the possibility of hierarchical advancement in the mystery ceremonies.

3. *Bureaucratic Irreligion*

It is likely that similar factors recommended Mithraism to civilian *officials,* for it was also very popular among them. Certainly, among government officials there have been found other incipient tendencies towards distinctively salvation type religions. One example of this may be seen in the pietistic German officials, a reflection of the fact that in Germany middle-class ascetic piety, exemplifying a characteristically bourgeois pattern of life, found its representation only among the officials, in the absence of a stratum of entrepreneurs. Another instance of the tendency of some government officials to favor the salvation type of religion appeared occasionally among certain really pious Prussian generals of the eighteenth and nineteenth centuries. But as a rule, this is not the attitude to religion of a dominant bureaucracy, which is always the carrier of a comprehensive sober rationalism and, at the same time, of the ideal of a disciplined "order" and security as absolute standards of value. A bureaucracy is usually characterized by a profound disesteem of all irrational religion, combined, however, with a recognition of its usefulness as a device for controlling the people. In Antiquity this attitude was held by the Roman officials, while today it is shared by both the civilian and military bureaucracy.[5]

The distinctive attitude of a bureaucracy to religious matters has been classically formulated in Confucianism. Its hallmark is an absolute lack of feeling of a need for salvation or for any transcendental anchorage for ethics. In its place resides what is substantively an opportunistic and utilitarian (though aesthetically refined) doctrine of conventions appropriate to a bureaucratic status group. Other factors in the bureaucratic attitude toward religion include the elimination of all those emotional and irrational manifestations of personal religion which go beyond the traditional belief in spirits, and the maintenance of the ancestral cult and of filial piety as the universal basis for social subordination. Still another ingredient of bureaucratic religions is a certain distance from the spirits, the magical manipulation of which is scorned by the enlightened official (but in which the superstitious one may participate, as is the case with spiritualism among us today). Yet both types of bureaucratic officials will, with contemptuous indifference, permit such spiritualistic activity to flourish as the religion of the masses (*Volksreligiosität*). Insofar as this popular religion comes to expression in recognized state rites, the official continues to respect them, outwardly at least, as a conventional obligation appropriate to his status. The continuous retention of magic, especially of the ancestral cult, as the guarantee of social obedience, enabled the Chinese bureaucracy to completely suppress all independent ecclesiastical development and all congregational religion. As for the European bureaucracy, although it generally shares such subjective disesteem for any serious concern with religion, it finds itself compelled to pay more official respect to the religiosity of the churches in the interest of mass domestication.

4. *Bourgeois Religiosity and Economic Rationalism*

If certain fairly uniform tendencies are normally apparent, in spite of all differences, in the religious attitude of the nobility and bureaucracy, the strata with the maximum social privilege, the real "middle" strata evince striking contrasts. Moreover, this is something quite apart from the rather sharp differences of status which these strata manifest within themselves. Thus, in some instances, merchants may be members of the most highly privileged stratum, as in the case of the ancient urban patriciate, while in others they may be pariahs, like impecunious wandering peddlers. Again, they may be possessed of considerable social privilege, though occupying a lower social status than the nobility or officialdom; or they may be without privilege, or indeed disprivileged, yet actually exerting great social power. Examples of the latter would be the Roman *ordo equester,* the Hellenic *metoikoi,* the medieval cloth merchants and other merchant groups, the financiers and great merchant princes of Babylonia, the Chinese and Hindu traders, and finally the bourgeoisie of the early modern period.

Apart from these differences of social position, the attitude of the commercial patriciate toward religion shows characteristic contrasts in all periods of history. In the nature of the case, the strongly mundane orientation of their life would make it appear unlikely that they have much inclination for prophetic or ethical religion. The activity of the great merchants of ancient and medieval times represented a distinctive kind of specifically occasional and unprofessional acquisition of money, e.g., by providing capital for traveling traders who required it. Originally seigneurial rulers, these merchants became, in historical times, an urban nobility which had grown rich from such occasional trade. Others started as tradesmen who having acquired landed property were seeking to climb into the families of the nobility. To the category of the commercial patriciate there were added, as the financing of public administration developed, the political capitalists whose primary business was to meet the financial needs of the state as purveyors and by supplying governmental credit, together with the financiers of colonial capitalism, an enterprise that has existed in all periods of history. None of these strata has ever been the primary carrier of an ethical or salvation religion. At any rate, the more privileged the position of the commercial class, the less it has evinced any inclination to develop an other-worldly religion.

The religion of the noble plutocratic class in the Phoenician trading cities was entirely this-worldly in orientation and, so far as is known, entirely non-prophetic. Yet the intensity of their religious mood and their fear of the gods, who were envisaged as possessing very sinister traits, were very impressive. On the other hand, the warlike maritime nobility of ancient Greece, which was partly piratical and partly commercial, has left behind in the *Odyssey* a religious document congruent with its own interests, which betrays a striking lack of respect for the gods. The god of wealth in Chinese Taoism, who is universally respected by merchants, shows no ethical traits; he is of a purely magical character. So, too, the cult of the Greek god of wealth, Pluto—indeed primarily of agrarian character—formed a part of the Eleusinian mysteries, which set up no ethical demands apart from ritual purity and freedom from blood guilt. Augustus, in a characteristic political maneuver, sought to turn the stratum of freedmen, with their strong capital resources, into special carriers of the cult of Caesar by creating the dignity of the *Augustalis*.[6] But this stratum showed no distinctive religious tendencies otherwise.

In India, that section of the commercial stratum which followed the Hindu religion, particularly all the banking groups which derived from the ancient state capitalist financiers and large-scale traders, belonged for the most part to the sect of the *Vallabhâchârîs*. These were adherents of the Vishnu priesthood of Gokulastha Gosain, as reformed by Vallabha Svami. They followed a form of erotically tinged worship of Krishna and Radha in which the cultic meal in honor of their savior was transformed into a kind of elegant repast. In medieval Europe, the great business organizations of the Guelph cities, like the *Arte di Calimala,* were of course papist in their politics, but very often they virtually annulled the ecclesiastical prohibition against usury by fairly mechanical devices which not infrequently created an effect of mockery. In Protestant Holland, the great and distinguished lords of trade, being Arminians in religion, were characteristically oriented to *Real-politik*, and became the chief foes of Calvinist ethical rigor. Everywhere, skepticism or indifference to religion are and have been the widely diffused attitudes of large-scale traders and financiers.

But as against these easily understandable phenomena, the acquisition of new capital or, more correctly, capital continuously and rationally employed in a productive enterprise for the acquisition of profit, especially in industry (which is the characteristically modern employment of capital), has in the past been combined frequently and in a striking manner with a rational, ethical congregational religion among the classes in question. In the business life of India there was even a (geographical) differentiation between the Parsees and the Jain sect. The former, adherents of the religion of Zoroaster, retained their ethical rigorism, particularly its unconditional injunction regarding truthfulness, even after modernization had caused a reinterpretation of the ritualistic commandments of purity as hygienic prescriptions. The economic morality of the Parsees originally recognized only agriculture as acceptable to God, and abominated all urban acquisitive pursuits. On the other hand, the sect of the Jains, the most ascetic of the religions of India, along with the aforementioned Vallabhacharis represented a salvation doctrine that was constituted as congregational religion, despite the antirational character of the cults. It is difficult to prove that very frequently the Islamic merchants adhered to the dervish religion, but it is not unlikely. As for Judaism, the ethical rational religion of the Jewish community was already in Antiquity largely a religion of traders or financiers.

To a lesser but still notable degree, the religion of the medieval Christian congregation, particularly of the sectarian type or of the heretical circles was, if not a religion appropriate to traders, nonetheless "bourgeois" religion, and that in direct proportion to its ethical rationalism. The closest connection between ethical religion and rational economic development—particularly capitalism—was effected by all the forms of ascetic Protestantism and sectarianism in both Western and Eastern Europe, viz., Zwinglians, Calvinists, Baptists, Mennonites, Quakers, Methodists, and Pietists (both of the Reformed and, to a lesser degree, Lutheran varieties); as well as by Russian schismatic, heretical, and rational pietistic sects, especially the Shtundists and Skoptsy, though in very different forms.[7] Indeed, generally speaking, the inclination to join an ethical, rational, congregational religion becomes more strongly marked the farther away one gets from those strata which have been the carriers of the type of capitalism which is primarily political in orientation. Since the time of Hammurabi political capitalism has existed wherever there has been tax farming, the profitable provisions of the state's political needs, war, piracy, large-scale usury, and colonization. The tendency toward affiliation with an ethical, rational, congregational religion is more apt to be found the closer one gets to those strata which have been the carriers of the modern rational enterprise, i.e., strata with middle-class economic characteristics in the sense to be expounded later.

Obviously, the mere existence of capitalism of some sort is not sufficient, by any means, to produce a uniform ethic, not to speak of an ethical congregational religion. Indeed, it does not automatically produce any uniform consequences. For the time being, no analysis will be made of the kind of causal relationship subsisting between a rational religious ethic and a particular type of commercial rationalism, where such a connection exists at all. At this point, we desire only to establish the existence of an affinity between economic rationalism and certain types of rigoristic ethical religion, to be discussed later. This affinity comes to light only occasionally outside the Occident, which is the distinctive seat of economic rationalism. In the West, this phenomenon is very clear and its manifestations are the more impressive as we approach the classical bearers of economic rationalism.

NOTES

1. The present and the following two sections constitute a single section in the German edition entitled "Status Groups, Classes and Religion."

2. Cf. Norman Cohn, *The Pursuit of the Millennium* (New York: Oxford University Press, 1957), esp. ch. X.

3. See Adolf Harnack, *Die Mission und Ausbreitung des Christentums* in den ersten drei Jahrhunderten (Leipzig: Hinrich, 1902), Part IV, esp. 539.

4. *Coge intrare* or *compelle intrare*, "to force (them) to join": the principle that justifies the use of force against heretics, or deceitful proselytizing; derived from a misinterpreted passage in Luc. 14:23. Cf. Soc. of Law, ch. VIII:*v*, n. 26.

5. I could make the observation that at the first appearance of von Egidy (Lieutenant-Colonel, Ret.) the Officers' Clubs entertained the expectation, inasmuch as the right of such criticism of orthodoxy was obviously open to any comrade, that His Majesty would seize the initiative in demanding that the old fairy tales, which no honest fellow could manage to believe, would not be served up at the military services any longer. But, naturally enough, when no such thing happened it was readily recognized that the church doctrine, just as it was, constituted the best fodder for the recruits. (Weber's note. Lt.-Col. Moritz von Egidy was cashiered in 1890 after publication of an attack on dogmatic Christianity. Cf. also Weber's contemporary observations in *Jugendbriefe*, 334–37.)

6. On the honor of the *seviri Augustales*, see below, ch. XVI:*v*, n. 29.

7. Cf. Karl Konrad Grass, *Die russischen Sekten* (2 vols., Leipzig: Hinrichs, 1907–14), I, 524ff. (on a Shtundo-Baptist group); II, *passim* (on the Skoptsy). Cf. also A. Leroy-Beaulieu, *The Empire of the Tsars* (London 1898), *passim*.

vi

The Religion of Non-Privileged Strata

1. *The Craftsmen's Inclination Toward Congregational and Salvation Religion*

When we move away from the strata characterized by a high degree of social and economic privilege, we encounter an apparent increase in the diversity of religious attitudes.

Within the petty-bourgeoisie, and particularly among the artisans, the greatest contrasts have existed side by side. These have included caste taboos and magical or mystagogic religions of both the sacramental and orgiastic types in India, animism in China, dervish religion in Islam, and the pneumatic-enthusiastic congregational religion of early Christianity, practiced particularly in the eastern half of the Roman Empire. Still other modes of religious expression among these groups are *deisidaimonia* as well as orgiastic worship of Dionysos in ancient Greece, Pharisaic fidelity to the law in ancient urban Judaism, an essentially idolatrous Christianity as well as all sorts of sectarian faiths in the Middle Ages, and various types of Protestantism in early modern times. These diverse phenomena obviously present the greatest possible contrasts to one another.

From the time of its inception, ancient Christianity was characteristically a religion of artisans. Its savior was a small-town artisan, and his missionaries were wandering journeymen, the greatest of them a wandering tent maker so alien to farmwork that in his epistles he actually employs in a reverse sense a metaphor relating to the process of grafting. The earliest communities of original Christianity were, as we have already seen, strongly urban throughout ancient times, and their adherents were recruited primarily from artisans, both slave and free. Moreover, in the Middle Ages the petty-bourgeoisie remained the most pious, if not always the most orthodox, stratum of society. But in Christianity as in other religions, widely different currents found a warm reception simultaneously within the petty-bourgeoisie. Thus, there were the ancient pneumatic prophecies which cast out demons, the unconditionally orthodox (institutionally ecclesiastical) religiosity of the Middle Ages, and the monasticism of the mendicant type. In addition, there were certain types of medieval sectarian religiosity such as that of the

Humiliati,[1] who were long suspected of heterodoxy, there were Baptist movements of all kinds, and there was the piety of the various Reformed churches, including the Lutheran.

This is indeed a highly checkered diversification, which at least proves that a uniform determinism of religion by economic forces never existed among the artisans. Yet there is apparent, in contrast to the peasantry, a definite tendency towards congregational religion, towards religion of salvation, and finally towards rational ethical religion. But this contrast is far from implying any uniform determinism. The absence of uniform determinism appears very clearly in the fact that the rural flatlands of Friesland provided the first localities for the popular dissemination of the Baptist congregational religion in its fullest form, while it was the city of Münster which became a primary site for the expression of its social revolutionary form.

In the Occident particularly, the congregational type of religion has been intimately connected with the urban middle classes of both the upper and lower levels. This was a natural consequence of the relative recession in the importance of blood groupings, particularly of the clan, within the occidental city. The urban dweller finds a substitute for blood groupings in both occupational organizations, which in the Occident as everywhere had a cultic significance, although no longer associated with taboos, and in freely created religious associations. But these religious relationships were not determined exclusively by the distinctive economic patterns of urban life. On the contrary, the causation might go the other way, as is readily apparent. Thus, in China the great importance of the ancestral cult and clan exogamy resulted in keeping the individual city dweller in a close relationship with his clan and native village. In India the religious caste taboo rendered difficult the rise, or limited the importance, of any soteriological congregational religion in quasi-urban settlements, as well as in the country. We have seen that in both India and China these factors hindered the city from developing in the direction of a community much more than they hindered the village.

Yet it is still true in theory that the petty-bourgeoisie, by virtue of its distinctive pattern of economic life, inclines in the direction of a rational ethical religion, wherever conditions are present for the emergence of a such religion. When one compares the life of a petty-bourgeois, particularly the urban artisan or the small trader, with the life of the peasant, it is clear that the former has far less connection with nature. Consequently, dependence on magic for influencing the irrational forces of nature cannot play the same role for the urban dweller as for the farmer. At the same time, it is clear that the economic foundation of the urban man's life has a far more rational character, viz., calculability and capacity for purposive manipulation. Furthermore, the artisan and in certain circumstances even the merchant lead economic existences which influence them to entertain the view that honesty is the best policy, that faithful work and the performance of obligations will find their reward and are "deserving" of their just compensation. For these reasons, small traders and artisans are disposed to accept a rational world view incorporating an ethic of compensation. We shall see presently that this is the normal trend of thinking among all non-privileged classes. The peasants, on the other hand, are much more remote from this notion of compensation and do not acquire it until the magic in which they are immersed has been eliminated by other forces. By contrast, the artisan is very frequently active in effecting the elimination of this very process of magic. It follows that the belief in ethical compensation is even more alien to warriors and to financial magnates who have economic interests in war and in the political manifestations of power. These groups are the least accessible to the ethical and rational elements in any religion.

The artisan is deeply immersed in magical encumbrances in the early stages of occupational differentiation. Every specialized "art" that is uncommon and not widely disseminated is regarded as a magical charisma, either personal or, more generally, hereditary, the acquisition and maintenance of which is guaranteed by magical means. Other elements of this early belief are that the bearers of this charisma are set off by taboos, occasionally of a totemic nature, from the community of ordinary people (peasants), and frequently that they are to be excluded from the ownership of land. One final element of this early belief in the magical charisma of every specialized art must be mentioned here. Wherever crafts had remained in the hands of ancient groups possessing raw materials, who had first offered their arts as intruders in the community and later offered their craftsmanship as individual strangers settled within the community, the belief in the magical nature of special arts condemned such groups to pariah status and stereotyped with magic their manipulations and their technology. But wherever this magical frame of reference has once been broken through (this happens most readily in newly settled cities), the effect of the transformation may be that the artisan will learn to think about his labor and the small trader will learn to think about his enterprise much more rationally than any peasant thinks. The craftsman in particular will have time and opportunity for reflection during his work in many instances, especially in occupations which are primarily of the indoor variety in our climate, for example, in the textile trades, which therefore are strongly infused with sectarian or religious trends. This is true to some extent even for the workers in modern factories with mechanized weaving, but very much more true for the weaver of the past.

Wherever the attachment to purely magical or ritualistic views has been broken by prophets or reformers, there has hence been a tendency for artisans, craftsmen and petty-bourgeois to incline toward a (often primitively) rationalistic ethical and religious view of life. Furthermore, their very occupational specialization makes them the bearers of an integrated pattern of life of a distinctive kind. Yet there is certainly no uniform determination of religion by these general conditions in the life of artisans and petty-bourgeois groups. Thus the small businessmen of China, though thoroughly calculating, are not the carriers of a rational religion, nor, so far as we know, are the Chinese artisans. At best, they follow the Buddhist doctrine of *karma,* in addition to magical notions. What is primary in their case is the absence of an ethically rationalized religion, and indeed this appears to have influenced the limited rationalism of their technology. This strikes us again and again. The mere existence of artisans and petty-bourgeois groups has never sufficed to generate an ethical religiosity, even of the most general type. We have seen an example of this in India, where the caste taboo and the belief in metempsychosis influenced and stereotyped the ethics of the artisan class. Only a congregational religiosity, especially one of the rational and ethical type, could conceivably win followers easily, particularly among the urban petty-bourgeoisie, and then, given certain circumstances, exert a lasting influence on the pattern of life of these groups. This is what actually happened.

2. *The Religious Disinclinations of Slaves, Day Laborers and the Modern Proletariat*

Finally, the classes of the greatest economic disability, such as slaves and free day-laborers, have hitherto never been the bearers of a distinctive type of religion. In the ancient Christian communities the slaves belonged to the petty-bourgeoisie in the cities. The Hellenistic slaves and the retinue of Narcissus mentioned in the Epistle to the Romans (presumably the infamous freedman of Emperor Claudius) were either relatively well-placed and independent domestic officials or service personnel belonging to very wealthy men. But in the majority of instances they were independent craftsmen who paid tribute to their master and hoped to save enough from their earnings to effect their liberation, which was the case throughout Antiquity and in Russia in the nine-teenth century. In other cases they were well-situated slaves of the state.

The religion of Mithra also included among its adherents numerous representatives of this group, according to the inscriptions. The Delphic Apollo (and presumably many another god) apparently functioned as a savings bank for slaves, attractive because of its sacred inviolability, and the slaves bought freedom from their masters by the use of these savings. According to the appealing hypothesis of Deissmann,[2] this was the image in Paul's mind in speaking of the redemption of Christians through the blood of their savior that they might be freed from enslavement by the law and by sin. If this be true (and of course the Old Testament terms for redemption, *gaal* and *pada,* must also be regarded as a possible source of the Christian concepts), it shows how much the missionizing effort of earliest Christianity counted upon the aspiring unfree petty-bourgeois group which followed an economically rational pattern of life. On the other hand, the "talking inventory" of the ancient plantation, the lowest stratum of the slave class, was not the bearer of any congregational reli-gion, or for that matter a fertile site for any sort of religious mission.

Handicraft journeymen have at all times tended to share the char-acteristic religion of the petty-bourgeois classes, since they are normally distinguished from them only by the fact that they must wait a certain time before they can set up their own shop. However, they evinced even more of an inclination toward various forms of unofficial religion of the sect type, which found particularly fertile soil among the lower occupational strata of the city, in view of their workaday deprivations, the fluctuations in the price of their daily bread, their job insecurity, and their dependence on fraternal assistance. Furthermore, the small artisans and craft apprentices were generally represented in the numerous secret or half-tolerated communities of "poor folk" that espoused congrega-tional religions, which were by turn revolutionary, pacifistic-communistic and ethical-rational, chiefly for the technical reason that wandering handicraft apprentices are the available missionaries of every mass con-gregational religion. This process is illustrated in the extraordinarily rapid expansion of Christianity across the tremendous area from the Orient to Rome in just a few decades.

Insofar as the modern proletariat has a distinctive religious position, it is characterized by indifference to or rejection of religion, as are broad strata of the modern bourgeoisie. For the modern proletariat, the sense of dependence on one's own achievements is supplanted by a conscious-ness of dependence on purely social factors, market conditions, and power relationships guaranteed by law. Any thought of dependence upon the course of natural or meteorological processes, or upon anything

that might be regarded as subject to the influence of magic or providence, has been completely eliminated, as Sombart has already demonstrated in fine fashion.[3] Therefore, the rationalism of the proletariat,
like that of the bourgeoisie of developed capitalism when it has come
into the full possession of economic power, of which indeed the proletariat's rationalism is a complementary phenomenon, cannot in the
nature of the case easily possess a religious character and certainly cannot easily generate a religion. Hence, in the sphere of proletarian rationalism, religion is generally supplanted by other ideological surrogates.

The lowest and the most economically unstable strata of the proletariat, for whom rational conceptions are the least congenial, and also
the proletaroid or permanently impoverished petty-bourgeois groups who
are in constant danger of sinking into the proletarian class, are nevertheless readily susceptible to being influenced by religious missionary
enterprise. But this religious propaganda has in such cases a distinctively
magical form or, where real magic has been eliminated, it has certain
characteristics which are substitutes for the magical-orgiastic supervention of grace. Examples of these are the soteriological orgies of the
Methodist type, such as are engaged in by the Salvation Army. Undoubtedly, it is far easier for emotional rather than rational elements of
a religious ethic to flourish in such circumstances. In any case, ethical
religion scarcely ever arises primarily in this group.

Only in a limited sense is there a distinctive class religion of disprivileged social groups. Inasmuch as the *substantive* demands for social
and political reform in any religion are based on god's will, we shall
have to devote a brief discussion to this problem when we discuss ethics
and natural law. But insofar as our concern is with the character of the
religion as such, it is immediately evident that a need for salvation in
the widest sense of the term has as one of its foci, but not the exclusive
or primary one, as we shall see later, disprivileged classes. Turning to
the "sated" and privileged strata, the need for salvation is remote and
alien to warriors, bureaucrats, and the plutocracy.

3. The Devolution of Salvation Religion From Privileged to Non-Privileged Strata

A religion of salvation may very well have its origin within socially
privileged groups. For the charisma of the prophet is not confined to
membership in any particular class; and furthermore, it is normally associated with a certain minimum of intellectual cultivation. Proof for

both of these assertions is readily available in the various characteristic prophecies of intellectuals. But as a rule, salvation religion changes its character as soon as it has reached lay groups who are not particularly or professionally concerned with the cultivation of intellectualism, and certainly changes its character after it has reached into the disprivileged social strata to whom intellectualism is both economically and socially inaccessible. One characteristic element of this transformation, a product of the inevitable accommodation to the needs of the masses, may be formulated generally as the emergence of a personal, divine or human-divine savior as the bearer of salvation, with the additional consequence that the religious relationship to this personage becomes the precondition of salvation.

We have already seen that one form of the adaptation of religion to the needs of the masses is the transformation of cultic religion into mere wizardry. A second typical form of adaptation is the shift into savior religion, which is naturally related to the aforementioned change into magic by the most numerous transitional stages. The lower the social class, the more radical are the forms assumed by the need for a savior, once this need has emerged. Hinduism provides an example of this in the *Kartabhajas,* a Vishnuite sect that took seriously the breakup of the caste taboo which in theory it shares with many salvation sects. Members of this sect arranged for a limited commensality of their members on private as well as on cultic occasions, but for that reason they were essentially a sect of common people. They carried the anthropolatric veneration of their hereditary *guru* to such a point that the cult became extremely exclusive. Similar phenomena can be found elsewhere among religions which recruited followers from the lower social strata or at least were influenced by them. The transfer of salvation doctrines to the masses practically always results in the emergence of a savior, or at least in an increase of emphasis upon the concept of a savior. One instance of this is the substitution for the Buddha ideal, viz., the ideal of exemplary intellectualist salvation into *Nirvana* by the ideal of a Bodhisattva, i.e., a savior who has descended upon earth and has foregone his own entrance into *Nirvana* for the sake of saving his fellow men. Another example is the rise in Hindu folk religion, particularly in Vishnuism, of salvation grace mediated by an incarnate god, and the victory of this soteriology and its magical sacramental grace over both the noble, atheistic salvation of the Buddhists and the ritualism associated with Vedic eduction. There are other manifestations of this process, somewhat different in form, in various religions.

The religious need of the middle and lower bourgeoisie expresses itself less in the form of heroic myths than in rather more sentimental legend, which has a tendency toward inwardness and edification. This corresponds to the peaceableness and the greater emphasis upon domestic and family life of the middle classes, in contrast to the ruling strata. This middle-class transformation of religion in the direction of domesticity is illustrated by the emergence of the god-suffused *bhakti* piety[4] in all Hindu cults, both in the creation of the Bodhisattva figure as well as in the cults of Krishna; and by the popularity of the edifying myths of the child Dionysos, Osiris, the Christ child, and their numerous parallels. The emergence of the bourgeoisie as a power which helped shape religion under the influence of mendicant monks resulted in the supplanting of the aristocratic *theotokos* of Nicola Pisano's imperialistic art by his son's genre depiction of the holy family, just as the Krishna child is the darling of popular art in India.[5]

The soteriological myth with its god who has assumed human form or its savior who has been deified is, like magic, a characteristic concept of popular religion, and hence one that has arisen quite spontaneously in very different places. On the other hand, the notion of an impersonal and ethical cosmic order that transcends the deity and the ideal of an exemplary type of salvation are intellectualistic conceptions which are definitely alien to the masses and possible only for a laity that has been educated along ethically rational lines. The same holds true for the development of a concept of an absolutely transcendant god. With the exception of Judaism and Protestantism, all religions and religious ethics have had to reintroduce cults of saints, heroes or functional gods in order to accommodate themselves to the needs of the masses. Thus Confucianism permitted such cults, in the form of the Taoist pantheon, to continue their existence by its side. Similarly, as popularized Buddhism spread to many lands, it allowed the various gods of these lands to live on as recipients of the Buddhist cult, subordinated to the Buddha. Finally, Islam and Catholicism were compelled to accept local, functional, and occupational gods as saints, the veneration of which constituted the real religion of the masses in everyday life.

4. *The Religious Equality of Women Among Disprivileged Strata*

The religion of the disprivileged strata, in contrast to the aristocratic cults of the martial nobles, is characterized by a tendency to allot equality to women. There is a great diversity in the scope of the religious participation permitted to women, but the greater or lesser, active or passive participation (or exclusion) of women from the religious cults is everywhere a function of the degree of the group's relative pacification or militarization (present or past). But the presence of priestesses, the prestige of female soothsayers or witches, and the most extreme devotion to individual women to whom supernatural powers and charisma may be attributed does not by any means imply that women have equal privileges in the cult. Conversely, equalization of the sexes in principle, i.e., in relationship to god, as it is found in Christianity and Judaism and, less consistently, in Islam and official Buddhism, may coexist with the most complete monopolization by men of the priestly functions and of the right to active participation in community affairs; men only are admitted to special professional training or assumed to possess the necessary qualifications. This is the actual situation in the religions to which reference has just been made.

The great receptivity of women to all religious prophecy except that which is exclusively military or political in orientation comes to very clear expression in the completely unbiased relationships with women maintained by practically all prophets, the Buddha as well as Christ and Pythagoras. But only in very rare cases does this practice continue beyond the first stage of a religious community's formation, when the pneumatic manifestations of charisma are valued as hallmarks of specifically religious exaltation. Thereafter, as routinization and regimentation of community relationships set in, a reaction takes place against pneumatic manifestations among women, which come to be regarded as irregular and morbid. In Christianity this appears already with Paul.

It is certainly true that every political and military type of prophecy —such as Islam—is directed exclusively to men. Indeed, the cult of a warlike spirit is frequently put into the direct service of controlling and lawfully plundering the households of women by the male inhabitants of the warrior house, who are organized into a sort of club. (This happens among the Duk-duk in the Indian archipelago and elsewhere in many similar periodic epiphanies of a heroic *numen*). Wherever an ascetic training of warriors involving the rebirth of the hero is or has been dominant, woman is regarded as lacking a higher heroic soul and is consequently assigned a secondary religious status. This obtains in most aristocratic or distinctively militaristic cultic communities.

Women are completely excluded from the official Chinese cults as well as from those of the Romans and Brahmins; nor is the religion of the Buddhist intellectuals feministic. Indeed, even Christian synods as late as the period of the Merovingians expressed doubts regarding the equality of the souls of women. On the other hand, in the Orient the characteristic cults of Hinduism and one segment of the Buddhist-Taoist sects in China, and in the Occident notably pristine Christianity but also later the pneumatic and pacifist sects of Eastern and Western Europe, derived a great deal of their missionizing power from the circumstance that they attracted women and gave them equal status. In Greece, too, the cult of Dionysos at its first appearance gave to the women who participated in its orgies an unusual degree of emancipation from conventions. This freedom subsequently became more and more stylized and regulated, both artistically and ceremonially; its scope was thereby limited, particularly to the processions and other festive activities of the various cults. Ultimately, therefore, this freedom lost all practical importance.

What gave Christianity its extraordinary superiority, as it conducted its missionary enterprises among the petty-bourgeois strata, over its most important competitor, the religion of Mithra, was that this extremely masculine cult excluded women. The result during a period of universal peace was that the adherents of Mithra had to seek out for their women a substitute in other mysteries, e.g., those of Cybele. This had the effect of destroying, even within single families, the unity and universality of the religious community, thereby providing a striking contrast to Christianity. A similar result was to be noted in all the genuinely intellectualist cults of the Gnostic, Manichean, and comparable types, though this need not necessarily have been the case in theory.

It is by no means true that all religions teaching brotherly love and love for one's enemy achieved power through the influence of women or through the feminist character of the religion; this has certainly not been true for the Indian *ahimsâ*-religiosity. The influence of women only tended to intensify those aspects of the religion that were emotional or hysterical. Such was the case in India. But it is certainly not a matter of indifference that salvation religions tended to glorify the non-military and even anti-military virtues, which must have been quite close to the interests of disprivileged classes and of women.

5. *The Differential Function of Salvation Religion for Higher and Lower Strata: Legitimation versus Compensation*

The specific importance of salvation religion for politically and economically disprivileged social groups, in contrast to privileged groups, may be viewed from an even more comprehensive perspective. In our discussion of status groups and classes [IX:6] we shall have a good deal to say about the sense of honor or superiority characteristic of the non-priestly classes that claimed the highest social privileges, particularly the nobility. Their sense of self-esteem rests on their awareness that the perfection of their life pattern is an expression of their underived, ultimate, and qualitatively distinctive *being;* indeed, it is in the very nature of the case that this should be the basis of their feeling of worth. On the other hand, the sense of honor of disprivileged classes rests on some guaranteed promise for the future which implies the assignment of some function, mission, or vocation to them. What they cannot claim to *be,* they replace by the worth of that which they will one day *become,* to which they will be called in some future life here or hereafter; or replace, very often concomitantly with the motivation just discussed, by their sense of what they *signify* and achieve in the world as seen from the point of view of providence. Their hunger for a worthiness that has not fallen to their lot, they and the world being what it is, produces this conception from which is derived the rationalistic idea of a providence, a significance in the eyes of some divine authority possessing a scale of values different from the one operating in the world of man.

This psychological condition, when turned outward toward the other social strata, produces certain characteristic contrasts in what religion must provide for the various social strata. Since every need for salvation is an expression of some distress, social or economic oppression is an effective source of salvation beliefs, though by no means the exclusive source. Other things being equal, strata with high social and economic privilege will scarcely be prone to evolve the idea of salvation. Rather, they assign to religion the primary function of *legitimizing* their own life pattern and situation in the world. This universal phenomenon is rooted in certain basic psychological patterns. When a man who is happy compares his position with that of one who is unhappy, he is not content with the fact of his happiness, but desires something more, namely the right to this happiness, the consciousness that he has earned his good fortune, in contrast to the unfortunate one who must equally have earned his misfortune. Our everyday experience proves that there exists just such a need for psychic comfort about the legitimacy or deservedness of one's happiness, whether this involves political success, superior economic status, bodily health, success in the game of love, or anything else. What the privileged classes require of religion, if anything at all, is this legitimation.

To be sure, not every class with high privilege feels this need in the same degree. It is noteworthy that martial heroes in particular tend to regard the gods as beings to whom envy is not unknown. Solon shared with ancient Jewish wisdom the same belief in the danger of high position. The hero maintains his superior position in spite of the gods and not because of them, and indeed he often does this against their wishes. Such an attitude is evinced in the Homeric and some of the Hindu epics, in contrast to the bureaucratic chronicles of China and the priestly chronicles of Israel, which express a far stronger concern for the legitimacy of happiness as the deity's reward for some virtuous human action pleasing to him.

On the other hand, one finds almost universally that unhappiness is brought into relation with the wrath or envy of either demons or gods. Practically every popular religion, including the ancient Hebrew, and particularly the modern Chinese, regards physical infirmity as a sign of magico-ritual or ethical sinfulness on the part of the unfortunate one, or (as in Judaism) of his ancestors. Accordingly, in these traditions a person visited by adversity is prohibited from appearing at the communal sacrifices of the political association because he is freighted with the wrath of the deity and must not enter in the circle of fortunate ones who are pleasing to him. In practically every ethical religion found among privileged classes and the priests who serve them, the privileged or disprivileged social position of the individual is regarded as somehow merited from the religious point of view. What varies is only the form by which good fortune is legitimized.

Correspondingly different is the situation of the disprivileged. Their particular need is for release from suffering. They do not always experience this need for salvation in a religious form, as shown by the example of the modern proletariat. Furthermore, their need for religious salvation, where it exists, may assume diverse forms. Most important, it may be conjoined with a need for just compensation, envisaged in various ways but always involving reward for one's own good deeds and punishment for the unrighteousness of others. This hope for and expectation of just compensation, a fairly calculating attitude, is, next to magic (indeed, not unconnected with it), the most widely diffused form of mass religion all over the world. Even religious prophecies, which rejected the more mechanical forms of this belief, tended as they underwent popularization and routinization to slip back into these expectations of compensation. The type and scope of these hopes for compensation and salvation varied greatly depending on the expectations aroused by the religious promises, especially when these hopes were projected from the earthly existence of the individual into a future life.

6. *Pariah People and* Ressentiment: *Judaism versus Hinduism*

Judaism, in both its exilic and post-exilic forms, provides a particularly important illustration of the significance of the content of religious promises. Since the Exile, as a matter of actual fact, and formally since the destruction of the Temple, the Jews became a pariah people in the particular sense presently to be defined. (The sense in which the Jews are a "pariah" people has as little to do with the particular situation of the pariah caste in India as, for example, the concept of "Kadi-justice" has to do with the actual legal principles whereby the *kadi* renders legal decisions.) In our usage, "pariah people" denotes a distinctive hereditary social group lacking autonomous political organization and characterized by internal prohibitions against commensality and intermarriage originally founded upon magical, tabooistic, and ritual injunctions. Two additional traits of a pariah people are political and social disprivilege and a far-reaching distinctiveness in economic functioning. To be sure, the pariah people of India, the disprivileged and occupationally specialized Hindu castes, resemble the Jews in these respects, since their pariah status also involves segregation from the outer world as a result of taboos, hereditary religious obligations in the conduct of life, and the association of salvation hopes with their pariah status. These Hindu castes and Judaism show the same characteristic effects of a pariah religion: the more depressed the position in which the members of the pariah people found themselves, the more closely did the religion cause them to cling to one another and to their pariah position and the more powerful became the salvation hopes which were connected with the divinely ordained fulfillment of their religious obligations. As we have already mentioned, the lowest Hindu castes in particular clung to their caste duties with the greatest tenacity as a prerequisite for their rebirth into a better position.

The tie between Yahweh and his people became the more indissoluble as murderous humiliation and persecution pressed down upon the Jews. In obvious contrast to the oriental Christians, who under the Umayyads streamed into the privileged religion of Islam in such numbers that the political authorities had to make conversion difficult for them in the interests of the privileged stratum, all the frequent mass conversions of the Jews by force, which might have obtained for them the privileges of the ruling stratum, remained ineffectual. For both the Jews and the Hindu castes, the only means for the attainment of salvation was to fulfill the special religious commandments enjoined upon the pariah people, from which none might withdraw himself without incurring the fear of evil magic or endangering the chances of rebirth for himself or his descendants. The difference between Judaism and Hindu caste religion is based on the type of salvation hopes entertained. From the fulfillment of the religious obligations incumbent upon him the Hindu expected an improvement in his personal chances of rebirth, i.e., the ascent or reincarnation of his soul into a higher caste. On the other hand, the Jew expected the participation of his descendants in a messianic kingdom which would redeem the entire pariah community from its inferior position and in fact raise it to a position of mastery in the world. For surely Yahweh, by his promise that all the nations of the world would borrow from the Jews but that they would borrow from none, had meant more than that the Jews would become small-time moneylenders in the ghetto. Yahweh instead intended to place them in the typical situation of citizens of a powerful city-state in Antiquity, who held as debtors and debt-slaves the inhabitants of nearby subject villages and towns. The Jew wrought in behalf of his actual descendants, who, on the animistic interpretation, would constitute his earthly immortality. The Hindu also worked for a human being of the future, to whom he was bound by a relationship only if the assumptions of the animistic doctrine of transmigration were accepted, i.e., his future incarnation. The Hindu's conception left unchanged for all time the caste stratification obtaining in this world and the position of his own caste within it; indeed, he sought to fit the future state of his own individual soul into this very gradation of ranks. In striking contrast, the Jew anticipated his own personal salvation through a revolution of the existing social stratification to the advantage of his pariah people; his people had been chosen and called by God, not to a pariah position but to one of prestige.

The factor of resentment (ressentiment), first noticed by Nietzsche,[6] thus achieved importance in the Jewish ethical salvation religion, although it had been completely lacking in all magical and caste religions. Resentment is a concomitant of that particular religious ethic of the disprivileged which, in the sense expounded by Nietzsche and in direct inversion of the ancient belief, teaches that the unequal distribution of mundane goods is caused by the sinfulness and the illegality of the privileged, and that sooner or later God's wrath will overtake them. In this theodicy of the disprivileged, the moralistic quest serves as a device for compensating a conscious or unconscious desire for vengeance. This is connected in its origin with the faith in compensation, since once a religious conception of compensation has arisen, suffering may take on the quality of the religiously meritorious, in view of the belief that it brings in its wake great hopes of future compensation.

The development of a religious conception of resentment may be supported by ascetic doctrines on the one hand, or by characteristic neurotic predispositions on the other. However, the religion of suffering acquires the specific character of ressentiment only under special circumstances. Ressentiment is not found among the Hindus and Buddhists, for whom personal suffering is individually merited. But the situation is quite different among the Jews.

The religion of the Psalms is full of the need for vengeance, and the same motif occurs in the priestly reworkings of ancient Israelite traditions. The majority of the Psalms are quite obviously replete with the moralistic legitimation and satisfaction of an open and hardly concealed need for vengeance on the part of a pariah people. (Some of these passages are admittedly later interpolation into earlier compositions, in which this sentiment was not originally present.) In the Psalms the quest for vengeance may take the form of remonstrating with God because misfortune has overtaken the righteous individual, notwithstanding his obedience to God's commandments, whereas the godless conduct of the heathen, despite their mockery of God's predictions, commandments and authority, has brought them happiness and left them proud. The same quest for vengeance may express itself as a humble confession of one's own sinfulness, accompanied by a prayer to God to desist from his anger at long last and to turn his grace once again toward the people who ultimately are uniquely his own. In both modes of expression, the hope is entertained that ultimately the wrath of God will finally have been appeased and will turn itself to punishing the godless foes in double measure, making of them at some future day the footstool of Israel, just as the priestly historiography had assigned to the Canaanite enemies a similar fate. It was also hoped that this exalted condition would endure so long as Israel did not arouse God's anger by disobedience, thereby meriting subjugation at the hands of the heathen. It may be true, as modern commentators would have it, that some of these Psalms express the personal indignation of pious Pharisees over their persecution at the hands of Alexander Jannaeus. Nevertheless, a distinctive selection and preservation is evident; and in any case, other Psalms are quite obviously reactions to the distinctive pariah status of the Jews as a people.

In no other religion in the world do we find a universal deity possessing the unparalleled desire for vengeance manifested by Yahweh. Indeed, an almost unfailing index of the historical value of the data provided by the priestly reworking of history is that the event in question, as for example the battle of Megiddo, does not fit into this theodicy of compensation and vengeance. Thus, the Jewish religion became notably a religion of retribution. The virtues enjoined by God are practiced for the sake of the hoped for compensation. Moreover, this was originally a collective hope that the people as a whole would live to see that day of restoration, and that only in this way would the individual be able to regain his own worth. There developed concomitantly, intermingled with the aforementioned collective theodicy, an individual theodicy of personal destiny which had previously been taken for granted. The problems of individual destiny are explored in the Book of Job, which was produced by quite different circles, i.e., the upper strata, and which culminates in a renunciation of any solution of the problem and a submission to the absolute sovereignty of God over his creatures. This submission was the precursor of the doctrine of predestination in Puritanism. The notion of predestination was bound to arise when the emotional dynamics of divinely ordained eternal punishment in hell was added to the complex of ideas just discussed, involving compensation and the absolute sovereignty of God. But the belief in predestination did not arise among the Hebrews of that time. Among them, the conclusion of the Book of Job remained almost completely misunderstood in the sense intended by its author, mainly, as is well known, because of the unshakeable strength of the doctrine of collective compensation in the Jewish religion.

In the mind of the pious Jew the moralism of the law was inevitably combined with the aforementioned hope for revenge, which suffused practically all the exilic and postexilic sacred scriptures. Moreover, through two and a half millennia this hope appeared in virtually every divine service of the Jewish people—a people indissolubly chained to religiously sanctified segregation from the other peoples of the world and divine promises relating to this world. From such a compensatory hope the Jews were bound to derive new strength, consciously or unconsiously. Yet as the Messiah delayed his arrival, this hope receded in the religious thinking of the intellectuals in favor of the value of an inner awareness of God or a mildly emotional trust in God's goodness as such, combined with a readiness for peace with all the world. This happened especially in periods during which the social condition of a community condemned to complete political isolation was tolerable. On the other hand, in epochs characterized by persecutions, like the period of the Crusades, the hope for retribution flamed up anew, either with a penetrating but vain cry to God for revenge, or with a prayer that the soul of the Jew might become as dust before the enemy who had cursed him. In the latter case there was no recourse to evil words or deeds, but only a silent waiting for the fulfillment of God's commandments and the cultivation of the heart so that it would remain open to God. To interpret *ressentiment* as the decisive element in Judaism would be an incredible aberration, in view of the many significant historical changes which Judaism has undergone. Nevertheless, we must not underestimate the influence of *ressentiment* upon even the basic characteristics of the Jewish religion. When one compares Judaism with other salvation religions, one finds that in Judaism the doctrine of religious resentment has an idiosyncratic quality and plays a unique role not found among the disprivileged classes of any other religion.

A theodicy of disprivilege, in some form, is a component of every salvation religion which draws its adherents primarily from the disprivileged classes, and the developing priestly ethic accommodated to this theodicy wherever it was a component of congregational religion based on such groups.

The absence of resentment, and also of virtually any kind of social revolutionary ethics among the pious Hindu and the Asiatic Buddhist can be explained by reference to their theodicy of rebirth, according to which the caste system itself is eternal and absolutely just. The virtues or sins of a former life determine birth into a particular caste, and one's behavior in the present life determines one's chances of improvement in the next rebirth. Those living under this theodicy experienced no trace of the conflict experienced by the Jews between the social claims based on God's promises and the actual conditions of dishonor under which they lived. This conflict precluded any possibility of finding ease in this life for the Jews, who lived in continuous tension with their actual social position and in perpetually fruitless expectation and hope. The Jews' theodicy of disprivilege was greeted by the pitiless mockery of the godless heathen, but for the Jews the theodicy had the consequence of transforming religious criticism of the godless heathen into ever-watchful concern over their own fidelity to the law. This preoccupation was frequently tinged with bitterness and threatened by secret self-criticism.

The Jew was naturally prone, as a result of his lifelong schooling, to casuistical meditation upon the religious obligations of his fellow Jews, on whose punctilious observance of religious law the whole people ultimately depended for Yahweh's favor. There appeared that peculiar mixture of elements characteristic of post-exilic times which combined despair at finding any meaning in this world of vanity with submission to the chastisement of God, anxiety lest one sin against God through pride, and finally a fear-ridden punctiliousness in ritual and morals. All these conflicts forced upon the Jew a desperate struggle, no longer for the respect of others, but for self-respect and a sense of personal worth. The struggle for a sense of personal worth must have become precarious again and again, threatening to wreck the whole meaning of the individual's pattern of life, since ultimately the fulfillment of God's promise was the only criterion of one's value before God at any given time.

Success in his occupation actually became one tangible proof of God's personal favor for the Jew living in the ghetto. But the conception of self-fulfillment (*Bewährung*) in a calling (*Beruf*) pleasing to god, in the sense of inner-worldly asceticism (*innerweltliche Askese*), is not applicable to the Jew. God's blessing was far less strongly anchored in a systematic, rational, methodical pattern of life for the Jew than for the

Puritan, for whom this was the only possible source of the *certitudo salutis*. Just as the Jewish sexual ethic remained naturalistic and anti-ascetic, so also did the economic ethic of ancient Judaism remain strongly traditionalistic in its basic tenets. It was characterized by a frank respect for wealth, which is of course missing in any system of asceticism. In addition, the entire system of outward piety had a ritualistic foundation among the Jews, and what is more, it was considerably interfused with the distinctive emotional mood of the religion. We must note that the traditionalistic precepts of the Jewish economic ethics naturally applied in their full scope only to one's fellow religionists, not to outsiders, which was the case in every ancient ethical system. All in all, then, the belief in Yahweh's promises actually produced within the realm of Judaism itself a strong component of the morality of *ressentiment*.

It would be completely erroneous to portray the need for salvation, theodicy, or congregational religion as something that developed only among disprivileged social strata or even only as a product of resentment, hence merely as the outcome of a "slave revolt in morality." This would not even be true of ancient Christianity, although it directed its promises most emphatically to the poor in spirit and in worldly goods. What results had to follow from the downgrading and rending asunder of the fabric of ritual laws (which had been purposefully composed to segregate the Jews from the outer world) and from the consequent *dissolution* of the link between religion and the caste-like position of the faithful as a pariah people, can be readily observed in the contrast between Jesus' prophecy and its immediate consequences. To be sure, the early Christian prophecy contained very definite elements of "retribution" doctrine, in the sense of the future equalization of human fates (most clearly expressed in the legend of Lazarus) and of vengeance (which is shown to be God's responsibility). Moreover, here too the Kingdom of God is interpreted as an earthly kingdom, in the first instance apparently a realm set apart particularly or primarily for the Jews, for they from ancient times had believed in the true God. Yet, it is precisely the characteristic and penetrating *ressentiment* of the pariah people which is neutralized by the implications of the new religious proclamation.

Not even Jesus' own warnings, according to the tradition, of the dangers presented by wealth to the attainment of salvation were motivated by asceticism. Certainly the motivation of his preaching against wealth was not resentment, for the tradition has preserved many evidences of Jesus' intercourse, not only with publicans (who in the Palestine of that period were mostly small-time usurers), but also with other well-to-do people. Furthermore, resentment cannot be regarded as the primary motivation of Jesus' doctrines regarding wealth, in view of the Gospels' impressive indifference to mundane affairs, an indifference based upon the power of eschatological expectations. To be sure, the rich young man was bidden unconditionally to take his leave of the world if he desired to be a perfect disciple. But it is stated that for God all things are possible, even the salvation of the wealthy [Matt. 19:21ff]. The rich man who is unable to decide to part with his wealth may nonetheless achieve salvation, despite the difficulties in the way. There were no "proletarian instincts" in the doctrine and teaching of Jesus, the prophet of acosmistic love who brought to the poor in spirit and to the good people of this world the happy tidings of the immediate coming of the Kingdom of God and of freedom from the domination of evil spirits. Similarly, any proletarian denunciation of wealth would have been equally alien to the Buddha, for whom the absolute precondition of salvation was unconditional withdrawal from the world.

The limited significance of the factor of *ressentiment,* and the dubiousness of applying the conceptual schema of "repression" almost universally, appear most clearly when Nietzsche mistakenly applies his scheme to the altogether inappropriate example of Buddhism. Constituting the most radical antithesis to every type of *ressentiment* morality, Buddhism clearly arose as the salvation doctrine of an intellectual stratum, originally recruited almost entirely from the privileged castes, especially the warrior caste, which proudly and aristocratically rejected the illusions of life, both here and hereafter. Buddhism may be compared in social provenience to the salvation doctrines of the Greeks, particularly the Neo-Platonic, Manichean, and Gnostic manifestations, even though they are radically different in content. The Buddhist *bhikshu* does not begrudge the entire world, not even a rebirth into paradise, to the person who does not desire *Nirvana.*

Precisely this example of Buddhism demonstrates that the need for salvation and ethical religion has yet another source besides the social condition of the disprivileged and the rationalism of the bourgeoisie, which is shaped by its way of life. This additional factor is intellectualism as such, more particularly the metaphysical needs of the human mind as it is driven to reflect on ethical and religious questions, driven not by material need but by an inner compulsion to understand the world as a meaningful cosmos and to take up a position toward it.

NOTES

1. The *Humiliati* were bourgeois lay ascetics who were barely tolerated from their emergence in the 12th century to their final suppression by the Counter-Reformation in the 16th century.

2. Gustav Adolf Deissmann, *Licht vom Osten* (Tübingen: Mohr, 1908), 234f.

3. See Werner Sombart, *Das Proletariat* (Frankfurt: Rütten und Loening, 1906), 75ff. and id., *Sozialismus und soziale Bewegung*, 1908, 6th ed., 25. (W)

4. Cf. Weber, *The Religion of India*, 306ff.

5. The *theotokos* is the regal Virgin; the term "imperialist" in the German text refers to the "proto-renaissance" style of Nicola Pisano (c. 1225–c. 1278). On this point, and the bourgeois trends, see Albert Brach, *Nicola und Giovanni Pisano und die Plastik des XIV. Jahrhunderts in Siena* (Strassburg: Heitz, 1904). Around 1904 there was a dispute about the origins of Nicola Pisano's style; one thesis derived it from the Imperial studios of Emperor Frederick II in Southern Italy; cf. Georg Swarzenski, *Nicolo Pisano* (Frankfurt: Iris, 1926). The *embourgeoisement* can be observed in Pisa in the contrast between Nicola's pulpit in the Baptistery (1259) and that made by Giovanni for the *Duomo* (1311). (Wi)

6. On *ressentiment* and the "slave revolt in morality," see Friedrich Nietzsche, *Werke* (Leipzig: Kröner, 1930), II, 38 and 98f.

vii
Intellectualism, Intellectuals, and Salvation Religion

1. Priests and Monks as Intellectualist Elaborators of Religion

The destiny of religions has been influenced in a most comprehensive way by intellectualism and its various relationships to the priesthood and political authorities. These relationships were in turn influenced by the provenience of the stratum which happened to be the most important carrier of the particular intellectualism. At first the priesthood itself was the most important carrier of intellectualism, particularly wherever sacred scriptures existed, which would make it necessary for the priesthood to become a literary guild engaged in interpreting the scriptures and teaching their content, meaning, and proper application. But no such development took place in the religions of the ancient city-states, and notably not among the Phoenicians, Greeks, or Romans; nor was this phenomenon present in the ethics of China. In these instances the development of all metaphysical and ethical thought fell into the hands of non-priests, as did the development of theology, which developed to only a very limited extent, e.g., in Hesiod.

By contrast, the development of intellectualism by the priesthood, was true to the highest degree in India, in Egypt, in Babylonia, in Zoro-astrianism, in Islam, and in ancient and medieval Christianity. So far as theology is concerned, the development of intellectualism by the priest-hood has also taken place in modern Christianity. In the religions of Egypt, in Zoroastrianism, in some phases of ancient Christianity, and in Brahmanism during the age of the Vedas (i.e., before the rise of lay asceticism and the philosophy of the Upanishads) the priesthood suc-ceeded in largely monopolizing the development of religious metaphysics and ethics. Such a priestly monopoly was also present in Judaism and Islam. But in Judaism it was strongly reduced by the strong impact of lay prophecy, and in Islam the very impressive power of the priesthood was limited by the challenge of Sufi speculation. In all the branches of Buddhism and Islam, as well as in ancient and medieval Christianity, it was the monks or groups oriented to monasticism who, besides the priests or in their stead, concerned themselves with and wrote in all the areas of theological and ethical thought, as well as in metaphysics and considerable segments of science. In addition, they also occupied themselves with the production of artistic literature. The cultic impor-tance of the singer played a role in bringing epic, lyrical and satirical poetry into the Vedas in India and the erotic poetry of Israel into the Bible; the psychological affinity of mystic and spiritual (*pneumatisch*) emotion to poetic inspiration shaped the role of the mystic in the poetry of both the Orient and Occident.

But here we are concerned, not with literary production, but rather the determination of the religion itself by the particular character of the intellectual strata who exerted a decisive influence upon it. The intel-lectual influence upon religion of the priesthood, even where it was the chief carrier of literature, was of quite varied scope, depending on which non-priestly strata opposed the priesthood and on the power position of the priesthood itself. The specifically ecclesiastical influence reached its strongest expression in late Zoroastrianism and in the religions of Egypt and Babylonia. Although Judaism of the Deuteronomic and exilic periods was prophetic in essence, the priesthood exerted a marked forma-tive influence upon the developing religion. In later Judaism, however, it was not the priest but the rabbi who exercised the decisive influence. Christianity was decisively influenced by the priesthood and by monas-ticism at the end of Antiquity and in the High Middle Ages, and then again in the period of the Counter-Reformation. Pastoral influences were dominant in Lutheranism and early Calvinism. Hinduism was formed and influenced to an extraordinary degree by the Brahmins, at least in its institutional and social components. This applies particularly to the caste system that arose wherever the Brahmins arrived, the social hierarchy of which was ultimately determined by the rank the Brahmins assigned to each particular caste. Buddhism in all its varieties, but particularly Lamaism, has been thoroughly influenced by monasticism, which has to a lesser degree influenced large groups in oriental Christianity.

2. High-Status Intellectuals as Religious Innovators

Here we are particularly concerned with the relationship to the priesthood of the non-ecclesiastical lay intelligentsia other than the monks, and in addition, with the relation of the intellectual strata to the religious enterprise and their position within the religious community. We must at this point establish as a fact of fundamental importance that all the great religious doctrines of Asia are creations of intellectuals. The salvation doctrines of Buddhism and Jainism, as well as all related doctrines, were carried by an intellectual elite that had undergone training in the Vedas. This training, though not always of a strictly scholarly nature, was appropriate to the education of Hindu aristocrats, particularly members of the Kshatriya nobility, who stood in opposition to the Brahmins. In China the carriers of Confucianism, beginning with the founder himself and including Lao Tzu, who is officially regarded as the initiator of Taoism, were either officials who had received a classical literary education or philosophers with corresponding training.

The religions of China and India display counterparts of practically all the theoretical variants of Greek philosophy, though frequently in modified form. Confucianism, as the official ethic of China, was entirely borne by a group of aspirants to official positions who had received a classical literary education, but it is true that Taoism became a popular enterprise of practical magic. The great reforms of Hinduism were accomplished by aristocratic intellectuals who had received a Brahminic education, although subsequently the organization of communities frequently fell into the hands of members of lower castes. Thus, the process of reform in India took another direction from that of the Reformation in Northern Europe, which was also led by educated men who had received professional clerical training, as well as from that of the Catholic Counter-Reformation, which at first found its chief support from Jesuits trained in dialectic, like Salmeron and Laynez. The course of the reform movement in India differed also from the reconstruction of Islamic doctrine by al-Ghazâlî [A.D. 1058–1111], which combined mysticism and orthodoxy, with leadership remaining partly in the hands of the official hierarchy and partly in the hands of a newly developed office nobility with theological training. So too, Manicheanism and Gnosticism, the salvation religions of the Near East, are both specifically religions of intellectuals. This is true of their founders, their chief carriers, and the character of their salvation doctrines as well.

In all these cases, in spite of various differences among the religions in question, the intellectual strata were relatively high in the social scale and possessed philosophical training that corresponded to that of the Greek schools of philosophy or to the most learned types of monastic or secular humanistic training of the late medieval period. These groups were the bearers of the ethic or the salvation doctrine in each case. Thus intellectual strata might, within a given religious situation, constitute an academic enterprise comparable to that of the Platonic academy and the related schools of philosophy in Greece. In that case the intellectual strata, like those in Greece, would take no official position regarding existing religious practice. They often ignored or philosophically reinterpreted the existing religious practice rather than directly withdrawing themselves from it. On their part, the official representatives of the cult, like the state officials charged with cultic responsibility in China or the Brahmins in India, tended to treat the doctrine of the intellectuals as either orthodox or heterodox, the latter in the cases of the materialistic doctrines of China and the dualist Sankhya philosophy of India. We cannot enter into any additional details here regarding these movements, which have a primarily academic orientation and are only indirectly related to practical religion. Our chief interest is rather in those other movements, previously mentioned, which are particularly concerned with the creation of a religious ethic. Our best examples in classical Antiquity are the Pythagoreans and Neo-Platonists. These movements of intellectuals have uniformly arisen among socially privileged strata or have been led or decisively influenced by men from these groups.

3. *The Political Decline of Privileged Strata and the Escapism of Intellectuals*

The development of a strong salvation religion by socially privileged groups normally has the best chance when demilitarization has set in for these groups and when they have lost either the possibility of political activity or the interest in it. Consequently, salvation religions usually emerge when the ruling strata, noble or middle class, have lost their political power to a bureaucratic-militaristic unitary state. The withdrawal of the ruling strata from politics, for whatever reason, also favors the development of a salvation religion. In such a case, the ruling strata come to consider their intellectual training in its ultimate intellectual and psychological consequences far more important for them than their practical participation in the external affairs of the mundane world. This does not mean that the salvation religions arise only at such times. On the contrary, the intellectual conceptions in question may sometimes arise without the stimulus of such anterior conditions, as a result of un-prejudiced reflection in periods of dynamic political or social change. But in that case such modes of thought tend to lead a kind of under-ground existence, normally becoming dominant only when the intel-lectuals have undergone depoliticization.

Confucianism, the ethic of a powerful officialdom, rejected all doc-trines of salvation. On the other hand, Jainism and Buddhism, which provide radical antitheses to Confucianist accommodation to the world, were tangible expressions of an intellectualist attitude that was utterly anti-political, pacifistic, and world-rejecting. We do not know, however, whether the sometimes considerable following of these two religions in India was increased by events of the times which tended to reduce pre-occupation with political matters. The pluralism of tiny states headed by minor Hindu princes before the time of Alexander, states lacking any sort of political dynamic in the face of the impressive unity of Brahman-ism (which was gradually forging to the front everywhere in India), was in itself enough to induce those groups of the nobility who had un-dergone intellectual training to seek fulfillment of their interests outside of politics. Therefore the scripturally enjoined world-renunciation of the Brahmin (as a *vanaprastha*—forest dweller—who foregoes his portion in old age) and the popular veneration accorded to him resulted in the evolution of non-Brahminic ascetics (*shramanas*). It is possible of course that the actual development went in the other direction, so that the recommendation of world-renunciation to the Brahmin who "has seen the son of his son" is the later of the two phenomena, and a borrowing. In any case, the *shramanas,* as the possessors of ascetic charisma, soon outstripped the official priesthood in popular esteem. This form of monas-tic apoliticism had been endemic among the nobles of India since very early times, i.e., long before apolitical philosophical salvation doctrines arose.

The Near Eastern salvation religions, whether of a mystagogic or prophetic type, as well as the oriental and Hellenistic salvation doctrines, whether of a more religious type or a more philosophical type of which lay intellectuals were the protagonists, were, insofar as they included the socially privileged strata at all, virtually without exception the consequence of the educated strata's enforced or voluntary loss of political influence and participation. In Babylonia the turn to salvation religion, intersected by components whose provenience was outside Babylonia, appeared first in Mandaeism. The religion of intellectuals in the Near East took this turn first through participation in the cult of Mithra and the cults of other saviors, and then through participation in the cults of Gnosticism and Manicheism, after all political interest had died off in the educated strata. In Greece there had always been salvation religion among the intellectual strata, even before the Pythagorean sect arose, but it did not dominate groups with decisive political power. The success of philosophical salvation doctrines and the propaganda of salvation cults among the lay elite during late Hellenic and Roman times parallels these groups' final turning aside from political participation. Indeed, the somewhat verbose "religious" interests of our German intellectuals of the present time are intimately connected with political frustrations that are responsible for their political indifference.

Quests for salvation which arise among privileged classes are generally characterized by a disposition toward an "illumination" mysticism, to be analyzed later, which is associated with a distinctively intellectual qualification for salvation. This brings about a strong devaluation of the natural, sensual, and physical, as constituting, according to their psychological experience, a temptation to deviate from this distinctive road to salvation. The exaggeration and fastidious refinement of sexuality, along with the simultaneous suppression of normal sexuality in favor of substitute abreactions, were determined by the life patterns of those who might be termed "nothing-but-intellectuals"; and these exaggerations and suppressions of sexuality occasionally played a role for which modern psychopathology has not yet formulated uniformly applicable rules. These phenomena are strongly reminiscent of certain phenomena, especially in the Gnostic mysteries, which clearly appear to have been sublimated masturbatory surrogates for the orgies of the peasantry. These purely psychological preconditions of the process whereby religion is irrationalized are intersected by the natural rationalistic need of intellectualism to conceive the world as a meaningful cosmos. Some typical outcomes are the Hindu doctrine of *karma* (of which more will be said presently) and its Buddhist variant; the Book of Job among the Hebrews, which presumably originated in aristocratic intellectual groups; and the comparable elements in Egyptian literature, in Gnostic speculation, and in Manichean dualism.

Once a salvation doctrine and an ethic of intellectualist origin has become a mass religion, an esotericism or aristocratic status ethic arises

that is adjusted to the needs of the intellectually trained groups. Mean-
while, however, the religion has become transformed into a doctrine
of a popular magical savior, thereby meeting the needs of the non-
intellectual masses. Thus in China, alongside the Confucianist status
ethic of the bureaucrats, who were completely uninterested in salvation,
Taoist magic and Buddhist sacramental and ritual grace survived in a
petrified form as the faith of the folk, though such beliefs were despised
by those who had received a classical education. Similarly, the Buddhist
salvation ethic of the monastic groups lived on alongside the magic and
idolatry of the laity, the continued existence of tabooistic magic, and the
new development of a savior religion within Hinduism. In Gnosticism
and its related cults the intellectualist religion took the form of mystagogy, with a hierarchy of sanctifications which the unilluminated were
excluded from attaining.

The salvation sought by the intellectual is always based on inner
need, and hence it is at once more remote from life, more theoretical
and more systematic than salvation from external distress, the quest for
which is characteristic of nonprivileged strata. The intellectual seeks in
various ways, the casuistry of which extends into infinity, to endow his
life with a pervasive meaning, and thus to find unity with himself, with
his fellow men, and with the cosmos. It is the intellectual who conceives
of the "world" as a problem of meaning. As intellectualism suppresses
belief in magic, the world's processes become disenchanted, lose their
magical significance, and henceforth simply "are" and "happen" but no
longer signify anything. As a consequence, there is a growing demand
that the world and the total pattern of life be subject to an order that
is significant and meaningful.

The conflict of this requirement of meaningfulness with the empirical realities of the world and its institutions, and with the possibilities
of conducting one's life in the empirical world, are responsible for the
intellectual's characteristic flight from the world. This may be an escape
into absolute loneliness, or in its more modern form, e.g., in the case of
Rousseau, to a nature unspoiled by human institutions. Again, it may be
a world-fleeing romanticism like the flight to the "people," untouched by
social conventions, characteristic of the Russian *narodnichestvo*. It
may be more contemplative, or more actively ascetic; it may primarily
seek individual salvation or collective revolutionary transformation of the
world in the direction of a more ethical status. All these doctrines are
equally appropriate to apolitical intellectualism and may appear as religious doctrines of salvation, as on occasion they have actually appeared.
The distinctive world-fleeing character of intellectualist religion also has
one of its roots here.

4. The Religious Impact of Proletarian, Petty-Bourgeois and Pariah Intellectualism

Yet the philosophical intellectualism of those classes that are usually well provided for socially and economically (particularly apolitical nobles or rentiers, officials, and incumbents of benefices whether of churches, monastic establishments, institutions of higher learning, or the like) is by no means the only kind of intellectualism, and frequently it is not the most important kind of intellectualism for the development of religion. For there is also a quasi-proletarian (proletaroid) intellectualism that is everywhere connected with aristocratic intellectualism by transitional forms and differs from it only in the character of its distinctive attitude. Members of this class include people at the edge of the minimum standard of living; small officials and incumbents of prebends, who generally are equipped with what is regarded as an inferior education; scribes, who were not members of privileged strata in periods when writing was a special vocation; elementary school teachers of all sorts; wandering poets; narrators; reciters; and practitioners of similar free proletaroid callings. Above all, we must include in this category the self-taught intelligentsia of the disprivileged ("negatively privileged") strata, of whom the classic examples are the Russian proletaroid peasant intelligentsia in Eastern Europe, and the socialist-anarchist proletarian intelligentsia in the West. To this general category there might also be added groups of a far different background, such as the Dutch peasantry as late as the first half of the nineteenth century, who had an impressive knowledge of the Bible, the petty-bourgeois Puritans of seventeenth-century England, and the religiously interested journeymen of all times and peoples. Above all, there must be included the classical manifestations of the Jewish laity, including the Pharisees, the Chassidim, and the mass of the pious Jews who daily studied the law.

It may be noted that pariah intellectualism, appearing among all proletaroid incumbents of small prebends, the Russian peasantry, and the more or less itinerant folk, derives its intensity from the fact that the groups which are at the lower end of, or altogether outside of, the social hierarchy stand to a certain extent on the point of Archimedes in relation to social conventions, both in respect to the external order and in respect to common opinions. Since these groups are not bound by the social conventions, they are capable of an original attitude toward the meaning of the cosmos; and since they are not impeded by any material considerations, they are capable of intense ethical and religious emotion. Insofar as they belonged to the middle classes, like the religiously self-taught petty-bourgeois groups, their religious needs tended to assume either an ethically rigorous or an occult form. The intellectualism of the journeyman stands midway between these [pariah and petty-bourgeois manifestations of intellectualism], and is significant because the itinerant journeyman is particularly qualified for missionizing.

In Eastern Asia and India, so far as is known, pariah intellectualism is practically non-existent, as is petty-bourgeois intellectualism. The latter requires the communal feeling of an urban citizenry, but this is absent. Both also lack the emancipation from magic, which is a prerequisite for them. Indeed, even those forms of religion that emerged out of the lower castes take their Gathas from the Brahmins. In China as well, there is no independent, unofficial intellectualism apart from the Confucian education. Confucianism is *the* ethic of the "noble" man (i.e., the "gentleman," as Dvořák[1] has correctly translated the term). Confucianism is quite explicitly a status ethic, or more correctly, a systematization of rules of etiquette appropriate to a dignified stratum the members of which have undergone literary training. The situation was not different in the ancient Levant and Egypt, so far as is known. There the intellectualism of the scribes, insofar as it lead to ethical and religious reflection, belonged entirely to the type of intellectualism which is sometimes apolitical but always aristocratic and anti-plebeian.

5. The Intellectualism of Higher- and Lower-Ranking Strata in Ancient Judaism

In ancient Israel, the author of the Book of Job assumed that upper-class groups are among the carriers of religious intellectualism. The Book of Proverbs and related works show traces in their very form of having been touched by the internationalization of the educated and apolitical higher strata resulting from their mutual contact with each other after Alexander's arrival in the East. Some of the dicta in Proverbs are directly attributed to a non-Jewish king, and in general the liturature stamped with the name of "Solomon" betrays marks of an international culture. Ben Sira's emphatic stress upon the wisdom of the fathers in opposition to Hellenization already demonstrates that there was a trend in this direction. Moreover, as Bousset[2] correctly pointed out, the "scribe" or "scriptural scholar" of that time who was learned in the law was, according to the Book of Ben Sira, a widely traveled and cultivated gentleman. There is throughout this book, as Meinhold has emphasized, a clearly expressed anti-plebeian line, quite comparable to that found among the Greeks: How can the peasant, the smith, or the potter have wisdom, which only leisure for reflection and dedication to study can produce?[3] Ezra is designated as the "first scribe," yet far older was the influential position of the priests, ideologists with a pure religious interest who had swarmed about the prophets, and without whom the imposition of the Book of Deuteronomy would never have taken place. On the other hand, the dominant position of the scribes, that means, those who know Hebrew and can interpret the divine commands, and whose position is almost equivalent to the Islamic mufti, arises much later than that of Ezra, the official creator of the theocracy, who had received his powers from the Persian emperor.

The social position of the scribes nevertheless underwent changes. At the time of the Maccabean commonwealth, piety—in essence a rather sober wisdom of life, as illustrated by the doctrine of xenophilia—was regarded as identical with education or "culture" (*musar, paideia*); the latter was the key to virtue, which was regarded as teachable in the same sense as among the Greeks. Yet the pious intellectuals of even that period, like the majority of the Psalmists, felt themselves to be in sharp opposition to the wealthy and proud, among whom fidelity to the law was uncommon, even though these intellectuals were of the same social class as the wealthy and proud. On the other hand, the schools of scriptural scholars of the Herodian period, whose frustration and psychological tension grew in the face of the obvious inevitability of subjugation to a foreign power, produced a proletaroid class of inter-preters of the law. These served as pastoral counselors, preachers and teachers in the synagogues, and their representatives also sat in the Sanhedrin. They influenced decisively the popular piety of those mem-bers (*chaberim*) of the Jewish community who were rigidly faithful to the law in the sense of the *perushim* (*pharisaioi*). In the Talmudic period, this functional activity developed into the rabbinate, a profession of congregational functionaries. Through this stratum there now ensued, in contrast to what had gone before, a tremendous expansion of petty-bourgeois and pariah intellectualism, such as we do not find among any other people. Philo already regarded "general public schools" for the diffusion of literacy and of systematic education in casuistical thinking as the hallmark of the Jews. It was the influence of this stratum that first supplanted, among urban Jews, the activity of the prophets by the cult of fidelity to the law and to the study of the sacred scriptures of the law.

This Jewish stratum of popular intellectuals, entirely remote from any connection with mystery religions, unquestionably occupied a lower social position than the strata of philosophers and mystagogues in Hel-lenistic societies of the Near East. But intellectualism was undoubtedly already diffused throughout the various social strata of the Hellenistic

Orient in pre-Christian times, and in fact produced in the various mysteries and cults of salvation, by allegory and speculation, dogmas similar to those generated by the Orphics, who generally seem to have belonged to the middle classes. These mysteries and soteriological speculations were certainly well known to a scriptural scholar of the Diaspora like Paul, who rejected them vigorously; it will be recalled that the cult of Mithra was widely diffused in Cilicia during the time of Pompey [ca. 60 B.C.] as a religion of pirates, although the epigraphic evidence for its existence specifically at Tarsus stems from the Christian era. It is quite likely that salvation hopes of different kinds and origins existed side by side in Judaism for a long period, especially in the provinces. Otherwise, it would have been impossible for Judaism to produce even in the period of the prophets, in addition to the idea of a future monarch of the Jewish people restored to power, the idea that another king of the poor folk would enter Jerusalem upon a donkey; and indeed it would have been difficult for the Jews to evolve their idea of the "son of man," an obvious linguistic product of Semitic grammar.

All in all, lay intellectualism, whether of the noble or the pariah kind, is involved in every complex soteriology which develops abstractions and opens up cosmic perspectives, going far beyond mythologies oriented to the mere processes of nature or to the simple prediction of the appearance at some future time of a good king who is already waiting somewhere in concealment.

6. The Predominance of Anti-Intellectualist Currents in Early Christianity

This scriptural scholarship, which is an instance of petty-bourgeois intellectualism, entered from Judaism into early Christianity. Paul, apparently an artisan like many of the late Jewish scriptural scholars (in sharp contrast to the intellectuals of the period of Ben Sira, who produced anti-plebeian wisdom doctrines), is an outstanding representative of this class in early Christianity, though of course other traits are also to be found in Paul. His *gnosis*, though very remote from that conceived by the speculative intellectuals of the Hellenistic Orient, could later provide many points of support for the Marcionite movement. Intellectualism rooted in a sense of pride that only those chosen by god understand the parables of the master was also strongly marked in Paul, who boasted that his true knowledge was "to the Jews a stumbling block and to the Greeks foolishness." Paul's doctrine of the dualism of flesh and spirit has some relationship to the attitudes toward sensuality typical of intellectualist salvation doctrines, but it is rooted in other conceptions. A somewhat superficial acquaintance with Hellenistic philosophy can be presumed in his thought. Above all, Paul's conversion was not merely a vision, in the sense of hallucinatory perception. Rather, his conversion was also recognition of the profound inner relationship between the personal fate of the resurrected founder of Christianity and the cultic ideologies of the general Oriental savior doctrines and conceptions of salvation (with which Paul was well acquainted), in which the promises of Jewish prophecy now found their place for him.

The argumentation of Paul's Epistles represents the highest type of dialectic found among petty-bourgeois intellectuals. Paul assumes a remarkable degree of direct "logical imagination" on the part of the groups he is addressing in such compositions as the Epistle to the Romans. It is most likely that it was not Paul's doctrine of justification which was taken over at the time, but rather his conception of the relationship between spirit and the community and his conception of the manner in which spirit is accommodated to the facts of the everyday world. The fierce anger directed against him by the Jews of the Diaspora, for whom his dialectical method must have appeared as a misuse of education, only shows how thoroughly just such a method corresponded to the mental attitude of the petty-bourgeois intellectual. This intellectualism was continued by the charismatic teachers (*didaskaloi*) in pristine Christian communities as late as the *Didache;* and Harnack found a specimen of its hermeneutic in the Epistle to the Hebrews.[4] But this intellectualism disappeared with the slow growth of the bishops' and presbyters' monopoly of the spiritual leadership of the community. In replacement of such intellectuals and teachers came first the intellectualist apologists, then the patristic church fathers and dogmatists, who had received a Hellenistic education and were almost all clerics, and then the emperors, who had a dilettante interest in theology. The culmination of this development was the emergence into power in the East, after victory in the iconoclastic struggle, of monks recruited from the lowest non-Greek social groups. Thenceforth it became impossible to eliminate completely from the Eastern church the type of formalistic dialectic common to all these circles and associated with a semi-intellectualistic, semi-primitive, and magical ideal of self-deification of the church.

Yet one factor was decisive for the fate of ancient Christianity. From its inception Christianity was a salvation doctrine in respect to its genesis, its typical carrier, and the religious way of life that appeared decisive to this carrier. From its very beginning, Christianity, notwithstanding the many similarities of its soteriological myth to the general Near Eastern pattern of such myths, from which it borrowed elements that it changed, took a position against intellectualism with the greatest possible awareness and consistency. Nor does it argue against the anti-intellectualism of Christianity that Paul took over the hermeneutical methodology of the scribes. Primitive Christianity took stands against both the ritualistic and legalistic scholarship of Judaism and the soteriology of the Gnostic intellectual aristocrats, and it most strongly repudiated ancient philosophy.

The distinctive characteristics of Christianity were its rejection of the Gnostic denigration of believers (*pistikoi*) and its affirmation that the exemplary Christians were those endowed with *pneuma,* the poor in spirit, rather than the scholars. Christianity also taught uniquely that the way to salvation is not derived from academic education in the Law, from wisdom about the cosmic or psychological grounds of life and suffering, from knowledge of the conditions of life within the world, from knowledge of the mysterious significance of sacramental rites, or from knowledge of the future destiny of the soul in the other world. To these hallmarks of Christianity must be added the fact that a considerable portion of the inner history of the early church, including the formulation of dogma, represented the struggle of Christianity against intellectualism in all its forms.

If one wishes to characterize succinctly, in a formula so to speak, the types representative of the various strata that were the primary carriers or propagators of the so-called world religions, they would be the following: In Confucianism, the world-organizing bureaucrat; in Hinduism, the world-ordering magician; in Buddhism, the mendicant monk wandering through the world; in Islam, the warrior seeking to conquer the world; in Judaism, the wandering trader; and in Christianity, the itinerant journeyman. To be sure, all these types must not be taken as exponents of their own occupational or material "class interests," but rather as the ideological carriers of the kind of ethical or salvation doctrine which rather readily conformed to their social position.

As for Islam, its distinctive religiosity could have experienced an infusion of intellectualism, apart from the official schools of law and theology and the temporary efflorescence of scientific interests, only after its penetration by Sufism, but the latter's orientation was not along intellectual lines. Indeed, tendencies toward rationalism were completely lacking in the popular dervish faith. In Islam only a few heterodox sects, which possessed considerable influence at certain times, displayed a distinctly intellectualistic character. Otherwise Islam, like medieval Christianity, produced in its universities tendencies towards scholasticism.

7. *Elite and Mass Intellectualism in Medieval Christianity*

It is imposisble to expatiate here on the relationships of intellectualism to religion in medieval Christianity. In any case this religion, at least as far as its sociologically significant effects are concerned, was not specifically oriented to intellectual elements. The strong influence of monastic rationalism upon the substantive content of the culture may be clarified only by a comparison of Occidental monasticism with that of the Near East and Asia, of which a brief sketch will be given later. The peculiar nature of Occidental monasticism determined the distinctive cultural influence of the church in the West. During the medieval period, Occidental Christianity did not have a religious lay intellectualism of any appreciable extent, whether of a petty-bourgeois or of a pariah character, although some religious lay intellectualism was occasionally found among the sects. On the other hand, the role of the educated classes in the development of the church was not a minor one. The educated strata of Carolingian, Ottonic, and Salic imperialism worked towards an imperial and theocratic cultural organization, just as did the Josephite monks in 16th century Russia.[5] Above all, the Gregorian reform movement and the struggle for power on the part of the papacy were carried forward by the ideology of an elite intellectual stratum that entered into a united front with the rising bourgeoisie against the feudal powers. With the increasing dissemination of university education and with the struggle of the papacy to monopolize, for the sake of fiscal administration or simple patronage, the enormous number of benefices which provided the economic support for this educated stratum, the ever-growing class of these "beneficiaries" turned against the papacy in what was at first an essentially economic and nationalistic interest in monopoly. Then, following the Schism, these intellectuals turned against the papacy ideologically, becoming the carriers of the conciliary reform movement and later of Humanism.

The sociology of the Humanists, particularly the transformation of a feudal and clerical education into a courtly culture based on the largesse of patrons, is not without inherent interest, but we are unable to linger over it at this point. The ambivalent attitude of the Humanists toward the Reformation was primarily caused by ideological factors. Insofar as Humanists placed themselves in the service of building the churches of either the Reformation or the Counter-Reformation, they played an extremely important, though not decisive, role in organizing church schools and in developing doctrine. But insofar as they became the carriers of particular religiosity (actually a whole series of particular types of faith), they remained without permanent influence. In keeping with their entire pattern of life, these Humanist groups of the classically educated were altogether antipathetic to the masses and to the religious sects. They remained alien to the turmoil and particularly to the demagogy of priests and preachers; on the whole they remained Erastian or irenic in temper, for which reason alone they were condemned to suffer progressive loss of influence.

In addition to sophisticated scepticism and rationalistic enlightenment, the Humanists displayed a tender religiousness, particularly in the Anglican group; an earnest and frequently ascetic moralism, as in the circle of Port Royal; and an individualistic mysticism, as in Germany during the first period and in Italy. But struggles involving realistic power and economic interests were waged, if not by outright violence, then at least with the means of demagogy, to which these Humanist groups were not equal. It is obvious that at least those churches desiring to win the participation of the ruling classes and particularly of the universities needed classically trained theological polemicists as well as preachers with classical training. Within Lutheranism, as a result of its alliance with the power of the nobility, the combination of education and religious activity rapidly devolved exclusively upon professional theologians.

Hudibras [Samuel Butler's mock-heroic poem, 1663–78] still mocked the Puritan groups for their ostensible philosophical erudition, but what gave the Puritans, and above all the Baptist sects, their insuperable power of resistance was not the intellectualism of the elite but rather the intellectualism of the plebeian and occasionally even the pariah classes, for Baptist Protestantism was in its first period a movement carried by wandering craftsmen or apostles. There was no distinctive intellectual stratum with a characteristic life pattern among these Protestant sects, but after the close of a brief period of missionary activity by their wandering preachers, it was the middle class that became suffused with their intellectualism. The unparalleled diffusion of knowledge about the Bible and interest in extremely abstruse and ethereal dogmatic controversies which was characteristic of the Puritans of the seventeenth century, even among peasants, created a popular religious intellectualism never found since, and comparable only to that found in late Judaism and to the religious mass intellectualism of the Pauline missionary communities. In contrast to the situations in Holland, parts of Scotland, and the American colonies, this popular religious intellectualism soon dwindled in England after the power spheres and the limits for seizing power had been tested and determined in the religious wars. However, this period formed the intellectualism of the educated in the Anglo-Saxon realm, marked as it is by a traditional deference toward a deistic-enlightened kind of religion, of varying degrees of mildness, which never reach the point of anti-clericalism (a phenomenon that we will not pursue at this point). Since this Anglo-Saxon mentality has been determined by the traditionalist attitudes and the moralistic interests of the politically powerful middle class, and thus by a religious plebeian intellectualism, it provides the sharpest contrast to the transformation of the basically aristocratic and court-centered education of the Latin countries into radical antipathy or indifference to the church.

8. *Modern Intellectual Status Groups and Secular Salvation Ideologies*

These Anglo-Saxon and Latin developments, which ultimately had an anti-metaphysical impact, contrast with the German brand of "non-political" elite education, which is neither apolitical nor anti-political.[6] This kind of education resulted from concrete historical events and had few (and mostly negative) sociological determinants. It was metaphysically oriented, but had very little to do with specifically religious needs, least of all any quest for salvation. On the other hand, the plebeian and pariah intellectualism of Germany, like that of the Latin countries, increasingly took a radically anti-religious turn, which became particularly marked after the rise of the economically eschatological faith of socialism. This development was in marked contrast to that in the Anglo-Saxon areas, where the most serious forms of religion since Puritan times have had a sectarian rather than an institutional-authoritarian character.

Only these anti-religious sects had a stratum of declassed intellectuals who were able to sustain a quasi-religious belief in the socialist eschatology at least for a while. This particular "academic" element receded to the extent that the workers took their interests into their own hands. It receded further because of the inevitable disillusionment with an almost superstitious veneration of science as the possible creator or at least prophet of social revolution, violent or peaceful, in the sense of salvation from class rule. So, too, it comes about that the only remaining variant of socialism in western Europe equivalent to a religious faith, namely syndicalism, can easily turn into a romantic game played by circles without direct economic interests.

The last great movement of intellectuals which, though not sustained by a uniform faith, shared enough basic elements to approximate a religion was the Russian revolutionary intelligentsia, in which patrician, academic and aristocratic intellectuals stood next to plebeian ones. Plebeian intellectualism was represented by the proletaroid minor officialdom, which was highly sophisticated in its sociological thinking and broad cultural interests; it was composed especially of the *zemstvo* officials (the so-called "third element"). Moreover, this kind of intellectualism was advanced by journalists, elementary school teachers, revolutionary apostles and a peasant intelligentsia that arose out of the Russian social conditions. In the eighteen-seventies, this movement culminated in an appeal to a theory of natural rights, oriented primarily toward agricultural communism, the so-called *narodnichestvo* (populism). In the nineties, this movement clashed sharply with Marxist dogmatics, but in part also aligned itself with it. Moreover, attempts were made to relate it, usually in an obscure manner, first to Slavophile romantic, then mystical, religiosity or, at least, religious emotionalism. Under the influence of Dostoevsky and Tolstoy, an ascetic and acosmistic patterning of personal life was created among some relatively large groups of these Russian intellectuals. We shall leave untouched here the question as to what extent this movement, so strongly infused with the influence of Jewish proletarian intellectuals who were ready for any sacrifice, can continue after the catastrophe of the Russian revolution (in 1906).

In Western Europe, ever since the seventeenth century, the viewpoints of Enlightenment religions produced, in both Anglo-Saxon and, more recently, Gallic culture areas, unitarian and deistic communities and communities of a syncretistic, atheistic, or free-church variety. Buddhistic conceptions, or what passed for such, also played some part in this development. In Germany, Enlightenment religious views found a hearing among the same groups that were interested in Freemasonry, namely those devoid of direct economic interests, especially university professors but also declassed ideologists and educated groups partly or wholly belonging to the proletariat. On the other hand, both the Hindu Enlightenment (Brahma-Samaj) and the Persian Enlightenment were products of contact with European culture.

The practical importance of such movements for the sphere of culture was greater in the past than now. Many elements conspire to render unlikely any serious possibility of a new congregational religion borne by intellectuals. This constellation of factors includes the interest of the privileged strata in maintaining the existing religion as an instrument for controlling the masses, their need for social distance, their abhorrence of mass enlightenment as tending to destroy the prestige of elite groups, and their well-founded rejection of any faith in the possibility that some new creed acceptable to large segments of the population could supplant the traditional creeds (from the texts of which everyone interprets something away, orthodoxy ten percent and liberals ninety percent). Finally, and above all, there is the scornful indifference of the privileged strata to religious problems and to the church. Performance of some irksome formalities does not constitute much of a sacrifice, inasmuch as everyone knows they are just that—formalities best performed by the official guardians of orthodoxy and the social conventions, and acted on in the interest of a successful career because the state requires them performed.

The need of literary, academic, or café-society intellectuals to include "religious" feelings in the inventory of their sources of impressions and sensations, and among their topics for discussion, has never yet given rise to a new religion. Nor can a religious renascence be generated by the need of authors to compose books on such interesting topics or by the far more effective need of clever publishers to sell such books. No matter how much the appearance of a widespread religious interest may be simulated, no new religion has ever resulted from such needs of intellectuals or from their chatter. The pendulum of fashion will presently remove this subject of conversation and journalism.

NOTES

1. See Rudolf Dvořak, *Chinas Religionen* (Münster: Aschendorff, 1895), vol. I, "Confucius und seine Lehre," 122; Dvořak uses the English term "gentleman"; cf. also *GAzRS*, I, 449.

2. See Wilhelm Bousset, *Die Religion des Judentums im neutestamentlichen Zeitalter* (Berlin: Reuther und Reichard, 1906), sec. ed., 187f.

3. Ecclesiasticus (i.e., *The Wisdom of Jesus ben Sirach*) xxxviii:25–39. The reference to Johannes Meinhold's writings could not be identified, but cf. his *Geschichte des jüdischen Volkes* (Leipzig: Quelle und Meyer, 1916), 63, which was probably published too late to be used here.

4. Cf. Adolf von Harnack, *Lehrbuch der Dogmengeschichte* (Tübingen: Mohr, 1909), vol. I, 104ff; on the *Didache* and the ancient Christian distinction between apostles, prophets and charismatic teachers, see *id.*, *Die Mission und Ausbreitung des Christentums in den ersten drei Jahrhunderten* (Leipzig: Hinrich, 1902), 237–51.

5. This refers to the so-called "Church Party" of the period of Ivan II and Vasilii III, around 1500. Its leader was Iosif Sanin, the abbot of Volokolamsk, who extolled the Muscovite rulers as the God-ordained secular arm of the church; it was during this time that the idea of Moscow as the Third (and last) Rome became established. Iosif and his followers, the "Josephites," fought both the rationalist heresy of the so-called Judaizers, a widespread and highly-placed anti-Trinitarian and anti-monastic movement, and the radical monastic movement of Nil Sorski who wanted the cloisters to abandon the lands and villages attached to them. The Josephites pressed for an improvement of monastic *mores*, but they defended the monastic landholdings against the secular interest of the Tsar as well as against otherwordly radicalism. Cf. D. S. Mirsky, *Russia: A Social His-*

tory (London: Cresset, 1931), 138; Günther Stöckl, *Russische Geschichte* (Stuttgart: Kröner, 1962), 218–30.

6. In German *unpolitisch* (non-political) usually refers to an attitude of proud disdain for any involvement in partisan activities and for the realities of parliamentary politics. Thomas Mann's nationalist aberration during the first World War, for example, was entitled *Reflections of a Non-Political Man* (*Betrachtungen eines Unpolitischen*). Weber attacked the "non-political" politics of the literati during the same period in his "Parliament and Government in a Reconstructed Germany" (see Appendix II). Since the literati tended to propagate grand, albeit unrealistic, political schemes, they were not "anti-political," and they were also not "apolitical" in an otherworldly religious sense.

viii
Theodicy, Salvation, and Rebirth

1 . Theodicy and Eschatology

Only Judaism and Islam are strictly monotheistic in principle, and even in the latter there are some deviations from monotheism in the later cult of saints. Christian trinitarianism appears to have a monotheistic trend when contrasted with the tritheistic forms of Hinduism, late Buddhism, and Taoism. Yet in practice, the Roman Catholic cult of masses and saints actually comes fairly close to polytheism. It is by no means the case that every ethical god is necessarily endowed with absolute unchangeableness, omnipotence, and omniscience—that is to say, with an absolutely transcendental character. What provides him with this quality is the speculation and the ethical dynamic of passionate prophets. Only the God of the Jewish prophets attained this trait in an absolute and consistent form, and he became also the God of the Christians and Muslims. Not every ethical conception of god produced this result, nor did it lead to ethical monotheism as such. Hence, not every approximation to monotheism is based on an increase in the ethical content of the god-concept. It is certainly true that not every religious ethic has crystallized a god of transcendental quality who created the universe out of nothing and directed it himself.

Yet the legitimation of every distinctively ethical prophecy has always required the notion of a god characterized by attributes that set him sublimely above the world, and has normally been based on the rationalization of the god-idea along such lines. Of course the manifestation and the significance of this sublimity may be quite different, depending in part on fixed metaphysical conceptions and in part on the expression of the concrete ethical interests of the prophets. But the more the development tends toward the conception of a transcendental unitary god who is universal, the more there arises the problem of how the extraordinary power of such a god may be reconciled with the imperfection of the world that he has created and rules over.

The resultant problem of theodicy is found in ancient Egyptian literature as well as in Job and in Aeschylus, but in very different forms. All Hindu religion was influenced by it in the distinctive way necessitated by its fundamental presuppositions; even a meaningful world order that is impersonal and super-theistic must face the problem of the world's imperfections. In one form or another, this problem belongs everywhere among the factors determining religious evolution and the need for salvation. Indeed, a recent questionnaire submitted to thousands of German workers disclosed the fact that their rejection of the god-idea was motivated, not by scientific arguments, but by their difficulty in reconciling the idea of providence with the injustice and imperfection of the social order.[1]

Now the problem of theodicy has been solved in various ways. These solutions stand in the closest relationship both to the forms assumed by the god-concept and to the conceptions of sin and salvation crystallized in particular social groups. Let us separate out the various theoretically pure types.

One solution is to assure a just equalization by pointing, through messianic eschatologies, to a future revolution in this world. In this way the eschatological process becomes a political and social transformation of this world. This solution held that sooner or later there would arise some tremendous hero or god who would place his followers in the positions they truly deserved in the world. The suffering of the present generation, it was believed, was the consequence of the sins of the ancestors, for which god holds the descendants responsible, just as someone carrying out blood revenge may hold an entire tribe accountable, and as Pope Gregory VII excommunicated descendants down to the seventh generation. Also, it was held that only the descendants of the pious could behold the messianic kingdom, as a consequence of their ancestors' piety. If it perhaps appeared necessary to renounce one's own experience of salvation, there was nothing strange in this. Concern about one's children was everywhere a definite fact of organic social life, pointing beyond the personal interest of an individual and in the direction of another world, at least a world beyond one's own death. For those who were alive, the exemplary and strict fulfillment of the positive divine commandments remained obligatory, in order to obtain for the individual himself the optimum opportunity for success in life by virtue of god's favor, and in order to obtain for his descendants a share in the realm of salvation. Sin is a breach of fidelity toward god and an impious rejection of god's promises. Moreover, the desire to participate personally in the messianic kingdom leads to further consequences: a tremendous religious excitation is generated when the establishment of the Kingdom of God here on earth appears imminent. Prophets repeatedly arose to proclaim the coming of the kingdom, but when such supervention of the messianic kingdom appeared to be unduly delayed, it was inevitable that consolation should be sought in genuine otherworldly hopes.

The germ of the conception of a world beyond the present one is already present in the development of magic into a belief in spirits. But it by no means follows that the existence of a belief in the souls of the dead always develops into a conception of a special realm of the dead. Thus, a very widespread view is that the souls of the dead may be incorporated into animals and plants, depending on the souls' different manners of life and death, and influenced by their clan and caste connections. This is the source of all conceptions regarding the transmigration of the soul. Where there exists a belief in a domain of the deceased —at first in some geographically remote place, and later above or beneath the earth—it by no means follows that the existence of the souls there is conceived as eternal. For the souls may be destroyed by violence, may perish as the result of the cessation of sacrifices, or may simply die, which is apparently the ancient Chinese view.

In keeping with the law of marginal utility, a certain concern for one's destiny after death would generally arise when the most essential earthly needs have been met, and thus this concern is limited primarily to the circles of the noble and the well-to-do. Only these groups and occasionally only the chieftains and priests, but never the poor and only seldom women, can secure for themselves life in the next world, and they do not spare great expenditures in doing so. It is primarily the example of these groups that serves as a strong stimulus for preoccupation with otherworldly expectations.

At this point there is as yet no question of retribution in the world to come. Where a doctrine of retributions arises, errors in ritual are deemed to be the principal causes of such unfortunate consequences. This is seen most extensively in the sacred law of the Hindus: whosoever violates a caste taboo may be certain of punishment in hell. Only after the god-concept has been ethicized does the god employ moral considerations in deciding the fate of human beings in the world to come. The differentiation of a paradise and a hell does not necessarily arise concomitantly with this development, but is a relatively late product of evolution. As otherworldly expectations become increasingly important, the problem of the basic relationship of god to the world and the problem of the world's imperfections press into the foreground of thought; this happens the more life here on earth comes to be regarded as a merely provisional form of existence when compared to that beyond, the more the world comes to be viewed as something created by god *ex nihilo*, and therefore subject to decline, the more god himself is conceived as subject to transcendental goals and values, and the more a person's behavior in this world becomes oriented to his fate in the next. At times, the hope for continued existence in the world beyond produces a direct inversion—in accordance with the formula, "the last shall be first"—of the primordial view in which it had held this to be a matter of concern only to the noble and the wealthy.

But this view has seldom been worked out consistently, even in the religious conceptions of pariah peoples. It did play a great role, however, in the ancient Jewish ethic. The assumption that suffering, particularly voluntary suffering, would mollify god and improve one's chances in the world to come is found sprinkled through and developed in many types of expectation regarding continued existence after death. These may arise from very diverse religious motivations, and may perhaps derive to some extent from the ordeals of heroic asceticism and the practice of magical mortification. As a rule, and especially in religions under the influence of the ruling strata, the converse view obtained, viz., that terrestrial differentiations of status could continue into the next world as well, for the reason that they had been divinely ordained. This belief is still apparent in the phrase current in Christian nations, "His late Majesty, the King."

However, the distinctively ethical view was that there would be concrete retribution of justice and injustice on the basis of a trial of the dead, generally conceived in the eschatological process as a universal day of judgment. In this way, sin assumed the character of a *crimen* to be brought into a system of rational casuistry, a *crimen* for which satisfaction must somehow be given in this world or in the next so that one might ultimately stand vindicated before the judge of the dead. Accordingly, it would have made sense to grade rewards and punishments into relative degrees of merit and transgression, which was still the case in Dante, with the result that they could not really be eternal. But because of the pale and uncertain character of a person's chances in the next world, by comparison with the realities of this world, the remission of eternal punishments was practically always regarded as impossible by prophets and priests. Eternal punishment, moreover, seemed to be the only appropriate fulfillments of the demand for vengeance against unbelieving, renegade, and godless sinners, especially those who had gone unpunished on earth.

2. Predestination and Providence

Heaven, hell, and the judgment of the dead achieved practically universal importance, even in religions for which such concepts were completely alien, such as ancient Buddhism. However, even though intermediate realms of existence, such as those depicted in the teachings of Zoroaster or in the Roman Catholic conception of purgatory, realms encompassing punishments which would only be undergone for limited durations, weakened the consistency of conceptions of eternal punishment, there always remained the difficulty of reconciling the punishment of human acts with the conception of an ethical and at the same time all-powerful creator of the world, who is ultimately responsible for these human actions himself. As people continued to reflect about the insoluble problem of the imperfections of the world in the light of god's omnipotence, one result was inevitable: the conception of an unimaginably great ethical chasm between the transcendental god and the human being continuously enmeshed in the toils of new sin. And this conception inevitably led to the ultimate conclusion, almost reached in the Book of Job, that the omnipotent creator God must be envisaged as beyond all the ethical claims of his creatures, his counsels impervious to human comprehension. Another facet of this emerging view was that God's absolute power over his creatures is unlimited, and therefore that the criteria of human justice are utterly inapplicable to his behavior. With the development of this notion, the problem of theodicy simply disappeared altogether.

In Islam, Allah was deemed by his most passionate adherents to possess just such a limitless power over men. In Christianity, the *deus absconditus* was so envisaged, especially by the virtuosi of Christian piety. God's sovereign, completely inexplicable, voluntary, and antecedently established (a consequence of his omniscience) determination has decreed not only human fate on earth but also human destiny after death. The idea of the determinism or predestination from all eternity of both human life on this earth and human fate in the world beyond comes to its strongest possible expression in such views. The damned might well complain about their sinfulness, imposed by predestination, in the same manner as animals might complain because they had not been created human beings, a notion expressly stated in Calvinism.

In such a context, ethical behavior could never bring about the improvement of one's own chances in either this world or the next. Yet it might have another significance, the practical psychological consequences of which would in certain circumstances be of even greater moment; it might be considered as a symptom or index of one's own state of religious grace as established by god's decree. For the absolute sovereignty of an omnipotent god compels a practical religious concern to try, at the very least, to penetrate god's design in individual cases. Above all, the need to ascertain one's own personal destiny in the world beyond is of paramount importance. Hence, concomitant with the tendency to regard god as the unlimited sovereign over his creatures, there was an inclination to see and interpret god's providence and his personal interposition everywhere in the world's process.

Belief in providence is the consistent rationalization of magical divination, to which it is related, and which for that very reason it seeks to devaluate as completely as possible, as a matter of principle. No other view of the religious relationship could possibly be as radically opposed to all magic, both in theory and in practice, as this belief in providence which was dominant in the great theistic religions of Asia Minor and the Occident. No other so emphatically affirms the nature of the divine to be an essentially dynamic activity manifested in god's personal, providential rule over the world. Moreover, there is no view of the religious relationship which holds such firm views regarding god's discretionary grace and the human creature's need of it, regarding the tremendous distance between god and all his creatures, and consequently regarding the reprehensibility of any deification of "things of the flesh" as a sacrilege against the sovereign god. For the very reason that this religion provides no rational solution of the problem of theodicy, it conceals the greatest tensions between the world and god, between the actually existent and the ideal.

3. *Other Solutions of Theodicy: Dualism and the Transmigration of the Soul*

Besides predestination, there are two other religious outlooks that provide systematically conceptualized treatment of the problem of the world's imperfections. The first is dualism, as expressed more or less consistently in the later form of Zoroastrianism, in the many forms of religion in Asia Minor influenced by Zoroastrianism, above all in the final form of Babylonian religion (containing some Jewish and Christian influences), and in Mandaeism and Gnosticism, down to the great ideas of Manicheism.

At the turn of the third century, Manicheism seemed to stand on the threshold of a struggle for world mastery, even in the Mediterranean area. According to the Manicheans, god is not almighty, nor did he create the world out of nothingness. Injustice, unrighteousness, and sin—in short, all the factors that have generated the problem of theodicy—result from the darkening of the luminous purity of the great and good gods through contact with the opposite autonomous powers of darkness, which are identified with impure matter. The dominance of these forces, which gives dominion over the world to some satanic power, has arisen through some primordial wickedness of men or of angels, or, as in the view of many Gnostics, through the inferiority of some subordinate creator of the world, e.g., Jehovah or the Demiurge. The final victory of the god of light in the ensuing struggle is generally regarded as certain, and this constitutes a deviation from strict dualism. The world process, although full of inevitable suffering, is a continuous purification of the light from the contamination of darkness. This conception of the final struggle naturally produces a very powerful eschatological emotional dynamic.

The general result of such views must be the enhancement of an aristocratic feeling of prestige on the part of the pure and elect. The conception of evil, which, on the assumption of a definitely omnipotent god, always tends to take a purely ethical direction, may here assume a strongly spiritual character. This is because man is not regarded as a mere creature facing an absolutely omnipotent power, but as a participant in the realm of light. Moreover, the identification of light with what is clearest in man, namely the spiritual, and conversely, the identification of darkness with the material and corporeal which carry in themselves all the coarser temptations, is practically unavoidable. This view, then, connects easily with the doctrine of impurity found in tabooistic ethics. Evil appears as soiling, and sin—in a fashion quite like that of magical misdeeds—appears as a reprehensible and headlong fall to earth from the realm of purity and clarity into that of darkness and confusion, leading to a state of contamination and deserved ignominy. In practically all the religions with an ethical orientation there are unavowed limitations of divine omnipotence in the form of elements of a dualistic mode of thought.

The most complete formal solution of the problem of theodicy is the special achievement of the Indian doctrine of *karma*, the so-called belief in the transmigration of souls. This world is viewed as a completely connected and self-contained cosmos of ethical retribution. Guilt and merit within this world are unfailingly compensated by fate in the successive

lives of the soul, which may be reincarnated innumerable times in animal, human, or even divine forms. Ethical merits in this life can make
possible rebirth into life in heaven, but that life can last only until one's
credit balance of merits has been completely used up. The finiteness of
earthly life is the consequence of the finiteness of good or evil deeds in
the previous life of a particular soul. What may appear from the viewpoint of retribution as unjust suffering in the present life of a person
should be regarded as atonement for sin in a previous existence. Each
individual forges his own destiny exclusively, and in the strictest sense
of the word.

The belief in the transmigration of souls has certain links with widely
diffused animistic views regarding the passage of the spirits of the dead
into natural objects. It rationalizes these beliefs, and indeed the entire
cosmos, by means of purely ethical principles. The naturalistic "causality"
of our habits of thought is thus supplanted by a universal mechanism of
retribution, for which no act that is ethically relevant can ever be lost.
The consequence for dogma is the complete dispensability, and indeed
unthinkableness, of an omnipotent god's interference with this mechanism, for the eternal world process provides for ethical obligations
through automatic functioning. The mechanism of retribution is, therefore, a consistent deduction from the super-divine character of the eternal
order of the world, in contrast to the notion of a god who is set over
the world, rules it personally, and imposes predestination upon it. In
ancient Buddhism, where this mechanistic notion of the eternal order
of the world has been developed with the greatest consistency, even the
soul is completely eliminated. What alone exists is the sum of individual
good or evil actions, which are relevant for the mechanisms of *karma*
and associated with the illusion of the ego.

But on their part, all actions are products of the eternally helpless
struggle of all created life, which by the very fact of its finite creation is
destined for annihilation; they all arise from the thirst for life, which
brings forth all questing for the world to come and all surrender to
pleasures here on earth. This thirst for life is the ineradicable basis of
individuation and creates life and rebirth as long as it exists. Strictly
speaking, there is no sin, but only offenses against one's own clear interest in escaping from this endless wheel, or at least in not exposing oneself to a rebirth under even more painful circumstances. The meaning
of ethical behavior may then lie, when modestly conceived, either in
improving one's chances in his next incarnation or—if the senseless
struggle for mere existence is ever to be ended—in the elimination of
rebirth as such.

In the doctrine of metempsychosis there is none of the bifurcation of the world that is found in the ethical dualistic religions of providence. The dualism of a sacred, omnipotent, and majestic god confronting the ethical inadequacy of all his creatures is altogether lacking. Nor is there, as in spiritualistic dualism, the bisection of all creation into light and darkness or into pure and clear spirit on the one side with dark and sullied matter on the other. Here, rather, is an ontological dualism, one contrasting the world's transitory events and behavior with the serene and perduring being of eternal order—immobile divinity, resting in dreamless sleep. Only Buddhism has deduced from the doctrine of the transmigration of souls its ultimate consequences. This is the most radical solution of the problem of theodicy, and for that very reason it provides as little satisfaction for ethical claims upon god as does the belief in predestination.

4. Salvation: This-Worldly and Other-Worldly

Only a few religions of salvation have produced a single pure solution of the problem of the relation of god to the world and to man from among the various possible pure types we have just sketched. Wherever such a pure type was produced it lasted for only a little while. Most religions of salvation have combined various theories, as a result of mutual interaction with each other, and above all in attempts to satisfy the diverse ethical and intellectual needs of their adherents. Consequently, the differences among various religious theories of god's relation to the world and to man must be measured by their degree of approximation to one or another of these pure types.

Now the various ethical colorations of the doctrines of god and sin stand in the most intimate relationship to the striving for salvation, the content of which will be different depending upon what one wants to be saved from, and what one wants to be saved for. Not every rational religious ethic is necessarily an ethic of salvation. Thus, Confucianism is a religious ethic, but it knows nothing at all of a need for salvation. On the other hand, Buddhism is exclusively a doctrine of salvation, but it has no god. Many other religions know salvation only as a special concern cultivated in narrow conventicles, frequently as a secret cult. Indeed, even in connection with religious activities which are regarded as distinctively sacred and which promise their participants some salvation that may be achieved only through these activities, the crassest utilitarian expectations frequently replace anything we are accustomed to term "salvation." The pantomimic musical mystery festivals of the great chthonic deities, which controlled both the harvest and the realm of the dead, promised to the participant in the Eleusinian mysteries who was ritually pure, first wealth and then improvement in his lot in the next world. But this was proclaimed without any idea of compensation, purely as a consequence of ritualistic devotion.

In the catalog of goods in the *Shih ching,* the highest rewards promised to the Chinese subjects for their correct performances of the official cult and their fulfillment of personal religious obligations are wealth and long life, while there is a complete absence of expectations in regard to another world and any compensation there. Again, it is wealth that Zoroaster, by the grace of his god, principally expects for himself and those faithful to him, apart from rather extensive promises relating to the world beyond. As rewards for the ethical conduct of its laity, Buddhism promises wealth and a long and honorable life, in complete consonance with the doctrines of all inner-worldly ethics of the Hindu religions. Finally, wealth is the blessing bestowed by God upon the pious Jew.

But wealth, when acquired in a systematic and legal fashion, is also one of the indices of the certification of the state of grace among Protestant ascetic groups, e.g., Calvinists, Baptists, Mennonites, Quakers, Reformed Pietists, and Methodists. To be sure, in these cases we are dealing with a conception that decisively rejects wealth (and other mundane goods) as a religious goal. But in practice the transition to this standpoint is gradual and easy. It is difficult to completely separate conceptions of salvation from such promises of redemption from oppression and suffering as those held forth by the religions of the pariah peoples, particularly the Jews, and also by the doctrines of Zoroaster and Muhammad. For the faithful, these promises might include world dominion and social prestige, which the true believer in ancient Islam carried in his knapsack[2] as the reward for holy war against all infidels; or the promises might include a distinctive religious prestige, such as that which the Israelites were taught by their tradition that God had promised them as their future. Particularly for the Israelites, therefore, God was in the first instance a redeemer, because he had saved them from the Egyptian house of bondage and would later redeem them from the ghetto.

In addition to such economic and political salvation, there is the very important factor of liberation from fear of noxious spirits and bad magic of any sort, which is held to be responsible for the majority of all the evils in life. That Christ broke the power of the demons by the force of his spirit and redeemed his followers from their control was, in the early period of Christianity, one of the most important and influential of its messages. Moreover, the Kingdom of God proclaimed by Jesus of Nazareth, which had already come or was held to be close at hand, [Lk. 11:20, Mk. 1:15] was a realm of blessedness upon this earth, purged of all hate, anxiety, and need; only later did heaven and hell appear in the doctrine. Of course, an eschatology oriented to a future in this world would show a distinct tendency to become a hope for the world beyond, once the Second Coming (*parousia*) was delayed. Henceforth, emphasis had to be shifted to the afterlife: those alive at present would not be able to see salvation during their lifetime, but would see it after death, when the dead would awaken.

The distinctive content of otherworldly salvation may essentially mean freedom from the physical, psychological, and social sufferings of terrestrial life. On the other hand, it may be more concerned with a liberation from the senseless treadmill and transitoriness of life as such. Finally, it may be focused primarily on the inevitable imperfection of the individual, whether this be regarded more as chronic contamination, acute inclination to sin, or more spiritually, as entanglement in the murky confusion of earthly ignorance.

Our concern is essentially with the quest for salvation, whatever its form, insofar as it produced certain consequences for practical behavior in the world. It is most likely to acquire such a positive orientation to mundane affairs as the result of a conduct of life which is distinctively determined by religion and given coherence by some central meaning or positive goal. In other words, a quest for salvation in any religious group has the strongest chance of exerting practical influences when there has arisen, out of religious motivations, a systematization of practical conduct resulting from an orientation to certain integral values. The goal and significance of such a pattern of life may remain altogether oriented to this world, or it may focus on the world beyond, at least in part. In the various religions, this has taken place in exceedingly diverse fashions and in different degrees, and even within each religion there are corresponding differences among its various adherents. Furthermore, the religious systematization of the conduct of life has, in the nature of the case, certain limits insofar as it seeks to exert influence upon economic behavior. Finally, religious motivations, especially the hope of salvation, need not necessarily exert any influence at all upon the manner of the conduct of life, particularly the manner of economic conduct. Yet they may do so to a very considerable extent.

The hope of salvation has the most far-reaching consequences for the conduct of life when salvation takes the form of a process that casts its shadow before it in this life already, or the form of a subjective process taking place completely in this world; hence, when this hope is tantamount to "sanctification" or leads to it or is a precondition of it. Sanctification may then occur as either a gradual process of purification or a sudden transformation of the spirit (*metanoia*), a rebirth.

The notion of rebirth as such is very ancient, and its most classical development is actually to be found in the spirit belief of magic. The possession of magical charisma almost always presupposes rebirth. The distinctive education of the magician himself, his specific pattern of life, and his distinctive training of the warrior hero are all oriented to rebirth and the insurance of the possession of magical power. This process is mediated by "removal" (*Entrückung*) in the form of ecstasy, and by the acquisition of a new soul, generally followed by a change of name. A vestige of these notions is still extant in the monastic consecration ceremony. Rebirth is at first relevant only to the professional magician, as a magical precondition for insuring the charisma of the wizard or warrior. But in the most consistent types of salvation religion it becomes a quality of devotional mood indispensable for religious salvation, an attitude which the individual must acquire and which he must make manifest in his pattern of life.

NOTES

1. See Adolf Levenstein, *Die Arbeiterfrage* (Munich: Reinhardt, 1912). Levenstein, a worker and self-taught researcher, who pioneered in the survey field, was publicly prodded by Weber into making a more detailed analysis of his results. See Weber, "Zur Methodik sozialpsychologischer Enqueten und ihrer Bearbeitung," *Archiv für Sozialwissenschaft*, 29, 1909, 949–58; cf. also Anthony R. Oberschall, *Empirical Social Research in Germany 1848–1914* (The Hague: Mouton, 1965) 94ff., and Paul Lazarsfeld and *id.*, "Max Weber and Empirical Social Research," *American Sociological Review*, 30:2, April 1965, 190f.

2. An allusion to the famous, but apocryphal statement attributed to Napoleon I: "Tout soldat français porte dans sa giberne le bâton de maréchal de France."

ix

Salvation Through The Believer's Efforts[1]

1. Salvation Through Ritual

The influence any religion exerts on the conduct of life, and especially on the conditions of rebirth, varies in accordance with the particular path to salvation which is desired and striven for, and in accordance with the psychological quality of the salvation in question.

Salvation may be the accomplishment of the individual himself without any assistance on the part of supernatural powers, e.g., in ancient Buddhism. In this case, one path to salvation leads through the purely ritual activities and ceremonies of cults, both within religious worship and in everyday behavior. Pure ritualism as such is not very different from magic in its effect on the conduct of life. Indeed, ritualism may even lag behind magic, inasmuch as magical religion occasionally produced a definite and rather thorough methodology of rebirth, which ritualism did not always succeed in doing. A religion of salvation may systematize the purely formal and specific activities of ritual into a devotion with a distinctive religious mood (*Andacht*), in which the rites to be performed are symbols of the divine. Then this religious mood is the truly redemptory quality. Once it is missing, only the bare and formal magical ritualism remains. This has happened as a matter of course again and again in the routinization of all devotional religions.

The consequences of a ritualistic religion of devotion may be quite diversified. The comprehensive ritualistic regimentation of life among pious Hindus, which by European standards placed extraordinary daily demands upon the devout, would have rendered virtually impossible the coexistence of a life of exemplary piety in the world with any intensive acquisitive economic activity, if these demands had been followed exactly. Such extreme devotional piety is diametrically opposite to Puritanism in one respect: such a program of ritualism could be executed completely only by a man of means, who is free from the burden of hard work. But this circumstance limiting the number of those whose conduct of life can be influenced by ritualism is to some extent avoidable, whereas another inherent limiting circumstance is even more basic to the nature of ritualism.

Ritualistic salvation, especially when it limits the layman to a spectator role, or confines his participation to simple or essentially passive manipulations, especially in situations in which the ritual attitude is sublimated as much as possible into a devotional mood, stresses the mood of the pious moment that appears to bring the salvation. Consequently, the possession of an essentially ephemeral subjective state is striven after, and this subjective state—because of the idiosyncratic irresponsibility characterizing, for example, the hearing of a mass or the witnessing of a mystical play—has often only a negligible effect on behavior once the ceremony is over. The meager effect such experiences frequently have upon everyday ethical living may be compared to the insignificant influence, in this respect, of a beautiful and inspiring play upon the theater public no matter how much it has been moved by it. All salvation deriving from mysteries has such an inconstant character as it purports to produce its effect *ex opere operato,* by means of an occasional devotional mood. There is no motivation for the believer's actual proof by deed, which might guarantee a rebirth.

On the other hand, when the occasional devotion induced by ritual is escalated into a continuing piety and the effort is made to incorporate this piety into everyday living, this ritualistic piety most readily takes on a mystical character. This transition is facilitated by the requirement that religious devotion lead to the participant's possession of a subjective state. But the disposition to mysticism is an individual charisma. Hence, it is no accident that the great mystical prophecies of salvation, like the Hindu and others in the Orient, have tended to fall into pure ritualism as they have become routinized. What is of primary concern to us is that in ritualism the psychological condition striven for ultimately leads directly away from rational activity. Virtually all mystery cults have this effect. Their typical intention is the administration of sacramental grace: redemption from guilt is achieved by the sheer sacredness of the manipulation. Like every form of magic, this process has a tendency to become diverted from everyday life, thereby failing to exert any influence upon it.

But a sacrament might have a very different effect if its distribution and administration were linked to the presupposition that the sacrament could bring salvation only to those who have become ethically purified in the sight of god, and might indeed bring ruin to all others. Even up to the threshold of the present time, large groups of people have felt a terrifying fear of the Lord's Supper (the sacrament of the Eucharist) because of the doctrine that "whoever does not believe and yet eats, eats and drinks himself to judgment." Such factors could exert a strong influence upon everyday behavior wherever, as in ascetic Protestantism, there was no central source for the provision of absolution, and where further participation in the sacramental communion occurred frequently, providing a very important index of piety.

In all Christian denominations, participation in sacramental communion is connected with a prescription of confession as the prelude to partaking of the Lord's Supper. But in assessing the importance of confession, everything depends upon what religious rules are prescribed as determining whether sacramental communion may be taken with profit to the participant. Only ritual purity was required for this purpose by the majority of non-Christian ancient mystery cults, though under certain circumstances the devotee was disqualified by grave blood guilt or other specific sins. Thus, most of these mysteries had nothing resembling a confessional. But wherever the requirement of ritual purity became rationalized in the direction of spiritual freedom from sin, the particular forms of control and, where it existed, of the confessional became important for the type and degree of their possible influence upon daily life. From the pragmatic point of view, ritual as such was in every case only an instrument for influencing the all-important extra-ritual behavior. So much is this the case that wherever the Eucharist was most completely stripped of its magical character, and where further no control by means of the confessional existed, e.g., in Puritanism, communion nevertheless exerted an ethical effect, in some cases precisely because of the absence of magical and confessional controls.

A ritualistic religion may exert an ethical effect in another and indirect way, by requiring that participants be specially schooled. This happened where, as in ancient Judaism, the fulfillment of ritual commandments required of the laity some active ritual behavior or some ritual avoidance of behavior, and where the formalistic side of the ritual had become so systematized into a comprehensive body of law that adequate understanding of it required special schooling. Philo emphasized already in ancient times that the Jews, in contrast to all other peoples, were trained from their earliest youth (along the lines of our public school system) and received a continuous intellectual training in systematic casuistry. Indeed, the literary character of Jewish law is responsible for the fact that even in modern times many Jews, e.g., those in Eastern Europe, have been the only people in their society to enjoy systematic popular education. Even in Antiquity, pious Jews had been led to equate persons unschooled in the law with the godless. Such casuistic training of the intellect naturally exerts an effect on everyday life, especially when it involves not only ritual and cultic obligations, as those of Hindu law, but also a systematic regulation of the ethics of everyday living as well. Then the works of salvation are primarily social achievements, distinctively different from cultic performances.

2. Salvation Through Good Works

The social achievements which are regarded as conducive to salvation may be of very different types. Thus, gods of war welcome into their paradise only those who have fallen in battle, or at least show them preference. In the Brahmin ethic the king was explicitly enjoined to seek death in battle once he had beheld his grandson. On the other hand, the social achievements in question may be works of "love for one's fellow men." But in either case systematization may ensue, and, as we have already seen, it is generally the function of prophecy to accomplish just this systematization.

A developing systematization of an ethic of "good works" may assume either of two very different forms. In the first major form of systematization of an ethic of good works, the particular actions of an individual in quest of salvation, whether virtuous or wicked actions, can be evaluated singly and credited to or subtracted from the individual's account. Each individual is regarded as the carrier of his own behavior pattern and as possessing ethical standards only tenuously; he may turn out to be a weaker or a stronger creature in the face of temptation, according to the force of the subjective or external situation. Yet it is held that his religious fate depends upon his actual achievements, in their relationship to one another.

This first type of systematization is consistently followed in Zoroastrianism, particularly in the oldest Gathas by the founder himself, which depict the judge of all the dead balancing the guilt and merit of individual actions in a very precise bookkeeping and determining the religious fate of the individual person according to the outcome of this accounting. This notion appears among the Hindus in an even more heightened form, as a consequence of the doctrine of *karma*. It is held that within the ethical mechanism of the world not a single good or evil action can ever be lost. Each action, being ineradicable, must necessarily produce, by an almost automatic process, inevitable consequences in this life or in some future rebirth. This essential principle of life-accounting also remained the basic view of popular Judaism regarding the individual's relationship to God. Finally, Roman Catholicism and the oriental Christian churches held views very close to this, at least in practice. The *intentio,* according to the ethical evaluation of behavior in Catholicism, is not really a uniform quality of personality, of which conduct is the expression. Rather, it is the concrete intent (somewhat in the sense of the *bona fides, mala fides, culpa,* and *dolus* of the Roman law) behind a particular action. This view, when consistently maintained, eschews the yearning for "rebirth" [in this life] in the strict sense of an ethic of inwardness. A result is that the conduct of life remains, from the viewpoint of ethics, an unmethodical and miscellaneous succession of discrete actions.

The second major form of systematization of an ethic of good works treats individual actions as symptoms and expressions of an underlying ethical total personality. It is instructive to recall the attitude of the more rigorous Spartans toward a comrade who had fallen in battle in order to atone for an earlier manifestation of cowardice—a kind of "redeeming duel" [as practiced by German fraternities]. They did not regard him as having rehabilitated his ethical status, since he had acted bravely for a specific reason and not "out of the totality of his personality," as we would term it. In the religious sphere too, formal sanctification by the good works shown in external actions is supplanted by the value of the total personality pattern, which in the Spartan example would be an habitual temper of heroism. A similar principle applies to social achievements of all sorts. If they demonstrate "love for one's fellow man," then ethical systematization of this kind requires that the actor possess the charisma of "goodness."

It is important that the specific action be really symptomatic of the total character and that no significance be attached to it when it is a result of accident. Thus, this ethic of inwardness (*Gesinnungsethik*), in its most highly systematized forms, may make increased demands at the level of the total personality and yet be more tolerant in regard to particular transgressions. But this is not always the case, and the ethic of inwardness is generally the most distinctive form of ethical rigorism. On the one hand, a total personality pattern with positive religious qualifications may be regarded as a divine gift, the presence of which will manifest itself in a general orientation to whatever is demanded by religion, namely a pattern of life integrally and methodically oriented to the values of religion. On the other hand, a religious total personality pattern may be envisaged as something which may in principle be acquired through training in goodness. Of course this training itself will consist of a rationalized, methodical direction of the entire pattern of life, and not an accumulation of single, unrelated actions. Although these two views of the origin of a religious total personality pattern produce very similar practical results, yet one particular result of the methodical training of the total personality pattern is that the social and ethical quality of actions falls into secondary importance, while the religious effort expended upon oneself becomes of primary importance. Consequently, religious good works with a social orientation become mere instruments of *self-perfection*: a methodology of salvation.

3. *Salvation Through Self-Perfection*

Now ethical religions are by no means the first to produce such a "methodology" of salvation. On the contrary, highly systematized procedures frequently played significant roles in those awakenings to charismatic rebirth which promised the acquisition of magical powers. This animistic trend of thinking entailed belief in the incarnation of a new soul within one's own body, the possession of one's soul by a powerful demon, or the removal of one's soul to a realm of spirits. In all cases the possibility of attaining superhuman actions and powers was involved. "Other-worldly" goals were of course completely lacking in all this. What is more, this capacity for ecstasy might be used for the most diverse purposes. Thus, only by acquiring a new soul through rebirth can the warrior achieve superhuman deeds of heroism. The original sense of "rebirth" as producing either a hero or a magician remains present in all vestigial initiation ceremonies, e.g., the reception of youth into the religious brotherhood of the phratry and their equipment with the paraphernalia of war, or the decoration of youth with the insignia of manhood in China and India (where the members of the higher castes are termed the "twice-born"). All these ceremonies were originally associated with activities which produced or symbolized ecstasy, and the only purpose of the associated training is the testing or arousing of the capacity for ecstasy.

Ecstasy as an instrument of salvation or self-deification, our exclusive interest here, may have the essential character of an acute mental aberration or possession, or else the character of a chronically heightened idiosyncratic religious mood, tending either toward greater intensity of life or toward alienation from life. This escalated, intensified religious mood can be of either a more contemplative or a more active type. It should go without saying that a methodical approach to sanctification was not the means used to produce the state of acute ecstasy. Rather, the various methods for breaking down organic inhibitions were of primary importance in producing ecstasy. Organic inhibitions were broken down by the production of acute toxic states induced by alcohol, tobacco, or other drugs which have intoxicating effects; by music and dance; by sexuality; or by a combination of all three—in short by orgy. Ecstasy was also produced by the provocation of hysterical or epileptoid seizures among those with predispositions toward such paroxysms, which in turn produced orgiastic states in others. However, these acute ecstasies are transitory in their nature and apt to leave but few positive traces on everyday behavior. Moreover, they lack the meaningful content revealed by prophetic religion.

It would appear that a much more enduring possession of the charismatic condition is promised by those milder forms of euphoria which may be experienced as either a dreamlike mystical illumination or a more active and ethical conversion. Furthermore, they produce a meaningful relationship to the world, and they correspond in quality to evaluations of an eternal order or an ethical god such as are proclaimed by prophecy. We have already seen that magic is acquainted with a systematic procedure of sanctification for the purpose of evoking charismatic qualities, in addition to its last resort to the acute orgy. For professional magicians and warriors need permanent states of charisma as well as acute ecstasies.

Not only do the prophets of ethical salvation not need orgiastic intoxication, but it actually stands in the way of the systematic ethical patterning of life they require. For this reason, the primary target of Zoroaster's indignant ethical rationalism was orgiastic ecstasy, particularly the intoxicating cult of the *soma* sacrifice, which he deemed unworthy of man and cruel to beasts. For the same reason, Moses directed his rationalized ethical attack against the orgy of the dance, just as many founders or prophets of ethical religion attacked "whoredom," i.e., orgiastic temple prostitution. As the process of rationalization went forward, the goal of methodically planned religious sanctification increasingly transformed the acute intoxication induced by orgy into a milder but more permanent *habitus,* and moreover one that was consciously possessed. This transformation was strongly influenced by, among other things, the particular concept of the divine that was entertained. The ultimate purpose to be served by the planned procedure of sanctification remained everywhere the same purpose which was served in an acute way by the orgy, namely the incarnation within man of a supernatural being, and therefore presently of a god. Stated differently, the goal was self-deification. Only now this incarnation had to become a continuous personality pattern, so far as possible. Thus, the entire procedure for achieving consecration was directed to attaining this possession of the god himself here on earth.

But wherever there is belief in a transcendental god, all-powerful in contrast to his creatures, the goal of methodical sanctification can no longer be self-deification in this sense and must become the acquisition of those religious qualities the god demands in men. Hence the goal of sanctification becomes oriented to the world beyond and to ethics. The aim is no longer to possess god, for this cannot be done, but either to become his instrument or to be spiritually suffused by him. Spiritual suffusion is obviously closer to self-deification than is instrumentality. This difference had important consequences for methodic sanctification itself, as we shall later explain. But in the beginning of this development there were important points of agreement between the methods directed at instrumentality and those directed at spiritual suffusion. In both cases the average man had to eliminate from his everyday life whatever was not godlike, so that he himself might become more like god. The primary ungodlike factors were actually the average *habitus* of the human body and the everyday world, as those are given by nature.

At this early point in the development of soteriological methodology of sanctification, it was still directly linked with its magical precursor, the methods of which it merely rationalized and accommodated to its new views concerning the nature of the superhuman and the significance of religious sanctification. Experience taught that by the hysteroid "deadening" of the bodies of those with special religious qualifications it was possible to render such bodies anesthetic or cataleptic and to produce in them by suggestion sundry actions that normal neurological functioning could never produce. It had also been learned from experience that all sorts of visionary and spiritual phenomena might easily appear during such states. In different persons, these phenomena might consist in speaking with strange tongues, manifesting hypnotic and other suggestive powers, experiencing impulses toward mystical illumination and ethical conversion, or experiencing profound anguish over one's sins and joyous emotion deriving from suffusion by the spirit of the god. These states might even follow each other in rapid succession. It was a further lesson of experience that all these extraordinary capacities and manifestations would disappear following a surrender to the natural functions and needs of the body, or a surrender to the distracting interests of everyday life. As the yearning for salvation developed, men everywhere drew [negative] inferences about the relationship of mental states to the natural functioning of the body and to the social and economic requirements of everyday life.

The specific soteriological methods and procedures for achieving sanctification are, in their most highly developed forms, practically all of Indian provenience. In India they were undoubtedly developed in connection with procedures for the magical coercion of spirits. Even in India these procedures increasingly tended to become a methodology of self-deification, and indeed they never lost this tendency. Self-deification was the prevalent goal of sanctification, from the beginnings of the *soma* cult of intoxication in ancient Vedic times up through the development of sublime methods of intellectualist ecstasy and the elaboration of erotic orgies (whether in coarser or more refined form, and whether actually enacted in behavior or only imaginatively enacted within the cult), which to this day dominate the most popular form of Hindu religion, the cult of Krishna. This sublimated type of intellectualist ecstasy and an attenuated method of orgiastic dervishism were introduced into Islam via Sufism. To this day Indians are still their typical carriers even as far afield as Bosnia (according to a recent statement by Dr. Frank).[2]

The two greatest powers of religious rationalism in history, the Roman church in the Occident and Confucianism in China, consistently suppressed this type of ecstasy in their domains. Christianity also sublimated ecstasy into semi-erotic mysticism such as that of Saint Bernard, fervent Mariolatry, the quietism of the Counter-Reformation, and the emotional piety of Zinzendorf. The specifically extraordinary nature of the experiences characteristic of all orgiastic cults, and particularly of all erotic ones, accounts for their having exerted no influence on everyday life, or at least in the direction of rationalization or systematization—as is seen clearly in the fact that the Hindu and (in general) the dervish religiosities produced no methodology that aimed at the control of everyday living.

4. *The Certainty of Grace and the Religious* Virtuosi

Yet the gap between unusual and routine religious experiences tends to be eliminated by evolution towards the systematization and rationalization of the methods for attaining religious sanctification. Out of the unlimited variety of subjective conditions which may be engendered by methodical procedures of sanctification, certain of them may finally emerge as of central importance, not only because they represent psychophysical states of extraordinary quality, but because they also appear to provide a secure and continuous possession of the distinctive religious acquirement. This is the *assurance of grace* (*certitudo salutis, perseverantia gratiae*). This certainly may be characterized by a more mystical or by a more actively ethical coloration, about which more will be said presently. But in either case, it constitutes the conscious possession of a lasting, integrated foundation for the conduct of life. To heighten the conscious awareness of this religious possession, orgiastic ecstasy and irrational, merely irritating emotional methods of deadening sensation are replaced, principally by planned reductions of bodily functioning, such as can be achieved by continuous malnutrition, sexual abstinence, regulation of respiration, and the like. In addition, thinking and other psychic processes are trained in a systematic concentration of the soul upon whatever is alone essential in religion. Examples of such psychological training are found in the Hindu techniques of Yoga, the continuous repetition of sacred syllables (e.g., *Om*), meditation focused on circles and other geometrical figures, and various exercises designed to effect a planned evacuation of the consciousness.

But in order to further secure continuity and uniformity in the possession of the religious good, the rationalization of the methodology of sanctification finally evolved even beyond the methods just mentioned to an apparent inversion, a planned limitation of the exercises to those devices which tend to insure continuity of the religious mood. This meant the abandonment of all techniques that are irrational from the viewpoint of hygiene. For just as every sort of intoxication, whether it be the orgiastic ecstasy of heroes, erotic orgies or the ecstasy of terpsichorean frenzies, inevitably culminates in physical collapse, so hysterical suffusion with religious emotionalism leads to psychic collapse, which in the religious sphere is experienced as a state of profound abandonment by god.

In Greece the cultivation of disciplined martial heroism finally attenuated the warrior ecstasy into the perpetual equableness of *sophrosyne*, tolerating only the purely musical, rhythmically engendered forms of *ekstasis*, and carefully evaluating the ethos of music for political correctness. In the same way, but in a more thorough manner, Confucian rationalism permitted only the pentatonic scale in music. Similarly, the monastic procedural plan for attaining sanctification developed increasingly in the direction of rationalization, culminating in India in the salvation methodology of ancient Buddhism and in the Occident in the Jesuit monastic order which exerted the greatest historical influence. Thus, all these methodologies of sanctification developed a combined physical and psychic regimen and an equally methodical regulation of the manner and scope of all thought and action, thus producing in the individual the most completely alert, voluntary, and anti-instinctual control over his own physical and psychological processes, and insuring the systematic regulation of life in subordination to the religious end. The goals, the specific contents, and the actual results of the planned procedures were very variable.

That people differ widely in their religious capacities was found to be true in every religion based on a systematic procedure of sanctification, regardless of the specific goal of sanctification and the particular manner in which it was implemented. As it had been recognized that not everyone possesses the charisma by which he might evoke in himself the experiences leading to rebirth as a magician, so it was also recognized that not everyone possesses the charisma that makes possible the continuous maintenance in everyday life of the distinctive religious mood which assures the lasting certainty of grace. Therefore, rebirth seemed to be accessible only to an aristocracy of those possessing religious qualifications. Just as magicians had been recognized as possessing distinctive magical qualities, so also the religious virtuosi who work methodically at their salvation now became a distinctive religious "status group" within the community of the faithful, and within this circle they attained what is specific to every status group, a social honor of their own.

In India all the sacred laws concerned themselves with the ascetic in this sense, since most of the Hindu religions of salvation were monastic. The earliest Christian sources represent these religious virtuosi as comprising a particular category, distinguished from their comrades in the congregation, and they later constituted the monastic orders. In Protestantism they formed the ascetic sects or pietistic conventicles. In Judaism they were the *perushim* (*Pharisaioi*), an aristocracy with respect to salvation which stood in contrast to *am haarez*. In Islam they were the dervishes, and among the dervishes the particular virtuosi were the authentic Sufis. In the [Russian] Skoptsy sect they constituted the esoteric community of the castrated. We shall later return to the important sociological consequences of these groups.

When methodical techniques for attaining sanctification stressed ethical conduct based on religious sentiment, one practical result was the transcendence of particular desires and emotions of raw human nature which had not hitherto been controlled by religion. We must determine for each particular religion whether it regarded cowardice, brutality, selfishness, sensuality, or some other natural drive as the one most prone to divert the individual from his charismatic character. This matter belongs among the most important substantive characteristics of any particular religion. But the methodical religious doctrine of sanctification always remains, in this sense of transcending human nature, an ethic of virtuosi. Like magical charisma, it always requires demonstration by the virtuosi. As we have already established, religious virtuosi possess authentic certainty of their sanctification only as long as their own virtuoso religious temper continues to maintain itself in spite of all temptations. This holds true whether the religious adept is a brother in a world-conquering order like that of the Muslims at the time of Umar or whether he is a world-fleeing ascetic like most monks of either the Christian or the less consistent Jainist type. It is equally true of the Buddhist monk, a virtuoso of world-rejecting contemplation, the ancient Christian, who was an exponent of passive martyrdom, and the ascetic Protestant, a virtuoso of the demonstration of religious merit in one's calling. Finally, this holds true of the formal legalism of the Pharisaic Jew and of the acosmistic goodness of such persons as St. Francis. This maintenance of the certainty of sanctification varied in its specific character, depending on the type of religious salvation involved, but it always —both in the case of the Buddhist *arhat* and the case of the early Christian—required the upholding of religious and ethical standards, and hence the avoidance of at least the most corrupt sins.

Demonstration of the certainty of grace takes very different forms, depending on the concept of religious salvation in the particular religion. In early Christianity, a person of positive religious qualification, namely one who had been baptized, was bound never again to fall into a mortal sin. "Mortal sin" designates the type of sin which destroys religious qualification. Therefore, it is unpardonable, or at least capable of remission only at the hands of someone specially qualified, by virtue of his possession of charisma, to endow the sinner anew with religious charisma (the loss of which the sin documented). When this virtuoso doctrine became untenable in practice within the ancient Christian communities, the Montanist group clung firmly and consistently to one virtuoso requirement, that the sin of cowardice remain unpardonable, quite as the Islamic religion of heroic warriors unfailingly punished apostasy with death. Accordingly, the Montanists segregated themselves from the mass church of the average Christians when the persecutions under Decius and Diocletian made even this virtuoso requirement impractical, in view of the interest of the priests in maintaining the largest possible membership in the community.

N O T E S

1. The present and the following two sections constitute a single section in the German edition, entitled "The Different Roads to Salvation and Their Influence on Conduct."
2. Perhaps C. Frank, author of *Studien zur babylonischen Religion*, I, 1911. (W)

X

Asceticism, Mysticism and Salvation

1. Asceticism: World-Rejecting and Inner-Worldly

As we have already stated at a number of points, the specific character of the certification of salvation and also of the associated practical conduct is completely different in religions which differently represent the character of the promised salvation, the possession of which assures blessedness. Salvation may be viewed as the distinctive gift of active ethical behavior performed in the awareness that god directs this behavior, i.e, that the actor is an instrument of god. We shall designate this type of attitude toward salvation, which is characterized by a methodical procedure for achieving religious salvation, as "ascetic." This designation is for our purposes here, and we do not in any way deny that this term may be and has been used in another and wider sense. The contrast between our usage and the wider usage will become clearer later on in this work.

Religious virtuosity, in addition to subjecting the natural drives to a systematic patterning of life, always leads to a radical ethico-religious critique of the relationship to society, the conventional virtues of which are inevitably unheroic and utilitarian. Not only do the simple, "natural" virtues within the world not guarantee salvation, but they actually place salvation in hazard by producing illusions as to that which alone is indispensable. The "world" in the religious sense, i.e., the domain of social relationships, is therefore a realm of temptations. The world is full of temptations, not only because it is the site of sensual pleasures which are ethically irrational and completely diverting from things divine, but even more because it fosters in the religiously average person complacent self-sufficiency and self-righteousness in the fulfillment of common obligations, at the expense of the uniquely necessary concentration on active achievements leading to salvation.

Concentration upon the actual pursuit of salvation may entail a formal withdrawal from the "world": from social and psychological ties with the family, from the possession of worldly goods, and from political, economic, artistic, and erotic activities—in short, from all creaturely interests. One with such an attitude may regard any participation in these affairs as an acceptance of the world, leading to alienation from god. This is "world-rejecting asceticism" (weltablehnende Askese).

On the other hand, the concentration of human behavior on activities leading to salvation may require participation within the world (or more precisely: within the institutions of the world but in opposition to them) on the basis of the religious individual's piety and his qualifications as the elect instrument of god. This is "inner-worldly asceticism" (innerweltliche Askese). In this case the world is presented to the religious virtuoso as his responsibility. He may have the obligation to transform the world in accordance with his ascetic ideals, in which case the ascetic will become a rational reformer or revolutionary on the basis of a theory of natural rights. Examples of this were seen in the "Parliament of the Saints" under Cromwell, in the Quaker State of Pennsylvania, and in the conventicle communism of radical Pietism.

As a result of the different levels of religious qualification, such a congery of ascetics always tends to become an aristocratic, exclusive organization within or, more precisely, outside the world of the average people who surround these ascetics—in principle, it is not different from a "class". Such a religiously specialized group might be able to master the world, but it still could not raise the religious endowment of the average person to its own level of virtuosity. Any rational religious associations that ignored this obvious fact were bound sooner or later to experience in their own everyday existence the consequences of differences in religious endowment.

From the point of view of the basic values of asceticism, the world as a whole continues to constitute a *massa perditionis*. The only remaining alternative is a renunciation of the demand that the world conform to religious claims. Consequently, if a demonstration of religious fidelity is still to be made within the institutional structure of the world, then the world, for the very reason that it inevitably remains a natural vessel of sin, becomes a challenge for the demonstration of the ascetic temper and for the strongest possible attacks against the world's sins. The world abides in the lowly state of all things of the flesh. Therefore, any sensuous surrender to the world's goods may imperil concentration upon and possession of the ultimate good of salvation, and may be a symptom of unholiness of spirit and impossibility of rebirth. Nevertheless, the world as a creation of god, whose power comes to expression in it despite its creatureliness, provides the only medium through which one's unique religious charisma may prove itself by means of rational ethical conduct, so that one may become and remain certain of one's own state of grace.

Hence, as the field provided for this active certification, the order of the world in which the ascetic is situated becomes for him a vocation which he must fulfill rationally. As a consequence, and although the enjoyment of wealth is forbidden to the ascetic, it becomes his vocation to engage in economic activity which is faithful to rationalized ethical requirements and which conforms to strict legality. If success supervenes upon such acquisitive activity, it is regarded as the manifestation of god's blessing upon the labor of the pious man and of god's pleasure with his economic pattern of life.

Any excess of emotional feeling for one's fellow man is prohibited as being a deification of the creaturely, which denies the unique value of the divine gift of grace. Yet it is man's vocation to participate rationally and soberly in the various rational organizations (*Zweckverbände*) of the world and in their objective goals as set by god's creation. Similarly, any eroticism that tends to deify the human creature is proscribed. On the other hand, it is a divinely imposed vocation of man "to soberly produce children" (as the Puritans expressed it) within marriage. Then, too, there is a prohibition against the exercise of force by an individual against other human beings for reasons of passion or revenge, and above all for purely personal motives. However, it is divinely enjoined that the rationally ordered state shall suppress and punish sins and rebelliousness. Finally, all personal secular enjoyment of power is forbidden as a deification of the creaturely, though it is held that a rational legal order within society is pleasing to god.

The person who lives as a worldly ascetic is a rationalist, not only in the sense that he rationally systematizes his own conduct, but also in his rejection of everything that is ethically irrational, esthetic, or dependent upon his own emotional reactions to the world and its institutions. The distinctive goal always remains the alert, methodical control of one's own pattern of life and behavior. This type of inner-worldly asceticism included, above all, ascetic Protestantism, which taught the principle of loyal fulfillment of obligations within the framework of the world as the sole method of proving religious merit, though its several branches demonstrated this tenet with varying degrees of consistency.

2. *Mysticism versus Asceticism*

But the distinctive content of salvation may not be an active quality of conduct, that is, an awareness of having executed the divine will; it may instead be a subjective condition of a distinctive kind, the most notable form of which is mystic illumination. This too is confined to a minority who have particular religious qualifications, and among them only as the end product of the systematic execution of a distinctive type of activity, namely contemplation. For the activity of contemplation to succeed in achieving its goal of mystic illumination, the extrusion of all everyday mundane interests is always required. According to the experience of the Quakers, God can speak within one's soul only when the creaturely element in man is altogether silent. All contemplative mysticism from Lao Tzu and the Buddha up to Tauler [c. 1300–1361] is in agreement with this notion, if not with these very words.

These beliefs may result in absolute flight from the world. Such a contemplative flight from the world, characteristic of ancient Buddhism and to some degree characteristic of all Asiatic and Near Eastern forms of salvation, seems to resemble the ascetic world view—but it is necessary to make a very clear distinction between the two. In the sense employed here, "world-rejecting asceticism" is primarily oriented to activity within the world. Only activity within the world helps the ascetic to attain that for which he strives, a capacity for action by god's grace. The ascetic derives renewed assurances of his state of grace from his awareness that his possession of the central religious salvation gives him the power to act and his awareness that through his actions he serves god. He feels himself to be a warrior in behalf of god, regardless of who the enemy is and what the means of doing battle are. Furthermore, his opposition to the world is felt, not as a flight, but as a repeated victory over ever new temptations which he is bound to combat actively, time and again. The ascetic who rejects the world sustains at least the negative inner relationship with it which is presupposed in the struggle against it. It is therefore more appropriate in his case to speak of a "rejection of the world" than of a "flight from the world." Flight is much more characteristic of the contemplative mystic.

In contrast to asceticism, contemplation is primarily the quest to achieve rest in god and in him alone. It entails inactivity, and in its most consistent form it entails the cessation of thought, of everything that in any way reminds one of the world, and of course the absolute minimization of all outer and inner activity. By these paths the mystic achieves that subjective condition which may be enjoyed as the possession of, or mystical union (*unio mystica*) with, the divine. This is a distinctive organization of the emotions which seems to promise a certain type of knowledge. To be sure, the subjective emphasis may be more upon the extraordinary content of this knowledge or more upon the emotional coloration of the possession of this knowledge; objectively, the latter is decisive.

The unique character of mystical knowledge consists in the fact that, although it becomes more incommunicable the more it is specifically mystical, it is nevertheless recognized as knowledge. For mystical knowledge is not new knowledge of any facts or doctrines, but rather the perception of an overall meaning in the world. This usage of "knowledge" is intended wherever the term occurs in the numerous formulations of mystics; it denotes a practical form of knowledge. Such *gnosis* is basically a "possession" of something from which there may be derived a new practical orientation to the world, and under certain circumstances even new and communicable items of knowledge. These items will constitute knowledge of values and non-values within the world. We are not interested here in the details of this general problem, but only in this negative effect upon "action" which can be ascribed to contemplation, in contrast to asceticism in our sense of the term.

Pending a more thorough exposition, we may strongly emphasize here that the distinction between world-rejecting asceticism and world-fleeing contemplation is of course fluid. For world-fleeing contemplation must originally be associated with a considerable degree of systematically rationalized patterning of life. Only this, indeed, leads to concentration upon the boon of salvation. Yet, rationalization is only an instrument for attaining the goal of contemplation and is of an essentially negative type, consisting in the avoidance of interruptions caused by nature and the social milieu. Contemplation does not necessarily become a passive abandonment to dreams or a simple self-hypnosis, though it may approach these states in practice. On the contrary, the distinctive road to contemplation is a very energetic concentration upon certain truths. The decisive aspect of this process is not the content of these truths, which frequently seems very simple to non-mystics, but rather the type of emphasis placed upon the truths. The mystical truths come to assume a central position within, and to exert an integrating influence upon, the total view of the world. In Buddhism, no one becomes one of the illuminated by explicitly affirming the obviously highly trivial formulations of the central Buddhist dogma, or even by achieving a penetrating understanding of the central dogma. The concentration of thought, together with the various other procedures for winning salvation, is only a means, not the goal. The illumination consists essentially in a unique quality of feeling or, more concretely, in the felt emotional unity of knowledge and volitional mood which provides the mystic with decisive assurance of his religious state of grace.

For the ascetic too, the perception of the divine through emotion and intellect is of central importance, only in his case feeling the divine is of a "motor" type, so to speak. This "feel" arises when he is conscious that he has succeeded in becoming a tool of his god, through rationalized ethical action completely oriented to god. But for the contemplative mystic, who neither desires to be nor can be the god's "instrument," but desires only to become the god's "vessel," the ascetic's ethical struggle, whether of a positive or a negative type, appears to be a perpetual externalization of the divine in the direction of some peripheral function. For this reason, ancient Buddhism recommended inaction as the precondition for the maintenance of the state of grace, and in any case Buddhism enjoined the avoidance of every type of rational, purposive activity, which it regarded as the most dangerous form of secularization. On the other hand, the contemplation of the mystic appears to the ascetic as indolent, religiously sterile, and ascetically reprehensible self-indulgence—a wallowing in self-created emotions prompted by the deification of the creaturely.

From the standpoint of a contemplative mystic, the ascetic appears, by virtue of his transcendental self-maceration and struggles, and especially by virtue of his ascetically rationalized conduct within the world, to be forever involved in all the burdens of created things, confronting insoluble tensions between violence and generosity, between matter-of-factness and love. The ascetic is therefore regarded as permanently alienated from unity with god, and as forced into contradictions and compromises that are alien to salvation. But from the converse standpoint of the ascetic, the contemplative mystic appears not to be thinking of god, the enhancement of his kingdom and glory, or the fulfillment of his will, but rather to be thinking exclusively about himself. Therefore the mystic lives in everlasting inconsistency, since by reason of the very fact that he is alive he must inevitably provide for the maintenance of his own life. This is particularly true when the contemplative mystic lives within the world and its institutions. There is a sense in which the mystic who flees the world is more dependent upon the world than is the ascetic. The ascetic can maintain himself as an anchorite, winning the certainty of his state of grace through the labors he expends in an effort to maintain himself as an anchorite. Not so the contemplative mystic. If he is to live consistently according to his theory, he must maintain his life only by means of what nature or men voluntarily donate to him. This requires that he live on berries in the woods, which are not always available, or on alms. This was actually the case among the most consistent Hindu *shramanas* (and it accounts also for the very strict injunction in all *bhikshu* regulations against receiving anything that has not been given freely).

In any case, the contemplative mystic lives on whatever gifts the world may present to him, and he would be unable to stay alive if the world were not constantly engaged in that very labor which the mystic brands as sinful and leading to alienation from god. For the Buddhist monk, agriculture is the most reprehensible of all occupations, because it causes violent injury to various forms of life in the soil. Yet the alms he collects consist principally of agricultural products. In circumstances like these, the mystic's inevitable feeling that he is an aristocrat with respect to salvation reaches striking expression, culminating in the mystic's abandonment of the world, the unilluminated, and those incapable of complete illumination, to their inevitable and ineluctable fate. It will be recalled that the central and almost sole lay virtue among the Buddhists was originally the veneration of the monks, who alone belonged to the religious community, and whom it was incumbent upon the laity to support with alms. However, it is a general rule that every human being "acts" in some fashion, and even the mystic perforce acts. Yet he minimizes activity just because it can never give him certainty of his state of grace, and what is more, because it may divert him from union with the divine. The ascetic, on the other hand, finds the certification of his state of grace precisely in his behavior in the world.

The contrast between the ascetic and mystical modes of behavior is clearest when the full implications of world-rejection and world-flight are not drawn. The ascetic, when he wishes to act within the world, that is, to practice inner-worldly asceticism, must become afflicted with a sort of happy closure of the mind regarding any question about the meaning of the world, for he must not worry about such questions. Hence, it is no accident that inner-worldly asceticism reached its most consistent development on the foundation of the Calvinist god's absolute inexplicability, utter remoteness from every human criterion, and un- searchableness as to his motives. Thus, the inner-worldly ascetic is the recognized "man of a vocation," who neither inquires about nor finds it necessary to inquire about the meaning of his actual practice of a voca- tion within the whole world, the total framework of which is not his responsibility but his god's. For him it suffices that through his rational actions in this world he is personally executing the will of god, which is unsearchable in its ultimate significance.

On the other hand, the contemplative mystic is concerned with perceiving the essential meaning of the world, but he cannot compre- hend it in a rational form, for the very reason that he has already con- ceived of the essential meaning of the world as a unity beyond all empirical reality. Mystical contemplation has not always resulted in a flight from the world in the sense of an avoidance of every contact with the social milieu. On the contrary, the mystic may also require of him- self the maintenance of his state of grace against every pressure of the mundane order, as an index of the enduring character of that very state of grace. In that case, even the mystic's position within the institutional framework of the world becomes a vocation, but one leading in an al- together different direction from any vocation produced by inner-worldly asceticism.

Neither asceticism nor contemplation affirms the world as such. The ascetic rejects the world's empirical character of creatureliness and ethical irrationality, and rejects its ethical temptations to sensual indulgence, to epicurean satisfaction, and to reliance upon natural joys and gifts. But at the same time he affirms individual rational activity within the institu- tional framework of the world, affirming it to be his responsibility as well as his means for securing certification of his state of grace. On the other hand, the contemplative mystic living within the world regards action, particularly action performed within the world's institutional framework, as in its very nature a temptation against which he must maintain his state of grace.

The contemplative mystic minimizes his activity by resigning him- self to the institutions of the world as it is, and lives in them incognito, so to speak, as those "that are quiet in the land" [Psalms, 35:20] have always done, since god has ordained once and for all that man must live in the world. The activity of the contemplative mystic within the world is characterized by a distinctive brokenness, colored by humility.

He is constantly striving to escape from activity in the world back to the quietness and inwardness of his god. Conversely, the ascetic, whenever he acts in conformity with his type, is certain to become god's instrument. For this reason the ascetic's humility, which he considers a necessary obligation incumbent upon a creature of god, is always of dubious genuineness. The success of the ascetic's action is a success of the god himself, who has contributed to the action's success, or at the very least the success is a special sign of divine blessing upon the ascetic and his activity. But for the genuine mystic, no success which may crown his activity within the world can have any significance with respect to salvation. For him, his maintenance of true humility within the world is his sole warranty for the conclusion that his soul has not fallen prey to the snares of the world. As a rule, the more the genuine mystic remains within the world, the more broken his attitude toward it becomes, in contrast to the proud aristocratic feeling with respect to salvation entertained by the contemplative mystic who lives apart from the world.

For the ascetic, the certainty of salvation always demonstrates itself in rational action, integrated as to meaning, end, and means, and governed by principles and rules. Conversely, for the mystic who actually possesses a subjectively appropriated state of salvation the result of this subjective condition may be anomism. His salvation manifests itself not in any sort of activity but in a subjective condition and its idiosyncratic quality. He feels himself no longer bound by any rule of conduct; regardless of his behavior, he is certain of salvation. With this consequence of mystical contemplation (with the feeling of πάντα μοι ἔξεστιν) Paul had to struggle; and in numerous other contexts the abandonment of rules for conduct has been an occasional result of the mystical quest for salvation.

For the ascetic, moreover, the divine imperative may require of human creatures an unconditional subjection of the world to the norms of religious virtue, and indeed a revolutionary transformation of the world for this purpose. In that event, the ascetic will emerge from his remote and cloistered cell to take his place in the world as a prophet in opposition to the world. But he will always demand of the world an ethically rational order and discipline, corresponding to his own methodical self-discipline. Now a mystic may arrive at a similar position in relation to the world. His sense of divine inwardness, the chronic and quiet euphoria of his solitary contemplative possession of substantively divine salvation, may become transformed into an acute feeling of sacred possession by or possession of the god who is speaking in and through him. He will then wish to bring eternal salvation to men as soon as they have prepared, as the mystic himself has done, a place for god upon earth, i.e., in their souls. But in this case the result will be the emergence of the mystic as a magician who causes his power to be felt among gods and demons; and this may have the practical consequences of the mystic's becoming a mystagogue, something which has actually happened very often.

If the mystic does not follow this path towards becoming a mystagogue, for a variety of reasons which we hope to discuss later, he may bear witness to his god by doctrine alone. In that case his revolutionary preaching to the world will be chiliastically irrational, scorning every thought of a rational order in the world. He will regard the absoluteness of his own universal acosmistic feeling of love as completely adequate for himself, and indeed regard this feeling as the only one acceptable to his god as the foundation for a mystically renewed community among men, because this feeling alone derives from a divine source. The transformation of a mysticism remote from the world into one characterized by chiliastic and revolutionary tendencies took place frequently, most impressively in the revolutionary mysticism of the sixteenth-century Baptists. The contrary transformation has also occurred, as in the conversion of John Lilburne to Quakerism.

To the extent that an inner-worldly religion of salvation is determined by contemplative features, the usual result is the acceptance of the given social structure, an acceptance that is relatively indifferent to the world but at least humble before it. A mystic of the type of Tauler completes his day's work and then seeks contemplative union with his god in the evening, going forth to his usual work the next morning, as Tauler movingly suggests, in the correct inner state. Similarly, Lao Tzu taught that one recognizes the man who has achieved union with the Tao by his humility and by his self-depreciation before other men. The mystic component in Lutheranism, for which the highest bliss available in this world is the ultimate *unio mystica*, was responsible (along with other factors) for the indifference of the Lutheran church towards the external organization of the preaching of the gospel, and also for that church's anti-ascetic and traditionalistic character.

In any case, the typical mystic is never a man of conspicuous social activity, nor is he at all prone to accomplish any rational transformation of the mundane order on the basis of a methodical pattern of life directed toward external success. Wherever genuine mysticism did give rise to communal action, such action was characterized by the acosmism of the mystical feeling of love. Mysticism may exert this kind of psychological effect, thus tending—despite the apparent demands of logic—to favor the creation of communities (*gemeinschaftsbildend*).

The core of the mystical concept of the oriental Christian church was a firm conviction that Christian brotherly love, when sufficiently strong and pure, must necessarily lead to unity in all things, even in dogmatic beliefs. In other words, men who sufficiently love one another, in the Johannine sense of mystical love, will also think alike and, because of the very irrationality of their common feeling, act in a solidary fashion which is pleasing to God. Because of this concept, the Eastern church could dispense with an infallibly rational authority in matters of doctrine. The same view is basic to the Slavophile conception of the community, both within and beyond the church. Some forms of this notion were also common in ancient Christianity. The same conception is at the basis of Muhammad's belief that formal doctrinal authorities can be dispensed with. Finally, this conception along with other factors accounts for the minimization of organization in the monastic communities of early Buddhism.

Conversely, to the extent that an inner-worldly religion of salvation is determined by distinctively ascetical tendencies, it always demands a practical rationalism, in the sense of the maximization of rational action as such, the maximization of a methodical systematization of the external conduct of life, and the maximization of the rational reorganization of the worldly arrangements (*Ordnungen*), whether monastic communities or theocracies.

3. *The Decisive Differences Between Oriental and Occidental Salvation*

The decisive historical difference between the predominantly oriental and Asiatic types of salvation religion and those found primarily in the Occident is that the former usually culminate in contemplation and the latter in asceticism. The great importance of this distinction, for our purely empirical consideration of religions, is in no way diminished by the fact that the distinction is a fluid one, recurrent combinations of mystical and ascetic characteristics demonstrating that these heterogeneous element may combine, as in the monastic religiosity of the Occident. For our concern is with the consequences for action.

In India, even so ascetical a planned procedure for achieving salvation as that of the Jain monks culminated in a purely contemplative and mystical ultimate goal; and in Eastern Asia, Buddhism became the characteristic religion of salvation. In the Occident, on the other hand, apart from a few representatives of a distinctive quietism found only in modern times, even religions of an explicitly mystical type regularly became transformed into an active pursuit of virtue, which was naturally ascetical in the main. Stated more precisely, there occurred along the way an inner selection of motivations which placed the primary preference upon some type of active conduct, generally a type pointing toward asceticism, and which implemented this motivational preference. Neither the mystical contemplativeness of St. Bernard and his followers, nor Franciscan spirituality, nor the contemplative trends among the Baptists and the Jesuits, nor even the emotional suffusions of Zinzendorf were able to prevent either the community or the individual mystic from attributing superior importance to conduct and to the demonstration of grace through conduct, though this was conceptualized very differently in each case, ranging from pure asceticism to attenuated contemplation. It will be recalled that Meister Eckehart finally placed Martha above Mary, notwithstanding the pronouncements of Jesus.[1]

But to some extent this emphasis upon conduct was characteristic of Christianity from the very outset. Even in the earliest period, when all sorts of irrational charismatic gifts of the spirit were regarded as the decisive hallmark of sanctity, Christian apologetics had already given a distinctive answer to the question of how one might distinguish the divine origin of the pneumatic achievements of Christ and the Christians from comparable phenomena that were of Satanic or demonic origin: this answer was that the manifest effect of Christianity upon the morality of its adherents certified its divine origin. No Hindu could make this kind of statement.

There are a number of reasons for this basic different between the salvation religions, Orient and Occident, but at this point it is only necessary to stress the following aspects of the distinction.

1. The concept of a transcendental, absolutely omnipotent god, implying the utterly subordinate and creaturely character of the world created by him out of nothing, arose in Asia Minor and was imposed upon the Occident. One result of this for the Occident was that any planned procedure for achieving salvation faced a road that was permanently closed to any self-deification and to any genuinely mystical possession of god, at least in the strict sense of the term, because this appeared to be a blasphemous deification of a mere created thing. The path to the ultimate pantheistic consequences of the mystical position was blocked, this path being always regarded as heterodox. On the contrary, salvation was always regarded as having the character of an ethical justification before god, which ultimately could be accomplished and maintained only by some sort of active conduct within the world. The certification of the really divine quality of the mystical possession of salvation (certification before the ultimate judgment of the mystic him-

self) could be arrived at through the path of activity alone. Activity in turn introduced into mysticism paradoxes, tensions, and the loss of the mystic's ultimate union with god. This was spared to Hindu mysticism. For the occidental mystic, the world is a "work" which has been created and is not simply given for all eternity, not even in its institutions, as in the view of the Asiatic mystic. Consequently, in the Occident mystical salvation could not be found simply in the consciousness of an absolute union with a supreme and wise order of things as the only true being. Nor, on the other hand, could a work of divine origin ever be regarded in the Occident as a possible object of absolute rejection, as it was in the flight from the world characteristic of the Orient.

2. This decisive contrast between oriental and occidental religions is closely related to the character of Asiatic salvation religions as pure religions of intellectuals who never abandoned the "meaningfulness" of the empirical world. For the Hindu, there was actually a way leading directly from insight into the ultimate consequences of the *karma* chain of causality, to illumination, and thence to a unity of knowledge and action. This way remained forever closed to every religion that faced the absolute paradox of a perfect god's creation of a permanently imperfect world. Indeed, in this latter type of religion, the intellectual mastery of the world leads away from god, not toward him. From the practical point of view, those instances of occidental mysticism which have a purely philosophical foundation stand closest to the Asiatic type.

3. Further to be considered in accounting for the basic distinction between occidental and oriental religion are various practical factors. Particular emphasis must be placed on the fact that the Roman Occident alone developed and maintained a rational law, for various reasons yet to be explained. In the Occident the relationship of man to god became, in a distinctive fashion, a sort of legally definable relationship of subjection. Indeed, the question of salvation can be settled by a sort of legal process, a method which was later distinctively developed by Anselm of Canterbury. Such a legalistic procedure of achieving salvation could never be adopted by the oriental religions which posited an impersonal divine power or which posited, instead of a god standing above the world, a god standing within a world which is self-regulated by the causal chains of *karma*. Nor could the legalistic direction be taken by religions teaching concepts of Tao, belief in the celestial ancestor gods of the Chinese emperor, or, above all, belief in the Asiatic popular gods. In all these cases the highest form of piety took a pantheistic form, and one which turned practical motivations toward contemplation.

4. Another aspect of the rational character of a methodical procedure for achieving salvation was in origin partly Roman, partly Jewish. The

Greeks, despite all the misgivings of the urban patriciate in regard to the Dionysiac cult of intoxication, set a positive value upon ecstasy, both the acute orgiastic type of divine intoxication and the milder form of euphoria induced primarily by rhythm and music, as engendering an awareness of the uniquely divine. Indeed, among the Greeks the ruling stratum especially lived with this mild form of ecstasy from their very childhood. Since the time when the discipline of the hoplites had become dominant, Greece had lacked a stratum possessing the prestige of the office nobility in Rome. Social relationships in Greece were in all respects simpler and less feudal. In Rome the nobles, who constituted a rational nobility of office of increasing range, and who possessed whole cities and provinces as client holdings of single families, completely rejected ecstasy, like the dance, as utterly unseemly and unworthy of a nobleman's sense of honor. This is obvious even in the terminology employed by the Romans to render the Greek word for ecstasy (*ekstasis*) into Latin: *superstitio*. Cultic dances were performed only among the most ancient colleges of priests, and in the specific sense of a round of dances, only among the *fratres arvales,* and then only behind closed doors, after the departure of the congregation. Most Romans regarded dancing and music as unseemly, and so Rome remained absolutely uncreative in these arts. The Romans experienced the same distaste towards the naked exercises in the *gymnasion,* which the Spartans had created as an arena for planned exercise. The Senate proscribed the Dionysiac cult of intoxication. The rejection by Rome's world-conquering military-official nobility of every type of ecstasy and of all preoccupation with individually planned procedures for attaining salvation (which corresponds closely to the equally strong antipathy of the Confucian bureaucracy towards all methodologies of salvation) was therefore one of the sources of a strictly empirical rationalism with a thoroughly practical political orientation.

As Christian communities developed in the Occident, they found this contempt for ecstatic procedures to be characteristic of all religion possible on essentially Roman territory. The Christian community of Rome in particular adopted this attitude against ecstasy quite consciously and consistently. In no instance did this community accept on its own initiative any irrational element, from charismatic prophecy to the greatest innovations in church music, into the religion or the culture. The Roman Christian community was infinitely poorer than the Hellenistic Orient and the community of Corinth, not only in theological thinkers but also, as the sources seem to suggest, in every sort of manifestation of the spirit (*pneuma*). Whether despite this lack of theology and *pneuma* or because of it, the soberly practical rationalism of Christianity, the most important legacy of Rome to the Christian church, almost everywhere set the tone of a dogmatic and ethical systematization of the faith, as is well known. The development of the methods for salvation in the Occident continued along similar lines. The ascetic requirements of the old Benedictine regulations and the reforms of Cluny are, when measured by Hindu or oriental standards, extremely modest and obviously adapted to novices recruited from the higher social circles. Yet, it is precisely in the Occident that *labor* emerges as the distinctive mark of Christian monasticism, and as an instrument of both hygiene and asceticism. This emphasis came to the strongest expression in the starkly simple, methodical regulations of the Cistercians. Even the mendicant monks, in contrast to their monastic counterparts in India, were forced into the service of the hierarchy and compelled to serve rational purposes shortly after their appearance in the Occident. These rational purposes included preaching, the supervision of heretics, and systematic charity, which in the Occident was developed into a regular enterprise (*Betrieb*). Finally, the Jesuit order expelled all the unhygienic elements of the older asceticism, becoming the most completely rational discipline for the purposes of the church. This development is obviously connected with the next point we are to consider.

5. The occidental church is a uniformly rational organization with a monarchical head and a centralized control of piety. That is, it is headed not only by a personal transcendental god, but also by a terrestrial ruler of enormous power, who actively controls the lives of his subjects. Such a figure is lacking in the religions of Eastern Asia, partly for historical reasons, partly because of the nature of the religions in question. Even Lamaism, which has a strong organization, does not have the rigidity of a bureaucracy, as we shall see later. The Asiatic hierarchs in Taoism and the other hereditary patriarchs of Chinese and Hindu sects were always partly mystagogues, partly the objects of anthropolatric veneration, and partly—as in the cases of the Dalai Lama and Tashi Lama—the chiefs of a completely monastic religion of magical character. Only in the Occident, where the monks became the disciplined army of a rational bureaucracy of office, did other-worldly asceticism become increasingly systematized into a methodology of active, rational conduct of life.

Moreover, only in the Occident was the additional step taken—by ascetic Protestantism—of transferring rational asceticism into the life of the world. The inner-worldly order of dervishes in Islam cultivated a planned procedure for achieving salvation, but this procedure, for all its variations, was oriented ultimately to the mystical quest for salvation of the Sufis. This search of the dervishes for salvation, deriving from

Indian and Persian sources, might have orgiastic, spiritualistic, or contemplative characteristics in different instances, but in no case did it constitute "asceticism" in the special sense of that term which we have employed. Indians have played a leading role in dervish orgies as far afield as Bosnia [cf. *ix*:3 above]. The asceticism of the dervishes is not, like that of ascetic Protestants, a religious ethic of vocation, for the religious actions of the dervishes have very little relationship to their secular occupations, and in their scheme secular vocations have at best a purely external relationship to the planned procedure of salvation. Even so, the procedure of salvation might exert direct effects on one's occupational behavior. The simple, pious dervish is, other things being equal, more reliable than a non-religious man, in the same way that the pious Parsee is prosperous as a businessman because of his strict adherence to the rigid injunction to be honest.

But an unbroken unity integrating in systematic fashion an ethic of vocation in the world with assurance of religious salvation was the unique creation of ascetic Protestantism alone. Furthermore, only in the Protestant ethic of vocation does the world, despite all its creaturely imperfections, possess unique and religious significance as the object through which one fulfills his duties by rational behavior according to the will of an absolutely transcendental god. When success crowns rational, sober, purposive behavior of the sort not oriented to worldly acquisition, such success is construed as a sign that god's blessing rests upon such behavior. This innerworldly asceticism had a number of distinctive consequences not found in any other religion. This religion demanded of the believer, not celibacy, as in case of the monk, but the avoidance of all erotic pleasure; not poverty, but the elimination of all idle and exploitative enjoyment of unearned wealth and income, and the avoidance of all feudalistic, sensuous ostentation of wealth; not the ascetic death-in-life of the cloister, but an alert, rationally controlled patterning of life, and the avoidance of all surrender to the beauty of the world, to art, or to one's own moods and emotions. The clear and uniform goal of this asceticism was the disciplining and methodical organization of conduct. Its typical representative was the "man of a vocation" or "professional" (*Berufsmensch*), and its unique result was the rational organization of social relationships.

NOTES

1. See Meister Eckehart (b. c. 1260, d. 1327), *Schriften* (Düsseldorf: Diederichs, 1959), Hermann Büttner, trans. and ed., p. 259ff.; this is his sermon on Luke 10:38.

xi

Soteriology or Salvation from Outside

1. Salvation Through the Savior's Incarnation and Through Institutional Grace

Another view regarding the attainment of salvation rejects the individual's own labors as completely inadequate for the purpose of salvation. From this point of view, salvation is accessible only as a consequence of the achievement of some greatly endowed hero, or even the achievement of a god who has become incarnate for this very purpose and whose grace will redound to the credit of his devotees, *ex opere operato.* Grace might become available as a direct effect of magical activities, or it might be distributed to men out of the excess of grace which had accumulated as a result of the human or divine savior's achievements.

Beliefs in salvation through the abundant grace accumulated by a hero's or incarnate god's achievement was aided by the evolution of soteriological myths, above all myths of the struggling or suffering god, who in his various possible manifestations had become incarnate and descended upon earth or even traveled into the realm of the dead. Instead of a god of nature, particularly a sun god who struggles with other powers of nature, especially with darkness and cold, and having won a victory over them ushers in the spring, there now arises on the basis of the salvation myths a savior who, like Christ, liberates men from the power of the demons. The savior type is further exemplified in the Gnostics' seven archons, who save men from enslavement to the astrological determinism of fate;[1] and in Gnosticism's savior, who at the command of the concealed and gracious god rescues the world from the corruption brought upon it by an inferior creator god (Demiurge or Jehovah). The savior, as in the case of Jesus, may save men from the hard-hearted hypocrisy of the world and its reliance on good works. Or again, the salvation may be from the oppressive consciousness of sin, arising from man's awareness of the impossibility of filling certain requirements of the law, as was the case with Paul and, somewhat differently, with Augustine and Luther. Finally, the salvation may be from the abysmal corruption of the individual's own sinful nature, as in

Augustine. In all these cases the savior led man upward toward a secure haven in the grace and love of a good god.

To accomplish these purposes the savior must fight with dragons or evil demons, depending on the character of the salvation in question. In some cases he is not able to engage in such battle right away—he is often a child completely pure of sin—and so he must grow up in concealment or must be slaughtered by his enemies and journey to the realm of the dead in order to rise again and return victorious. From this particular belief may develop the view that the death of the savior is a tributary atonement for the power achieved over the souls of men by the devil as a result of men's sins. This is the view of earliest Christianity. Or the death of the savior may be viewed as a means of mollifying the wrath of god, before whom the savior appears as an intercessor for men, as in the cases of Christ, Muhammad, and other prophets and saviors. Again, the savior may, like the ancient bearer of salvation in magical religions, bring man forbidden knowledge of fire, technical arts, writing, or possibly the lore requisite for subjugating demons in this world or on the way toward heaven, as in Gnosticism. Finally, the decisive achievement of the savior may be contained, not in his concrete struggles and sufferings, but in the ultimate metaphysical root of the entire process. This ultimate metaphysical basis would of course be the incarnation of a god as the only device for bridging the gap between god and his creatures. This metaphysical conception constituted the culmination of Greek speculation about salvation, in Athanasius. The incarnation of god presented men with the opportunity to participate significantly in god, or as Irenaeus had already phrased it, "enabled men to become gods." The post-Athanasian philosophical formula for this was that god, by becoming incarnate, had assumed the essence (in the Platonic sense) of humanity. This formula points up the metaphysical significance of the concept of *homoousios* [i.e., of the Son who is "of the same substance" as the Father, the formulation of the Nicaean Creed].

According to another view, the god might not be content with one single act of incarnation, but as a result of the permanence of the world, which is practically axiomatic in Asiatic thought, he might become incarnate at various intervals or even continuously. Belief in continuous incarnation is the principal force of the *Mahayana* Buddhist idea of the *Bodhisattva*, though this idea is related to occasional utterances of the Buddha himself, in which he apparently expressed a belief in the limited duration of his doctrine on earth. Furthermore, the Bodhisattva was occasionally represented as a higher ideal than the Buddha, because the Bodhisattva forgoes his own entrance into *Nirvana*, which has only exemplary significance, to prolong his universal function in the service of mankind. Here again, the savior "sacrifices" himself. But just as Jesus was superior in his own time to the saviors of other competing soteriological cults, by virtue of the fact that he had been an actual person whose resurrection had been observed by his apostles, so the continuously corporeal and living incarnation of god in the Dalai Lama is the logical conclusion of every incarnation soteriology. But even when the divine distributor of grace lives on as an incarnation, and especially when he does not linger continuously on earth, certain more tangible means are required to maintain the adherence of the mass of the faithful, who wish to participate personally in the gifts of grace made available by their god. It is these more tangible instruments of grace, exhibiting a wide variety, which exert a decisive influence on the character of the religion.

Of an essentially magical nature is the view that one may incorporate divine power into himself by the physical ingestion of some divine substance, some sacred totemic animal in which a mighty spirit is incarnated, or some host that has been magically transformed into the body of a god. Equally magical is the notion that through participation in certain mysteries one may directly share the nature of the god and therefore be protected against evil powers. This is the case of sacramental grace.

Now the means of acquiring these divine blessings may take either a magical or a ritualistic form, and in either case they entail, not only belief in the savior or the incarnate living god, but also the existence of human priests or mystagogues. Moreover, the manner in which this divine grace is distributed depends in considerable measure on whether certifying proofs of the personal possession of charismatic gifts of grace are required of these earthly intermediaries between man and the savior. If certifying proofs are required, a religious functionary who no longer shares in such a state of grace, as for example a priest living in mortal sin, cannot legitimately mediate this grace by officiating at the sacraments. Such a strict consistency in the principle of charismatic distribution of grace was maintained by the Montanists, Donatists, and in general all those religious communities of Antiquity that based the organization of their church on the principle of prophetic-charismatic leadership. The outcome of this view was that not every bishop who occupied an office or possessed other credentials, but only those bishops who manifested the verification of prophecy or other witnesses of the spirit, could effectively distribute divine grace. This was at least the case when what was required was the distribution of grace to a penitent who had fallen into mortal sin.

When we leave this requirement, we are dealing with an altogether different notion of the distribution of grace. Now salvation supervenes by virtue of the grace which is distributed on a continuous basis by some institutional organization that has either divine or prophetic credentials for its establishment. For this type of operation we shall reserve the appellation of "institutional grace" (Anstaltsgnade). The institution may exert its power directly through purely magical sacraments or through its control over the accumulation of supernumerary achievements performed by officials or devotees, achievements which produce divine blessing or grace.

Wherever institutional grace operates consistently, three basic principles are involved. The first is extra ecclesiam nulla salus: salvation cannot be obtained apart from membership in a particular institution vested with the control of grace. The second principle is that it is not the personal charismatic qualification of the priest which determines the effectiveness of his distribution of divine grace. Third, the personal religious qualification of the individual in need of salvation is altogether a matter of indifference to the institution which has the power to distribute religious grace. That is, salvation is universal; it is accessible to other than the religious virtuosi. Indeed the religious virtuoso may easily fall into spiritual danger with respect to chances of salvation and the genuineness of his religious profession—and actually cannot fail to fall into this danger—if instead of relying ultimately on institutional grace he seeks to attain grace by his own unaided power, treading his own pathway to God. In this theory, all human beings are capable of finding salvation if they but obey god's requirements enough for the accession of grace distributed by the church to suffice for their attainment of salvation. The level of personal ethical accomplishment must therefore be made compatible with average human qualifications, and this in practice means that it will be set quite low. Whoever can achieve more in the ethical sphere, i.e., the religious virtuoso, may thereby, in addition to insuring his own salvation, accumulate good works for the credit of the institution, which will then distribute them to those in need of good works.

The viewpoint we have just described is the specific attitude of the Catholic church and determines its character as an institution of grace, which developed throughout many centuries but has been fixed since the time of Gregory the Great [ca. 600]. In practice, however, the viewpoint of the Catholic church has oscillated between a relatively magical and a relatively ethical and soteriological orientation.

The manner in which the dispensation of charismatic or of institutional grace influences the actual conduct of life of the adherents depends upon the preconditions which are attached to the granting of the means of grace. Thus there are similarities here to ritualism, to which sacramental and institutional grace dispensation accordingly show close affinity. Ethical religiosity is affected in the same direction in yet another respect, which may be of considerable significance: Every type of actual dispensation of grace by a person, regardless of whether his authority derives from personal charismatic gifts or his official status within an institution, has the net effect of weakening the demands of morality upon the individual, just as does ritualism. The vouchsafing of grace always entails an inner release of the person in need of salvation; it consequently facilitates his capacity to bear guilt and, other things being equal, it largely spares him the necessity of developing an individual pattern of life based on ethical foundations. The sinner knows that he may always receive absolution by engaging in some occasional religious practice or by performing some religious rite. It is particularly important that sins remain discrete actions, against which other discrete deeds may be set up as compensations or penances. Hence, value is attached to concrete individual acts rather than to a total personality pattern produced by asceticism, contemplation, or eternally vigilant self-control, a pattern that must constantly be demonstrated and determined anew. A further consequence is that no need is felt to attain the *certitudo salutis* by one's own powers, and so this category, which may in other circumstances have such significant ethical consequences, recedes in importance.

For the reasons just discussed, the perpetual control of an individual's life pattern by the official—whether father confessor or spiritual director—empowered to distribute grace, a control that in certain respects is very effective, is in practice very often cancelled by the circumstance that there is always grace remaining to be distributed anew. Certainly the institution of the confessional, especially when associated with penances, is ambivalent in its effects, depending upon the manner in which it is implemented. The poorly developed and rather general method of confession which was particularly characteristic of the Russian church, frequently taking the form of a collective admission of iniquity, was certainly no way to effect any permanent influence over conduct. Also, the confessional practice of the early Lutheran church was undoubtedly ineffective. The catalog of sins and penances in the Hindu sacred scriptures makes no distinction between ritual and ethical sins, and enjoins ritual obedience (or other forms of compliance which are in line with the status interests of the Brahmins) as virtually the sole method of atonement. As a consequence, the pattern of everyday life could be influenced by these religions only in the direction of traditionalism. Indeed, the sacramental grace of the Hindu *gurus* even further weakened any possibility of ethical influence.

The Catholic church in the Occident carried through the Christianization of Western Europe with unparalleled force, by virtue of an unexampled system of confessionals and penances, which combined the techniques of Roman law with the Teutonic conception of fiscal expiation (*Wergeld*). But the effectiveness of this system in developing a rational plan of life was quite limited, even apart from the inevitable hazards of a loose system of dispensations. Even so, the influence of the confessional upon conduct is apparent "statistically," as one might say, in the impressive resistance to the two-children-per-family system among pious Catholics, though the limitations upon the power of the Catholic church in France are evident even in this respect.

A tremendous historical influence was actually exerted by the absence in Judaism and ascetic Protestantism of anything like the confessional, the dispensation of grace by a human being, or magical sacramental grace. This historical influence favored the evolution of an ethically rationalized pattern of life (*ethisch rationalen Lebensgestaltung*) in both Judaism and ascetic Protestantism, despite their differences in other respects. These religions provide no opportunity, such as the confessional or the purveyance of institutional grace, for obtaining release from sins. Only the Methodists maintained at certain of their meetings, the so-called "assemblages of the dozens," a system of confessions which had even comparable effects, and in that case the effects were in an altogether different direction. From such public confessions of sinfulness there developed the semi-orgiastic penitential practices of the Salvation Army.

Institutional grace, by its very nature, ultimately and notably tends to make obedience a cardinal virtue and a decisive precondition of salvation. This of course entails subjection to authority, either of the institution or of the charismatic personality who distributes grace. In India, for example, the *guru* may on occasion exercise unlimited authority. In such cases the resulting pattern of conduct is not a systematization from within, radiating out from a center which the individual himself has achieved, but rather is nurtured from some center outside the self. The content of the pattern of life is not apt to be pushed in the direction of ethical systematization, but rather in the reverse direction.

Such external authority, however, increases the elasticity of concrete sacred commandments and thus makes it easier to adjust them in practice to changed external circumstances, though in a direction different from that of a *Gesinnungsethik*. An example of this elasticity is provided by the Catholic church of the nineteenth century in its non-enforcement (in practice) of the prohibition against usury, despite the prohibition's ostensibly eternal validity on the basis of biblical authority and papal decretals. To be sure, this was not accomplished openly by outright in-validation, which would have been impossible, but by an innocuous directive from the Vatican office to the confessional priests that thence-forth they should refrain from inquiring during confession concerning infractions of the prohibition against usury, and that they should grant absolution for this infraction as long as it could be taken for granted that if the Holy See should ever return to the older position the con-fessants would obediently accept such a reversal. There was a period in France when the clergy agitated for a similar treatment of the problem presented by families having only two children. Thus, the ultimate re-ligious value is pure obedience to the institution, which is regarded as inherently meritorious, and not concrete, substantive ethical obligation, nor even the qualification of superior moral capacity achieved through one's own methodical ethical actions. Wherever the pattern of institu-tional grace is carried through consistently, the sole principle integrating the life pattern is a formal humility of obedience, which like mysticism produces a characteristic quality of brokenness or humility in the pious. In this respect, the remark of Mallinckrodt that the freedom of the Catholic consists in being free to obey the Pope appears to leave universal validity for systems of institutional grace.[1a]

2. Salvation Through Faith Alone and Its Anti-Intellectual Consequences

Salvation, however, may be linked with faith. Insofar as this concept is not defined as identical with subjection to practical norms, it always presupposes some attribution of truth to certain metaphysical data and some development of dogmas, the acceptance of which becomes the distinctive hallmark of membership in the particular faith. We have already seen that dogmas develop in very different degrees within the various religions. However, some measure of doctrine is the distinctive differential of prophecy and priestly religion, in contrast to pure magic. Of course even pure magic presupposes faith in the magical power of the magician, and, for that matter, the magician's own faith in himself and his ability. This holds true of every religion, including early Chris-tianity. Thus, Jesus taught his disciples that since they doubted their own power they would be unable to cure victims of demonic possession. Whosoever is completely persuaded of his own powers possesses a faith that can move mountains. On the other hand, the faith of those who demand magical miracles exercises a compulsive influence upon magic, to this very day. So Jesus found himself unable to perform miracles in his birthplace and occasionally in other cities, and "wondered at their disbelief." He repeatedly declared that he was able to heal the crippled and those possessed by demons only through their belief in him and his power [Mk. 10:51–52]. To some degree this faith was sublimated in an ethical direction. Thus, because the adulterous woman believed in his power to pardon sins, Jesus was able to forgive her iniquities.

On the other hand, religious faith developed into an assertion of intellectual propositions which were products of ratiocination, and this is what primarily concerns us here. Accordingly, Confucianism, which knows nothing of dogma, is not an ethic of salvation. In ancient Islam and ancient Judaism, religion made no real demands with respect to dogma, requiring only, as primeval religion does everywhere, belief in the power (and hence also in the existence) of its own god, now regarded by it as the only god, and in the mission of this god's prophets. But since both these religions were scriptural (in Islam the Koran was believed to have been divinely created), they also insisted upon belief in the substantive truth of the scriptures. Yet, apart from their cosmogonic, mythologic, and historical narratives, the biblical books of the law and the prophets and the Koran contain primarily practical commandments and do not inherently require intellectual views of a definite kind.

Only in the non-prophetic religions is belief equivalent to sacred lore. In these religions the priests are still, like the magicians, guardians of mythological and cosmogonic knowledge; and as sacred bards they are also custodians of the heroic sagas. The Vedic and Confucian ethics attributed full moral efficacy to the traditional literary educations obtained through schooling which, by and large, was identical with mere memorized knowledge. In religions that maintain the requirement of intellectual understanding there is an easy transition to the philosophical or gnostic form of salvation. This transition tends to produce a tremendous gap between the fully qualified intellectuals and the masses. But even at this point there is still no real, official dogmatics—only philosophical opinions regarded as more or less orthodox, e.g., the orthodox *Vedanta* or the heterodox *Sankhya* in Hinduism.

But the Christian churches, as a consequence of the increasing intrusion of intellectualism and the growing opposition to it, produced an unexampled mass of official and binding rational dogmas, a theological faith. In practice it is impossible to require both belief in dogma and the universal understanding of it. It is difficult for us today to imagine that a religious community composed principally of petty-bourgeois members could have thoroughly mastered and really assimilated the complicated contents of the Epistle to the Romans, for example, yet apparently this must have been the case. This type of faith embodied certain dominant soteriological views current among the group of urban proselytes who were accustomed to meditating on the conditions of salvation and who were to some degree conversant with Jewish and Greek casuistry. Similarly, it is well known that in the sixteenth and seventeenth centuries broad petty-bourgeois strata achieved intellectual mastery over the dogmas of the Synods of Dort and Westminster, and over the many complicated compromise formulae of the Reformation churches. Still, under normal conditions it would be impossible for such intellectual penetration to take place in congregational religions without producing one of the following results for all those not belonging to the class of the philosophically knowledgeable (Gnostics). These less knowledgeable people, including the "hylics" and the mystically unilluminated "psychics," would either be excluded from salvation or limited to a lesser-order salvation reserved for the non-intellectual pious (*pistikoi*). These results occurred in Gnosticism and in the intellectual religions of India.

A controversy raged in early Christianity throughout its first centuries, sometimes openly and sometimes beneath the surface, as to whether theological *gnosis* or simple faith (*pistis*) is the higher religious quality, explicitly or implicitly providing the sole guarantee of religious salvation. In Islam, the Mu'tazilites held that a person who is "religious" in the average sense, and not schooled in dogma, is not actually a member of the real community of the faithful. A decisive influence was everywhere exerted on the character of religion by the relationships between the theological intellectuals, who were the virtuosi of religious knowledge, and the pious non-intellectuals, especially the virtuosi of religious asceticism and the virtuosi of religious contemplation, who equally regarded "dead knowledge" as of negligible value in the quest for salvation.

Even in the Gospels themselves, the parabolic form of Jesus' message is represented as being purposefully esoteric. To avoid the appearance of an esotericism propagated by an intellectualist aristocracy, religious faith must base itself upon something other than a real understanding and affirmation of a theological system of dogma. As a matter of fact, every prophetic religion has based religious faith upon something other than real understanding of theology, either at the very outset or at a later stage when it has become a congregational religion and has generated dogmas. Of course the acceptance of dogmas is always relevant to religious faith, except in the views of ascetics and more especially mystical virtuosi. But the explicit, personal recognition of dogmas, for which the technical term in Christianity is *fides explicita,* was required only with reference to those articles of faith which were regarded as absolutely essential, greater latitude being permitted in regard to other dogmas. Protestantism made particularly strict demands upon belief in dogma, because of its doctrine of justification by faith. This was especially, though not exclusively, true of ascetic Protestantism, which regarded the Bible as a codification of divine law. This religious requirement was largely responsible for the intensive training of the youth of the Protestant sects and for the establishment of universal public schools like those of the Jewish tradition. This same religious requirement was the underlying reason for the familiarity with the Bible on the part of the Dutch and Anglo-Saxon Pietists and Methodists (in contrast to the conditions prevalent in the English public schools, for example), which aroused the amazement of travelers as late as the middle of the nineteenth century. Here, the people's conviction about the unequivocally dogmatic character of the Bible was responsible for the far-reaching demand that each man know the tenets of his own faith. In a church rich in dogmas, all that may be legitimately required in respect to the mass of dogmas is *fides implicita*, viz., a general readiness to subject one's own convictions to religious authority. The Catholic church has required this to the greatest possible degree, and indeed continues to do so. But a *fides implicita* is no longer an actual personal acceptance of dogmas; rather, it is a declaration of confidence in and dedication to a prophet or to the authority of an institution. In this way, faith loses its intellectual character.

Religion retains only a secondary interest in intellectual matters once religious ethics has become predominantly rational. This happens because the mere assertion of intellectual propositions falls to the lowest level of faith before a *Gesinnungsethik*, as Augustine among others maintained. Faith must also take on a quality of inwardness. Personal attachment to a particular god is more than knowledge and is therefore designated as "faith." This is the case in both the Old and New Testaments. The faith which was "accounted to Abraham to righteousness" was no intellectual assertion of dogmas, but a reliance upon the promises of God. For both Jesus and Paul, faith continued to hold the same central significance. Knowledge and familiarity with dogmas receded far into the background.

In a church organized as an institution, it works out in practice that the requirement of *fides explicita* is limited to priests, preachers, and theologians, all of whom have been trained in dogmatics. Such an aristocracy of those trained and knowledgeable in dogmatics arises within every religion that has been systematized into a theology. These persons presently claim, in different degrees and with varying measures of success, that they are the real carriers of the religion. The view that the priest must demonstrate his capacity to understand more and believe more than is possible for the average human mind is still widely diffused today, particularly among the peasantry. This is only one of the forms in which there comes to expression in religion the status qualification resulting from special education that is found in every type of bureaucracy, be it political, military, ecclesiastical, or commercial. But even more fundamental is the aforementioned doctrine, found also in the New Testament, of faith as the specific charisma of an extraordinary and purely personal reliance upon god's providence, such as the shepherds of souls and the heroes of faith must possess. By virtue of this charismatic confidence in god's support, the spiritual representative and leader of the congregation, as a virtuoso of faith, may act differently from the layman in practical situations and bring about different results, far surpassing normal human capacity. In the context of practical action, faith can provide a substitute for magical powers.

This anti-rational inner attitude characteristic of religions of unlimited trust in god may occasionally produce an acosmistic indifference to obvious practical and rational considerations. It frequently produces an unconditional reliance on god's providence, attributing to god alone the consequences of one's own actions, which are interpreted as pleasing to god. In Christianity and in Islam, as well as elsewhere, this anti-rational attitude is sharply opposed to knowledge and particularly to theological knowledge. Anti-rationality may be manifested in a proud virtuosity of faith, or, when it avoids this danger of arrogant deification of the creaturely, it may be manifested in an unconditional religious surrender and a spiritual humility that requires, above all else, the death of intellectual pride. This attitude of unconditional trust played a major role in ancient Christianity, particularly in the case of Jesus and Paul and in the struggles against Greek philosophy, and in modern Christianity, particularly in the antipathies to theology on the part of the mystical spiritualist sects of the seventeenth century in Western Europe and of the eighteenth and nineteenth centuries in Eastern Europe.

At some point in its development, every genuinely devout religious faith brings about, directly or indirectly, that "sacrifice of the intellect" in the interests of a trans-intellectual, distinctive religious quality of absolute surrender and utter trust which is expressed in the formula *credo non quod sed quia absurdum est.* The salvation religions teaching belief in a transcendental god stress, here as everywhere, the inadequacy of the individual's intellectual powers when he confronts the exalted state of the divinity. Such a turning away from knowledge, based on faith in a transcendental god's power to save, is altogether different from the Buddhist's renunciation of knowledge concerning the world beyond, which is grounded simply in his belief that such knowledge cannot advance contemplation that alone brings salvation. It is also altogether different in essence from skeptical renunciation of the possibility of understanding the meaning of the world, which indeed it is inclined to combat much more harshly than it combats the Buddhist form of renunciation of knowledge. The skeptical point of view has been common to the intellectual strata of every period. It is evident in the Greek epitaphs and in the highest artistic productions of the Renaissance, such as the works of Shakespeare; it has found expression in the philosophies of Europe, China, and India, as well as in modern intellectualism.

Deliberate belief in the absurd, as well as in triumphant joy expressed in the sermons of Jesus over the fact that the charisma of faith has been granted by God to children and minors rather than to scholars, typifies the great tension between this type of salvation religion and intellectualism. Nevertheless, this type of religion constantly seeks to adapt intellectualism to its own purposes. As Christianity became increasingly penetrated by Greek forms of thought, even in Antiquity but far more strongly after the rise of universities in the Middle Ages, it came to foster intellectualism. The medieval universities were actually centers for the cultivation of dialectics, created to counterbalance the achievements of the Roman jurists on behalf of the competing power of the Empire.

Every religion of belief assumes the existence of a personal god, as well as his intermediaries and prophets, in whose favor there must be a renunciation of self-righteousness and individual knowledge at some point or other. Consequently, religiosity based on this form of faith is characteristically absent in the Asiatic religions. We have already seen that faith may assume very different forms, depending on the direction in which it develops. To be sure, despite all diversities, a striking similarity to contemplative mysticism characterizes all religions of faith oriented to salvation which are found among peaceful groups, though it does not characterize ancient Islam and the religion of Yahweh, in both of which the primordial trust of the warrior in the tremendous power of his own god was still dominant. This similarity to contemplative mysticism derives from the fact that when the substantive content of salvation is envisaged and striven after as redemption, there is always at least a tendency for salvation to evolve into a primarily emotional relationship to the divine, a *unio mystica*. Indeed, the more systematically the "attitudinal" character of the faith is developed, the more easily may outright antinomian results ensue, as occurs in every type of mysticism.

The great difficulty of establishing an unequivocal relationship between ethical demands and a religion based on faith, i.e., a genuine salvation religion based on an attitude of utter trust, was already demonstrated by the Pauline Epistles, and even by certain contradictions in the utterances of Jesus, as those utterances are recorded in the tradition. Paul struggled continually with the immediate consequences of his own views, and with their very complicated implications. The consistent development of the Pauline doctrine of salvation by faith achieved in the Marcionite doctrines definitively demonstrated the antinomian consequences of Paul's teaching.[2] As increasing stress was placed upon salvation by faith, there was generally but little tendency for an active ethical rationalization of the pattern of life to take place within everyday religion, although the opposite was the case for the prophet of such a religion. Under certain circumstances, salvation by faith can have directly antirational effects in concrete cases as well as in principle. A minor illustration of this is found in the resistance of many religious Lutherans to entering into insurance contracts, on the ground that such action would manifest an irreligious distrust of God's providence. The wider importance of this problem lies in the fact that every rational and planned procedure for achieving salvation, every reliance on good works, and above all every effort to surpass normal ethical behavior by ascetic achievement, is regarded by religion based on faith as a wicked preoccupation with purely human powers.

Wherever the conception of salvation by faith has been developed consistently, as in ancient Islam, trans-worldly asceticism and especially monasticism have been rejected. As a result, the development of belief in salvation by faith may directly augment the religious emphasis placed upon vocational activity within the world, as actually happened in the case of Lutheran Protestantism. Moreover, religion based on faith may also strengthen the motivations for a religiously positive evaluation of vocations within the world, particularly when such religion also devalues the priestly grace of penance and sacrament in favor of the exclusive importance of the personal religious relationship to god. Lutheranism took this stand in principle from its very outset, and strengthened the stand subsequently, after the complete elimination of the confessional. The same effect of the belief in faith upon vocational motivations was particularly evident in the various forms of Pietism, which were given an ascetic cast by Spener and Francke, but which had also been exposed to Quaker and other influences of which they themselves were not too well aware.

Moreover, the German word for "vocation" (*Beruf*) is derived from the Lutheran translation of the Bible. The positive evaluation of ethical conduct within one's worldly calling, as the only mode of life acceptable to god, was central in Lutheranism from the very beginning. But in Lutheranism, good works did not enter into consideration as the real basis for the salvation of the soul, as in Catholicism, nor did good works provide the intellectual basis for the recognition that one had been reborn, as in ascetic Protestantism. Instead, certainty of salvation was derived in Lutheranism from the habitual feeling of having found refuge in God's goodness and grace. Hence, Lutheranism taught, as its attitude toward the world, a patient resignation toward the world's institutional structures. In this regard, Lutheranism presents a striking contrast to those religions—especially those forms of Protestantism—which required for the assurance of one's salvation either a distinctive methodical pattern of life or a demonstration of good works, such as was known as *fides efficax* among the Pietists and as *amal* among the Muslim Kharijis, and an equally striking contrast to the virtuosi religions of ascetic sects.[3]

Lutheranism lacks any motivation toward revolutionary attitudes in social or political relationships and any inclination toward rational reformist activity. Its teaching requires one to maintain, both within the world and against it, the substance of the salvation promised by one's faith, but does not require one to attempt a transformation of the world in any rationalized ethical direction. The Lutheran Christian has all that is needful for him, if only the word of God is proclaimed pure and clear; the remaking of the eternal order of the world and even the remaking of the church is a matter of indifference, an *adiaphoron*. To be sure, this emotionalist quality of the faith, which is relatively indifferent to the world, but in contrast to asceticism also "open" to it, was the product of a gradual development. It is difficult for such an emotionalist faith to generate anti-traditionalist, rational patterns of conduct, and it lacks any drive toward the rational control and transformation of the world.

"Faith," in the form known to the warrior religions of ancient Islam and of Yahwism, took the form of simple allegiance to the god or to the prophet, along the lines that originally characterize all relationships to anthropomorphic gods. Faithfulness is rewarded and disloyalty punished by the god. This personal relationship to the god takes on other qualities when the carriers of salvation religion become peaceful groups, and more particularly when they become members of the middle classes. Only then can faith as an instrument of salvation take on the emotionally tinged character and assume the lineaments of love for the god or the savior. This transformation is already apparent in exilic and postexilic Judaism, and is even more strongly apparent in early Christianity, especially in the teachings of Jesus and John. God now appears as a gracious master or father of a household. But it is of course a vulgar xi]   Soteriology or Salvation from Outside   5 7 1

error to see in the *paternal* quality of the god proclaimed by Jesus an intrusion of non-Semitic religion, on the argument that the gods of the (generally Semitic) desert peoples "create" mankind whereas the Greek deities "beget" it. For the Christian god never thought of begetting *men* —the phrase "begotten and not created (γεννηθέντα μὴ ποιηθέντα) is precisely the distinctive predicate of the trinitarian, deified, Christ which sets him off from humankind; moreover, even though the Christian god surrounds mankind with superhuman love, he is by no means a tender modern "daddy," but rather a primarily benevolent, yet also wrathful and strict, regal patriarch, such as was also the Jewish god.

In any case, the emotional content of religions of faith may be deepened whenever the followers of these religions substitute the view that they are children of god for the ascetic view that they are merely his instruments. The result may be a strong tendency to seek the integration of one's pattern of life in subjective states and in an inner reliance upon god, rather than in the consciousness of one's continued ethical probation. This tendency may even further weaken the practical, rational character of the religion. Such an emotional emphasis is suggested by the "language of Canaan" which came to expression with the renaissance of Pietism, that whining cadence of typical Lutheran sermons in Germany which has so often driven strong men out of the church.

A completely anti-rational effect upon the conduct of life is generally exerted by religions of faith when the relationship to the god or the savior exhibits the trait of passionate devotion, and consequently whenever the religion has a latent or manifest tinge of eroticism. This is apparent in the many varieties of love of god in Sufism, in the Canticles type of mysticism of St. Bernard and his followers, in the cult of Mary and the Sacred Heart of Jesus, in other comparable forms of devotionalism, and finally in the characteristic manifestations of emotionally suffused Pietism within Lutheranism, such as the movement of Zinzendorf. However, its most striking manifestation occurs in the characteristically Hindu religiosity of love (*bhakti*) which from the fifth and sixth centuries on supplanted the proud and noble intellectualistic religion of Buddhism, becoming the popular form of salvation religion among the masses of India, particularly in the soteriological forms of Vishnuism. In this Hindu religiosity of love, devotion to Krishna, who had been apotheosized from the *Mahabharata* to the status of a savior, and more especially devotion to the Krishna child, is raised to a state of erotically tinged devotion. This process takes place through the four levels of contemplation: servant love, friendship love, filial or parental love, and, at the highest level, a piety tinged with definite eroticism, after the fashion of the love of the *gopis* (the love of Krishna's mistresses for him). Since the procedure enjoined by this religion as necessary for salvation is essentially hostile to the concerns of everyday life, it has always presupposed some degree of sacramental intermediation in the achievement of grace, by priests, *gurus,* or *gosains.* In its practical effects, this religion is a sublimated counterpart of the Shakti religion, which is popular among the lowest social strata in India. The religion of Shakti is a worship of the wives of gods, always very close to the orgiastic type of religion and not infrequently involving a cult of erotic orgies, which of course makes it utterly remote from a religion of pure faith, such as Christianity, with its continuous and unshakeable trust in God's providence. The erotic element in the personal relationship to the savior in Hindu salvation religion may be regarded as largely the technical result of the practices of devotion; whereas, in marked contrast, the Christian belief in providence is a charisma that must be maintained by the exercise of the will of the believer.

3. Salvation Through Belief in Predestination

Finally, salvation may be regarded as a completely free, inexplicable gift of grace from a god absolutely unsearchable as to his decisions, who is necessarily unchanging because of his omniscience, and utterly beyond the influence of any human behavior. This is the grace of predestination. This conception unconditionally presupposes a transcendental creator god, and is therefore lacking in all ancient and Asiatic religions. It is also lacking in warrior and heroic religions, since they posit a super-divine fate, whereas the doctrine of predestination posits a world order or regime which is rational from god's point of view even though it may appear irrational to human beings. On the other hand, a religion of predestination obliterates the goodness of god, for he becomes a hard, majestic king. Yet it shares with religions of fate the capacity for inducing nobility and rigor in its devotees. It has this effect in spite of the fact, or rather because of the fact, that only in respect to this kind of god is the complete devaluation of all the powers of an individual a prerequisite for his salvation by free grace alone.

Dispassionate and sober ethical men like Pelagius might believe in the adequacy of their own good works. But among the prophets and founders of religions, predestination has been the belief of men animated by a drive to establish rationally organized religious power, as in the case of Calvin and Muhammad, each of whom felt that the certainty of his own mission in the world derived less from any personal perfection than from his situation in the world and from god's will. In other cases, e.g., Augustine and also Muhammad, the belief in predestination may arise as a result of recognizing the necessity for controlling tremendous passions and feeling that this can be accomplished only, if at all, through a power acting upon the individual from without and above. Luther, too, knew this feeling during the terribly excited period after his difficult struggle with sin, but it receded in importance for him after he had achieved a better adjustment to the world.

Predestination provides the individual who has found religious grace with the highest possible degree of certainty of salvation, once he has attained assurance that he belongs to the very limited aristocracy of salvation who are the elect. But the individual must find certain indices (*Symptome*) by which he may determine whether he possesses this incomparable charisma, inasmuch as it is impossible for him to live on in absolute uncertainty regarding his salvation. Since god has deigned to reveal at least some positive injunctions for the type of conduct pleasing to him, the aforementioned indices must reside, in this instance as in the case of every religiously active charisma, in the decisive demonstration of the capacity to serve as one of god's instruments in fulfilling his injunctions, and that in a persevering and methodical fashion, for either one possesses predestined grace or one does not. Moreover, the assurance of this grace is not affected by any particular transgressions of the individual in question. The ultimate certainty of one's salvation and one's continuance in a state of grace, notwithstanding disparate transgressions which the man predestined to salvation commits in the same way that all other sinful creatures commit transgressions, is provided by one's knowledge that, despite these particular errors, one's behavior is acceptable to god and flows out of an inner relationship based on the mysterious quality of grace—in short, salvation is based on a central and constant quality of personality.

Hence, the belief in predestination, although it might logically be expected to result in fatalism, produced in its most consistent followers the strongest possible motives for acting in accordance with god's pattern. Of course this action assumed different forms, depending upon the primary content of the religious prophecy. In the case of the Muslim warriors of the first generation of Islam, the belief in predestination often produced a complete obliviousness to self, in the interest of fulfillment of the religious commandment of a holy war for the conquest of the world. In the case of the Puritans governed by the Christian ethic, the same belief in predestination often produced ethical rigorism, legalism, and rationally planned procedures for the patterning of life. Discipline acquired during wars of religion was the source of the unconquerableness of both the Islamic and Cromwellian cavalries. Similarly, innerworldly asceticism and the disciplined quest for salvation in a vocation pleasing to God were the sources of the virtuosity in acquisitiveness characteristic of the Puritans. Every consistent doctrine of predestined grace inevitably implied a radical and ultimate devaluation of all magical, sacramental, and institutional distributions of grace, in view of god's sovereign will, a devaluation that actually occurred wherever the doctrine of predestination appeared in its full purity and maintained its strength. By far the strongest such devaluation of magical and institutional grace occurred in Puritanism.

Islamic predestination knew nothing of the "double decree"; it did not dare attribute to Allah the predestination of some people to hell, but only attributed to him the withdrawal of his grace from some people, a belief which admitted man's inadequacy and inevitable transgression. Moreover, as a warrior religion, Islam had some of the characteristics of the Greek *moira* in that it developed far less the specifically rational elements of a world order and the specific determination of the individual's fate in the world beyond. The ruling conception was that predestination determined, not the fate of the individual in the world beyond, but rather the uncommon events of this world, and above all such questions as whether or not the warrior for the faith would fall in battle. The religious fate of the individual in the next world was held, at least according to the older view, to be adequately secured by the individual's belief in Allah and the prophets, so that no demonstration of salvation in the conduct of life is needed. Any rational system of ascetic control of everyday life was alien to this warrior religion from the outset, so that in Islam the doctrine of predestination manifested its power especially during the wars of faith and the wars of the Mahdi. The doctrine of predestination tended to lose its importance whenever Islam became more civilianized, because the doctrine produced no planned procedure for the control of the workaday world, as did the Puritan doctrine of predestination.

In Puritanism, predestination definitely did affect the fate of the individual in the world beyond, and therefore his assurance of salvation was determined primarily by his maintenance of ethical integrity in the affairs of everyday life. For this reason, the belief in predestination assumed greater importance in Calvinism as this religion became more bourgeois than it had been at the outset. It is significant that the Puritan belief in predestination was regarded by authorities everywhere as dangerous to the state and as hostile to authority, because it made Puritans skeptical of the legitimacy of all secular power. It is interesting to note by way of contrast that in Islam the family and following of Umar, who were denounced for their alleged secularism, were followers of the belief in predestination, since they hoped to see their dominion, which had been established by illegitimate means, legitimized by the predestined will of Allah.

Clearly, every use of predestination to determine concrete events in history, rather than to secure one's orientation to one's place in the world beyond, immediately causes predestination to lose its ethical, rational character. The belief in predestination practically always had an ascetic effect among the simple warriors of the early Islamic faith, which in the realm of ethics exerted largely external and ritual demands, but the ascetic effects of the Islamic belief in predestination were not rational, and for this reason they were repressed in everyday life. The Islamic belief in predestination easily assumed fatalistic characteristics in the beliefs of the masses, viz., *kismet,* and for this reason predestination did not eliminate magic from the popular religion.

Finally, the Chinese patrimonial bureaucracy, in keeping with the character of its Confucian ethic, considered knowledge concerning destiny or fate to be indissolubly associated with sophistication. On the other hand, Confucianism permitted destiny to assume certain fatalistic attributes in the magical religion of the masses, though in the religion of the educated it assumed approximately a middle position between providence and *moira.* For just as the *moira,* together with the courage to endure it, nurtured the heroic pride of warriors, so also did predestination feed the "pharisaical" pride of the heroes of middle-class asceticism.

But in no other religion was the pride of the predestined aristocracy of salvation so closely associated with the man of a vocation and with the idea that success in rationalized activity demonstrates god's blessing as in Puritanism (and hence in no other religion was the influence of ascetic motivation upon the attitude toward economic activity so strong). Predestination too is a belief of virtuosi, who alone can accept the thought of the everlasting "double decree." But as this doctrine continued to flow into the routine of everyday living and into the religion of the masses, its dour bleakness became more and more intolerable. Finally, all that remained of it in occidental ascetic Protestantism was a vestige, a *caput mortuum:* the contribution which this doctrine of grace made to the rational capitalistic temperament, the idea of the methodical demonstration of vocation in one's economic behavior.

The neo-Calvinism of Kuyper no longer dared to maintain the pure doctrine of predestined grace.[4] Nevertheless, the doctrine was never completely eliminated from Calvinism; it only altered its form. Under all circumstances, the determinism of predestination remained an instrument for the greatest possible systematization and centralization of the *Gesinnungsethik.* The "total personality," as we would say today, has been provided with the accent of eternal value by "God's election," and not by any individual action of the person in question.

There is a non-religious counterpart of this religious evaluation, one based on a mundane determinism. It is that distinctive type of "guilt" and, so to speak, godless feeling of sin which characterizes modern secular man precisely because of his own *Gesinnungsethik*, regardless of its metaphysical basis. Not that he has *done* a particular deed, but that by virtue of his unalterable qualities, acquired without his cooperation, he "*is*" such that he *could* commit the deed—this is the secret anguish borne by modern man, and this is also what the others, in their "pharisaism" (now turned determinism), blame him for. It is a "merciless" attitude because there is no significant possibility of "forgiveness," "contrition," or "restitution"—in much the same way that the religious belief in predestination was merciless, but at least it could conceive of some impenetrable divine rationality.

NOTES

1. Cf. Wilhelm Bousset, *Hauptprobleme der Gnosis* (Göttingen: Vandenhoeck, 1907), ch. I. Since Weber used Bousset's work on *Die Religion des Judentums* (1906), it appears likely that Bousset was also one of his major sources on gnosticism.

1a. Hermann Mallinckrodt (1821–74) was one of the founders of the Catholic Center Party and one of its most vociferous spokesmen; he was a member of the *Reichstag* from 1867 until 1871. His sister Pauline founded the congregation of the "Sisters of Christian Love."

2. Cf. Adolf von Harnack, *Lehrbuch der Dogmengeschichte* (Tübingen: Mohr, 1931), vol. I, 292–309. This is the fourth edition of the 1909 publication, and another of Weber's major sources.

3. On the Kharijis, see Chantepie et al., *op cit.*, vol. I, 682ff.; on *amal*, see C. H. Becker, *Islamstudien*, vol. I, 165, 167. (W)

4. On Abraham Kuyper, Dutch theologian and Minister of the Interior (1901–05), see Weber, "The Protestant Sects. . . .," in Gerth and Mills, *op. cit.*, 452f.

xii

Religious Ethics and the World: Economics

1 . Worldly Virtues and the Ethics of Ultimate Ends

The more a religion of salvation has been systematized and internalized in the direction of an ethic of ultimate ends (*Gesinnungsethik*), the greater becomes its tension in relation to the world. This tension between religion and the world appears in a less consistent fashion and less

as a matter of principle, so long as the religion has a ritualistic or legalistic form. In these earlier stages, religions of salvation generally
assume the same forms and exert the same effects as those of magical
ethics. That is to say, a salvation religion generally begins by assigning
inviolable sanctity to those conventions received by it, since all the followers of a particular god are interested in avoiding the wrath of the
deity, and hence in punishing any transgression of the norms enjoined
by him. Consequently, once an injunction has achieved the status of a
divine commandment, it rises out of the circle of alterable conventions
into the rank of sanctity. Henceforth, the regulations enjoined by the
religion are regarded, like the arrangements of the cosmos as a whole, as
eternally valid—susceptible of interpretation, but not of alteration, unless
the god himself reveals a new commandment.

In this stage, the religion exercises a stereotyping effect on the entire
realm of legal institutions and social conventions, in the same way that
symbolism stereotypes certain substantive elements of a culture and prescription of magical taboos stereotypes concrete types of relationships to
human beings and to goods. The sacred books of the Hindus, Muslims,
Parsees and Jews, and the classical books of the Chinese treat legal
prescriptions in exactly the same manner that they treat ceremonial and
ritual norms. The law is sacred law. The dominance of law that has
been stereotyped by religion constitutes one of the most significant limitations on the rationalization of the legal order and hence also on the
rationalization of the economy.

Conversely, when ethical prophecies have broken through the stereotyped magical or ritual norms, a sudden or a gradual revolution may take
place, even in the daily order of human living, and particularly in the
realm of economics. It must be admitted, of course, that there are limits
to the power of religion in both spheres. It is by no means true that religion is always the decisive element when it appears in connection with
the aforementioned transformation. Furthermore, religion nowhere creates certain economic conditions unless there are also present in the
existing relationships and constellations of interests certain possibilities
of, or even powerful drives toward, such an economic transformation.
It is not possible to enunciate any general formula that will summarize
the comparative substantive powers of the various factors involved in
such a transformation or will summarize the manner of their accommodation to one another.

The needs of economic life make themselves manifest either through
a reinterpretation of the sacred commandments or through their casuistic
by-passing. Occasionally we also come upon a simple, practical elimination of religious injunctions in the course of the ecclesiastical dispensation of penance and grace. One example of this is the elimination

within the Catholic church of so important a provision as the prohibition against usury even *in foro conscientiae* (concerning which we shall have more to say presently), but without any express abrogation, which would have been impossible. Probably the same process will take place in the case of another forbidden practice, *onanismus matrimonialis,* viz., the limitation of offspring to two children per family.

The frequent ambivalence or silence of religious norms with respect to new problems and practices like the aforementioned results in the unmediated juxtaposition of the stereotypes' absolute unalterableness with the extraordinary capriciousness and utter unpredictability of the same stereotypes' validity in any particular application. Thus, in dealing with the Islamic *shar'iah* it is virtually impossible to assert what is the practice today in regard to any particular matter. The same confusion obtains with regard to all sacred laws and ethical injunctions that have a formal ritualistic and casuistical character, above all the Jewish law.

But the systematization of religious obligations in the direction of an ethic based on inner religious faith (*Gesinnungsethik*) produces a situation that is fundamentally different in essence. Such systematization breaks through the stereotypization of individual norms in order to bring about a meaningful total relationship of the pattern of life to the goal of religious salvation. Moreover, an inner religious faith does not recognize any sacred law, but only a "sacred inner religious state" that may sanction different maxims of conduct in different situations, and which is thus elastic and susceptible of accommodation. It may, depending on the pattern of life it engenders, produce revolutionary consequences from within, instead of exerting a stereotyping effect. But it acquires this ability to revolutionize at the price of also acquiring a whole complex of problems which becomes greatly intensified and internalized. The inherent conflict between the religious postulate and the reality of the world does not diminish, but rather increases. With the increasing systematization and rationalization of social relationships and of their substantive contents, the external compensations provided by the teachings of theodicy are replaced by the struggles of particular autonomous spheres of life against the requirements of religion. The more intense the religious need is, the more the world presents a problem. Let us now clarify this matter by analyzing some of the principal conflicts.

Religious ethics penetrate into social institutions in very different ways. The decisive aspect of the religious ethic is not the intensity of its attachment to magic and ritual or the distinctive character of the religion generally, but is rather its theoretical attitude toward the world. To the extent that a religious ethic organizes the world from a religious perspective into a systematic, rational cosmos, its ethical tensions with the social institutions of the world are likely to become sharper and more principled; this is the more true the more the secular institutions (*Ordnungen*) are systematized autonomously. A religious ethic evolves that is oriented to the rejection of the world, and which by its very nature completely lacks any of that stereotyping character which has been associated with sacred laws. Indeed, the very tension which this religious ethic introduces into the human relationships toward the world becomes a strongly dynamic factor in social evolution.

2. Familial Piety, Neighborly Help, and Compensation

Those cases in which a religious ethic simply appropriates the general virtues of life within the world require no exposition here. These general virtues naturally include relationships within the family, truthfulness, reliability, and respect for another person's life and property, including wives. But the accentuation of the various virtues is characteristically different in different religions. Confucianism placed a tremendous stress on familial piety, a stress which was motivated by belief in magic, in view of the importance of the family spirits. This familial piety was cultivated in practice by a patriarchal and patrimonial-bureaucratic political organization. Confucius, according to a dictum attributed to him, regarded "insubordination as more reprehensible than brutality," which indicates that he expressly interpreted obedience to family authorities very literally as the distinctive mark of all social and political qualities. The directly opposite accentuation of general virtues of life is found in those more radical types of congregational religion which advocate the dissolution of all family ties. "Whosoever cannot hate his father cannot become a disciple of Jesus."

Another example of the different accentuations of virtues is the stress placed on truthfulness in the Hindu and Zoroastrian ethics, whereas the Decalogue of the Judeo-Christian tradition confines this virtue to judicial testimony. Even further from the Hindu and Zoroastrian requirements of truthfulness is the complete recession of the obligation of veracity in favor of the varied injunctions of ceremonious propriety found in the status ethic of the Confucian Chinese bureaucracy. Zoroastrianism forbids the torture of animals, as a consequence of the founder's campaign against orgiastic religion. Hindu religion goes far beyond any other in absolutely prohibiting the slaying of any living thing, a position that is based on conceptions of animism and metempsychosis.

The content of every religious ethic which goes beyond particular magical prescriptions and familial piety is primarily determined by two simple motives that condition all everyday behavior beyond the limits of the family, namely, just retaliation against offenders and fraternal assistance to friendly neighbors. Both are in a sense compensations: the offender deserves punishment, the execution of which mollifies anger; and conversely, the neighbor is entitled to assistance. There could be no question in Chinese, Vedic, or Zoroastrian ethics, or in that of the Jews until postexile times, but that an enemy must be compensated with evil for the evil he has done. Indeed, the entire social order of these societies appears to have rested on just compensation. For this reason and because of its accommodation with the world, the Confucian ethic rejected the idea of love for one's enemy, which in China was partly mystical and partly based on notions of social utility, as being contrary to the interests of the state. The notion of love for one's enemy was accepted by the Jews in their postexile ethic, according to the interpretation of Meinhold, but only in the particular sense of causing their enemies all the greater humiliation by the benevolent attitude exhibited by the Jews. The postexile Jews added another proviso, which Christianity retained, that vengeance is the proper prerogative of God, who will the more certainly execute it the more man refrains from doing so himself.

Congregational religion added the fellow worshipper and the comrade in faith to the roster of those to whom the religiously founded obligation of assistance applied, which already included the blood-brother and the fellow member of clan or tribe. Stated more correctly, congregational religion set the co-religionist in the place of the fellow clansman. "Whoever does not leave his own father and mother cannot become a follower of Jesus." This is also the general sense and context of Jesus' remark that he came not to bring peace, but the sword. Out of all this grows the injunction of brotherly love, which is especially characteristic of congregational religion, in most cases because it contributes very effectively to the emancipation from political organization. Even in early Christianity, for example in the doctrines of Clement of Alexandria, brotherly love in its fullest extent was enjoined only within the circle of fellow believers, and not beyond.

The obligation to bring assistance to one's fellow was derived—as we saw [Part Two, ch. III:2]—from the neighborhood group. The nearest person helps the neighbor because he may one day require the neighbor's help in turn. The emergence of the notion of universal love is possible only after political and ethnic communities have become considerably intermingled, and after the gods have been liberated from connection with political organizations to become universal powers. The extension of the sentiment of love to include the followers of alien religions is more difficult when the other religious communities have become competitors, each proclaiming the uniqueness of its own god. Thus, Buddhist tradition relates that the Jainist monks expressed amazement that the Buddha had commanded his disciples to give food to them as well as to Buddhist monks.

3. *Alms-Giving, Charity, and the Protection of the Weak*

As economic differentiation proceeded, customs of mutual neighborly assistance in work and in meeting immediate needs were transformed into customs of mutual aid among various social strata. This process is reflected in religious ethics at a very early time. Sacred bards and magicians, the professional groups which first lost their contact with the soil, lived from the bounty of the rich. Consequently, the wealthy who share their plenty with religious functionaries receive the praises of the latter at all times, while the greedy and miserly have curses hurled at them. Under the economic conditions of early, natural agricultural economies, noble status is conferred, not just by wealth, but also by a hospitable and charitable manner of living, as we shall see later on. Hence, the giving of alms is a universal and primary component of every ethical religion, though new motivations for such giving may come to the fore. Jesus occasionally made use of the aforementioned principle of compensation as a source of motivation for giving to the poor. The gist of this notion was that god would all the more certainly render compensation to the giver of alms in the world beyond, since it was impossible for the poor to return the generosity. To this notion was added the principle of the solidarity of the brothers in the faith, which under certain circumstances might bring the brotherliness close to a communism of love.

In Islam, the giving of alms was one of the five commandments incumbent upon members of the faith. Giving of alms was the "good work" enjoined in ancient Hinduism, in Confucianism, and in early Judaism. In ancient Buddhism, the giving of alms was originally the only activity of the pious layman that really mattered. Finally, in ancient Christianity, the giving of alms attained almost the dignity of a sacrament, and even in the time of Augustine faith without alms was not regarded as genuine.

The impecunious Muslim warrior for the faith, the Buddhist monk, and the impoverished fellow believers of ancient Christianity, especially those of the Christian community in Jerusalem, were all dependent on alms, as were the prophets, apostles, and frequently even the priests of salvation religions. In ancient Christianity, and among Christian sects as late as the Quaker community, charitable assistance was regarded as a sort of religious welfare insurance, and was one of the most important factors in the maintenance of the religious community and in missionary enterprises. Hence, when congregational religion lost its initial sectarian drive, charity lost its significance to a greater or lesser degree and assumed the character of a mechanical ritual. Still, charity continued to survive in principle. In Christianity, even after its expansion, the giving of alms remained so unconditionally necessary for the achievement of salvation by the wealthy that the poor were actually regarded as a distinctive and indispensable "status group" within the church. The rendering of assistance naturally developed far beyond the giving of alms, and so the sick, widows, and orphans were again and again described as possessing particular religious value.

The relationships among brothers in the faith came to be characterized by the same expectations which were felt between friends and neighbors, such as the expectations that credit would be extended without interest and that one's children would be taken care of in time of need without any compensation. Many of the secularized organizations which have replaced the sects in the United States still make such claims upon their members. Above all, the poor brother in the faith expects this kind of assistance and generosity from the powerful and from his own master. Indeed, within certain limitations, the powerful personage's own interests dictated that he protect his own subordinates and show them generosity, since the security of his own income depended ultimately on the good will and cooperation of his underlings, as long as no rational methods of control existed. On the other hand, the possibility of obtaining help or protection from powerful individuals provided every pauper, and notably the sacred bards, with a motive to seek out such individuals and praise them for their generosity. Wherever patriarchal relationships of power and coercion determined the social stratification, but especially in the Orient, the prophetic religions were able, in connection with the afore-mentioned purely practical situation, to create some kind of protectorate of the weak, i.e., women, children, slaves, etc. This is especially true of the Mosaic and Islamic prophetic religion.

This protection can also be extended to relationships between classes. To exploit unscrupulously one's particular class position in relation to less powerful neighbors in the manner typical of precapitalist times—through the merciless enslavement of debtors and the aggrandizement of land holdings, processes that are practically identical—meets with considerable social condemnation and religious censure, as being an offense against group solidarity. Similar objections apply to the maximum utilization of one's purchasing power in acquiring consumer goods for the speculative exploitation of the critical condition of those in less favorable positions. On the other hand, the members of the ancient warrior nobility tend to regard as a parvenu any person who has risen in the social scale as a result of the acquisition of money. Therefore, the kind of avarice just described is everywhere regarded as abominable from the religious point of view. It was so regarded in the Hindu legal books, as well as in ancient Christianity and in Islam. In Judaism, the reaction against such avarice led to the creation of the characteristic institution of a jubilee year in which debts were cancelled and slaves liberated, to ameliorate the conditions of one's fellow believers. This institution was subsequently construed as the "sabbatical year," a result of theological casuistry and of a misunderstanding on the part of those pious people whose provenience was purely urban. Every systematization in the direction of a *Gesinnungsethik* crystallized from all these particular demands the distinctive religious mood or state known as "charity" (*caritas*).

4. Religious Ethics, Economic Rationality and the Issue of Usury

The rejection of usury appears as an emanation of this central religious mood in almost all ethical systems purporting to regulate life. Such a prohibition against usury is completely lacking, outside of Protestantism, only in the religious ethics which have become a mere accommodation to the world, e.g., Confucianism; and in the religious ethics of ancient Babylonia and the Mediterranean littoral in which the urban citizenry (more particularly the nobility residing in the cities and maintaining economic interests in trade) hindered the development of a consistent caritative ethics. The Hindu books of canonical law prohibit the taking of usury, at least for the two highest castes. Among the Jews, collecting usury from "members of the tribe" (*Volksgenossen*) was prohibited. In Islam and in ancient Christianity, the prohibition against usury at first applied only to brothers in faith, but subsequently became unconditional. It seems probable that the proscription of usury in Christianity is not primary in that religion. Jesus justified the biblical injunction to lend to the impecunious on the ground that God will not reward the lender in transactions which present no risk. This verse was then misread and mistranslated in a fashion that resulted in the prohibition of usury: μηδένα ἀπελπίζοντες was mistranslated as μηδέν, which in the Vulgate became *nihil inde sperantes*.[1]

The original basis for the thoroughgoing rejection of usury was generally the primitive custom of economic assistance to one's fellows, in accordance with which the taking of usury "among brothers" was undoubtedly regarded as a serious breach against the obligation to provide assistance. The fact that the prohibition against usury became increasingly severe in Christianity, under quite different conditions, was due in part to various other motives and factors. The prohibition of usury was not, as the materialist conception of history would represent it, a reflection of the absence of interest on capital under the general conditions of a natural economy. On the contrary, the Christian church and its servants, including the Pope, took interest without any scruples even in the early Middle Ages, i.e., in the very period of a natural economy; even more so, of course, they condoned the taking of interest by others. It is striking that the ecclesiastical persecution of usurious lending arose and became ever more intense virtually as a concomitant of the incipient development of actual capitalist instruments and particularly of acquisitive capital in overseas trade. What is involved, therefore, is a struggle in principle between ethical rationalization and the process of rationalization in the domain of economics. As we have seen, only in the nineteenth century was the church obliged, under the pressure of certain unalterable facts, to remove the prohibition in the manner we have described previously.

The real reason for religious hostility toward usury lies deeper and is connected with the attitude of religious ethics toward the imperatives of rational profitmaking. In early religions, even those which otherwise placed a high positive value on the possession of wealth, purely commercial enterprises were practically always the objects of adverse judgment. Nor is this attitude confined to predominantly agrarian economies under the influence of warrior nobilities. This criticism is usually found when commercial transactions are already relatively advanced, and indeed it arose in conscious protest against them.

We may first note that every economic rationalization of a barter economy has a weakening effect on the traditions which support the authority of the sacred law. For this reason alone the pursuit of money, the typical goal of the rational acquisitive quest, is religiously suspect. Consequently, the priesthood favored the maintenance of a natural economy (as was apparently the case in Egypt) wherever the particular economic interests of the temple as a bank for deposit and loans under divine protection did not militate too much against a natural economy.

But it is above all the impersonal and economically rationalized (but for this very reason ethically irrational) character of purely commercial relationships that evokes the suspicion, never clearly expressed but all the more strongly felt, of ethical religions. For every purely personal relationship of man to man, of whatever sort and even including complete enslavement, may be subjected to ethical requirements and ethically regulated. This is true because the structures of these relationships depend upon the individual wills of the participants, leaving room in such relationships for manifestations of the virtue of charity. But this is not the situation in the realm of economically rationalized relationships, where personal control is exercised in inverse ratio to the degree of rational differentiation of the economic structure. There is no possibility, in practice or even in principle, of any caritative regulation of relationships arising between the holder of a savings and loan bank mortgage and the mortgagee who has obtained a loan from the bank, or between a holder of a federal bond and a citizen taxpayer. Nor can any caritative regulation arise in the relationships between stockholders and factory workers, between tobacco importers and foreign plantation workers, or between industrialists and the miners who have dug from the earth the raw materials used in the plants owned by the industrialists. The growing impersonality of the economy on the basis of association in the market place follows its own rules, disobedience to which entails economic failure and, in the long run, economic ruin.

Rational economic association always brings about depersonalization, and it is impossible to control a universe of instrumentally rational activities by charitable appeals to particular individuals. The functionalized world of capitalism certainly offers no support for any such charitable orientation. In it the claims of religious charity are vitiated not merely because of the refractoriness and weakness of particular individuals, as it happens everywhere, but because they lose their meaning altogether. Religious ethics is confronted by a world of depersonalized relationships which for fundamental reasons cannot submit to its primeval norms. Consequently, in a peculiar duality, priesthoods have time and again protected patriarchalism against impersonal dependency relations, also in the interest of traditionalism, whereas prophetic religion has broken up patriarchal organizations. However, the more a religious commitment becomes conscious of its opposition to economic rationalization as such, the more apt are the religion's virtuosi to end up with an anti-economic rejection of the world.

Of course, the various religious ethics have experienced diverse fates, because in the world of facts the inevitable compromises had to be made. From of old, religious ethics has been directly employed for rational economic purposes, especially the purposes of creditors. This was especially true wherever the state of indebtedness legally involved only the *person* of the debtor, so that the creditor had to appeal to the filial piety of the heirs. An example of this practice is the impounding of the mummy of the deceased in Egypt [to shame his descendants into paying his debts]. Another example is the belief in some Asiatic religions that whoever fails to keep a promise, including a promise to repay a loan and especially a promise guaranteed by an oath, would be tortured in the next world and consequently might disturb the quiet of his descendants by evil magic. In the Middle Ages, as Schulte has pointed out,[2] the credit standing of bishops was particularly high because any breach of obligation on their part, especially of an obligation assumed under oath, might result in their excommunication, which would have ruined a bishop's whole existence. This reminds one of the credit-worthiness of our lieutenants and fraternity students [which was similarly upheld by the efficacy of threats to the future career].

By a peculiar paradox, asceticism actually resulted in the contradictory situation already mentioned on several previous occasions, namely that it was precisely its rationally ascetic character that led to the accumulation of wealth. The cheap labor of ascetic celibates, who underbid the indispensable minimum wage required by married male workers, was primarily responsible for the expansion of monastic businesses in the late Middle Ages. The reaction of the middle classes against the monasteries during this period was based on the "coolie" economic competition offered by the brethren. In the same way, the secular education offered by the cloister was able to underbid the education offered by married teachers.

The attitudes of a religion can often be explained on grounds of economic interest. The Byzantine monks were economically chained to the worship of icons, and the Chinese monks had an economic interest in the products of their workshops and printing establishments. An extreme example of this kind is provided by the manufacture of alcoholic liquors in modern monasteries, which defies the religious campaign against alcohol. Factors such as these have tended to work against any consistent religious opposition to worldly economic activities. Every organization, and particularly every institutional religion, requires sources of economic power. Indeed, scarcely any doctrine has been belabored with such terrible papal curses, especially at the hands of the greatest financial organizer of the church, John XXII, as the doctrine that Christ requires poverty of his true followers, a doctrine which enjoys scriptural authority and was consistently espoused by the Franciscan Spirituals (*Franziskanerobservanten*).[3] From the time of Arnold of Brescia and down through the centuries, a whole train of martyrs died for this doctrine.

It is difficult to estimate the practical effect of Christianity's prohibition of usury, and even more difficult to estimate the practical effect of Christianity's doctrine with respect to economic acquisition in business, viz., *deo placere non potest*.[4] The prohibitions against usury generated legalistic circumventions of all sorts. After a hard struggle, the church itself was virtually compelled to permit undisguised usury in the charitable establishments of the *montes pietatis* when the loans were in the interests of the poor; this became definitively established after Leo X [1513–21]. Furthermore, emergency loans for businesses at fixed rates of interest were provided during the Middle Ages by allocating this function to the Jews.

We must note, however, that in the Middle Ages fixed interest charges were rare in the entrepreneurial contracts extending business credit to enterprises subject to great risk, especially overseas commerce (credit contracts which in Italy also used the property of wards). The more usual procedure was actual participation in the risk and profit of an enterprise (*commenda, dare ad proficuum de mari*), with various limitations and occasionally with a graduated scale such as that provided in the Pisan *Constitutum Usus*.[5] Yet the great merchant guilds nevertheless protected themselves against the protest of *usuraria pravitas* by expulsion from the guild, boycott, or blacklist—punitive measures comparable to those taken under our stock exchange regulations against protests of contract. The guilds also watched over the personal salvation of the souls of their members by providing them with indulgences (as did the Florentine *Arte di Calimala*) and by innumerable testamentary gifts of conscience money or endowments.

The wide chasm separating the inevitabilities of economic life from the Christian ideal was still frequently felt deeply. In any case this ethical separation kept the most devout groups and all those with the most consistently developed ethics far from the life of trade. Above all, time and again it tended to attach an ethical stigma to the business spirit, and to impede its growth. The rise of a consistent, systematic, and ethically regulated mode of life in the economic domain was completely prevented by the medieval institutional church's expedient of grading religious obligations according to religious charisma and ethical vocation and by the church's other expedient of granting dispensations. (The fact that people with rigorous ethical standards simply could not take up a business career was not altered by the dispensation of indulgences, nor by the extremely lax principles of the Jesuit probabilistic ethics after the Counter-Reformation.) A business career was only possible for those who were lax in their ethical thinking.

The inner-worldly asceticism of Protestantism first produced a capitalistic ethics, although unintentionally, for it opened the way to a career in business, especially for the most devout and ethically rigorous people. Above all, Protestantism interpreted success in business as the fruit of a rational mode of life. Indeed, Protestantism, and especially ascetic Protestantism, confined the prohibition against usury to clear cases of complete selfishness. But by this principle it now denounced interest as uncharitable usury in situations which the Roman church itself had, as a matter of practice, tolerated, e.g., in the *montes pietatis*, the extension of credit to the poor. It is worthy of note that Christian business men and the Jews had long since felt to be irksome the competition of these institutions which lent to the poor. Very different was the Protestant justification of interest as a legitimate form of participation by the provider of capital in the business profits accruing from the money he had lent, especially wherever credit had been extended to the wealthy and powerful—e.g., as political credit to the prince. The theoretical justification of this attitude was the achievement of Salmasius [*de usuris*, 1638].

One of the most notable economic effects of Calvinism was its destruction of the traditional forms of charity. First it eliminated unsystematic almsgiving. To be sure, the first steps toward the systematization of charity had been taken with the introduction of fixed rules for the distribution of the bishop's fund in the later medieval church, and with the institution of the medieval hospital—in the same way that the poor tax in Islam had rationalized and centralized almsgiving. Yet random almsgiving had still retained its qualification in Christianity as a "good work." The innumerable charitable institutions of ethical religions have always led in practice to the creation and direct cultivation of mendicancy, and in any case charitable institutions tended to make of charity a purely ritual gesture, as the fixed number of daily meals in the Byzantine monastic establishment or the official soup days of the Chinese. Calvinism put an end to all this, and especially to any benevolent attitude toward the beggar. For Calvinism held that the inscrutable God possessed good reasons for having distributed the gifts of fortune unequally. It never ceased to stress the notion that a man proved himself exclusively in his vocational work. Consequently, begging was explicitly stigmatized as a violation of the injunction to love one's neighbor, in this case the person from whom the beggar solicits.

What is more, all Puritan preachers proceeded from the assumption that the idleness of a person capable of work was inevitably his own fault. But it was felt necessary to organize charity systematically for those incapable of work, such as orphans and cripples, for the greater glory of God. This notion often resulted in such striking phenomena as dressing institutionalized orphans in uniforms reminiscent of fool's attire and parading them through the streets of Amsterdam to divine services with the greatest possible fanfare. Care for the poor was oriented to the goal of discouraging the slothful. This goal was quite apparent in the social welfare program of the English Puritans, in contrast to the Anglican program, so well described by H. Levy.[6] In any case, charity itself became a rationalized "enterprise," and its religious significance was therefore eliminated or even transformed into the opposite significance. This was the situation in consistent ascetic and rationalized religions.

Mystical religions had necessarily to take a diametrically opposite path with regard to the rationalization of economics. The foundering of the postulate of brotherly love in its collision with the loveless realities of the economic domain once it became rationalized led to the expansion of love for one's fellow man until it came to require a completely unselective generosity. Such unselective generosity did not inquire into the reason and outcome of absolute self-surrender, into the worth of the person soliciting help, or into his capacity to help himself. It asked no questions, and quickly gave the shirt when the cloak had been asked for. In mystical religions, the individual for whom the sacrifice is made is regarded in the final analysis as unimportant and exchangeable; his individual value is negated. One's "neighbor" is simply a person whom one happens to encounter along the way; he has significance only because of his need and his solicitation. This results in a distinctively mystical flight from the world which takes the form of a non-specific and loving self-surrender, not for the sake of the man but for the sake of the surrender itself—what Baudelaire has termed "the sacred prostitution of the soul."

NOTES

1. "Do not expect anything from it" instead of "Do not deprive anybody of hope." Weber relied on the painstaking analysis of Luke 6:35 by Adalbert Merx, *Die Evangelien des Markus und Lukas* (Berlin: Reimer, 1905), 223ff. Weber mentions Merx below, ch. XV:10:D; cf. also *Economic History*, ch. 21 and p. 274.

2. See Aloys Schulte, *Geschichte des mittelalterlichen Handels und Verkehrs zwischen Westdeutschland und Italien* (Leipzig: Dunker & Humblot, 1900), I, 263ff.

3. In the 15th century the Franciscans of the Strict Observance developed into a congregation that was privileged over the Conventuals. On these *Franziskanerobservanten* see *Religion in Geschichte und Gegenwart* (Tübingen 1910), IV. Cf. also Benjamin Nelson, "Max Weber's Sociology of Religion," *American Sociological Review*, 30:4, Aug. 1965, 596f. On the issue of usury in general, see Nelson's follow-up of Weber, *The Idea of Usury* (New York 1949).

4. The complete formulation reads: "Home mercator vix aut nunquam deo

potest placere"—"A merchant can hardly or never please God." The passage became important through the *Decretum Gratiani* (about 1150 A.D.). Cf. Weber, *Wirtschaftsgeschichte*, sec. ed., J. Winckelmann, ed. (1958), 305, and Nelson's article, *loc. cit.*

5. Cf. Weber, *Handelsgesellschaften*, ch. IV, "Pisa. Das Sozietätsrecht des Constitutum Usus," reprinted in *GAzSW*, 386–410.

6. See Hermann Levy, *Economic Liberalism* (London: Macmillan, 1913), ch. VI; first published in German in 1902.

xiii

Religious Ethics and the World: Politics

1. *From Political Subordination to the Anti-Political Rejection of the World*

Every religiously grounded unworldly love and indeed every ethical religion must, in similar measure and for similar reasons, experience tensions with the sphere of political behavior. This tension appears as soon as religion has progressed to anything like a status of equality with the sphere of political associations. To be sure, the ancient political god of the locality, even where he was an ethical and universally powerful god, existed merely for the protection of the political interests of his followers' associations.

Even the Christian God is still invoked as a god of war and as a god of our fathers, in much the same way that local gods were invoked in the ancient *polis*. One is reminded of the fact that for centuries Christian ministers have prayed along the beaches of the North Sea for a "blessing upon the strand" (i.e., for numerous shipwrecks). On its part the priesthood generally depended upon the political association, either directly or indirectly. This dependence is especially strong in those contemporary churches which derive support from governmental subvention. It was particularly noteworthy where the priests were court or patrimonial officials of rulers or landed magnates, e.g., the *purohita* of India or the Byzantine court bishops since Constantine. The same dependence also arose wherever the priests themselves were either enfeoffed feudal lords exercising secular power (e.g., as during the medieval period in the Occident), or scions of noble priestly families. Among the Chinese and Hindus as well as the Jews, the sacred bards, whose compositions were practically everywhere incorporated into the scriptures, sang the praises of heroic death. According to the canonical books of the Brahmins, a heroic death was as much an ideal obligation of the Kshatriya caste member at the age when he had "seen the son of his son" as withdrawal from the world into the forests for meditation was an obligation of members of the Brahmin caste. Of course, magical religion had no conception of a religious war. But for magical religion, and even for the ancient religion of Yahweh, political victory and especially vengeance against the enemy constituted the real reward granted by god.

The more the priesthood attempted to organize itself as a power independent of the political authorities, and the more rationalized its ethic became, the more this position shifted. The contradiction within the priestly preaching, between brotherliness toward fellow religionists and the glorification of war against outsiders, did not as a general rule decisively stigmatize martial virtues and heroic qualities. This was so because a distinction could be drawn between just and unjust wars. However, this distinction was a product of pharisaical thought, which was unknown to the old and genuine warrior ethics.

Of far greater importance was the rise of congregational religions among politically demilitarized peoples under the control of priests, such as the Jews, and also the rise of large and increasingly important groups of people who, though comparatively unwarlike, became increasingly important for the priests' maintenance of their power position wherever they had developed into an independent organization. The priesthood unquestioningly welcomed the characteristic virtues of these classes, viz., simplicity, patient resignation to trouble, humble acceptance of existing authority, and friendly forgiveness and passivity in the face of injustice, especially since these virtues were useful in establishing the ascendancy of an ethical god and of the priests themselves. These virtues were also complementary to the special religious virtue of the powerful, namely magnanimous charity (*caritas*), since the patriarchal donors desired these virtues of resignation and humble acceptance in those who benefited from their assistance.

The more a religion became congregational, the more did political circumstances contribute to the religious transfiguration of the ethics of the subjugated. Thus, Jewish prophecy, in a realistic recognition of the external political situation, preached resignation to the domination by the great powers, as a fate apparently desired by God. The domestication of the masses was assigned to priests by foreign rulers (for the first time systematically by the Persians), and later indigenous rulers followed suit. As religion became more popularized, this domestication provided ever stronger grounds for assigning religious value to the essentially feminine virtues of the ruled; moreover, the activities of the priests themselves were distinctively unwarlike and women had everywhere shown a particular susceptibility to religious stimuli. However, this "slave revolt" in the realm of morality, a revolt organized by priests, was not the only internal force of pacification. In addition, by its own logic, every ascetic, and especially every mystic, quest for individual salvation, took this line. Certain typical external situations also contributed to this development, e.g., the apparently senseless changes of limited and ephemeral small political power structures in contrast to universalistic religions and relatively unitary social cultures such as that of India. Two other historical processes operating in the opposite direction also contributed to the same development: universal pacification and the elimination of all struggles for power in the great world empires, and particularly the bureaucratization of all political dominion, as in the Roman Empire.

All these factors removed the ground from under the political and social interests involved in a warlike struggle for power and involved in a social class conflict, thus tending to generate an antipolitical rejection of the world and to favor the development of a religious ethic of brotherly love that renounced all violence. The power of the apolitical Christian religion of love was not derived from interests in social reform, nor from any such thing as "proletarian instincts," but rather from the complete loss of such secular concerns. The same motivation accounts for the increasing importance of all salvation religions and congregational religions from the first and second century of the [Roman] Imperial period. This transformation was carried out, not only or even primarily by the subjugated classes with their slave revolt *in ethicis,* but by educated strata which had lost interest in politics because they had lost influence or had become disgusted by politics.

The altogether universal experience that violence breeds violence, that social or economic power interests may combine with idealistic reforms and even with revolutionary movements, and that the employment of violence against some particular injustice produces as its ultimate result the victory, not of the greater justice, but of the greater power or cleverness, did not remain concealed, at least not from the intellectuals who lacked political interests. This recognition continued to evoke the most radical demands for the ethic of brotherly love, i.e., that evil should not be resisted by force, an injunction that is common to Buddhism and to the preaching of Jesus. But the ethic of brotherly love is also characteristic of mystical religions, because their peculiar quest for salvation fosters an attitude of humility and self-surrender as a result of its minimization of activity in the world and its affirmation of the necessity of passing through the world incognito, so to speak, as the only proven method for demonstrating salvation. Indeed, from the purely psychological point of view, mystical religion must necessarily come to this conclusion by virtue of its characteristically acosmistic and non-specific experience of love. Every pure intellectualism bears within itself the possibility of such a mystical development.

On the other hand, inner-worldly asceticism can compromise with the facts of the political power structures by interpreting them as instruments for the rationalized ethical transformation of the world and for the control of sin. It must be noted, however, that the coexistence is by no means as easy in this case as in the case where economic acquisitive interests are concerned. For public political activity leads to a far greater surrender of rigorous ethical requirements than is produced by private business activity, since political activity is oriented to average human qualities, to compromises, to craft, and to the employment of other ethically suspect devices and people, and thereby oriented to the relativization of all goals. Thus, it is very striking that under the glorious regime of the Maccabees, after the first intoxication of the war of liberation had been dissipated, there arose among the most pious Jews a party which preferred alien hegemony to rule by the national kingdom. This may be compared to the preference found among some Puritan denominations for the subjection of the churches to the dominion of unbelievers, because genuineness of religion can be regarded as proven only in such churches. In both these cases two distinct motives were operative. One was that a genuine commitment in religion could be truly demonstrated only in martyrdom; the other was the theoretical insight that the political apparatus of force could not possibly provide a place for purely religious virtues, whether uncompromising rational ethics or acosmistic fraternalism. This is one source of the affinity between inner-worldly asceticism and the advocacy of the minimization of state control such as was represented by the laissez-faire doctrine of the "Manchester school."

2. *Tensions and Compromises Between Ethics and Politics*

The conflict of ascetic ethics, as well as of the mystically oriented temper of brotherly love, with the apparatus of domination which is basic to all political institutions has produced the most varied types of tension and compromise. Naturally, the polarity between religion and politics is least wherever, as in Confucianism, religion is equivalent to a belief in spirits or simply a belief in magic, and ethics is no more than a prudent accommodation to the world on the part of the educated man. Nor does any conflict between religion and politics exist wherever, as in Islam, religion makes obligatory the violent propagation of the true prophecy which consciously eschews universal conversion and enjoins the subjugation of unbelievers under the dominion of a ruling order dedicated to the religious war as one of the basic postulates of its faith, without recognizing the salvation of the subjugated. For this is obviously no universalistic salvation religion. The practice of coercion poses no problem, as god is pleased by the forcible dominion of the faithful over the infidels, who are tolerated once they have been subjugated.

Inner-worldly asceticism reached a similar solution to the problem of the relation between religion and politics wherever, as in radical Calvinism, it represented as God's will the domination over the sinful world, for the purpose of controlling it, by religious virtuosi belonging to the "pure" church. This view was fundamental in the theocracy of New England, in practice if not explicitly, though naturally it became involved with compromises of various kinds. Another instance of the absence of any conflict between religion and politics is to be found in the intellectualistic salvation doctrines of India, such as Buddhism and Jainism, in which every relationship to the world and to action within the world is broken off, and in which the personal exercise of violence as well as resistance to violence is absolutely prohibited and is indeed without any object. Mere conflict between concrete demands of a state and concrete religious injunctions arises when a religion is the pariah faith of a group that is excluded from political equality but still believes in the religious prophecies of a divinely appointed restoration of its social level. This was the case in Judaism, which never in theory rejected the state and its coercion but, on the contrary, expected in the Messiah their own masterful political ruler, an expectation that was sustained at least until the time of the destruction of the Temple by Hadrian.

Wherever congregational religions have rejected all employment of force as an abomination to god and have sought to require their members' avoidance of all violence, without however reaching the consistent conclusion of absolute flight from the world, the conflict between religion and politics has led either to martyrdom or to passive anti-political sufferance of the coercive regime. History shows that religious anarchism has hitherto been only a short-lived phenomenon, because the intensity of faith which makes it possible is in only an ephemeral charisma. Yet there have been independent political organizations which were based, not on a purely anarchistic foundation, but on a foundation of consistent pacifism. The most important of these was the Quaker community in Pennsylvania, which for two generations actually succeeded, in contrast to all the neighboring colonies, in existing side by side with the Indians, and indeed prospering, without recourse to violence. Such situations continued until the conflicts of the great colonial powers made a fiction of pacifism. Finally, the American War of Independence, which was waged in the name of basic principles of Quakerism (though the orthodox Quakers did not participate because of their principle of non-resistance), led to the discrediting of this principle even inwardly. More-over, the corresponding policy of the tolerant admission of religious dissidents into Pennsylvania brought even the Quakers there to a policy of gerrymandering political wards, which caused them increasing un-easiness and ultimately led them to withdraw from co-responsibility for the government.

Typical examples of completely passive indifference to the political dimension of society, from a variety of motives, are found in such groups as the genuine Mennonites, in most Baptist communities, and in nu-merous other sects in various places, especially Russia. The absolute renunciation of the use of force by these groups led them into acute conflicts with the political authorities only where military service was demanded of the individuals concerned. Indeed, attitudes toward war, even of religious denominations that did not teach an absolutely anti-political attitude, have varied in particular cases, depending upon whether the wars in question were fought to protect the religion's free-dom of worship from attack by political authority or fought for purely political purposes. For these two types of war, two diametrically oppo-site slogans prevailed. On the one hand, there was the purely passive sufferance of alien power and the withdrawal from any personal partici-pation in the exercise of violence, culminating ultimately in personal martyrdom. This was of course the position of mystical apoliticism, with its absolute indifference to the world, as well as the position of those types of inner-worldly asceticism which were pacifistic in principle. But even a purely personal religion of faith frequently generated political indifference and religious martyrdom, inasmuch as it recognized neither a rational order of the outer world pleasing to God, nor a rational domination of the world desired by God. Thus, Luther completely re-jected religious revolutions as well as religious wars.

The other possible standpoint was that of violent resistance, at least to the employment of force against religion. The concept of a religious revolution was consistent most with a rationalism oriented to an ascetic mastery of mundane affairs which taught that sacred institutions and institutions pleasing to God exist within this world. Within Christianity, this was true in Calvinism, which made it a religious obligation to defend the faith against tyranny by the use of force. It should be added, however, that Calvin taught that this defense might be undertaken only at the initiative of the proper authorities, in keeping with the character of an institutional church. The obligation to bring about a revolution in behalf of the faith was naturally taught by the religions that engaged in wars of missionary enterprise and by their derivative sects, like the Mahdists and other sects in Islam, including the Sikhs— a Hindu sect that was originally pacifist but passed under the influence of Islam and became eclectic.

The representatives of the two opposed viewpoints just described sometimes took virtually reverse positions toward a political war that had no religious motivation. Religions that applied ethically rationalized demands to the political realm had necessarily to take a more fundamentally negative attitude toward purely political wars than those religions that accepted the institutions of the world as "given" and relatively indifferent in value. The unvanquished Cromwellian army petitioned Parliament for the abolition of forcible conscription, on the ground that a Christian should participate only in those wars the justice of which could be affirmed by his own conscience. From this standpoint, the mercenary army might be regarded as a relatively ethical institution, inasmuch as the mercenary would have to settle with God and his conscience as to whether he would take up this calling. The employment of force by the state can have moral sanction only when the force is used for the control of sins, for the glory of God, and for combating religious evils—in short, only for religious purposes. On the other hand, the view of Luther, who absolutely rejected religious wars and revolutions as well as any active resistance, was that only the secular authority, whose domain is untouched by the rational postulates of religion, has the responsibility of determining whether political wars are just or unjust. Hence, the individual subject has no reason to burden his own conscience with this matter if only he gives active obedience to the political authority in this and in all other matters which do not destroy his relationship to God.

The position of ancient and medieval Christianity in relation to the state as a whole oscillated or, more correctly, shifted its center of gravity from one to another of several distinct points of view. At first there was a complete abomination of the existing Roman empire, whose existence until the very end of time was taken for granted in Antiquity by everyone, even Christians. The empire was regarded as the dominion of Anti-Christ. A second view was complete indifference to the state, and hence passive sufferance of the use of force, which was deemed to be unrighteous in every case. This entailed active compliance with all the coercive obligations imposed by the state, e.g., the payment of taxes which did not directly imperil religious salvation. For the true intent of the New Testament verse about "rendering unto Caesar the things which are Caesar's" is not the meaning deduced by modern harmonizing interpretations, namely a positive recognition of the obligation to pay taxes, but rather the reverse: an absolute indifference to all the affairs of the mundane world.

Two other viewpoints were possible. One entailed withdrawal from concrete activities of the political community, such as the cult of the emperors, because and insofar as such participation necessarily led to sin. Nevertheless, the state's authority was accorded positive recognition as being somehow desired by God, even when exercised by unbelievers and even though inherently sinful. It was taught that the state's authority, like all the institutions of this world, is an ordained punishment for the sin brought upon man by Adam's fall, which the Christian must obediently take upon himself. Finally, the authority of the state, even when exercised by unbelievers, might be evaluated positively, due to our condition of sin, as an indispensable instrument, based upon the divinely implanted natural knowledge of religiously unilluminated heathens, for the social control of reprehensible sins and as a general condition for all mundane existence pleasing to God.

3. *Natural Law and Vocational Ethics*

Of these four points of view, the first two mentioned belong primarily to the period of eschatological expectation, but occasionally they come to the fore even in a later period. As far as the last of the four is concerned, ancient Christianity did not really go beyond it in principle, even after it had been recognized as the state religion. Rather, the great change in the attitude of Christianity toward the state took place in the medieval church, as the investigations of Troeltsch have brilliantly demonstrated.[1] But the problem in which Christianity found itself involved as a result, while not limited to this religion, nevertheless generated a whole complex of difficulties peculiar to Christianity alone, partly from internal religious causes and partly from the operation of non-religious factors. This critical complex of difficulties concerned the relationship of so-called "natural law" to religious revelation on the one hand, and to positive political institutions and their activities on the other.

We shall advert again to this matter briefly, both in connection with our exposition of the forms of religious communities and in our analysis of the forms of domination [below, ch. XV: 14]. But the following point may be made here regarding the theoretical solution of these problems as it affects personal ethics: the general schema according to which religion customarily solves the problem of the tension between religious ethics and the non-ethical or unethical requirements of life in the political and economic structures of power within the world is to relativize and differentiate ethics into "organic" (as contrasted to "ascetic") *ethics of vocation.* This holds true whenever a religion is dominant within a political organization or occupies a privileged status, and particularly when it is a religion of institutional grace.

Christian doctrine, as formulated by Aquinas for example, to some degree assumed the view, already common in animistic beliefs regarding souls and the world beyond, that there are purely natural differences among men, completely independent of any effects of sin, and that these natural differences determine the diversity of status destinies in this world and beyond. Troeltsch has correctly stressed the point that this formulation of Christian doctrine differs from the view found in Stoicism and earliest Christianity of an original golden age and a blissful state of anarchic equality of all human beings.[2]

At the same time, however, religion interprets the power relationships of the mundane world in a metaphysical way. Human beings are condemned—whether as a result of original sin, of an individual causality of *karma,* or of the corruption of the world deriving from a basic dualism—to suffer violence, toil, pain, hate, and above all differences in class and status position within the world. The various callings or castes have been providentially ordained, and each of them has been assigned some specific, indispensable function desired by god or determined by the impersonal world order, so that different ethical obligations devolve upon each. The diverse occupations and castes are compared to the constituent portions of an organism in this type of theory. The various relationships of power which emerge in this manner must therefore be regarded as divinely ordained relationships of authority. Accordingly, any revolt or rebellion against them, or even the raising of vital claims other than those corresponding to one's status in society, is reprehensible to god because they are expressions of creaturely self-aggrandizement and pride which are destructive of sacred tradition. The virtuosi of religion, be they of an ascetic or contemplative type, are also assigned their specific responsibility within such an organic order, just as specific functions have been allocated to princes, warriors, judges, artisans, and peasants. This allocation of responsibilities to religious virtuosi is intended to produce a treasure of supernumerary good works which the institution of grace may thereupon distribute. By subjecting himself to the revealed truth and to the correct sentiment of love, the individual will achieve, and that within the established institutions of the world, happiness in this world and reward in the life to come.

For Islam, this organic conception and its entire complex of related problems was much more remote, since Islam rejected universalism, regarding the ideal status order as consisting of believers and unbelievers or pariah peoples, with the former dominating the latter. Accordingly, Islam left the pariah peoples entirely to themselves in all matters which were of indifference to religion. It is true that the mystical quest for salvation and ascetic virtuoso religion did conflict with institutional orthodoxy in the Muslim religion. It is also true that Islam did experience conflicts between sacred and profane law, which always arise when positive sacred norms of the law have developed. Finally, Islam did have to face certain questions of orthodoxy in the theocratic constitution. But Islam did not confront the ultimate problem of the relationship between religious ethics and secular institutions, which is a problem of religion and natural law.

On the other hand, the Hindu books of law promulgated an organic, traditionalistic ethic of vocation, similar in structure to medieval Catholicism, only more consistent, and certainly more consistent than the rather thin Lutheran doctrine regarding the *status ecclesiasticus, politicus,* and *oeconomicus.* As we have already seen, the status system in India actually combined a caste ethic with a distinctive doctrine of salvation. That is, it held that an individual's chances of an ever higher ascent in future incarnations upon earth depend on his having fulfilled the obligations of his own caste, be they ever so disesteemed socially. This belief had the effect of inducing a radical acceptance of the social order, especially among the very lowest castes, which would have most to gain in any transmigration of souls.

On the other hand, the Hindu theodicy would have regarded as absurd the medieval Christian doctrine, as set forth for example by Beatrice in the *Paradiso* of Dante, that the class differences which obtain during one's brief span of life upon earth will be perpetuated into some "permanent" existence in the world beyond. Indeed, such a view would have deprived the strict traditionalism of the Hindu organic ethic of vocation of all the infinite hopes for the future entertained by the pious Hindu who believed in the transmigration of souls and the possibility of an ever more elevated form of life upon this earth. Hence, even from the purely religious point of view, the Christian doctrine of the perpetuation of class distinctions into the next world had the effect

of providing a much less secure foundation for the traditional stratification of vocations than did the steel-like anchorage of caste to the altogether different religious promises contained in the doctrine of metempsychosis.

The medieval and the Lutheran traditionalistic ethics of vocation
actually rested on a general presupposition, one that is increasingly rare,
which both share with the Confucian ethic: that power relationships in
both the economic and political spheres have a purely personal character. In these spheres of the execution of justice and particularly in
political administration, a whole organized structure of personal relations
of subordination exists which is dominated by caprice and grace, indignation and love, and most of all by the mutual piety and devotion
of masters and subalterns, after the fashion of the family. Thus, these
relationships of domination have a character to which one may apply
ethical requirements in the same way that one applies them to every
other purely personal relationship.

Yet as we shall see later, it is quite certain that the "masterless
slavery" (Wagner) of the modern proletariat, and above all the whole
realm of the rational institution of the state—that "rascal, the state"
(*Racker von Staat*) so heartily abominated by romanticism—no longer
possess this personalistic character.[3] In a personalistic status order it is
quite clear that one must act differently toward persons of different
status. The only problem that may arise on occasion, even for Thomas
Aquinas, is how this is to be construed. Today, however, the *homo
politicus*, as well as the *homo oeconomicus,* performs his duty best when
he acts without regard to the person in question, *sine ira et studio,* without hate and without love, without personal predilection and therefore
without grace, but sheerly in accordance with the impersonal duty imposed by his calling, and not as a result of any concrete personal relationship. He discharges his responsibility best if he acts as closely as
possible in accordance with the rational regulations of the modern power
system. Modern procedures of justice impose capital punishment upon
the malefactor, not out of personal indignation or the need for vengeance, but with complete detachment and for the sake of objective norms
and ends, simply for the working out of the rational autonomous lawfulness inherent in justice. This is comparable to the impersonal retribution of *karma,* in contrast to Yahweh's fervent quest for vengeance.

The use of force within the political community increasingly assumes the form of the *Rechtsstaat.* But from the point of view of religion, this is merely the most effective mimicry of brutality. All politics
is oriented to *raison d'état,* to realism, and to the autonomous end of

maintaining the external and internal distribution of power. These goals, again, must necessarily seem completely senseless from the religious point of view. Yet only in this way does the realm of politics acquire a peculiarly rational mystique of its own, once brilliantly formulated by Napoleon, which appears as thoroughly alien to every ethic of brotherliness as do the rationalized economic institutions.

The accommodation that contemporary ecclesiastical ethics is making to this situation need not be discussed in detail here. In general the compromise takes form through reaction to each concrete situation as it arises. Above all, and particularly in the case of Catholicism, the accommodation involves the salvaging of ecclesiastical power interests, which have increasingly become objectified into a *raison d'église*, by the employment of the same modern instruments of power employed by secular institutions.

The objectification of the power structure, with the complex of problems produced by its rationalized ethical provisos, has but one psychological equivalent: the vocational ethic taught by asceticism. An increased tendency toward flight into the irrationalities of apolitical emotionalism in different degrees and forms, is one of the actual consequences of the rationalization of coercion, manifesting itself wherever the exercise of power has developed away from the personalistic orientation of heroes and wherever the entire society in question has developed in the direction of a national "state." Such apolitical emotionalism may take the form of a flight into mysticism and an acosmistic ethic of absolute goodness or into the irrationalities of non-religious emotionalism, above all eroticism. Indeed, the power of the sphere of eroticism enters into particular tensions with religions of salvation. This is particularly true of the most powerful component of eroticism, namely sexual love. For sexual love, along with the "true" or economic interest, and the social drives toward power and prestige, is among the most fundamental and universal components of the actual course of interpersonal behavior.

NOTES

1. See Ernst Troeltsch, "Das stoisch-christliche Naturrecht und das moderne profane Naturrecht" (1911), in *Aufsätze zur Geistesgeschichte und Religionssoziologie* (Tübingen: Mohr, 1924), 179. (W)

2. *Id.*, "Epochen und Typen der Sozialphilosophie des Christentums" (1911), *op. cit.*, 133.

3. The term "herrenlose Sklaverei" is attributed to the economist Adolf Wagner (1835–1917), a proponent of the Christian welfare state. "Racker von Staat" had in Weber's time become a humorous expression; it was a favorite

phrase of the romantic king Frederick William IV of Prussia (1840–61). The words were allegedly spoken by a peasant whose personal petition the king had turned down in the name of state and order; the peasant is supposed to have said: "I knew in advance that it would not be my beloved King who would confront me but that *Racker von Staat.*"

xiv

Religious Ethics and the World: Sexuality and Art

1. *Orgy versus Chastity*

The relationship of religion to sexuality is extraordinarily intimate, though it is partly conscious and partly unconscious, and though it may be indirect as well as direct. We shall focus on a few traits of this relationship that have sociological relevance, leaving out of account as being rather unimportant for our purposes the innumerable relationships of sexuality to magical notions, animistic notions, and symbols. In the first place, sexual intoxication is a typical component of the orgy, the religious behavior of the laity at a primitive level. The function of sexual intoxication may be retained even in relatively systematized religions, in some cases quite directly and by calculation. This is the case in the *Shakti*-religion of India, after the pattern of the ancient phallic cults and rites of the various functional gods who control reproduction, whether of man, beast, cattle, or grains of seed. More frequently, however, the erotic orgy appears in religion as an undesired consequence of ecstasy produced by other orgiastic means, particularly the dance. Among modern sects, this was still the case in the terpsichorean orgy of the Khlysty. This provided the stimulus for the formation of the Skoptsy sect, which, as we have seen, then sought to eliminate this erotic by-product so inimical to asceticism.[1] Various institutions which have often been misinterpreted, as for example temple prostitution, are related to orgiastic cults. In practice, temple prostitution frequently fulfilled the function of a brothel for traveling traders who enjoyed the protection of the sanctuary. (In the nature of the case, the typical client of brothels to this very day remains the traveling salesman.) To attribute extraordinary sexual orgies to a primordial and endogamous promiscuity obtaining in the everyday life of the clan or tribe as a generic primitive institution is simple nonsense.

The intoxication of the sexual orgy can, as we have seen, be sublimated explicitly or implicitly into erotic love for a god or savior. But there may also emerge from the sexual orgy, from temple prostitution, or from other magical practices the notion that sexual surrender has a religious meritoriousness. This aspect of the matter need not interest us here. Yet there can be no doubt that a considerable portion of the specifically anti-erotic religiosity, both mystical and ascetic, represents substitute satisfactions of sexually conditioned physiological needs. What concerns us in this religious hostility to sexuality is not the neurological relationships, important aspects of which are still controversial, but rather the meaning which is attributed to sex. For this meaning which underlies religious antipathy to sex in a given case may produce quite diverse results in actual conduct, even if the neurological factor remains constant. Even these consequences for action are of only partial interest here. The most limited manifestations of the religiously grounded antipathy to sexuality is cultic chastity, a temporary abstinence from sexual activity by the priests or participants in the cult prior to the administration of sacraments. A primary reason for such temporary abstinence is usually regard for the norms of taboo which for various magical and spiritualistic reasons control the sexual sphere. The details of this matter do not concern us here.

On the other hand, the permanent abstinence of charismatic priests and religious virtuosi derives primarily from the view that chastity, as a highly extraordinary type of behavior, is a symptom of charismatic qualities and a source of valuable ecstatic abilities, which qualities and abilities are necessary instruments for the magical control of the god. Later on, especially in Occidental Christianity, a major reason for priestly celibacy was the necessity that the ethical achievement of the priestly incumbents of ecclesiastical office not lag behind that of the ascetic virtuosi, the monks. Another major reason for the emphasis upon the celibacy of the clergy was the church's interest in preventing the inheritance of its benefices by the heirs of priests.

At the level of ethical religion, two other significant attitudes of antipathy to sexuality developed in place of the various types of magical motivation. One was the conception of mystical flight from the world; this conception interpreted sexual abstinence as the central and indispensable instrument of the mystical quest for salvation through contemplative withdrawal from the world, in which sexuality, the drive that most firmly binds man to the animal level, constitutes the most powerful temptation. The other basic position was that of asceticism.

Rational ascetic alertness, self-control, and methodical planning of life are threatened the most by the peculiar irrationality of the sexual act, which is ultimately and uniquely unsusceptible to rational organization. These two motivations have frequently operated together to produce hostility toward sexuality in particular religions. All genuine religious prophecies and all non-prophetic priestly systematizations of religion without exception concern themselves with sexuality from such motives as we have just discussed, generally terminating in hostility toward sexuality.

2. The Religious Status of Marriage and of Women

Religion primarily desires to eliminate the sexual orgy (the "whoredom" denounced by the Jewish priests), in keeping with prophetic religion's general attitude toward orgies, which we have described already. But an additional effort is made by religion to eliminate all free sexual relationships in the interest of the religious regulation and legitimation of marriage. Such an effort was even made by Muhammad, although in his personal life and in his religious preachments regarding the world beyond he permitted unlimited sexual freedom to the warrior of the faith. It will be recalled that in one of his *suras* he ordained a special dispensation regarding the maximum number of wives permitted for himself. The various forms of extra-marital love and prostitution, which were legal before the establishment of orthodox Islam, have been proscribed in that religion with a success scarcely duplicated elsewhere.

World-fleeing asceticism of the Christian and Hindu types would obviously have been expected to evince an antipathetic attitude toward sex. The mystical Hindu prophecies of absolute and contemplative world-flight naturally made the rejection of all sexual relations a prerequisite for complete salvation. But even the Confucian ethic of absolute accommodation to the world viewed irregular sexual expression as an inferior irrationality, since irregular behavior in this sphere disturbed the inner equilibrium of a gentleman and since woman was viewed as an irrational creature difficult to control. Adultery was prohibited in the Mosaic Decalogue, in the Hindu sacred law, and even in the relativistic lay ethics of the Hindu monastic prophecies. The religious preaching of Jesus, with its demand of absolute and indissoluble monogamy, went beyond all other religions in the limitations imposed upon permissible and legitimate sexuality. In the earliest period of Christianity, adultery and whoredom were almost regarded as the only absolute mortal sins. The *univira* was regarded as the hallmark of the Christian community in the Mediterranean littoral area, which had been educated by the Greeks and the Romans to accept monogamy, but with free divorce.

Naturally, the various prophets differed widely in their personal attitudes toward woman and her place in the community, depending on the character of their prophecy, especially on the extent to which it corresponds to the distinctively feminine emotionality. The fact that a prophet such as the Buddha was glad to see bright women sitting at his feet and the fact that he employed them as propagandists and missionaries, as did Pythagoras, did not necessarily carry over into an evaluation of the whole female sex. A particular woman might be regarded as sacred, yet the entire female sex would still be considered vessels of sin. Yet practically all orgiastic and mystagogic religious propagandizing, including that of the cult of Dionysos, called for at least a temporary and relative emancipation of women, unless such preachment was blocked by other religious tendencies or by specific resistance to hysterical preaching by women, as occurred among the disciples of the Buddha and in ancient Christianity as early as Paul. The admission of women to an equality of religious status was also resisted due to monastic misogyny, which assumed extreme forms in such sexual neurasthenics as Alfonsus Liguori [1696–1787]. Women are accorded the greatest importance in sectarian spiritualist cults, be they hysterical or sacramental, of which there are numerous instances in China. Where women played no role in the missionary expansion of a religion, as was the case in Zoroastrianism and Judaism, the situation was different from the very start.

Legally regulated marriage itself was regarded by both prophetic and priestly ethics, not as an erotic value, but in keeping with the sober view of the so-called "primitive peoples," simply as an economic institution for the production and rearing of children as a labor force and subsequently as carriers of the cult of the dead. This was also the view of the Greek and Roman ethical systems, and indeed of all ethical systems the world over which have given thought to the matter. The view expressed in the ancient Hebrew scriptures that the young bridegroom was to be free of political and military obligations for a while so that he might have the joy of his young love was a very rare view. Indeed, not even Judaism made any concessions to sophisticated erotic expression divorced from sexuality's natural consequence of reproduction, as we see in the Old Testament curse upon the sin of Onan (*coitus interruptus*). Roman Catholicism adopted the same rigorous attitude toward sexuality by rejecting birth control as a mortal sin. Of course every type of religious asceticism which is oriented toward the control of this world, and above all Puritanism, limits the legitimation of sexual expression to the aforementioned rational goal of reproduction. The anomistic and semi-orgiastic types of mysticism were led by their universalistic feeling of love into only occasional deviations from the central hostility of religion toward sexuality.

Finally, the evaluation of normal and legitimate sexual intercourse, and thus the ultimate relationship between religion and biological phenomena, by prophetic ethics and even ecclesiastical rational ethics is still not uniform. Ancient Judaism and Confucianism generally taught that offspring were important. This view, also found in Vedic and Hindu ethics, was based in part on animistic notions and in part on later ideas. All such notions culminated in the direct religious obligation to beget children. In Talmudic Judaism and in Islam, on the other hand, the motivation of the comparable injunction to marry seems to have been based, in part at least, like the exclusion of unmarried ordained clergy from the lower ecclesiastical benefices in the Eastern churches, on the conception that sexual drives are absolutely irresistible for the average man, for whom it is better that a legally regulated channel of expression be made available.

These beliefs in the inevitability of sexual expression correspond to the attitude of Paul and to the relativity of lay ethics in the Hindu contemplative religions of salvation, which proscribe adultery for the *upasakas*. Paul, from mystical motivations which we need not describe here, esteemed absolute abstinence as the purely personal charisma of religious virtuosi. The lay ethic of Catholicism also followed this point of view. Further, this was the attitude of Luther, who regarded sexual expression within marriage simply as a lesser evil enjoined for the avoidance of whoredom. Luther construed marriage as a legitimate sin which God was constrained not to notice, so to speak, and which of course was a consequence of the ineluctable concupiscence resulting from original sin. This notion, similar to Muhammad's notion, partly accounts for Luther's relatively weak opposition to monasticism at first. There was to be no sexuality in Jesus' kingdom to come, that is, in some future terrestrial regime, and all official Christian theory strongly rejected the inner emotional side of sexuality as constituting concupiscence, the result of original sin.

Despite the widespread belief that hostility toward sexuality is an idiosyncracy of Christianity, it must be emphasized that no authentic religion of salvation had in principle any other point of view. There are a number of reasons for this. The first is based on the nature of the evolution that sexuality itself increasingly underwent in actual life, as a result of the rationalization of the conditions of life. At the level of the peasant, the sexual act is an everyday occurrence; primitive people do not regard this act as containing anything unusual, and they may indeed enact it before the eyes of onlooking travelers without the slightest feeling of shame. They do not regard this act as having any significance beyond the routine of living. The decisive development, from the point of view of the problems which concern us, is the sublimation of sexual expression into an eroticism that becomes the basis of idiosyncratic sensations, hence generates its own unique values and transcends everyday life. The impediments to sexual intercourse that are increasingly produced by the economic interests of clans and by status conventions are the most important factors favoring this sublimation of sexuality into eroticism. To be sure, sexual relations were never free of religious or economic regulations at any known point in the evolutionary sequence, but originally they were far less surrounded by bonds of convention, which gradually attach themselves to the original economic restrictions until they subsequently become major restrictions on sexuality.

The influence of modern ethical limitations upon sexual relations, which is alleged to be the source of prostitution, is almost always interpreted erroneously. Professional prostitution of both the heterosexual and homosexual types (note the training of *tribades*) is found even at the most primitive levels of culture, and everywhere there is some religious, military, or economic limitation upon prostitution. However, the absolute proscription of prostitution dates only from the end of the fifteenth century. As culture becomes more complex, there is a constant growth in the requirements imposed by the clan in regard to providing security for the children of a female member, and also in the living standards of young married couples. Thereby another evolutionary factor becomes necessarily important. In the formation of ethical attitudes the emergence of a new and progressively rationalized total life pattern, changing from the organic cycle of simple peasant existence, has a far stronger influence but one less likely to be noticed.

3. The Tensions Between Ethical Religion and Art

Just as ethical religion, especially if it preaches brotherly love, enters into the deepest inner tensions with the strongest irrational power of personal life, namely sexuality, so also does ethical religion enter into a strong polarity with the sphere of art. Religion and art are intimately related in the beginning. That religion has been an inexhaustible spring for artistic expressions is evident from the existence of idols and icons of every variety, and from the existence of music as a device for arousing ecstasy or for accompanying exorcism and apotropaic cultic actions.

Religion has stimulated the artistic activities of magicians and sacred bards, as well as the creation of temples and churches (the greatest of artistic productions), together with the creation of religious paraments and church vessels of all sorts, the chief objects of the arts and crafts. But the more art becomes an autonomous sphere, which happens as a result of lay education, the more art tends to acquire its own set of constitutive values, which are quite different from those obtaining in the religious and ethical domain.

Every unreflectively receptive approach to art starts from the significance of the *content,* and that may induce formation of a community. But the conscious discovery of uniquely esthetic values is reserved for an intellectualist civilization. This development causes the disappearance of those elements in art which are conducive to community formation and conducive to the compatibility of art with the religious will to salvation. Indeed, religion violently rejects as sinful the type of salvation within the world which art *qua* art claims to provide. Ethical religions as well as true mysticisms regard with hostility any such salvation from the ethical irrrationalities of the world. The climax of this conflict between art and religion is reached in authentic asceticism, which views any surrender to esthetic values as a serious breach in the rational systematization of the conduct of life. This tension increases with the advance of intellectualism, which may be described as quasi-esthetic. The rejection of responsibility for ethical judgment and the fear of appearing bound by tradition, which come to the fore in intellectualist periods, shift judgments whose intention was originally ethical into an esthetic key. Typical is the shift from the judgment "reprehensible" to the judgment "in poor taste." But this unappealable subjectivity of all judgments about human relationships that actually comes to the fore in the cult of estheticism, may well be regarded by religion as one of the profoundest forms of idiosyncratic lovelessness conjoined with cowardice. Clearly there is a sharp contrast between the esthetic attitude and religio-ethical norms, since even when the individual rejects ethical norms he nevertheless experiences them humanly in his knowledge of his own creatureliness. He assumes some such norm to be basic for his own conduct as well as another's conduct in the particular case which he is judging. Moreover, it is assumed in principle that the justification and consequences of a religio-ethical norm remain subject to discussion. At all events, the esthetic attitude offers no support to a consistent ethic of fraternalism, which in its turn has a clearly anti-esthetic orientation.

The religious devaluation of art, which usually parallels the religious devaluation of magical, orgiastic, ecstatic, and ritualistic elements in favor of ascetic, spiritualistic, and mystical virtues, is intensified by the rational and literary character of both priestly and lay education in scriptural religions. But it is above all authentic prophecy that exerts an influence hostile to art, and that in two directions. First, prophecy obviously rejects orgiastic practices and usually rejects magic in general. Thus, the primal Jewish fear of images and likenesses, which originally had a magical basis, was given a spiritualistic interpretation by Hebrew prophecy and transformed in relation to a concept of an absolute and transcendental god. Second, somewhere along the line there arose the opposition of prophetic faith, which is centrally oriented to ethics and religion, to the work of human hands, which in the view of the prophets could promise only illusory salvation. The more the god proclaimed by the prophets was conceived as transcendental and sacred, the more insoluble and irreconcilable became this opposition between religion and art.

On the other hand, religion is continually brought to recognize the undeniable "divinity" of artistic achievement. Mass religion in particular is frequently and directly dependent on artistic devices for the required potency of its effects, and it is inclined to make concessions to the needs of the masses, which everywhere tend toward magic and idolatry. Apart from this, organized mass religions have frequently had connections with art resulting from economic interests, as, for instance, in the case of the traffic in icons by the Byzantine monks, the most decisive opponents of the caesaropapist Imperial power which was supported by an army that was iconoclastic because it was recruited from the marginal provinces of Islam, still strongly spiritualistic at that time. The imperial power, in turn, attempted to cut off the monks from this source of income, hoping thus to destroy the economic strength of this most dangerous opponent to its plans for domination over the church.

Subjectively too, there is an easy way back to art from every orgiastic or ritualistic religion of emotionalism, as well as from every mystic religion of love that culminates in a transcendence of individuality—despite the heterogeneity of the ultimate meanings involved. Orgiastic religion leads most readily to song and music; ritualistic religion inclines toward the pictorial arts; religions enjoining love favor the development of poetry and music. This relationship is demonstrated by all our experience of Hindu literature and art; the joyous lyricism of the Sufis, so utterly receptive to the world; the canticles of St. Francis; and the immeasurable influences of religious symbolism, particularly in mystically formed attitudes. Yet particular empirical religions hold basically different attitudes toward art, and even within any one religion diverse attitudes toward art are manifested by different strata, carriers, and

structural forms. In their attitudes toward art, prophets differ from mystagogues and priests, monks from pious laymen, and mass religions from
sects of virtuosi. Sects of ascetic virtuosi are naturally more hostile to art
on principle than are sects of mystical virtuosi. But these matters are not
our major concern here. At all events, any real inner compromise between the religious and the esthetic attitudes in respect to their ultimate
(subjectively intended) meaning is rendered increasingly difficult once
the stages of magic and pure ritualism have been left behind.

In all this, the one important fact for us is the significance of the
marked rejection of all distinctively esthetic devices by those religions
which are rational, in our special sense. These are Judaism, ancient
Christianity, and—later on—ascetic Protestantism. Their rejection of
esthetics is either a symptom or an instrument of religion's increasingly
rational influence upon the conduct of life. It is perhaps going too far
to assert that the second commandment of the Decalogue is the decisive
foundation of actual Jewish rationalism, as some representatives of influential Jewish reform movements have assumed. But there can be no
question at all that the systematic prohibition in devout Jewish and
Puritan circles of uninhibited surrender to the distinctive form-produc-
ing values of art has effectively controlled the degree and scope of artistic productivity in these circles, and has tended to favor the development of intellectualist and rational controls over life.

NOTE

1. The *Khlysty* ("flagellants" or, in another explanation, a derisory distortion
of their self-designation as *Kristy*, "Christs" or "People of God") were a clan-
destine Russian sect in existence at least since the 17th century. Their services,
involving ecstatic dance, were claimed by their persecutors to have culminated
in sexual orgies (*svalnii grech*, a ritual of "Christian loving"); cf. K. K. Grass,
Die russischen Sekten, I (1907), 434ff., who discounts the accusations. The
Skoptsy ("castrators"), an offshoot of the above group founded in the 1770s,
aspired to purification through various degrees of self-emasculation. See also A.
Leroy-Beaulieu, *The Empire of the Tsars* (London 1896), III.

XV

The Great Religions and the World

1. Judaism and Capitalism

Judaism, in its postexilic and particularly its Talmudic form, belongs among those religions that are in some sense accommodated to the world. Judaism is at least oriented to the world in the sense that it does not reject the world as such but only rejects the prevailing social rank order in the world.

We have already made some observations concerning the total sociological structure and attitude of Judaism. Its religious promises, in the customary meaning of the word, apply to this world, and any notions of contemplative or ascetic world-flight are as rare in Judaism as in Chinese religion and in Protestantism. Judaism differs from Puritanism only in the relative (as always) absence of systematic asceticism. The ascetic elements of the early Christian religion did not derive from Judaism, but emerged primarily in the heathen Christian communities of the Pauline mission. The observance of the Jewish law has as little to do with asceticism as the fulfillment of any ritual or tabooistic norms.

Moreover, the relationship of the Jewish religion to both wealth and sexual indulgence is not in the least ascetic, but rather highly naturalistic. For wealth was regarded as a gift of God, and the satisfaction of the sexual impulse—naturally in the prescribed legal form—was thought to be so imperative that the Talmud actually regarded a person who had remained unmarried after a certain age as morally suspect. The interpretation of marriage as an economic institution for the production and rearing of children is universal and has nothing specifically Jewish about it. Judaism's strict prohibition of illegitimate sexual intercourse, a prohibition that was highly effective among the pious, was also found in Islam and all other prophetic religions, as well as in Hinduism. Moreover, the majority of ritualistic religions shared with Judaism the institution of periods of abstention from sexual relations for purposes of purification. For these reasons, it is not possible to speak of an idiosyncratic emphasis upon sexual asceticism in Judaism. The sexual regulations cited by Sombart do not go as far as the Catholic casuistry of the seventeenth century and in any case have analogies in many other casuistical systems of taboo.[1]

Nor did Judaism forbid the uninhibited enjoyment of life or even of luxury as such, provided that the positive prohibitions and taboos of the law were observed. The denunciation of wealth in the prophetic books, the Psalms, the Wisdom literature, and subsequent writings was evoked by the social injustices which were so frequently perpetrated against fellow Jews in connection with the acquisition of wealth and in violation of the spirit of the Mosaic law. Wealth was also condemned in response to arrogant disregard of the commandments and promises of God and in response to the rise of temptations to laxity in religious observance. To escape the temptations of wealth is not easy, but is for this reason all the more meritorious. "Hail to the man of wealth who has been found to be blameless." Moreover, since Judaism possessed no doctrine of predestination and no comparable idea producing the same ethical effects, incessant labor and success in business life could not be regarded or interpreted in the sense of certification, which appears most strongly among the Calvinist Puritans and which is found to some extent in all ascetic Protestant religions, as shown in John Wesley's remark on this point.[2] Of course a certain tendency to regard success in one's economic activity as a sign of God's gracious direction existed in the religion of the Jews, as in the religions of the Chinese and the lay Buddhists and generally in every religion that has not turned its back upon the world. This view was especially likely to be manifested by a religion like Judaism, which had before it very specific promises of a transcendental God together with very visible signs of this God's indignation against the people he had chosen. It is clear that any success achieved in one's economic activities while keeping the commandments of God could be, and indeed had to be, interpreted as a sign that one was personally acceptable to God. This actually occurred again and again.

But the situation of the pious Jew engaged in business was altogether different from that of the Puritan, and this difference remained of practical significance for the role of Judaism in the history of the economy. Let us now consider what this role has been. In the polemic against Sombart's book, one fact should not have been seriously questioned, namely that Judaism played a conspicuous role in the evolution of the modern capitalistic system. However, this thesis of Sombart's book needs to be made more precise. What were the *distinctive* economic achievements of Judaism in the Middle Ages and in modern times? We can easily list: moneylending, from pawnbroking to the financing of great states; certain types of commodity business, particularly retailing, peddling, and produce trade of a distinctively rural type; certain branches of wholesale business; and trading in securities, above all the brokerage of stocks. To this list of Jewish economic achievements should be added:

money-changing; money-forwarding or check-cashing, which normally accompanies money-changing; the financing of state agencies, wars, and the establishment of colonial enterprises; tax-farming (naturally excluding the collection of prohibited taxes such as those directed to the Romans); banking; credit; and the floating of bond issues. But of all these businesses only a few, though some very important ones, display the forms, both legal and economic, characteristic of modern Occidental capitalism (as contrasted to the capitalism of ancient times, the Middle Ages, and the earlier period in Eastern Asia). The distinctively modern legal forms include securities and capitalist associations, but these are not of specifically Jewish provenience. The Jews introduced some of these forms into the Occident, but the forms themselves have perhaps a common Oriental (probably Babylonian) origin, and their influence on the Occident was mediated through Hellenistic and Byzantine sources. In any event they were common to both the Jews and the Arabs. It is even true that the specifically modern forms of these institutions were in part Occidental and medieval creations, with some specifically Germanic infusions of influence. To adduce detailed proof of this here would take us too far afield. However, it can be said by way of example that the Exchange, as a "market of tradesmen," was created not by Jews but by Christian merchants. Again, the particular manner in which medieval legal concepts were adapted to the purposes of rationalized economic enterprise, i.e., the way in which partnerships *en commandite, maone,* privileged companies of all kinds and finally joint stock corporations were created,[3] was not at all dependent on specifically Jewish influences, no matter how large a part Jews later played in the formation of such rationalized economic enterprises. Finally, it must be noted that the characteristically modern principles of satisfying public and private credit needs first arose *in nuce* on the soil of the medieval city. These medieval legal forms of finance, which were quite un-Jewish in certain respects, were later adapted to the economic needs of modern states and other modern recipients of credit.

Above all, one element particularly characteristic of modern capitalism was strikingly—though not completely—missing from the extensive list of Jewish economic activities. This was the organization of industrial production (*gewerbliche Arbeit*) in domestic industry and in the factory system. How does one explain the fact that no pious Jew thought of establishing an industry employing pious Jewish workers of the ghetto (as so many pious Puritan entrepreneurs had done with devout Christian workers and artisans) at times when numerous proletarians were present in the ghettos, princely patents and privileges for the establishment of any sort of industry were available for a financial remuneration, and areas of industrial activity uncontrolled by guild monopoly were open? Again, how does one explain the fact that no modern and distinctively industrial bourgeoisie of any significance emerged among the Jews to employ the Jewish workers available for home industry, despite the presence of numerous impecunious artisan groups at almost the threshold of the modern period?

All over the world, for several millennia, the characteristic forms of the capitalist employment of wealth have been state-provisioning, tax-farming, the financing of colonies, the establishment of great plantations, trade, and moneylending. One finds Jews involved in just these activities, found at all times and places but especially characteristic of Antiquity, just as Jews are involved in those legal and entrepreneurial forms evolved by the Middle Ages but not by them. On the other hand, the Jews were relatively or altogether absent from the new and distinctive forms of modern capitalism, the rational organization of labor, especially production in an industrial enterprise of the factory type. The Jews evinced the ancient and medieval business temper which had been and remained typical of all genuine traders, whether small businessmen or large-scale moneylenders, in Antiquity, the Far East, India, the Mediterranean littoral area, and the Occident of the Middle Ages: the will and the wit to employ mercilessly every chance of profit, "for the sake of profit to ride through Hell even if it singes the sails." But this temper is far from distinctive of modern capitalism, as distinguished from the capitalism of other eras. Precisely the reverse is true. Hence, neither that which is new in the modern economic *system* nor that which is distinctive of the modern economic *temper* is specifically Jewish in origin.

The ultimate theoretical reasons for this fact, that the distinctive elements of modern capitalism originated and developed quite apart from the Jews, are to be found in the peculiar character of the Jews as a pariah people and in the idiosyncrasy of their religion. Their pariah status presented purely external difficulties impeding their participation in the organization of industrial labor. The legally and factually precarious position of the Jews hardly permitted continuous and rationalized industrial enterprise with fixed capital, but only trade and above all dealing in money. Also of fundamental importance was the subjective ethical situation of the Jews. As a pariah people, they retained the double standard of morals which is characteristic of primordial economic practice in all communities: what is prohibited in relation to one's brothers is permitted in relation to strangers. It is unquestionable that the Jewish ethic was thoroughly traditionalistic in demanding of Jews an attitude of sustenance toward fellow Jews. Although the rabbis made concessions in these matters, as Sombart correctly points out, even in regard to

business transactions with fellow Jews, this amounted merely to concessions to laxity, whereby those who took advantage of them remained
far behind the highest standards of Jewish business ethics. In any case,
it is certain that such behavior was not the realm in which a Jew could
demonstrate his religious merit.

However, for the Jews the realm of economic relations with
strangers, particularly economic relations prohibited in regard to fellow
Jews, was an area of ethical indifference. This is of course the primordial economic ethic of all peoples everywhere. That this should have
remained the Jewish economic ethic was a foregone conclusion, for even
in Antiquity the stranger confronted the Jew almost always as an enemy.
All the well-known admonitions of the rabbis enjoining fairness especially toward Gentiles could not change the fact that the religious law
prohibited taking usury from fellow Jews but permitted it in transactions
with non-Jews. Nor could the rabbinical counsels alter the fact, which
again Sombart has rightly stressed, that a lesser degree of exemplary
legality was required by the law in dealing with a stranger, i.e., an
enemy, than in dealing with another Jew, in such a matter as taking
advantage of an error made by the other party. In fine, no proof is
required to establish that the pariah condition of the Jews, which we
have seen resulted from the promises of Yahweh, and the resulting
incessant humiliation of the Jews by Gentiles necessarily led to the
Jewish people's retaining a different economic morality for its relations
with strangers than with fellow Jews.

2. *Jewish Rationalism versus Puritan Asceticism*

Let us summarize the mutual relatedness in which Catholics, Jews,
and Protestants found themselves in regard to economic acquisition. The
devout Catholic, as he went about his economic affairs, found himself
continually behaving—or on the verge of behaving—in a manner that
transgressed papal injunctions. His economic behavior could be ignored
in the confessional only on the principle of *rebus sic stantibus*, and it
could be permissible only on the basis of a lax, probabilistic morality.
To a certain extent, therefore, the life of business itself had to be regarded as reprehensible or, at best, as not positively favorable to God.
The inevitable result of this Catholic situation was that pious Jews were
encouraged to perform economic activities among Christians which if
performed among Jews would have been regarded by the Jewish community as unequivocally contrary to the law or at least as suspect from
the point of view of Jewish tradition. At best these transactions were

permissible on the basis of a lax interpretation of the Judaic religious code, and then only in economic relations with strangers. Never were they infused with positive ethical value. Thus, the Jew's economic conduct appeared to be permitted by God, in the absence of any formal contradiction with the religious law of the Jews, but ethically indifferent, in view of such conduct's correspondence with the average evils in the society's economy. This is the basis of whatever factual truth there was in the observations concerning the inferior standard of economic legality among Jews. That God crowned such economic activity with success could be a sign to the Jewish businessman that he had done nothing clearly objectionable or prohibited in this area and that indeed he had held fast to God's commandments in other areas. But it would still have been difficult for the Jew to demonstrate his ethical merit by means of characteristically modern business behavior.

But this was precisely the case with the pious Puritan. He could demonstrate his religious merit through his economic activity because he did nothing ethically reprehensible, he did not resort to any lax interpretations of religious codes or to systems of double moralities, and he did not act in a manner that could be indifferent or even reprehensible in the general realm of ethical validity. On the contrary, the Puritan could demonstrate his religious merit precisely in his economic activity. He acted in business with the best possible conscience, since through his rationalistic and legal behavior in his business activity he was factually objectifying the rational methodology of his total life pattern. He legitimated his ethical pattern in his own eyes, and indeed within the circle of his community, by the extent to which the absolute —not relativized—unassailability of his economic conduct remained beyond question. No really pious Puritan—and this is the crucial point —could have regarded as pleasing to God any profit derived from usury, exploitation of another's mistake (which was permissible to the Jew), haggling and sharp dealing, or participation in political or colonial exploitation. Quakers and Baptists believed their religious merit to be certified before all mankind by such practices as their fixed prices and their absolutely reliable business relationships with everyone, unconditionally legal and devoid of cupidity. They believed that precisely such practices promoted the irreligious to trade with them rather than with their own kind, and to entrust their money to the trust companies or limited liability enterprises of the religious sectarians rather than those of their own people—all of which made the religious sectarians wealthy, even as their business practices certified them before their God.

By contrast, the Jewish law applying to strangers, which in practice was the pariah law of the Jews, enabled them, nothwithstanding innumerable reservations, to engage in dealings with non-Jews which the Puritans rejected violently as showing the cupidity of the trader. Yet the pious Jew could combine such an attitude with strict legality, with complete fulfillment of the law, with all the inwardness of his religion, with the most sacrificial love for his family and community, and indeed with pity and mercy toward all God's creatures. For in view of the operation of the laws regarding strangers, Jewish piety never in actual practice regarded the realm of permitted economic behavior as one in which the genuineness of a person's obedience to God's commandments could be demonstrated. The pious Jew never gauged his inner ethical standards by what he regarded as permissible in the economic context. Just as the Confucian's authentic ideal of life was the gentleman who had undergone a comprehensive education in ceremonial esthetics and literature and who devoted lifelong study to the classics, so the Jew set up as his ethical ideal the scholar learned in law and casuistry, the intellectual who continuously immersed himself in the sacred writings and commentaries at the expense of his business, which he very frequently left to the management of his wife.

It was this intellectualist trait of authentic late Judaism, with its concern with literary scholarship, that Jesus revolted against. His criticism was not motivated by "proletarian" instincts, which some have attributed to him, but rather by his type of piety and his type of obedience to the law, both of which were appropriate to the rural artisan or the inhabitant of a small town, and constituted his basic opposition to the virtuosi of legalistic lore who had grown up on the soil of the *polis* of Jerusalem. Members of such urban legalistic circles asked "What good can come out of Nazareth?"—the kind of question that might have been posed by any dweller of a metropolis in the classical world. Jesus' knowledge of the law and his observance of it was representative of that average lawfulness which was actually demonstrated by men engaged in practical work, who could not afford to let their sheep lie in wells, even on the Sabbath. On the other hand, the knowledge of the law obligatory for the really pious Jews, as well as their legalistic education of the young, surpassed both quantitatively and qualitatively the preoccupation with the Bible characteristic of the Puritans. The scope of religious law of which knowledge was obligatory for the pious Jew may be compared only with the scope of ritual laws among the Hindus and Persians, but the Jewish law far exceeded these in its inclusion of ethical prescriptions beyond merely ritual and tabooistic norms.

The economic behavior of the Jews simply moved in the direction of least resistance which was permitted them by these legalistic ethical norms. This meant in practice that the "acquisitive drive," which is found in varying degrees in all groups and nations, was here directed primarily to trade with strangers, who were usually regarded as enemies. Even at the time of Josiah and certainly in the post-exilic period, the pious Jew was an urban dweller, and the entire Jewish law was oriented to this urban status. Since the orthodox Jew required the services of a ritual slaughterer, he had necessarily to live in a community rather than in isolation. Even today residential clustering is characteristic of orthodox Jews when they are contrasted with Jews of the Reform group, as for example in the United States. Similarly, the Sabbatical year, which in its present form is probably a product of post-exilic urban scholars learned in the law, made it impossible for Jews to carry on systematic intensive cultivation of the land. Even at the present time, German rabbis endeavor to apply the prescription of the Sabbatical year to Zionist colonization in Palestine, which would be ruined thereby. In the age of the Pharisees a rustic Jew was of second rank, since he did not and could not observe the law strictly. Jewish law also prohibited the participation of Jews in the banquets of the guilds, in fact, all commensality with non-Jews; in Antiquity as well as in the Middle Ages commensality was the indispensable foundation for any kind of civic integration in the surrounding world. On the other hand, the Jewish institution of the dowry, common to the Orient and based originally on the exclusion of daughters from inheritance, favored the establishing of the Jewish groom at marriage as a small shopkeeper. Traces of this phenomenon are still apparent in the relatively undeveloped class consciousness of Jewish shop clerks.

In all his other dealings, as well as those we have just discussed, the Jew—like the pious Hindu—was controlled by scruples concerning his Law. As Guttmann has correctly emphasized, genuine study of the Law could be combined most easily with the occupation of moneylending, which requires relatively little continuous labor.[4] The outcome of Jewish legalism and intellectualist education was the Jew's methodical patterning of life and his rationalism. It is a prescription of the Talmud that "A man must never change a practice." Only in the realm of economic relationships with strangers, and in no other area of life, did tradition leave a sphere of behavior that was relatively indifferent ethically. Indeed, the entire domain of things relevant before God was determined by tradition and the systematic casuistry concerned with its interpretation, rather than determined by rational purposes derived from natural law and oriented without further presupposition to methodical plans of action. The "rationalizing" effect of the Jewish fear of God's Law is thoroughly pervasive but entirely indirect.

Self-control—usually accompanied by alertness, equableness, and serenity—was found among Confucians, Puritans, Buddhist and other types of monks, Arab sheiks, and Roman senators, as well as among Jews. But the basis and significance of self-control were different in each case. The alert self-control of the Puritan flowed from the necessity of his subjugating all creaturely impulses to a rational and methodical plan of conduct, so that he might secure his certainty of his own salvation. Self-control appeared to the Confucian as a personal necessity which followed from his disesteem for plebeian irrationality, the disesteem of an educated gentleman who had received classical training and had been bred along lines of propriety and dignity. On the other hand, the self-control of the devout Jew of ancient times was a consequence of the preoccupation with the Law in which his mind had been trained, and of the necessity of his continuous concern with the Law's precise fulfillment. The pious Jew's self-control received a characteristic coloring and effect from the situation of being piously engaged in fulfilling the Law. The Jew felt that only he and his people possessed this law, for which reason the world persecuted them and imposed degradation upon them. Yet this law was binding; and one day, by an act that might come suddenly at any time but that no one could accelerate, God would transform the social structure of the world, creating a messianic realm for those who had remained faithful to His law. The pious Jew knew that innumerable generations had awaited this messianic event, despite all mockery, and were continuing to await it. This produced in the pious Jew a certain anxious wakefulness. But since it remained necessary for him to continue waiting in vain, he nurtured his feelings of self-esteem by a meticulous observance of the law for its own sake. Last but not least, the pious Jew had always to stay on guard, never permitting himself the free expression of his passions against powerful and merciless enemies. This repression was inevitably combined with the aforementioned inevitable effect of the feeling of *ressentiment* which derived from Yahweh's promises and the resulting unparalleled sufferings of this people.

These circumstances basically determined the rationalism of Judaism, but this is not "asceticism" in our sense. To be sure, there are ascetic traits in Judaism, but they are not central. Rather, they are byproducts of the law or products of the peculiar tensions of Jewish piety. In any case, ascetic traits are of secondary importance in Judaism, as are any mystical traits developed within this religion. We need say nothing more here about Jewish mysticism, since neither cabalism, Chassidism nor any of its other forms—whatever symptomatic importance they held for Jews—produced any significant motivations toward practical behavior in the economic sphere.

The ascetic aversion of pious Jews toward everything esthetic was originally based on the second commandment of the Decalogue, which actually prevented the once well-developed angelology of the Jews from assuming artistic form. But another important cause of aversion to things esthetic is the purely pedagogic and jussive character of the divine service in the synagogue, even as it was practiced in the Diaspora, long before the disruption of the Temple cult. Even at that time, Hebrew prophecy had virtually removed plastic elements from the cult, effectively extirpating orgiastic, orchestral, and terpsichorean activities. It is of interest that Roman religion and Puritanism pursued similar paths in regard to esthetic elements, though for reasons quite different from the Jewish reasons. Thus, among the Jews the plastic arts, painting, and drama lacked those points of contact with religion which were elsewhere quite normal. This is the reason for the marked diminution of secular lyricism and especially of the erotic sublimation of sexuality, when contrasted with the marked sensuality of the earlier Song of Solomon. The basis of all this is to be found in the naturalism of the Jewish ethical treatment of sexuality.

All these traits of Judaism are characterized by one overall theme: that the mute, faithful, and questioning expectation of a redemption from the hellish character of the life enforced upon the people who had been chosen by God (and definitely chosen, despite their present status) was ultimately refocused upon the ancient promises and laws of the religion. Conversely, it was held—there are corresponding utterances of the rabbis on this point—that any uninhibited surrender to the artistic or poetic glorification of this world is completely vain and apt to divert the Jews from the ways and purposes of God. After all, even the purpose of the creation of this world had already on occasion been problematical to the Jews of the later Maccabean period.

Above all, what was lacking in Judaism was the decisive hallmark of the inner-worldly type of asceticism: an integrated relationship to the world from the point of view of the individual's conviction of salvation (*certitudo salutis*), which nurtures all else. Again in this important matter, what was ultimately decisive for Judaism was the pariah character of the religion and the promises of Yahweh. An ascetic management of this world, such as that characteristic of Calvinism, was the very last thing of which a traditionally pious Jew would have thought. He could not think of methodically controlling the present world, which was so topsy-turvy because of Israel's sins, and which could not be set right by any human action but only by some free miracle of God that could not be hastened. He could not take as his "mission," as the sphere of his religious "vocation," the bringing of this world and its very sins under the rational norms of the revealed divine will, for the glory of God and as an identifying mark of his own salvation. The pious Jew had a far more difficult destiny to overcome than did the Puritan, who could be certain of his election to the world beyond. It was incumbent upon the individual Jew to make peace with the fact that the world would remain recalcitrant to the promises of God as long as God permitted the world to stand as it is. The Jew's responsibility was to make peace with this recalcitrancy of the world, while finding contentment if God sent him grace and success in his dealings with the enemies of his people, toward whom he must act soberly and legalistically, in fulfillment of the injunctions of the rabbis. This meant acting toward non-Jews in an objective or impersonal manner, without love and without hate, solely in accordance with what was permissible.

The frequent assertion that Judaism required only an external observance of the Law is incorrect. Naturally, this is the average tendency; but the requirements for real religious piety stood on a much higher plane. In any case, Judaic law fostered in its adherents a tendency to compare individual actions with each other and to compute the net result of them all. This conception of man's relationship to God as a bookkeeping operation of single good and evil acts with an uncertain total (a conception which may occasionally be found among the Puritans as well) may not have been the dominant official view of Judaism. Yet it was sufficient, together with the double-standard morality of Judaism, to prevent the development within Judaism of a methodical and ascetic orientation to the conduct of life on the scale that such an orientation developed in Puritanism. It is also important that in Judaism, as in Catholicism, the individual's activities in fulfilling particular religious injunctions were tantamount to his assuring his own chances of salvation. However, in both Judaism and Catholicism, God's grace was needed to supplement human inadequacy, although this dependence upon God's grace was not as universally recognized in Judaism as in Catholicism.

The ecclesiastical provision of grace was much less developed in Judaism, after the decline of the older Palestinian confessional (*teshubah*), than in Catholicism. In practice, this resulted in the Jew's having a greater religious responsibility for himself. This responsibility for oneself and the absence of any mediating religious agency necessarily made the Jewish pattern of life more systematic and personally responsible than the corresponding Catholic pattern of life. Still, the methodical control of life was limited in Judaism by the absence of the distinctively ascetic motivation characteristic of Puritans and by the continued presence of Jewish internal morality's traditionalism, which in principle remained unbroken. To be sure, there were present in Judaism numerous single stimuli toward practices that might be called ascetic, but the unifying force of a basically ascetic religious motivation was lacking. The highest form of Jewish piety is found in the religious mood (*Stimmung*) and not in active behavior. How could it be possible for the Jew to feel that by imposing a new rational order upon the world he would become the human executor of God's will, when for the Jew this world was thoroughly contradictory, hostile, and—as he had known since the time of Hadrian—impossible to change by human action? This might have been possible for the Jewish freethinker, but not for the pious Jew.

Puritanism always felt its inner similarity to Judaism, but also felt the limits of this similarity. The similarity in principle between Christianity and Judaism, despite all their differences, remained the same for the Puritans as it had been for the Christian followers of Paul. Both the Puritans and the early Christians always looked upon the Jews as the people who had once been chosen by God. But the unexampled activities of Paul had the following significant effects for early Christianity. On the one hand, Paul made the sacred book of the Jews into one of the sacred books of the Christians, and at the beginning the only one. He thereby erected a stout fence against all intrusions of Greek, especially Gnostic, intellectualism, as Wernle in particular has pointed out.[5] But on the other hand, by the aid of a dialectic that only a rabbi could possess, Paul here and there broke through what was most distinctive and effective in the Jewish law, namely the tabooistic norms and the overpowering messianic promises. Since these taboos and promises linked the whole religious worth of the Jews to their pariah position, Paul's breakthrough was fateful in its effect. Paul accomplished this breakthrough by interpreting these promises as having been partly fulfilled and partly abrogated by the birth of Christ. He triumphantly employed the highly impressive proof that the patriarchs of Israel had lived in accordance with God's will long before the issuance of the Jewish taboos and messianic promises, showing that they found blessedness through faith, which was the surety of God's election.

The dynamic power behind the incomparable missionary labors of Paul was his offer to the Jews of a tremendous release, the release provided by the consciousness of having escaped the fate of pariah status. A Jew could henceforth be a Greek among Greeks as well as a Jew among Jews, and could achieve this within the paradox of faith rather than through an enlightened hostility to religion. This was the passionate feeling of liberation brought by Paul. The Jew could actually free himself from the ancient promises of his God, by placing his faith in the new savior who had believed himself abandoned upon the cross by that very God.

Various consequences flowed from this rending of the sturdy chains that had bound the Jews firmly to their pariah position. One was the intense hatred of this one man Paul by the Jews of the Diaspora, sufficiently authenticated as fact. Among the other consequences may be mentioned the oscillations and utter uncertainty of the early Christian community; the attempt of James and the "pillar apostles" to establish an ethical minimum of law which would be valid and binding for all, in harmony with Jesus' own layman's understanding of the law; and finally, the open hostility of the Jewish Christians. In every line that Paul wrote we can feel his overpowering joy at having emerged from the hopeless "slave law" into freedom, through the blood of the Messiah. The overall consequence was the possibility of a Christian world misison.

The Puritans, like Paul, rejected the Talmudic law and even the characteristic ritual laws of the Old Testament, while taking over and considering as binding—for all their elasticity—various other expressions of God's will witnessed in the Old Testament. As the Puritans took these over, they always conjoined norms derived from the New Testament, even in matters of detail. The Jews who were actually welcomed by Puritan nations, especially the Americans, were not pious orthodox Jews but rather Reformed Jews who had abandoned orthodoxy, Jews such as those of the present time who have been trained in the Educational Alliance, and finally baptized Jews. These groups of Jews were at first welcomed without any ado whatsoever and are even now welcomed fairly readily, so that they have been absorbed to the point of the absolute loss of any trace of difference. This situation in Puritan countries contrasts with the situation in Germany, where the Jews remain— even after long generations—"assimilated Jews." These phenomena clearly manifest the actual kinship of Puritanism to Judaism. Yet precisely the non-Jewish element in Puritanism enabled Puritanism to play its special role in the creation of the modern economic temper, and also to carry through the aforementioned absorption of Jewish proselytes, which was not accomplished by nations with other than Puritan orientations.

3. *The This-Worldliness of Islam and Its Economic Ethics*

Islam, a comparatively late product of Near Eastern monotheism, in which Old Testament and Jewish-Christian elements played a very important role, "accommodated" itself to the world in a sense very different from Judaism. In the first Meccan period of Islam, the eschatological religion of Muhammad developed in pietistic urban conventicles which displayed a tendency to withdraw from the world. But in the subsequent developments in Medina and in the evolution of the early Islamic communities, the religion was transformed from its pristine form into a national Arabic warrior religion, and even later into a religion with very strong status emphasis. Those followers whose conversion to Islam made possible the decisive success of the Prophet were consistently members of powerful families.

The religious commandments of the holy war were not directed in the first instance to the purpose of conversion. Rather, the primary purpose was war "until they (the followers of alien religions of the book) will humbly pay the tribute (*jizyah*)," i.e., until Islam should rise to the top of this world's social scale, by exacting tribute from other religions. This is not the only factor that stamps Islam as the religion of masters. Military booty is important in the ordinances, in the promises, and above all in the expectations characterizing particularly the most ancient period of the religion. Even the ultimate elements of its economic ethic were purely feudal. The most pious adherents of the religion in its first generation became the wealthiest, or more correctly, enriched themselves with military booty—in the widest sense—more than did other members of the faith.

The role played by wealth accruing from spoils of war and from political aggrandizement in Islam is diametrically opposed to the role played by wealth in the Puritan religion. The Muslim tradition depicts with pleasure the luxurious raiment, perfume, and meticulous beard-coiffure of the pious. The saying that "when god blesses a man with prosperity he likes to see the signs thereof visible upon him"—made by Muhammad, according to tradition, to well-circumstanced people who appeared before him in ragged attire—stands in extreme opposition to any Puritan economic ethic and thoroughly corresponds with feudal conceptions of status. This saying would mean, in our language, that a wealthy man is obligated "to live in keeping with his status." In the Koran, Muhammad is represented as completely rejecting every type of monasticism (*rahbaniya*), though not all asceticism, for he did accord respect to fasting, begging, and penitential mortification. Muhammad's attitude in opposition to chastity may have sprung from personal motivations similar to those apparent in Luther's famous remarks which are so expressive of his strongly sensual nature; i.e., in the conviction, also found in the Talmud, that whoever has not married by a certain age must be a sinner. But we would have to regard as unique in the hagiology of an ethical religion of salvation Muhammad's dictum expressing doubt about the ethical character of a person who has abstained from eating meat for forty days; as well as the reply of a renowned pillar of ancient Islam, celebrated by some as a Mahdi, to the question why he, unlike his father Ali, had used cosmetics for his hair: "In order to be more successful with women."

But Islam was never really a religion of salvation; the ethical concept of salvation was actually alien to Islam. The god it taught was a lord of unlimited power, although merciful, the fulfillment of whose commandments was not beyond human power. An essentially political character marked all the chief ordinances of Islam: the elimination of private feuds in the interest of increasing the group's striking power against external foes; the proscription of illegitimate forms of sexual behavior and the regulation of legitimate sexual relations along strongly patriarchal lines (actually creating sexual privileges only for the wealthy, in view of the facility of divorce and the maintenance of concubinage with female slaves); the prohibition of usury; the prescription of taxes for war; and the injunction to support the poor. Equally political in character is the distinctive religious obligation in Islam, its only required dogma: the recognition of Allah as the one god and of Muhammad as his prophet. In addition, there were the obligations to journey to Mecca once during a lifetime, to fast by day during the month of fasting, to attend services once a week, and to observe the obligation of daily prayers. Finally, Islam imposed such requirements for everyday living as the wearing of distinctive clothing (a requirement that even today has important economic consequences whenever savage tribes are converted to Islam) and the avoidance of certain unclean foods, of wine, and of gambling. The restriction against gambling obviously had important consequences for the religion's attitude toward speculative business enterprises.

There was nothing in ancient Islam like an individual quest for salvation, nor was there any mysticism. The religious promises in the earliest period of Islam pertained to this world. Wealth, power, and glory were all martial promises, and even the world beyond is pictured in Islam as a soldier's sensual paradise. Moreover, the original Islamic conception of sin has a similar feudal orientation. The depiction of the prophet of Islam as devoid of sin is a late theological construction, scarcely consistent with the actual nature of Muhammad's strong sensual passions and his explosions of wrath over very small provocations. Indeed, such a picture is strange even to the Koran, just as after Muhammad's transfer to Medina he lacked any sort of tragic sense of sin. The original feudal conception of sin remained dominant in orthodox Islam, for which sin is a composite of ritual impurity, ritual sacrilege (*shirk*, i.e., polytheism), disobedience to the positive injunctions of the prophet;

and the violation of status prescriptions by infractions of convention or etiquette. Islam displays other characteristics of a distinctively feudal spirit: the obviously unquestioned acceptance of slavery, serfdom, and polygamy; the disesteem for and subjection of women; the essentially ritualistic character of religious obligations; and finally, the great simplicity of religious requirements and the even greater simplicity of the modest ethical requirements.

Islam was not brought any closer to Judaism and to Christianity in decisive matters by such Islamic developments as the achievement of great scope through the rise of theological and juristic casuistry, the appearance of both pietistic and enlightenment schools of philosophy (following the intrusion of Persian Sufism, derived from India), and the formation of the order of dervishes (still today strongly under Indian influence). Judaism and Christianity were specifically bourgeois-urban religions, whereas for Islam the city had only political importance. A certain sobriety in the conduct of life might also be produced by the nature of the official cult in Islam and by its sexual and ritual commandments. The petty-bourgeois stratum was largely the carrier of the dervish religion, which was disseminated practically everywhere and gradually grew in power, finally surpassing the official ecclesiastical religion. This type of religion, with its orgiastic and mystical elements, with its essentially irrational and extraordinary character, and with its official and thoroughly traditionalistic ethic of everyday life, became influential in Islam's missionary enterprise because of its great simplicity. It directed the conduct of life into paths whose effect was plainly opposite to the methodical control of life found among Puritans, and indeed, found in every type of asceticism oriented toward the control of the world.

Islam, in contrast to Judaism, lacked the requirement of a comprehensive knowledge of the law and lacked that intellectual training in casuistry which nurtured the rationalism of Judaism. The ideal personality type in the religion of Islam was not the scholarly scribe (*Literat*), but the warrior. Moreover, Islam lacked all those promises of a messianic realm upon earth which in Israel were linked with meticulous fidelity to the law, and which—together with the priestly doctrine of the history, election, sin and dispersion of the Jews—determined the fateful pariah character of the Jewish religion.

To be sure, there were ascetic sects among the Muslims. Large groups of ancient Islamic warriors were characterized by a trend toward simplicity; this prompted them from the outset to oppose the rule of the Umayyads. The latter's merry enjoyment of the world presented the strongest contrast to the rigid discipline of the encampment fortresses in which Umar had concentrated Islamic warriors in the conquered domains; in their stead there now arose a feudal aristocracy. But this was the asceticism of a military caste, of a martial order of knights, not of monks. Certainly it was not a middle-class ascetic systematization of the conduct of life. Moreover, it was effective only periodically, and even then it tended to merge into fatalism. We have already spoken of the quite different effect which is engendered in such circumstances by a belief in providence. Islam was diverted completely from any really methodical control of life by the advent of the cult of saints, and finally by magic.

4. *The Other-Worldliness of Buddhism and Its Economic Consequences*

At the opposite extreme from systems of religious ethics preoccupied with the control of economic affairs within the world stands the ultimate ethic of world-rejection, the mystical illuminative concentration of authentic ancient Buddhism (naturally not the completely altered manifestations Buddhism assumed in Tibetan, Chinese, and Japanese popular religions). Even this most world-rejecting ethic is "rational," in the sense that it produces a constantly alert control of all natural instinctive drives, though for purposes entirely different from those of inner-worldly asceticism. Salvation is sought, not from sin and suffering alone, but also from ephemeralness as such; escape from the wheel of *karma*-causality into eternal rest is the goal pursued. This search is, and can only be, the highly individualized task of a particular person. There is no predestination, but neither is there any divine grace, any prayer, or any religious service. Rewards and punishments for every good and every evil deed are automatically established by the *karma*-causality of the cosmic mechanism of compensation. This retribution is always proportional, and hence always limited in time. So long as the individual is driven to action by the thirst for life, he must experience in full measure the fruits of his behavior in ever-new human existences. Whether his momentary situation is animal, heavenly, or hellish, he necessarily creates new chances for himself in the future. The most noble enthusiasm and the most sordid sensuality lead equally into new existence in this chain of individuation (it is quite incorrect to term this process transmigration of souls, since Buddhist metaphysics knows nothing of a soul). This process of individuation continues on as long as the thirst for life, in this world or in the world beyond, is not absolutely extinguished. The process is but perpetuated by the individual's impotent struggle for his personal existence with all its illusions, above all the illusion of a distinctive soul or personality.

All rational purposive activity is regarded as leading away from salvation, except of course the subjective activity of concentrated contemplation, which empties the soul of the passion for life and every connection with worldly interests. The achievement of salvation is possible for only a few, even of those who have resolved to live in poverty, chastity, and unemployment (for labor is purposive action), and hence in mendicancy. These chosen few are required to wander ceaselessly—except at the time of the heavy rains—freed from all personal ties to family and world, pursuing the goal of mystical illumination by fulfilling the injunctions relating to the correct path (*dharma*). When such salvation is gained, the deep joy and tender, undifferentiated love characterizing such illumination provides the highest blessing possible in this existence, short of absorption into the eternal dreamless sleep of *Nirvana,* the only state in which no change occurs. All other human beings may improve their situations in future existences by approximating the prescriptions of the rule of life and by avoiding major sins in this existence. Such future existences are inevitable, according to the *karma* doctrine of causality, because the ethical account has not been straightened out, the thirst for life has not been "abreacted," so to speak. For most people, therefore, some new individuation is inevitable when the present life has ended, and truly eternal salvation remains inaccessible.

There is no path leading from this only really consistent position of world-flight to any economic ethic or to any rational social ethic. The universal mood of pity, extending to all creatures, cannot be the carrier of any rational behavior and in fact leads away from it. This mood of pity is the logical consequence of contemplative mysticism's position regarding the solidarity of all living, and hence transitory, beings. This solidarity follows from the common *karma*-causality which overarches all living beings. In Buddhism, the psychological basis for this universal pity is the religion's mystical, euphoric, universal, and acosmistic love.

Buddhism is the most consistent of the salvation doctrines produced before and after by the intellectualism of educated Indian strata. Its cool and proud emancipation of the individual from life as such, which in effect stood the individual on his own feet, could never become a popular salvation faith. Buddhism's influence beyond the circle of the educated was due to the tremendous prestige traditionally enjoyed by the *shramana,* i.e., the ascetic, which possessed magical and anthropolatric traits. As soon as Buddhism became a missionizing popular religion, it duly transformed itself into a savior religion based on *karma* compensation, with hopes for the world beyond guaranteed by devotional techniques, cultic and sacramental grace, and deeds of mercy. Naturally, Buddhism also tended to welcome purely magical notions.

In India itself, Buddhism succumbed, among the upper classes, to a renascent philosophy of salvation based on the Vedas; and it met competition from Hinduistic salvation religions, especially the various forms of Vishnuism, from Tantristic magic, and from orgiastic mystery religions, notably the *bhakti* piety (love of god). In Lamaism, Buddhism became the purely monastic religion of a theocracy which controlled the laity by ecclesiastical powers of a thoroughly magical nature. Wherever Buddhism was diffused in the Orient, its idiosyncratic character underwent striking transformation as it competed and entered into diverse combinations with Chinese Taoism, thus becoming the region's typical mass religion, which pointed beyond this world and the ancestral cult and which distributed grace and salvation.

At all events, no motivation toward a rational system for the methodical control of life flowed from Buddhist, Taoist, or Hindu piety. Hindu piety in particular, as we have already suggested, maintained the strongest possible power of tradition, since the presuppositions of Hinduism constituted the most consistent religious expression of the organic view of society. The existing order of the world was provided absolutely unconditional justification, in terms of the mechanical operation of a proportional retribution in the distribution of power and happiness to individuals on the basis of their merits and failures in their earlier existences.

All these popular religions of Asia left room for the acquisitive drive of the tradesman, the interest of the artisan in sustenance (*Nahrungs-Interesse*), and the traditionalism of the peasant. These popular religions also left undisturbed both philosophical speculation and the conventional status-oriented life patterns of privileged groups. These status-oriented patterns of the privileged evinced feudal characteristics in Japan; patrimonial-bureaucratic, and hence strongly utilitarian features in China; and a mixture of knightly, patrimonial, and intellectualistic traits in India. None of these mass religions of Asia, however, provided the motives or orientations for a rationalized ethical transformation of a creaturely world in accordance with divine commandments. Rather, they all accepted this world as eternally given, and so the best of all possible worlds. The only choice open to the sages, who possessed the highest type of piety, was whether to accommodate themselves to the Tao, the impersonal order of the world and the only thing specifically divine, or to save themselves from the inexorable chain of causality by passing into the only eternal being, the dreamless sleep of Nirvana.

"Capitalism" existed among all these religions, of the same kind as in Occidental Antiquity and the medieval period. But there was no development toward modern capitalism, nor even any stirrings in that direction. Above all, there evolved no "capitalist spirit," in the sense that is distinctive of ascetic Protestantism. But to assume that the Hindu, Chinese, or Muslim merchant, trader, artisan, or coolie was animated by a weaker "acquisitive drive" than the ascetic Protestant is to fly in the face of the facts. Indeed, the reverse would seem to be true, for what is distinctive of Puritanism is the rational and ethical limitation of the quest for profit. There is no proof whatever that a weaker natural "endowment" for technical economic rationalism was responsible for the actual difference in this respect. At the present time, all these people import this "commodity" as the most important Occidental product, and whatever impediments exist result from rigid traditions, such as existed among us in the Middle Ages, not from any lack of ability or will. Such impediments to rational economic development must be sought primarily in the domain of religion, insofar as they must not be located in the purely political conditions, the structures of domination, with which we shall deal later.

Only ascetic Protestantism completely eliminated magic and the supernatural quest for salvation, of which the highest form was intellectualist, contemplative illumination. It alone created the religious motivations for seeking salvation primarily through immersion in one's worldly vocation (Beruf). This Protestant stress upon the methodically rationalized fulfillment of one's vocational responsibility was diametrically opposite to Hinduism's strongly traditionalistic concept of vocations. For the various popular religions of Asia, in contrast to ascetic Protestantism, the world remained a great enchanted garden, in which the practical way to orient oneself, or to find security in this world or the next, was to revere or coerce the spirits and seek salvation through ritualistic, idolatrous, or sacramental procedures. No path led from the magical religiosity of the non-intellectual strata of Asia to a rational, methodical control of life. Nor did any path lead to that methodical control from the world accommodation of Confucianism, from the world-rejection of Buddhism, from the world-conquest of Islam, or from the messianic expectations and economic pariah law of Judaism.

5. Jesus' Indifference Toward the World

The second great religion of world-rejection, in our special sense of the term, was early Christianity, at the cradle of which magic and belief in demons were also present. Its Savior was primarily a magician whose magical charisma was an ineluctable source of his unique feeling of individuality. But the absolutely unique religious promises of Judaism contributed to the determination of the distinctive character of early Christianity. It will be recalled that Jesus appeared during the period of the most intensive messianic expectations. Still another factor contributing to the distinctive message of Christianity was its reaction to the unique concern for erudition in the Law characteristic of Jewish piety. The Christian evangel arose in opposition to this legalistic erudition, as a non-intellectual's proclamation directed to non-intellectuals, to the "poor in spirit." Jesus understood and interpreted the "law," from which he desired to remove not even a letter, in a fashion common to the lowly and the unlearned, the pious folk of the countryside and the small towns who understood the Law in their own way and in accordance with the needs of their own occupations, in contrast to the Hellenized, wealthy and upper-class people and to the erudite scholars and Pharisees trained in casuistry. Jesus' interpretation of the Jewish law was milder than theirs in regard to ritual prescriptions, particularly in regard to the keeping of the Sabbath, but stricter than theirs in other respects, e.g., in regard to the grounds for divorce. There already appears to have been an anticipation of the Pauline view that the requirements of the Mosaic law were conditioned by the sinfulness of the superficially pious. There were, in any case, instances in which Jesus squarely opposed specific injunctions of the ancient tradition.

Jesus' distinctive self-esteem did not come from anything like a "proletarian instinct" but from the knowledge that the way to God necessarily led through him, because of his oneness with the Godly patriarch. His self-esteem was grounded in the knowledge that he, the non-scholar, possessed both the charisma requisite for the control of demons and a tremendous preaching ability, far surpassing that of any scholar or Pharisee. This self-esteem involved the conviction that his power to exorcise demons was operative only among the people who believed in him, even if they be heathens, not in his home town and his own family and among the wealthy and high-born of the land, the scholars, and the legalistic virtuosi—among none of these did he find the faith that gave him his magical power to work miracles. He did find such a faith among the poor and the oppressed, among publicans and sinners, and even among Roman soldiers. It should never be forgotten that these charismatic powers were the absolutely decisive components in Jesus' feelings concerning his messiahship. These powers were the fundamental issue in his denunciation of the Galilean cities and in his angry curse upon the recalcitrant fig tree. His feeling about his own powers also explains why the election of Israel became ever more problematical to him and the importance of the Temple ever more dubious, while the rejection of the Pharisees and the scholars became increasingly certain to him.

Jesus recognized two absolutely mortal sins. One was the "sin against the spirit" committed by the scriptural scholar who disesteemed charisma and its bearers. The other was unbrotherly arrogance, such as the arrogance of the intellectual toward the poor in spirit, when the intellectual hurls at his brother the exclamation "Thou fool!" This anti-intellectualist rejection of scholarly arrogance and of Hellenic and rabbinic wisdom is the only "status element" of Jesus' message, though it is very distinctive. In general, Jesus' message is far from being a simple proclamation for every Tom, Dick, and Harry, for all the weak of the world. True, the yoke is light, but only for those who can once again become as little children. In truth, Jesus set up the most tremendous requirements for salvation; his doctrine has real aristocratic qualities.

Nothing was further from Jesus' mind than the notion of the universalism of divine grace. On the contrary, he directed his whole preaching against this notion. Few are chosen to pass through the narrow gate, to repent and to believe in Jesus. God himself impedes the salvation of the others and hardens their hearts, and naturally it is the proud and the rich who are most overtaken by this fate. Of course this element is not new, since it can be found in the older prophecies. The older Jewish prophets had taught that, in view of the arrogant behavior of the highly placed, the Messiah would be a king who would enter Jerusalem upon the beast of burden used by the poor. This implies no "social equalitarianism." Jesus lodged with the wealthy, which was ritually reprehensible in the eyes of the virtuosi of the law, and when he bade the rich young man give away his wealth, Jesus expressly enjoined this act only if the young man wished to be "perfect," i.e., a disciple. Complete emancipation from all ties of the world, from family as well as possessions, such as we find in the teachings of the Buddha and similar prophets, was required only of disciples. Yet, although all things are possible for God, continued attachment to Mammon constitutes one of the most difficult impediments to salvation into the Kingdom of God —for attachment to Mammon diverts the individual from religious salvation, the most important thing in the world.

Jesus nowhere explicitly states that preoccupation with wealth leads to unbrotherliness, but this notion is at the heart of the matter, for the prescribed injunctions definitely contain the primordial ethic of mutual help which is characteristic of neighborhood associations of poorer people. The chief difference is that in Jesus' message acts of mutual help have been systematized into *Gesinnungsethik* involving a fraternalistic sentiment of love. The injunction of mutual help was also construed universalistically, extended to everyone. The "neighbor" is the one nearest at hand. Indeed, the notion of mutual help was enlarged into an acosmistic paradox, based on the axiom that God alone can and will reward. Unconditional forgiveness, unconditional charity, unconditional love even of enemies, unconditional suffering of injustice without requiting evil by force—these demands for religious heroism could have been products of a mystically conditioned acosmism of love. But it must not be overlooked, as it so often has been, that Jesus combined acosmistic love with the Jewish notion of retribution. God alone will one day compensate, avenge, and reward. Man must not boast of his virtue in having performed any of the aforementioned deeds of love, since his boasting would preempt his subsequent reward. To amass treasures in heaven one must in this world lend money to those from whom no repayment can be expected; otherwise, there is no merit in the deed. A strong emphasis upon the just equalization of destinies was expressed by Jesus in the legend of Lazarus and elsewhere. From this perspective alone, wealth is already a dangerous gift.

But Jesus held in general that what is most decisive for salvation is an absolute indifference to the world and its concerns. The kingdom of heaven, a realm of joy upon earth, utterly without suffering and sin, is at hand; indeed, this generation will not die before seeing it. It will come like a thief at night; it is already in the process of appearing among mankind. Let man be free with the wealth of Mammon, instead of clutching it fast; let man render unto Caesar that which is Caesar's— for what profit is there in such matters? Let man pray to God for daily bread and remain unconcerned for the morrow. No human action can accelerate the coming of the kingdom, but man should prepare himself for its coming. Although this message did not formally abrogate the law, it did place the emphasis throughout upon religious sentiment. The entire content of the law and the prophets was condensed into the simple commandment to love God and one's fellow man, to which was added the one far-reaching conception that the true religious mood is to be judged by its fruits, by its faithful demonstration (*Bewährung*).

The visions of the resurrection, doubtless under the influence of the widely diffused soteriological myths, generated a tremendous growth in pneumatic manifestations of charisma; in the formation of communities, beginning with Jesus' own family, which originally had not shared Jesus' faith; and in missionary activity among the heathens. Nascent Christianity maintained continuity with the older Jewish prophecies even after the fateful conversion of Paul had resulted in a breaking away from the pariah religion. As a result of these developments, two new attitudes toward the world became decisive in the Christian missionary communities. One was the expectation of the Second Coming, and the other was the recognition of the tremendous importance of charismatic gifts of the spirit. The world would remain as it was until the master would come. So too the individual was required to abide in his position and in his calling (κλῆσις), subordinate to the authorities, save where they demanded of him that he perpetrate a sinful deed.[6]

N O T E S

1. See Werner Sombart, *The Jews and Modern Capitalism* (London: Fischer Unwin, 1913), 230ff.

2. Cf. Weber, *Protestant Ethic*, 175.

3. On the *commenda* and the *commandite*, see Weber, *Handelsgesell-schaften* (1889), 1924 reprint in *GAzSW*, 339ff, and *Economic History*, ch. 17, "Forms of Commercial Enterprise." The *maona* comprised various types of associations employed in Italian cities for the running of a fleet or the exploitation of an overseas colony.

4. See Julius Guttmann, "Die Juden and das Wirtschaftsleben," *AfS*, vol. 36, 1913, 149ff. This is a critique of Sombart's book. (W)

5. Paul Wernle, *The Beginnings of Christianity* (New York: Putnam, 1904), vol. II, ch. IX, esp. 192f.

6. According to notes in the manuscript, this section was to have been expanded further. (W)

VII

THE MARKET: ITS IMPERSONALITY AND ETHIC *(Fragment)*[1]

Up to this point we have discussed group formations that rationalized their social action only in part, but for the rest had the most diverse structures—more amorphous or more rationally organized, more continuous or more intermittent, more open or more closed. In contrast to all of them stands, as the archetype of all rational social action (*rationales Gesellschaftshandeln*), consociation (*Vergesellschaftung*) through exchange in the *market*.

A market may be said to exist wherever there is competition, even if only unilateral, for opportunities of exchange among a plurality of potential parties. Their physical assemblage in one place, as in the local market square, the fair (the "long distance market"), or the exchange (the merchants' market), only constitutes the most consistent kind of market formation. It is, however, only this physical assemblage which allows the full emergence of the market's most distinctive feature, viz., dickering. Since the discussion of the market phenomena constitutes essentially the content of economics (*Sozialökonomik*), it will not be presented here. From a sociological point of view, the market represents a coexistence and sequence of rational consociations, each of which is specifically ephemeral insofar as it ceases to exist with the act of exchanging the goods, unless a norm has been promulgated which imposes upon the transferors of the exchangeable goods the guaranty of their lawful acquisition as warranty of title or of quiet enjoyment. The completed barter constitutes a consociation only with the immediate partner. The preparatory dickering, however, is always a social action (*Gemeinschafts-handeln*) insofar as the potential partners are guided in their offers by the potential action of an indeterminately large group of real or imaginary competitors rather than by their own actions alone. The more this is true, the more does the market constitute social action. Furthermore, any act of exchange involving the use of money (sale) is a social action simply because the money used derives its value from its relation to the potential action of others. Its acceptability rests exclusively on the expectation that it will continue to be desirable and can be further used as a means of payment. Group formation (*Vergemeinschaftung*) through the use of money is the exact counterpart to any consociation through rationally agreed or imposed norms.

Money creates a group by virtue of material interest relations between actual and potential participants in the market and its payments. At the fully developed stage, the so-called money economy, the resulting situation looks as if it had been created by a set of norms established for the very purpose of bringing it into being. The explanation lies in this: Within the market community every act of exchange, especially monetary exchange, is not directed, in isolation, by the action of the individual partner to the particular transaction, but the more rationally it is considered, the more it is directed by the actions of all parties potentially interested in the exchange. The market community as such is the most impersonal relationship of practical life into which humans can enter with one another. This is not due to that potentiality of struggle among the interested parties which is inherent in the market relationship. Any human relationship, even the most intimate, and even though it be marked by the most unqualified personal devotion, is in some sense relative and may involve a struggle with the partner, for instance, over the salvation of his soul. The reason for the impersonality of the market is its matter-of-factness, its orientation to the commodity and only to that. Where the market is allowed to follow its own autonomous tendencies, its participants do not look toward the persons of each other but only toward the commodity; there are no obligations of brotherliness or reverence, and none of those spontaneous human relations that are sustained by personal unions. They all would just obstruct the free development of the bare market relationship, and its specific interests serve, in their turn, to weaken the sentiments on which these obstructions rest. Market behavior is influenced by rational, purposeful pursuit of interests. The partner to a transaction is expected to behave according to rational legality and, quite particularly, to respect the formal inviolability of a promise once given. These are the qualities which form the content of market ethics. In this latter respect the market inculcates, indeed, particularly rigorous conceptions. Violations of agreements, even though they may be concluded by mere signs, entirely unrecorded, and devoid of evidence, are almost unheard of in the annals of the stock exchange. Such absolute depersonalization is contrary to all the elementary forms of human relationship. Sombart has pointed out this contrast repeatedly and brilliantly.[2]

The "free" market, that is, the market which is not bound by ethical norms, with its exploitation of constellations of interests and monopoly positions and its dickering, is an abomination to every system of fraternal ethics. In sharp contrast to all other groups which always presuppose some measure of personal fraternization or even blood kinship, the market is fundamentally alien to any type of fraternal relationship.

At first, free exchange does not occur but with the world outside of the neighborhood or the personal association. The market is a relationship which transcends the boundaries of neighborhood, kinship group, or tribe. Originally, it is indeed the only peaceful relationship of such kind. At first, fellow members did not trade with one another with the intention of obtaining profit. There was, indeed, no need for such transactions in an age of self-sufficient agrarian units. One of the most characteristic forms of primitive trade, the "silent" trade [cf. ch. VIII:*ii*:2], dramatically represents the contrast between the market community and the fraternal community. The silent trade is a form of exchange which avoids all face-to-face contact and in which the supply takes the form of a deposit of the commodity at a customary place; the counteroffer takes the same form, and dickering is effected through the increase in the number of objects being offered from both sides, until one party either withdraws dissatisfied or, satisfied, takes the goods left by the other party and departs.

It is normally assumed by both partners to an exchange that each will be interested in the future continuation of the exchange relationship, be it with this particular partner or with some other, and that he will adhere to his promises for this reason and avoid at least striking infringements of the rules of good faith and fair dealing. It is only this assumption which guarantees the law-abidingness of the exchange partners. Insofar as that interest exists, "honesty is the best policy." This proposition, however, is by no means universally applicable, and its empirical validity is irregular; naturally, it is highest in the case of rational enterprises with a stable clientele. For, on the basis of such a stable relationship, which generates the possibility of mutual personal appraisal with regard to market ethics, trading may free itself most successfully from illimited dickering and return, in the interest of the parties, to a relative limitation of fluctuation in prices and exploitation of momentary interest constellations. The consequences, though they are important for price formation, are not relevant here in detail. The fixed price, without preference for any particular buyer, and strict business honesty are highly peculiar features of the regulated local neighborhood markets of the medieval Occident, in contrast to the Near and Far East. They are, moreover, a condition as well as a product of that particular stage of capitalistic economy which is known as Early Capitalism. They are absent where this stage no longer exists. Nor are they practiced by those status and other groups which are not engaged in exchange except occasionally and passively rather than regularly and actively. The maxim of *caveat emptor* obtains, as experience shows, mostly in transactions involving feudal strata or, as every cavalry officer knows, in horse trading among comrades. The specific ethics of the market place is alien to them. Once and for all they conceive of commerce, as does any rural community of neighbors, as an activity in which the sole question is: who will cheat whom.

The freedom of the market is typically limited by sacred taboos or through monopolistic consociations of status groups which render exchange with outsiders impossible. Directed against these limitations we find the continuous onslaught of the market community, whose very existence constitutes a temptation to share in the opportunities for gain. The process of appropriation in a monopolistic group may advance to the point at which it becomes closed toward outsiders, i.e., the land, or the right to share in the commons, may have become vested definitively and hereditarily. As the money economy expands and, with it, both the growing differentiation of needs capable of being satisfied by indirect barter, and the independence from land ownership, such a situation of fixed, hereditary appropriation normally creates a steadily increasing interest of individual parties in the possibility of using their vested property rights for exchange with the highest bidder, even though he be an outsider. This development is quite analogous to that which causes the co-heirs of an industrial enterprise in the long run to establish a corporation so as to be able to sell their shares more freely. In turn, an emerging capitalistic economy, the stronger it becomes, the greater will be its efforts to obtain the means of production and labor services in the market without limitations by sacred or status bonds, and to emancipate the opportunities to sell its products from the restrictions imposed by the sales monopolies of status groups. Capitalistic interests thus favor the continuous extension of the free market, but only up to the point at which some of them succeed, through the purchase of privileges from the political authority or simply through the power of capital, in obtaining for themselves a monopoly for the sale of their products or the acquisition of their means of production, and in thus closing the market on their own part.

The breakup of the monopolies of status groups is thus the typical immediate sequence to the full appropriation of all the material means of production. It occurs where those having a stake in the capitalistic system are in a position to influence, for their own advantage, those communities by which the ownership of goods and the mode of their use are regulated; or where, within a monopolistic status group, the upper hand is gained by those who are interested in the use of their vested property interests in the market. Another consequence is that the scope of those rights which are guaranteed as acquired or acquirable by the coercive apparatus of the property-regulating community becomes limited to rights in material goods and to contractual claims, including claims to contractual labor. All other appropriations, especially those of customers or those of monopolies by status groups, are destroyed. This state of affairs, which we call free competition, lasts until it is replaced by new, this time capitalistic, monopolies which are acquired in the market through the power of property. These capitalistic monopolies differ from monopolies of status groups[3] by their purely economic and rational character. By restricting either the scope of possible sales or the permissible terms, the monopolies of status groups excluded from their field of action the mechanism of the market with its dickering and rational calculation. Those monopolies, on the other hand, which are based solely upon the power of property, rest, on the contrary, upon an entirely rationally calculated mastery of market conditions which may, however, remain formally as free as ever. The sacred, status, and merely traditional bonds, which have gradually come to be eliminated, constituted restrictions on the formation of rational market prices; the purely economically conditioned monopolies are, on the other hand, their ultimate consequence. The beneficiary of a monopoly by a status group restricts, and maintains his power against, the market, while the rational-economic monopolist rules through the market. We shall designate those interest groups which are enabled by formal market freedom to achieve power, as market-interest groups.

A particular market may be subject to a body of norms autonomously agreed upon by the participants or imposed by any one of a great variety of different groups, especially political or religious organizations. Such norms may involve limitations of market freedom, restrictions of dickering or of competition, or they may establish guaranties for the observance of market legality, especially the modes or means of payment or, in periods of interlocal insecurity, the norms may be aimed at guaranteeing the market peace. Since the market was originally a consociation of persons who are not members of the same group and who are, therefore, "enemies," the guaranty of peace, like that of restrictions of permissible modes of warfare, was ordinarily left to divine powers.[4] Very often the peace of the market was placed under the protection of a temple;

later on it tended to be made into a source of revenue for the chief or prince. However, while exchange is the specifically peaceful form of acquiring economic power, it can, obviously, be associated with the use of force. The seafarer of Antiquity and the Middle Ages was pleased to take without pay whatever he could acquire by force and had recourse to peaceful dickering only where he was confronted with a power equal to his own or where he regarded it as shrewd to do so for the sake of future exchange opportunities which might be endangered otherwise. But the intensive expansion of exchange relations has always gone together with a process of relative pacification. All of the "public peace" arrangements of the Middle Ages were meant to serve the interests of exchange.[5] The appropriation of goods through free, purely economically rational exchange, as Oppenheimer has said time and again, is the conceptual opposite of appropriation of goods by coercion of any kind, but especially physical coercion, the regulated exercise of which is the very constitutive element of the political community.

NOTES

1. The title is by the present editor; all notes are by Rheinstein. (R)

2. DIE JUDEN UND DAS WIRTSCHAFTSLEBEN (1911, Epstein tr. 1913, 1951, s.t. THE JEWS AND MODERN CAPITALISM); DER BOURGEOIS (1913); HÄNDLER UND HELDEN (1915); DER MODERNE KAPITALISMUS, vol. III, Part I, p. 6; see also DEUTSCHER SOZIALISMUS (1934) (Geiser tr. s.t. A NEW SOCIAL PHILOSOPHY, 1937). Revulsion against the so-called "de-humanization" of relationships has constituted an important element in the German neo-romanticism of such groups and movements as the circle around the poet Stefan George, the youth movement, the Christian Socialists, etc. Through the tendency to ascribe this capitalistic spirit to the Jews and to hold them responsible for its rise and spread, these sentiments became highly influential in the growth of organized anti-Semitism and, especially, National-Socialism.

3. Such as the monopoly of guild members to sell certain goods within the city, or the monopoly of the lord of a manor to grind the grain of all peasants of the district, or the monopoly of the members of the bar to give legal advice, a monopoly which was abolished in most Continental countries in the nineteenth century.

4. On market peace, cf. S. RIETSCHEL, MARKT UND STADT (1897); H. PIRENNE, VILLES, MARCHÉS ET MARCHANDS AU MOYEN ÂGE (1898).

5. On such medieval peace arrangements (Landfrieden), which were aimed at the elimination of feuds and private wars and which occurred either as non-aggression pacts concluded, often with ecclesiastical or royal coöperation, between barons, cities, and other potentates, or were sought to be imposed on his unruly subjects by the king, see Quidde, Histoire de la paix publique en Allemagne au moyen âge (1929), 28 RECUEIL DES COURS DE L'ACADÉMIE DE DROIT INTERNATIONAL 449.